OCCASIONS OF SIN

ALSO BY DIARMAID FERRITER

The Transformation of Ireland 1900–2000
Judging Dev: A reassessment of the life and legacy of Éamon de Valera

OCCASIONS OF SIN

SEX AND SOCIETY
IN MODERN IRELAND

DIARMAID FERRITER

P
PROFILE BOOKS

First published in Great Britain in 2009 by
Profile Books Ltd
3A Exmouth House
Pine Street
Exmouth Market
London ECIR OJH
www.profilebooks.com

1 3 5 7 9 10 8 6 4 2

Typeset in Garamond by MacGuru Ltd
info@macguru.org.uk

Printed and bound in Great Britain by
Clays, Bungay, Suffolk

A CIP catalogue record for this book is available from the British Library.

ISBN 978 1 86197 918 6

For Enya, Ríona and Saorla, Loves of My Life

CONTENTS

ACKNOWLEDGEMENTS

The research and writing of this book was greatly facilitated by my being awarded an Irish Research Council for the Humanities and Social Sciences (IRCHSS) Government of Ireland Staff Fellowship for the academic year 2006–7. I am extremely grateful to the IRCHSS for the time and space it afforded me to spend lengthy bouts of time in the archives that house the material on which this book is based. The staff of those archives, in particular the National Archives of Ireland, the National Library of Ireland, the Dublin Diocesan Archives and the Public Record Office of Northern Ireland, deserve the utmost thanks for all that they have done for me and all that they continue to do for countless researchers, as custodians of our archival treasures. I am also grateful to the staffs of the libraries at University College Dublin, St Patrick's College, Drumcondra and Trinity College Dublin. My former colleagues at St Patrick's College, Marion Lyons, Daire Keogh, Matthew Stout, Carla King and especially James Kelly, provided an atmosphere of collegiality and warmth and practical support, while my colleagues in the School of History and Archives, University College Dublin, have done likewise; I remain in their collective debt. This book was completed at Boston College, Massachusetts, where Bob O'Neill, Tom Hachey, the staff of the Burns and O'Neill Libraries, and the friendship of those involved in the Irish Studies Programme at Connolly House – particularly Robert Savage, Kevin Kenny, Joe Nugent, Jim Smyth and Marjorie Howes – made my year there memorable and special.

Deirdre McMahon made invaluable suggestions on reading the manuscript; I am very grateful for her repeated generosity and insights. Margaret MacCurtain was also generous with her wisdom and experience. Catríona Crowe's advice, suggestions, insights and friendship were, as always, stimulating and unique. Catríona, with her colleagues Ken Martin and Brendan Martin, kindly facilitated access to the courts archive, an invaluable source for researchers. Greg Prendergast's long-term and intense friendship has meant a great deal, both for its quality and hilarity, as has the special bond with Kevin Maher and the companionship, over many years, of Stephen Cullinane, Paul Rouse, Mark Duncan, Carmel, Ronan and Karen Furlong.

To my cherished and marvellous parents, Nollaig and Vera, my siblings Cian, Tríona and Muireann, my in-laws Tom, Anne, Lucy and Catherine Maher, Deirdre Mulligan, Lar Joyce and my nephews and nieces Luan, Síofra, Rachel and Shane, once again, thank you from the bottom of my heart. Your support, friendship, love and tolerance are hugely appreciated.

Various other individuals, by providing assistance, advice, friendship, diversion, support and levity, have assisted me in the last few years and I want to record my gratitude to: Hugh Brady, Anne, Carla, Melanie and Tom Briggs, Aisling and Eugene Cadden, Peter Casey, Bernadette Comerford, Rose Cottam, Catherine Cox, Mary Daly, Fergus D'Arcy, Pauric Dempsey, Noelle Dowling, Colleen Dube, Jeff Dudgeon, Sophie Duncan, Adrienne Egan, Alan English, Anne Enright, Lisa Finnegan, Roy Foster, Rachel Furlong, Teri Garvey, Tom Garvin, Grainne Gavigan, Tom Halpin, Lorelei Harris, Philip Harvey, Seamus Helferty, David Heron, Lucy Hogan, Ann Marie Hourihane, Aideen Ireland, Lar Joye, Anne Marie Kearney, Finola Kennedy, Philip King, Cormac Kinsella, Michael Laffan, Pat Leahy, Joe Lee, June Levine, Gerry Lyons, Sandra McAvoy, Eileen McDevitt, Ivar McGrath, James McGuire, Ciaran Mac Murchaidh, Yvonne Marshall, Peter Mooney, Eve Morrison, Paul Murphy, William Murphy, Mairin Nic Eoin, Ronan O'Brien, Nuala O'Connor, Theresa O'Farrell, Eunan O'Halpin, Mary Pluck, Fiona Poole, Antoinette Prout, Heather Randall, Jennifer Redmond, Noemi Rigney, Susanna Riordan, Declan Roe, John Rouse, Louise Ryan, Peter Straus, Mary Shine Thompson, Tony and Catherine Sweeney, Michelle Thomas, Colm Toibin, Pauric Travers, Martin Walsh, Tonie Walsh, David Whelan.

Once again, Peter Carson and his colleagues at Profile Books, Penny Daniel, Andrew Franklin and Ruth Killick, deserve my gratitude for their patience, skill and help. I am very fortunate to have had a very efficient copy editor, Sally Holloway, and I am deeply grateful for her precision and insight.

This is another book that could not have been written without the love, support, guidance, scepticism and generosity of Sheila Maher, the most important person in my life and a compassionate, broad-minded, intelligent, powerful, brave and invigorating force of nature. My debt to you is immeasurable. Our three daughters, Enya, Ríona and Saorla, have changed everything and brought mayhem and ecstasy to our lives. We wouldn't have it any other way. This book is dedicated to them, and the coming times.

INTRODUCTION

This book was researched and written during a time when it appeared that there was an unprecedented amount of sexual indulgence in Ireland. By the beginning of the twenty-first century Ireland seemed to be in the throes of a delayed sexual revolution, as a country long accustomed to a strict policing of sexual morality had carnally come of age. In conjunction with this, it became commonplace to satirise the values of earlier decades that had seemingly inhibited and repressed the libido of the Irish. A series of television programmes transmitted on RTÉ, Ireland's national broadcaster, in the summer of 2008, *Sex and Sensibility*, suggested that by the 1990s Ireland had 'finally joined the carnal mainstream'. This conclusion was reached after a backward glance, accompanied by an incredulous tone, at many of the debates and controversies associated with sexual activity in general, and contraception in particular, in previous decades.[1]

Such programmes tend to contrive a neat historical symmetry – in this case, the emergence from the sexual dark ages towards liberation – and though there is some truth in such a thesis, it does scant justice to the complexity of Irish sexual history. Likewise, if the infamous comment of Fine Gael politician Oliver J. Flanagan, who announced on an Irish television programme in the early 1960s that 'there was no sex in Ireland before television',[2] were true, this would be a much shorter book than it is, given that Irish television broadcasts only commenced on New Year's Eve, 1961.

Sometimes, there appears to be an assumption that we know a lot more about our sexual history than we actually do. During an interview in 2003 about the life and career of John Charles McQuaid, the Catholic Archbishop of Dublin from 1940 to 1972, and the most powerful prelate of his generation, historian and Dominican nun Margaret MacCurtain suggested it was an exaggeration to see an obsession with sex as McQuaid's major preoccupation. She added, 'I think the history of the repression of sex in Ireland in the 1940s and 1950s has yet to be written about.'[3]

How does the historian set about researching that history and themes associated with sexuality, such as contraception, sexual abuse and crime, abortion, infanticide, illegitimacy, censorship, prostitution and homosexuality, these being the themes that dominate this book? At the outset, it is important to acknowledge that the sexual history of Ireland is just as complicated and multilayered as the sexual history of many other countries. Perhaps the real challenge is to identify the degree to which there are aspects of the Irish sexual experience that were unique. Does sexuality really have national characteristics? Or, as historian Anthony Copley asks in his study of France's sexual history, is there such a thing as 'national sexual morality'?[4]

Common sense, he suggests, permits the historian to use the convenient shorthand of there being 'a distinctly French contribution to the debate on sexual morality'. This book also takes that liberty and examines the distinctly Irish contribution, while acknowledging that such a contribution needs to be framed in a broader international context and that the sexual is always about the individual as well as social constructions, discourses and struggles for power that are part of society's quest for control over the individual.[5]

Michel Foucault, the French philosopher, sociologist and historian of sexuality, saw the role of the intellectual as 'laying bare the mechanisms of such power' in order to discover the role played by guilt and the means by which sexual conduct became 'an object of moral solicitude'.[6] Ireland's sexual history must also be placed in the context of European nationalism and the quest for 'respectable' sexuality; part of an international struggle to cope with the perceived evils of modernity, increased industrialisation, political upheaval and the construction of middle-class norms of the body and of sexual behaviour.[7] Irish sociologist Tom Inglis, who has published extensively on aspects of Irish sexuality, has suggested that Foucault's theories about sex being 'the most subtle, most penetrative form of discipline and control' have a limited application to Ireland. He has acknowledged that there is much that Foucault wrote about sexuality that is relevant to Ireland, including a discourse of sexuality centred on the policing of bodies in marriage, family and property relations, the extent to which sex becomes an issue between the state and the individual, and a public issue 'articulated within a whole web of discourses'. But in Ireland, according to Inglis, 'alternative or resistant discourses were relatively absent' and 'transgressions were limited'. In Ireland, the deployment of sexuality remained, until the end of the twentieth century, within what Foucault terms the 'thematic of sin'.[8] Inglis further suggests that when Foucault writes of sex being 'taken charge of, tracked down as it were, by a discourse that aimed to allow it no obscurity, no respite', this process cannot be applied to Ireland to the same extent as elsewhere because there was not 'the same quantity of discourses concerned with sex' which Foucault argues was characteristic of the West, and that he failed to map out the relationship between the religious and sexual spheres of a country's social life.[9]

The archival material on which this book is based suggests that Inglis exaggerates Irish exceptionalism in this regard. While acknowledging the influence of Catholicism and the 'thematic of sin', this book uncovers numerous discourses that were independent of, or in opposition to, the Church, and shows that the state in its reports was not always just framing its observations or comments in the context of religious sensibilities. Issues such as the appropriateness of state intervention, civil rights, public health and living conditions also played their part. Neither was there a shortage of transgressions, both illegal behaviours – sexual crime and abuse – and legal but perceived as socially trangressive, such as unmarried motherhood.

Inglis has also maintained that 'the absence of physical affection, an obsession with sex and an emphasis on self-denial have been central to what makes the Irish different.' The notion of sex being the greatest sin was 'inculcated deeper and lasted longer in the bodies and souls of the Irish than among the rest of the West'.[10] The Irish society Inglis grew up in in the 1950s was, he insists, 'a society of guilt, secrecy, darkness and oppression [in which] the body was a source of awkwardness, guilt, shame and embarrassment' and where individual difference and initiative were strangled.[11] But there were also dissent, different opinions, double standards and a more complex sexual identity and practice than Inglis allows for. None the less, Inglis has raised interesting questions and challenges for historians and sociologists, particularly with his suggestion that 'what is missing in a Foucauldian analysis is an understanding of the Irish sensibility about sex; the particular way the "game of sexuality" was played in Ireland'.[12]

That Irish 'sensibility' was frequently commented on throughout the

twentieth century. It was common during the earlier decades of Irish independence to assert, as General Eoin O'Duffy, the commissioner of the Irish
police force, the Garda Síochana, did in 1930, that in other countries 'moral
standards are much lower'. But at the same time, there were numerous commissions, inquiries and private reflections that suggested Irish sexual morality was by no means as pure as was imagined – O'Duffy going as far as to
suggest (in contradiction of his first assertion) that public indecency was
'more prevalent here than in Britain'.[13] The report of the Carrigan Committee, which examined the laws relating to sexual offences and juvenile prostitution in 1930, was unequivocal in its assertion of moral decline in the early
years of the Irish Free State:

> The testimony of all witnesses, clerical, lay, and official, is striking in its
> unanimity that degeneration in the standard of social conduct has taken
> place in recent years. It is attributed primarily to the loss of parental
> control and responsibility during a period of general upheaval, which
> have not been recovered since the revival of settled conditions. This is
> due largely to the introduction of new phases of popular amusement,
> which, being carried on in the Saorstát [Free State] in the absence of
> supervision, and of the restrictions found necessary and enforced by law
> in other countries, are the occasions of many abuses baneful in their effect
> upon the community generally and are the cause of the ruin of hundreds
> of young girls, of whom many are found in the streets of London, Liv-
> erpool and other cities and towns in England ... gross offences are rife
> throughout the country of a nature from which it could formerly claim
> a degree of immunity that may perhaps have lulled into a state of false
> security. Frank recognition of this fact will, we believe, create a state
> of healthy public opinion helpful to the government purging the State
> from these evils. In seeking remedies for the disease, it appears to us from
> the suddenness with which it has manifest itself, to be due to indigenous
> conditions, and we think the cure is to be found by the application of
> home remedies.[14]

As is apparent from these assertions, it was assumed that in terms of sexual
morality Ireland was different to other countries. There was a delusion Ireland was immune from certain sexual problems; they were deemed to be
'foreign vices', usually associated with England. Marjorie Howes has asserted
that 'since independence sexuality has been an important if somewhat

confusing marker of Irish national difference'.[15] It was also often highly ambivalent and paradoxical. In 1941 in *The Bell* magazine, a contributor on the subject of censorship suggested that 'the average Irish mind has not, and perhaps never had, a properly balanced outlook on sex. Either it runs away from sex or it runs after it; it never seems able to stand and look at it objectively. Will it ever learn?'[16] The following year, in the same magazine, an unemployed man sharing a cigarette in a Dublin tenement struggled to get his companion to open up: 'Irish people do not talk about their private affairs; they do not express their feelings; they usually talk of something beside the point.' And yet, at the very same time, on the street below, two men were walking together arm in arm, 'seeking some darker place'.[17] In relation to another dominant theme in this book – child abuse – Angela Bourke has made the point that 'the Bishops had apparently been so exquisitely trained to see things from a particular, special Irish angle, that they could no longer recognise and react as human beings to what was staring them in the face'.[18]

The many illustrations of moral panic uncovered in this book are by no means unique to Ireland. Other European countries and the United States went through similar panics at various times in the nineteenth and twentieth centuries. None the less, it was often asserted that the solutions applied to other countries were not relevant to Ireland, particularly in light of its religious composition; by the middle of the twentieth century, just over 94 per cent of the population was Catholic. In a state that became quite confessional, public condemnation seemed to be more pronounced than elsewhere, and sexual suspicion and class resentment made for a potent mix, summed up by the view of a priest in Offaly, who wrote to the Minister for Justice in 1932. Irish people, he suggested, 'say not what they think, but what they feel they ought to think, if they are to be as good as their neighbours. Then there is in all of us the propensity to lament in public for other people's sins.'[19] But it is also the case that some dismissed the alarmist and grave tone of the reports of moral decline, and did little to implement proposals for improvement when they were suggested.

A history of sexuality raises questions not just of religion and morality but also about public health, the attitude of the medical profession to reproduction, the operation of the criminal law system, the application of legislation, the age of consent, demographics, living standards and conditions, education, the role of the family and patriotism, and ultimately the uses and abuses of power. This book thus explores a wide variety of issues that shaped and regulated Irish sexual life, and also examines whether or not the approach to these issues was different in Northern Ireland than in the twenty-six counties that became the Republic in 1949.

Continued condemnation of sexual excess or deviance suggests there was a significant gulf between the rhetoric of Irish chastity and the reality. In 1953, Father Tom Fitzgerald, a native of Tipperary who was working as a prison chaplain in the East End of London, was quoted in an English newspaper expressing scepticism that the Irish were any more chaste than their English counterparts. An Irish woman was restrained at home, he suggested, 'only by outward convention, not by anything deep within herself'.[20] Despite this, there was a continued articulation of the myth that 'anything which tends to keep the Irish together reduces the risk of moral lapse',[21] revealing a striking double standard; the belief that there were no such lapses at home in Ireland. In truth, the Irish solution was to hide and deny those who had 'lapsed'.

A history of sexuality also has to navigate the theme of Church–state relations, and in this regard the personal archive of John Charles McQuaid, used extensively in this book, is highly revealing. There is little doubt that there were many Irish politicians during the twentieth century who saw themselves as Catholics first and legislators second, and that this influenced their stance on issues of sexual morality. Research into twentieth-century Irish history in the National Archives reveals many examples of the Church being consulted on impending legislation relating to such areas. Indeed, given what is now known about sexual abuse by clerics, it is ironic that the Church was continually being looked to for guidance on legislation that was supposed to protect Irish citizens from sexual immorality.

But the Hierarchy was not always strident or, on the surface, demanding. What is most striking is the extent to which politicians continually asked for guidance. When a government committee investigated and compiled a report on the incidence of venereal disease in the Free State in 1927, a meeting was arranged between a government representative and Archbishop Byrne of Dublin, who was 'hesitant in giving an opinion either for or against publication' of the VD report but, after pressure from the government representative, 'made it clear he rather favoured postponement of publication'. The government acquiesced.[22] In 1932, Minister for Justice James Geoghegan met the Bishops to discuss changes in the law relating to the age of consent and prostitution and informed them he wanted a bill 'which would bring the law into accord with the best Catholic practice and teaching on these subjects'. Bishop Daniel Keane, secretary to the Hierarchy, duly asked for any heads of a bill to be 'communicated' to him.[23]

But the portrayal of the state as consistently demonstrating a cowering deference is a simplification of the complex distribution of power in Ireland. There is a danger in isolating individual letters and brandishing them as evidence that twentieth-century Ireland was a Catholic theocracy in all but name. Politicians frequently consulted members of *all* churches when legislating for so-called moral issues. It is also the case that the label 'Church–state clash' is often misleading. Those with a determination to oppose or impose change were frequently lay groups who brought the Church on board, as happened with the Irish Medical Association during the 'mother and child' controversy in 1951 and with the Catholic lay lobbyists who pressed for a pro-life amendment to the constitution in 1983. In both cases, powerful but unrepresentative lay organisations sought to highlight the supposed danger to Catholic morals if certain proposals were either not adopted or accepted.

There was also scepticism on the part of some politicians and civil servants throughout the century as to the extent to which the state could, or should, be involved in policing sexual morality. Stephen Roche, for example, the Secretary of the Department of Justice in the 1930s, wrote, 'Personally, my habit of thought is to be rather sceptical as to the results of state intervention in these matters.'[24] Fifty years after Irish independence, some were looking for solutions that involved neither side losing face, or as Patrick Cogan, a former TD, told the Taoiseach Jack Lynch in 1971, two things 'have got to be avoided ... 1. The Catholic Church must not appear to overrule the state. 2. The Catholic Church must not appear to be defeated.'[25] This advice was offered during a period of intense public and private debate about contraception but it was also relevant to other issues, including abortion.

The perspective of Church leaders and legislators only tells part of the story, and this book is filled with the voices of victims and perpetrators of sexual abuse, violence and assault. It makes extensive use of the Circuit Court archive in particular, and the archive of its predecessor before 1922, the Quarter Sessions Court. The recounting of experiences as revealed in the depositions and witness statements prepared for court cases is essential in order to get some sense of how sexual crime impacted on individuals and communities, the language used to express what was experienced, the vulnerability of the victims and a sense of what went on behind closed doors. These also underline the extent to which social and sexual experiences were gendered. When these crimes were publicised it was invariably girls and women rather than boys and men who were seen as sexual deviants. In 1936, for example, the *Cork Examiner* reported that a judge referred to two teenage girls being used for sex in the backstreets of Cork city as 'two little girls who were a positive danger to the people of Cork'.[26] Likewise, though a woman who was raped and impregnated could insist that the male defendant was 'responsible for me going to have a baby', juries often did not see it that way.[27]

The court records and proceedings reveal many other things: the underdevelopment of psychology in Ireland, which continued to be associated with institutional treatment rather than psychotherapy or other forms of treatment;[28] and the fact that there was little audience for sexologist Sigmund Freud, his work on the frequency of sexual abuse in childhood and how damaging the psychological consequences can be. To cope, many had to 'freeze the traumatic experiences and then dissociate' and 'because they had spent a lifetime building up defences to keep these experiences at bay, they were only too ready to disavow them if they were met with scepticism or ridicule'.[29] The court records also reveal a constant vulnerability of children to sexual assaults, the role of alcohol in the attacks and the extent to which living conditions facilitated sexual abuse – in 1926, 78,934 people – that is, nearly a quarter of the total population of Dublin city – were housed in one-roomed tenements.[30]

There was also a lack consistency in sentencing and a harsher attitude displayed in relation to assaults on young boys than assaults on young girls. There was an abundance of cases not proceeded with, evidence of the audacity of some abusers, the resilience and suffering of their victims, the targeting of domestic servants, the secret gay geography of Dublin city, and the extent to which gay men were targeted not just for sexual assaults on minors but also for consensual adult sex. There was also a multitude of guilty verdicts 'with a strong recommendation to mercy', suggesting those sitting in judgment on sexual crimes were not devoid of charity.

Reading these court records also places the historical researcher in a somewhat delicate position, summed up well by historian Sandra McAvoy: one becomes conscious of the extent to which one is 'a privileged eavesdropper on statements sometimes made in periods of extreme stress – recounting moments of extraordinary intimacy. This is a problem that arises with varying degrees of intensity depending on the category of material involved.'[31]

While it is true that there was little open discussion before the 1970s about sexual crime, it is not true that there was no awareness of it; parents, doctors, judges, juries and charity workers were aware. But it is likely parents and police were ignorant of the extent of the emotional and psychological trauma it caused, and failed to grasp that an assault of a very young child was different to that of an older girl or adult woman. There was little will to confront these issues, a reluctance neatly summed up by the writer Francis Hackett, who spent a decade living in Ireland: 'about the problems of sex they pretend to be doves when they are in fact ostriches'.[32] He made this assertion in an article for an American publication in 1945; Irish writer Frank O'Connor chose to do likewise four years later, when he referred to infanticide in Ireland as 'appallingly common', for which he drew opprobrium and accusations of treachery.[33]

An over reliance on sources relating to sexual crime also presents the historian with a dilemma. Does the history of sex in Ireland have to be a history of criminal sexual activity? Tom Inglis suggests that 'if we go back into the archives to find who wrote what about pleasure we can find numerous diatribes about the evils of sex and drink, but very few about its pleasures'.[34] Paul Ferris, the historian of sex in twentieth-century Britain, has pointed out that 'the history of sex is written from the point of view of what went wrong, not of how much people enjoyed it ... it is the suffering that is spelt out.'[35]

In the absence of accounts of the joys of sex, this remains a problem, but this book seeks to frame the discussion of sex in as broad a context as possible and includes memoirs, literature, magazine articles, private diaries, the archives of voluntary organisations, moments of levity and reminders that the history of sex cannot be divorced from the history of other dominant themes in post-Famine Irish history – land, religion and identity, in particular.

There were also battles won in the quest for sexual liberation and the struggle to force a confrontation of truths long denied and buried, and ultimately successful challenges to 'the ignorance and prejudice of professed Christians' when it came to understanding the plight of sexual minorities.[36] The donation of the Irish Queer Archive to the National Library of Ireland has allowed the story of the Irish gay rights movement to be fully documented for the first time from primary sources. Its struggle was successful to the point where Ireland's best-known gay rights activist, David Norris, could confidently assert in 1994 that 'the vast majority of Irish people don't want to be interfering in other people's sex lives.'[37] From the early 1970s, the Irish women's movement also successfully began the process by which sexual violence came to be seen as a social problem, though the backlash against women's rights in the 1980s was an indication that these gains could be halted, interrupted and resented. This book also assesses the extent to which a sexual liberalism based on individual rights experienced elsewhere in the West in the 1960s and 1970s was delayed in coming to Ireland.

In dissecting the debates about contraception and abortion, the decriminalisation of homosexuality, the impact of clerical abuse scandals and the revelations of a bishop fathering a child, it is worth considering how 'all these, whether progressive social changes or disturbing revelations, have given an urgency to the issues of gender and sexuality and have been accompanied by a growing intellectual awareness of the extent to which social experience, past and present, is gendered'.[38]

This book is also a chronicle of a vanished era, when the language associated with sex was overwhelmingly negative and judgemental; a time when condemnations and warnings abounded and there were deemed to be sexual traps and temptations around every corner. In Brian Moore's novel *Fergus* (1971), Father Kinneally, who taught the main protagonist Fergus English when he was a student, is asked by Fergus many years later if it was true that he had once cut all the corset and brassière advertisements out of magazines on the school dentist's waiting-room table: 'There were young boys looking at those suggestive drawings,' Father Kinneally said. 'I thought it wise. Remember, an occasion of sin is an occasion of sin, even if it is not intended to be.'[39]

By the beginning of the twenty-first century, it seemed that 'the fear of being too sexual has been replaced with a fear of not being sexual enough'.[40] In detailing the forces that shaped and regulated sexual life and the ways in which sexuality was explained and experienced in the twentieth century, this book tells the story of that evolution in Irish attitudes and practices.

1845–1922

'All of us know that Irish women are the most virtuous in the world'

Writing to the playwright John Millington Synge on 14 January 1907, Lady Gregory, one of the directors of the Abbey Theatre in Dublin, announced starkly: 'I feel we are beginning the fight of our lives ... we must make no mistakes.'[1] At the time, rehearsals were being held for the Abbey's production of Synge's new play, *The Playboy of the Western World*. The first performance was on 26 January 1907, and so began one of the most controversial episodes in Irish theatre history. By the third act, the audience was in uproar. For the second night's performance, a section of the audience protested so loudly that the play was inaudible. The following night, the police were summoned to the theatre and arrests were made. Newspapers called for the play to be withdrawn and devoted much attention to the disturbances.

On the surface, this seemed to be a story of a pious nationalist audience reacting spontaneously and angrily to a play that depicted violence, the celebration of patricide and sexual frankness, most notably in the line spoken by the Playboy, Christy Mahon, that he would have no other woman but Pegeen Mike, even if offered 'a drift of Mayo girls standing in their shifts. [underwear].'[2] 'Blasphemy' and 'blackguardism' were among the more polite terms used by male playgoers 'who agreed that it was fortunate they had left their wives at home'. It was probably Synge's mocking of heroism that upset the male audience; Christy Mahon seems an unlikely hero – more of a comic buffoon, and a vain liar with it – but the fact that he is 'tokenised as a sex object and a tomboy of the village girls' would indicate a high level of sexual depriva-tion of the Mayo women that they could find such a flawed man a hero.[3] The literary theorist Declan Kiberd has pointed out that by the time the play trav-elled to the west of Ireland, 'the audiences were bored rather than annoyed, complaining that you could see such carry on any day in any shebeen.'[4]

The disturbances and protests are usually referred to as 'The Playboy Riots', which is something of an exaggeration. What was witnessed was mostly verbal disapproval, some drunkenness and the odd scuffle, mostly outside the theatre; there was no furniture broken and no physical attacks on the cast. But the police were called to the second and third performances to remove protestors and some of them were subsequently fined. One his-torian of the Irish theatre, Chris Morash, told the Synge Summer School in 1999, 'Throughout the affair it is possible to trace a thread of drunken hilar-ity weaving its way through the more serious strands.'

The 'more serious strands' were linked to Synge's genius for translating dialect and depicting the dignity and wildness of the west of Ireland. He did this in a way that was unparalleled, and informed by direct experience. As far as his defenders were concerned he was bravely holding a mirror to Ire-land in all its contradictions; he had spent several summers immersed in the west of Ireland, and observed at close hand the kind of characters he wrote about. In contrast, some scholars have disputed the notion that the language he used functions in a subversive way, and point out that the play was not aimed at 'the oppressed', but at a middle-class audience; that the presenta-tion of the rural Gael as some sort of 'exotic throwback' was arrogant and romanticised the marginalisation of such communities and their language.[5]

Synge was unapologetic and, like all artists, recognised that a hostile response is infinitely preferable to indifference. As he wrote to his lover, the actress Molly Allgood, 'Now we'll be talked about. We're an event in the history of the Irish stage.'[6]

Although the poet W. B. Yeats, Lady Gregory and Synge may have formed an at times uneasy alliance (despite her public defence of Synge, Lady Gregory disliked him and the play), it was an alliance that was of huge benefit to Irish cultural life, highlighting the importance of facing difficult questions about language, violence, identity and sexuality. On the surface, it was that last issue – sexuality – that dominated a lot of the reaction. As Synge put it himself, 'I had restored sex to the stage and the people were so surprised they saw sex only.'[7]

An earlier play of Synge's, *The Shadow of the Glen* (1903), in which a woman abandons a loveless marriage with an older man in order to elope with a tramp (she chooses the tramp with the line, 'You've a fine bit of talk stranger and it's with yourself I will go'), led to the oft-quoted response of Arthur Griffith, founder of the fledgling Sinn Féin movement: 'all of us know that Irish women are the most virtuous in the world', while the *Freeman's Journal* castigated *The Playboy* as 'unmitigated protracted libel'.[8]

This is a view that is inconsistent with Synge's own contention in the preface to *The Playboy* that 'anyone who has lived in real intimacy with the Irish peasantry will know that the wildest sayings and ideas in the play are tame indeed'. As he asserted in relation to another of his plays, *The Well of the Saints*, produced by the Abbey in 1905, 'what I write of country life I know to be true and I most emphatically will not change a syllable because A, B or C may think they know better than I do'.[9]

These are again references to the time Synge had spent in the west of Ireland observing remote poor communities full of rich language and a curious mixture of wildness and dignity, passion and restraint. But Kiberd's comments about the casualness of the response of the west of Ireland audiences to *The Playboy*, and Synge's own adamant defence of his portrayal of that society, do not tell the whole story about the communities' self awareness of the force of human behaviour and sexuality.

When he published his account of the Aran islands in the same year that *The Playboy* was first performed, Synge was not quite as direct about sexual frankness; instead, he made it clear that the community he had observed was full of sexual tension and coyness, interrupted by occasional frankness, such as from the girl he encountered who 'told me with seriousness, as if speaking of a thing that surprised herself, and should surprise me, that she was very fond of the boys'.[10] Another character, 'Old Mourteen', wandered off into tedious matters of theology, repeating long prayers and sermons in Irish he had heard from priests, but when they came to a slate house and Synge asked him who was living in it, his tone and demeanour changed:

'A kind of schoolmistress', he said; then his old face puckered with a gleam of pagan malice.

'Ah, master', he said. 'Wouldn't it be fine to be in there, and to be kissing her.'[11]

Synge noticed many other things on the islands: medleys of rude puns and jokes 'that meant more than they said', and an obsession with marriage or the lack of it. 'The women were over excited and when I tried to talk to them they crowded round me and began jeering and shrieking at me because I'm not married.' He concluded in relation to the men:

> the greatest merit they see in a woman is that she should be fruitful and bring them many children. As no money can be earned by children on the island this one attitude shows the immense difference between these people and the people of Paris [another place where Synge had spent some time]. The direct sexual instincts are not weak on the island, but they are so subordinated to the instincts of the family that they rarely lead to irregularity. The life here is still at an almost patriarchal stage, and the people are nearly as far from the romantic moods of love as they are from the impulsive life of the savage.[12]

Despite Synge's defiance in the face of adverse reaction to his plays, his personal view of women's assertiveness seems to have been conservative. Máirtín O'Direáin, a native of the Aran islands and one of the leading poets working in the Irish language in the twentieth century, remarked that Synge's letters to his fiancée Molly Allgood reveal a patronising attitude: 'He is easily shocked if women do not conform to a traditional mode of behaviour, yet his heroines transcend such limitations.'[13]

Another observer of island life with direct experience of those communities was Tomás O'Criomhthainn, whose book *An tOileánach* (*The Islander*) based on his experiences on the Blasket islands, off the coast of Kerry, was published in 1929. His work also suggests that in the unit of the family the parents came first and were inviolate, and that the sexual instinct was subordinated to the family, though it was seen as a healthy instinct. O'Criomhthainn wrote of dancing at night and uninhibited encounters with girls on the mountain, but he also boasted that sexual irregularity had never occurred on the mountain. He was, however, quiet about what went on behind closed doors, and in the institution of marriage. He turned away from the girl of his heart ('the most lovely girl on blessed earth at that time') and watched as a marriage with another girl was arranged, in John McGahern's words, 'as if he were observing a separate person, a person in a drama. What interests him most is the pull and tug of the different family factions as they battle to decide which girl will get him ... once it was arranged [in 1878] we hear no more about the marriage.'[14]

'Keeping the lovely Irish girl lovely, for many decades to come'

Synge's and O'Criomhthainn's observations were insightful and honest in so far as their eyes could see, and they touched on some of the themes, ambiguities, contradictions and priorities associated with sexual identity and sexual secrecy in the post-Famine period in Ireland. But the notion that sexual instincts were entirely subordinated to the instincts of the family and that they rarely led to irregularity is far from a true picture of Irish sexuality in the late nineteenth and early twentieth centuries. Arthur Griffith's assertions about the uniqueness of Irish female virtue were, of course, facile, a reflection of another theme of the post-Famine period – the idealisation of the chaste woman whose ambitions lay solely in the direction of homemaking and marriage.

The piety of Griffith and others is also a reminder that any attempt to analyse the themes of sex and sexuality during this period must involve the critical interrogation of rhetoric that, if not downright dishonest, was delusional, leaving the historian of Irish sexuality with the task of comparing public rhetoric with private reality, in so far as the sources available allow the historian to reach and analyse that private reality. Griffith's indignant rhetoric, as pointed out by the novelist Anne Enright, proved remarkably durable: 'we did a mean job of keeping the lovely Irish girl lovely, for many decades to come'.[15] But the truth was that, in private, much was being done to undermine the 'virtue' of Irish women and, indeed, men, and hypocrisy abounded. Yeats must have enjoyed telling the tale of Synge informing him about the *Playboy* protestors: 'A young doctor has just told me that he can hardly keep himself from jumping on to a seat and pointing out in that howling mob those whom he is treating for venereal disease.'[16]

There was a general decline in interpersonal violence in the early twentieth century, but sexual violence was increasing. As pointed out by the historian Mark Finnane, 'various legal categories of assault also show a pronounced decline. These tendencies were not unique to Ireland, although the longer-term trend was towards a level of violence very low by international standards. Yet there was at least one exception: in prosecutions for rape and sexual assault.'[17]

Many 'irregular' sexual practices occurred within families, and many people did not subordinate their sexual 'instincts' to the 'instincts' of the family. These were often hidden, and one of the few places where the historian can find them is in the surviving records of the court cases that heard evidence of sexual crime. This, of course, only gives part of the picture, as it is likely the majority of sexual crimes were unreported, but it does provide a place to start when trying to unravel the complicated and often criminal aspects of sexual power in Ireland.

At the height of the *Playboy* controversy, it had been commented in the *Irish Times* that, 'It is as if we looked into a mirror for the first time and found ourselves hideous. We fear to face the thing. We shrink at the word for it. We scream.'[18] This was not necessarily a reference to sex and sexuality, but more a comment on the combined ingredients that made up Synge's play, but it could just as well have been a comment on the attitude to sexual 'irregularities'. The reaction to what Synge had done highlights the tendency to deny, but also the determination to hide issues of sexuality and keep them as private as possible. One woman wrote to the *Freeman's Journal* in shocked indignation at the use of the word 'shift', signing herself 'a western girl', and insisting that a woman would not say this 'even to herself'.[19] But whatever the infrequency with which matters sexual were discussed in public, or depicted through drama, there was little room for censorship in the depositions and witness statements that were prepared for court cases, and in the courts' archival records the historian is able to find a degree of frankness unavailable elsewhere.

Hiding evidence of sexuality or sexual activity was the norm in Ireland, as elsewhere, in the early twentieth century. This was particularly true in relation to women, particularly 'fallen women' – prostitutes and unmarried mothers – some of whom ended up in the Magdalen asylums. Established in the eighteenth century, these institutions housed 'penitents' (usually prostitutes) who were urged to stay until their characters were reformed. More restrictive and difficult to leave by the end of the nineteenth century, by the twentieth century they had largely become homes for unmarried mothers. It was estimated there were forty-five 'selected fallen women' at the Magdalen asylum in New Ross in Wexford in 1901, for example, while in the same year at a Magdalen home in Cork there were 196 'vagrant' girls. The home was drawing from the state 'the substantial sum of £3,157 per year',[20] an indication of another enduring theme in relation to perceived sexual transgression – the collusion of state, society and religious orders in seeking to remove from public circulation perceived threats to a conservative moral order. Women who were sexually active could be conveniently hidden – and many of them were – while the men who engaged in sex with them could generally carry on regardless. Mary Costello, a journalist who wrote a series of articles on Dublin's penitentiaries for *The Lady of the House*, a popular middle-class women's magazine, referred in 1897 to [Irish] women with 'pleasure-craving temperaments', as well as to the fact that 'there is no branch of state service for which religious communities are more especially fitted, and in which they succeed more notably, than in the rescue of fallen women'.[21]

There was, however, little attention focused on the men who impregnated the unmarried women; there were no 'fallen men' in Ireland. The exception was when men were successfully prosecuted for sexual crimes against women. Another reason the courts records are so valuable is that the men were legally obliged to respond to the allegations made against them, meaning it is possible to gain some insight into how they viewed their own actions. But any such insights, and any further elaboration on Irish sexuality generally, need to be framed in the broader context of Irish celibacy, marriage, fertility and economic and social patterns and customs in the late nineteenth century.

'Irish society enjoys no mean place in the history of sexuality'

The Famine of the 1840s, resulting in the death of over 1 million people and the emigration of over 2 million in the decade 1846–55, was an event that impacted significantly on Irish sexual behaviour and on marriage and fertility. It resulted in a rise in the age at marriage, a low marriage rate and declining birth rate, though fertility remained high, declining after 1881, as it did in most other European countries. But the increase in marriage age and celibacy rates 'were more significant demographically', and Irish fertility levels after the turn of the twentieth century remained high by contemporary European standards. The marriage rate per 1,000 of the population stood at 5.10 in the period 1864–70, dropping to 4.02 for the period 1881–90,[22] while those born between 1896 and 1910 'displayed the greatest reluctance to marry of any Irish generation'.[23]

According to the census of 1911, Irish women married for 20–24 years duration gave birth to an average of 5.87 live children. In Dublin city and suburbs, the figure was 5.60. Class differences were apparent in terms of the fertility of professional, semi-skilled and labouring couples, and the research of Cormac O'Gráda has established that by 1911 many Irish couples, even in rural areas, were practising some form of family planning, with 'the leaders in family limitation' larger farmers, those in non-agricultural occupations,

and Protestants. In the Pembroke township in south Dublin city, professional couples had the smallest families: 3.7 children for those married
20–29 years, compared with 9.47 for semi-skilled and 7.64 for labouring
couples.[24] Surviving letters from Ireland received by British family planning
campaigner Marie Stopes in the second decade of the twentieth century
indicate a middle-class desire for information on contraception (to be sent
to them secretly), as well as ignorance about sexual problems.[25]

Liam Kennedy has suggested that 'Irish society enjoys no mean place
in the history of sexuality' because, while features of the Irish demographic
trend can be found elsewhere, the way in which they combined in Ireland
was unique.[26] Internationally, there was much alarm expressed in the nineteenth century about the dangers of over-population (in contrast to the eighteenth century, when population growth was often seen as a precondition of
economic growth). There were many advocates of the Malthusian doctrine
of 'moral restraint', which became an acceptable expression of 'early Victorian anxiety about sexuality and reproduction'. The philosopher and political
economist John Stuart Mill had preached in 1845 about how tragic it was
that 'the lower orders produced such a devastating torrent of babies'.[27] The
rediscovery of Malthus, a growing awareness of contraception techniques
and an expectation of higher living standards prompted a worldwide movement advocating 'prudent' family planning and 'enlightened parenthood' in
the late nineteenth and early twentieth centuries, which also involved international contacts and conferences. Societies filled with 'sexual reformers'
emerged in Germany (1889), France (1896), Spain (1904) and Italy (1913),
among other countries. These were by no means mass movements; indeed,
they faced public hostility and political repression and there was also a certain backlash as middle-class opponents rallied to reassert 'the sexual status
quo and Victorian social values'. There was, however, an alarm over decreasing birth rates, while in countries like Italy a resurgence of nationalism and
colonialism became linked to the fertility debate and perceptions of national
grandeur and decline, and the term 'race suicide' was increasingly employed
in Europe and the United States.[28]

In some respects, Ireland remained aloof from such debate and pressures, partly because of its colonial status, but more importantly because of
the Famine – a reminder that it is necessary to be somewhat cautious about
applying Foucault's theory of sexuality to the Irish situation. As Tom Inglis has argued,[29] when looking at Foucault's ideas, specifically his notion of
the deployment of sexuality, or the sense in which an approach to sexuality

that was originally marked by a scarcity of discourse 'was taken charge of, tracked down as it were, by a discourse that aimed to allow it no obscurity, no respite' and indicative of a new 'political, economic and technical incitement to talk about sex',[30] it is doubtful if they can realistically be applied to Ireland in the post-Famine period.

'Sexually shutting up or shipping out'

Control of sex and sexual relations was central to the creation and maintenance of power and the social order, as recognised by both Freud and Foucault, and, in the Irish context, the attitudes adopted by the new class of farmers (see below) and the desire to control marriage, supported by the Catholic Church, was a reflection of such power.[31] As a result of the Famine, the preoccupation with sexuality, marriage and fertility and population as issues between the state and the individual had come to Ireland later than in other countries. Given the dramatic reduction in population (between 1841, when the population of the thirty-two counties stood at over 8 million, and 1901, the population declined by approximately 50 per cent in the area that is now the Republic and 25 per cent in what is now Northern Ireland), and the late age of marriage, it is understandable that these debates and discourses were not going to carry the same weight in Ireland as elsewhere in the late nineteenth century.

More important in the Irish context was the changing rural class structure, a reluctance to subdivide larger farms, and the land war of the 1870s and 1880s which ultimately led to an almost universal shift to peasant proprietorship in the early twentieth century – all of which were crucial in changing attitudes to marriage. One farm in four disappeared as a result of the Famine, the decline being concentrated in holdings of less than 15 acres. The 'cottier' class – that is, those on the lowest rung of the social ladder – were virtually wiped out. The average size of a farm increased and, in the words of the historian Joe Lee, 'it became increasingly difficult to marry a little above or a little beneath oneself. The range of social choice for bidders in the marriage market narrowed. Farmers' children preferred celibacy to labourers and increasing longevity of parents reinforced the drift towards late marriage.'[32] Inglis describes this more starkly: it was a choice of 'sexually shutting up or shipping out'.[33]

Sons waiting to inherit farms became older than their brides, and many wives inevitably in due course became widows. According to Lee, these women – 'victims of largely loveless matches' – projected their 'frustrated capacity for affection on to their sons', whom they were reluctant to see marry and even more reluctant to hand over their farms to. The integrity of the family was thus 'ruthlessly sacrificed' to economic priorities. It was observed that 'the average Irish peasant ... takes unto himself a mate with as clear a head, as placid a heart and as steady a nerve as if he were buying a cow at Ballinasloe fair'.

Such an approach, argues Lee, was sanctified by a Catholic Church that was 'in any case powerless to challenge the primacy of economic man over the Irish countryside'.[34] In his classic portrait of Irish peasant society, K. H. Connell suggests that 'an apparent aversion to marriage is perhaps the most intriguing trait acquired – or required – in Irish peasant society under the impact of famine and land legislation. The trend towards longer, if not lifelong, celibacy probably set in with the imminence of the famine.' He, too, insists that a wariness of marriage was rooted in a reluctance to divide land, and so was economic in origin.[35] The Famine, it is argued, accentuated the trends of arranged marriages, few illegitimate births and a strict code of sexual behaviour: the 'match' (arranged marriage) became more generally accepted, those without land found it more difficult to get wives, and there was a steady increase in celibacy. David Fitzpatrick notes that 'just before the Famine about one-tenth of Irish 50-year-olds were unmarried, a proportion which increased to one quarter before the First World War.'[36]

But Fitzpatrick disputes the notion that Ireland was uniquely sexually repressed, pointing out that celibacy, postponed marriage and arranged matches 'were all commonplace among European peasant populations' at the time, and that 'in most past societies, the pursuits of love and marriage were strictly separated'. This is also a point underlined by Timothy Guinnane, who stresses that by the late nineteenth century some areas of Portugal, Austria and Germany had celibacy rates comparable to or even higher than Ireland's, and that the Irish 'were not alone in resorting to sexual abstinence and celibacy in order to control fertility'.[37]

But Fitzpatrick's comments about the 'rarity of crimes arising (at least in part) from sexual frustration', though they may apply to the late nineteenth century (he points out that rape peaked at 114 reports in 1844, reaching a nadir of 10 in 1888) do not apply to the twentieth century on the basis of the evidence in the courts files. Nor does the contention that 'the Irish seldom landed their sexual frustrations on each other'.[38] But there is truth in the idea that when emigration was blocked, the Irish marriage system 'became inefficient and markedly repressive' because 'Irish boys and girls lost their essential freedom to choose between alternative sets of constraints in Ireland and the urban world'.[39] In 1907, the marriage rate stood at 4.8 per 1,000, 40 per cent below that of England and Wales, and 35 per cent below Scotland. In June 1907, the *Farmers Journal* concluded that men preferred 'the selfish ease of bachelor life', and, more curiously, that 'women are no longer attractive'. If a woman was married, Father Bernard O'Reilly advised in his book *The Mirror of True Womanhood* (1877) ('a book of instruction for women in the world') that she should display no vanity and should not please 'any eye but that of her husband'.[40]

In any case, statistics concerning marriage and childbirth and reported rates of sexual crime only tell part of the story, as K. H. Connell acknowledged in 1968. Figures

> might of course be deceptive. Irish seasonal labourers, it has been said, fathered more children in Glasgow or Liverpool than in the Rosses or Achill; abortion and infanticide were sometimes practised; priests, parents and public opinion all did their bit to make legitimate births of illegitimate conceptions and pregnant Irish girls, harshly regarded at home, sometimes had their babies in England.[41]

'Those shadowy but potent figures of males who set women on a downward course to vilification'

In certain parts of the country there was an apparent surge in illegitimate births in the post-Famine period, particularly in places that had been devastated by starvation and disease. In Kilrush, County Clare, for example, illegitimate births accounted for one in ten of all births recorded, whereas before the Famine the ratio was 'barely one in a hundred in most years'. Eviction and poverty may have resulted in some women bartering sex for food and shelter, and men may have taken advantage of straitened times to abscond when normally they may have stood by and married their pregnant partners.

It is also possible that Kilrush's status as a port town was a factor, as such towns were sometimes associated with prostitution and illegitimacy. But, as pointed out by Paul Gray and Liam Kennedy, this is only part of the story; the real reason for the high figures was the number of illegitimate children born in the workhouses. An examination of the Catholic baptismal register for Kilrush reveals that almost two out of every three births for the period 1850–75 were to women from the workhouse. The Kilrush workhouse served the whole union, not just the parish of Kilrush, thus 'the apparently inflated levels of illicit sexuality in Kilrush after the Famine arise primarily from a quirk of registration rather than from a radical shift in sexual behaviour on the part of Clare men and women'. This raises questions about the validity of parish registers for information on illegitimacy, 'not just for Ireland but for other societies where the institutionalised provision of welfare might affect the recording of illegitimate births'.[42]

These qualifications are a reminder of the difficulty of drawing conclusions about sexual behaviour based on incomplete records or samples of records. Sean Connolly has suggested that in 1864, the first year official statistics became available, the proportion of illegitimate to total births was 3.8 per cent and in the first seven years of civil registration it remained constant at 3.2 per cent – a very low figure by European standards. The rate in France was between 6 and 7 per cent, in Scotland between 6 and 9 per cent, Germany between 8 and 9 per cent and in England and Wales between 5 and 6 per cent.[43]

One thing was clear in nineteenth-century Ireland, however. 'While unmarried and pregnant women suffered stigmatisation and degradation under both the workhouse system and in the larger society, men appeared largely to have escaped notice or sanction ... if there are few clues as to the unmarried mothers in Kilrush who graced the parish records, albeit briefly, even less is known of those shadowy but potent figures of males who set women on a downward course to vilification, destitution and disgrace.'[44]

But the workhouses did provide a safety net of sorts in the single mother's battle for survival in a hostile moral climate. A Bastardy Act had been introduced in Britain in 1863, which enabled a board of guardians to recover the cost of maintenance of illegitimate children from putative fathers when a child under 14 years was in receipt of relief from the poor rates, but the local authority could not sue for maintenance unless the mother of the child made an affidavit declaring him to be the father. After the creation of the Irish Free State in 1922, these provisions in the 1863 Act were not inherited by Ireland, and 'consequently, no body of law dealing fully with such matters was inherited by the Saorstát'.[45]

'Victorianism is a greatly underestimated influence on sexual attitudes here'

A reluctance to replicate British legislation highlighted the tendency in Ireland to sometimes ignore or avoid issues to do with sexuality, pregnancy and illegitimacy. By the time Irish sexuality was being tentatively explored, written and spoken about in the 1970s, it was common for Irish scholars to look back to the Victorian era to trace the origins of an Irish prudery or repression in relation to matters of the flesh and the degree to which it inhibited writing about sex. Historian John A. Murphy suggested to Rosita Sweetman, who published in 1979 the groundbreaking account of changing attitudes to sex in Ireland, *On Our Backs*, that 'Victorianism is a greatly underestimated influence on sexual attitudes here'.[46] When researching her book, Sweetman found the 'blanket of silence' in relation to sexual issues striking, but historians, sociologists and others have made efforts in the intervening period to try and establish just how important that Victorian culture was, despite the contention of Irish novelist John McGahern in 1995 that 'you almost can't write about sex, like you can't write about happiness, because in a way it's private and it's mechanical'.[47]

Tom Inglis, in surveying the historiography of modern Ireland, makes the point that the history of Irish sexuality remains a secret and hidden area. What has existed to date in the established survey histories of modern Ireland are brief and general references to sexual frustration and a preoccupation with sexual morality, without actually telling us much, if anything 'about the sexual lives and practices of Irish people in the twentieth century ... it is as if the old Catholic Church strategy of not referring directly to sex and sexuality – for fear that it might offend or undermine the innocent – still guides what historians research and write about'.[48] Those comparing the sexual habits of different European countries have suggested that the lack of research into sexual questions in Ireland 'contrasts with the lengthy British tradition of reflecting (though often with moral opprobrium) on facets of national sexual mores'. Complicating such reflections on Ireland are the themes of Ireland's status as a colony of the British Empire, Catholicism and the law and the issue of the extent to which 'one response to British cultural hegemony was to take even further the sexual tenets of high Victorian morality'.[49]

But by the beginning of the twenty-first century, the editors of volume 4 of *The Field Day Anthology of Irish Writing*, dealing with women's writing and traditions, were able to compile a substantial section on women and sexuality, incorporating personal testimony, official reports, literature and confessional modes of address. What seems on first glance to be very much about the 'wrongs of woman' is in fact much more than that and incorporates a large range of experiences: 'There are stories of violence, poverty, coercion, children abused and murdered, women beaten, raped, abandoned, forced into unwanted sexual liaisons, including marriage, traded, enslaved and exploited. There are also narratives of desire and of the affections and examples of transgressive behaviour that defied or subverted the conventions of each period.'[50]

These accounts, which encompass a wide range of sexual behaviour and sexual attitudes, highlight not only how a study of sexuality can be enhanced by the examination of demography and personal experience, but also the extent to which sexuality might have national characteristics. Editor Siobhán Kilfeather concludes that 'writing on Ireland suggests that it does.'[51] This focus on a variety of discourses – also a central feature of the current book – is a reminder of the dangers of generalisations about the 'denial' of and 'silence' about sex in Ireland. Much of the work of Tom Inglis, for example, has been built around a framework that emphasises the endurance of 'practices of chastity, humility, piety and self-denial' born of an oppressive Catholic culture that led to Irish Catholics being 'flat, awkward, embarrassed, shameful, guilty and communicatively incompetent about sex.'[52] Sex, he maintains, was only talked about in the context of 'the natural law of God' and confined to religious discourse.

Inglis is correct in his assertion that in mapping changes in the history of sexuality it is necessary to 'detail local formations and discontinuities' (as acknowledged by Foucault), but he exaggerates the lack of discourses in Ireland, which are traceable through a variety of sources. By responding to his own challenge to scholars – to write a history of Irish sexuality by examining biographies, diaries, letters and literature[53] – and adding other layers, such as state papers, court records and the documents of voluntary organisations, this book ultimately raises doubts about the validity of Inglis's assertions about blanket denial and wholesale absence of a variety of discourses.

'Sex posed a far more severe threat than the landlord to the security and status of the family'

Given the historic ties between Britain and Ireland, and Ireland's status as a British colony until 1922, it is also necessary to consider the impact of British culture and law on Irish sexual morality, particularly in the nineteenth century, as discourses on sexuality evolved. If it is true Victorianism was a paramount influence, how did it manifest itself in terms of attitudes to sexual behaviour? Undoubtedly in the post-Famine period, as Siobhán Kilfeather points out, representations of sexuality became more polarised 'between versions of the authentic Ireland as a realm of purity and versions which insist that the true Irish character is ribald and promiscuous'.[54] Tom Inglis has argued that the sexuality that came to be embodied in Ireland in the nineteenth century was similar to that embodied by the middle classes in Victorian Britain, but what was different 'was how long this Victorian regime lasted and how deeply it seeped into the minds and bodies of the Irish'. There was a policing of pleasure and desires in families, schools and communities[55] and 'classical Victorian moralism spread upwards and downwards from the new bourgeoisie', initially through evangelical religious movements, on to a preoccupation with conservative forms of dress and social habits. Its spread in Ireland 'was slow and uneven in places', and the low marriage rate in Ireland 'led to an enormous cultural contradiction: the home and motherhood were promoted as the natural vocation for women, and yet women were denied access to this role'.

In 1978, historian Joe Lee wrote trenchantly about what this meant in practice:

> It was therefore crucial to maintain the economic dominance of the new order that all thoughts of marriage in Ireland should be banished from the minds of the majority of Irish youth. Temptation must not be placed in their way. Sex, therefore, must be denounced as a satanic snare, in even what had been its most innocent pre-famine manifestations. Sex posed a far more severe threat than the landlord to the security and status of the family. Boys and girls must be kept apart at all costs.[56]

This, and the observations by Inglis, create the impression of a degree of 'moral panic', precisely the phrase used by the pioneering historian of sexuality Jeffrey Weeks, who saw the fashioning of a repressive familial ideology as a species of 'moral panic' and a defence mechanism against change and modernisation; at a time of uncertainty, morality was at a premium.[57]

In reality, as recognised by Anthony Copely, the Victorians were 'divided and contradictory' in their attitudes towards questions of sexual morality, which creates 'sheer difficulties' for historians in generalising about this issue.[58] Inglis has suggested that over the course of the nineteenth century 'external constraints on sexual behaviour slowly became combined with internal self-control',[59] but an examination of neglected Irish court records for the late nineteenth century would suggest that there is a tendency to exaggerate such internal control. In the 1890s, the Crown legal books highlight cases of indecent assault on males, concealment of birth, indecent exposure, sodomy, bestiality and attempted rape. Typical sentences handed down to those convicted were between 4 and 12 months' hard labour for indecent assault, 5–8 months for indecent exposure, up to five years for sodomy, 2–3 months for concealment of birth, and 18 months for the attempted rape of a girl under the age of 13.[60] As with all court cases, these represented only a tiny fraction of actual crimes that occurred.

Not everyone relied on the legal system to deal with transgressors and perceived transgressors; nor were all the accused male. Angela Bourke's fascinating account of the murder of Bridget Cleary in rural Tipperary in 1895 details the fate suffered by a woman who was not conforming to social expectations. Deemed to be 'away with the fairies' and burnt to death on that account, there were rumours that Cleary had a lover, with contemporary newspapers reporting her husband as saying, 'she used to meet an egg-man on the low road'. A dressmaker, who was therefore unusually economically independent, she was sexually attractive, confident and dissatisfied with her marriage, and it is possible her buttocks were burnt as a result of sexual misconduct, though this cannot be proven. While it is unlikely that her murder was deliberate or premeditated, it is likely that in supposedly burning her 'to get her back from the fairies' her killers, including her husband and other members of her family who were convicted and imprisoned, were also settling other scores, her husband well aware that 'a childless marriage was unusual, even shameful' and that, combined with her refusal to conform, increased the resentment towards her.[61]

'Without any material interference with the so-called "liberty of the subject"'

There was also an anxiety in the post-Famine period about prostitution and venereal diseases (VD), concerns not unique to Ireland, but perhaps the guilt and fear of infection with sexually transmitted diseases took on 'a particular inflection in the Irish context from the memory of the Famine'. In addition, newspapers of the nineteenth century were beginning to uncover secrets and unapproved methods of sexual expression: 'The sensational reporting of sex crimes, for example, while sometimes apparently sympathetic to the victims, tends to reinforce the idea that the middle-class home is a woman's only safe haven and that any form of female adventure will be punished. Prostitution and disease become the focus of journalistic and bureaucratic investigation.'[62] One example of this was James Greenwood's account in the *Pall Mall Gazette* in the 1860s of the prostitutes at the Curragh military camp in Kildare, known as the 'Wrens'. Greenwood interviewed some of these women, who were living in squalor, but recorded their observations that even this was preferable to the alternative due to 'the horror the women have of the workhouse'.[63] Many of them lived all year round in the furze bushes, the only groundcover on the plain, and were of concern due to their perceived impact on the health of soldiers, but 'while the resulting venereal diseases would make a soldier unfit for duty, and subject to official censure, the condition of the women was their own problem'. There were some attempts at prosecution for rape and assaults on these prostitutes in the 1860s, but few details are available.[64]

Rescuing and policing prostitutes became a particular preoccupation in the nineteenth century, and statistics would suggest that such activities led to a reduction in their visibility. In 1838 there were 2,410 convictions for solicitation in the Dublin Metropolitan District; in 1863 the number had risen to 2,888, but by 1899 convictions were at a low of 487.[65] Maria Luddy suggests there were in the region of 1,700 prostitutes in Dublin in the 1830s; in 1845 William Logan, a mission worker, was reliably informed that in Cork that year there were 85 regular brothels and 356 'public prostitutes'.[66] Their numbers were bolstered by the presence of British soldiers, and this continued to be relevant well into the twentieth century; in 1901 the Irish census recorded the presence of 21,000 soldiers and officers, nearly 4,000 militia men and yeomanry and over 2,000 members of the Royal Navy and Royal Marines, mostly of British origin. By 1921, the forces of the

Crown in Ireland amounted to 15,000 troops and 17,000 police.[67]

The opening of a Lock hospital for the treatment of syphilis in 1869 resulted in the rehabilitation of many patients. Con Costello points out that the official military view of the problem of prostitution, in particular in the Curragh region, was that it was 'a necessary evil ... if the women, of whom it was estimated in 1865 there were 500 in the locality, were regarded as a nuisance, especially as they invaded the camp plains at night and displayed themselves openly on the plains, it was accepted that if they lived more discretely and away from the camp they would be tolerated'.[68] The passing of Contagious Diseases Acts (CDAs) in the 1860s (the first of three statutes was passed in 1864, suspended in 1883 and repealed in 1886), through which women could be incarcerated against their will, led to the imposition of personal and geographic restrictions on women's freedom, permitted the compulsory inspection of prostitutes for venereal disease in certain military camps in England and Ireland, and reduced the activities of the prostitutes. But they did not disappear and their presence was still being commented on when the Irish army moved into the Curragh barracks in 1922.[69]

From the late nineteenth century there were a number of groups active in campaigning for reform of the laws against prostitution and for raising the age of consent. The only parts of Ireland to which the CDAs applied were the Curragh camp and its immediate neighbourhood, the municipal borough of Cork and the town of Queenstown. The acts were robustly defended by a manual of public health for Ireland edited by physicians to the leading Dublin hospitals and published in 1875. The physicians believed that, owing to formidable results in reducing the incidence of venereal diseases in places like Dover, the acts should be extended to the civil population in cities like London and Dublin. They maintained this was done 'without any material interference with the so-called "liberty of the subject". It was also pointed out that 'Prostitution and the keeping of houses of ill fame are not in any way legalised by the enforcement of the Contagious Diseases Act, although there is a popular belief that such is the fact'; the prostitute 'is prevented from inflicting physical injury on herself and others, or the children of herself and others, for the disease is hereditary, by arrest and detention until harmless'. The acts were directly compared to the law on public drunkenness: 'A drunkard is prevented by the state from inflicting injury upon himself or his neighbours when drunk by his arrest and confinement.'[70]

Elizabeth Malcolm has argued that the CDAs helped to encourage all the major churches to assert that prostitution and female sexuality generally 'were moral issues, not public health ones to be controlled by the state through the medium of the police'.[71] Women could be detained and forcibly treated for up to three months and doctors and police could lay information before a magistrate in a closed court that they believed a woman was a prostitute with VD; the magistrate could then summons the woman and order her detention. The CDAs appear to have encouraged Protestant and Catholic clergy alike to patrol the cities, looking for those 'in danger'. Though clerical opinion on the merits of the CDAs was divided, and there was a reluctance to speak openly about a sexual issue, it did seem to encourage the clergy 'to move against prostitution in a more concerted manner than previously' and to assert their own teaching about sexual mores more forcefully. Men did not face the same opprobrium as women, who were deemed to be already so degraded that further indignities did not matter.[72]

Josephine Butler, one of the English women who protested against the laws in question, attended the annual general meeting of the National Association for the Repeal of the Contagious Diseases Act in Dublin in 1878, and in 1886 announced the formation of a new organisation that would assist in the 'purification of the moral standard of society'.[73] She also maintained that Irish people were naturally more chaste and virtuous than other peoples.[74] This would not seem to be the case if the activities of prostitutes and their clients are anything to go by; Maria Luddy has suggested that the fact that the 'Curragh Wrens' remained active until at least the early part of the twentieth century would suggest there was no absolute sanction against prostitution in nineteenth-century Ireland: 'While all women who worked as prostitutes were exposed to the rhetoric of condemnation from the police, local community and the clergy, society was relatively at ease ignoring the problem as long as it was hidden from public view'.[75] A rescue mission home in Dublin pronounced a success rate of 65 per cent in 1899, but in the same year the Dublin by Lamplight Institution recorded a 70 per cent failure rate, and by the end of the nineteenth century few 'outcast' women 'could escape the rescue net'.[76] This conclusion of Luddy's is somewhat at odds with her contention that society was ignoring the problem with relative ease. Perhaps the truth was that rescue workers and reformers were more interested in some prostitutes than others. A concerted 'rescue operation' was also evident a few decades later when the Catholic Legion of Mary, established in Dublin in 1921, began to campaign for the closure of the brothels in the area known colloquially as Monto in the vicinity of Montgomery Street – then an extensive brothel and tenement quarter. Frank Duff, the Legion's

founder, recalled his discovery of the prostitution issue in Dublin and his
first visit to a brothel:

> For a moment, I did not realise where I was. Then I saw, and I was so
> intimidated that I actually backed out without uttering a word. My
> retreat was typical of the attitude to the problem at the time. We were
> not without constant reminders of the existence of the problem and
> of the menace it afforded. Other than by the Magdalen asylums, the
> problem was untouched in Dublin.[77]

It has been estimated that in 1868 there were 132 brothels in the city and at
least 1,000 prostitutes: 'Prostitution in Dublin was unregulated by police
control, a situation at the time unique in Britain or Ireland as remarked on
in the 1903 edition of *Encyclopaedia Britannica*.'[78] The Irish census of 1911
includes a return for a house on Purdon Street in Monto which may have
been a brothel; other well-known brothels were around the docks and in
the southern inner city, while prostitutes also pedalled their trade in more
fashionable areas such as Grafton Street, Stephen's Green, Sackville Street
and Harcourt Street, and 'for all the condemnation of their occupation,
the women were generally considered to be decent, unfortunate and kind,
forced into a life on the streets through circumstance'. The presence of so
many prostitutes was determined at least in part by the significant military
presence in the city and in 1911 'the military do not seem to have disappointed prostitutes seeking business judging by the inmates of the isolation
ward at the Royal Military Infirmary'.[79]

'The three rush out of the gallery into the open air'

Monto is celebrated as Nighttown in the Circe episode of James Joyce's
Ulysses (1922); and Joyce himself had no shortage of carnal knowledge and
experience when it came to the women of the night. His brother Stanislas
referred to his familiarity with the prostitute world of Dublin, while the
psychologist Carl Gustav Jung commented that Joyce knew more about
women 'than the Devil's grandmother'. Seeking to shock, Joyce would ask,
'What did Christ know about life? He died at 33 and he never tried to live
with a woman.' In *A Portrait of the Artist as a Young Man* (1916), some of the
details of Joyce's nocturnal habits are revealed to priestly ears:

   – With women, my child?

   – Yes, Father.

   – Were they married women, my child?

He did not know. His sins trickled from his lips, one by one, trickled in shameful drops from his soul.

The Priest was silent. Then he asked:

   – How old are you, my child?

   – Sixteen, Father.[80]

Joyce's private letters to his lover Nora Barnacle were full of uninhibited sexuality. One such letter, written during their second separation in December 1909 and described as 'a torrential outpouring of sexual imagery and feeling', set a world record at Sotheby's in London in 2004 when it sold for a staggering £240,800. Although Barnacle initiated the correspondence, this particular letter testifies to Joyce's self-described 'ungovernable lust', with 'his glands in a pandemonium'. Writer Edna O'Brien describes the exchange of letters between Barnacle and Joyce as a 'scalding marathon', but perhaps Joyce was not free of Catholic guilt; the following day he wrote to his lover again wondering whether he should apologise for 'the extraordinary letter I wrote you last night'.[81]

In 2003, one Joyce scholar suggested there was traditionally 'an abiding reluctance to concede that sexual masochism runs like a core through the centre of Joyce and is the impetus for his writing'; that in terms of the history of sexuality, he was situated at a time of 'profoundly changing attitudes and tactics of control' regarding perceptions of sexuality and conflicts about marriage, chastity, reproduction, feminism and censorship. For Joyce, these themes forged his conscience and were also important because of his immersion in Irish Catholicism during his youth.[82] Virtually all of his formal education was at the hands of the Jesuits. He probably gave serious consideration to the prospect of becoming one himself, but religion became for him a 'very troublesome burden'. He later told Barnacle that in 1898, the same year he finished at the Jesuit's Belvedere School, he 'left the Catholic Church, hating it most fervently'. Until the 1950s, due to his controversial writings, the Jesuits were not keen to acknowledge their former pupil. When researching his biography of Joyce in 1937, Herbert Gorman visited Clongowes, the Jesuit school Joyce attended between 1888 and 1891, where he was advised to 'breathe not his name' if he wanted to gain admittance.[83]

Joyce was interested in scientific, legal and underground discourses on sexuality, while the speech of 'perverse desire' flows unrestrained in *Finnegans Wake* (1939).[84] The vastness of the Joyce industry and the quantity of analysis has ensured that there are many Joyces to choose from when it comes to sexuality. For some, he subverted the discourses of sexology; for others, he was contradictory in claiming both ignorance of Freud and insisting he rejected Freud passionately and unequivocally. He has been praised for his intimate knowledge of the female psyche but has also been condemned for a view of women that is stereotypical and reductive; woman emerges in Joyce's work as 'virgin or whore, Madonna or temptress', but 'usually within a problematic context of maternity'. He can also be viewed as a writer who deliberately and comically deflated 'sex-role stereotypes of masculine prowess and feminine passivity'.[85]

Joyce's preoccupation with 'virgin or whore' reflected a much broader societal concern about the perceived transgressions of certain women. Since the eighteenth century, the Magdalen asylums mentioned by Frank Duff had been used to rescue and reform 'fallen women'. Often called Magdalen laundries because the women were put to work washing clothes, by the early twentieth century there were at least twenty-three such institutions and, unlike in earlier times, they seemed to be more preoccupied with 'wayward daughters' and unmarried mothers than prostitutes. Maria Luddy has pointed out that 'both the Catholic public and the religious communities colluded in removing these "shameful objects" from public view'. An abstract from a report of the Magdalen asylum at High Park in Drumncondra for 1881 gives an indication of how they were viewed and perceived:

> To hope that those whose lives have been passed in sin and degradation, whose study has been to deceive and whose hearts are hardened by evil habits, should return to the path of virtue without continued efforts against the temptation to relax, would be to anticipate a miracle ... how many steps they have to retrace! How much to sacrifice and combat![86]

As pointed out by James Smith, the archival records of the Magdalen laundries are not available after 1900 and, although initially it was the women themselves who made the decision to stay, it is clear that in the post-Famine period the laundries helped to reinforce the ideology of women's respectability and modesty, the primacy of the domestic sphere, a desire to marry and readiness to confine her sexuality to marriage.[87]

Women, in this sense, were depicted as fragile, delicate creatures whose nature had to be protected, ideas instilled by Church and mothers. However, there were also, as Tom Inglis suggests, economic issues: women who transgressed through sexual promiscuity, including the mothers of illegitimate children, presented a challenge to the economic stability of men newly converted to the benefits of capital accumulation, hence the reason why such women were increasingly monitored, supervised and suppressed.[88]

Perhaps the reaction to them was also an implicit recognition that, as pointed out by Dympna McLoughlin, there was a wide range of sexual relationships in nineteenth-century Ireland. These directly challenged the notion of a country of exceptional chastity and prudery; though it is clear that by the end of the nineteenth century there was diminishing tolerance of any kind of sexual diversity and 'the triumph of respectability' had been achieved, by which women's sexuality was 'totally contained in marriage'. Women, since they were believed to have no sexual desire, were 'compensated with a superior moral nature ... this belief made women into a moral army; not only were they responsible for their own shortcomings, they were also responsible for the shortcomings of their men folk.'[89]

According to official statistics, as seen earlier, Ireland was a country with a low marriage rate, high marital fertility, minimal illegitimacy, frequent emigration and an abundance of celibacy. But McLoughlin raises some interesting questions about the gulf between the theory and the practice of Irish sexuality: 'Was the constant articulation of the purity of Irish women a warning to them rather than an accurate reflection of reality? Why was there a thriving trade in prostitution? Why was there the preponderance of the "gentlemen's miss"? ("She never became an outcast ... there was a kind of grudging admiration of this woman's economic astuteness") and is it really conceivable that all, or even most details of illegitimacy and illicit sexual contact would be found in the official records of the age? And what of the economics of the emerging middle class and the economic impact of an "unvirtuous daughter" ... a woman of this class who became pregnant outside marriage could never redeem herself.'[90]

Much of the articulation of that 'purity' came from priests, and it is the thunderous clerics of post-Famine Ireland who have received much attention regarding what they said and did and wrote on these matters. The leading role of the priest in blocking immorality was also dependent on support from key respectable members of the lay community and the necessity for them to lead by example. K. H. Connell suggests that 'priests' teaching was the more telling because of their observing, more scrupulously, perhaps, than some of their continental colleagues, their vows of chastity'.[91] The novelist George Moore wrote a sketch concerning the Irish priest in his book *Parnell and His Island* (1887) in which chaste priests were deemed worthy of psychological analysis because they were men 'who live so well and have so much leisure [and] keep women at bay, especially as so many of them live in such close proximity with their housekeepers ... [it] seems to reflect on the general sexual devitalisation of Irishmen ... that they sin and elude discovery, no one who knows the country, every eye fixed upon them, would believe for a moment'.[92] In a further story, *Letter to Rome*, published in 1903, Moore returned to the issue of clerical celibacy, suggesting secular priests should be allowed to father children in order to counteract the effects of emigration; they would also father children of the best stock as 'the priests live in the best houses, eat the best of food'.[93] In Moore's 1905 novel *The Lake*, Father Oliver Gogarty falls in love with the music teacher Nora Glynn and then denounces her from the pulpit when she is seduced.[94]

In the early twentieth century, some priests were already looking to the past with nostalgia about the operation of a stricter moral code, in contrast to the decadence they perceived to be a feature of modern times. Tom Garvin points out that the most widely read Catholic author of the era, Canon Patrick Sheehan, was appalled at the character of the literature, both popular and intellectual, coming in to Ireland from England, and wanted to see more 'Christian idealism'. He may have seen priests as the main line of defence against 'neo-paganism', but he also looked to women to lead by example. In his book *Under the Leaders and the Stars*, published in 1903, 'He tells with evident approval and hope an anecdote of a lady and her two daughters who visit the National Gallery in Dublin, evidently for the first time "with that eager look which people assume when they expect something delightful". When they see the classical nude statuary, however, they seem "transfixed into marble themselves, so tense [are] their surprise and horror". The three rush out of the gallery into the open air.'[95]

Writing in 1904, the Jesuit Father Michael Phelan lamented that

> Fifty years ago the priests of Ireland often had recourse to rough methods with the people. Even the aid of the blackthorn stick was occasionally invoked as an effective method of securing conviction. Yet, on the morrow, all was forgotten and the people would die for the man who had punished them.
>
> Let the priest of today but thwart the grandchildren of that

generation, even in a small matter, and mark the rancour ... the spirit
that Catholic Ireland had fifty years ago is sadly changed today.[96]

In his book *Ireland in the New Century* (1904), Horace Plunkett maintained
that at the beginning of the twentieth century, excessive sexual surveillance
by rural priests and older members of the community was driving people
to emigrate: 'in some parishes the Sunday cyclist will observe that strange
phenomenon of a normally light-hearted peasantry marshalled in male
and female groups along the road, eyeing one another in dull wonderment
across the forbidden space'.[97] But Plunkett's analysis was simplistic. The suppression of Irish sexual instincts was more complicated than the image of a
Catholic Church snuffing out pleasure and physical instinct in a population
that was instinctively joyful when it came to sexuality would suggest. Sexuality could also be expressed violently and criminally, and it was often neighbours and police, not priests, who got to observe what went on in some of
those forbidden spaces.

'That bitch, that wicked whore ...'

Some of the above writers were also questioning, often indirectly, whether
there was a particularly chaste Irish character. Undoubtedly the famine
played a role in this; as a result of it, 'the contexts for sexual expression
and reproduction were profoundly changed'.[98] The scandal surrounding
the public airing of the domestic arrangements of Charles Stewart Parnell,
the iconic Home Rule leader who died in 1891, was also of relevance in
terms of private intrigue, public comment and controversy about sexual
morality.

There was nothing novel about Irish politicians having affairs with
women they were not married to; W. B. Yeats famously asserted of Daniel
O'Connell, the Irish nationalist who won emancipation for Irish Catholics
in 1829, that during his career 'you could not throw a stick over a workhouse
wall without hitting one of his children'. This was delightful exaggeration,
but there is enough evidence to suggest some of the stories about his sexual proclivities were true.[99] When Captain Willie O'Shea, the husband of
Katherine O'Shea with whom Parnell lived and had three children, filed a
petition for divorce in December 1889, citing Parnell as co-respondent, Parnell could have been reasonably confident that he would weather the storm.

Knowledge of his love affair was widespread, and he believed he had not deceived anyone. The divorce case began on 15 November 1890 and only lasted two days but, unfortunately for them, 'the evidence presented the two lovers in the most squalid light; most ludicrous of all, it was alleged that Parnell had on occasions evaded the Captain by departing rapidly down a fire escape'.[100]

It has commonly been assumed that once the Irish Catholic Bishops set their faces against Parnell he was doomed; but the affair did not have that neat symmetry. It was, rather, the 'non-conformist conscience' in England that openly reacted against him, in regard to which the attitude of Prime Minister William Gladstone was pivotal. The Bishops, not for the last time in relation to issues of sexual morality, came on board afterwards. None the less, it was the divorce case that brought down Parnell, and historians ever after have been left to speculate about what lay at the root of his infatuation with O'Shea. Undoubtedly there was passion, but in the words of F. S. L. Lyons, 'tender domesticity was much more the key note' of their love affair. Ultimately, suggests Lyons, 'it is impossible to be sure how much of the final destructive rage was devotion to Katherine and how much injured pride at his own rejection by his followers'.[101]

Despite the fascination with the case, Katherine, who outlived Parnell by thirty years, remained quite elusive, despite four biographies, the most recent of which was published in 2008.[102] What did this saga of Parnell's forced downfall reveal? That love affairs between well-known people are rarely as dramatic, interesting or romantic as myth would suggest. That publicly Parnell compromised O'Shea by bringing her into his private sitting room at Cannon Street hotel; that he was happy to live in her home at her expense and at the risk of exposing their affair; that she did not initiate a divorce from her husband because she wanted to inherit her aunt's money; that she was no feminist icon, but had access to high-ranking politicians, which she was determined to exploit.[103] It is also clear she could be vain, annoying and frivolous; that she used Parnell to advance her husband's career; that O'Shea may have believed he was the father of Parnell's children. Parnell's letters, as originally revealed by Katherine's own memoirs, were mundane, sentimental and sometimes juvenile. Overall, in the words of Anne Dolan, there was more in this affair that was 'sordid and selfish than sincere'.[104]

What significance or relevance did the affair have beyond how it destroyed Parnell and O'Shea? It was a reminder that blind eyes were often turned; that British 'liberalism' and Victorian morality had a heavy influence on Irish affairs and attitudes; that the Irish Catholic Church was becoming more adept at spotting opportunities to assert its leadership role in terms of the 'character' and morality of a future Home Rule Ireland; that certain behaviours would be tolerated as long as they remained hidden; and that people will give in to physical passion regardless of the consequences. Perhaps it also facilitated a discourse about a woman's status in relationships and in society generally in terms of what was and was not acceptable. Katherine became an outcast and died in poverty; she had often been referred to as 'Kitty', a name used by Parnell's enemies as a form of insult (it was also a slang term for a prostitute at the time). She was, for many, 'that bitch, that wicked whore', as a character in *Ulysses* calls her. In contrast, Parnell's place in history was assured, even if the affair troubled many of his adoring followers. Maria Luddy tells the tale of a devoted Parnellite woman who, when Parnell falls from grace, 'cannot bring herself to take his picture down from the wall and yet, cannot continue to venerate the image of an adulterer. Her solution is to leave the picture hanging, but turn it to the wall.'[105]

In the broader context of women's status, what was initially more evident in England than Ireland in the late nineteenth century was the emergence of feminists vocally campaigning for women's rights and knowledge of contraception. The birth rate in England fell continuously from 1871 to 1900, most notably among the middle and professional classes, and in 1878 Annie Besant and Charles Bradlaugh published *The Fruits of Knowledge*, which addressed the issue of birth control. There was no Irish equivalent publication; but nor were there the paintings of sexualised nudes or erotic photographs. Neither should the degree of liberalisation in England be exaggerated, as Besant and Bradlaugh were prosecuted under obscenity laws. There was also a lack of articulation of the sexual frustration identified by Irish writers; in *Grania*, a novel published in 1892, Emily Lawless suggested 'the mere fact of giving utterance to a complaint on the subject gave her a sense not merely of having committed a hideous breach of common decency, but of having actually crossed the line that separates sanity from madness'.[106]

What was also evident from the late nineteenth and early twentieth century was the extent to which, in conjunction with the cultural revival that promoted the Irish language, literature, games and customs, there was an underlining of the difference between Irish 'values' and practices and what 'others did'. J. J. Sheehan's *A Guide to Irish Dancing* (1902) warned dancers:

Don't hug your partner around the waist English fashion. When
swinging, hold her hands only. A bow to your partner at the end would
be amiss, but be careful to avoid any straining after 'deportment'. Leave
that to the Seoníní [Little John, i.e. John Bull – a term of derision for
those who aped foreign customs]. In short, be natural, unaffected, easy –
be Irish, and you'll be alright.[107]

But when it came to the application of the law, different 'values' in Ireland and England – if such existed – did not matter, as the same laws applied
in both countries. Changes in the law governing sexual offences were crucial in raising more awareness about sexual crime and in ensuring a greater
degree of prosecutions – a further indication of the extent of 'moral policing' in the late nineteenth and early twentieth century and an illustration
of a greater awareness of child sexual abuse in Victorian England. The 1861
Offences Against The Person Act had confirmed the age of consent at 12,
made carnal knowledge of a girl under 10 a felony and carnal knowledge of
a girl between the ages of 10 and 12 a misdemeanour, with indecent assault
or attempted rape of a girl under 12 punishable by up to two years' imprisonment. The act also provided for penal servitude for life in rape cases. This act
was amended in 1875 to raise the age of consent to 13.

The Criminal Justice Amendment Act of 1885 suggests awareness of
sexual abuse and sexual violence, though an undeveloped understanding of
their physical and psychological effects.[108] It has, however, been described
as a 'lasting monument' to the efforts of reform groups, and a reflection
of the impact made by popular journalist W. T. Stead, who had published
articles in the *Pall Mall Gazette* depicting an epidemic of child prostitution.
The Labouchère Amendment to that act, named after Henry Labouchère,
the MP who introduced it, placed all homosexual practice outside the law
by making it an offence for males to engage in acts of 'gross indecency' in
public or private, irrespective of age (the offence of buggery had existed for
several hundred years, though in theory it was a 'gender neutral offence'[109]).
It provided for a term of imprisonment not exceeding two years, with or
without hard labour, for any male person guilty of an act of gross indecency
with another male person in public or in private. The 1885 act was in fact
'the latest in a twenty-five year series of legislation that raised the age of
consent and delineated the penalties for sexual offences against women and
minors'. It raised the age of consent to 16; sexual assaults on girls under the
age of 13 were deemed felonious and assaults on girls between 13 and 16 were

deemed misdemeanours.[110] The Punishment of Incest Act was not passed until 1908.

Given that 'the study of sexual offences is, in many ways, a study in social values',[111] the preponderance of new legislation in the late Victorian and early Edwardian period would suggest that social values were undergoing a serious change, with an understandable concentration on women, who constituted (as they still do) the vast majority of victims of sexual violence. In the words of legal historian Thomas O'Malley, 'there is perhaps no period in the history of these islands which has exercised a more lasting influence on the law governing sexual offences than the last quarter of the nineteenth century'.[112]

'A fetish for respectability'

Developments in the United Kingdom and elsewhere in Europe at this time in relation to awareness of sex and sexuality were manifold, but there was an inevitable difference of emphasis in different countries, given that Europe contained 'a complex patchwork of sexual cultures'.[113] Most European countries around the turn of the century 'faced an opening up of sexual possibilities and at the same time a strengthening of sexual codes. Literature and the arts became focal points for laxer attitudes towards sex, whereas at the same time new laws were promulgated to restrain what was seen as sexual licence.'[114] Britain had a long history of fits of 'moral panic' and in the late nineteenth and early twentieth century there were 'white slave panics' and an emerging middle class with a 'fetish for respectability', while there was also 'the suppression of female-influenced oral traditions by a largely male-dominated literature discourse with the rise of print culture'.[115] It is interesting in this context that in the 1970s and 1980s when there were many bitter debates about sexuality and the politics of procreation in Ireland, an older woman who attended a women's health seminar in Dublin in 1979 organised by the Contraception Action Programme 'claimed that the earliest Irish-language editions of Peig Sayers' account of her life on the Blasket Islands [published in 1936 and regarded as an important autobiography in the context of women's experiences in isolated rural environments] included a reference to a primitive form of cap, or diaphragm, made from sheep's wool. This reference was later purged.'[116]

The dichotomy between social purity and the movement for sex reform based on the new sexology (for which an interest in homosexuality was the main starting point) was reflected in the publication at the turn of the century of Henry Havelock Ellis's multi-volume studies of the psychology of sex, but this did not provoke much public debate. Ellis had worked on his studies in the 1890s, was seen as a dangerous radical, and for many years 'only one part of the *Studies*, which eventually ran to seven volumes, was published in Britain, and that was quickly suppressed'. It had actually first appeared in Germany, 'a country with an active – many Englishmen would have said, a disgusting – interest in sex'.[117]

The discussion of eugenics, however, did impact on Ireland, reflected in the formation in 1911 of a Belfast Eugenics Society, whose president approved of the vigour of forced sterilisation to prevent the birth of the 'unfit'.[118] The French also played a leading role in cataloguing and describing sexual 'perversions', with pioneers like Alfred Binet writing about inversion, fetishism, bestiality and sadism, while in Austria in 1905, Sigmund Freud published his three essays on the theory of sexuality. Freud and the various theories associated with him were generally resisted in both British and Irish psychiatry, but were greeted with more enthusiasm by the educated public. The popularisation of Freud by the British lay press began as early as 1912; by the end of that decade, 'a large quantity of material about psychoanalysis had been written by and for the educated lay public'. The medicopsychological community were attracted to his theory of the unconscious but 'strongly disapproving of his sexual theories'.[119]

The legal emphasis differed according to location; there was a harsher tone to France's sexology but a legislature of relative tolerance. There was an eroticisation of marriage and women's clothes, but there was also an energetic censorship, and, after the First World War, a clampdown on abortionists and birth control information.[120] In Italy, support for birth control came from 'individual socialists, libertarians and anarchists', but there was both a reticence about publicly debating the issue and a certain moral ambivalence: in 1913, an attempted prosecution against the publishers of a manual entitled *The Art of Not Having Children* (which sold 27,000 copies) was rejected; the jury found it 'immoral', but nothing in it 'obscene'.[121]

In Dutch society, the influence of Catholic and orthodox Calvinist groups was disproportionately large, and the state's involvement in matters of sexuality grew stronger towards the end of the nineteenth century. As a result, in the first two decades of the twentieth century such groups took over political power, rejected a 'scientific' or 'medical' approach to sexuality and prostitution, and introduced the 'moral laws' of 1911 that included regulations against birth control, prostitution and homosexuality – although, unlike in Britain and Germany, homosexual practice between adults was not criminalised. There was, however, a climate of repression and condemnation in relation to all sexuality outside of marriage and a relatively high birth rate due to the influence of Christian views on Dutch social life.[122] This religious influence was important in Ireland, also; although marital fertility rates declined after 1880, they were still high in the early twentieth century and though, economically, celibacy represented a 'sensible option' for many Irish men, religious views were likely to have influenced this also.[123] What Ireland shared with the Netherlands was the fact that the activities of lawmakers and the Church resulted 'not so much in more chastity among the population but rather in an intensification of attention to sexuality and a guilt-ridden perception of it'.[124]

Inevitably, such a climate in Ireland also ensured that much of that sexual activity became criminal or hidden, and this presented difficulties in trying to secure prosecutions. The Crown file books for the north and south of Ireland record a lot of instances of *Nolle Prosequi* (a decision not to proceed) in relation to cases involving allegations of sexual crime, suggesting difficulty in prosecuting these cases and problems in securing witnesses. Even when prosecutions were successful, there were contemporary criticisms of 'the curious scale of values' employed when sentencing for sexual crimes: 'One report highlighted cases in which an indecent assault on a girl under 16 and the theft of bacon were equally punished with six months' hard labour, while in the same court the theft of clothes and £13. 10s. brought twelve months with hard labour.'[125] The Crown books also reveal the degree to which children were being sexually assaulted; many cases of incest appear, as do cases relating to infanticide, buggery, gross indecency, unlawful carnal knowledge and indecent assault.

A typical jury during these years consisted of male well-off members of society, such as vintners, merchants, bankers, publicans and jewellers, while many were just listed as 'gent'.[126] The preponderance of men and the prevailing view of the status of women, as well as comments from judges about 'the natural, irresistible impulse animating the man', ensured that the women who appeared in court as witnesses or victims were at a distinct disadvantage – so much so that in 1914 the Irish feminist Marion Duggan was quoted in the newspaper of the Irish suffragette movement, *The Irish Citizen*, as contending, 'Every man is innocent until proved guilty; every girl and woman

witness against a man is guilty of perjury until proved innocent.' According
to Sandra McAvoy, this is also indicative of a feminist belief that existing
criminal law legislation on such issues as age of consent and sexual assault
'reflected double standards of sexual morality, excused male sexual aggression and exposed woman and girl victims to further abuse in the courts'.[127]
It was to be twenty years, however, before those laws were changed in what
became the Irish Free State, in contrast to Britain, where a criminal law
amendment committee was established in 1912. Like their British counterparts in the second decade of the twentieth century, Irish feminists formed
'women watching the court committees'; the Irish Women's Reform League
(IWRL) argued the importance of female jurors, particularly in view of
the widely held belief, as asserted by one judge, that sexual matters should
be dealt with by 'men of the world'. In response, Marion Duggan wrote, 'I
decline to believe any sensible man or woman could think that men understand little girls of 15 better than a jury of responsible women would ... we
want mixed juries in these cases.'[128]

This was particularly significant given that a separate category of
offence existed for unlawful carnal knowledge of girls above the age of 13
and under the age of 16; such cases were also frequently prosecuted. The
feminists highlighted many of the difficulties with these and other sexual
crime cases, including the problem that the defence of belief that a girl
was of age made it almost impossible to bring a successful unlawful carnal
knowledge prosecution. A six-month statutory time limit also meant that
prosecutions were difficult if a girl's visible pregnancy was the first evidence
that a crime had occurred. Concern was expressed about the impact on child
abuse cases of the rule that defendants could not be convicted on the basis
of a child's uncorroborated evidence. In cases of sexual crime (as with treason and perjury) it was also a rule of practice to warn juries of the danger of
convicting on the evidence of a single witness – the victim – which many
juries took as an instruction to acquit, even if there was no reason to doubt
the victim's testimony.[129] The Irish feminist demands reflected an international challenge to the male sexual exploitation of women but, as elsewhere,
it was also a challenge that went into decline; the intervention of sexology
'reinforced the patriarchal model of sexuality by endowing it with scientific
legitimation and subverted the further development of the feminist model
of sexuality. What feminists had argued was political, sexologists redefined
as natural and asserted could not be changed.'[130]

The categories of sexual assault that feature prominently in the archive of court records, and are used extensively throughout this book, are: acts of rape and other sexual assaults rendered criminal by the absence of consent; exploitative acts even when consent existed (for example in relation to girls under the age of 17); and incest and homosexuality, deemed criminal irrespective of consent.[131] In the twenty years prior to the establishment of the Irish Free State, numerous sexual crimes were dealt with by the Crown quarter sessions and Crown Commission legal hearings, the forerunners of the district and circuit court hearings of the Irish Free State. In the Crown books of these trials in Dublin, cases of indecent exposure, gross indecency, indecent assault, buggery and unlawful carnal knowledge were so commonplace that, in August 1920, the clerk of the Dublin commission courts wrote to the Chief Secretary's office on behalf of the Lord Justices, drawing attention to a motion adopted at a committee meeting of the Dublin White Cross Association: 'That the Dublin White Cross Association desires to enter its most solemn protest against young people of both sexes being permitted to remain in the Dublin Commission Courts during the hearing of cases of sexual irregularities to the grave danger of their morals.'[132] Newspapers did carry reports of sexual crime court cases, though were careful in the language they used; unlawful carnal knowledge, for example, was frequently referred to as 'criminal assault' and less frequently as a 'completed act'.[133]

Sexual assaults were also perpetrated by those of tender age. The extension of the Borstal system to Ireland in 1906 marked a 'revolutionary new phase' in the treatment of young offenders. In 1910, the gaol at Clonmel was reconstituted as a Borstal institution, regarded as a courageous penal innovation in the treatment of the juvenile offender. Between August 1910 and December 1914, 235 inmates were committed, 69 of them from Dublin, most from labouring backgrounds, having been found guilty of larceny. Offences of a sexual nature were perpetrated by 8 boys, and 'while this is not a high figure it is comparatively greater than more mainstream offences'.[134]

'I was drunk and lay down beside the cow'

Those with a predilection for sex with animals also found themselves before the courts; although not appearing very regularly, bestiality cases cropped up in both the north and south of Ireland. In Dublin in August 1900, a man employed on a farm in County Dublin was accused of an 'unnatural offence', or more formally it was alleged he 'did attempt feloniously to have a venereal affair with a certain animal, to wit, a hen and with the same hen unlawfully did attempt to commit and perpetrate that detestable and abominable crime of buggery not to be named amongst Christians'. The witness, who had known the defendant for five years, described arriving on the unfortunate scene: 'I was behind his back and let a scream and he turned away and he dropped the hen and was all exposed ... It was the "croaks" of the hen that brought me to the spot ... his wife came out and said in his presence: "That old vagabond is after ill using the hen."' The witness subsequently had the hen killed and buried, but not before she had brought it to the police station. The defendant was bailed for £50.[135]

On another occasion, during the Belfast Spring Assizes of 1915, a man was charged with 'the abominable crime of bestiality with a cow'. A constable described how he had been on duty at 2.45 a.m. on the Ormeau Road and saw the accused

in a field to the right of the road known as Galwally Park. There were a number of cows in that field. The greater number of them were lying down. I saw the prisoner go over to 3 cows that were lying down. He walked around behind them and they got up and walked away. He then went to a fourth cow that was lying down and sat down on the grass behind the cow. I saw him put his hands down to the spare of his trousers, then put his hand on the hindermost part of the cow. This cow did not get up. I was about 30 or 40 yards away. I ran back to the Ormeau Road and came over Galwally Park and got to the other side of a paling. The prisoner was then about a yard or 2 off me. He had his person exposed and had it in the private part of the cow and was pushing in and out. The prisoner saw me and then got up. His trousers were open and his person exposed. I crossed the paling and brought the prisoner to the Ormeau Road. The prisoner had some drink taken but could walk steady. I met Sergeant Richard Moore and I charged the prisoner with the above offence and cautioned him. He said, 'What's that you charge me with?' I then repeated the charge and he said, 'I had nothing to do with the cow. I was drunk and lay down beside the cow.' Sergeant Moore accompanied me to the Police Office with the prisoner and I was present when the sergeant examined the trousers and vest worn by the prisoner and I saw cow manure on the spare of his trousers and short cows hairs on the vest.

The prisoner was well used to the company of cows; the constable noted that 'he is in the dairy business'.[136]

'A young girl seduced under promise of marriage'

There was also much focus in the late nineteenth and early twentieth centuries on the concept of child welfare. The Prevention of Cruelty to Children Act, which came into operation in 1904, deemed it illegal 'to cause or encourage the seduction or prostitution of a girl under 16 years of age' or 'to reside in or frequent any disorderly house'.[137] Thomas O'Malley has suggested that the new laws 'reflected an idealised vision of childhood typical of the late Victorian era'.[138] Judging by contemporary comment on the 1908 Children's Act, the same could be said of that legislation, which was warmly welcomed by child protection groups. As the National Society for the Prevention of Cruelty to Children (NSPCC) put it, it made the society 'a far greater power for good in the cause of children' and ensured its work 'hitherto but partially known, to be now an epistle known and read of all men'.[139]

Officially, children were beginning to be noticed as individuals susceptible to neglect and ill treatment. In Edwardian England, social investigators like Charles Booth and Seebohm Rowntree were attempting to quantify poverty and analyse its causes and characteristics. The emergence of legislation and protective organisations would suggest a premium was placed on the life of children that had not existed previously, reflected in Ireland in 1889 with the emergence of the Dublin Society for the Prevention of Cruelty to Children (DSPCC). Members of the Dublin Corporation and societies such as the DSPCC and the Women's National Health Association sought to implement public health and welfare schemes for mothers, infants and children, and, though they were also resented by some as middle- and upper-class interfering philanthropists, they did improve the lives of many. One of the arguments used in an attempt to prevent the establishment of the DSPCC was a repudiation of any claim that Dublin children were maltreated. It was even suggested that to admit the existence of cruelty would destroy the image of Ireland as the 'maternal isle'.[140] Just over 300 people were charged with neglect of children in 1900. By 1918 that figure had been reduced to 150.

The 1908 Children's Act was regarded as a fundamental step in extending child protection, incorporating in one statute a host of laws and piecemeal legislation that emphasised the social rights of children. In practice, it was more parent-centred (in the sense of bringing them to account for neglect) than child-centred. Crucially, it also dictated that 'the courts should be agencies for the rescue as well as the punishment of children'. [141] It was this act that was relied on in dealing with the problems of child welfare in Ireland for most of the twentieth century. Children were afforded a status in the Democratic Programme of the first Dáil in 1919, which placed the care of children as 'the first duty of the Republic' (as opposed to the constitution of 1937, which sought to protect 'the family' from interference from the state). [142]

The reports of the Dublin Aid Committee of the NSPCC for the early twentieth century give an overview of the problems children were facing and the extent of the threat to them due to the activities of neglectful parents and 'immoral surroundings'. Most of the cases it dealt with came under headings of 'neglect', 'starvation', 'ill-treatment', 'abandonment' and 'exposure', but 'immoral surroundings' was also listed as a category, and most had been reported by the public. The overall number of cases investigated by the society during the year 1904–5 was 1,625, involving the welfare of 4,300 children, of whom 4,162 were legitimate and 45 illegitimate. The overwhelming majority of cases investigated came under the headings 'neglect and starvation' (1,424). There were 29 cases under the heading 'immoral surroundings', similar in number to those relating to 'abandonment' (37) and 'exposure' (30); however, the number of such cases had been increasing since the late nineteenth century. Between 1889 and 1905, the total number of cases investigated was 79, but in the year 1904–5 alone there were 30, suggesting either that this was a growing problem or that there was simply more awareness of it. [143] Excessive drinking was the chief cause of child neglect and the reports are notable for their constant mention of women addicted to drink, and the fact that so many women were 'confirmed drunkards'. [144]

There are also many reports of violence against children and, although sexual abuse is not specifically mentioned, it is inconceivable that this was not a feature of the abuse experienced. Dirt, squalor, disease, starvation, rags and sores make frequent appearances in these reports; but the society was also proud of its record in redressing wrongs, and it published a suspiciously high number of case studies with happy endings. It claimed in 1910 that, due to its activities over the previous twenty-one years, 52,685 children had had their 'wrongs redressed'. [145] The reports also detail the plight of deserted pregnant girls. In 1914 the society intervened to induce the father of an

illegitimate child to marry the mother and gave the following details of how
this was done:

> B.2760: A young girl seduced under promise of marriage had an illegiti-
> mate child about three weeks old when the case came under notice. The
> man refused to carry out his promise to marry the girl after the birth of
> the child and her mother, on whom she was dependent, turned her out
> and refused to provide anything for her and the child. With much dif-
> ficulty and largely owing to the interposition of the brother of the girl,
> the Inspector induced the mother to allow the girl to stay in the house
> with the child. The inspector then saw the father and brought him and
> the girl together again, with the result that they were married shortly
> afterwards.[146]

Another case, reported in the same year, detailed the case of a mother
and children deserted:

> B.2781: A man and a woman lived together unmarried for a number of
> years and had 5 children, of whom four were alive at the time the case
> came under notice, one being a baby six months old. The man was a
> tradesman earning 38 shillings a week. The home was of the most unsuit-
> able description and, as the man had deserted her, the woman was unable
> to provide even food for the children. The inspector induced the man
> to help for a little time, but the woman having taken to drink and evil
> courses, steps were taken to place the three elder children in schools on
> the ground of immoral surroundings. After the magistrates advice, the
> inspector succeeded in getting the sister in charge to take the baby into
> a convent home.[147]

In 1911, details were given of another child rescued from 'immoral surroundings', which would suggest that the inspectors were often operating
under a degree of risk to their own safety, and that it was necessary for them
to literally grab children in danger, in this case, from what was likely to have
been a brothel:

> C.689: A complaint having been made to the society that a child of five
> was being brought up in immoral surroundings, an officer was sent to
> investigate the case. Matters were found to be as stated, the child having

been put out to nurse when 2 years of age. The case presented no little difficulty. Acting on instructions the officer obtained the mother's sanction
to have the little girl placed in an industrial school. On going to the
house to remove the child his action was hotly contested by a number of
bad characters, but he forced his way through them, took the child in his
arms and conveyed her to the police court, where she was committed to
an Industrial School until she attained the age of 16.[148]

In 1901, for every 1,000 children under the age of 14, 6 were in industrial
schools in Ireland; the corresponding figures for Scotland and England were
3 and just over 1.[149] First established in 1868, based on those already in existence in England and Scotland, these schools, largely run by religious orders,
incarcerated children under the age of 14 who were neglected, orphaned,
abandoned, deemed to be out of control, delinquent or living in unsuitable
conditions. Given what is now known about the manner in which industrial schools were run and the violence and abuse experienced by some of
the inmates, it is easy to be cynical about the wisdom of placing children as
young as five in such institutions in order to save them from 'immoral surroundings', but the contemporary view was that industrial schools, although
by no means an adequate substitute for a safe and loving family home, were
a far better alternative to a precarious existence outside, or, as the NSPCC
noted in 1907, they were institutions 'where they will be well educated and
given a start in life'.[150]

It was known that children, particularly in the larger cities, were in danger of drifting into prostitution or being subjected to sexual abuse, often as
a result of poverty or neglectful parents. The Ulster Children's Aid Society
was to the fore in highlighting this problem in Belfast; in 1910 a speaker on
their behalf, Dr Purves, delivered a sermon in which he referred to 'Vagrancy
and the moral dangers arising from it ... a disgraceful blot on the reputation
of Belfast'.[151] The main concern was to get such children placed in industrial
schools.

'I did not tell my mother at first because I was afraid she'd beat me'

As mentioned earlier, there is no direct mention of sexual abuse in these
reports, but it is inconceivable that some children living in what were
described as 'immoral surroundings', including, presumably, brothels, were

not sexually abused. Although language referring to, or describing, child sexual abuse had few public airings, it is clear that it was not just an issue 'discovered and constructed' in the 1970s. In his book *Child Sexual Abuse in Victorian England*, L. A. Jackson notes that, although the term 'child abuse' was not used in the late nineteenth and early twentieth century, other euphemisms such as 'moral corruption, immorality, tampering, white slavery, juvenile prostitution and ruining' were.[152] But the court files give some indication of the extent of child abuse, and the often frank language that was used to describe it. A case heard at the Belfast Spring Assizes in 1900 concerned a 17-year-old girl who had allegedly been seduced against her will by a man from Shankill who had promised her work in a factory and offered her accommodation. The accused effectively took her, in his own words, as 'my wife', but when the girl addressed the accused in court, she maintained: 'You asked me if I had nobody belonging to me. I told you I had no mother but I had a father. I told you I had no place to go ... you told me you had a house of your own ... I was willing to go to bed. I was not willing that you should have connection [sex] with me.'[153]

It was not unusual for priests to be informed before the police, but it was frequently to their mothers that the victims first turned. Often, it was neighbours who carried out the crime. In July 1900, a 19-year-old man was accused of attempted carnal knowledge with a neighbour, a girl under the age of 13, who had gone out to collect the cows. He allegedly raped her at Shangan Hill, Dunsaghley, County Dublin ('when he got off me he said I would have a young one in the morning'). When informed, her mother told the priest, but was slow to get the law involved because 'at first she did not realise how serious it was'.[154]

There also seems to have been public awareness of the dangers that paedophiles posed: in 1902 a gardener in the Phoenix Park in Dublin gave evidence in the case of a man on an indecent assault charge against two girls aged 5 and 9 who had been playing with a skipping rope in the park. The man had sat in the park for two hours. When he groped the children the gardener challenged him, saying, 'Only I thought you belonged to the children I would have stopped you by force.'[155]

Many of the cases relating to indecent assaults on children highlight the degree of overcrowding in Dublin city. Housing statistics suggest that little progress was made in this regard in the opening decade of the twentieth century. While just under 40 per cent of the population had exclusive occupancy of a house or cottage in 1901, the number of families living in what was described as 'fourth-class accommodation' (one room and one window) in Dublin was 21,429 in 1901 and 20,564 in 1911.[156] In February 1903, a 22-year-old man was accused of carnally knowing a 9-year-old girl at a house in Dorset Street in Dublin city, one of many rooms in lodging houses occupied by whole families. The accused man's sister was a friend of the victim's mother and was in another room in the house when the assault took place. According to the victim, he abused her in a room 'while a baby cried in the cradle'. He left the country before the arrest warrant was issued but was later arrested when 'in hiding and evading arrest', after which he retorted, 'I don't care what happens to myself, but this will kill my father and mother.' It subsequently emerged that the child had contracted gonorrhoea but she had delayed telling her mother about the abuse: 'I was afraid and ashamed.'[157] The man was convicted and sentenced to nine months' imprisonment with hard labour.[158]

Also in February 1903, a man who identified himself as a clergyman from the 'Dominican convent Tallaght' was found by a jury not to be capable of pleading after he had been accused of the indecent assault and attempted carnal knowledge in Templeogue, County Dublin, of an 11-year-old girl, who had been on an errand for her mother in the company of her 6-year-old brother. The girl told the hearing he was 'a low sized man dressed like a priest. He asked me to pray for him' and that this was the second time he had assaulted her. The girl described what happened after the assault: 'I went home because I hit my little brother Joseph [because] he said he'd tell his mother what the priest did to me. I did not tell my mother at first because I was afraid she'd beat me.' The priest, according to the arresting constable, did not seem to understand the nature of the charge against him, and the case was not proceeded with, presumably due to his unsound mind: 'I noticed the demeanour of the prisoner was indifferent at the time of his arrest.'[159]

A case heard the following day related to the indecent assault of a 9-year-old girl living in Beresford Street who had been assaulted by a 19-year-old man at a mock wake: 'He raised up my clothes and he put his "mickey" over to mine and hurt me ... I was afraid to cry for fear he'd hit me ... he gave me ½ d. before he did the dirty thing to me. I went with my sister aged 6 and bought sweets in Malones.'[160] In 1908, the owner of a shop in Marlborough Street was accused of the indecent assault of a 9-year-old girl at the back of the shop, after which, according to the girl, 'he gave me three sweets'. The victim was a friend of the defendant's daughter. Before the charge sheet was read to him, he said, 'If I have injured the girl, charge me.' The police sergeant did not notice any signs that he had been drinking: 'I wouldn't say he was in the horrors.' He was bailed for £20 and subsequently found guilty and imprisoned for four months with hard labour.[161]

In Anne Street, Cork, in 1908, a young girl was subjected to a terrifying sexual attack very close to her house by a man who was known to the family. The girl had been playing on the street with her younger sister, near a hall in Cork Street:

> He said come over here in the hall and I will give you a penny. I said I would not go. He then dragged me over to the hall. When he took me into the hall he grabbed me by the neck. He then threw me down on the ground. He opened his trousers, he went down on top of me, he put his hand underneath my clothes. He hurted me by being down on top of me. I felt him pressing something against me. I cried. When I was there some time I heard my mother call my name. He said to come back again. He said to me not to tell anyone, that he would give me the penny.

The accused insisted that he had been with his wife and family at the time of the alleged incident. The girl's mother, however, claimed she had seen him at the corner of the street and that 'I knew the man before. I know him for about 10 years. We never had any quarrel.'[162] The man was found guilty.[163]

'She told me a man met her down the street in Meath Street and gave her a penny'

That women forced to work due to economic circumstances frequently featured as witnesses in harrowing cases concerning the sexual abuse of their children after the children had been left unattended serves as an indication of the extent to which child abuse was a direct product of poverty and lack of parental supervision. In almost all cases, the families knew the perpetrator; sometimes the assailant was even a member of the family. In 1911, a man was prosecuted for the indecent assault of his 6-year-old niece. It emerged from the medical evidence that the child was suffering from secondary, acquired rather than congenital, syphilis. The mother's evidence was as follows:

I go out cleaning and take the youngest child with me and I leave K. in charge of M. A. About 6 weeks ago I noticed the child M. A. I took her up to look at the heel, which had a bruise and noticed the bottom of her stomach black. I examined her private part and saw she was in a bad state. She told me a man met her down the street in Meath Street and gave her a penny. I brought her to Mercer's Hospital and from that to the Coombe. I brought her back to Mercers where she was detained.

When the girl's uncle was charged and cautioned, he replied to the constable, 'What will I get for this? Do you think I will get three years? My sister is the cause of this. She knew I had this disease.'[164]

There were many similar cases in early twentieth-century Dublin; paedophiles were clearly targeting young girls in the inner city. The victims were frequently offered small amounts of money or sweets, and it was usually the mothers who were either confided in, noticed a change in their daughter's behaviour or mood, or spotted physical evidence that something had changed or was wrong. Countless such cases could be cited. What is striking are the similarities between them, the extent to which neighbours and families were the perpetrators, as well as a preponderance of soldiers; the very young age of the victims; the occurrence of many of the assaults in broad daylight in densely populated areas, the speed with which the Dublin Metropolitan Police apprehended those discovered and how quickly they reacted; and the relatively light sentences that were imposed on those convicted. In March 1911, a 41-year-old man with three previous convictions for assaulting minors (for which he had received sentences of between two weeks and one month) was challenged by the mother of a 5-year-old victim:

I said to defendant I saw you putting your hand up under my child's clothes and he said I was a dangerous woman and when he said that I struck him in the face with my open hand and I took my child downstairs and I examined her and found red marks about her private part. I sent for the police. I told defendant to stop there until I got a policeman to charge him and he said, 'You can do so.' He remained there 'till the policeman came. My daughter told me about 5 or 10 minutes after the occurrence that this man put his hand up her clothes and asked her would she like a penny.

The man was convicted and imprisoned for twelve months with hard labour.[165]

In 1919, another case of indecent assault against a 5-year-old child produced evidence from witnesses who observed the accused in Waterford Street sexually assaulting the child, but 'he had a lot of children around him and was trying to encourage them in'. Members of the public accosted him.[166] During the same Crown session, a 47-year-old man 'in uniform' was charged with the indecent assault of two children, aged 9 and 11, in O'Connell Avenue. He had lured them up a lane way with the promise of sixpence. One of the girls was asked by her uncle why she was crying 'and she said she did not like to tell me what happened down the lane'.[167]

Many of the sentences imposed for such assaults seem relatively light. In August 1917, a man convicted of indecent assault on a girl aged less than 13 received three months' imprisonment. In May 1918, the sentence of one month's hard labour was imposed for gross indecency. Those on rape charges were dealt with more severely; a 5-year penal servitude sentence was imposed for that crime in November 1920.[168] Many of the cases occurred within families living in tenements, so the contention that 'sexual crimes were virtually unknown'[169] in Dublin's tenements does not withstand scrutiny.

'Dancing was the cause of many a bastard and he wanted none in his parish'

As well as a concern for child welfare, as reflected in the activities of the DSPCC, the status of illegitimate mothers and their children was also something that preoccupied charitable proselytising organisations and priests. Reactions to mothers of illegitimate children on the part of members of the clergy was influenced by their training at Ireland's national seminary at Maynooth, as depicted in the works of George Moore in novels such as *The Lake*. One of his characters comments: 'You were the typical priest who looks upon women as the deadly peril and the difficulty of temporal life.' To which the priest replies: 'I remember how at Maynooth the tradition was always to despise women.'[170] Many contemporary writers wrote of the preoccupation priests had with 'the evils of company keeping', and a preference for boys and girls to walk on opposite sides of the road. As a priest says from the altar in Moore's short story 'Home Sickness' in his collection *The Untilled Field* (1903): 'Keeping company is not the custom of the country.'[171] In that book,

Moore elaborates on the contribution the priests were making to sexual repression. In 'Julia Cahill's Curse' he writes of Father Madden, who

> put down the crossroad dances because he said dancing was the cause of many a bastard and he wanted none in his parish. Now there was no dancer like Julia; the boys used to gather around to see her dance and who ever walked with her under the hedges in the summer could never think about another woman. The village was cracked about her, so I suppose the priest was right. He had to get rid of her. But I think he mightn't have been as hard on her as he was.[172]

David Fitzpatrick has drawn attention to a case that reached the Enniskillen Petty Sessions in 1908 concerning a returned Irish emigrant from the United States who engaged a cattle dealer to source him a wife. When he discovered the dealer had sourced him a wife 'with a past' (the dealer maintained she had only 'happened with a bit of a mistake') he was awarded 10 shillings in compensation, despite having boasted to the court of having several previous wives in America.[173]

One of the easiest ways to blacken a character's name was to suggest an association with illegitimacy. When P. D. Kenny, a controversial Catholic and nationalist journalist who edited the *Irish Peasant* newspaper and later allied himself with the Unionist cause, settled at his home place in County Mayo after working as a journalist in Edwardian England, he was attacked from the pulpit because of his critical views of Catholicism, Irish rural society and land agitation. He was subjected to 'a whispering campaign' that 'spoke of illegitimate children and abandoned wives in England', though he was ultimately not excluded from the Irish-Ireland movement.[174]

Many unmarried mothers were destitute and, according to official figures in 1905, there were 2,129 unmarried mothers and 2,764 illegitimate and deserted children (1,454 boys and 1,310 girls) in Irish workhouses. In 1914 William Rodden, organising secretary in Ireland for the NSPCC, pointed out that in England and Scotland, because of the Bastardy Act of 1863, 'girls who have been wronged have got the remedy within themselves if they wish to take advantage of it and I ask the question – why is this remedy denied to Irish girls?' – a reference to the fact that, while the father could be compelled to pay for maintenance in England and Scotland, this did not apply to Ireland where, for many, the only refuge was in the workhouse.[175]

There was a further law in Britain in 1914 (and Northern Ireland in

1924) enabling the mother of an illegitimate child to get an affiliation order from the district court compelling the father to make a contribution to the support of the child until the child reached 16 years of age 'of an amount not exceeding in any case twenty shillings per week',[176] and it was a version of this legislation that was introduced in the Free State in 1930. But in the late nineteenth and early twentieth century, for the mother of an illegitimate child, abandoned by the father, such recourses were largely academic. The law in relation to seduction was quite clearly designed to cater for the better off, even though the overwhelming majority of women affected were poorer, and in the absence of a putative father willing to marry them, or in a case of the father denying parenthood or simply disappearing, there was little the woman could do except depend on charity.

Whatever the law said, there was little ambiguity when it came to the operation of moral judgements in relation to illegitimacy; the idea of 'moral policing' became well established, and much of it was tied into religion and the attitude of clergy. As K. H. Connell noted in the late 1960s in his essays on Irish peasant society, mothers of illegitimate children would have been very fortunate not to be shunned due to the lack of tolerance for 'failure in chastity'.[177] Many were forced into begging or prostitution and the memories of those who were interviewed for the Irish Folklore Commission in the 1930s, some of whom had grown up in the post-Famine period, were that the 'stain' of illegitimacy 'never wears off' and could last for generations. Referring to a table published in 1908 detailing the percentage of illegitimacy to total births in fifteen countries, in which the Irish figure was the lowest, Connell concluded that 'the incidence of extra-marital relations has been relatively low in Ireland – astonishingly low for a people marrying so little and late'.[178] But these figures do not tell the full story and do not take into account 'shotgun' weddings, infanticide and the number of Irish women travelling abroad to have babies.

Unmarried mothers were repeatedly referred to as 'fallen' or 'offending' women, terms that remained in use for many decades. The handbook for Catholic social workers in Dublin in the 1940s, for example, referred to homes for unmarried mothers who were 'principally first offenders' and others who were 'girls in danger'.[179]

There was also a 'rescue and maternity' home in Belfast, about which William Wallace, a Belfast Poor Law guardian, stated that 'out of 262 births in the Belfast Maternity Home for the year ended June 1902, 155 were illegitimate, or 50 per cent of them born in the workhouse'.[180] It was also observed that three-quarters of the unmarried mothers who, with their children, obtained relief in the Belfast workhouse 'were either domestic servants, or girls employed in warehouses, mills and the like'.[181]

In 1912, the Report of the Registrar General revealed that the total number of recorded births for that year was 101,035, of which 98,188 (97.2 per cent) were legitimate and 2,847 illegitimate (2.8 per cent), the latter figure being 0.2 per cent above the corresponding average for the previous ten years. It was noted that 'these results bear favourable comparison with the returns for most other countries', including England, where the illegitimacy rate was 4.2 per cent in 1911. There was some discrepancy between the different provinces; Ulster was the highest with 3.8 per cent, Leinster 2.9 per cent, Munster 2.3 per cent and Connaught 0.7 per cent. The divergence in these figures could be explained partly by pregnancy migration:

> Most of the mothers of illegitimate children in the South Dublin Union come from the country, being sent away from their homes or places of residence. The children are born in Dublin and the illegitimacy is put down to it, or to the province of Leinster, whereas the woman may have come from Munster, Ulster or Connaught.[182]

Charitable organisations with church backing took on the task of 'rescuing' the unmarried mothers and their children in the late nineteenth and early twentieth centuries under the banner of anti-proselytism. The first annual report of the Irish bureau of the International Catholic Girls Protection Society, based in Mountjoy Square, Dublin, was published in 1913 and detailed the attempts to help Catholic girls, with the initial assistance of a £100 donation from the Catholic Archbishop of Dublin in 1912. It was contended that many of these girls 'leave home through foolish motives, others, compelled by circumstances [a frequent euphemism for pregnancy], pass through Dublin on their way, without help or direction – sometimes with no fixed destination'.[183] Another group, the Catholic Protection and Rescue Society of Ireland (CPRSI), based in Molesworth Street, Dublin, was established in 1913 'by a committee of Catholic gentleman' and published annual reports from 1914. It was chiefly concerned with religious rather than physical salvation, claiming that 'enormous sums – between £60,000 and £70,000 a year – are being spent in Ireland by Protestant proselytising organisations'.

The CPRSI acknowledged the work that was being done by institutions like the Sacred Heart Home, and various Catholic maternity societies, 'but such institutions and societies have been local in their activity and limited in their objectives ... some hundreds of Catholic and expectant unmarried mothers drift annually into Dublin and other large cities. Their children and themselves have hitherto fallen for the most part into the hands of the proselytisers, as there is no large Catholic body which will take care of such mothers or look after their children.'[184] It also published typical case studies, profiling the situations young women had found themselves in. The following descriptions are typical of the era: 'Father deserted when he knew of Mother's trouble', or 'Mother leading an immoral life', or 'Father a drunkard'. The perceived ever-present dangers of conversion were also elucidated: 'Protestants traced her whereabouts and tried to get the baby', or 'girl would have been adopted by an Aunt (a Protestant)'.[185]

The society made it clear that religious welfare should be of primary consideration, prioritised above that of physical or mental well-being, and its report for 1915 was defensive about this approach: 'Our sole object is to protect the faith of our Catholic poor. We do not seek to make converts, or to relieve distress or to protect and rescue from a sinful life. All these are admirable works and we have been blamed for refusing to undertake them. But we have been compelled to refuse. Our society was established for a different and we cannot help thinking, a more important purpose – the preservation of the faith.'[186] That year, the society dealt with 275 cases.

'A parcel lying in a bed of nettles'

One solution to the problem of illegitimate children was the killing of newborn babies – referred to as infanticide, or 'concealment of birth' – which was a very common practice in the late nineteenth and early twentieth centuries, and continued well beyond then. Penal codes introduced in various European countries had long recognised infanticide as a serious crime; unified Italy's first penal code, for example, provided for heavy sentences for those guilty of infanticide.[187] It has been observed in relation to infanticide cases in England during the late Victorian period that there were 'a wide variety of other voices present in these narratives';[188] such voices can be found in the Irish cases also. Depositions were not confined to medical or legal professionals, but included the statements of unmarried mothers and their employers and relatives. The Crown Books for Armagh, incorporating the Spring, Summer and Winter Assizes, list five cases of infanticide for that region between 1890 and 1916.[189] Infanticide cases were also common in County Down in the early 1900s.[190] In the Belfast Winter Assizes of 1904, a woman was accused of killing the baby she had given birth to at the maternity hospital in the Belfast Union workhouse. She left the hospital three weeks later, but the baby was found dead the next day, 'a parcel lying in a bed of nettles' off the Ravenhill Road. The accused was a domestic servant who had gone to the workhouse to have her baby. In her own words:

> I may as well tell the truth. When I left the Union I came down by the Ormeau Road and through the Ormeau Park. The child was sick and vomiting. When I came out to the Ravenhill Road, I turned up towards Ballynafeigh and I left it down beside some nettles in a new avenue off the Ravenhill Road ... I took the train to Bangor and returned to my service ... what do you think will happen to me for this or will I get transported?[191]

It appears that some women charged with infanticide were treated compassionately, or perhaps occasionally given the benefit of the doubt. In 1918 a woman accused of concealing a birth in Dublin city 'by secretly placing the dead body of said child in a bucket' was attended to by the same maternity nurse who had attended at the birth of her previous nine children. According to the medical evidence she had suffered considerable haemorrhaging and appeared 'dazed'. When asked where her child was, 'she said the child must have fallen in the bucket at the birth and that she didn't hear it cry'. The woman was found not guilty.[192] But it was unusual for married mothers of so many children to be accused of infanticide or concealment of birth; much more common were young unmarried mothers who panicked, alone, or acted with the assistance of relatives. In December 1900, a 23-year-old hospital cook was found not guilty of the murder of her newborn infant. She had been sharing a room with another employee in Foley's Hotel, Wicklow Street, at the time and, having given birth in a toilet, placed the baby's body in a tin box, wrapped it in a towel with a portion of the towel in its mouth. The medical evidence was that the child had been asphyxiated, but the jury decided the woman was not responsible for her actions at the time. The woman with whom she had been sharing said simply, 'I had not noticed that the defendant was pregnant.'[193] (It was not unusual for women to successfully conceal their pregnancies to full term.)

In 1914, a woman staying at a lodging house in Upper Gloucester Street, Dublin, locked her prematurely newborn twins in a trunk in a room that she was sharing with two others. She had given birth to them in the room in the dark; one of her roommates maintained she did not know the woman was pregnant. The defendant did not wish to say anything when charged, except 'when I was not sick I did not tell anyone about them. Only they died I would not have locked them up in my trunk.'[194] This case contains details that were common to many: women moving from lodging house to lodging house, enduring pregnancy and childbirth in the dark, without privacy and away from their homes, and frequently trying to hide their pregnancies, especially from their employers.

'The "scientific" camp still had to deal with the "moral" camp'

Another issue that was receiving considerable attention in the early twentieth century was venereal diseases (sometimes referred to as 'the black plague'). As Maria Luddy highlights, considerable advances had been made in their treatment, including the Wasserman test for syphilis, introduced in 1906, but there was still very little public discussion of the issue in Ireland: 'the use of Salvarsan and its derivatives, and the knowledge available about the prevention of venereal diseases, did not lead to any great level of enlightenment on the issue; the "scientific" camp still had to deal with the "moral" camp.'[195] J. V. O'Brien suggests that of the 1,984 deaths from venereal disease recorded in Ireland between 1899 and 1916, 69 per cent of the victims were children under five years of age, inherited syphilis being the main killer.[196] At the dispensary in Sir Patrick Dun's hospital from August 1904 to October 1908, the number of VD consultations suggest 'a high rate of infection as in Dublin too many VD sufferers would not have resorted to medical institutions, but would have relied on the many "quack" or patent remedies then available'.[197] In 1914, figures given by the Irish Registrar General suggested a high death rate in Dublin from syphilis, at 1.47 per 10,000, compared with only 0.51 in Belfast and 0.76 in London, but 'given the reluctance of Dublin hospitals to accept VD patients, this could have been due to lack of adequate treatment facilities as much as to high rates of infection'.[198]

The British government had not done enough to combat VD in the late nineteenth and early twentieth centuries; indeed 'the publication of the word "Syphilis" in 1913 was a major breakthrough', but the impact of the

First World War meant that it could be ignored no longer.[199] A Royal Commission on VD which sat between 1913 and 1916 heard evidence from Dr Brian O'Brien, chief medical inspector to the Irish local government board. He believed that VD had declined in Ireland, and that syphilis was almost non-existent outside of urban areas because, in his words, 'there was very little immorality' in rural Ireland. He attributed the prevalence of syphilis in Dublin to poverty, bad housing, the tendency of 'girls who go wrong' to drift to the city and the fact that Dublin was a refuge for people 'who are doing no good for themselves'.[200]

The commission's report led to the Public Health (Prevention and Treatment of Disease) (Ireland) Act of 1917, whereby a county council, provided it gave consent, could be an agency for dealing with the disease. In October 1917, circulars were sent to local authorities to inform them of details concerning the diagnosis and treatment of VD, with a promise of 75 per cent financial aid for any schemes they embarked upon. In the event, suitable schemes were formulated in only six counties: Dublin, Louth, Westmeath, Monaghan, Kildare and Wicklow, while during the War of Independence the schemes in Louth and Westmeath fell into abeyance.[201] By the early 1920s, two out of twelve wards at Dr Steeven's hospital in Dublin were available for VD treatment and 'arrangements are so organised as to prevent the VD patients being distinguished from the other inmates of the hospital'. In the year 1921–2, 10,624 people attended as outpatients.[202]

'People who can do these things must be dead to all sense of shame'

Another issue about which there was little public discussion was homosexuality, but the trial of Oscar Wilde in 1895 and other high-profile scandals ensured that an awareness of homosexual offences became more widespread. In that sense, the Wilde trial was 'far more influential in constructing popular and even medical attitudes' about homosexuality, and an expression such as 'an unspeakable of the Oscar Wilde sort' became more representative of the public's vague notions about homosexuality than sexologists Havelock Ellis and Edward Carpenter's 'inverts', 'intermediates' and 'uranians'.[203]

Wilde's relationship with Alfred Douglas, a son of the Marquis of Queensbury, enraged the latter, who wrote a note to Wilde accusing him of 'posing as a Somdomite [sic]'. Wilde's solicitor subsequently applied for a warrant for the arrest of Queensbury for libel. But what began as a libel suit against Queensbury evolved quickly into an examination of the morality of Wilde's art and then into the 'gross indecency' of his relationships with younger, working-class men. As a major media event with a famous author in the dock accused of homosexual offences and a cross-class cast, it was assured significant coverage, not just in Britain and Ireland, but across Europe. Wilde's biographer Richard Ellmann observes that 'as the French newspapers commented with some bewilderment, in England sodomy ranked only one step below murder'.[204]

The trial can also be seen as the second major scandal (after the Cleveland Street Affair of 1889–90, which had involved messenger boys and postal clerks who had prostituted themselves to rich men) featuring cross-class liaisons which 'heightened tensions about the extent of consumer sexuality ... The overlap of sexuality and signs of wealth, like the champagne dinners and silver cigarette cases that Wilde gave to his working-class lovers, seemed indicative of the developing consumer culture of sexuality in which the sexual consumer could find all sorts of articles and individuals to meet his tastes (as feminists and socialists quite rightly pointed out). The contrast between the rich and the poor – Wilde's boys, the postal clerks in the Cleveland Street scandal ... and the commodities that passed between them created an explosive situation that played out politically as well as sexually. This rift took place where physical desires merged with consumer longings.'[205]

What was also striking at the time was the public opprobrium, the prison sentence imposed (two years with hard labour, Wilde having been convicted of 'gross indecency'), the damning language, and the fact that there was almost universal praise for the guilty verdict from the press. Wilde, who despite his formidable performance and fortitude in the dock, denied everything sexual, later reflected that the closing speech of the prosecution was 'an appalling denunciation ... like a thing out of Tacitus, like a passage in Dante, like one of Savonarda's indictments of the Popes at Rome'. Mr Justice Willis in his summing-up included the observation that 'it is the worst case I have ever tried', and concluded:

> The crime of which you have been convicted is so bad that one has to put stern restraint upon one's self to prevent one's self from describing it in a language I would rather not use, the sentiments which must rise to the breast of every man of honour who has heard the details of these two terrible trials ... It is no use for me to address you. People who can do

these things must be dead to all sense of shame and one cannot hope to produce any effect upon them.[206]

When writing to the Home Secretary in 1896 Wilde referred to the offences for which he was imprisoned as 'forms of sexual madness', but in truth he was unrepentant. According to J. B. Lyons, 'This concession to the outraged mores of his time was motivated to attract official sympathy and failed to do so. After his release he gave full rein to his imagination, reassured by the liberality of France.'[207]

Publicly, because of the stigma attached to homosexuality, there seemed little appetite for remembering Oscar Wilde both as an Irishman and as a gay man. Reflecting on a revival in studies of Wilde in the 1990s, Declan Kiberd suggests: 'Just as Wilde's Irishness poses some problems for those who considered that he had been conclusively assimilated to English dramatic tradition, so now his gayness is offering a challenge to some who would otherwise be happy – after all these years – to reclaim him for Ireland. For these essentialist souls you can be gay or you can be Irish, but you cannot be both at the same time ... there would be little point in recovering Wilde's Irish elements if this were to be done at the cost of denying his sexual identities.'[208]

But perhaps this ignores the extent to which Wilde 'came to be seen by subsequent Irish authors as a disruptive figure of anti-colonial resistance and that this reconstruction mitigated his aberrant homosexuality for those writers and indeed for their society. Even the powerfully homophobic culture that twentieth-century Ireland was to develop located strategies by which the unspeakable Oscar could be reclaimed as Wilde, the Irish rebel.'[209]

A 'crisis of sexual identity and male privilege' has also been identified as a feature of Victorian England in the 1890s, accompanied by the advent of sexology in the same decade; meanwhile, as exemplified most obviously by the Wilde trial, a 'public contest' over the meaning of masculinity took place in the press and courts. One conclusion drawn is that journalism and trials enabled a male 'hegemonic culture to subordinate the new self-consciousness of men who desired other men'; another is that a sensationalising populist press provided space to generate scandals, but had also made possible 'the marketing of Wilde's persona' on which he based his career. Richard Dellamora has identified a 'literature of masculine crisis' seen in such books as Wilde's own *Picture of Dorian Gray* (1890) and Henry James's *The Beast in the Jungle* (1903), through which a 'homosexual existence' was both visible and vocal.

Jeff Weeks suggests the possible outcome of many of these different elements and the consequences of the 1885 legislation criminalising all homosexual acts had already been vividly demonstrated the preceding summer when 'a full-scale homosexual scandal involving high officials in Dublin Castle' occurred.[210] This is a reference to the allegation by Irish nationalist politician William O'Brien in his newspaper *United Ireland* that Dublin Castle administrators and officers had engaged in homosexual activities – which gave a public airing of a widely held private view that 'homosexual vice was rampant in official circles in Ireland'.[211] Gustavus Cornwall, the secretary of the General Post Office, sued O'Brien for libel, but the move backfired as evidence brought against Cornwall and others resulted in them being tried for indecency and sodomy. A number were found guilty and imprisoned; Cornwall was acquitted, but resigned his post in Dublin Castle, 'for having, as one Dublin wag put it, tampered with her majesty's males'.[212]

The extensive condemnation of homosexuality in the Irish media was accompanied by the nationalist contention that it was a 'foreign' vice. But, as pointed out by Eibhear Walshe, the coverage of the Wilde trials was different in Ireland than in England, as Irish media coverage of the Wilde trials 'drew out an ambivalent and often contradictory contestation around Wilde's sexual sin from within Irish cultural discourse. The Irish newspapers struck a markedly differing note from that of their British counterparts.'[213] Because he was an Irishman, the discourse about homosexuality became more circumspect and instead concentrated on 'nationalist outrage at British legal injustice', with Wilde's defence subsequently presented as 'one of the great Irish anti-imperialist speeches from the dock' (his mother, Speranza, was also a revered nationalist). Irish newspapers at the time of Wilde's trial were very reticent about naming the crime or giving the details; direct mention of homosexuality was avoided, reference instead being made to certain 'abominations' with hints at 'a queer community hidden within artistic and theatrical circles' and many comments made on his flamboyant appearance and dress and physical arrogance, so that 'the defendant's body becomes the site upon which the trial's sexual significance can be inscribed'.[214]

'Sodom and Gomorrah were destroyed by fire but
Dublin castle still stands'

Another controversy that sparked allegations of homosexuality in Dublin's
ruling establishment was the theft of the Crown Jewels of the Order of St
Patrick for the use of the Lord Lieutenant in Ireland in his capacity as Grand
Master of the Order. The disappearance of the jewels coincided with the
visit of King Edward VII to Dublin in 1907. Though 'documented allusions
to homosexual activity at the Office of Arms are oblique and names are
seldom used',[215] the custodian of the arms, Sir Arthur Vicars, and his staff,
including Frank Shackleton (who Vicars believed was responsible for the
theft), came under intense scrutiny, with suggestions of lack of security and
after-hours hospitality at the Bedford Tower in Dublin Castle for selected
males. An attempt was made to break Vicars' resolve by circulating rumours
that he was homosexual. Confidential files on high-society homosexuals
which linked Vicars with other men, including Lord Aberdeen, were leaked
within perhaps another political context – the hope of destroying the moral
reputation of Aberdeen, a Home Rule supporter.[216] Shackleton became the
chief suspect: 'the reasoning was that, even if he had not actually stolen the
jewels himself (he was out of the country when they were taken) he might,
under threat of exposure as a homosexual, have been blackmailed into supplying the thieves with the sort of help and information that had ensured the
success of their operation'.[217]

In any case, it was deemed imperative to clear out the staff 'without
giving a clue that there were any motives other than the justifiable removal
of an incompetent administration', though this did not stop newspapers in
places as far away as New York making references to orgies and gangs of
'aristocratic degenerates' and the declaration that 'Sodom and Gomorrah
were destroyed by fire but Dublin Castle still stands'.[218] Police investigations
and a Vice-regal Commission of Inquiry failed to lead to any arrests or the
recovery of the jewels. Vicars was dismissed for negligence.

It has been suggested that the Irish language stories of Patrick Pearse,
who came to prominence as one of the leaders of the Easter Rising in 1916,
were influenced by Oscar Wilde, though little acknowledgement was made
of this, or of the tone of his poem '*A Mhic Bhig Na gCleas*' ('Little Lad of
the Tricks'), which was described much later as 'a poem of far more explicit
homosexuality than any written by Wilde' and one that contained 'a palpable presence of same-sex desire'.[219] This may be an exaggeration: Pearse was

probably asexual, and his poetic focus on young men and boys probably had more to do with the Edwardian fascination with the cult of youthful masculinity than his own sexuality. It has also been suggested that the notion that Pearse was sexually attracted to boys is based only on the above mentioned Irish language poem and that 'to produce the desired effect, it is translated naively into English where then the suggestive undercurrent of the English word "tricks" can be brought into play. One poem – one in translation at that – makes a meagre and unsteady crutch for an argument. Poetry does not allow itself to be interpreted with the cold precision algebra does.'[220] The translated verse that some believe contains the evidence of an erotic interest in young boys is as follows:

> There is a fragrance in your kiss
> That I have not found yet
> In the kisses of women
> Or in the honey of their bodies.[221]

In truth, Pearse had no experience of 'the honey' of women's bodies. As recounted by Ruth Dudley Edwards, he was ill at ease with women, and 'after adolescence, passion between men and women ceased to figure in his writings'. Tales of an engagement to a young Gaelic League activist were construed after his death; in reality he 'had not the slightest inclination to take a wife'. The English translation of the above poem 'caused alarm among his more worldly friends', some of whom explained to him the 'ignoble construction' that could be placed on it, which left Pearse hurt and bewildered.[222]

'Edward was a bachelor before he left his mother's womb'

In 1929, when Denis Gwynn published his life of the nationalist and leading figure of the Irish cultural renaissance Edward Martyn, he wrote nothing of Martyn's private life, and soon afterwards Martyn's personal papers were lost, possibly destroyed 'given that they may well have revealed the complexity of Edward's sexual nature or even his latent Paganism'.[223] Martyn's cousin George Moore showed no such restraint in laying bare Martyn's private life in his trilogy *Hail and Farewell*, published between 1911 and 1914:

> Edward was a bachelor before he left his mother's womb ... if the boy is
> a natural boy with a healthy love of sex, in his body, the wife or mistress
> will redeem him from his mother, but if there be no such love in him he
> stands in great danger.

Throughout the book Moore lampoons what he considers to be Martyn's misogyny and his love of boys, but as Madeleine Humphreys' 2007 biography of Martyn argues, while all his life Martyn liked men and boys, by the time Moore's book was published most of his friends were strong, independent-minded women whom he respected and who, in turn, held him in great affection.[224] His was a life that certainly lacked intimacy:

> There is no evidence that he ever accepted the responsibility of physical
> love and all his early writings suggest a strong aversion of women. Such
> sentiment was well suited to Oxford University in 1879 when the cult
> of Hellenism was the *Zeitgeist*. Edward read for a degree in *Literae
> Humaniores* [classics] (which he did not achieve) where the emphasis
> was on the work of Johann Joachim Winkelmann, who believed that
> true beauty must always be male and never could be female.

This influence was apparent in his later work but, in publishing what he did, Moore did not acknowledge any emotional development in Martyn and in portraying Martyn as a 'loveable duffer' discounted his cousin's 'genuine and serious contribution to the artistic movements of the era'.[225]

Alongside artistic reflections on the nature of masculinity and same sex desire, internationally, the development of sexology also ensured greater attention was given to homosexuality. In 1912, a homosexual emancipation movement in the Netherlands, the Dutch Scientific Humanitarian Committee, followed the German example of Magnus Hirschfeld in maintaining that it was a congenital condition which had to be accepted as a natural phenomenon, though an ensuing backlash followed that was part of the wider condemnation of all extra marital sex.[226] Meanwhile, in France there was a certain contemptuousness in descriptions of homosexuality and disdain shown towards Freud's theory that the libido was not programmed for any particular combination of sexual direction but gained its orientation in the course of an individual's life experience.[227]

'A strange aberration which had little to do with the character of the man'

Much has been made of the homosexuality of Irish patriot Sir Roger Casement, who was executed for treason after the 1916 Rising. Casement is remembered for his campaigns against the brutalisation of indigenous peoples in the Congo and the Amazon (for which he received a knighthood) and his Irish nationalism (he resigned from the consular service in 1913), but he 'remains a hot topic much less on account of his public acts than because he left behind him a set of diaries describing his promiscuous gay sex life in explicit detail. A final indignity for Casement was that a rectal examination by the Pentonville Prison medical officer on his corpse after he had been hanged found, in the medic's words, "unmistakeable evidence of the practices to which, it was alleged, the prisoner in question had been addicted".[228] The authenticity of the diaries is generally, though not unanimously, accepted. The debate over the authenticity of his 'black diaries' has raged for decades 'and will probably never be resolved to everyone's satisfaction', but forensic tests and handwriting analysis conducted in 2002 confirm what most Casement scholars believe – that 'beyond reasonable doubt Roger Casement did indeed write the diaries'.[229]

The most voluminous biography of Casement to date, published in 2008, concludes that they are genuine and remarks that 'when old "discrepancies" or "contradictions" have been found to be no longer sustainable, the forgery school has continued to reinvent itself by discovering new ones ... the overall content of the diaries fits comfortably with Casement's movements during the relevant years ... the patterns of sexuality revealed in the volumes, though causing shock to many, are familiar to gay observers.'[230]

Casement left behind a revealing gay geography of the many places where he spent time. According to his diaries, the gay cruising areas in Belfast were at the Albert Clock (and 'the Custom's House toilet'), Botanic Gardens, Ormeau Park and the Giant's Ring as well as in 'an elegant iron edifice' in Victoria Square and at the gasworks. The GNR station in Great Victoria Street and DuBarry's bar at the docks were also 'recognised haunts, the latter, as in other cities, being shared with prostitutes.'[231] Casement's diaries have prompted imaginative reconstructions of his sex life, depicting a man 'lusting after transient pleasures with young male bodies'.

The homosexual exploits recounted in Casement's diaries for 1903, 1910 and 1911 reveal 39 such entries for 1903, 70 in 1910 and 'several hundred'

in 1911; scrawled jottings in pen and pencil describing anonymous casual
encounters, usually with young men and teenagers, 'frequently recording
size of genitals and price paid'. But this level of promiscuity is not unusual
when compared with the recorded experiences of Edward Stevenson, an
American writer in London in the early twentieth century, and John May-
nard Keynes, the economist, 'who kept a detailed record of his homosexual
encounters between 1906 and 1915'.[232] Plenty were willing to sell their bodies for cash payments as an income supplement and Casement's sexual journey incorporated London, Paris, Dublin, Belfast and Lisbon amongst other
places.

In the summer of 1916, when the details of the diaries became public,
an editorial in the *Daily Express* insisted that if those attempting to turn
him into a martyr read the diaries, 'no man – and certainly no minister of
religion – would ever mention Casement's name again without loathing and
contempt', while the British Home Secretary, Herbert Samuel, when writing a letter to his wife about the unpleasant Cabinet meeting in which it
was decided not to reprieve Casement after he was sentenced to be hanged,
observed that 'had Casement not been a man of atrocious moral character,
the situation would have been even more difficult'. A Dublin clergyman in
whose parish Casement had lived in 1914 suggested to the Home Office that
he be confined to a criminal lunatic asylum.[233]

'Trying to do a bit of Oscar Wilde on me'

Homosexuality, of course, was by no means confined to Dublin Castle or
the aristocracy. The Crown files at commission for the County and City
of Dublin in April 1903 detail the case of a 32-year-old man accused of
attempted buggery ('that detestable and abominable crime called buggery',
to give it its full legal title) with a young soldier on 22 February 1903, during
which the ghost of Wilde made an appearance. Later, when in the dock for
the crime of shoplifting, the alleged victim said the accused 'was trying to do
a bit of Oscar Wilde on me', or, as the policeman's deposition put it,

> As Defendant was going over to sign the charge sheet the soldier P. said,
> 'That's the man who tried to Oscar Wilde me and he gave me money and
> drink to get me out of the house and he told me to come back tomorrow
> night and he'd give me plenty more.'[234]

The alleged victim had been standing outside the soldiers' home in Parkgate Street, Dublin, when the defendant asked him for a light and if he wanted to go for a drink. They proceeded to O'Connell Street, where they boarded a tram for Terenure where the accused had a shop; both had whiskey and the sexual advances allegedly began:

> He asked me to take my belt off and sit down. He tried to open the front of my trousers and once succeeded in doing so. He caught me by the private parts through the trousers. He opened his own trousers and exposed his person. He tried to get his private part against my body and I shoved him away several times. He gave me money and a bottle of whiskey. When he saw that it was of no use he told me to go away. He was playing about me all the time I was in the shop – catching hold of me. I don't remember leaving the shop. There is no part of my body sore today. He attempted to commit this crime with me.

The alleged victim was arrested for shop-breaking later that night, and was found to have whiskey and money in his possession. He maintained he 'told nobody about Defendant's indecent conduct till I was in the dock'. The soldier's belt, gloves and stick had been left behind in the house.

Some details of this case mirror what emerged in many other trials: the attempt by an older man to seduce a younger one; the promise of a reward – whether food, drink or money; drunkenness; and allegation and counter-allegation in the wake of the event. Some cases involved more violence, particularly where young boys were involved.

On the same day in court as the previous case, a 38-year-old man was accused of buggering a 10-year-old boy in a wood near Blandchardstown in County Dublin. The victim had met the accused a few times in the vicinity in November 1902 when he had been asking directions. The child accompanied him to the wood and then according to the victim's description:

> He knocked me down, threw me on my face, pulled off my trousers and took off his own, he lay on top of me, kissed me, hurt me and wet me behind. He said don't tell anyone about this or I will take your life and I told nobody about what happened as I was afraid.

Nine days later, the boy was again taken to the wood by the accused and again was dragged and knocked down: 'He turned me on my face and lay on the top of me and kissed me and said the mouse was in.' But this time someone disturbed them. The medical evidence was inconclusive; the doctor found 'no mark of any violence upon him; it might be possible for penetration to take place without leaving any mark or any visible signs'. The accused, who had been 'constantly on the road looking for work', was found guilty; he had been imprisoned four times previously for vagrancy and loitering.[235]

It appears it was common for gay men to lure young boys with the promise of money for services rendered. This most frequently happened in densely populated areas, as revealed in the case of a man who lured an 8-year-old boy into a water closet in the back yard of a tenement house in Great Britain Street, Dublin, in February 1900. He was formally charged with 'procuring the commission of an act of gross indecency'. The evidence of the arresting policeman was as follows:

> I cautioned him. He said in reply I'm guilty but I thought it was for begging you wanted me. I may as well tell you all. I met two little fellows in Green Street on Saturday evening. One of them was a little red-headed fellow. I brought them to Britain Street to a hall there and in the back yard there is a closet. I brought in the little fellow, shut the door. I got him to rub my mickie until the milk came. It was the divil tempted me to do it. I did not think it was any harm. Don't be hard on me for my poor old mother's sake who is a cripple.[236]

The man was sentenced to eight months' imprisonment with hard labour.

In contrast to the furtive activities of that tenement dweller, in December 1904 a man who had been 'going about Sandymount all the evening drinking' the previous month was charged with sexually assaulting three teenage boys, after he had emerged in a drunken state from Moroney's public house on Sandymount Road. The advances occurred 'opposite the public house; there was plenty of light there', so there was no shortage of witnesses, the most important of whom were the boys, who were well aware of what the man was attempting to do: 'Defendant asked me would I toss him off ... he didn't offer me any money.' Meanwhile another witness saw the man 'put his hand twice on [one boy's] private parts outside his clothes', this witness commenting 'to toss me off means two men together, just the same as a man and a woman'. Another of the boys' depositions noted: 'Defendant tipped me twice in my privates and offered me sixpence to toss him off.' The defendant was bailed for fifty pounds, but was subsequently convicted and sentenced to six months' imprisonment with hard labour.[237]

One of the notable features of the court records concerning older men's assaults on young boys is the number of witnesses who emerged. In 1911, a 40-year-old man with one previous conviction for assault was accused of the indecent assault of a 6-year-old boy at Greek Street in Dublin city, where it was alleged he had taken a boy into the toilet. Lavatories seem to have been common venues for such assaults, which is unsurprising given the lack of private accommodation and the fact that so many different people were sharing single buildings and single rooms. It also explains, given the high population densities of such areas, why many of these men were observed, caught and ultimately brought to trial. In this case, the WC was in a back yard and the perpetrator locked the door and remained there for half an hour. The defendant 'said the child lost a cap and he was looking for it', while in her statement the mother of the child 'saw a crowd after the defendant' when they had returned from the WC. The doctor remarked that there were 'no marks whatever on the child', though it should be noted that medical evidence of injury was not necessary for there to be a conviction.

Many of the cases of indecency between males, whether consensual or not, seem to have occurred in lavatories. In May 1910 two men were accused of gross indecency in a toilet at the back of the Royal Oak public house in Dublin. It was a double closet in the back yard; unbeknownst to the men, they were being observed by a witness in the other closet, who said he 'stood on the seat and saw McG. with his trousers down, L. beside him and L. was on top of McG. McG's chest was leaning on the seat of the closet and his rump exposed to L. who put his penis funnel into McG.'s rump'. McG insisted he was not a consenting party; he was a 19-year-old recruit from the Highland Light Infantry and a native of Glasgow who had met the accused, L, a 60-year-old man, at Kingsbridge railway station; McG claimed that L had taken his train ticket. He continued:

> We both left the station and I went across the bridge and into a public house. He stood me a drink and I took a bottle of Bass and I can't say what he had himself. I wanted to go to the lavatory and did so and he came in at my back. I was using the closet when he came in and the lower part of my body was undressed. I had not put the catch on the closet door. When he came in he said, 'It's alright'; he put his arms around me and then ill-used me; he took out his private part and he put it into my

backside hole. I shouted and I resisted as well as I could and two men put their heads over the partition and said it was wrong or words to that effect and to get out of that. Accused then ran out of the lavatory and I went to the bar and the accused man was not there. I came out and I met the two men and they told me not to let him off, to charge him. The next time I saw him was in the bar of the same public house again and he stood a drink. I took a bottle of Bass and we went along the riverside ... and three men were with us.

Both men were found guilty.[238]

There are a number of interesting aspects to this case: the witnesses; the youth and probable confusion of the victim; the fact that he was prepared to drink with the accused after the first alleged assault; the fact that men appeared to be moving around together in groups; and, once again, the level of drunkenness. An appendix to the prison calendar reveals that McG was considered suitable for Borstal, it being noted, 'His associates are of bad character and he has not been sober or industrious and he appears to be drifting into criminal habits.'[239] Under the Prevention of Crime Act of 1908, young offenders between the ages of 16 and 21 could be sent to Borstal rather than prison.

Another lavatory, this time a public urinal in East Sussex Street, featured in a case later that month. This time the charge was commission of an act of gross indecency and the procuring of the same. The defendant was a 24-year-old former junior clerk in the Navy, now living at the Linen Hall barracks in Dublin, who was said by a witness to have been in the urinal with 'an elderly man':

When I went in defendant and another male were in it. As soon as I went in I noticed both men were open together, the front of their trousers was open, their private parts were exposed. Defendant more exposed than the other. The other man had a hold of defendant by the private part. I can't say if defendant had a hold of the other man. The other man came round to me and put his hand over me. I said, 'How dare you, you old scoundrel' ... I didn't follow either of the men. I was just exposed when the other man made to touch me. I had never seen that before.

The witness informed a police constable who identified the defendant and followed him to another urinal at Wood Quay, another urinal at Essex Street and yet another at Wellington Quay. The defendant 'kept loitering around Essex Street', but it was clearly difficult to catch him in the act, as he was found not guilty.[240]

'He gave me a silver penny after he did that'

Children were frequent targets of abusers. It was not uncommon for a number of children to be targeted by the abuser, who was often a neighbour, or already known to the children. In November 1909 a man was charged with gross indecency with a 7-year-old boy at a 'closet' in Grassmarble Lane; two other children, aged 9 and 11, also gave evidence of having been abused by the same man. The 7-year-old described how 'he made me get up on his back before that and do bad things on his back. He gave me a silver penny after he did that. I spent it and got a halfpenny change and gave it to my mother ... when I went home I got sick and vomited and told my mother what happened to me.' The 9-year-old boy referred to the defendant 'putting his fork against my back and pulling me everyway'.[241] The case was not proceeded with.[242]

Soldiers also appeared frequently in the sex cases heard at the Dublin commission hearings. In October 1915 two soldiers, one aged 40, the other 34, were handed over to the custody of a constable in College Street by the military authorities and detained for drunkenness. Later on, when giving evidence on a charge of indecency with a male person, the constable described looking into the cell:

> I saw that Mr K., having L.'s persons in his hand. They were both lying side by side on the cell floor ... I saw Mr K. with his trousers down below his hips, his back was turned towards L. and L.'s pinnus was inserted in Mr K.'s backside. I could see plainly it was inside ... they were under the influence of drink still but knew what they were doing.

Both were charged and had nothing to say: 'both then seemed sober'. One of the men had a previous conviction for indecent behaviour in Belfast in 1907. However, both were found not guilty, despite graphic evidence of their activities from three witnesses. It would appear that witnesses' responses to questions asked about their drunkenness may have secured their acquittal:

'Did the soldiers intelligibly understand what they were doing?'
'No.'
'Was what they were doing substantially caused by intoxication?'
'Yes.'[243]

Others were undoubtedly experiencing homosexuality in more rarefied atmospheres and there were concerted attempts to prevent this. There seemed to be a belief in Victorian Britain and Ireland in the late nineteenth century that masturbation was something of a gateway to homosexuality, with the result that, for some, 'trouser pockets were sewn up and lavatory doors removed to create virtual Victorian sexual concentration camps'.[244]

'Perfect weekends'

There was no public discussion of lesbianism, though Emma Donoghue has pointed out that 'at least two dozen Irish writers from the late eighteenth to the late twentieth century have touched on lesbian themes in their works'.[245] Rosa Mulholland's *The Tragedy of Chris* (1903) tells the story of Chris, a young flower seller who saves another girl, Sheelia, from beggary. They become devoted partners, living together and fostering a child, though their activities are never presented as sexual or deviant. One passage describes Chris being kissed 'with passion ... yielding to the embrace and allowing her poor, thin face to be kissed and held close to Sheelia's womanly shoulder'.[246] Edith Somerville, partner of Martin Ross (Violet Martin), wrote about the significance of their relationship in her *Irish Memories* (1917): 'For most boys and girls the varying yet invariable flirtations and emotional episodes of youth, are resolved and composed by marriage. To Martin and to me was opened another way and the flowering of both our lives was when we met each other.'[247]

There was no such frankness in the writings of Kathleen Lynn, a doctor who was active in the suffrage movement, vice-president of the Irish Women's Workers Union and medical director of the Irish Citizen Army, and who was elected to the executive of Sinn Féin in 1917. She established St Ultan's hospital for children in Dublin in 1919 with Madeleine ffrench-Mullan, the nurse and deeply committed political and social activist, suffragist, republican and Sinn Féin councillor with whom she shared both her political work and her personal life. They lived together in Rathmines in Dublin. Lesbians writing in the twenty-first century, including Marie Mulholland, whose perceptive biography of Lynn was published in 2002, have found themselves embroiled in 'an academic wrestling match; that is, the debate on whether women from a past century whose domestic and intimate lives revolved around other women could be described as lesbian and whether those intimacies took sexual expression ... Was an enduring affection between two spinsters a positive alternative to the confinement of traditional nineteenth- and early twentieth-century marriage?'[248]

There has been pressure, in this sense, to find incontrovertible evidence of a physical relationship between the two women, but Mulholland concludes that this is the wrong approach, as medical and social constraints placed on women's relationships 'would have seriously impeded any explicit acknowledgement of sexual intimacy' and because 'the evidence is found throughout the emotional, professional, public and private dimensions of Kathleen's life and is rarely hidden'. The two women shared a home for almost three decades and Kathleen's diary entries contain intimate and loving references to Madeleine and to their loving domestic environment. They stole time together to be alone, had 'perfect weekends' in Wicklow: 'no man ever made a dent in their commitment to one another ... in fact, no man was ever allowed to get that close'.[249] What is also clear is that Lynn and ffrench-Mullan were just one of a number of female couples involved in the political and social movements of early twentieth-century Ireland who established a 'lasting, committed political and domestic relationship with another woman, such as Eva Gore Booth (sister of Constance Markievicz) and Esther Roper, Louie Bennett of the Irish Women's Workers Union and Helen Chevenix [trade unionist and pacifist]'.[250]

It has also been argued by a London lesbian history group that 'it is ... a misleading belief ... that the term lesbian refers solely to a sexual practice and not to a mode of life in which a woman's political, intellectual, emotional, social and sexual energies are focused on other women'.[251] What Lynn and ffrench-Mullan's partnership amounted to was a 'vibrant and determined lesbian approach to living and loving', highlighted by historians like Mulholland 'because it mirrors so much of my own and that of my lesbian friends'.[252] This might be seen as an attempt to read history backwards, but Mulholland's measured account of Lynn's life and diaries suggests she does not fall into that trap. What is striking in many of these partnerships is the absolute confidence these women had in their mutual love and their determination to live together as they saw fit; whether or not theirs were physical relationships is perhaps the wrong preoccupation.

'Immorality is promoted by overcrowded dwellings'

Legal historian Thomas O'Malley has highlighted the preoccupation of moral reformers with identifying and punishing perceived sexual deviancy, while neglecting the social and economic conditions that created the environment in which the crimes occurred. This is borne out by the fact that so many of the sexual crime cases concern poorer parts of Dublin city and residents of overcrowded tenements. Such living conditions were identified on many occasions as being conducive to sexual abuse. According to the census of 1911, 26,000 families lived in inner city tenements, 20,000 of them in just one room. In Henrietta Street, an astonishing 835 people lived in just 15 houses.[253] A housing inquiry in 1914 found both that 16 members of Dublin Corporation, the city authority, owned tenements and that members of the Corporation intervened to prevent the enforcement of regulations against their properties.[254]

As early as 1875, a manual of public health published in Dublin identified overcrowding as a contributory factor to the spread of sexually transmitted diseases, and the solution was deemed to lie in comfortable dwellings rather than legislation:

> Immorality is promoted by overcrowded dwellings and the too close contact of the sexes in the wretched homes of the working classes, in many of which decency is totally disregarded.[255]

Giving evidence to the commission on the relief of unemployment in the 1920s, E. P. McCarron, the secretary of the Department of Local Government and Public Health, highlighted the fact that in 1913 there were 5,322 tenements in Dublin occupied by 87,305 people, with 20,108 families occupying one-roomed tenements; even in the mid 1920s, there were 78,934 people living in one-roomed tenements, meaning 'nearly a quarter of the total population of Dublin city consists of families housed in one-roomed tenements'. The number of people resident in single rooms was 68,100 in 1913 and 78,934 in 1926. One Irish doctor involved in maternity and child welfare work wrote to contraception pioneer Dr Marie Stopes in February 1919 outlining his fears about overburdened mothers, and wondering whether there was any possibility of her sending him a leaflet he could distribute among the labouring classes about limiting the size of their families: 'I am one of a great many others who have tried in all the first-class chemists in Dublin for the appliances you recommend and have been met with an indignant denial of stocking any such things.'[256]

In February 1928 the Revd D. Hall, director of the Association for the Housing of the Very Poor, maintained, 'the conditions are hellish. Sin creeps in and young people with bad habits infect others. You will find from cases in the law courts that it is out of such places come people who have really degenerated. It seems to me that flats only make it possible for a number of bad-minded people to associate with and corrupt others, unless there is some other influence to help them.'[257]

'He said from the bed that I should bring back his Mayflower'

Many of the legal cases of the early twentieth century reflect the extent to which living conditions contributed to sexual crime. In April 1900 a man was found guilty of raping his sister-in-law, a 16-year-old girl, on the Clonliffe Road in Dublin. She was on her way to the Gardiner Street church, and had just emerged from six years in a convent in Cashel. He told her not to tell her sister of the rape 'as he would have to leave the country for America'. The night before the rape he had assaulted her, and she noted that 'I sleep in the same room as he and his wife'. The doctor gave evidence of 'considerable violence' to her genital area caused by 'forcible connection'.[258]

Nor was it unusual, given the overcrowding, for parents to sleep in the same beds as their children, or for widowed fathers to begin sexually abusing their daughters: in 1900 a Dublin widower was accused of carnal knowledge of his 5-year-old daughter; or, as it was put in the evidence of the police officer who arrested him, he was charged with 'assaulting her and making the child a wife of himself' (there was no incest act until 1908). After the death of his wife three years previously the man had moved to lodgings with his sister in Blessington Place, Dublin, where he and the child slept together. The sister gave evidence to the effect that she had heard cries of pain from the child:

> I went into the room and took the child from him and I said to the defendant that if he did not conduct himself he'd have to leave. I went back to the bed and still the child kept crying. I made that statement before I knew what had occurred to the child.

After she had taken the child from the room 'he said from the bed that

I should bring back his Mayflower'. The following day the sister talked to
the child:

> She said that Father was lying on her. I asked her what way he was lying
> on her and she said her father put his joker to her. I never heard her use
> the word joker before. I asked her where did he put it and she pointed to
> her private parts. She said her father told her that if she was to tell Auntie
> or Uncle that he'd kill her and that if she didn't tell he wouldn't kill her.

The witness's husband challenged the father and threw him out of the
house:

> I said he wouldn't get the child until he suffered the penalty for trying to
> make his child a W—[Whore] and told him never to show his face near
> my door again. I told him he was making a W— of his child ... he said
> he'd take her in spite of me and put her into a school.

The father subsequently returned drunk to the house with two companions. At the hearing, the evidence of the child was accepted, she being
'a child of tender years but being, in the opinion of the court, of sufficient
intelligence to justify the reception of her evidence'. Her evidence was that
'he hurt me with his joker between my legs where I do my "pee". He hurt
me much and more than once.' The medical evidence supported the child's
testimony and the man received a sentence of five years' penal servitude.[259]

Overcrowded living conditions also meant that, on occasion, children
had to witness the sexual abuse of adults, or were in the vicinity when it
occurred. In 1908, a man was accused of the attempted rape of his sister in a
case that sheds much light on contemporary living conditions. Her deposition included the following details:

> I am married. My husband is in the country [ie, in a rural area, away from
> Dublin city] at present. Defendant is my brother and has lodged with me
> in my tenement for last 4 or 5 weeks. I slept in my bed with my children.
> He slept on the floor. I was awakened this morning by my brother lying
> on top of me. He was stripped in his shirt under the clothes. He was
> trying to put his person into me. I jumped up and cried out. He got out
> of the bed and went back and lay down where he had been lying and in
> about ½ an hour he got up and came to me and said, 'I hope you are not

going to tell anything about this.' I said nothing. I got up as soon as I could about 4 a.m. and went to the police station.

When charged, the defendant replied, 'If I done it, it must have been in my sleep I did it.' He insisted the alleged victim had come in drunk that night and 'was so drunk she imagined this thing we done. It is not the first time I have had to stop her in drink.' He was found not guilty.[260]

Many victims of what in 1908 legally became the crime of incest were subjected to rape over extended periods, an abuse sustainable because of the absence of a mother and the fear of being sent away. In 1919 a case was heard in Dublin involving a man accused of having unlawful carnal knowledge of his daughter, aged 14; the girl had also given a statement to the NSPCC. The girl, her brother and her father, who was separated from their mother, were occupying two upstairs rooms in a house in St Alban's Road, Dublin, which they shared with six other adults. While her father and brother shared a room, the girl was given her own room, but her father had repeatedly come into her room early in the morning and raped her. The family had been at the house for three months. According to the girl:

> I did not say anything to him. I was afraid to say anything to him. My father has done the same thing to me every second morning and some-times every third morning while we have been living in our present residence. On some mornings I refused to let my father into the bed to me and on one of those occasions that I refused to let him into the bed to me I remember in the night of that day when he came home from work my father threatened to send me away to a school.

From the victim's evidence, it emerged that the girl had been living with her mother, but when the father returned home from the army, he took her to live with him. However, he was only allowed to do so when the mother was satisfied her brother would also be there, suggesting she knew her daughter needed protection of some kind. The abuse continued, however, and the child was careful to stifle her cries so as not to alert the other residents, because, as she commented, 'he knew I was afraid of going into a home'. The girl insisted she be given the key to her bedroom and locked it at night:

> He knocked at my door the following morning but I refused to let him

in. He then got a chisel and tried to open the door. He failed to open the
door though he broke the chisel in the attempt.

But the father subsequently took the key back and the abuse continued.
When the girl informed her mother, she took her in for a few weeks and
the child was subsequently sent to stay with her aunt in the Rialto area.
The medical evidence ('no trace of hymen left') made it clear she had been
penetrated.[261]

In Belfast, during the 1914 Winter Assizes, a case of a man accused of
unlawful carnal knowledge of his 12-year-old daughter was heard. The suspicions of the child's stepmother had been aroused:

> Defendant takes a good deal of drink. He is barely ever sober. About 3
> weeks ago when I was changing the sheets of defendant's bed I saw blood
> on them. I asked my stepdaughter ... how the blood came to be there and
> if there had been any woman in the place but she did not say anything.

When the case was heard, the child gave evidence of the abuse and
commented that 'about 2 years ago another person did the same thing to
me'. When the father was cross-examining his daughter, he attempted to
portray her as a liar who was sexually active:

> When Mrs Smith ... said she could not keep you out of the stable from
> the boys didn't you own up to a man having to do with you about two
> years ago?

To which she answered, 'Yes.'

It was clear from the kind of language used by the father that he believed
a 10-year-old girl could take full responsibility for sexual relations, if not be
the prime instigator. More extraordinary was the doctor's evidence in this
case, in which he gave an explanation as to why her left ovary was slightly
congested:

> From the condition of the child I would say that there had been
> attempted sexual intercourse by a male person, but not complete. The
> same symptoms might be shown by dirt and neglect or by masturbation.
> The child looks like a masturbator.[262]

'He said I had no right to lock the door ...
when I resisted he called me a whore'

K. H. Connell's study of Irish peasant society highlights 'failure in chastity' on the part of servant girls, due to the fact that so many servants were obliged, for want of accommodation, to sleep together, but he correctly identifies that it was often the servants' employers who perpetrated the sexual abuse.[263] This is something also noted by Mona Hearn in her study of life for domestic servants in Dublin in the late nineteenth and early twentieth centuries. In 1911 domestic servants were the largest group of employed women outside of the manufacturing sector; there were 125,783 female indoor servants, of whom 47 per cent were under the age of 25, and 92 per cent were unmarried. It was a class of employment that appealed to unskilled and semi-skilled parents because it came with board and lodgings for their offspring. Many of the advertisements for servant girls stipulated that they were to have 'no followers' (boyfriends), while no spouse was a rule in many houses. The women frequently worked 16-hour days with just one half day per week off for their own pursuits.

The former servants interviewed by Hearn in 1980 made it clear that employers sometimes hired women who had illegitimate children, but also that 'sexual exploitation of servants by masters and sons of the house was not uncommon. Former servants had experience of masters who made sexual overtures to them or to other servants.'[264] The court records illustrate that this was indeed the case; and given that court cases only represent the tip of the iceberg, the fact that there was a large number of cases heard involving the sexual exploitation and abuse of servants shows that the problem was a recurring one. What is clear is not only that employers took advantage of these girls (sometimes when their wives were 'confined' due to childbirth) but that they did so under the assumption that allowing themselves to be used for sex was part of the girls' job description. These girls were also often seen as legitimate targets for sexual abuse outside of the house.

In 1900, a domestic servant named Margaret, who had only been employed in the house of the wealthy defendant in Grovesnor Square in Dublin for five days, alleged he assaulted her while his wife was in bed 'expecting her confinement'. Apparently, the 'master of the house ... had been drinking all the week'. Margaret alleged that he grabbed her hands, pulled them behind her and said, 'when he had not his own wife he would like to have me or some other woman and that he would like to leave me the same way as his wife'; he placed his hands under her clothes and tried to knock her to the floor: 'I said I would tell the mistress of the house and that I would not put up with such ways.' Next she went to her bedroom, a room off the kitchen, and locked the kitchen door. 'He said I had no right to lock the door ... when I resisted he called me a whore.' The defendant spent three days attempting to have his way, trying a variety of ruses, and 'all this time my mistress was ill in bed'. On Sunday night 'he caught hold of me in the kitchen and tried to force me to drink whiskey', while on Monday morning when she was attending to her housework 'he came in and he offered me five shillings if I would get into the bed with him. I made no answer but walked out of the room and left him there.' When Margaret told of the harassment to a friend of hers who came to visit, her friend agreed to stay the night; at 3 a.m., the predator again pounced but the two girls barricaded the door. Having informed the mistress the next day of her husband's behaviour, the girls left the house and sought an arrest warrant. The nurse who was looking after the mistress of the house maintained, 'the house is a small one and I never heard the slightest commotion or screams of any kind. If there were any, I would have heard them.' The defendant was bailed for £20.[265]

On the same day, two young men were accused of the rape of a domestic servant employed in Clontarf. The girl knew the two men and had occasionally walked with them. The alleged rape occurred in a field between the Howth and Malahide roads. According to the servant's deposition, one of the men

> came up and got hold of me by the arm and asked me was there any chance of something which I understood to mean badness and I said no ... he then pulled me by the arm to the field at the end of the lane where he threw me down, lifted up my clothes, exposed my person, opened his clothes, took out his person, lay down on top of me and put his person into mine, while I kept resisting my best and screamed. I believe he was lying on me for ten minutes. I was very frightened and screamed as well as I could but I think I could not be heard very far.

When he had finished, the man encouraged his friend to rape her also, which 'would only be a few minutes', though this rape was interrupted by people approaching the field. When the girl escaped and told her employer, 'she told me to tell the priest and then go to the sergeant'.

According to the employer, the victim returned home and 'complained that she had been ill treated by someone up the road. I did not think at the time it was so serious. While she was making the complaint my husband came into the room and she left and went out ... she was a very quiet kind of girl who did not appear anxious to go out. I am surprised to hear that she had two sweethearts.'[266]

At Glanmire Road in Cork in 1919 a widower with four teenage children who employed a domestic servant girl was accused of attempted carnal knowledge of the employee. Her deposition tells a tale that would be almost comical were it not for the trauma she had experienced:

I slept in the attic. I went to bed last night at 11 ¼ p.m. This morning at 2 a.m. I was awoken by feeling something under my bedclothes. I asked 'Who is that?' I then saw it was defendant. He said, 'It's the boss.' I saw he was dressed in his sleeping garments. I said, 'What do you want with me?' He said, 'I want to see the time.' I said, 'The clock is there, sir.' He then said, 'You know damn well what I mean. You have often been out with a soldier.' He then threw himself on the bed and [on] top of the clothes and of me. I got away to the side of the bed but he had me. He also tried to put his hand on my private parts. I struggled, I defeated him in his object. He said several times that he would stick a knife through me if I made a sound of noise. He said, 'Will you come down to my room there?' I said, 'Yes' but I did not mean to do it. I wanted to get him away so that I could get out of the house. He asked me how long I would be and I said, 'I'll be down in 10 minutes, sir' ... He said, before he left, 'If you are not down in 10 minutes I'm coming up again.' He also said, 'If you do as I tell you, you won't be sorry for it and I'll take care of you' ... After he left I got up and dressed myself. I threw my trench coat out of the skylight thinking it would fall to the front door. It got caught in the roof. I stole down the stairs and got out the back door and reported the matter to police on duty on the top of Bridge Street.

The response of the accused, who owned a shop in Patrick Street, Cork, was, 'It is all blackmail. There's not a word of truth in it.'[267]

A case in Dublin in 1914 involved a charge of attempted rape against a defendant who employed the 16-year-old victim as a servant. The employer initially assaulted the girl in the kitchen and then later came to her bedroom, situated next to it. According to the victim, in the bedroom 'he only pressed against me'; he told her 'he'd buy me anything I'd want and anytime

I wanted money for sweets I was to ask him'. But on another occasion she claimed he came to her bedroom and raped her, after saying he would give her a shilling. This was by no means a straightforward case. The victim was accused of being dismissed from previous employment 'for stopping out all night'; her mother's evidence ('she said he didn't have sexual intercourse with her') contradicted her own; and it emerged that the mother wanted her to drop the case 'because defendant is an old man'. The mother also referred to a case two years previously in which the alleged victim 'had a charge against a prostitute who brought her away to a married man. The woman was charged for trying to procure my daughter and got 7 months. My daughter never met that man.'

The doctor called to give evidence said he could not find evidence of injury 'of any sort' and noted that 'she corrected the statement she made to the police after I had examined her, and another servant maintained that "she swore she'd have Mr B. up, that she was paid for a case before and would be paid again".' It was also maintained that she 'demanded a couple of pounds or she'd charge him'.[268]

'It was all a sup of drink'

Young men often acted violently and in collusion with each other when carrying out some sex assaults. In 1906, two men aged 21 and 23 were accused of raping a servant who had worked for three years in the employment of one of the men's fathers. It also emerged during the trial that the servant had, in the words of the father, 'been living with me as my wife and occupies the same bed with me, for 3 years past'. It was alleged the two men had attacked the woman in the loft of some stables in the grounds of the house, in Mercer Street, Dublin, on St Stephen's Day, 1905. Her deposition included the following:

> He said I want a 'f—' off the cow. When I was down he said to the man M., 'Hold her till I get a fuck off her', whereupon the defendant M. held my hands while T. opened his trousers and exposed himself, raised my clothes, lay on top of me and had connection with me. I struggled. T. said if I opened my mouth he'd take my life. When he was finished I thought I was free. I tried to get up and went about half a yard, when he said, 'I'll give you this you fucking cow' and he gave me a blow of his fist on the left eye, marking it as it now appears. I fell then. T. held me down

while M. lay on me and had connection with me and I did all I could to resist them both and cried for mercy.

The defendants claimed the woman had invited them to the loft for whiskey and had consented to what happened. When one of the defendants was arrested, he replied simply, 'It was all a sup of drink.' One doctor who examined the alleged victim found no signs of rape, adding that 'it would be possible that a woman accustomed to sexual intercourse would show no signs of such connection', though another doctor examined her and a bloody cloth, noting that 'assuming this woman was not a virgin, unless considerable violence were used in having connection with E. I cannot understand why these blood stains were on this cloth'.

The father also gave a statement in which he referred to the defendants drinking in the Swan pub, and later Peter's pub in Aungier Street, but when he confronted his son, he 'wanted to charge him to a policeman but the policeman would not take the charge owing to the crowd'. He added that there 'was never any quarrel or difference' between himself and his son over the victim's presence in the house. This case seemed to indicate that the son believed that the woman was a legitimate target for his sexual advances on the grounds of her status as an unmarried live-in servant who was prepared to share his father's bed. Both men were acquitted.[269]

Some women employed in other capacities were also taken advantage of by their employers, with evidence in some cases of considerable violence being used. In 1918, a man was accused of raping a 25-year-old female employee in the backroom of a jeweller's shop in Mary Street where she worked. Her deposition, sworn against the defendant and his brother, also highlights something that was common to many of these cases – the reluctance of the victim to confide in other people about their experiences, and their sense of isolation:

I had no parents to tell about this. I went to see my brother. I didn't tell him on the Monday, Wednesday or Thursday. It didn't occur to me to tell a constable or doctor. I had not in my mind that I wanted to see a doctor, but I wanted to see someone to tell first. I told my employer the following morning that I'd have to leave, that his brother had attempted me also ... I know men to speak to through business. I don't know any other men ... I didn't want to complain to anyone. I lived with my sister all the time this was going on.

She added poignantly that she needed protection but that 'my sister could give me none'. Eventually she told her brother. The victim's greatest fear in all this was being left without a reference from her assailant: 'I said I wanted to leave and I asked him to give me a reference and stamp my card' – which he refused to do, so she felt she had no option but to continue working there.

Medical evidence about whether a woman had been raped or not was often inconclusive and doctors were equivocal, but in this instance it was quite clear that force had been used. The victim's brother was furious, but also indicated that it was very difficult for victims to confide: 'She was too ashamed to tell me more ... I did not report the matter to the police but I gave certain advice to my sister ... she was living with my mother all her life, up until when my mother died ... I think my sister is about 25 years of age.'[270] The defendant was found guilty of what was reported in the *Irish Times* as 'an assault'.[271]

The brother's evidence is very revealing of what happened to many Irish families: a sense of remove from siblings was common because of the young age at which boys went to work; there was also a resultant dependence of young girls on their mothers. The sense of dislocation and vulnerability that often came with the death of a parent is palpable in many of these cases, as is the degree to which victims struggled to find a language for the abuse they had experienced. But what also stands out is the bravery of these many women in taking these cases to court and subjecting themselves to the trauma of giving evidence.

Women were also doubly vulnerable when pregnancy occurred as a result of rape and sexual assault, and indeed, the distress caused by discovering a pregnancy sometimes took precedence over the abuse issue, if not from the victim's perspective, at least on the part of her parents. In 1902, a 16-year-old girl who was working part time as a cleaner and chambermaid in the Eagle House pub and bed and breakfast in Dundrum village, County Dublin, where her mother also worked, was raped by the assistant barman who forced her to drink alcohol before attacking her: 'He put his body into mine and did all he wanted. The drink he had for me made me stupid. It was port wine. I didn't know there would be any harm and told nobody.' The girl's mother confronted the rapist in the presence of his parents, who denied it; the mother insisted, 'he had brought her to disgrace ... I told him she was going to have a baby for him and that there was no-one down to it only him ... the first question I asked P. was what are you going to do with my J. I meant what arrangements was he going to make; was he going to marry her and for the support of the baby.'

The prosecution was dropped.[272]

Although the Public Record Office of Northern Ireland has a more restrictive policy than the National Archives of Ireland regarding the release of files relating to criminal trials dealing with sexual offences, with an embargo of 75 or 100 years imposed on many of them, the Crown Books that list the cases heard and the verdicts and sentences imposed there indicate the frequency of sexual crime in the early twentieth century. There were many instances of cases of unlawful carnal knowledge not being proceeded with, suggesting such cases were difficult to prove. In Belfast those convicted of indecent assault on young girls were usually sentenced to twelve months' hard labour, as happened to two men convicted of that offence in the summer of 1914; the girls were aged 6 and 9 respectively.[273] Cases heard on 20 July 1914 included indecency, bestiality and rape.[274]

The County of Londonderry Assizes Crown Book for the first quarter of the twentieth century gives a good indication of the range of sexual crimes prosecuted and the pattern of sentencing. During the Spring Assizes of 1911 a man accused of unlawful carnal knowledge of a 15-year-old girl who was found guilty 'with a strong recommendation to mercy' received a sentence of one month's imprisonment with hard labour. The following year another case, also involving the assault on a 15-year-old girl, resulted in the jury disagreeing; the jury disagreed at the second trial also, while at the third trial a *Nolle Prosequi* was entered. The following spring another man convicted of indecent assault was given a sentence of three months with hard labour, while in the spring of 1916 a man convicted of the assault and unlawful carnal knowledge of a 10-year-old girl was given the unusually severe sentence of seven years' penal servitude.[275]

'And at any rate isn't a hornyman'

While court cases highlight the degree of violence, deception and fear involved in criminal sexual activity, there was another private world of Irish sexuality which by contrast was about consent, choice and, occasionally, liberation. There were those who chose not to follow the sexual orthodoxy of the early twentieth century. Lady Gregory, for example, one of the founders of the National Theatre and widow of the nineteenth-century politician William Gregory, sailed to the United States in 1911 at the age of 59 and engaged in a passionate love affair with John Quinn, a wealthy New York lawyer eighteen years her junior. In the words of novelist Colm Tóibín, she managed to combine on that trip 'foreign travel, a great political cause and secret passion'.[276]

In contrast, Margaret Cousins, a suffragette and feminist cultural critic involved in the Celtic revival, like her contemporaries the poet W. B. Yeats and the scholar Douglas Hyde, was interested in the occult and theosophy with its belief that each soul changed sex as it was reincarnated. Living in a non-sexualised marriage, and a practising vegetarian, she found sex degrading and shameful. She was 'revolted' by 'certain of the techniques of nature connected with sex', wanting a more artistic method of continuance of the human race than sexual intimacy. The solution to the 'curse' of enforced motherhood and conjugal rights as a result of which the woman 'suffers shame to her inner feelings and a hardening of nature through bitterness of spirit, thus degenerating the female form', was 'the attainment of the state of the Blessed Virgin' which could be won by men and women alike, Christ being the perfect 'man woman'. As a theosophical devotee, Cousins migrated to India in 1915, where she became immersed in feminism and nationalism.[277] Her attitudes are a reminder that the 'anti-sensualism' that is ascribed to the Victorian and Edwardian eras was not just something driven by the 'lip service Puritanism of the bourgeoisie', nor by 'the asceticism of evangelicals'; it also emanated from 'secularist and progressive quarters' which included those involved in the women's rights movement.[278]

Yeats, however, saw the role of sex rather differently, and the exceptionally detailed dissection of his life and career by Roy Foster makes clear the degree to which his sexual concerns were very much interconnected with his theatrical, magical, poetical and political concerns. Yeats's interest in the occult was a significant dimension to his relationship with Maud Gonne in the late 1890s, his correspondence making it clear that he thought he had entered into a mystical marriage with her. They communicated 'astrally and chemically with mescalin and hashish'. Foster wryly observes that 'unsurprisingly, visions followed'. Yeats seems to have finally consummated his affair with Maud in 1908. In 1913, he also made an appeal to a medium to discover if his then mistress was pregnant, as she had alleged; when the spirit revealed that she was lying – and she was – it bolstered his belief in the power of the medium.

Appealing to a medium, however, was not the answer to all of Yeats's sexual concerns, as he continued to experience frustration and doubts. He had a difficult relationship with the English heiress Annie Horniman;

others, too, remained unconvinced of his sexual vitality and prowess. Oliver Gogarty penned a limerick about the plight of Horniman:

What a pity it is that Miss Horniman,
When she wants to secure or suborn a man,
Should choose Willie Yeats,
Who still masturbates,
And at any rate isn't a hornyman.[279]

Yeats himself suffered guilt about his own sexual inadequacies, his longings for Gonne and the failure of his affair with his friend Olivia Shakespear. He wrote in 1897 that he was 'tortured by sexual desire and disappointed love. Often as I walked in the woods at Coole it would have been a relief to have screamed aloud. When desire became an unendurable torture, I would masturbate, and that, no matter how moderate I was, would make me ill.'[280]

'There will be a great rush for all the heroes when you return.
All the girls will want you'

Little attention has been focused on the impact the all-encompassing nationalism and republicanism had on the romantic and sexual passions of the young generation who were consumed with the political struggle that came to dominate their lives. The private lives of the icons of Irish nationalism were not explored much by historians owing to lack of source material. In his memoir of his father's life, Risteárd Mulcahy, son of Richard Mulcahy, the IRA's chief of staff during the War of Independence, recalled of his mother, who married Richard in 1919: 'I cannot recall her ever expressing any details to me about their relationship except on one occasion in her later years when she confessed that he was a very passionate man.'[281] There was some surprise recently when private letters written by the most enduring and best-known Irish politician of the twentieth century, Éamon de Valera, revealed a side to him at odds with his dour stereotype. In December 2000 Gardaí seized eighteen love letters written by de Valera to his wife Sinéad, which were being advertised for auction, but which, it was understood, had been stolen in the mid 1970s from the de Valera family home in Blackrock. The owners, who had bought them in England some years previously in an effort to ensure their return to Ireland, were unaware of their dubious provenance. De Valera wrote the letters between 1911 and 1920 from Mountjoy jail, Lincoln jail and from the US during his mission there in 1919–20, while five letters were written from Tawin Island, off the coast of Galway, where he ran a Gaelic League college during the summers of 1911–13.[282]

One of them, from 1911, included the lines:

> I need a kiss, urgently ... I want to press my wife to my heart, but we are 150 miles apart. Darling, do you think of me at all? Can you sleep without those long limbs wrapped around you? Those same limbs are longing to be wrapped around you again – two weeks – fourteen days – how can I endure it? You do not know how sorrowful I am ...

The publicity surrounding the uncovering of the letters caused a stir because they seemed to offer a previously unopened window on the private man who, for many, represented 'the epitome of joyless rectitude'. Journalist Cian Óhéigeartaigh notes wryly, 'Just when we were getting used to the idea that our parents had sex and enjoyed it, a further imaginative effort is called for.'[283] But as John A. Murphy points out, when the letters first came to light, 'the only people who were gobsmacked by such eroticism were those who had deluded themselves that Dev wasn't human (i.e., sexual) in the first place'.[284]

The premature deaths and incarcerations of young men that were experienced as a result of war in Ireland undoubtedly prevented many a romance from blossoming. In 1953, in a statement given to the Bureau of Military History (BMH) which collected witness accounts of those involved in the Irish War of Independence, Elizabeth Colbert, sister of Con Colbert, who was executed for his role in the 1916 Rising, recalled that he was a man in love with a woman as well as his political movement:

> I went to a Ceilidhe [Irish dance] with Con shortly before the Rising ... In the course of the evening he said to me, 'I'll show you the nicest girl in Dublin.' He introduced me to Lucy Smith. I think he was in love with her and would probably have married her if he had lived. She was a nice, gentle, refined girl, a member of Cumman na mBan and a great worker in the movement. She afterwards married Tom Byrne of Boer War fame who was also keen on her at the same time. He was Con's rival.

Elizabeth got to know Lucy Smith well, and Smith subsequently showed her the love letters Con had sent her, though she did not reveal the last message that Con communicated to her through Father Albert, who attended him just before his execution. Ultimately, it seems, the struggle for freedom took precedence over romance:

> He cycled all over Ireland organising companies ... he was very serious where work for Ireland was concerned and that was why I never thought he was taking an interest in girls. So I was surprised when I found out that he had been writing love letters to Lucy Smith and thinking very seriously about her. He also gave Lucy a copy book containing several scraps of paper with poems scribbled on them. I don't know whether they are his own composition. They are all about Ireland and its struggle for freedom and the sufferings it endured from the English.[285]

Many other statements given to the BMH underline the importance of the Gaelic League, established in 1893 to promote the Irish language, in organising social events and in creating an environment conducive to the meeting of the sexes. These social occasions, particularly the dances, undoubtedly initiated numerous romances. For some, the enthusiasm for the language movement 'was a fad, not unrelated to the emancipation of women and the advent of the bicycle'.[286]

David Fitzpatrick's biography of Harry Boland, who accompanied Éamon de Valera to the United States during the War of Independence and became a close friend of Michael Collins, highlights the degree to which letter writing became important for those seeking romance in the midst of war. In the aftermath of the 1916 Rising the letters Boland wrote from Lewes jail contain many reminiscences of the socialising that was part of the GAA and Gaelic League circles, as he recalled matches, walks and moonlit swims. The GAA becomes a shorthand for youth, friendship and romance, while rumours of marriage prompted jocose comments. Inquiries were made as to whether there was 'anything going on for you in the "coortin line"'.[287] Fitzpatrick concluded from this correspondence that 'Games provided the entrée to a busy social scene, clubbishly exclusive yet internally democratic, in which high-minded, firm-bodied youngsters could flirt, marry or simply find easy companionship'. The letters also contain many references to prayer and God, faith and piety, but women also emerge from these letters as often assertive and flirtatious. It was recognised that, given the shift in public

opinion after the 1916 Rising, participation in that event would add significantly to a boy's sex appeal; Boland's sister wrote to him in 1917: 'There will
be a great rush for all the heroes when you return. All the girls will want
you.'[288]

Boland was certainly not short of female admirers. While in the United
States he developed a close friendship with Stephen O'Mara and his family, and was particularly drawn towards O'Mara's wife's sister, Kitty O'Brien,
who came from Limerick but who lived for a time in Washington. They
flirted and played golf together, and she wrote to him as he prepared to
return to Ireland:

> You never knew how much I loved you – did you, Harry? Until you
> started going away. What a wet, red-eyed object I was today! Ah well,
> I'm not the only unhappy female who will weep for the Irish ambassador
> this week.

This letter is a further demonstration of the extent to which certain Irish
women of this era could be very frank about their feelings and passions,
and is particularly interesting in retrospect, as 'his sportive yet sentimental
admirer, under the more severe name Kate O'Brien, was to become a much-
censored novelist and in due course an icon of Irish lesbianism.'[289]

Yet the world of the Irish republican was often during this period a
male world, and brotherly love was one facet of the 'social and emotional
world of a Gaelic athlete', which, in some instances, was quite homoerotic.
After Boland returned to Ireland from the United States in late August 1921,
Collins and Boland, according to Frank O'Connor, 'indulged in endless
horseplay, delighted to be together again'.[290] It wasn't that they were exclusive wrestling partners (Boland records a wrestle with de Valera also), but in
their case the physical tussles seem to have been a regular and important part
of their relationship.

This rough and tumble between Irish republicans and their supporters
seems to have been quite common. In his statement to the Bureau of Military History, Eamon (Ned) Broy recounts in great detail incidents and long
conversations with Michael Collins in tones of hero worship that occasionally border on the homoerotic. In January 1921 a number of IRA officers
were invited to a dinner given by James Mark Sullivan, an Irish-American
living in Dublin, at which Broy was also present:

Mick was persuaded to recite 'the Lisht', which he did with his own inimitable accent. When he was finished, there was a rush for him by everybody in the place to seize him. I was very proud of the fact that he fell into my arms ...[291]

Many others had an equally high opinion of Collins and their commitment to him endured. His contemporary Richard Mulcahy, who commanded the military forces of the provisional government during the civil war, was so incensed by a 1969 novel by the Irish-American Constantine Fitzgibbon, *High Heroic*, on page one of which Collins is featured getting out of bed with a prostitute, that he pressed the Minister for Justice to refuse Fitzgibbon his naturalisation papers, denouncing his 'foul penmanship'. He failed to stop Fitzgibbon becoming an Irish citizen.[292]

Although Irish censors later tried to deny that there was any sexual misbehaviour during the Irish War of Independence, it did feature as part of the conflict. Irish women formed sexual liaisons with British soldiers and not everyone was pleased to see them leave the country in 1922. Alongside celebratory photographs of troops marching from barracks, the *Freeman's Journal* newspaper of 3 March 1922 published a photograph of nine young Irishwomen standing on the quayside at the North Wall waving to a ship carrying soldiers back to England. The caption read:

> The girls they left behind. In spite of the fact that they were alien soldiers, some of the younger generation of Irishwomen were attracted to the khaki uniforms ... as in the continental war, peoples of ravished districts formed alliances with the enemy.[293]

But many more were glad to see the British soldiers depart, particularly those women who had been subjected to sexual assault as part of the war. Sources such as the *Irish Bulletin*, Sinn Féin's news and propaganda sheet outlining British military atrocities, refer to rape,[294] though there was a perceived conflict between the need to protect female modesty and the urge to publicise brutality. In April 1921 the *Irish Bulletin* devoted a special edition to 'outrages on Irish women', which explicitly used the word 'rape' and broke taboo with its frank statements from victims, while suggesting there were other victims who were not prepared to see their names and addresses published. At this stage the *Irish Bulletin* seemed to think the urge to record the brutality outweighed the need to protect the women's modesty.[295]

Republicans and British soldiers cut off girls' hair and women dressed in night attire faced uniformed and armed men. There was a tendency for republicans to suggest that 'no girls, except the unfortunates' would meet British soldiers, but the British in turn distributed leaflets that suggested republican men were 'safely hidden in the bedrooms of their female admirers in Dublin ... many of our once pure Irish girls have lost their virtue in the abnormal lives they are leading'.[296]

'A heavy drinker, plain and vulgar'

Kitty Kiernan, the girlfriend of Michael Collins, certainly did not appear to be one of them. Collins was a smoking, drinking, charming, boyish sex symbol who was mobbed in London during the 'Collinsmania' surrounding the Treaty period. David Fitzpatrick in 2003 referred to him as 'a practised strategist of seduction',[297] but his most recent biographer, Peter Hart, can find no credible evidence that he was sexually active; indeed, some have wondered what he was doing with Kiernan at all, and the evidence for sexual liaisons between Collins and Lady Lavery is thin and unconvincing.[298]

The love triangle between Boland, Collins and Kiernan was fascinating and ultimately quite painful, particularly for Boland, who had first met Kiernan in 1918 – in the words of Fitzpatrick, she was a 'stylish, spirited and worldly lass ... one of four famously nubile sisters who held court in their brother's hotel, entertaining and captivating myriad Sinn Féiners and volunteers'. Boland corresponded with her while in the United States, but she was sometimes a lot more vague and non-committal than him. In reality, as Boland realised, she was keeping her options open regarding Collins: 'I need not say to you how much I love him and I know he has a warm spot in his heart for me and I feel sure in no matter what manner our triangle may work out, he and I shall always be friends.'[299] Boland did his best to get Kitty to commit to him ('I know exactly all your emotions and your ways and feel that I could sympathise with you in your sadness and laugh at you in your gladness') and even got his mother to write to her, but the more ardent he became, the further she retreated towards Collins, though hers and Collins's relationship was hardly the romance of the century.

The correspondence that survived between Collins and Kiernan raised a question for historian Deirdre McMahon, which was 'how long their marriage would actually have lasted before Collins, goaded beyond endurance by her endless prattle about frocks, hats and beaux, finally throttled her'.[300] McMahon's pertinent question is a reminder that this supposedly great romance was perhaps not all it appeared. In May 2007 letters exchanged in the 1940s between Moya Llewelyn Davis, who spied for and hid Collins during the War of Independence, and P. S. O'Hegarty, a leading Sinn Féin figure from that era, were auctioned. They appear to give some insight into Collins's relationship with Kiernan, though the caveat has to be added that for Davis, Collins 'was the love of her life' and so she was hardly an objective observer. Perhaps she resented that Collins was engaged to Kiernan, but she described Kitty as 'a heavy drinker, plain and vulgar', and maintained Collins had pleaded with her to 'make a lady' of Kiernan, whom he believed was 'brainless'. Explaining how Collins had got engaged to Kiernan, Davis also maintained that 'I believe he never had any sexual experience. I got the impression he was still virginal.'[301]

Any search for sex in the memoirs and biographies written by Irish republicans of this era will be in vain; the same is true of the Bureau of Military History. What the reader gets, instead, is a depiction of chivalrous masculinity, brotherhood and camaraderie, or, as Florence O'Donoghue wrote in his biography of IRA general Liam Lynch, 'thoughts of love and marriage he put aside so that nothing might stand between him and complete dedication in service to the duty he envisaged'.[302]

'We must above all have healthy laughter, nor must we be ashamed to love'

When looking back on this period in 1982, veteran nationalist C. S. 'Todd' Andrews accepted he and his colleagues 'had not had a normal adolescence' and had never known a girl who was more than a passing acquaintance:

> [My] boyhood and early manhood, spent as they were in all-male schools, football clubs and the IRA, had left me emotionally immature in the matter of inter-sex relations ... which was at that time the not uncommon experience of a man of nearly 23 years of age, as I was when I came home from the civil war. I was far from ignorant of the argot of the physiology of sex. I knew all the slang words used to describe the human anatomy, male and female – I knew all the slang words used to describe the variations of the love-making process. But I knew nothing about women

beyond their home-making functions and their ability to provide some of the services required to support the IRA military operations.[303]

Andrews also dwelt on this subject in correspondence with Seán O'Faoláin after the publication of the latter's autobiography, *Vive Moi!*, in 1965. In reading the book, and specifically O'Faoláin's account of his time as an IRA volunteer and his relationship with his future wife Eileen, Andrews found much with which to empathise. In a letter of congratulations to O'Faoláin he commented:

> I was especially interested in your adventure with Eileen in Paris. It is impossible to explain to outsiders that such a trip could have taken place in all 'innocence'; the absence of sexual relations between the men and women of the movement was one of its most peculiar features. I suppose all revolutionaries are basically Puritanical, otherwise they wouldn't be revolutionaries.[304]

There was a tendency to believe that sexual activity and its consequences, such as sexually transmitted diseases, were the responsibility of the English who had tarnished a pure Ireland. Father Devane, a Jesuit priest who made many interventions in the inquiries into sexual activity in the Free State in the 1920s, suggested in 1926 that 'In the past few years we have had wave after wave of men passing over the country ... it will be found that *in many cases*, the girls who acted as camp followers to Black and Tans, etc. ... were the same who pursued the Free State troops, conveying in not a few cases infection.'[305]

In *Midsummer Night's Madness*, Seán O'Faoláin's collection of short stories published in 1932 (and banned by the Censorship Board), the story 'The Small Lady' mocks the self-proclaimed heroism of IRA men who, at the outset, celebrate in verse the capture and execution of an English female spy, Bella. She is a lonely colonel's wife trapped in Ireland and longing for sexual passion and the narrative favours her passion (and perhaps Protestant liberal morality) over the IRA men.[306] When he was recounting civil war anecdotes to fellow writer Francis Hackett in 1932, Frank O'Connor recalled the time he was ordered as part of an IRA active service unit to 'shoot all servant girls flirting with [Free] Staters'. A commandant revoked the order; 'Thanks be to Jesus,' said a fellow soldier. 'I'd intended to shoot the soldiers and then meself.'[307]

There has been a conscious attempt in recent years to subject IRA actions during the War of Independence to a fresh and critical scrutiny; to highlight the cold-blooded violence that was a part of that war, and the extent to which some of its activities were sectarian. There was, for instance, considerable controversy generated by a documentary in November 2007 on the killing of two brothers, Richard and Abraham Pearson, at Coolacrease, County Offaly, in June 1921.[308] Historian Brian Hanley made the observation that the programme and the reaction to it highlighted 'the extent to which comment about the War of Independence is still driven by present-day, ideological concerns'. The programme implied that the brothers, substantial farmers and members of the evangelical Cooneyite sect, were murdered for sectarian and land-grabbing motives, even though there is evidence to suggest they were killed because they had previously fired on IRA volunteers. 'Nor do the medical records support the programme's contention that there was sexual mutilation involved (i.e. that the Pearsons were deliberately shot in the genitals and buttocks) but rather that this was a botched execution carried out by inexperienced volunteers.'[309] The British military court of inquiry evidence, which was not included in the documentary, suggested there were no injuries to the genitals:

> Dr F. W. Woods examined Richard Pearson and found a superficial wound in the left shoulder; a deep but not life-threatening wound in the right groin (which is farther from the genitals than an ear lobe is from the brain); another in the right buttock; superficial wounds in the left lower leg; and about six glancing wounds in the back.
>
> Lt Col. C. R. Woods RAMC (an army doctor) examined Abraham Pearson and found extensive wounds on left cheek, left shoulder, left thigh and lower third of left leg. In addition there was a wound through the abdomen.[310]

Alongside these ugly and brutal episodes there was an idealism, which in retrospect often seems naive, that suffused many of the young Irish revolutionaries during these years, and some did turn their minds to the question of the moral climate they hoped to see prevail in the 'new' Ireland. Desmond Ryan, who became a well-established and highly regarded journalist and writer, had been a pupil of Patrick Pearse at St Enda's school in Dublin and took part in the 1916 Rising, after which he was interned. Following his release he began to keep a private diary ('a record of all my opinions,

prejudices and petulances') which was permeated by the ghost of Patrick
Pearse, to whom his devotion was absolute and, to the modern eye, homoerotic: '... that last splendid vision of him, proud, confident and gallant, in
his green tunic, head erect, staring undaunted at dismay and defeat. Perhaps
that vision obsesses me ... the memory of Pearse, my own highly diverting –
to others – love affair.'[311]

Many of Ryan's nocturnal digressions were centred on the notion of
Ireland being 'purified and sweetened by the physical and mental agonies'
of the Irish revolution, but he also bemoaned the fact that, despite being
surrounded by 'good comrades', his life lacked intimacy ('I feel awfully alone
... I have no intimate friends'), and he was often plagued by self-doubt and
a 'want of self-confidence, a very ugly, provoking and dangerous beast'.[312]
But Ryan expressed certainty about many things, particularly the virtue of
Pearse, the Rising and the quest for political independence (despite getting
temporarily 'fed up with demonstrations and meetings'). He often wrote
late into the night, and on one occasion reflected at length on 'the question
of sex and the part it plays in our lives. It is a question no healthy minded
man or woman should hesitate to face honestly ... let us away with snigger-
ing or prudery alike.'[313]

A committed supporter of women's rights, Ryan's major preoccupation
was with prostitution, 'that vile and intolerable thing' that should 'move any
man of honour to wrath and bitterness ... I can understand the puritans and
kill joys a trifle better when I consider that tragic and loathsome procession
of the streets.' He suggested that prostitution was 'largely economic' in its
'source and patrons' and that ultimately as women 'rise into economic security undoubtedly the evil will be on the way to ultimate extinction'.

While suggesting, like many of his contemporaries, that 'something
serious is amiss with current morality', Ryan also insisted that a balance
needed to be struck and hypocrisy avoided in approaching sexual matters
generally:

> We must sweep compromise aside. Let us insist upon one standard of
> morality for men and women and by one standard we mean what we
> say; monogamy or free love, one of two quite intelligible things. But
> let there be no white-sepulchred morality plus a system that connotes
> personal degradation for man and woman, disease for the race and the
> vilest of human exploitation ... we must be human and reverent, neither
> prudes nor brutes. We must respect women. We must demand for them

all the rights we claim for ourselves. We must not condemn in them what
we condone in men. We must above all have healthy laughter nor must
we be ashamed to love ... circumstances, training, temperament influence the final decision we all make upon the questions of religion and
morality. Upon them for the present, I reserve an open mind.[314]

Such an approach to issues of sexuality was rarely in evidence in the
Free State that was created five years after Ryan's diary entries.

1922–40

*'The future of the country is bound up with the dignity
and purity of the women of Ireland'*

During the decade after the creation of the Irish Free State in 1922, it was frequently maintained that sexual morality was in decline and that perceived moral failings needed to be tackled by a joint alliance of state, Catholic Church and voluntary lay Catholic groups in an effort to recover a historic (or mythical) Irish chasteness. Sexuality was something that was discussed quite regularly in private, but there was also no shortage of public preaching on the subject. The Jesuit Father Michael Garahy's Lenten lectures in 1922 included one on 'The Collapse of Chastity', while the Irish Bishops' Lenten pastoral of 1924 referred to the 'existence of many abuses' in the context of morality and decency. Maintaining this trend, in 1926 a sermon by Dr Gilmartin, the Archbishop of Tuam, referred to the fashion in women's immodest dress and suggested 'the future of the country is bound up with the dignity and purity of the women of Ireland'.[1]

This was another indication, in the words of Maria Luddy, that the 'redemption of chaste reproductive sexuality is prescribed as the antidote to moral bankruptcy; women must return to the home; to the domestic sphere'.[2] Nor was the notion that the country needed to redeem itself articulated solely by Catholic preachers. The year after Gilmartin's sermon, an editorial in the *Irish Times* (which had a mostly Protestant readership) lamented that

> Throughout the centuries, Ireland has enjoyed a high reputation for the cardinal virtues of social life. She was famous for her men's chivalry and for her women's modesty. Today, every honest Irishman must admit that this reputation is in danger ... our first need is full recognition of the fact that today the nation's proudest and most precious heritage is slipping from its grasp.[3]

This was the sort of language which echoed that being used in other parts of Europe after the First World War. Angus McLaren's history of twentieth-century sexuality suggests the 'purveyors of sexual panic', in constructing 'a sexual other', were keen to alert the public to the 'social rather than the strictly sexual threat posed by the deviant', and that the war did not simply create new sexual worries but 'gave greater credibility to moralists who had argued for some time that sexual misdemeanours imperiled national well-being'. Internationally during this period, social crises were 'read' by the middle class as sexual crises, which in some countries involved 'collapsing all youth problems into the problems of sexuality'.[4] Discussions of sexuality were also coloured by the notions that conventional gender roles were under assault and that war and the mobilisation it entailed weakened family structures. In London in 1918, *The Times* condemned

> the 'tolerance of evil ... no public man or woman can afford unnecessary contact with questionable companions. In the days before the war there was growing in London, beyond any sort of question, that passion for excitement and for the latest novelty which is always the familiar beginning of a corrupt society.[5]

In Ireland, some of this concern was due to the number of children being born outside of marriage. Between 1912 and 1927, figures based on total annual births showed a 29 per cent increase in illegitimate births. Notwithstanding, illegitimate births were described in the annual report of the Registrar General for the Free State in 1922 as 'less than that recorded for other countries'. This was asserted in light of figures that suggested 2.6 per cent of births in that year were illegitimate. From 1920 to 1930, the average number of illegitimate births per annum in the twenty-six counties was deemed to be 1,706. But this rose to 1,853 between 1926 and 1929.[6] These figures do not take into consideration 'shotgun' weddings, pregnancy emigration, abortion and infanticide.[7]

During the early years of the Free State's existence, a number of other issues relating to sexual activity surfaced. With the obvious exceptions of sermons and pastorals, most fears were expressed in private and a tone of panic was frequently evident about the perceived degeneration of Irish sexual morality, the practices associated with it, and the consequences of it. Some of the legislative initiatives and public pronouncements relating to policing the morals of Ireland in the 1920s and 1930s are well known: fiery Lenten pastorals; the censorship of films and literature deemed to be obscene; the outlawing of the importation of contraceptives; the restrictions on public dances, and the efforts of religious groups such as the Legion of Mary to eradicate prostitution and brothel-keeping in Dublin city. Others are less well known: the suppression of the Carrigan Committee Report (see below) into the operation of the criminal law; inquiries into the spread of VD and sexually transmitted diseases; fears about the operations of 'vice' rings in some of the larger cities; worries about the high levels of infanticide, mostly as a result of sex outside marriage; internal government memorandums on the age of consent for sexual activity; the perceived need for female Gardaí; and the treatment of women and children by the judicial system.

Government inquiries resulted in the unpublished 'Report of the Interdepartmental Committee of Inquiry Regarding Venereal Disease' (1926) and the *Report of the Committee on the Criminal Law Amendment Acts (1880–85) and Juvenile Prostitution* (1931), known as the Carrigan Committee Report. Other, published reports included the *Report of the Committee on Evil Literature* (1927) and the *Report of the Commission of Inquiry on the Relief of the Sick and Destitute Poor* (1927). As pointed out by Maria Luddy, the work of the Interdepartmental Ad Hoc Committee on the Suppression of Prostitution of 1947–8, which also remained unpublished, similarly provides much information on sexual activity in the 1920s and 1930s.[8]

Internationally, governments during the interwar period, particularly authoritarian regimes, became preoccupied with the regulation of sexual behaviour, a behaviour that Sigmund Freud, the founder of psychoanalysis, had suggested was the product of a variety of psychic combinations and developmental processes, rather than the result of one fundamental reproductive instinct; indeed, it was widely believed that only authoritarian regimes would be in a position to control (and manipulate) such perceived threats and diverse sexual instincts and their consequences.[9]

The irony of all the focus on sexual morality in Ireland is that it was being conducted in a country where, in terms of official statistics, there was very little sexual activity. In 1926, 72 per cent of Irish men between the ages of 25 and 43 were unmarried, as were 53 per cent of women of that age. In 1936, census figures indicated that one-quarter of Irish women never married and 25 per cent of Irish men remained permanently celibate (in 1937, 29 per cent of Irish men aged 45 or over had never married). These were trends that did not alter significantly until the 1950s, meaning that 'Ireland had the highest rates of postponed marriage and permanent celibacy of any western country that kept such records'. A high percentage of males in rural areas were classified as 'assisting relatives' – that is, sons and brothers of farmers normally not in a position to marry.[10] Mary Daly has observed that in 1926 the son of an English farmer aged 20–34 working with his father on the family farm 'was four times more likely to be married than his Irish counterpart'.[11]

The reasons for this extensive celibacy are manifold, including: late marriage; concern about standards of living (in 1936 the majority of farmhouses consisted of 3 or 4 rooms); the land inheritance system (men not marrying until their non-inheriting siblings had emigrated – a situation exacerbated by the collapse of emigration in the 1930s); the likelihood that those most inclined to rebel against Irish sexual culture were the ones most likely to emigrate; and the influence of the Catholic Church. But it was not a simple case of the Church 'exhorting the large proportions of unmarried people to chastity' as 'Many priests encouraged early and universal marriage and were ignored'[12] – a reminder of the dangers of exaggerating the Church's control over sexuality.

Those who did marry continued to have large families. In 1926 a farming couple married for twenty years or more had an average of six children, but that in itself condemned many of their offspring to celibacy, if, as was normal practice, only one was assigned ownership of the farm.[13] Conrad Arensberg and S. T. Kimball, who based their book *Family and Community in Ireland* (1968) on research conducted in County Clare in the 1930s, describe Irish rural practices as 'unique among civilised peoples', in that marriage was primarily about the transfer of economic control, land ownership and advance in status. The system of land transfer and inheritance also created difficulties for those family members still living at home when the land was transferred or when those inheriting the land could not find marriage partners, while co-habitation with parents-in-law led to much strife. Arensberg and Kimball assert that the solution to the crisis of rural marriage was 'beyond the reach of ordinary measures'.[14]

'He was just as perfect as I could have ever imagined and more than ever like a lovely big black cat'

But in some respects, contradictory signals were being sent about Irish sexual behaviour. As Marjorie Howes has pointed out, 'some observers of Irish sexual culture thought the Irish uniquely, laudably chaste, others sensed corruption and exhorted them to be more chaste, and, somewhat later, still others worried that they were excessively unnaturally chaste'. In reality, 'Irish sexual culture was almost certainly more diverse and less isolated than many commentators thought.'[15]

The private diaries from the 1920s of Rosamund Jacob, a feminist, Sinn Féin activist and writer who lived in Dublin and had a relationship with Irish republican Frank Ryan, provide some evidence of the veracity of Howe's observations. Jacob rejected the idea that for women, 'it is unreasonable of them to wish both mind and body to be used and pleased'.[16] Like many others, she enjoyed the social scene centred around ceilidhs in Dublin city in the 1920s; indeed, the reader of her diaries is introduced to a dizzying array of non-stop late-night dances: 'not having got to bed til 6 ... we had a lovely dance but I couldn't get a properly long swing out of him though it was fast enough ... He kept me for [the last dance] and it was delicious – he didn't dance at all like a tired man.'[17]

Initially, some of Jacob's friends referred to her attraction to Ryan as a 'weakness'; she also wrote of 'the unmentionable things' in November 1927, as well as recording tension between herself and her flatmates when Ryan stayed overnight and slept in the sitting room. Her flatmate Dorothy MacArdle was in a wild temper: 'I was to tell "that young man" he was never to do it again – it was indecent – no flat for a man to be in ... I never thought she was such a prude.'[18] Jacob recorded her growing feelings for Ryan – 'a continual pleasure to the eye and ear' – though she came to lament his immaturity and the fact that the conversations he instigated when women were around had 'a kind of mechanical air' about them.[19]

Ultimately, Ryan was not a satisfying, consistent or mature lover; he also had religious scruples about physical contact with an unmarried woman and was far too consumed with his myriad political activities to give time to the relationship. Reviewing her year at the end of 1928, Jacob recorded, 'I didn't get one long evening with him, but I had three quarters of an hour in heaven ... I had one real taste of love, and now and then half an hours substitute for it which I enjoyed more than I used to but I've had ten years loneliness and jealousy in one.'[20] In July of that year she had asked him to stay the night:

> He was perfect – didn't shirk it – shut the door, refused with obvious reasons, looking painfully miserable – admitted he'd like to – any man would like to accept such an invitation – I didn't argue it, he was so unhappy over it – then he did take me and kiss me and when I made to stop he pulled me down on the sofa and lay there, holding me tight, partly on top of me, his face against mine, all hot and panting and deliciously excited, showing most plainly how tempted he was, for more than half an hour – absolute heaven and he was just as perfect as I could have ever imagined and more than ever like a lovely big black cat.[21]

At the end of 1929 she was once again frustrated: 'As to the black panther. I had hell from him, in suspense, disappointment and starvation, but I had a few heavenly hours to make up – but if only his soul was more friendly – I sometimes feel that as he wants me physically he doesn't want me to talk to – the shyness and the sense of sin he seems to get and I helpless to prevent it.'[22] By the mid 1930s, contact had fizzled out; in the few years previously there was 'an absolute famine of him' and, because of his travels and imprisonment, in 1932 'I had only 3 spots of love, the last one the best.' There were also three encounters the following year, and she maintained that she 'will be better for it forever', but at the end of 1934, while 'he was here for love 4 times and for other things a couple of times – I wonder will I ever know a little more about him in his own soul?'[23] The depths she yearned for were never reached.

'About the problems of sex they pretend to be doves when in fact they are ostriches'

The Irish authorities were not unique in their preoccupation with sexual morality. Senia Pašeta has pointed out that the 'almost hysterical denunciations in the 1920s and 1930s ... reflected broader European and North

American panic about the supposed erosion of moral codes' in the aftermath of the First World War (and, in Ireland's case, the War of Independence and civil war). It would be unwise to contend that Irish measures against film, literature, divorce and birth control were 'unparalleled, especially as Irish politicians looked very closely at foreign legislation before drawing up their own'. None the less, Pašeta also suggests it would be 'absurd to fail to recognise the specificity of some of these measures' which differed from 'international initiatives in important ways'. The most striking of these was in relation to birth control, which was prohibited 'with little or no recourse to the demographic and eugenic concerns and debates that underpinned similar legislation in continental Europe'. In Ireland, it was clear, 'moral concerns were paramount'.[24] Internationally, concerns about the activities of the 'modern girl' were also widespread. In Italy in the 1920s, for example, the traditional courtship pattern with strict parental control gradually lost its influence, there was 'panic' about the blurring of gender identities, and the Church defeated proposals to introduce sex education in schools. In Britain concerns were voiced about the circulation of American 'pulp' magazines and there were rows about sex education in the schools and, although it was assumed that the better off had access to birth control knowledge unavailable to working-class women, inquiries received by Marie Stopes 'suggest that ignorance about contraception was rife throughout the social spectrum'.

There was also much emphasis on family values and birth control issues as a result of the rise of Fascism on the continent and a strong emphasis on 'pro-natalism' and the perceived urgent need for women to have more children.[25] In Spain, there was conflict between Catholics and those seeking a much more open discussion of sexuality. A royal decree denounced a conference on eugenics as 'a pornographic bonanza', but it was also significant that there was a Spanish branch of the World League for Sex Reform (WLSR). In the context of the Spanish Civil War of 1936–9 the Bishops crusaded against 'godless, lawless, immoral red Spain'. The founder of the Fascist party the Falange denounced the left before the civil war as a group that 'undermined the family, substituted in Russia by free love, by collective canteens, by facilities for divorce and abortion. Have you not heard Spanish girls recently shouting "Children, yes, husbands, no!?"'[26]

Partly because of the lack of ideological gulfs in politics, the Irish experience differed from its continental counterparts in some respects. In Italy, for example, 'socialism was the first major non-religious – and often provocatively irreligious – popular movement in Italian history', an assertion that cannot be made about any significant Irish political movement. There was no pronounced early twentieth-century 'crisis of secularisation', or a radicalism strongly asserted alongside a strong and authoritative Catholic Church.[27]

The change of government in 1932, when Fianna Fáil ousted Cumann na nGaedheal from power, did not matter much in the context of attitudes to sexual morality. The wife of the critic Francis Hackett, Signe Toksvig, a neglected Danish writer who wrote in English and was author of *Eve's Doctor* (1937) – a 'gynaecological novel' banned in Ireland which contains oblique criticism of clerical Catholic views on childbirth and birth control – wrote diaries during her stay in the country from 1926 to 1937. They contain withering comments on what she regarded as the suffocating impact of Irish Catholicism, or the preponderance of what she described in an entry in December 1930 as the 'dreary, craw-thumping, fast-keeping bourgeois'.[28] She also recorded in her diaries in February 1932 that she and Hackett were 'mildly excited' about the general election that year, 'hoping not so much Fianna [Fáil] would get in as that holy Willie's [William Cosgrave] gang would be booted out'. But she recognised that 'of course we shall be *snorting* with rage at the new one'.[29]

What remained constant, however, was the prevalence of sexual crimes and the determination to prosecute them. Once again, it is in the court files that the evidence can be found which makes a mockery of the pretence that Ireland was exceptionally chaste and virtuous when it came to expressions of sexuality. This was something commented on by Hackett, a well-known Irish-born but largely US-based literary critic and author of *Ireland: A Study in Nationalism* (1918), when he wrote an article on Ireland for the *American Mercury* magazine in January 1945. Hackett was initially concerned with providing a critique of Irish neutrality and living standards, but he also focused much of his skilfully expressed ire on the Irish denial of sex in the 1920s and 1930s, during which he and Toksvig both fell foul of the censorship laws. Along with what he referred to as a 'mythical' neutrality, he maintained:

Equally fantastic is de Valera's desire to lock up the Irish in their innocence and purity. By suppressing the crimes report [the report of the Carrigan Committee], full of awkward facts, he strove before the war to maintain another myth; in the same way, he abolished prophylaxis for the army, ignoring the increase of syphilis which was bound to follow and which did follow. He was not allowed to monopolise hypocrisy.

Both political parties linked with the Church in all sorts of prohibitions and inhibitions. About the problems of sex they pretend to be doves when in fact they are ostriches. A Jesuit father took it upon himself to decide where, and for how long, the young were to dance. The Bishops came out against late parties, mixed bathing, night rides, communism, lipstick and legs. The list of censored books previous to the war already exceeded a thousand.

Perhaps more interesting was the manner in which Hackett wove his personal experience into his harsh assessment. He was no detached observer, but someone who had direct insight into the underbelly of sexual activity and crime:

As for the sexual morbidity, I can testify from my own observation as a juror in Wicklow, where I lived from 1929 to 1937, that de Valera closes his eyes to facts. During quarter sessions, the panel had these cases to try: first, a village girl accused of throwing her newborn baby out of a railway carriage; second, a seller of soda water charged with homosexuality on twenty counts, pleading guilty, third, a village elder accused of criminal assault on two children under twelve, pleading guilty. Fourth, a romping athletic youth, accused of raping a girl under sixteen, found guilty. In Clare, at the same time, the Judge had so many sex cases, in de Valera's own stronghold, that he called it the Dirty Assize. Rape, infanticide, homosexuality, even incest, crop up all over the country.[30]

Hackett was not exaggerating; these crimes were indeed cropping up all over the country and were on the increase in the 1920s.

When Hackett showed some of their regular visitors, including Cumann na nGaedheal minister Desmond FitzGerald, a cartoon of a priest riding an ass labelled Ireland, 'at once they got stiff, defensive, mum, ridiculous.'[31] The following year Toksvig and Hackett went on one of their long walks in which they discussed whether or not they could continue to live in Ireland, given that 'the psyche of the country is so stinkingly Catholic and reactionary that it is insufferable. Anything in the way of base reaction is possible here.'[32] Hackett was exceptionally hostile to de Valera because he felt he embodied everything that was puritanical about Ireland, recording in his diary in March 1932, 'my antagonism to Dev is an antagonism to illiberation, sex repression and ugliness'. The following week he read a short story from Seán O'Faoláin's new book *Midsummer Night Madness* (1932), which was banned by the Censorship Board: 'It is melodramatic, but these boys have a sense of beauty. And as I think of Dev & Co. what they completely lack is the loyalty to sensuous beauty which frees a man from Puritanism.'[33]

'I love you utterly … my life, my breath my sun and air and wind'

But for all the caustic comments made by Hackett and Toksvig about the politicians they encountered, not all were able or willing to reconcile their private behaviour with the sexual ethos of the new Free State. Cumann na nGaedheal's Minister for Home Affairs (later Justice), Kevin O'Higgins, for example, fell deeply in love with Hazel Lavery, the society hostess and wife of the artist John Lavery, who had become a confidante of a number of Irish politicians in the early 1920s. A biography of Hazel by Sinead McCoole, published in 1996, reveals the depth of O'Higgins's feelings for her, a love and devotion she accepted and which also involved her censoring some of his letters. O'Higgins, who had fasted for six months before his marriage and with a reputation as a devoted family man, often melted in her presence. In November 1924, he wrote, 'When I do see you it will be as it always is, my poor old stunted brain will be unable to send any coherent instruction.'[34]

Such correspondence was in stark contrast to his public persona, as 'the deeply religious hard man of the cabinet' who had considered a vocation to the priesthood and backed legislative discrimination against women when it came to jury service. In contrast to the cold logic he used to justify his political initiatives, his correspondence with Lavery reveals a man entranced, burning with desire and desperately emotional:

> I want you – all the enchantments … sight and sounds and the touch of you. I want to hold you to me and hear you say again and again and again that you love me and are [mine] forever … I love you utterly … my life, my breath my sun and air and wind.[35]

The surviving fragments of these letters cannot be taken as definitive proof of a physical affair; while his daughter referred to them as 'indisputable' evidence of her father's infatuation with Lavery, he was one of many she corresponded intimately with. O'Higgins's most recent biographer, John McCarthy, has trod carefully around the subject. At one stage, O'Higgins wrote to Lavery: 'God help me. I loved the highest when I saw it and fate placed it out of reach. You have been so sweet with me' – words that could be interpreted as implying physical consummation was not something he could bring himself to attempt due to religious or moral scruples. The fasting before his marriage may have been in vain, given that Lavery insisted that many of his letters to her were 'bearing in no complimentary manner on married life in general and his own in particular'. McCarthy makes the fair point that the obvious emotional infidelity was also due to the context of 'a young man drawn from the innocent social circles of middle- and upper-middle-class Catholic Ireland of the early twentieth century into the vortex of London high society in the 1920s'.[36] Perhaps it also allowed him to escape the tumultuous, bitter and violent atmosphere of civil war Ireland and the huge political and personal pressure he and his colleagues were under in the 1920s, which culminated in his murder by IRA members in 1927.

'To me it is appalling ... a young man who would indulge in the things alleged against him is a serious menace to the community'

While much has been made of the legislative milestones in Ireland in relation to contraception and censorship, little attention has been devoted to the other issues Hackett listed, which were of more significance in terms of their impact on individuals, families, neighbours and communities – and these were only the cases that came to court (circuit courts were first established by Dáil Eireann in 1920 and were formally established by the Free State under the 1924 Courts of Justice Act; less serious cases were dealt with at district court level, while more serious cases were tried at the Central Criminal Court). In 2007, American researcher Moira Maguire, having examined all available circuit court records (records are not complete for all counties) between 1924 and 1960, established that there were 1,500 sexual assault cases. If contemporary suggestions that reported cases represented less than 15 per cent of actual cases are accurate, and given that the number of cases proceeded with is higher than the 1,500 documented, it is fair to assume that the number of sexual assaults that occurred throughout the country between the 1920s and the 1960s exceeded 10,000. Of the 1,500 sexual assault cases detailed in available court records, 81 per cent of the victims were aged 17 or younger, 55 per cent were between the ages of 14 and 17, 18 per cent were between the ages of 10 and 13, and 8 per cent were aged 9 or younger.[37]

Many of these cases were reported in newspapers, though the language used was often circumspect and barristers had a tendency to announce they would not 'go into the gruesome details of the cases' in their summings-up (newspapers gave more elaborate coverage to slander actions, manslaughter trials and disputes over money and inheritances).[38] But circuit court judges were vocal about the extent of sexual crime and its implications, while maintaining (in the context of the time) their humanity, as did juries. In 1936, for example, Judge O'Donnell at the Cork circuit court, referring to an 18-year-old male found guilty on four charges 'concerning girls under age', addressed the jury in a passage that was reported in the *Cork Examiner* newspaper:

> Young men of this type are a problem. To me it is appalling ... a young man who would indulge in the things alleged against him is a serious menace to the community and a danger to himself. To me the trouble is: what is best for young men of this type? Whatever punishment I may inflict is not enough. A cure under care, protection and discipline in the hope that they may be weaned away from conduct of this kind – that of course is the thing we would all wish for.

To the jury, who added a rider to their verdict recommending mercy on grounds of age and health, he said he hoped 'they would never again have to come to court to listen to such cases as it had been theirs and his misfortune to listen to during the present criminal sitting'. But he consented to the jurors' wish and sentenced the defendant to two years in prison.[39]

During sentencing for other convicted sex offenders on the same day, including a man sentenced to five years for 'indecency' with another male (the convicted man had previously served seven years for a similar offence), another two young men bound over to keep the peace for 'indecency' with the man sentenced to five years, and a father jailed for three years for incest ('a broken man' on a disability pension after military service in the First World War), described as 'one of the most serious crimes it was possible to commit', the same judge commented that most of these cases were 'due to the conditions under which the poor lived, bad housing and poverty'. He urged the rich in the community to help the poor and expressed the hope that those who felt 'a Christian duty to help the unfortunate' would assist them on their release, praising the good work Catholic lay groups did in the community.[40]

'Having regard to the nature of the offence with which he is charged'

The circuit court cases during the 1920s and 1930s suggest a high degree of sexual frustration, violence and abuse, but the verdicts delivered and the number of prosecutions abandoned also suggest that it was difficult for many victims to get justice. This is underlined by the high number of acquittals in relation to rape and carnal knowledge cases in particular. In Dublin city circuit court, for example, the criminal trials record book shows that on 18 October 1927, of the 92 cases listed, ten were sexual crime cases, including indecent assaults on young girls and boys, attempted buggery, gross indecency and rape. Of the four cases of indecent assault, two *Nolle Prosequis* were entered, one defendant was found not guilty by direction because there was no corroboration of the child's evidence, and the defendant that was found guilty of the carnal knowledge of a girl under 13 was fined £30 in lieu of six months' hard labour.

A man convicted of attempted buggery was sentenced to twelve months' hard labour, suggesting that, on occasion, consenting sex between males was dealt with more harshly than the crime of unlawful carnal knowledge of girls under 13. Another man convicted of gross indecency with a boy under the age of 6 was found guilty by the jury but with a 'strong recommendation to mercy', and was bound over to keep the peace for two years. Two men convicted of buggery were sentenced to three years' and one year's hard labour respectively, while another convicted of gross indecency was given a suspended twelve-month sentence on the condition he paid £25 towards the cost of prosecution and that he left the country. The man accused of rape was found not guilty by direction.[41]

These records reveal that more than 10 per cent of cases listed that day (10 out of 92) were sex crimes, and that homosexuality and indecent assault on girls predominated. The cases listed for January and October 1928 tell a similar tale: a man convicted of the carnal knowledge of a girl under the age of 14 was sentenced to four months' hard labour, while a man convicted of gross indecency with another man was sentenced to fifteen months' hard labour. Although obviously the circumstances of the cases varied, it is difficult to find consistency in the sentencing: one man convicted of the unlawful carnal knowledge of a 7-year-old girl was sentenced to ten years' penal servitude.

There was a large number of attempted prosecutions for gross indecency in Dublin in 1928, but it was difficult to secure convictions. Of the six cases listed, one defendant was found guilty and bound to keep the peace for two years, another found not guilty by direction, the jury disagreed in another case, a *Nolle Prosequi* was entered in another, another defendant was found guilty and sentenced to fifteen months' hard labour, and another bound to keep the peace for two years. A young man who pleaded guilty to the indecent assault of a boy under 13 was sent to the Borstal in Clonmel, County Tipperary, for three years. As a result of the indecent assault cases, one man convicted of the indecent assault of a male under 13 years was sentenced to five years' penal servitude while another was found not guilty. A *Nolle Prosequi* was entered in another, as happened in a case involving a man accused of carnal knowledge of his 15-year-old sister. It appears that in some of these cases there was no counsel for the defence, and that it was also sometimes difficult to get parents to appear in defence of the accused.[42]

In the 1930s, if anything, it became even more difficult to prosecute men for sexual offences. The Dublin city state files for the circuit court commencing on 14 January 1938 list seven cases of attempted carnal knowledge with young girls, for which only one defendant was found guilty. This underlines the extent to which the odds were stacked against women when it came to prosecutions for unlawful carnal knowledge, and may be an indication that the evidence of children was not taken seriously enough. The ages of the alleged victims ranged from 8½ years to 16 years. It has been maintained that due to statutes passed in England and Scotland in 1922 and 1928 and in Northern Ireland in 1923, 'the law with regard to sexual offences against young persons was relatively more lenient in the 26 counties'[43] – one of the reasons for the setting-up of the Carrigan Committee.

Overall, of the forty-one cases listed in the issue papers of Dublin circuit court in January 1938, eight were cases of sexual crime, but there were only two convictions – the one mentioned above for unlawful carnal knowledge, and another in which a man was convicted of buggery 'on the seashore in the vicinity of Woodbrook in County Dublin'.[44]

But a survey of some of the other sentencing does suggest a lot of leniency was shown: in April 1922, a man convicted of indecent assault on three males received a four-month sentence.[45] As in the 1920s, there seemed to be little consistency throughout the 1930s in relation to sentencing. The calendar of prisoners sent for trial at the Dublin circuit court commencing on 14 January 1938 includes the case of a 34-year-old man convicted of gross indecency with another male. He had previous convictions, having served a sentence of five years' penal servitude for buggery, but for the 'assault and battery of a female' he received only two months' imprisonment.

Sexual crime was also prevalent outside of Dublin. Those convicted of such crimes at Galway circuit court from October 1927 to June 1930 were given the following sentences: buggery with a sheep: three years' penal servitude; indecent assault of a girl under 14: eighteen months; attempted buggery: three years; indecent assault of a girl under the age of 8: four years. Overall statistics reveal that there were 142 criminal cases heard by the Galway circuit court during these years, ten of them for sexual offences, in which five of the defendants were found not guilty and five guilty. Typical sentences for other common offences included fifteen months for robbery with personal violence, thirteen months for receiving stolen goods, fifteen months for the larceny of £20, and two years in a Borstal for stealing a bottle of whiskey.[46]

Certain patterns and trends are discernable: the first is that defendants seemed just as likely to be acquitted as convicted for sexual offences; homosexual offences were often dealt with more severely than sexual assaults against female children; and overall between 8 and 10 per cent of the cases being tried were for sexual offences; there was an abundance of *Nolle Prosequis*; and juries often disagreed, prompting retrials. These patterns were broadly applicable to the circuit court in Dublin for the year 1928, when there were 192 indictments, sixteen of which were for sexual offences: four defendants were found not guilty; the juries disagreed in another two cases, three *Nolle Prosequis* were entered, and seven defendants were found guilty. Of those found guilty, one man convicted of gross indecency was bound over to keep the peace for two years, another convicted of the carnal knowledge of a girl under 14 was sentenced to four months' hard labour, a man convicted of the indecent assault of a male under 13 was sentenced to five years' (his father failed to appear in his defence), while another young man convicted of the same offence was sentenced to Clonmel Borstal for three years (even though ten years later a 19-year-old man charged with gross indecency with another male person was not sent to Clonmel because, according to the circuit court Borstal reports, 'having regard to the nature of the offence with which he is charged, he is not considered a suitable case for treatment in the Borstal institution'; the same reason was cited for not sending a 21-year-old man convicted of unlawful carnal knowledge to Clonmel).[47]

An adult male convicted of gross indecency with another man was sentenced to fifteen months, while another convicted of unlawful carnal knowledge of a 7-year-old girl received ten years' penal servitude.[48] During the same circuit court sittings, three prosecutions for gross indecency failed.

This would indicate that there was active homosexual activity in Dublin city, that those who engaged in it were being arrested and brought to trial, but also that it was not always easy to secure convictions.

Many of the files would suggest that sexual crimes involving gay men were treated as being in a different league. The calendar of prisoners for trial at Dublin circuit court commencing on 14 January 1938 includes the criminal record of a 34-year-old man who was convicted of gross indecency with a male person; he had nine previous convictions, including assault and battery of a woman, for which he had received two months' hard labour, and a conviction of buggery for which he had been sentenced to five years' penal servitude.[49]

The patterns of sexual crime and sentencing of cases in Northern Ireland were similar: bestiality, infanticide and indecent assault cropped up in the Crown quarter sessions in County Down, infanticide being particularly common from the 1900s to the 1940s.[50] The Crown Book at Assizes for the county of Londonderry in the 1920s provides an overview of typical crimes and sentencing during that decade: twelve months' hard labour for carnal knowledge of a girl under 13; twelve sex crime cases in the Summer Assizes of 1922; and in the Summer Assizes of 1925 a one-month suspended sentence for indecent assault on a 17-year-old girl, as well as regular not guilty verdicts for rape and assault. At the Summer Assizes of 1926, there were three sex cases, with two defendants found not guilty and one found guilty – a man convicted of the sexual assault of an 8-year-old girl who was sentenced to nine months' hard labour. This conforms to a regular pattern.[51]

Meanwhile, not all gunfire in Belfast in 1921 was to do with sectarianism: a crowd of people chased and restrained a man on the Antrim Road in Belfast in May 1921 when a woman was shot and wounded by her former boyfriend in broad daylight. The victim had been taking music lessons:

> I had been keeping company with him and had had a dispute sometime before. I passed by without speaking to him. I then heard quick footsteps behind me and I heard 2 shots. I knew I was shot but I did not feel any pain at the time. I saw blood on my dress. I looked around and saw the prisoner running towards Atlantic Avenue. He did not say anything before he fired the shot.[52]

*'Cases come before the courts not infrequently which one would not like
to discuss with the feminine members of one's own family'*

Many of the court cases also required the evidence of witnesses, including
children, which means they give some insight into how these crimes were
perceived, how they were presented and spoken about, and how victims
interacted with their families and their communities once the crimes – or
alleged crimes – had taken place. Francis Hackett also highlights how awareness and rhetoric about sexual crime and sexual morality seemed to operate at two levels: public denunciation and private prosecution; the voices
from the pulpit and the Bishops and the decisions of the juries and from the
benches.

What factors influenced those typical decisions from the benches
and the juries in the 1920s? Firstly, the cases were heard almost exclusively
before all-male juries. In 1924 legislation was enacted which, while retaining women's right to serve on a jury, gave them exemption on demand. Few
were empanelled and very few served. In 1927, the government proposed
the extreme measure of removing women from jury service altogether, but
a compromise was reached that they would be exempted but allowed to
serve if they so chose, a situation similar to that in some states in the US at
the time (and a significant achievement for the women's groups that forced
the amendment to the original outright exemption). The *Irish Independent*
claimed 'real' women did not want to serve on juries in any case, as it would
take them away from 'the bosoms of their families, from their cherished
household duties, from the preparation of their husbands' dinners ... to take
their places on juries to decide matters entirely foreign to their experience
and often beyond their comprehension'.[53] Similar sentiments were expressed
in the US Congress.

The introduction of the 1927 legislation provided one of the few opportunities for discussion of sexual crime, particularly rape, to be placed on the
official record. When the Juries Bill was debated in the Dáil in February
1927, Minister for Justice Kevin O'Higgins justified the government's proposal on the basis that

> Extremely unpleasant cases come before the courts, cases of indecent
> assault, of rape, and, occasionally, of sodomy, and so on, and I would
> not take the administrative decision of subjecting women officials to a
> task of taking down verbatim evidence given in cases of that kind. That

consideration applies equally in the matter of juries. I do not want to overstress it, but it is a fact that cases come before the courts not infrequently which one would not like to discuss with the feminine members of one's own family.[54]

Major Bryan Cooper elaborated on the issue of rape in rejecting the proposal to excuse women from service:

> As a rule, there is only one witness in a case of rape, and that witness is the person on whom the rape was committed. It is very much easier for a woman to tell whether or not another woman is telling the truth than it is for a man. I would go so far as to say that it is almost impossible for a man to tell whether a woman is telling the truth or not.[55]

Thomas Johnson, however, the leader of the Labour Party, saw the proposal to restrict female jury service as creating a further sense of grievance on the part of women, and maintained that 'privileges and obligations' should be the same for all citizens. On the subject of what was and was not appropriate for women to hear, he argued that in cases such as rape and sexual assault, there were inevitably going to be women in the dock or in the witness box, and 'If the woman in the dock or in the witness box has to suffer all the indignities, indelicacies and indecencies that come out in court, I think it is not too much to expect a woman in the jury box to undergo the same ordeal.'[56]

When women were undergoing their legal ordeals, court files suggest that particulars of each individual case were weighed, and humanity was not absent in reaching verdicts. The Crown Book at Quarter Sessions (what evolved into the circuit court book) for Dublin in the early 1920s includes, for instance, a case in March 1922 in which a woman convicted of concealing a birth by placing her baby in a parcel in a drawer in a house in Ranelagh was 'discharged without punishment'.[57]

Some of the capital murder cases also involved sexual motives, notably the case of Annie Walsh, who was hanged following the murder of her husband in 1924 – the only woman hanged after the foundation of the Free State. It was a classic triangle of young wife, old husband and young lover. The murder of Moll (Mary) McCarthy in November 1940 was another case in which sex featured strongly. Living in poverty in a prosperous farming area of Tipperary, between 1921 and 1940 she had seven children out of wedlock, six of the seven reputed fathers being local residents. Historian Brendan O'Cathaoir has suggested that McCarthy was 'a paradox in a rigidly Catholic society'; her unorthodox lifestyle became a source of local tension and as a result of pressure from parishioners the local priest condemned her from the altar. The police investigation following the discovery of her body at a neighbouring farm was hampered by lack of co-operation from the local community and an innocent farm worker, Harry Gleeson, was framed for the killing – a move probably orchestrated by the father of McCarthy's youngest child, who feared exposure. Seán MacBride, one of the lawyers defending Gleeson, suggested McCarthy was the 'victim of a perverted sense of morality bred by a civilisation which, nominally based on Christianity', lacked most of its essentials. O'Cathaoir observes that 'the one person to show moral courage was Anna Cooney, a leading member of the Legion of Mary. She took possession of Moll McCarthy's body and arranged for its burial in her own family plot.'[58]

'La perfecta casada'

Many aspects of the Irish sexual experience remained constant in the 1920s and 1930s. Capital murder cases with a sexual element were rare, but the sexual crimes detailed at circuit court level occurred frequently. What was significant was the gulf between the sexual crimes revealed in court cases and the official Free State desire to present Ireland as a pure and virginal country. Some senior Church and state figures who became alarmed because the sordid sexual underworld conflicted so obviously with their self-image and desired perception, called into question the extent to which laws and religious teaching were being obeyed and seemed to highlight something of an anarchic streak when it came to sexual expression.

There is nothing uniquely Irish about this. Perhaps what is unusual is how it contrasted so strongly with the strict public moral, religious and political code. There are a lot of parallels with Spain in the aftermath of the Spanish Civil War, with a similar focus on a post-revolutionary 'moral crusade'. In Spain in the 1940s Francoist notions of decency were enforced and promoted, with Catholic teaching to the fore, though the perceived need in Spain for 'rechristianisation' may not have been quite as pronounced in Ireland. Nor did hatred of the Church in Ireland run as deep as it did in Spain, given the shared religious sensibilities of most Irish nationalists (though some Irish republicans refused to forgive the Catholic Church for its denunciation of republicans during the civil war).

Spanish national renewal, as in Ireland, 'required a wide range of preventative measures: divorce, abortion and non-religious marriage were banned; censorship of words and pictures was enforced'; much emphasis was put on the family as a source of social stability, male authority was reinforced within the family with the re-introduction of the 1889 civil code, and homosexuality was 'fiercely repressed' – a harbinger of which had been the murder of the gay playwright and poet Frederico Garcia Lorca at the start of the civil war.[59]

In Franco's Spain contraception was banned, unmarried women aged between 17 and 35 were required to undertake six months' social services where they were indoctrinated with Falangist values, and in the quest for the perfect woman ('*La perfecta casada*') women were seen 'as both the source of all virtue and of all vice in society'. Censorship was excessive, with many foreign films 'mutilated beyond recognition ... such prudery extended even to painting the limbs of women in short skirts'.[60] The decree which created Francoist Spain's board of film censors stipulated that 'on moral questions the vote of the representative of the church shall be especially worthy of respect', while professional boxing matches were kept out of newsreels on the grounds that they showed naked male torsos – vests were painted on by the *Retocadores* (retouchers), who were 'employed by every newspaper and magazine' until the 1950s,[61] an extremism not quite matched in Ireland. In the summer of 1936, for example, the *Cork Examiner* newspaper ran a front page advertisement for summer lingerie wear, with readers informed that the sketch of the scantily clad woman 'is of a very attractive and dainty vest and knicker set in cellular lock nut'.[62]

'About half an hour after the child being born I got out and went to Tom Cleary's and milked the cows'

There was continuing concern in Ireland with issues that had been prevalent since the post-Famine era, most notably illegitimacy, and it is clear the fear of being branded the parent of an illegitimate child drove young women to desperation. In December 1938 a 21-year-old woman from Mountjoy Place in Dublin city was prosecuted for attempted suicide. The doctor at the city's Mater hospital who treated her gave evidence that she had been brought in to have her stomach pumped after drinking Jeyes cleaning fluid. Her statement was made in hospital:

> I am 21 years of age and am not employed. About last September I began to keep company with a man whose name and address I do not wish to make known. Shortly afterwards intimacy between myself and this man took place as a result of which I am now pregnant. About a fortnight ago I realised I was pregnant. I was examined by Dr Spain, Mater Hospital Dispensary, and he told me I was pregnant. When Dr Spain told me that I became distressed and decided to take poison. On Tuesday 14 December I bought 3 pence worth of Jeyes fluid in a bottle and between 10 and 11 p.m. same date I was passing through Gardiner Lane and decided to take the fluid. The bottle was a 'baby Jameson' and was about three quarters full. I drank the contents of the bottle and threw the empty bottle away ... about 11.30 p.m. same date I walked to the Mater Hospital where I was treated and detained.[63]

The defendant, who pleaded guilty, was bound over to keep the peace on condition that 'she shall go to the Union Hospital, St Patrick's Home Pelletstown Dublin, and remain there for whatever period the authorities deem necessary'.[64]

Many other women carried their babies to full term and then attempted to conceal the births or kill their newborn; infanticide was very common, but, as mentioned earlier, there was a degree of mercy shown when the women were prosecuted. In 1925 a young woman was charged with infanticide at New Docks in Galway city. Two days prior to giving birth she had applied for a position as kitchen maid at the Skeffington Arms hotel in Eyre Square. She was given the job but could not get up for work and was sacked, after which she gave birth in a disused house on the docks. A 'crowd of men' gathered around the house and the baby's body was found with marks around its neck and covered in stones. She told the Garda, 'I cannot remember whether the baby was alive when born as I became partly unconscious after giving birth.' According to the doctor, 'I asked her was she married and she said no.'[65]

In March 1935, a young woman living alone with her widowed mother in Cork gave birth and buried the baby thirty yards from their cottage. She initially insisted she had influenza, but then admitted, 'It was dead a long time I think as my stomach used to be awfully cold. That's all that happened, only I buried it then when it was dead, out in the field down by the side of a ditch. I covered it with clay and sods.'[66] In 1927 at Ballinamona, near Hospital in County Limerick, a Garda acting on 'information received' (highlighting the difficulty of keeping secrets in a small rural community) gave evidence about a grim discovery: 'I found in the grove the dead body of a male infant concealed in a cardboard sausage box tied with a piece of rope; the box appeared to be there for some time as the grass underneath it had withered.' The statement of the mother of the child is very revealing, not only about the extent to which women could carry babies to full term, either without anyone knowing or else with an agreed silence on the issue, but also the loneliness of the women involved and their determination to get back to a normal routine immediately:

> About the 30th or 31st March 1927 a child was born to me in my own house about 4 o'clock in the evening. No one knew the child was born, not even my mother. The child never moved or stirred and I don't know whether the child was born alive or dead. I rolled it up in a sheet and put it under the bed. I left it there for about 3 days and then put it into a box and about 2 days afterwards I brought it to Ballynamona and left it in a wood. About half an hour after the child being born I got out and went to Tom Cleary's and milked the cows. I meant to leave the baby in the churchyard at Hospital but there were two women standing at the chapel gate when I was passing.

She subsequently went to the doctor and, according to his statement, 'wanted a certificate to take to the Guards that she had not been delivered of a child recently. On examination I told her I could not give her the certificate and that in my opinion she was recently delivered of a child.' After a postmortem, the doctor was 'satisfied the child was born dead'.[67] The woman was found guilty of concealment of birth and was discharged on entering into her own recognisances.[68] Although twelve women were sentenced to death for the murder of an illegitimate infant between 1922 and 1949 (seven were unmarried mothers), juries in trials of infanticide and concealment of birth usually recommended mercy: a woman convicted of concealment of birth in Dublin in 1927, for example, was bound over to keep the peace for two years; and of the seven unmarried mothers sentenced to death between 1922 and 1949, five were recommended to mercy because of the 'exceptional' and 'overwhelming' circumstances at the birth, and some were deemed to be suffering from temporary insanity.[69]

Infanticide continued to crop up regularly in the 1920s at the General Assizes in Armagh, Down and Londonderry.[70] At the Spring Assizes for County Londonderry in February 1925 a woman convicted of the concealment of birth was found guilty of 'placing its dead body behind a certain curtain and basket' and received a three-month suspended sentence.[71] In Londonderry in 1925, a woman convicted of the concealment of her baby's birth 'by placing its dead body behind a certain curtain and basket' was also sentenced to three months, suspended on condition she kept the peace.[72]

Historian Louise Ryan has highlighted that, despite the degree of self-censorship of Irish newspapers in the 1920s, they frequently carried stories of marital breakdown, child abuse and infanticide, and that 'to judge from the pages of the *Cork Examiner* infanticide was a weekly, if not a daily reality in Ireland'. In the month of August 1925, for example, four discovered cases of infanticide were reported; the reports were brief, factual and non-judgemental.[73] The same perhaps could be said of the doctors' and Garda statements in the courts files, partly because they were aware of the desperate circumstances of the women involved, partly because such cases were so common as not to unduly shock, and also, by 1943, it was being suggested at government level that infanticide be made a non-capital offence, as in England.[74]

But in one case cited by Ryan the judge found it 'rather unfortunate' that the jury opted for a verdict of manslaughter instead of 'wilful murder', and on occasion juries were ready to give the defendants the benefit of the doubt in the absence of conclusive medical proof. As the plight of servant girls or mothers with already more children than they could afford to feed were highlighted, economic and social realities clashed with moral and legal niceties, and the divergence between social laws and social practices became apparent. In the words of Ryan, 'The courtroom provided an environment where the private worlds of desperate decisions, made in heartbreaking circumstances, encountered the public world of uncompromising law and order.'[75]

'She gave birth to a male child on the mountainside without any skilled or other attendance'

But the law was not always uncompromising, as the records of the cases forwarded to the government in order for death sentences to be commuted make clear. In one such case, relating to a woman from Roscommon in 1935, the judge recommended mercy because 'of [the] age and sex of the convicts and the circumstances of the case'.[76] The sentence was commuted. In February 1929, a judge also strongly recommended mercy in the case of a 21-year-old Kerry woman, described by the medical officer as being 'of low mental calibre', who had killed her baby after she gave birth alone on the side of a mountain. The unmarried daughter of a labourer, she had been on the way to the county home 'for her confinement' when 'she gave birth to a male child on the mountainside without any skilled or other attendance ... the accused had no assistance and after the birth she appears to have placed the baby in a stream where it was found some two days afterwards ... The act was committed immediately after birth when the accused must have still been suffering from the pangs and subsequent prostration of child birth.'

The judge was emphatic about the need for mercy to be shown towards the woman's plight, given that executions were normally expected to take place one month after conviction. 'She was living at home at the time and she stated in her evidence that she was terrified of her mother. May I suggest that this is a case in which the mental condition of the accused, who is quite a young girl, may be seriously prejudiced by her remaining for any considerable time under sentence of death.' He also referred to the difficulties of the jury in the case, giving a rare glimpse of how they reacted to these cases when deliberating. According to court records, 'The jury had a difficulty in arriving at their verdict and informed the Judge that their difficulty was as to the state of mind of the woman at the time of the act. The judge having explained to them that the onus of proof that [the] prisoner was unable to appreciate her actions at the time she committed the crime lay on the defence, which however had not established such proof.' The jury gave a verdict of guilty 'with a strong recommendation to mercy having regard to the exceptional circumstances'.[77]

A similar plea was made by the judge in the case of an unmarried 22-year-old woman who had given birth in Mullingar hospital and was convicted of drowning her baby daughter in the local canal: 'It is a case in which the strain of a capital sentence, if continued for any length of time, may have serious results on the physical and mental health of the prisoner.'[78]

In December 1938, the Court of Criminal Appeal heard the case of a Monaghan woman who had been sentenced to death for killing her newborn granddaughter through drowning. The defence counsel referred to 'the shame which was brought upon householders by the birth of an illegitimate child. That is a fact, of course, of which we were all aware ... it is a natural thing to try and avoid.' The trial judge took issue with that assertion, insisting that the life of a baby was 'as sacred in the eyes of our law as the life of any adult person'. He also said, 'One hears a good deal of discussion from time to time about child murder ... It may be a natural thing to try and hide the birth of an illegitimate child, but it is not to be suggested that it is a natural thing to kill the child for the purpose of hiding its birth.' The woman's death sentence was commuted to penal servitude for life.[79]

But there was much more to this case than most infanticide cases. The report of the investigating Garda noted that the accused had herself given birth to an illegitimate child in her youth when employed as a domestic servant, and a few years later had married a widower thirty years her senior, with whom she had seven children. Her eldest daughter had also given birth to an illegitimate child, four years previously. The case created much consternation at government level, and one of the reasons it was being investigated in the appeal court was 'in view of the reputation of the family'. It also transpired that when she became pregnant the daughter was under the age of 17; her boyfriend, a 16-year-old labourer, was charged with unlawful carnal knowledge. The Garda reports, which amount to a trawl through the sexual history of the accused woman and her family, also reveal much about attitudes at the time to those deemed to be sexually deviant, the extent to which they could be socially ostracised, the light in which rape was viewed, and the degree to which the woman was being sentenced not just for the crime of which she was charged but for the sheer brazenness of her sexual activity, deemed deviant in the extreme:

> M.S. had the reputation of being of loose moral character. It is freely stated in the locality that her husband – J.S. – was not the father of some of the younger members of the family. After his death a number of men, whose relations with Mrs S. from the moral aspect were suspected, frequented the house. Of these, one is reputed to be the father of several of the children and one of another of them. The result of all this was that in later years the family were largely shunned by their neighbours. This woman is a rough masculine type, appears to be below the average in intelligence and did not appear to worry in the least as to the views, or opinions, regarding her which were held by neighbours ... she was a very hardworking industrious woman and the family, although not well housed or clothed, appeared to be well fed.[80]

The 16-year-old labourer charged with the unlawful carnal knowledge of this woman's daughter (it happened outside Monaghan town 'on the ground by the side of the road') that led ultimately to infanticide was acquitted at Monaghan circuit court in October 1938 due to inconsistencies in the daughter's evidence. He contended, 'I never done any harm to any girl I went with. There was plenty of fellows with her [before] me.' There was also a comment by the investigating Garda attached to the file: 'It is interesting to observe the apparent simplicity with which the girl was seduced and the unrepentant attitude and youth of the seducer – an interesting commentary of itself of the type of people involved.'[81]

'Offences against very young girls show a deplorable increase'

It is significant that the judge in the case above referred to there being 'a good deal of discussion' about infanticide. But amongst whom and where? There was little appetite, it would seem, for a public discussion of the issues surrounding the concealment of births. But there was consternation at government level in March 1936 when Justice Hanna, a judge at the Central Criminal Court, speaking at a function in Dublin on St Patrick's Day, observed that regarding 'concealment of the birth of illegitimate children – tantamount in many cases to child murder – we have a notably high figure of 49 cases in the last statistical year'. He also commented on the regularity of indecent sexual assault cases (237 cases) and suggested rather cryptically that when clergy 'solemnly avow that certain forms of entertainment tend to the demoralisation of their young parishioners, their opinion should have more weight than appears to have been given to it in some quarters'.[82]

The Department of Justice took Hanna's comments very seriously, so much so that a memorandum by its intelligence division was drawn up in response. The secretary of the Department of Justice, Stephen Roche, suggested Hanna 'drew conclusions from insufficient data' and was only using the statistical abstract, adding that what he meant by 'normal standards' he did not specify. In fact, according to Roche, infanticide and rape offences were decreasing; there was 'no appreciable change' regarding indecent assault on females, 'but unnatural offences and offences against young girls show a definite tendency to increase'. Triennial figures were then cited as follows:

Infanticide (including abortion): 1927–9 (223 cases), 1930–32 (194) and 1933–5 (163).

Unnatural offences, including indecency with males: 1927–9 (99), 1930–32 (154), 1933–5 (256).

Rape: 1927–9 (69), 1930–32 (44), 1933–5 (41).

Indecent assault on females: 1927–9 (245), 1930–32 (243), 1933–5 (243).

Offences against young girls: 1927–9 (86), 1930–32 (92), 1933–5 (132).[83]

As with all such statistics, they only tell part of the story. Justice Hanna had said that 'It is clear ... that in the Free State the normal standard has been far exceeded in sexual offences, dishonesty in business, offences against public order and in juvenile crime', though significantly it was the mention of sexual offences that prompted a response (and it was a private one) from the Department of Justice. Roche asserted that it was 'impossible to discern any fixed trend', adding:

> The position in regard to sexual crime involving as it does an increase in sexual perversion, whether in the form of unnatural crime or offences against children, has led me to consider whether the relatively satisfactory figures in regard to concealment of birth and offences against fully grown women might really be taken as an indication that at least in one direction the general trend of sexual morality was towards an improvement. Prima Facie, the only information readily available, viz. the statistics for illegitimacy does not support this view.[84]

Officially, as has been previously mentioned, between 1926 and 1929 the numbers of illegitimate births had risen gradually to an annual average of 1,853; in 1926, the secretary of the Committee for the Reform of the Laws Relating to the Protection of Women and Young Girls informed the Minister for Justice that rescue societies were under severe pressure 'so much has the number of unmarried mothers increased during the last few years', and it was widely believed that 'unregistered births of illegitimate children possibly exceeded those registered'.[85]

In the year 1929–30, the infant mortality rate of illegitimate children was 295 per 1,000 registered births, compared with 307 in 1928, whereas the general infant mortality rate was 70 per 1,000. 'This meant that in the year 1929, 5 out of every 17 illegitimate children died in their first year. More than half of the deaths occurred within the first 2 months of life and were probably associated with ante-natal conditions inseparable from the circumstances attendant on the plight in which the mothers found themselves.'[86] The following year the figure was reduced to 251, 'the lowest rate recorded by the Registrar General since such mortality was classified separately in 1923', but in Northern Ireland the figure was 140, and in England and Wales 105, giving some indication of how far behind the Irish Free State lagged.[87]

'By appropriate training and example, self-respect is restored'

The solution to the problem of illegitimate births was believed to lie in the establishment of antenatal homes for expectant unmarried mothers and institutions where the mother and children 'might be maintained together for at least the first year of the child's life' (the idea being that the child could then be fostered). It was also believed that such homes were necessary 'where by appropriate training and example, self-respect is restored', preventing the women from staying in county homes at the expense of the ratepayers, or 'drifting into a life of degradation'. In the summer of 1922, proposals that unmarried mothers go to institutions other than workhouses (now referred to as county homes) were raised by religious orders, the main concern being, it seems, that at that time such women were 'not segregated' from more 'hardened sinners'. The state's acceptance of such proposals laid the foundation for the infrastructure of religious order-run mother and baby homes that operated from 1922 until the 1970s. As James Smith points out, 'the rehabilitative function of the nineteenth-century Magdalen was thus siphoned off to the new mother and baby institutions'.[88]

The priority was to avoid mixing 'redeemable' and 'unreformable' sinners (those who had had more than one illegitimate pregnancy), with the 'unreformable' being sent to the Magdalens (along with the 'mentally deficient'). As there was no female Borstal, the Magdalens were deemed suitable. James Smith observes that between 1926 and 1964 there were at least 211 instances of women charged with murder, concealment of birth (an act of 1949 made this a non-capital offence) and, after 1949, infanticide. Most who received suspended sentences for infanticide went to Magdalen asylums, in theory 'voluntarily', since women could not be legally remanded in that manner until 1960, though the prison authorities actively facilitated such committals.[89]

*The Report of the Commission on the Relief of the Destitute Poor Includ-
ing the Insane Poor* (1925–6) was frank about the stigma associated with
illegitimacy, but also about the danger to children's welfare: 'the illegitimate
child, being the proof of the Mother's shame is, in most cases, sought to be
hidden at all costs'; it was often arranged for someone to take the child, but
'if a lump sum is paid or if the periodical payment lapse, the child becomes
an encumbrance on the foster mother, who has no interest in keeping it
alive'. It was as stark as that. (Concern in this regard ultimately led to tighter
regulations under the Registration of Maternity Homes Act of 1934.) The
report of the commission offered further justification for a two-tiered institutional response to the two classes of unmarried mothers, by calling for
newly funded residential institutions for 'first offenders' where the women
would stay for a year, fulfil unpaid domestic duties and care for their child,
after which they could return home or go into domestic service. Three
homes – in Cork, Tipperary and Westmeath – received a capitation grant
from their local authorities and government grants were provided for the
maternity homes attached, while three additional homes were managed by
Catholic nuns but operated directly by local authorities.[90] Regarding one
home in Cork, it was observed, 'The matron of Bessborough reports that a
number of the girls are very weak willed and have to be maintained in the
home for a long period to safeguard them against a second lapse.'[91]

'She had committed a mortal sin, fornication, and unless she had a piece of luck she might be going to have a baby'

What is never mentioned in these reports is how many of the women were
pregnant as a result of rape, but it is clear from the court records that for
some this was indeed the case. Regardless of whether the men were convicted or not, these women were forced to undergo a period of incarceration,
having already been the victims of serious assaults. It is little wonder some
chose to leave the country altogether and the prevalence of such emigration
caused tension between English and Irish charity workers. As identified by
Lindsey Earner Byrne, 'it was also perceived as a national embarrassment,
reflecting not just the harshness of the moral code in Ireland, but its abject
failure to control sexual behaviour.'[92] By the 1930s, the Irish Hierarchy
'half-heartedly and under considerable pressure' sanctioned a repatriation
scheme. It was reluctant because such emigration was seen as convenient

by state and society alike, as it saved money and preserved the illusion at home of chastity. Reports sent to Archbishop Byrne in the 1920s concerning the work of the Port and Station Worker Society reveal that, between 1922 and 1927, of the 3,420 women the society helped at the English ports, 2,292 were Irish. By 1938, the London Crusade and Rescue Society received 356 requests for assistance from Irish unmarried mothers, eighty of whom admitted conception in Ireland. Such figures touched 'only the fringe of the problem'. Meanwhile at home, in the same year, residents of upmarket Herbert Avenue in Dublin collectively protested against the establishment of a home for unmarried mothers there.[93]

Some Irish women abroad, many of whom worked in domestic service, also became pregnant and abandoned, or if they thought they were pregnant must have endured great fear of exposure and shame, not to mention reflection on the extent to which the fact that they were in a less religious country was responsible for the predicament in which they found themselves. These fears were very effectively described in Norah Hoult's *Bridget Kiernan* (1928), the story of an Irish domestic servant in England who succumbs to the charms of an Englishman who has his way with her and then abandons her: 'she'd never forgive him for that never ... She had her pride and even if he wanted to marry her she wouldn't.' Bridget has to navigate the hostility of her working environment (and clashes with the mistress of the house) as well as the confusion engendered by Irish Catholic guilt. But there is a smattering of defiance born of a foreign environment that has slightly emboldened her:

> Well, here she was, Bridget Mary Kiernan, aged twenty-five, in a pretty plight and she might as well face it here and now. She had committed a mortal sin, fornication, and unless she had a piece of luck she might be going to have a baby. All because of that good-for-nothing fellow, Jim – Jim, with his lovely blue suit, and smart figure and wavy fair hair, and laughing blue eyes. And his warm lips that held yours till they seemed to draw you out of yourself into a great fire and confusion. Stop now! A lively-looking lad enough, maybe, but he had gone now and left her forever. Deserted her! Deserted – that was the word they called it ... It was her own fault in a way because she hadn't chosen to take heed of his style of talking ... she couldn't really see now that it was such a terrible thing as the way in which people talked about it. But, of course, it was badness, and she'd been bad, she had so ... all that a poor ignorant girl

the like of herself could do was to be good and leave the matters to the
priests and learned people to settle ... she had never been to confession
the whole year long she had been in England ... it was so different here
where no one seemed to have any religion at all ...[94]

In 1932, 'Miss Johnnie', a girl who helped with housework in the home of
Francis Hackett and Signe Toksvig, would not admit to her pregnancy and,
when it was medically confirmed, lied about the father, 'naming a mysterious chauffeur in Donegal'. She had the baby in a home 'and drops out of the
Hackett household'.[95]

Irish language scholar Phil O'Leary has highlighted how some writers in the Irish language in the early years of the Free State confronted the
theme of illegitimacy, amongst them Eamonn Mac Giolla Iasachta, who
served as a Free State senator. His book *Cúrsaí Thomáis* (1927) attracted criticism for its frank treatment of sexual topics, including prostitution, illegitimacy and (indirectly) abortion, and also for its unconventional approach to
Catholicism and the clergy. Another writer in Irish, Una Bean Uí Dhíocsa
(Elizabeth Rachel Dix), in her book *Cailín na Gruaige Duinne* (1932), dealt
'honestly and forthrightly' with the subjects of marital breakdown and postnatal depression.[96] In the realm of Irish language autobiographical writing,
Pádraig Ua Maoileoin's *Macadúna* (2001) is unusual in its frank treatment
of sexual matters; the author, born in 1913 and raised in the Kerry Gaeltacht
(Irish-speaking district), observed adults indulging in masturbation and
sexual intercourse in the open air. He makes the point that a child who grew
up in close proximity to animals was aware of the mechanics of sex, though
it was not until he was older that he understood its true significance; as a
child, the awareness of sexual differences between men and women aroused
interest but not anxiety.[97]

After his death in 2002, Ua Maoileoin was described as a character
who had been 'outwardly Rabelaisian ... inwardly staunchly religious', but
no puritan. As he wrote himself, '*Nír chuaigh Piúratánachas an Bhéarla I
bhfeidhm riamh ar an nGaeltacht*' ('The puritanism of the English language
never had an affect on the Gaeltacht').[98]

It was also pointed out in *The Bell* magazine in 1941 that the Irish language contains 'a remarkably abundant and varied vocabulary for sex terms
and that Gaelic writers have seldom hesitated to make use of them'. An Irish
priest gave as a reason for extending and preserving the use of the Irish language in Church 'that it was so much easier to speak plainly about the Sixth

Commandment [You Shall Not Commit Adultery] without shocking people, when one used Gaelic'.[99]

'That's a nice thing that's wrong with you'

One noteworthy aspect of some of the courts files from the 1930s is that the men who impregnated some of the girls who ended up in mother and baby homes were being arrested and charged. It was also common for the defendants to present these young women as promiscuous and responsible for their pregnancies. A case heard by Judge E. J. McElligott in Tralee, County Kerry in 1939, related to a 16-year-old girl from Castleisland who had given birth to twin babies in November 1938. It was alleged that the husband of the woman who employed her was the father; the man was, according to his wife, a violent drunkard. When he was confronted 'he said it was not his, that there were others besides themselves ... that's a nice thing that's wrong with you'. There was also mention during the case of someone having suggested 'a mustard bath', an obvious reference to an abortificient, which both women denied had ever been discussed.

The victim's mother, living in a labourer's cottage with eight other children (two more had died), commented, 'she asked me not to tell her father as he'd kill her' (this was a very common reaction, which left the victim under further threat of violence). The twins were stillborn. Significantly, during this case, in order for the charge to proceed, it was necessary for the girl's age to be verified. As was again common, fathers often could not remember when their children had been born, or indeed the order in which they were born; but in this case, the mother was also forced to admit 'my first child was born about a fortnight before my marriage. I was not going to deny that to anyone.' The father's statement recalled the circumstances of the girl's birth:

> I had no ticket for Nurse Kerins who is and was the public nurse for poor people. I have little remembrance of the birth of others of my children, as there was not any excitement on the occasion of their births. I remember the date of the birth of my eldest son Thomas. He was born on 15 July. I cannot say what year he was born ... I remember the date in his case because he was born on St Swithin's day and because he was the first boy to live. I am not able to say the exact age of E. I do not remember the year of her birth. I remember the date, the 9th November, because

of the difficulty I had with her case going a few times to the nurse and
going at night time into Castleisland when Free State soldiers were in
the town.[100]

The defendant was found not guilty on all charges.

A number of factors seem to have recurred in these cases; not guilty
verdicts, despite the pregnancies; the characters of the barely literate girls
being called into question; and the frequency of the alleged victims knowing
their alleged perpetrators very well. A 1936 case relating to events in Shrule,
County Mayo and heard at Ballinrobe in the district court area of Kilinaine
dealt with a charge of unlawful carnal knowledge of a 15-year-old girl by her
next-door neighbour: 'he is a distant relative of mine and the members of
his family and himself constantly visit my house and me theirs'. She alleged
he had assaulted her when they were alone in the barn: 'I did not resist. I
was then a schoolgirl and I did not know what the consequences of this
connection might be.' This was followed by a number of further assaults.
In recounting her story, the victim gave an indication as to why she was
on the receiving end of such sexual frustration, common in isolated rural
areas: 'There are no other young boys in the village except my brothers and
defendant.'

The girl subsequently went to work as a domestic servant: 'I did not
know I was about to have a baby until a month before it was born, when
Nurse Dooley told me.' Three weeks before the baby was born the defendant
and his father called at the house where she worked. The father commented,
'This is a nice sort of thing, leaving this upon this poor innocent boy that
has nothing.' The victim replied, 'It was him', to which she alleged the defendant's father replied, 'Shut up or I will smash your face.'

On the day her baby was born, the girl was sent to a home in Castlebar
('I had nobody attending me when the baby was born'). The father of the
victim, who mentioned that he and his sons were always out in the fields,
working 'for long continuous hours' (during which the alleged rapes took
place), gave evidence that 'N. was never at a dance and she was always in the
house for the saying of the rosary every night ... I did not bring my daughter
home for her confinement. She refused to come home with me.' The defendant was found not guilty, another decision that suggested many of these
girls were simply not believed or that the defendants were given the benefit
of the doubt.[101]

[handwritten: x father = 'begetter' / 'kill' daughter   x mother ? 'conceiver']

[handwritten: " in sin I was conceived"]

'I told him I'd be ruined. he said I wouldn't,
not the way he had done it'

During the 1920s an Illegitimate Children (Affiliation Orders) Bill was drafted and became law in 1930 to make it easier to compel fathers to contribute to the support of their children. This legislation was a response to the pressures of various people, including the Jesuit priest and social activist Richard Devane, who made representations on the subject to emphasise the necessity of placing the burden of maintenance on the father. The Free State did not inherit any law on this issue from Westminster; as the law stood prior to 1930, the only redress open to the mother was that 'her parent, guardian or employer may institute a civil action for seduction based on the legal fiction of loss of service'. The difficulty with this was that it was costly and 'of no avail unless the putative father is a "good mark" and has means or property ... moreover, where the employer is the father even this remedy is not readily available because the fiction breaks down except by recourse to a certain amount of subterfuge'.

In the memorandum for the Department of the Taoiseach on this subject, there was a degree of charitable thinking, perhaps even sympathy towards unmarried mothers:

Many unfortunate unmarried mothers are denied the shelter of their own families and it is possible that some of them, who might otherwise reform, drift into the prostitute class in a spirit of despair induced by the hardships they suffer. It can be readily appreciated that girls of the domestic servant class who get into difficulty find themselves in a position of great hardship trying to earn their living and to maintain an illegitimate child away from their ordinary place of work. A weekly contribution from the father of the child would ease this situation considerably. It is not impossible too, that the ability to obtain an affiliation order may lessen the number of cases of infanticide.[102]

[handwritten: x 'love'!]

Young women employed as domestic servants also continued to appear in court cases relating to sexual crime, though not as frequently as they had earlier in the twentieth century. In October 1927, a man was accused of raping a maid employed by his widowed mother in Stoneybatter, Dublin, for a wage of 8 shillings per week. He entered the servant's room and, according to her statement, 'said he felt cold and shut the door and gave me a cigarette to smoke. I said I didn't know how to smoke I'd get sick. He said "Go on, all girls smoke". He threw his arms around me and threw me down on the bed. He put his knee on my knee to keep me from kicking.' He then raped her. 'I told him I'd be ruined. He said I wouldn't, not the way he had done it, that he had done it dozens of times before ... I didn't tell my mother, neither then nor later, I was afraid to tell her.' The maid did, however, tell her fiancé, who reported the rape. The victim also mentioned that 'I was in Goldenbridge industrial school about 7 years. My mother was living in Dublin while I was in the school.'[103] The defendant was found not guilty.

living with!!

'Nothing is being done by legislation in this country to help them to cope with this evil'

One question on which the government began to receive submissions during this period was the manner in which the legal system dealt with women and children in relation to sexual crime, as well as the linked issue of the age of consent, both of which were central to the deliberations of the committee that reported on the Criminal Law Amendment Acts of 1880–85 and Juvenile Prostitution, otherwise known as the Carrigan Committee Report. It contains an extensive overview of sexual activity and perceived sexual activity in Ireland in the 1920s. Many had been lobbying for the age of consent to be raised to 18 years, and for new legislation to deal with juvenile prostitution, and the formation of the Carrigan Committee in June 1930 was the government's response. The committee included both a Catholic and a Protestant cleric, a female commissioner of the Dublin Poor Law Union and the matron of the Coombe hospital. Oral evidence was received from twenty-nine witnesses, eighteen of whom were women, which amounted to 'an unprecedented engagement by any committee of inquiry with the views of women'. It explored such topics as public indecency, birth control, censorship, illegitimacy, brothels and female police officers.[104]

The age of consent was something that the League of Nations had raised with the Irish government in 1926; three years earlier, Louie Bennett of the Irish Women's Workers Union corresponded with the government about the possibility of raising the age of consent to 18, as it was 'of vital importance to the moral safety of the youth of the nation'.[105] The following year the Irish Women Citizens' Association also insisted, in correspondence with the Attorney General's office, that the consent of those under the age of 18 should not be a defence to a charge, a reminder of the extent to which women's organisations from the 1920s to the 1940s took it upon themselves to exert pressure concerning such issues:

> Our association feels very strongly that it is unjust to hold young persons entirely responsible for their own moral conduct until they have passed out of the chaotic stages of adolescence and the period of curiosity. Both boys and girls are entitled to a much greater degree of protection from the state than they receive at present and we feel that the protection should be equal for both. With reference to girls in particular, it is the experience of all who have taken part in rescue or patrol work either as voluntary workers or in the official capacity of women police, that if girls can be prevented from slipping into prostitution until they have reached the age of 18 the probability of their ever doing so is greatly reduced.[106]

A memorandum from the Attorney General's office was more blunt, contending that 'the age of consent must be raised so as to protect the innocent, the ignorant and the giddy. England and Northern Ireland have raised it to 16. In the USA, eighteen states have set down 18 as the age of consent and in Australasian states the age is 16 and 17 – generally the former age. Social workers and medical men who have studied this question state definitely that 16 is the age of greatest danger for a girl.' It concluded that the age of consent should be raised to 18 in Ireland. It also noted that 'strong representations have been made to this department regarding the weakness of the existing law for dealing with prostitutes', and that as a result of them being sent to prison, 'no attempt at redemption is made'. It was believed girls under 21 should be sent to 'the existing female reformatories'. It was also claimed that 'it is well known that many prostitutes are seriously mentally deficient'.[107]

Legislative change in England in 1928 and in Northern Ireland in 1923 meant that the law with regard to sexual offences against young people was now more lenient in the Free State than it was in the United Kingdom. As the situation existed in the Irish Free State in 1926 (in which the minimum age at which marriage was legal was 12 for females and 14 for males; if the couple were under the age of 21, parental permission was necessary, though its absence did not make the marriage void), the age of consent was 16, and if the girl was under the age of 13 the crime was punishable as a felony. At that time, a man who was charged with carnal knowledge of a girl under 16 could be acquitted if he satisfied the jury that he had reasonable cause to believe the girl was over 16, a defence abolished in Northern Ireland and restricted in the UK, where it was only permitted for young men up to the age of 23. Eventually the age of 17, rather than the Carrigan Committee's proposed 18, was adopted as the age of consent.

In the 1920s an organisation was set up in Dublin specifically dedicated to 'the reform of the laws relating to the protection of women and girls'. Its honorary secretary requested a meeting with the Department of Justice in 1926 as 'at the present time the rescue societies are almost overwhelmed, so much has the number of unmarried mothers increased during the last few years. It is simply appalling to anyone doing social work, to feel that nothing is being done by legislation in this country to help them to cope with this evil.'[108]

The Department of Justice was not initially interested in confronting the issue. It was not until 1930 that the Minister for Justice begin asking individuals whether they would be prepared to serve on a committee to look at the age of consent and young prostitutes.[109] When the minister asked William Carrigan, a retired senior barrister, to chair such a committee, he added optimistically that 'the work of the Committee would be rendered simple by the fact that there is already a valuable English report on this very subject published in 1926'.[110] It was certainly not envisaged that it would be a lengthy inquiry, nor that it would become a milestone in the history of the Irish state legislating for sexual matters. The findings of the committee ultimately led to the Criminal Law Amendment Act of 1935, which raised the age of consent to 17 and banned the sale and importation of contraceptives.

The Carrigan report saga has assumed an added significance in light of the revelations from the late twentieth century about the extent of sexual abuse in Irish society and controversies over the age of consent (see chapter 5). James Smith has suggested that the Carrigan Committee's deliberations and the reactions to its report can be seen as the 'the origins of Ireland's containment culture', the desire to hide sexual transgressions and prevent public discussions of them.[111] But this is far too neat a conclusion, as is the contention that the committee arrived at a 'hegemonic discourse' in response to perceived sexual immorality.

Did it also reveal that the state willingly abdicated its responsibility for matters sexual to the Catholic Church and established 'a precedent for Church–state management of socio-sexual controversies', as James Smith suggests?[112] It was not that simple, and sweeping assertions about the impact

Immaculate Conception → negative influence? view of women

Post 1921

of Carrigan have often been made through the prism of what was revealed in the 1990s as opposed to the environment of the 1930s. None the less, it is difficult to refute Smith's contention that 'the discourse on "sexual immorality" marginalised the real-life sexual practice that resulted in single motherhood *pregnancy* and illegitimacy while it simultaneously elided the pervasive reality of rape, incest and paedophilia'.[113]

The evidence presented by the women's organisations shows they had a very different attitude to the concept of welfare and what was needed to protect people – in contrast to the report, which raised the possibility of flogging for those convicted of sexual crime and the blacklisting of those convicted of public indecency (though this was something the Minister for Justice was clearly not happy about). In January 1933, the Attorney General's notes referred to the possibility of 'whipping for all offenders and publication of names of offenders'.[114]

Perhaps prompting such extremity was the view articulated by Garda Commissioner Eoin O'Duffy, when giving evidence to the Carrigan Committee, that a serious rot had set in; that the outlook of young people in Ireland had changed over the previous ten years 'and the morally depraved who would then be exorcised from society are now regarded as rather clever and interesting'.[115] Evidence of a considerable rise in the number of illegitimate births in the 1920s was given and a heavy reliance was placed on the evidence of voluntary lay groups working with unmarried mothers. Such evidence should also be viewed in the context of the campaign waged by the Irish Catholic Bishops against what was often termed 'a loosening of morals', with the motor car and dance halls identified as chief facilitators of this. Legislation restricting the number of dance hall licences was passed in 1935. The report also highlighted the way in which the prevailing judicial processes operated to the detriment of children by not being victim-oriented *children* but rather often seeing children as accomplices to crime. It concluded: 'the frequency of assaults on children is to some degree attributable to the impunity on which culprits may reckon under this protection'.[116] It also recommended that the age of consent be raised to 18, that the 'reasonable cause to believe' clause be abolished, and that female Borstals be established.

The apparent moral weakness of adolescents was also a theme that emerged during the evidence given to the committee, but witnesses distinguished between those girls who were foolish, innocent and 'easy prey' and those who were well informed about sexual matters but did not have a formal education and so were destined to become unmarried mothers. In the *conscious love ?*

view of Dermot Gleeson, a district justice in County Clare, lack of parental responsibility, dance halls and indecent conduct in public were 'at the root of nearly all the moral evil in rural areas, especially to young persons'.[117]

In relation to prostitution, there was much consensus about the reasons why women got involved – dance halls, adolescent turbulence, a bad home environment and 'feeble-mindedness'. A greater emphasis was placed on the need for preventive rather than rescue work; the committee suggested no one under the age of 21 should be charged as a common prostitute, that laws against solicitation should be broadened, and that men found in brothels should be prosecuted for 'aiding and abetting'.[118]

*'Morality crimes should now be dealt with
from an Irish point of view.'*

Garda Commissioner Eoin O'Duffy gave some of the most frank and revealing evidence to the committee. In a detailed and strongly worded report he asserted: 'There was an alarming amount of sexual crime increasing yearly, a feature of which was the large number of cases of criminal interference with girls and children from 16 years downwards, including many cases of children under 10 years.' The Gardaí estimated that only about 15 per cent of such cases were prosecuted because of

children Ireland ?

1. The anxiety of parents to keep them secret in the interests of their children, the victims of such outrages, which overcame the desire to punish the offenders.
2. The reluctance of parents to subject their children to the ordeal of appearing before a public court to be examined and cross-examined.
3. The actual technical embarrassments in the way of a successful prosecution of such offenders owing to (a) the difficulty of proof, from the private nature of the offence, usually depending on the evidence of a single witness, the child; (b) the existing law, or the rule of practice in such cases, requiring corroboration, or requiring the judge to warn the jury of the danger of convicting the accused upon the uncorroborated evidence of the witness.[119]

O'Duffy's memorandum gave an extensive overview of the issue of sexual morality in the Free State which was completely at odds with that society's image of itself, partly, he suggested, because they were relying on English laws: 'outlook in such matters here being fundamentally different ... morality crimes should now be dealt with from an Irish point of view. The present state of the law is disgraceful in a Christian country.' Women, he maintained, were deliberately being made drunk 'with a view to have carnal knowledge of them' and indecent exposure 'is fairly common in the suburbs of Dublin and even in the most rural areas. It is more a form of insanity than a criminal offence.'

As well as calling for female Gardaí 'for intimate investigations' and dealing with juvenile prostitution, he detailed court cases to back up his contentions. Between 1924 and 1929 in Dublin city, there were 72 indecent assaults on females reported, and 13 prosecutions 'for reported defilement of girls under 10'. According to his figures, in 1927 there were 133 prosecutions of sexual assault of females nationally (up from 88 the previous year), nearly a quarter of which involved offences against girls under the age of 10. Between 1927 and 1929 more than a third involved offences against girls under the age of 13. In the year 1928–9 there were 78 convictions for 'gross indecency' between males nationwide (45 in Dublin city). In relation to these, he noted, 'We believe, however, this is only a small percentage of the actual cases.' Clearly, this reflected a determination by the Gardaí to focus on sexual offences generally.[120]

O'Duffy also referred to unlawful carnal knowledge of young girls as a particular problem 'in tenement buildings'.[121] An official in the Department of Justice later commented on this, to the effect that

> the children of the poorer classes are less protected than in Great Britain. In Dublin, the necessity in the case of many families living in tenements for the parents, both father and mother, to leave the children to look after themselves in the daytime while they themselves went out to earn their livelihood, was a constant source of danger. In rural districts girls of fourteen years are sent out to service, which deprives them of the protection they had with their parents.[122]

Sentences imposed ranged between twelve months' and five years' hard labour, the more severe sentences being reserved for cases involving homosexuality or incest.

Judging by the court records, O'Duffy's alarmist tone was justified. O'Duffy also referred to prosecutions for sexual offences in the Free State for the first nine months of 1930. There had been 34 prosecutions, most of them successful; they included indecent assault, carnal knowledge and rape, homosexuality, bestiality ('sodomy of a mare donkey') and incest. Seven involved indecent assault or rape of girls under the age of 10.

Of the 29 witnesses who gave evidence to the committee only 6 were members of the clergy. Father Richard Devane suggested there was no attempt to understand female psychology in relation to morality; perhaps there was no other country 'where the woman is always handed down and the man dealt with so leniently'.[123] But most of the focus was not on the social realities that facilitated sexual abuse, incest and pregnancy, but what was visible. As well as the emphasis on prosecution revealed in O'Duffy's evidence and the concern about the judicial process requiring corroboration of a single witness and juries being warned of convicting the accused on uncorroborated evidence, parents' anxiety to protect their children from court proceedings was also raised.[124]

Irish female doctors expressed concern that the official statistics on illegitimacy failed to reflect 'the actual conditions of the country'. The women's organisations that gave evidence emphasised prevention, care and welfare rather than punishment. They also highlighted the failure to educate women about their bodies, as did Judge F. Gleeson of Ennis district court, who criticised a lack 'in knowledge of physical facts'.[125] The women suggested that Irish girls were more immature and less knowledgeable than their English counterparts, but all their recommendations were ignored, as were calls for sex education.

They also recognised that an inhospitable atmosphere contributed to prostitution, infanticide and emigration. Dr Angela Russell of the Irish Women Citizens and Local Government Association (IWCLGA) suggested that prostitution accounted for only '20% of the immorality' in contemporary Ireland, trying in vain to establish a distinction between extramarital sexual practice and sexual abuse and prostitution.[126] Although these witnesses believed in institutionalisation (county homes housed 2,105 unmarried mothers in 1928), they also were speaking as twentieth-century social workers. James Smith has suggested that 'their attention to rehabilitation, education and spiritual reform, on the one hand, and alternative forms of institutional confinement on the other, signals a transitional moment in sociological thinking; assumptions of late nineteenth-century Victorian philanthropy were giving way to emerging trends in professional work'.[127] Complicating this was their backing for mother and baby homes and their high praise of Magdalen laundries, which it is now apparent was misplaced, but at the time such institutions were regarded as better for the women than the county homes.

'We need to preserve the young from the contagion around them'

The Carrigan Committee Report had revealed much about the reality and the perception of immoral conduct; one of its key phrases was that 'we need to preserve the young from the contagion around them', as Monsignor Michael Browne of Maynooth College wrote in November 1932.[128] Another key assertion was, in the words of O'Duffy, that 'indecent conduct between men and women in public is, at the moment, a serious problem':

> men and women may be seen lying on one another and carrying on indecent movements continuously – no more restraint than the lower creation ... police say the women are usually the boldest and most indifferent ... such conduct is more prevalent here than in Britain or on the Continent where the moral standards are much lower ... the [dance] halls are situated deliberately, I would say, some distance from the villages and the conduct carried on in the fields around is very bad indeed.[129]

What these extracts reveal is an unremitting pessimism about the Irish moral character, an obsession with what was visible as opposed to what was not, a belief that the Irish were different, and little mention of what went on in private, or the need for compassion or education. ✳   *I*

The Department of Justice concluded that 'unless these statements are exaggerated (as they may easily have been owing to the anxiety of the Rev. gentlemen concerned to present a strong case to the committee) the obvious conclusion to be drawn is that the ordinary feelings of decency and the influence of religion have failed in this country and that the only remedy is *I* by way of police action'.[130]

What all agreed on was the need to keep discussion of these issues behind closed doors, which was why the report of the Carrigan Committee was never made public on the advice of the Department of Justice. A memorandum compiled by the department – in which there were insightful criticisms of the report but an overestimation of the extent to which the harbingers of doom and the chroniclers of indecency were exaggerating – stated

that the obvious conclusion to be drawn from the report was that 'decency
and morality had faded', that policing was the only remedy, and that 'it was
clearly undesirable that such a view of conditions in the Saor Stát [Free
State] be given wide circulation'.[131] Also significantly, as the critical memorandum from the Department of Justice noted, there was no evidence heard
'from a single circuit or high court judge, a surprising omission considering
that the committee recommends radical changes in legal procedure and in
the method of trying certain offenders'.[132]

After a change of government in 1932, it was left to the new Fianna Fáil
Minister for Justice, James Geoghegan, to consider what the state should do
in terms of legislating for the Carrigan proposals. Monsignor Browne commented in a letter to Geoghegan that 'girls under 18 need protection especially from employers or foremen', many of whom used alcohol to 'stupefy'
their victims. On the age of consent, he added that 'if I could get only 17 I
would take it', but that it should be 18.[133] As to whether the report should be
made public, he argued that

> publication of the report would not create a good impression. It would
> lead many to say, as the report suggests, that the influence of religion has
> failed in this country. They would be partly right. Religion has failed to
> neutralise the aphrodisiac influence of cinema, drama and literature on
> a great number of young people ... we need to preserve the young from
> the contagion around them ... the report reads like a 'scare' and therefore
> one is at least unconsciously prejudiced by it.

He maintained that publication would 'rejoice our enemies, I admit; but the
more I consider it the more I see the need of wakening people up and the
dangers of suppression', an indication that not all felt that change had to be
advanced only through private discussion.[134]

'Minimum sentences are dangerous things'

Father J. Canavan, a Jesuit based in Tullamore, was more sceptical about the
report, contending that such issues should not be discussed in public, as he
believed those involved in commissions exaggerated the moral state of the
country

in order not to be outdone by the general public in the zeal for morality ...
It would be far better if a bill dealing with the matters reported on by
the commission could be passed into law without public discussion in
the Dáil. A judge or two, a lawyer or two, a well-balanced priest or two,
an experienced police officer, meeting in private, and all sharing the
Catholic view on the moral gravity of sexual offences, could give government much helpful advice.[135]

This seemed to be a view the politicians accepted. In October 1932, a memorandum presented to the Minister for Justice strongly recommended that
the report should not be published due to its sweeping statements about the
decline of morality in the Free State, to which publication would give wide
currency.[136]

The memorandum from the Department of Justice reflecting on the
Carrigan Committee Report also expressed reservations about raising the
age of consent, not least because it would result in a lot more prosecutions;
it argued that 'it is not unlikely that the final result will not be a police protection, but a forced marriage', and there could also be a situation in which a
girl looked older than her years. The memorandum acknowledged that the
abolition of the 'reasonable cause to believe' would protect 'young reprobates', but 'the defenders of the provision might say that it confers a measure
of protection on unsophisticated young men against the wiles of designing
hussies. Either remark is mere vituperation and unhelpful. The parties may
be "reprobates" or "hussies" or both, but it is certain that the blame is not
invariably on one side.' It was observed that the authors of the report 'are
silent as to what should be done with two persons both under 18'.

This memorandum acknowledged that the current age of consent was
too low and argued that it should be 16, but that 'the committee's proposal
is a drastic one. Any indecent gesture by a boy of 18 years with a girl a few
months younger, even though provoked by the girl, would render him liable
to two years hard labour and a whipping', adding that 'minimum sentences
are dangerous things'.[137]

The views outlined in this memorandum, which appear to have been
Geoghegan's own (he was a lawyer by training), were quite incisive and
enlightened. He was opposed to what he regarded as some of the more hysterical attitudes to sexual crimes. He was not convinced that whipping for
all offences was necessary, neither was he persuaded by the idea that 'the
court would be bound to order whipping'. His memorandum was harshly

critical of the tone of moral panic emanating from the committee's report. He did not believe that its members faced their task 'in a judicial and impartial frame of mind'; he also felt they were unduly and unhealthily preoccupied with increasing penalties, creating new offences and removing the safeguards that existed for persons charged.[138]

There are many reasonable arguments in Geoghegan's memorandum and it is a reminder of the danger of simplifying attitudes to sex and its discussion during these decades; not all shared the view that laws regarding sexual transgression needed to be so severe. But Geoghegan, like his contemporaries, perhaps got too fixated on the question of the activities of 16 to 18-year-olds, and was certainly inclined to attribute more blame to females than was justified. It is clear from the court records that women were rarely equally to blame when it came to sexual assault.

Another memorandum in the files of the Department of Justice stated that the testimony of children could not be trusted: 'It is understood that many competent authorities have grave doubts as to the value of children's evidence. A child with a vivid imagination may actually live in his mind the situation as he invented it and will be quite unshaken by severe cross-examination.' The Bishop of Limerick, Daniel Keane, requested that Geoghegan send him copies of the report so the Hierarchy could discuss it. The minister complied in October 1932, and the following month Keane advised against publication, as he feared 'a good deal of unsavoury correspondence in the Press'.[139] In December Geoghegan, in a letter to Keane, who wanted him to keep the Hierarchy notified of all proposed heads of a bill, referred to the problem of 'conduct on or alongside highways which is unseemly but falls short of gross indecency.'[140]

The prevailing view was that public debate on the morality of the country was out of bounds and inappropriate. Economist and historian Finola Kennedy has commented that 'To pose one specific question – if Carrigan had been debated in public, would public awareness of the prevalence of child sexual abuse have ensured that the relevant authorities took appropriate action? If, as Bentham said, "publicity is the soul of justice", perhaps the answer to the question is in the affirmative.'[141]

Following the change of government, James Geoghegan got cross-party co-operation in an attempt to come up with legislation; he also sought counsel from the Church. He concluded ('ironically', according to Smith) that the report was too drastic and unworkable.[142] (Why ironically? It just goes to show that opinion was not unanimous and that many felt the moral panic was highly exaggerated). Subsequently, the Irish Hierarchy made clear the issues they wanted to see addressed, including the banning of contraceptives, the age of consent being raised to 18 years and the licensing of dance halls. An informal committee of Dáil deputies met eight times, but did not give a copy of proposals to the Hierarchy for review, claiming that would be 'a breach of privilege'. The committee rejected the more extreme Carrigan proposals, including whipping and blacklisting.

Subsequently, the 1935 Criminal Law Amendment Act (CLAA), which raised the age of consent to 17, abolished the 'reasonable cause to believe' clause contained in the 1885 Act (in other words, it stipulated no defence was possible for having sex with a girl under the age of 15 once her age and the act of sex were confirmed) and prohibited the sale and importation of contraceptives (see below). Unlawful carnal knowledge of a girl between 15 and 17 years was now a misdemeanour, not a felony, as was attempted unlawful carnal knowledge of a girl under 15 years. Tellingly, the act used the phrase 'only attempted carnal knowledge', revealing the contemporary leniency that existed in this regard, implying that attempted carnal knowledge of a girl under 15 might constitute a 'minor offence'. The act, which also included a public indecency provision to protect 'the morals of the community', passed both houses of the Oireachtas in February 1935 with little debate, as did the Public Dance Halls Act.

When Father Richard Devane corresponded in 1934 with Alison Neilans, the General Secretary of the Association for Moral and Social Hygiene in England, on the proposed CLAA, he noted that penalties for prostitution would be a fine of 40 shillings for a first offence but for a second or subsequent offences up to six months' imprisonment, commenting that 'the purpose is to allow the girl (to) come back to the normal. I intend to try and have such girls sent (if in prison) to the hospital as pathological cases and dealt with accordingly – as in Vienna and Soviet Russia.' He added, 'There has been general apathy as regards all these problems, especially among women. A few educated women have been interested and their number has been very limited indeed.'[143] Significantly, most of the parliamentary debate on the issue took place in committee. The provision that abolished the 'reasonable cause to believe' was challenged successfully in the Supreme Court in 2006, which declared that it was unconstitutional that a person be deprived of an opportunity to plead that he had made an honest mistake as to the age of a girl with whom he had consensual sex. (See Chapter 5.)

'Turkey, the land of the veil and purdah, has women police'

The Joint Committee of Women's Societies and Social Workers (JCWSSW), which had evolved out of a meeting in Ely Place in March 1935 between groups of women 'interested in social welfare', with representatives from nine different organisations, expressed concerns about the implications of the 1935 legislation. The committee quickly grew to comprise representatives of sixteen organisations, including the Women's National Health Association, the Irish Women Workers Union, the Irish Countrywomen's Association, the Irish Mothers Union and the National University Women's Graduate Association. Its initial concern had been with the CLAA, but it was also concerned with the age of consent. It demanded that laws on solicitation be the same for men as for women, and that all offences against children be tried in camera – a proposed amendment that had been previously rejected. The joint committee's stance on the question of solicitation was interesting in light of the private correspondence between Devane and Neilans mentioned above; Neilans had suggested in 1934 that the clause relating to prostitution was flawed as the terms '"common prostitute" and "purposes of prostitution" only apply to women. Moreover, this clause means that certain women, and only women, can be arrested for loitering and soliciting.'[144]

Members of the JCWSSW were determined and, for their era, quite radical women who were remarkably persistent in relation to a few set objectives, including the demand that the Gardaí employ females – a campaign that was to last for over twenty years. They also decided at their first meeting 'to organise a rota of women who would attend the children's court and trials for solicitation'.[145] In the autumn of 1935 they expressed their dissatisfaction at the Minister for Justice's continued refusal to meet them, particularly in view of their belief that 'it is the duty of a responsible minister to hear and weigh the opinions of such a representative and experienced body of women on a matter of vital public importance'.[146] They maintained that the CLAA 'omits to give adequate protection to girls of a certain age', and suggested in some respects it lagged behind similar legislation in Northern Ireland. They also criticised the lack of female probation officers and insisted women should be eligible for jury service on the same terms as men.[147] In December 1935, the minister eventually received a deputation; he would not give a commitment on amending the CLAA, but did promise to investigate the possibility of female police officers. This proved to be a frustrating crusade for the organisation, which was looking for 25 female police officers in

Dublin, 9 in Cork and 5 each in Limerick, Waterford and Galway. In May 1939, they pointed out to the Department of Justice that 'Turkey, the land of the veil and Purdah, has women police' and that they existed in a further 28 countries worldwide, which clearly made them better equipped to deal with women and children.

Stephen Roche, the secretary of the Department of Justice, remained dismissive, advising his minister that 'the agitation for women police is an artificial business without any real roots in the country'.[148] In the previous year, senior Gardaí in Cork had expressed a desire to see female police, but despite that in July 1938 Roche had expressed his scepticism 'as to the utility of female officers'.[149]

In relation to sexual offences, the women's committee was also concerned at the manner in which cases of solicitation were tried and sentences imposed, highlighting the double standards prevalent in relation to the sentencing of men and women for sexual offences:

> In the Dublin criminal court on February 6th [1936], 2 men accused of serious offences against a girl under 16 years of age were sentenced, one to 3 months and the other to 4 months hard labour, whereas women brought before the district court on charges of solicitation were sentenced to 6 months imprisonment.[150]

It also pointed out that 'members of the committee reported that they had attended the courts and that when women are brought up on charges of solicitation it is usual to take the evidence of the policeman only; that the women are not questioned and that 6 months imprisonment is the usual sentence. In cases of larceny or drunkenness the accused are generally questioned.' It appeared to the committee that Section 16 of the CLAA allowed for a situation where 'prostitutes are arrested under summary powers, which apparently allows of no defence'.[151]

The women also frequently expressed their concerns about the welfare of children who came before the courts and their escort to industrial schools by policemen, but they were satisfied that the conditions within the industrial schools were more than adequate. In April 1939, Mary Kettle, the chairwoman of the JCWSSW, visited Artane industrial school and, in a report to the society, 'paid tribute to the excellence of the arrangements there, not only for the education and training of the children, but for their health and general upbringing'.[152] The JCWSSW also seemed satisfied with the treatment of prostitutes in Magdalen asylums and was positive in its appraisal of conditions in reformatory schools, too. In relation to the Magdalen asylum in Gloucester Street, it was noted that the girls 'are well treated and in Gloucester Street some ... spend their whole lives in the institution, permission being given them to remain if they like. Many of these girls come from the country and the nuns report that a large number are sub-normal.'[153] Unlike the industrial and reformatory schools, Magdalen asylums were not governed by state legislation, did not receive state grants and rejected any form of government regulation or inspection.

'The legionnaires picket the streets between 8 p.m. and 11.30 p.m. each night'

The clauses in the CLAA reflected the culmination of considerable comment on the issue of prostitution since the formation of the Free State. Father Richard Devane, the Jesuit mentioned earlier, was optimistic in the 1920s that because British soldiers were no longer stationed in Dublin, the prostitution problem could be solved 'with comparative ease'.[154] One of the challenges to his misguided assumption was that the women involved were quite well integrated and 'accepted within the community', and that they worked over a broader geographic spread than the Monto area (Montgomery Street was subsequently renamed Foley Street). Many had no fixed address; of the 78 women arrested and imprisoned from 1 September to 20 October 1924, 48 fell into that category. One woman had 30 previous convictions. The women ranged in age from 19 to 50, a range that had changed little from the nineteenth century. [155]

In 1925 the commissioner of the Dublin Metropolitan Police suggested that until that year the brothels in the Monto area operated without 'much let or hindrance on the part of the police authorities', and he argued that the law as it stood 'respects too much the liberty of the subject'; brothel keepers were generally fined, which he saw as a form of licensing of prostitution.[156] There was a tendency to assume that one of the reasons prostitution needed to be tackled was because women working as prostitutes were the chief spreaders of venereal disease. Indeed, the incidence of VD became a serious preoccupation in the 1920s and 1930s, prompting a government inquiry on the issue in 1924. (See below.) But it was a voluntary religious group, the Legion of Mary, established by the Catholic and charitable activist Frank

Duff in 1921, rather than the state or the police, that had done most to clamp down on prostitution in the Monto area in the mid 1920s.

In 1922 Duff opened the Sancta Maria hostel at 76 Harcourt Street as a refuge for prostitutes in premises given to him by the politician W. T. Cosgrave. The hostel remained open until the 1970s. In August 1935, the secretary of the Department of Local Government and Public Health gave information to the Department of External Affairs on the work of the Legion of Mary over the previous decade in combating prostitution through the Sancta Maria hostel, noting that 'the legionnaires picket the streets between 8 p.m. and 11.30 p.m. each night … the chief difficulty experienced with the girls residual in the hostel arises from their craving for intoxicating drink'. It was observed that since its opening in 1922, 324 prostitutes had entered the hostel, 'of these, 229 have made good and 95 have been failures', with some moving on to the Magdalen asylums.[157]

Duff estimated that there were 200 girls working there in 1922, but that by 1925 the number had fallen to 40. Underpinning his account of the fall of Monto, *Miracles on Tap* (1960), is, according to Anne Enright, 'the sense that women themselves knew that they were out of joint with the times'.[158] In July 1922, Duff took the first group of 23 'girls' off in a charabanc for a weekend retreat in Baldoyle, stopping briefly to pick up a Franciscan at Adam and Eve's church on the quays. 'As we go,' he wrote,

we are brushing by history … I bound creditably from my perch and run across the road to the door. If I had thought to look across the Liffey – as all those I left behind me were now doing, I would have witnessed a pitiful sight. Portions of the former proud walls of the Four Courts, the central law courts of Ireland, were being pulled down by great gangs of men with ropes. Civil War had just been raging, and these dangerously tottering walls were part of its grim heritage. And even during the short time I was away, our great adventure was in peril: the result of that striking scene playing upon supercharged nerves and galvanising into life that old terror to which reference has already been made, that a government plot was in operation against them. What were those soldiers stalking about with rifles for and looking – many of them – in the direction of the vivid-coloured charabanc? Did they not look as if they were going to shoot at it?[159]

*'They go on a spree, and fall victim to the two things that men have
fallen victims to from the beginning of time – wine and women'*

The Monto clampdown was preceded by public references by Dublin priests
to the activities of prostitutes. A Lenten mission in February 1925 galvanised
members of the Legion of Mary and the Society of Saint Vincent de Paul
to spread the message that prayers were necessary to end a 'great local evil'.
Brothel owners were cajoled into shutting down their premises voluntarily,
but it was the agreement of the Gardaí to force the recalcitrant that led to
a raid in March 1925 during which more than 100 people were arrested,
after which it was believed that the problem of the 'open brothel' no longer
existed.[160]

Significantly, Frank Duff faced difficulties in trying to obtain official
endorsement from the Hierarchy for his work, including the operation of
his three hostels – the Sancta Maria, the Regina Coeli (opened in 1930),
and the Morning Star for down-and-out men. The latter was opened in 1927
but Duff had to wait until 1940 before he obtained an interview with the
Archbishop of Dublin, Dr Byrne, regarding episcopal sanction for the work
of the Legion.

Duff was an ecumenist before his time, which did not always endear
him to the Catholic Hierarchy. He was also adamant that unmarried
mothers be encouraged to keep their babies, in which respect, in the words
of Finola Kennedy, his work was 'so far ahead of its time ... he wrote to the
Archbishop complaining about a particular social worker and the phrase
he used was "she is shovelling children into these orphanages" and he was
trying to provide an alternative'.[161] When the Regina Coeli hostel opened to
receive homeless women in October 1930, among the first to seek admission
were an unmarried mother and her child. According to Finola Kennedy, 'So
began what was then a revolutionary means of helping women, who had no
other support, to bring up their children themselves.'[162]

Duff, in giving evidence to the committee inquiring into VD, referred
to the 'horrors' of Dublin's red light district, which he and others maintained
was internationally notorious. Duff also contended, 'it is not too much to
say that one half of the largest parish in the city, numbering 60,000 persons,
was, more or less, corrupted by the spectacle of open vice, and to a large
extent, too, drawn into the whirl of it'.[163]

Towards the end of the twentieth century, former residents of the Dublin tenements recalled the activities of prostitutes in the early decades of the

Free State in 'seven or eight kip houses' and bouncers or pimps who were labelled 'whore's bullies'. There was also a belief that 'the Guards couldn't do anything'. There were female pimps, or 'madams', who ran the 'kip' houses on Purdon and Railway Street: 'they were Dublin people and they all stuck together'. Some treated the women who did not bring in enough money harshly and, according to Jem King, who moved to Corporation Street in 1916, they encouraged the prostitutes to 'rob the men ... when I was a young lad I saw many a sailor, probably after travelling the seven seas, come home here and lose all his money in the kip houses.' However, King also recalled that Becky Cooper, one of the madams, was 'very good to the poor'.[164]

The prostitutes themselves were not ostracised by the tenement communities ('they had a bad occupation but they was very very decent, very kind'); more ire was directed towards the madams than to the 'poor girls that suffered all the hardship ... the girls were gentle girls ... they were no trouble at all ... the girls never carried on in front of the children ... The madams gave them a terrible scourging life and the only ones that looked after them were the people of Monto.'[165] There were also myths about what happened to them behind closed doors, particularly those who contracted syphilis and were treated at the Lock hospital on Townsend Street. It was believed by some that when they had incurable syphilis 'They used to smother them. They couldn't cure them; smother them to take them out of their pain, or give them some kind of needle. They were that far-gone and at that time there was no cure. They wouldn't do them all. Just an odd one. They'd be nearly gone dead before they'd do it.'[166]

In 1926, a particularly disturbing case occurred in which a medical doctor and a former Garda superintendent were charged with the murder of Lily O'Neill, a prostitute also known as 'Honour Bright'. She was found dead near the Dublin mountains as a result of a shotgun wound. According to contemporary newspaper reports, she was 'compelled to seek her livelihood on the streets at night'.[167] She was seen getting into a car with the two men in the vicinity of St Stephen's Green. William Carrigan acted as prosecuting counsel and described the murder as 'a sordid tale of debauchery by a pair of moral degenerates'. Despite testimony from witnesses who saw the three together, and evidence that one of the men owned two revolvers, both men were acquitted after their defence counsel, Joe O'Connor, appealed to the jury: 'Is it because they go on a spree, and fall victim to the two things that men have fallen victims to from the beginning of time – wine and women – that you are not to judge them by ordinary standards, but to treat them as human vampires?'[168] The jury took less than five minutes to reach its decision. Bright, as Anne Enright notes, had changed her mind at the last minute about attending one of the original retreats for prostitutes organised by Frank Duff because she 'did not want to leave her baby'. Testimony at her murder trial made it clear that although Monto was quiet, 'business was still brisk' outside the Shelbourne hotel at St Stephen's Green, where girls and jarveys (hackney coach drivers) provided a 'once around the Green' service for gentlemen at the end of their evening. Accounts of the trial, as well as interviews with former residents of Monto, 'make it clear that the Dublin poor had a great sympathy for the "unfortunate girls" working in their midst, and that many of the better-off were equally slow to judge'.[169]

'One need only imagine the feelings of a new bride, roughly awakened and questioned'

A preoccupation with prostitutes working indoors was something that emerged during the Department of Justice's research for members of the Criminal Law Amendment Act Committee. A memorandum concerning the issue of warrants to search brothels noted that 'no such power exists at present and the police are forced to rely on "shebeen" warrants obtained on the ground that drink is being illegally sold', and that it was 'undesirable to have to rely on what is really a subterfuge'. But there was another warning in November 1933 about what exactly constituted a brothel, and a civil servant worked himself into quite a lather about the implications of an indiscriminate approach to catching prostitutes plying their trade in more respectable institutions:

> It is easy to be led astray by the word 'brothel'. On first glance, one naturally associates it with the brothel as it was known in Dublin, a disorderly house with a number of prostitutes and billies in it, where men resorted for drink [and] women ... one is inclined to forget that the term 'brothel' includes establishments of quite other types. It applies also to a genuine hotel to which the proprietor habitually allows prostitutes to bring their customers. Such an hotel may have in addition to the illegal trade, a bona fide business with people who are unaware of what is going on. The execution of a 'brothel' search warrant in such a place might have most unpleasant consequences. Under the warrant, the police would

have power to, and indeed must, enter all the bedrooms and question the occupants. It would be annoying for a man sleeping by himself, but one need only imagine the feelings of a new bride, roughly awakened and questioned, not too gently, as to whether she is a prostitute or married to the man who is with her. Such an intrusion would be bitterly resented.[170]

Another preoccupation of the 1920s and 1930s was that while there were Borstals for boys, there were no similar institutions for female offenders; prostitutes were sent to a common prison where 'no attempt at redemption is made'. In response, the Attorney General suggested that 'the existing female reformatories would be suitable as homes' and that some prostitutes should be in homes instead of prisons as 'it is well known that many prostitutes are seriously mentally deficient'.[171] But the assistant secretary of the Department of Education, noting that there had been 37 female committals to reformatory schools between 1918 and 1923, insisted in January 1925 that these places were not suitable for prostitutes, as most of the inmates were placed in them for the crime of larceny. The Minister for Education was also opposed on the grounds that those committing sexual offences were a different class of criminal and he feared 'the influence which this type of girl would undoubtedly exert on the existing inmates of these schools ... It is suggested that the Magdalen asylums might possibly be available for the purpose in contemplation.'[172] This was an indication that the government was keen to ensure that the responsibility for these issues could be placed on the voluntary and religious sectors; it was not for the state, it seemed, to rescue 'fallen women'.

'The RUC are so busy having joy rides with the ladies'

In Northern Ireland, there were allegations in the 1920s that the police themselves were not beyond reproach when it came to the use of prostitutes. In 1925, for example, there was a series of complaints about the immorality of police in Dunamanagh, County Tyrone, with correspondence sent to the Prime Minister James Craig alleging that the sergeant in charge of the district was seen regularly in the company of prostitutes. A similar letter was sent by 'one of the disgusted ratepayers' to the Duke of Abercorn, the first Governor of Northern Ireland, claiming two members of the local Royal Ulster Constabulary were using the services of a prostitute in a local licensed

premise: 'this sort of conduct is enough to contaminate the largest city in
the British Isles with filth and disease, let alone a little village'. The county
inspector in Strabane referred to such allegations as 'a tissue of falsehoods'
written by a resident with an agenda concerning a criminal trial her brother
had been involved in. But allegations persisted from other quarters as well,
including a claim from a resident contained in a letter to Home Affairs minister Dawson Bates in October 1927 to the effect that an RUC constable 'has
been having carnal knowledge of a little girl about 14 years or thereabouts,
[she] is about to become a mother ... the RUC are so busy having joy rides
with the ladies'.[173]

Availing themselves of the services of prostitutes seems to have been
almost a rite of passage for those who became iconic Irish writers, among
them James Joyce (recounted in the previous chapter) and Samuel Beckett.
In 1969 the American scholar Lawrence Harvey controversially analysed
Beckett's inner psychology to deduce aspects of Beckett's sexuality from it
and found that voyeurism and infantilism, as well as a reluctance to engage
in physical sex except with prostitutes, were key parts of Beckett's sexuality. His biographer Anthony Cronin agrees that Beckett 'had difficulty in
associating the act of sex with other forms of emotional involvement'. When
Beckett was a student at Trinity College, Cronin notes that 'prostitution
was carried on so openly that a shocked Encyclopaedia Britannica contributor compared Dublin adversely to the south of Europe and Algeria. The
brothels catered for all trades and classes, including students, who got a cut
rate in some establishments.' One of the more select venues was Becky Coo-
pers, which survived 'sudden official closure in March 1926', but as a result
of which prostitutes were forced 'into shabbier hotels, including the Grose-
venor Hotel on Westland Row near the back gate of Trinity, which Belacqua
also frequents in More Pricks Than Kicks'.[174]

Beckett's experience of prostitutes began in Dublin and continued in
Paris, and 'at rare moments in the right company he would assert that these
were the only satisfactory sexual conjunctions there were'. In his first novel
Murphy (1938), the vital statistics of the prostitute Celia are given a page
to themselves and are constantly referred to, suggesting she was based on
first-hand knowledge of prostitutes at the lower ends of London's Kings and
Fulham Roads.[175]

'Contrary to the currently accepted opinion,
VD was widespread throughout the country'

Alongside prostitution, sexually transmitted diseases were also the subject of much discussion both at government level and among those involved in 'rescue work' during the 1920s and 1930s. The government's interdepartmental committee of inquiry into venereal disease was constituted in December 1924 and reported in February 1926. Its specific terms of reference were 'to make inquiries as to the steps, if any, which are desirable to secure that the extent of VD may be diminished'. It held 14 meetings, heard from 24 witnesses and received written statements from Dublin hospitals, the Royal College of Physicians, prison services, Gardaí, social workers interested in prostitution, Cork and Galway hospitals, and the senior district justice for the metropolitan district.[176] After hearing the evidence, the report's authors concluded, 'contrary to the currently accepted opinion, VD was widespread throughout the country and that it was disseminated largely by a class of girl who could not be regarded as a prostitute'.[177]

The committee, which had been primarily concerned with the problem of VD in the army, also commented on sexually transmitted diseases as a wider issue in Irish society, but added caveats regarding its own function. Discussing how the issue of the spread of VD related to public morality, the committee decided, would 'lead us outside the subject with which we were appointed to deal', as it would raise the issue of sex education ('This would be a *Reductio ad Absurdum*'). It also concluded that, while it was concerned with public health and 'public decency', 'the extent to which the state can interfere to promote morality is strictly limited; we feel that the only hope of any marked improvement in this respect lies in the activity of moral agents'. Such moral agents were deemed to be the Catholic Church and the voluntary agencies working under its auspices.

The report included some startling statistics, including the fact that Dublin's death rate from syphilis per 10,000 of the population was 1.47 – double that of London at 0.73. At the time there were only two VD clinics in the entire country, both in Dublin, in contrast to England and Wales, where there were 192 treatment centres. In Dr Steeven's hospital, VD outpatient attendance rose from 10,624 in 1921–2 to 19,531 in 1924–5. In Sir Patrick Dun's hospital it almost doubled from 3,737 to 6,545. The report called for a system of confidential notification for VD, and the authors agreed 'with the expressed views of all authorities on VD that the most certain method of reducing its incidence and preventing its spread is by the general adoption of a system of prophylaxis, or the application of preventive remedies after exposure. But considering the present state of public opinion, we refrain from recommending such a system.' During this period the word 'prophylaxis' was used not just to refer to condoms but sometimes in the form 'moral prophylaxis' (abstinence) or 'chemical prophylaxis' (disinfection following exposure to infection).

'Conveyed by apparently decent girls throughout the country'

The situation in the army was alarming and constituted 'a serious menace to the health of the nation'. Underlining the fact that it was not prostitutes who were the main carriers was the statistic that revealed they constituted only 30 per cent of the women passing on the disease and were mainly confined to Dublin. It was also noted that 90 per cent of soldiers who contracted the disease were 'infected by women who were not prostitutes', and that the army definition of a prostitute was far too wide, as 'a woman was classed as a prostitute if the smallest reward – even a bottle of stout – was given to her by the soldier'. The real worry was that VD appeared to be 'conveyed by apparently decent girls throughout the country. There is a considerable danger to the innocent sections of the community, because these so-called amateurs mix with all sections and include nurses, maids, cooks, etc.' Typically, it was believed that voluntary religious organisations would have to be in the vanguard of any moves to counteract this threat, and that the encouragement of other outlets, including sport and hard work, was necessary to neutralise sexual frustration.

It was also observed that war and social disturbance was often followed by a rise in VD, while a Jesuit priest, Father Richard Devane, noted in his evidence the waves of soldiers who had passed over Ireland: 'Black and Tans, British soldiers, Auxiliaries, Irregulars, Free State troops – all of whom have been living under war conditions, with all that means in a soldier's life, as far as vice is concerned.'[178] Tom Garvin quotes Francis Hackett's account of 'de Valera's Ireland' published in the *American Mercury* in 1945 which suggested the government had abolished the weekly prophylactic issue ('rubbers') in the army 'at the behest of the Catholic Church in 1932', while, in Hackett's words, 'ignoring the increase in syphilis which was bound to follow and did follow'. As Garvin wryly comments, 'perhaps it was just as well that the Irish army remained small during most of the period'.[179] But confronting this problem in the army remained a preoccupation; the secretary of the Department of Defence was anxious in 1933 to get VD statistics 'in connection with an examination of the army prophylaxis system with a view to arriving at what might be called a "risk" figure in order to get a value figure for prophylaxis in reducing this risk'[180] – correspondence which calls into question the assertion that the issue of prophylaxis for soldiers had been discontinued as a result of orders from the Church in 1932.

The VD report included the view both that prostitution needed to be suppressed and that there should be tougher laws, including 'imprisonment without the option of a fine, even on the first offence' because fines had become 'simply an expense of the trade and are regarded as such', often paid by the girls' employers. But the report disputed that the police needed more power to deal with brothels, suggesting 'there is now no problem of the open brothel in Dublin and it occurred to us that it would be impossible that such an establishment could be maintained for any period without its existence coming to the knowledge of the police'.[181]

This assessment was in stark contrast to the evidence given to the Carrigan Committee by Eoin O'Duffy in October 1930, when he suggested

> the brothel keeper and the prostitutes are not more hampered in their calling today than they were 100 years ago. They are as free to carry on their activities in London or Dublin as in Paris, the only difference being that in Paris they are legalised and subjected to frequent medical examination as a precaution against the spread of VD ... the existing law was made by Englishmen, and the general conditions, and outlook in such matters here being fundamentally different, it is unsuitable for application to this country.[182]

There was also concern expressed in the VD committee's report about the 'lack of interest of the medical profession' evidenced by the 'insignificant number' who sought instruction in the methods of dealing with VD or took advantage of the facilities for obtaining free supplies of Salvarsan, the drug used to treat syphilis. In 1924, the Free State did not accede to an international agreement for the treatment of VD among seamen, which committed the parties who signed to maintain in each of their principal ports services for the treatment of VD 'without distinction of nationality'. By the summer of 1930, and in light of the interdepartmental committee report, the Department of Local Government and Public Health informed the Minister for

External Affairs that Ireland was now ready to be a part of this agreement, as arrangements for the treatment of VD were 'now available in the ports of Cork, Dublin and Waterford and in all seaports in Dublin, Louth, Waterford and Wexford'.[183]

The government agreed in March 1926 to the request that the report be put on sale as a government publication,[184] but subsequently the Department of Local Government and Public Health asked the advice of Archbishop Byrne of Dublin as to whether the report should be published. Although the members of the committee 'believed it should be published', neither the Archbishop nor the government wanted that to happen. Dr Byrne suggested postponing publication, but if the situation did not improve 'he would not object to publication'.[185] According to Dr McDonnell, who served on the committee and was medical inspector of the Department of Local Government and Public Health, who interviewed the Archbishop, 'the only comment His Grace made upon the substance of the committee's findings was that he was greatly surprised to learn that the chief disseminators of infection were non-prostitutes'.[186]

The inquiry into VD and the evidence submitted to it has recently been subjected to detailed analysis by two historians, Susannah Riordan and Philip Howell, in the context of the politics of both prostitution and public health. Howell has suggested that the committee preferred a solution which would have involved legal regulation of prostitution, as was common in other European countries such as Italy, but that this was rejected in favour of a system of 'moral regulation', marked by elements of 'Catholic social purity'.[187] Riordan has refuted this contention and has argued that, despite the preoccupation with perceived 'national moral decay', the issue of VD was approached in the context of public health, and that the military evidence presented to the committee 'reflected four years of experimentation with different means of combating its VD problem'.[188] Given the paucity of statistics relating to civilian infection, significant weight was given to the military statistics and Riordan highlights that the army medical service had moved successfully from an emphasis on the control of prostitution to the use of chemical prophylaxis. It is also the case, as outlined above, that the committee did not see its role as presiding over a broad investigation of public morality, and it resisted the insistence of Frank Duff and Father Devane that VD be equated with prostitution.[189] Given the many layers to this issue, it is probably fair to assert that the 'politics of prostitution' and the 'politics of public health' were not mutually exclusive.

The report made a number of recommendations but, with the exception of the issue of notification of the disease, little interest was shown in implementing them. As mentioned above, the government did accede to the international agreement on the treatment of merchant seamen, but this probably had more to do with 'the campaign for a seat on the League of Nations Council than to the Department of Local Government and Public Health's zeal in combating VD'.[190]

'Castlebar I: "one case in 30 years"; Castlebar II: "never seen"'

In the districts outside the counties in which approved schemes for treating VD were in operation, grants were available to deal with VD through the supply of Salvarsan solutions, providing the doctors were trained to deal with the condition and were prepared to compile reports giving details of the treatment administered. But according to the VD report there was 'little demand on the state grant for this service, the cost in 1923–4 being only £1.5s.7d. and there being no expenditure therein in 1924–5'.[191] This could have been because medics in more isolated areas rarely came across cases, or, more likely, because sufferers were reluctant to come forward for treatment, due to the difficulty of obtaining it anonymously. The Department of Local Government and Public Health required medical officers in dispensary districts to make returns on the incidence of VD; the reports from West Mayo in 1926 included:

'Castlebar I: 'one case in 30 years' Castlebar II: 'never seen'
Achill I: 'Very occasionally, it is brought from England or Scotland'
Ballycastle: '2 cases of gonorrhoea (both non residents) in 26 years'
Ballina I: 'none in district: medical officer sees an occasional sailor with
   it'[192]

Individual sufferers also found themselves writing letters in desperation to the Minister for Local Government and Public Health. In May 1932 a woman wrote from Sligo: 'I am suffering from it and was advised to write to you and that my letter would be treated as strictly confidential', to which the reply was that since there were 'no approved' arrangements in County Sligo it would be necessary for her either to travel elsewhere or to get the local GP to order Salvarsan preparations from the department.[193]

E. J. Banks, the secretary at Dr Steeven's hospital, returned figures which showed that the incidence of the disease continued to rise into the 1930s. In 1927–8, the number of cases dealt with at Dublin treatment centres was 1,575 males and 662 females; in 1932–3 the figures were 1,719 males and 675 females.[194]

Some sufferers found it a better option to cross the border for treatment. In June 1934 the Donegal Board of Health got a bill from Belfast Corporation, 'stated to be apportioned share of expenses in respect of treatment of patients under the VD scheme'. They refused to pay it because they were unaware of any such scheme.[195] VD also raised certain ethical issues for doctors. The medical officer in Ennis wrote to the department in March 1934: 'I have been treating a case of syphilis in an adult male in my district. On last Saturday this man told me confidentially the name of the female who infected him. I shall be obliged if you will instruct me, what steps I am to take to deal with this woman.' The secretary of the department replied that it would be open to the doctor 'if he deems fit and is satisfied with the information received to offer treatment to the person concerned.'[196]

The same medical officer faced a subsequent dilemma when he had to consult another doctor about a syphilis case and asked the Clare Board of Health to cover the expenses involved, but they deferred consideration of the matter 'mainly because I did not state the patient's name. I do not wish to expose the poor devil of a patient to public odium.' This doctor felt he was on something of a crusade, being determined to 'in a large measure wipe out the scourge of syphilis in this area'.[197]

Another recurring problem was that some local authorities, for example Leitrim, frequently refused to pay the Dublin hospitals for treatment of natives of their counties in the capital on the grounds that they had no VD schemes and therefore no budget for such payments.[198] Other local authorities consistently refused to consider such schemes; the county secretary for Limerick wrote to the minister in 1927 to inform him he had raised the issue with the Board of Public Health and Assistance but 'no action' was taken. It subsequently voted against the adoption of a scheme but was eventually persuaded to introduce one in 1931, having been strongly urged to do so by the county medical officer, Dr James McPolin, for the sake of children whose parents could transmit the disease to them, leading to 'severe mental defects'.

McPolin accepted the need for the utmost confidentiality for patients, which was significant because the Limerick Board of Public Health minutes actually named VD sufferers, as this extract shows: 'M.H., poor person, in this district is suffering from VD and should be sent to Dublin for treatment.' McPolin did not approve of the burying of heads in sand:

> It is an absolutely certain fact that VD exists in the county area. We are
> all very liable to shut our eyes to such a fact. This arises because of the
> existence of a moral stigma usually associated with the mode of infec-
> tion. This attitude of mind is liable to lead us astray.[199]

The Legion of Mary's Sancta Maria rescue society induced many females to get treatment for VD; it also provided a medical officer and after care. In 1938 it was estimated that 'more than 75% of the persons with whom the society gets in touch are suffering from VD'. As one of the volunteers pointed out to the Department of Local Government and Public Health, 'This society is the only body in this country carrying out all the activities outlined above.'[200]

'A form of depravity that is spreading with malign vigour'

Giving his evidence to the Carrigan Committee, Eoin O'Duffy had maintained that current sentencing for sexual crime was 'farcical' and 'disgraceful in a Christian country'.[201] To his credit, he highlighted problems few others were prepared to point out, particularly in regard to paedophilia. He gave the brief particulars of some cases of indecent assault, unlawful carnal knowledge, sodomy of young boys, and bestiality, with most resulting in prison sentences of between twelve and sixteen months. In June 1930, one 23-year-old man was convicted of committing 'buggery with a mare donkey' and was sentenced to eighteen months' hard labour, suggesting sex with animals was deemed to be a more serious crime than sex with children.[202] O'Duffy drew particular attention to a rise in homosexual crimes in his submission, observing, 'I think power should be given to a district justice to deal summarily with this offence as well as on indictment.'

He referred to the figures for homosexual offences for the years 1928–9 – 86 prosecutions and 78 convictions – but added, 'we believe, however, this is only a small percentage of the actual cases.'[203] Of the 47 prosecutions in Dublin city, 45 resulted in conviction; the figures cited for Waterford were 15 (15 convictions), Limerick 2 (1), Cork 10 (7), while Mayo and Galway both had 1 prosecution and 1 conviction, suggesting such crimes were both more prevalent in and pursued more rigorously in the cities. O'Duffy also suggested that homosexual activity 'is a form of depravity that is spreading with malign vigour'.

According to Chrystel Hug's history of the politics of sexual morality in Ireland, the Department of Justice ignored O'Duffy's pleas for more action. 'From then on, silence fell on this issue, as on other issues of sexual ethics. The spirit of the English Puritan laws was in tune with the new Catholic-inspired Irish laws and neither were questioned until the 1970s'.[204] That assertion is exaggerated. The Gardaí and the courts certainly did not ignore homosexuality. Thomas O'Malley highlights the extent to which homosexual crimes were actively pursued; quoting from the prison reports, he cites figures in relation to 'a surprisingly high number of committals to prison for sexual offences' in the period 1927–61 (rape: 86; indecent assault: 852; gross indecency: 215; indecency with males: 435), noting that the number of committals for indecency with males was 'particularly remarkable'.[205] This may be partly explained by recidivist offending by some individuals – and the calendar of prisoners where previous convictions are recorded would indeed suggest this was the case – but another point that has to be considered is the strong determination to entrap and pursue gay men engaging in homosexual activity.

There has been much interest in O'Duffy's own sexuality and suggestions over the years that he was homosexual. He continually stressed the virtues of clean living, preached 'the gospel of national virility', and fostered the cult of personality and an obsession with 'manliness'. Fearghal McGarry, who has written the definitive biography of O'Duffy, is cautious of drawing conclusions about his sexuality – he could not find any direct evidence of O'Duffy's homosexuality. There are no recorded contemporaneous references to it but plenty of third-hand accounts. In his position as manager of the Irish Olympic Team in 1932 O'Duffy could also be justified in having, as he did, many photographs of semi-clothed, muscular young athletes.[206]

Interest in O'Duffy's sexuality also persisted because so much of his rhetoric was at odds with his own habits. The obsession with moral regeneration, improved national virility and the need to cleanse society was promoted by a man who smoked and drank heavily, was overweight and died at only 54. In the same way, in Italy, a fat and bald Mussolini did not live up to 'the official image of the *Duce* as a young and virile specimen of Italian manhood'.[207]

The evidence that O'Duffy was actively gay is not there, but it is fair to conclude that McGarry detects fire behind the smoke, and it is reasonable to suggest that perhaps O'Duffy sublimated his sexuality into military camaraderie, uniforms, discipline and 'manly organisations'; and turned his personal 'crisis' into the very thing he publicly dedicated himself to eradicating, which ultimately took its toll on his mental and physical health – though McGarry warns that it should not be taken as the sole key to his personality.[208] O'Duffy can certainly be credited with overseeing a successful, committed and relatively disciplined police force; perhaps he was also all the more determined to pursue sexual crimes due to his own obsessions.

'In the name of the Blessed Virgin and St Joseph, let me off, I am a businessman!'

The court cases dealing with homosexual crimes reveal the mostly hidden sexual lives of gay men; there is no mention of lesbianism. In 1921 the British parliament rejected a bill on lesbianism, seemingly convinced of the argument that the measure would make women aware that such acts existed, and it was certainly not going to be confronted in Ireland. It is to literature rather than the courts' files that one must look for any accounts of eroticism between women. The novelist Elizabeth Bowen, for example, 'presents a range of erotic relations between women', sometimes as ambiguous, flirtatious kinds of friendships, as found in *The Hotel* (1927), in which a young girl becomes infatuated with a sophisticated older woman. Women are also bound together by infatuation in *Devoted Ladies* (1934), which presents different versions of love between women, though none are presented as explicitly lesbian.[209]

But for gay men, the charges of gross indecency, indecency with males, sodomy and buggery were commonplace, particularly in the cities, with occasional prosecutions in rural areas too. Darkened cinemas were obvious places for gay men to attempt to seek sex, sometimes targeting young boys. In April 1922, a man accused at the Dublin city commission of the indecent assault of three young boys at a cinema replied, when charged, 'How could I interfere with 3 boys sitting in the same seat?' Abuse had allegedly occurred at the picture house in North Mary Street, where the man had apparently been seen attempting to open the buttons of the boys' trousers; the boys called the manager, who contacted the police. The casual tone of the testimony of the cinema usher, who saw him, might indicate that this was something of a regular occupational hazard for him: 'I saw him with his hand on the front of the trousers of the second chap. I cautioned defendant and said if he didn't behave himself I'd have him removed.' He seemed 'sensible and not drunk'.[210] The man was found guilty and sentenced to four months imprisonment with hard labour.[211]

As seen in the previous chapter, gay men were also likely to be caught in the act in public lavatories. In Dublin city in 1927 a man was accused of the buggery of another man after a Garda on duty at North Wall Quay between 12 a.m. and 1 a.m. observed them 'leaning over bridge, looking towards Custom House Docks talking' and followed them as they began to walk. They entered a public lavatory in Guild Street where the Garda 'looked through holes in it' and saw them engaged in sexual activity ('his penis was put in E.'s rump'). It transpired that one of the men was an American sailor, the other a bar worker in O'Connell Street, who insisted, 'I let no man do such an abominable offence with me', but at his trial he pleaded guilty to attempted buggery and received a sentence of twelve months with hard labour.[212]

At the same court session, a man was found not guilty of gross indecency with a 7-year-old boy from Abbey Street. The defendant had approached the boy on Bachelor's Walk and allegedly lured him to the Phoenix Park and assaulted him. According to the boy, 'when he was done then he threw water over me, and then he gave me a halfpenny and some cigarette pictures'. The boy claimed he had been encouraged to go with the man by another young boy. The boy's mother also gave evidence: 'I said where are you after being? He wouldn't answer. I said "tell me the truth or I'll shoot you." Another one of my sons said he was after begging off a man on the quay.'[213] The defendant was found not guilty, as there was no corroboration of the child's evidence.

Another case, perceived as less severe, was also heard at this time, when a Free State soldier was found guilty of gross indecency with a 6-year-old boy ('he took me into the room and took out his Dooley and asked me to hold it tight') having first attempted to get the boy's sister to touch him. The soldier was found guilty 'with a strong recommendation to mercy' and bound over to keep the peace for two years.[214] It is likely that this assault was considered on the lesser scale, but perhaps his status as a soldier was also a factor. Significantly, the sexual crime cases from this session were put into circuit court office envelopes and sealed and labelled 'private', while the cases for other crimes were not.

In the same year, 1927, a man was convicted of attempting to procure an act of gross indecency from another man; after pleading guilty he was sentenced to twelve months' hard labour and fined £25. This is a particularly interesting case because the defendant, a businessman from Kildare who obviously travelled to Dublin to meet other men for sex, was set up by a Garda detective, who maintained he had needed to use a public lavatory in O'Connell Street: 'My attention was attracted to him because when I went down the steps he stared me. I stared at him.' They then chatted outside, walked together and the defendant invited the Garda for a drink. The detective replied that he could not meet him that night, but would meet him on another night and they arranged to meet the following week. 'I then shook hands with him and he said, "I hope there will be something doing" and I said, "We'll have to wait and see as Asquith said."'

The detective, 'acting on instructions', arranged to meet the man at the same place. According to the detective, 'I spoke about the weather. He then said, "I heard of a very good place at the back of the bank in Fleet Street. Will we go there?"' On the way to Fleet Street, the defendant unintentionally gave the detective more rope by commenting, 'I met a very nice man from Ballsbridge about 3 weeks ago on O'Connell Bridge who asked me to go with him.' He also said 'that the lavatory in the Winter Gardens of Theatre Royal was a great place – you would only have to stop there a few minutes and you would meet somebody'.

When the two men arrived at the lavatory on Parliament Row, the defendant, having 'struck a match', opened the trousers of the detective:

> Then he opened his own clothes, took out his person and said, 'Isn't that a fine big one. That may give you a horn. Look at that.' I looked and then stood outside the lavatory, told him I was a detective officer and that he was under arrest. He then said, 'In the name of the Blessed Virgin and St Joseph, let me off, I am a businessman and there's no place for me now only the workhouse.' I said, 'No' I would not allow him to go. He lay down on the ground. I told him it was no use, to stop his fooling and come along and he then came with me and on the way several times he asked me to let him go.

The defendant had also said something significantly revealing before it became apparent that he was a victim of entrapment: 'People have a great time here in the city. We can do nothing in the country. We are being watched everywhere.'[215]

In March 1928, another two men were charged with attempting to procure an act of gross indecency at a urinal in Upper Hatch Street. Two Gardaí had 'concealed ourselves in a position overlooking urinal ... and kept place under observation for some time'. They described the men going in and out of the urinal, furtively glancing, making eye contact, waiting for other men to disappear. When the Gardaí arrested them, one of them said, 'I hope my people won't hear about this. I will tell you all the truth about what happened.' He pleaded guilty, was bound to keep the peace for two years 'and come up for sentence if called upon', while the other, a commercial traveller, insisted 'no such thing at all took place'. He was found not guilty.[216]

Older gay men also came before the courts as a result of investigations of their relationships with younger men. One such case was heard in Dublin in 1928, when two men were charged with buggery and indecent assault; both men, who had engaged in consensual sex, were found not guilty by direction. The older man lived in Upper Erne Street in Dublin city. Two Gardaí, obviously acting on a tip off, knocked on the house's back door and were admitted. Both men agreed to make statements. The younger man, aged 18, was unemployed and had met the older man, aged 62 and an ex British soldier, at the Tivoli theatre: 'he said he would give me a few nights lodgings if I liked'.

The men slept together regularly, the younger man describing in detail in his statement the kind of sex they had, using a language that was frank and juvenile. He maintained: 'I did not know it was any harm. I have done the same with other men before I met P. I have seen 3 other fellows in the room with P.' The older man denied any impropriety: 'we both slept in the one bed. I wanted the boy for company. I never touched the boy indecently ... I occupy the back kitchen in the house. It is a tenant house. I took this boy in for kindnesses.' He also mentioned that he had boys from 'Keoghs barracks and Grand Canal Company' and added that 'the last man I had was sent to the Richmond Asylum'.[217]

'You are grand ... I'd love to be up you'

In 1935, a number of men from the Bandon area of County Cork were pardoned on charges of attempted sodomy and gross indecency. One of them, a 31-year-old man, employed with his father in a prominent local business, was found guilty, even though he was supported by letters from character witnesses, including the chairman of Bandon Town Commissioners, to the effect that he was 'honest, industrious, hardworking. He belongs to a most respectable family.' What became clear from the evidence, though, was that there were an unusually high number of other men involved. He was charged with 20 counts of indecency with 6 different men, at locations all over Bandon: 'at the Green in Bandon, at the cinema, Market Street, Bandon, at Shinagh Bandon, at Carhue, Bandon, at Cottage Hospital Lane, Bandon ... at Burlington Quay, Bandon.'

The deposition of one of the victims, a 15-year-old choirboy at the Bandon Catholic church, revealed that the man was targeting the cinema: 'I know the accused. He used to be in the box at Parnell's cinema. About a year and a half ago I went to the pictures with him. He used to pay for me going in. I remember the first time we went to the pictures. We sat in the back seat stairs.' The boy then revealed that the defendant had forced him to perform oral sex on him on a number of occasions at the cinema: 'this first happened about a year and a half ago. It happened about 3 or 4 times since. It last happened about the first of last month. The name of the picture that was on that night was *What Price Hollywood*.'

As well as the targeting of young boys, an unusual amount of detail emerged during this trial about the clandestine sexual activities of young men in their twenties and thirties, meeting for consensual homosexual activity, going for walks, one young man being regarded by the others 'as a topper at the game'. Another defendant, a married 33-year-old printer, was said by another boy to have

> asked me to go out the road for a walk and I would have a bit of sport with him and that he would give me a tanner. I went down the road about 6 yards. I saw boys coming after us and I said I would not go, that I would be ashamed. I turned back and said I would not go at all. About a quarter of an hour after I saw the accused go out the road with B.S. [another defendant]. They went down the lane near the ball alley. I, with other boys, followed them. We heard them talking and we fired stones at them ... I know the accused all my life.

The defendant admitted: 'For a number of years I have been given to self abuse and have on number of occasions committed acts of indecency, that is, got boys to pull my private part for me. I have never put my private part into the back private part of any body.' He then listed the names and addresses of six boys he had got to do this for him. Another two defendants, also found guilty of attempted sodomy and also pardoned, were both 22 years old. All these men had known each other for years and, although some of the sexual activity was more serious than others, there also seems to have been a good deal of experimenting going on, or 'blackguarding' as one of them described it. Another gave evidence of having sex with seven men, and offered frank admissions of his level of sexual activity, including the fact that he had 'a bit of Vaseline': 'H. went away to town before me and I followed him about 5 minutes after ... he said to me you are grand ... I'd love to be up you.' In total, seven men were charged; it is not clear from the records why, but they were all pardoned.[218]

The following year, 1936, a hairdresser working at James Street in Cork city was convicted of an act of gross indecency with a 16-year-old boy (who was also charged) after he had cut his hair. He had previously been convicted of attempted sodomy in 1928 and had been sentenced to seven years' penal servitude. According to the evidence of his fellow accused he had cut his and another boy's hair and then asked him to call on his own one day, which he did:

> He asked me used I go with girls. He then opened his trousers and took out his private part and told me to take it in my hand. He told me he would give me 4 pence if I would pull it for him. We sat down on the side of the bed and I kept pulling his private part until something happened that I wouldn't like to say. He then got me to take out my private part and he did the same thing to me. When I was going away then he gave me four pence. He told me not to say anything about it, that it was between me and himself.[219]

The defendant was sentenced to five years' penal servitude.[220] His co-accused was found guilty and bound over to keep the peace for two years. However, it was noted in the newspaper report of the sentencing hearing that: 'at 14 years [he] went to work with a farmer who paid him the munificent wage of 2s. weekly. He was homeless in Cork when he fell under the influence of D.'[221] During the same sitting, a 50-year-old man who had 'held good positions in Dublin' was sentenced to two years' hard labour for indecency with another man.[222]

In the same year, two men were found not guilty of gross indecency at St Anne's churchyard off Roman Street in Cork the previous November. A plain clothes Garda gave evidence that he had discovered them in a doorway together. When asked what they were doing one of them replied, 'We are having a pump [urinating]. We were at the Damer at the Arcadia. We had a few drinks.' However, one of the men ran off, resisted arrest, kicked the Garda when he caught him and tore his coat. Another Garda 'examined the doorway for any trace of urine and the ground was quite dry'.[223]

'Rather sceptical as to the results of state interference in these matters'

It is likely that the Gardaí involved in pursuing homosexual crime in Cork were part of the 'vice squad' that was mentioned in Department of Justice correspondence relating to concern about the growing number of sexual offences coming to light in Cork city. From 1935 a 'special squad detained for duty in this connection' had been in operation, or as J. J. Hanigan, the chief superintendent of the Gardaí in Cork, labelled it, 'a special vice squad'.[224] Concerns continued to be expressed about criminal sexual activity in Cork over the next few years. In a memorandum Stephen Roche prepared for the department in July 1938, in the context of the possible appointment of women police, he referred to a 'rather alarming document' received the previous month which suggested that 'offences against morality were increasing in that city to a really serious extent', that more women needed to be appointed as probation officers, and that female police were also necessary.

Several Catholic priests, Protestant and Presbyterian clergymen and representatives of other social and religious organisations in the city signed the document. Roche elaborated:

> On the other hand, it was not signed by the Bishop (Dr Cohalan). I learned afterwards that the Bishop knew of it and didn't like it. I wrote to the local DJ [District Justice] Mr D. B. Sullivan and his reply confirmed, in strong terms, the suggestion that there was something seriously wrong in Cork and in particular he referred to the number of young girls who had come before him in connection with offences of this class, their apparent shamelessness and their readiness to commit perjury. I then asked assistant Justice [Henry] McCarthy, in whose ability and discretion I have great confidence, to go down to Cork and investigate matters on the spot (he had just returned from Geneva where he had been representing our government at a women and children protection

conference). In sum, he seems to think that both the local justice and the petitioners have exaggerated the gravity of the situation but that there is a lot of immorality and need for some action. Personally, my habit of thought is to be rather sceptical as to the results of state interference in these matters. I have the feeling that the rising generation in Cork are going Pagan despite all that the churches and the teachers and the voluntary organisations can do; the situation cannot be served by the appointment of a few more state officers, whether men or women. So far as I can see, what the petitioners are really looking for is a body of special police who will patrol the streets of Cork, asking young girls where they are going and sending them home if they are not satisfied with the answers. There is no power in law for any officer to do this and the general theory of the law is that people can be as immoral as they like provided they do not come up against some special provision of the law.[225]

Such frankness was unusual, and Roche touched upon a number of issues that were relevant to the degree of 'moral panic', which had been highlighted in the VD and Carrigan reports of earlier years. He seemed to be sceptical about how justified such panics were, how far the law could extend, and conscious that there was a need for the state to be mindful of the civil rights of its citizens – a preoccupation of officials in the Department of Justice that had already surfaced in relation to the issue of brothels. There was also an underlying sense of the state wanting to wash its hands of this, on the grounds that if the first line of defence – the Catholic Church – could not prevent these activities, how was the state going to deal with them? But it is also likely the bishop would not have wanted to sign the petition because he would have been loathe to admit that Cork was an exceptionally immoral city, and because such an admission would have suggested that the Church was not doing a very effective job in policing sexual activity.

The report that Henry McCarthy compiled referred to 112 cases of VD treated at the Cork city clinic between April 1936 and March 1937, with 95 new cases from 1 April 1937 to March 1938, 'all these cases were men, for there is no clinical treatment available in the city for women'. Abortion was on the increase, but illegitimate births were not. He acknowledged that prosecutions for immoral offences increased between 1935 and 1937, but that was because from 1935 a 'special squad [was] detailed for duty in this connection'. He also referred to 'ex-industrial school boys drifting into the city', and some young girls spending the night 'on foreign ships in the Port'. McCarthy reiterated that the bishop had seen no cause for alarm and that one priest 'informed me he had signed it because he was pressed to do so, and not from any real sense of conviction.

McCarthy concluded, in a fascinating observation on class and sex:

> I am satisfied that there is nothing in the moral state of the city which, apart from conditions in other cities, calls for any special attention. It seems true that the morals, especially of the more well to do people, have deteriorated here, as in other places, and those who are less favourably circumstanced have not been slow to follow their example, but that the young people who are obliged to spend most of their time in the lanes and streets have become deplorably immoral I do not believe, nor could I find the slightest justification for such a contention.[226]

Neither was he convinced of the need for female police. He also cited the returns for offences of immorality committed in the districts of Cork City North and South from 1934 to 1937, which revealed there were 52 cases relating to buggery and gross indecency, 1 incest case a year in 1934–6, 2 cases of 'bathing in the nude', a single rape, 6 cases of prostitution and 4 cases of indecent assault on a male, figures which once again illustrate either how homosexual offences were being prioritised above others, or that these offences were more likely to be committed outdoors and therefore noticed. He also offered a social profile of the offenders: 'The persons apprehended in connection with the different offences range in age from 15 to 72 years and include persons of different occupations in life, principally labourers, unemployed, ex-British soldiers, national army soldiers, commercial travellers, messenger boys, altar boys, parish clerk, etc.'[227]

The Garda chief superintendent in Cork referred to the success of the 'special vice squad' mentioned above to explain the increases, as well as to 'the trend of modern times' and the recurrence of these type of offences 'amongst youths who have become initiated and are of low mentality', while prostitution was deemed to be partly attributable to lack of parental supervision 'and to a lesser extent to modern customs and conveniences which provide greater facilities for both normal and abnormal intercourse between members of the opposite sex'.[228] There was a refusal by the state to take on board serious concerns, particularly with regard to the demand for women police, and a belief that voluntary organisations had a tendency to exaggerate, or were interfering upper-class do-gooders.

The reaction of Bishop Daniel Cohalan, whatever his motives, was commented on by the writer and native of Cork Seán O'Faoláin, who, in his book *An Irish Journey*, published in 1940, referred to 'these poor homeless lovers' on the corner of Cork streets, 'the shawled girls and their boys make love, the shawl is wrapped tight around them both and under it they lean in tight embrace'. He referred to a 'society' (of St Jude) to root them out and a movement to introduce 'women police into Cork – mainly to stop 'this natural, passionate, innocent, human' courtship: 'I say to his eternal credit that the Bishop ... has consistently frowned on the Manichaens. He snuffed out the society of St Jude.'[229]

'Wait till you feel something tickle you'

O'Faoláin was being naive if he thought that innocent courting was all that was going on in the streets and lanes of Cork. As the court archives make clear there were much more sinister forces at work, and it is notable that during the private correspondence about events in Cork, and the determination to dismiss it as exaggerated, there was little discussion of one of the most prevalent sexual crimes – indecent assault against young children, prosecutions for which were proceeded with in circuit courts in all parts of the country.

There were features that were common to most of these cases. The children invariably knew their attackers, some of whom were in a position of power over them; much violence was employed; many were easy targets because of parental absence, many were terrified to let other adults know what was going on; and many were vulnerable due to the preponderance of large families, making it difficult for them to find space to make their grievances known, or highlight the crimes against them.

Like all children in such situations these found it difficult to find a language that could adequately describe what had happened to them, and many who were sent away from home, whether to employment, on service, or merely on a message, were prey to the designs of older men who would often offer them the inducement of sweets or small amounts of money. As mentioned before, the cases that came to court were likely to have been only a fraction of those that actually occurred, making it realistic to conclude that this was a very serious and prevalent problem.

'Silence and secrecy' is a fair description of the approach to the issue of childhood female sexuality in Ireland in the 1930s and the 1940s.[230] A survey in the *Irish Journal of Feminist Studies* based on the reminiscences of thirteen women born into actively Catholic families between 1923 and 1940 makes it clear that there was 'a growing discrepancy between devotional practice and social experience, albeit discreet', that Catholic religious observation was widespread, but 'its lessons were neither universally enjoyed nor acted on', and that perhaps what was more significant than confession was silence. Girls who were taken on religious missions and retreats at the age of 14 or so certainly heard an awful lot about the 'unbridled passions of men', but there was also 'a very heavy emphasis on that and how it was women; women had the moral responsibility of holding that in check'.

Attempts to gain any clarity about these issues were discouraged and discussion of the facts of life was virtually non-existent. Only when mothers were confronted with the reality of their daughter's menstruating would they issue any kind of advice, and then 'it was usually a strongly worded warning against the dangers inherent in physical intimacy with boys' and what would happen to 'fallen women'. Regarding sons, veteran suffragette and feminist Hanna Sheehy Skeffington was very much an exception to the rule in giving her son a copy of Marie Stope's banned *Married Love* as a wedding present in 1935.[231]

Of course, the widely believed solution to this was to keep boys and girls apart at all times. In 1934, the headmaster of Blackrock College and future Archbishop of Dublin, John Charles McQuaid, made it clear in public that he regarded any proposal to encourage mixed athletics, for example, as a 'monstrous suggestion'. He wrote a letter to the *Irish Press* suggesting that 'mixed athletics and all cognate immodesties are abuses that rightminded people reprobate, wherever and whenever they exist'.[232] This was a protest against a proposal by the National Athletic and Cycling Association to promote mixed sports, a decision they decided not to implement, McQuaid insisting that no boy from his college would participate in sport with girls 'no matter what attire they may adopt'. A teacher at Marino College in Dublin wrote to McQuaid to congratulate him on his stance against 'the pagan proposal', hoping it would achieve 'an awakening of vigilance on the part of the heads of all Catholic schools' and the false arrogance of 'lay claimants to be guides in the training of youth'. Joseph Walsh, future Archbishop of Tuam, expressed the hope in a letter to McQuaid that 'you will be long spared to lead the way whenever similar perils threaten our country'.[233] Little did he know just how long McQuaid would be spared, or the powerful position he would assume six years later.

Many factors need to be kept in mind in relation to young girls and sexuality, but one that was not being tackled, and rarely mentioned, was the issue of their sexual abuse. How did the victims react to the crimes and deal with the fall-out as reflected in the court records, and just how common was the crime of sexual abuse of young girls? Girls working as domestic servants were still very vulnerable, as revealed by a case at Galway Central Criminal Court in June 1924, in which a 14-year-old girl gave evidence of being assaulted at a time when the wife of the house she worked in, at Salthill, County Galway, was sick in bed:

> I was boiling some milk for her. Mr McC. caught hold of me, pulled my legs apart and had connection with me at the stove. After those occurrences he used to fiddle about with me. He used put his hands under my clothes and on my private part. I complained to my sister after the first time he had assaulted me, but I did not tell her the whole truth as I thought she would understand all about it. He used follow me upstairs but I used make away from him ... I knew it was wrong. I wiped up the delph then ... I went to confession and I told my sister the whole story.

The defendant, who was married '3 or 4 years', was sent for trial in the Central Criminal Court in Dublin.[234]

The circuit court files for Dublin in 1927 document the experience of another girl under 15 whose female employer sent her to a doctor in Aungier Street to collect medicine. She alleged the doctor put his leg under her clothes: 'I began to cry; he said "wait till you feel something tickle you".' This happened on a few occasions, with the doctor using the medicine as a bargaining tool: 'on each occasion I was there some people were sitting outside the partitions.'

The family circumstances of this girl were typical of those sent out to be domestic servants at a young age. Her father, a labourer who had not worked for four years, and three siblings were living in one room. Another doctor, after examining her, concluded she had not been a virgin when the alleged assault had taken place and could find 'nothing to corroborate her story'. The father gave evidence to the effect that 'she didn't run away. I was always abusing her for going with soldiers. I heard Dr O'N's evidence that [the] girl was not a virgin. I can't explain that.' The case files also include a note signed by her father: 'I hereby agree to take £50 as full payment for stopping proceedings against Dr M. F. for alleged assault on my daughter.'[235] A *Nolle Prosequi* was entered.

In Cork in 1935, a 21-year-old man who had been in Greenmount industrial school in Cork until the age of 16 and had previous convictions for larceny gave evidence of having sex with a 14-year-old girl down the backs of various streets in Cork city. A Garda had observed them near Railway Street. The man admitted, 'I had connection with M. W. about 5 times altogether and I paid her sixpence each time.' The evidence of the Garda suggested that this girl was effectively seen as an amateur prostitute: 'I have seen at least five other boys having connection with the same girl and in the same places.' Another defendant charged with assaulting her was just under 17; he was deemed not to be suitable for Borstal, because he was not regarded as the 'criminal type' and because of his previous 'good' character: 'his father, who is intemperate and of the rowdy type, probably takes little interest in him. Nothing definite is known as to his associates but he is charged jointly with an elder youth in the present case. He has never been in regular employment.'

No such detailed observations were offered in the case of the girl; the doctor who examined her and another girl saw no signs of virginity: 'I would say the girls were accustomed to sexual intercourse. They appeared to be common prostitutes.' The alleged victim said she wanted the money 'for chips'.[236] The following year the same man was charged with the unlawful carnal knowledge of the other girl, who was 16. He admitted having sex with her at a gateway in Queen Street for sixpence: 'Yes, I did interfere with the girl. E. W. was with her twice and J. S. once. I know the girl goes round with other men. She came up and told me what she got by going with other men.'[237] The man was sentenced to six months' imprisonment without hard labour (the judge believed 'he would be much better off in prison' than on the streets), while the girls were referred to by the judge, as reported by the *Cork Examiner*, as 'two little girls who were a positive danger to the people of Cork'.[238]

'It was my fault, but I have to blame the children a lot'

The following year, also in Cork city, an 18-year-old man was convicted of the unlawful carnal knowledge and indecent assault of two sisters, aged 7 and 8, at the Erin Piper's band room in the city. The father's deposition recalled that 'up to that day my daughters were normal children, never making a complaint. When I returned home I observed that M. was crying and I asked her why she was crying and she said she would be afraid to tell because I would beat her. She then told me how a man above in the band room rose up her clothes and put his no.1 into her body. She told me he had done the same to C.' The 8-year-old sister also gave evidence, 'being a child of tender years aged about 9 and not in the opinion of the court understanding the nature of an oath, but being of sufficient intelligence in the opinion of the court to justify the reception of her evidence, she understanding the duty of speaking the truth'.

According to her, the defendant, a playing member of the band for the previous eight months, had promised them toys and a penny. The medical examination confirmed the abuse of one of the sisters. According to the defendant's statement, 'They were the cause of I doing it, if any bloody children come near me again I will tear their heads off ... It was my fault, but I have to blame the children a lot.' Having seen him urinate in a bucket, 'the young B. girl said that my private part was bigger than her brother's'. The defendant was found guilty on all counts with a recommendation to 'mercy on account of his youth and health', though the details of his ill health do not appear in the records. The judge sentenced him to two years in prison, though according to the court record book he was subsequently pardoned.[239]

At the district court area of Dingle in County Kerry in June 1936, a man was accused of the indecent assault of a 5-year-old girl at Strand Street in Dingle, at a shed in the back of Flaherty's pub, while three of her friends were also there: 'he lifted me up in his arms and he rubbed me there and he put a thing in there ... he gave me a penny after rubbing me. He threw a penny on the floor and said stay there now ... I bought sweets with the penny ... I ate them all myself ... I did not tell because I was ashamed to tell.' This trial was adjourned after two hours because, according to the judge, E. J. McElligott, it was obvious that the court interpreter, despite being a trained Irish speaker, could not understand the native Irish speakers. As the judge subsequently wrote: 'It was abundantly clear that he found it impossible to understand the Irish spoken by Sergeant Gleeson, one of the principal witnesses for the state. I do not know if Sergeant Gleeson is a "native" speaker; under the circumstances it was imperative on me to adjourn the trial, especially as only one member of the jury professed to have any knowledge of the language.'[240] The following year a *Nolle Prosequi* was entered in this case on the instruction of the Attorney General.

Some notable absences from court cases in relation to the sexual abuse of children – particularly in view of what was learnt at the end of the twentieth century – are clerics. This is significant in the context of the evidence of Brother David Gibson, Province leader of St Mary's Province in Ireland, given to the Commission to Inquire into Child Abuse (see Chapter 3) in July 2004, which revealed that from the 1930s onwards there was evidence of abuse in institutions run by the Christian Brothers, and that thirty internal formal trials of abusers were kept secret at a time when it was a criminal offence to withhold information on a crime, and that they were withholding this information at a time when the Gardaí were actively pursuing such criminals.[241]

'Mixed bathing by strangers, all night dancing in farm houses, company keeping'

Alcohol features in many of these cases, but drinking was also something that may have stymied overall sexual activity in Ireland. In his novel *The Saint and Mary Kate* (1932), Frank O'Connor drew attention to the havoc drink abuse wreaked in Irish family life when the character Mary Kate begins to realise the truth of an Irish adage – that 'behind all the love of women for man lies a secret sorrow', that of excessive drinking. It undoubtedly created a sexual incapacity, to the point that 'where the charms of women are concerned, a son of Erin couldn't care less'.[242]

Notwithstanding, village celebrations, wakes and dance halls sometimes provided a backdrop to sexual crime court cases, and there was no shortage of condemnation of their ill-effects. Those in the 'first line of defence' were certainly busying themselves, especially the Redemptorists, a congregation of priests established in Italy specifically for the work of parish missions and who first arrived in Ireland in 1851. As Brendan McConvery, the archivist of the Irish Redemptorist Province, has highlighted, Redemptorists were required to keep a record of all the work they did outside the monastery. This was entered into a 'mission chronicle' which included descriptions of various parishes and the state of religious practice they found, as well as comments on 'principal abuses of the place', of which there were plenty. In order to counteract these, parish missions (of which there were 164 in 1933) were held, usually lasting a fortnight and consisting of an early morning Mass said each day, a short practical instruction, followed by the main mission service

in the evening with a full sermon lasting nearly an hour, visitation to homes
and the 'opportunity for a more earnest mission confession.'[243] There was
also a blessing of holy objects on the final night.

It sounds exhausting, which was precisely the intended effect as the
missioners battled socialism, communism and, of course, the greatest sin of
all – lust. In the Cork–Kerry area in the 1920s and 1930s, they conducted
running battles with dance hall owners and promoters. Those who refused
to close their halls were denounced publicly at the end of the mission, effectively being declared public sinners, as the congregations were invited to
pray for their conversion – an indication perhaps that the missioners did not
always get their way. The use of motor cars was also castigated for facilitating
easier travel to dance halls and seaside resorts by young people.

The Redemptorists also campaigned against 'immodest dress' such
as swimwear and the new fashion of women wearing slacks. Summer was
regarded as a particularly dangerous time; in 1927, missioners referred to the
Ballybunion resort in County Kerry as having a reputation for 'much public immorality and marriages of necessity'. In Roundstone, County Galway,
abuses were noted such as 'mixed bathing by strangers, all night dancing in
farm houses, company keeping ... the Parish Priest formed a vigilance committee to stamp out mixed bathing. Visitors had introduced men's dress for
women but the Legion of Mary is going to deal with this scandal.'[244]

'Conduct that in other countries is confined to the brothels is to be seen without let or hindrance on our public roads'

According to sociologist James Smyth, the dance hall was 'one obsession
[that] remained constant and central', as was unsupervised dancing of any
sort during the 1920s and 1930s: 'this popular rural pastime became a classic terrain of fantasy projection and pseudo-knowledge involving a potent
brew of alleged sources of evil and degradation'.[245] The rhetoric of moral
degeneration concerning dancing was not unique to Ireland; it was common in England, Europe and North America also, but there is a tendency to
believe it took on a 'unique configuration' in Ireland during these decades,
underlined by a discourse of ruin and sin. One of the leading cheerleaders in
this regard was Bishop O'Doherty of Galway, who maintained in 1924 that
'the dances indulged in were not the clean, healthy, national Irish dances.
They were, on the contrary, importations from the vilest dens of London,

Paris and New York, direct and unmistakable incitements to evil thought and evil desires.'

Another critic was the Jesuit priest Father Richard Devane, who noted approvingly that 'Havana, the capital of Cuba, is virtually danceless', while jazz music (referred to disparagingly as 'nigger music') was seen as threatening because of its association with black and African sexuality.[246]

Concerts, card-playing and dancing were often housed in the public libraries. The Swords Library Committee carried a motion in March 1923 to the effect that 'promiscuous dancing in the Swords Library is prohibited, but Irish dancing can be carried on as usual'.[247] The statutes from the Maynooth National Synod in 1927 had made it clear that 'late at night' was considered to be midnight and that 'proceeds from public dances (a) which are of doubtful character, or (b) which are continued till late at night are not to be devoted to any ecclesiastical purpose'.[248] The fact that people were travelling distances to such dances was frowned upon by Cardinal MacRory in 1931, as was the loss of parental control. The dance hall legislation, eventually introduced as the 1935 Public Dance Halls Act, which was patchily enforced, required organisers of dances to get the sanction of clergy, police and judiciary.[249]

The critics of dances also turned their attention elsewhere; some maintained there was nowhere more dangerous when it came to sexual assaults than an Irish ditch, field or country road – which was true. When he made a submission to the Carrigan Committee, the Revd John Flannagan, parish priest of Fairview in Dublin, stated that 'conduct that in other countries is confined to the brothels is to be seen without let or hindrance on our public roads'.[250] His comments were regarded with scepticism by the Department of Justice, but they were not that wide of the mark, to judge by the frequency with which roads are mentioned in witness depositions as the venues for sexual assault. But it was also true that some contemporaries thought public dancing was being unduly targeted; the Department of Justice's response to the Carrigan Committee's proposals was curt: 'their suggestions amount almost to a suppression of public dancing'.[251]

'He stood up and said he had no sweets, but that he would give them to me the next day'

A court case heard in Limerick in October 1927 concerned the rape of a woman ('I am about 21 years') following a dance in Milltown, Croagh, County Limerick. The daughter of the victim's employer reported that the defendant, a boy who had been hired by the victim's employer for occasional labour, had previously been violent. The victim had been accosted by him as she left the dance; two other men approached them to remonstrate with him, asking him to let the girl go, to which he replied, 'I won't until she accounts for herself first.' During the court hearing the victim was questioned about her contacts with boys, a line of questioning common to almost all of these rape cases; in reply she said that she 'knew another boy: I walked with him one night'. The local man who had put up bail for the defendant withdrew it, saying he now believed the man would abscond, after which he was put in prison in Limerick before his trial. He was found not guilty of rape but guilty of indecent assault.[252]

A case heard ten years later, in October 1937, in Tralee recounted a night of heavy drinking by the 22-year-old son of a shopkeeper in Knocknagoshel who was charged with the unlawful carnal knowledge of a girl under the age of 15 on the day of the village sports and pattern (during which a Mass was often said in a house in the village). He had been drinking in various pubs throughout the evening and then attended two different dances, between visits to the pubs: 'I went from one dance hall to the other all night and I went in home about 6 a.m. and went to bed ... we were all kind of merry. I was drunk.' The alleged victim was the 12-year-old daughter of a local Garda who had been in the vicinity of one of the dances at about 10 p.m. Her mother's statement noted, 'she told me he told her to lift up her clothes. I formed a conclusion from that.' The girl said she had been raped in a ditch in a field. The medical evidence of Dr John Coffey, former assistant master in Holles Street hospital in Dublin, was that a semen stain had been found on the girl's chemise; he also found marks, stained knickers and a discharge (and added 'conception can take place in my opinion in a girl even younger than 12 years with or without full intercourse taking place, that is without penetration'). But he added that 'outside these marks I found on her I found nothing definite [to indicate] that she had been violated. She was not suffering from shock.' The state pathologist, Dr John McGrath, confirmed semen stains, but the accused was found not guilty.[253]

These cases, particularly in such small communities, must have had serious consequences for relations between neighbours and friends, as the victims were almost always known to the perpetrators, and the making of statements and the giving of evidence involved so many different members of the community. Many of the assaults also highlight a broader social context, in particular the poor standard of living, which made some children vulnerable; due to economic circumstances they were frequently sent out to work at a very young age with sexually frustrated older men.

In January 1937, a labourer and father of nine children gave evidence at a trial of a man found guilty of nine counts of the unlawful carnal knowledge (but not rape) of a 13-year-old girl. Of the nine children, two were away in service, one of them was living with his grandmother and six were living with the labourer and his wife. The father, who commented, 'I don't know the date of birth of my daughter. I know she is 13 years of age', witnessed the abuse taking place in a local field: 'I had suspicions from the position I saw my daughter in. I continued on ... I made no report to the Guards for 10 days.' It might seem extraordinary that a father would appear so reluctant to act when he witnessed a man sexually assaulting his daughter in a field in broad daylight, but there were three issues here: the difficulty of finding a language to discuss what was happening; the desire to deny it; and the fact that the defendant was well known to him. The accused was in the victim's house on the day of the alleged incident 'speaking about the dole forms'.

The mother subsequently went to the house of the accused and confronted him, saying he had 'shamed and disgraced my little girl' – a common way of placing the shame on the victim as well as the perpetrator. The mother subsequently took her daughter to the doctor, who confirmed the abuse. The victim's testimony included this account:

> I was sent by mother to the house of the accused for the purpose of saving hay with him ... after a time he stood up and said he had no sweets, but that he would give them to me the next day ... when he came off me he said to me, 'That's your father down the road' and he ducked down and told me to stoop down too and I did.[254]

'I know the sin of it and I wouldn't go any further'

Many other children were assaulted by neighbours while they were out on errands for their parents, though convictions were difficult in the absence of adult witnesses. A man from Louisburgh, County Mayo, was accused of the unlawful carnal knowledge of his 14-year-old neighbour while she was on an errand to Louisburgh village with her 10-year-old brother in February 1936.

According to her testimony, on the way home they met the defendant, who got off his bicycle,

> and without saying anything he caught a hold of me by putting his left arm around me and brought me over to a stack of turf that was on the roadside and pressed me against the stack of turf. He then lifted up my dress ... the accused opened the front of his trousers and took out his pencil – by that I mean his private part and he put it into my private part ... I offered no resistance. I was crying all the time. I did not shout out for help. My brother was standing on the road all this time crying.

When she got home, the girl merely told her mother that the man had caught hold of her and torn her dress, not about the sexual assault, 'because I was ashamed to do so. I know the accused for a few years, since I was a child, as he was in the habit of visiting our house.'

Medical examinations were often hampered due to the delay between assaults happening and the child informing an adult, which also seems to have acted as a hindrance to prosecution: the girl in this case was examined two weeks after the alleged assault. The doctor at the Louisburgh dispensary 'found that the result of the examination was on the whole negative as regards coitus'.[255] The jury failed to agree a verdict.

In another Mayo case from the 1930s a man from Castlebar was accused of indecently assaulting a 15-year-old neighbour, but in this case the assault happened after the man had left the local pub at 11 p.m. He went across the bog and sat on a wall near the victim's house. The girl's father, who knew the defendant, later gave evidence that 'I knew that he had been spreading turf in the bog that day'. The defendant, who said afterwards, 'If I was as wise as I am now I wouldn't go near any house', recalled what prompted him to break into the house and enter the bedroom where the victim shared a bed with her sister:

> Often during that week I had impressions of M.McD. I am a next door neighbour of the McD.'s. On the night I had this impression and then I was sitting on the wall and saw the light in the girl's room quenching. I sat near the window for about half an hour. I got a stick and then I rose the window. I took off the boots first. I went in to the bedroom then and I had no intention of doing anything to either of them. After that I just rose the clothes off one of them. I partly discovered then that it was M.

was in it. I only wanted to leave my hand on her and I'd be satisfied then. I just put my hand on her private and I was satisfied then. I know the sin of it and I wouldn't go any further.[256]

Like other provincial newspapers, the weekly *Mayo News* devoted much space to district and circuit court hearings and the reports – often very detailed – named both the defendants and the victims involved in these kind of cases. In the above case, the state solicitor pointed out that 'in the local papers it was stated that the accused was accused of indecent assault ... he would like to have this corrected, as no indecent assault took place. It was only attempted assault.' The judge asked the journalists in court to make this point clear in their reports.[257]

Incest also occurred, though such cases do not appear that frequently in the court records. In 1935 an illiterate Cork grandfather was sentenced to two years' penal servitude for the indecent assault of his 11-year-old grand-daughter and to three years for incest with his daughter, the sentences to run concurrently. The jury in the case had recommended mercy owing to the age of the defendant, who was 76. The abuse of the daughter had occurred in 1918. In the more recent case the granddaughter had been living with the grandparents, having previously lived with her aunt, when the abuse took place. She had been impregnated by her grandfather and gave birth to a baby that only survived for a few days, after which she was admitted to Bessborough House in Cork, the mother and baby home run by the Sisters of the Sacred Heart of Jesus and Mary. Four of the defendant's daughters gave evidence against him.[258]

'On the landings and dark hallways of the tenements you could always get a grope or a squeeze'

Living conditions undoubtedly influenced the amount of sexual activity and abuse in urban Ireland, but some were later to lament lost opportunities for sexual indulgence as a result of the demise of tenement living. While the new Fianna Fáil government in 1932 was anxious to proclaim its Catholic credentials and made a practice of asking the bishop of the diocese to bless a new factory or housing estate,[259] the writer Brendan Behan decried the move away from tenement city living to the new suburbs as a regretful development in the context of his burgeoning sexuality. According to his biographer, Michael O'Sullivan, 'He used to say wryly that de Valera's housing reforms had ruined his ordinary sexual development; that the move from the slums out to the windy spaces and semi-detached houses of Crumlin had come at a crucial age and had been disastrous ... on the landings and dark hallways of the tenements you could always get a grope or a squeeze and at fourteen he was just getting the hang of things ... when the move came along.'[260]

For older former residents of the tenements, interviewed by Kevin Kearns for his oral history of tenement life in Dublin, memories of the policing of sexual activity were common: 'You had a priest called Fr Crosbie and he used to go up the laneway with a stick and any courting couples he'd see he'd hit them with a stick.' Another interviewee maintained that adultery was 'quite common' and that when a woman confessed to priests that she had not complied with her husband's sexual desires, 'they'd tell you to get out! I'm not giving you absolution!'

Some, because of ignorance about sex, were 'like lambs to the slaughter' on their wedding nights, and there was a tone of anger about this emanating from the women who were reminiscing, as there was about the practice of women being 'churched' after they had given birth to be purified, 'the way it was you were like a fallen woman' even in marriage. 'I thought I was a dirty woman because I had the child,' recalled one tenement dweller.[261]

But the real stigma was reserved for unmarried mothers, and suicide could result – there were frequent prosecutions for attempted suicide in Dublin courts in the early twentieth century.[262]

As mentioned earlier, there was also a concern that the presence of more motor cars in Ireland could facilitate increased sexual activity. Car ownership was a middle-class privilege and it was not possible to restrict a car's use or legislate for the behaviour in it; as James Smyth notes, 'the ingenious solution was to define a motor car as a street in the paragraph dealing with soliciting and importuning in the Public Dance Halls Act: "the word street in this section (shall) include a motor car, carriage or other vehicle".' This allowed the police to 'treat a car as a public place and use their discretion as to the nature of behaviour within', which prompted Senator Mahaffey to suggest that a wheelbarrow was a street and could therefore be used for an immoral purpose.[263]

Smyth notes that 'the motor car was seen as an instrument of seduction in the hands of unscrupulous males'. It was for some. A rape case, particularly horrific due to the victim's psychological as well as physical trauma, was heard in Galway in May 1935, and at its centre was a car, a Model Y Ford Babyford 8 horsepower. A man claiming to be a machine agent called at the house of a 24-year-old woman in Salthill and told her she was needed urgently at her husband's workplace as he had had a serious accident. After she had got into his car he told her her husband was dead. In the words of her deposition, 'he stopped the car opposite a public house on the left side and he asked me to have a drink. I declined to drink. He drove on.' The man subsequently raped her in the car for fifteen minutes while she resisted. He then drove her home; 'on the way back he proffered me a £1 note and said he'd see me again'. She refused the money and went straight to Salthill barracks.[264] The jury in this trial failed to reach a verdict and it was ordered that the trial be transferred to the Central Criminal Court. The following month, a man convicted of rape in the Galway circuit court was sentenced to three years' penal servitude.[265]

'The morals of the poultry yard'

Access to information about sex and treatment for sexually transmitted diseases was not helped by the censorious attitude that existed in the 1920s and 1930s, although the link is not as straightforward as has sometimes been presented. Not withstanding, it became quickly apparent that free speech in the new Free State in the 1920s would rest on shaky foundations. Signe Toksvig, in one of the many angry entries in her Irish diaries, recorded in 1931 that 'it is so strange to be living where ordinary free thinking is treated as indecent contraband'.[266] Censorship in Ireland may have been highly centralised and severe, but it was not unique – Australia had one of the strictest censorship systems in the world in the 1920s, while in France laws existed to punish the writing and distribution of birth control information and to punish severely abortionists and the women who sought them out.[267]

In Italy in 1922, the fascist government organised an anti-pornography campaign on the grounds that 'it was necessary to save the energy spent in the search for sexual pleasure in order to reconstruct the nation'. But the Italian League of Decency was not always successful; when the liberal novelist Dino Segre was accused of being pornographic after the publication of *The Chastity Belt* in 1921, many fascist intellectuals stood up for him and, while there was censorship of birth control, unorthodox books that dealt with sexual pleasure, such as Edorado Tinto's *Dictionary of Sexology* (1932–4), were still being published. The fascist penal code made propaganda in favour of birth control a crime, but it did not prevent a decline in birth rates in the 1930s.[268]

The idea that the political chaos of early twentieth-century Ireland had resulted in a moral crisis was one shared on both sides of the border, as Peter Martin's perusal of a great variety of archival sources in *Censorship and the Two Irelands* (2006) makes clear. Sex, or 'the morals of the poultry yard', to use the memorable phrase of the Irish film censor James Montgomery, was not the only concern; the censorship process was also about the interaction between Church, state and the power (often resented) of social reform movements and lobby groups. While active state intervention was much less pronounced in Northern Ireland, in the excessively centralised censorship process of the Free State, much doubt, confusion and resentment existed about how to define indecency. Indeed, in reaction to the debate over how to define indecency in the context of the Censorship of Publications Act of 1929, there were many who shared the view articulated by Fianna Fáil politician Seán Lemass that there was nothing intrinsically wrong with sexual passion. The original proposed definition of indecency as 'calculated to excite sexual passion or to suggest or to excite sexual immorality, or in any other way to corrupt or deprave' was widely criticised as being too vague and the amended wording that became law did not include the phrase 'calculated to excite sexual passion'.[269]

It was clear that ultimately Irish literary censorship 'was about sexuality more than anything else',[270] but the appetite on the part of the state for stringent censorship should not be exaggerated. Peter Martin makes the observation that 'the government's eventual decision to introduce legislation that it clearly did not want was a tribute to the organisation, skill and sheer bloody-mindedness of the moral reformers'.[271] Both jurisdictions were perhaps more comfortable with issues of political censorship, strict security laws and a distaste for left-wing movements, which, as Martin again observes, was out of all proportion to their actual presence on the island. But in other areas attitudes were more complicated – despite the stereotype of Catholic hidebound reaction and triumphalism, there was admiration in some Protestant quarters in Northern Ireland for the Free State's more active and systematic film censorship, and equally there was widespread frustration within the Free State's censorship of publications board which frequently felt unappreciated and misunderstood. There were many undercurrents of unofficial complaints and bullying; in this context the wry comment of

James Montgomery in 1934 that 'there are at least one million censors in Ireland, I am only the official censor' is illuminating.[272]

The Committee on Evil Literature was established by Minister for Justice Kevin O'Higgins in 1926 to consider and report on 'whether it is necessary or advisable in the interest of the public morality to extend the existing powers of the state to prohibit or restrict the sale and circulation of printed matter'. It consisted of three laymen and two clergymen, one Roman Catholic, one Church of Ireland. A statement circulated to members of the committee regarding existing laws suggested there was no satisfactory legal definition of the words 'obscene' and 'indecent'. Representations have been made that the law should be framed so as to cover things that while not grossly obscene or indecent are merely so, and to include all matters which may be subversive of public morals or tend to corrupt the minds of youthful or impressionable persons'.[273]

The papers of the secretary of the Committee on Evil Literature give a comprehensive overview of the submissions made between February and May 1926 by individuals and organisations who were anxious to see censorship legislation advanced, including the Dublin Christian Citizenship Council, the Irish Vigilance Association and the Catholic Headmasters Association (CHA).[274] The CHA wanted the establishment of a 'censorship or vigilance committee' to draw up a list of 'immoral publications', while the Christian Brothers provided a list of 'some objectionable papers and periodicals – *News of the World, The People, Vogue* and *Girl's Companion'*. The Christian Brother representatives made it clear that their main target was material imported from England – a long-time preoccupation of advocates of greater censorship. They referred to 'gilded filth; papers that publish answers to the letters of young men and women relating to sexual intercourse; papers that publish nauseous details of divorce proceedings; papers and books containing advertisement of certain drugs and instruments which urge people to the most monstrous crimes'.[275] The following month, the Garda Commissioner, Eamon Coogan, informed the secretary of the Department of Justice that, in his view, 'the existing acts are inadequate' regarding obscenity.[276]

A prominent Jesuit who supported increased censorship, Father Richard Devane, wrote to committee member Revd. J. Dempsey to inform him that Dean Herbert Kennedy, the senior official of Dublin's landmark Church of Ireland Christchurch Cathedral ('I got some Protestants interested') had written to him 'saying many conscientious "Christian" people believe in this practice ... Frank Duff has a choice collection of catalogues, ads and books dealing with this unsavoury matter.' He also cited countries which had strong legislation on birth control propaganda, such as Belgium, France and Sweden. Devane's submission also contained copies of *Family Limitation* (1914) by the American birth control activist Margaret Sanger, and *A Letter to Working Mothers* (1919) by Marie Stopes.[277]

'A handful of Calvinists mad with Sexphobia'

There was considerable opposition to the proposed terms of the censorship legislation, in particular from the Irish literary world. The nationalist writer George Russell, for example, put pressure on the government through the pages of his *Irish Statesman*, publishing a piece by the eminent playwright George Bernard Shaw in November 1928 which suggested that Ireland 'having broken England's grip on her ... slips back into the Atlantic as a little grass patch in which a few million moral cowards are not allowed to call their souls their own by a handful of morbid Catholics, mad with Heresyphobia, unnaturally combining with a handful of Calvinists mad with Sexphobia (both being in a small and intensely disliked minority of their own co-religionsists)'. But Russell himself opted, unlike Shaw, to lobby for amendments rather than to seek to have the proposal entirely dropped. He received assurances the legislation would be applied sparingly to literature and that private associations could not refer books to the censorship board. But he had few qualms about the automatic banning of books on birth control, a position supported by his friend Senator Oliver St John Gogarty, who in his contribution to the debate maintained:

> No one who has any care for a nation's welfare can for one moment countenance contraceptive practices which are a contradiction of a nation's life. In England, the condition of the miners and the unemployed is as it is because England has allowed its capital to go into yellow, brown and black labour, so that the government tolerates clinics for education in the practice of contraception.[278]

The Censorship Act of 1929 consisted of four parts: the first covering the application of new definitions of 'obscene' and 'indecent'; the second establishing a censorship of publications board consisting of five members appointed by the Minister for Justice for five years; part three stated that it was unlawful to print 'any indecent matter the publication of which would be calculated to injure public morals, or any indecent medical, surgical or physiological details the publication of which would be calculated to injure public morals'; the final part made it unlawful to print, publish, sell or distribute any publication which advocated 'or might reasonably be supposed to advocate the unnatural prevention of conception or miscarriage or any method, treatment, or appliance to be used for such prevention or procurement'.[279]

Even before the passing of the Censorship Act, those who sought to surreptitiously sell birth control literature were leaving themselves open to the possibility of prosecution under existing law. A bookseller at 59 Upper Stephen Street in Dublin city, for instance, was indicted for having Margaret Sanger's booklet for sale on 14 February (!) 1928. He had, apparently, 'sold and uttered and published an obscene libel in the form of a booklet entitled *Family Limitation*'; it was also noted that the book's publisher had been prosecuted in Britain for selling the same book by 'the late government', but that since then, 'largely as a consequence', public opinion had changed. By the late 1920s, the women's conference of the British Labour Party was practically unanimous in favouring birth control for working-class mothers and the Ministry of Health had confirmed it was legal to disseminate information on it. No such liberalism was to prevail in Dublin; Sanger's booklet included advertisements for 'cheap, racy and passionate novels to suit young and old' and prophylaxis – 'prevention is better than cure: rubber goods to suit all'. A woman, acting under the instruction of the Garda metro division, had entered the shop and asked for the 10d. booklet. 'He had it on top of the counter but some other books were on top of it ... It wasn't exposed.' She added, under cross-examination, 'I haven't read the book.' The defendant pleaded guilty, 'acknowledged himself to be bound to the state for the sum of £50' and was ordered to pay £30 towards the cost of prosecution.[280]

'The requirement to set off and cancel obscenities and indecencies by calculation of literary excellence'

The advocates of greater censorship were persistent in their insistence that not enough was being done, and after the passing of the act they continued to lobby the government for amendments. The Catholic Truth Society (CTS) was particularly active in this regard, insisting in 1938, for example, that the censorship board should contain thirty members instead of five. The Department of Justice rejected the idea that censorship was not severe enough, noting that the representations from the CTS were based on 'the assumption that the Censorship Act has failed. With this the minister does not agree. The Censorship of Publications Board has functioned only since February 1930 and already 1,048 books and 20 periodicals publications have been permanently prohibited.' Most of the books were detected by the staff of the board, obtained from the Library of *The Times* or submitted by the customs authorities. Significantly, it was observed that 'only a fraction of the number of books examined by the board are sent in by members of the public' – a reminder that such Catholic activists were not as representative of public opinion as they liked to believe.

The Department of Justice also got to the heart of what these groups wanted by rejecting the idea that 'it should be made possible to prohibit a book for being indecent merely and not necessarily in its "general tendency" indecent as is prescribed in the act'.[281] The board felt undervalued, with an insufficient budget (its allocation for the purchase of 'suspected books' was £15 per annum), and complained that as a statutory body it did not receive enough attention or get invited to enough official events.

The idea of ignoring consideration of the 'general tendency' of publications was also a viewpoint the censorship board came around to, on the grounds, as they put it in 1940, that it is 'utterly wrong in principle in as much as it postulates the supremacy of the aesthetic over the ethical'. The minister rejected its arguments, as he did the unintentionally hilarious contention of the board that 'the requirement to set off and cancel obscenities and indecencies by calculation of literary excellence is one that cannot possibly be complied with in the absence of any book of mathematical tables stating how much of moral viciousness is to be cancelled by so much of artistic excellence'.[282]

Another frequent complaint from the censorship crusaders was that not enough was being done to prevent the publicising of information on contraception. Greta Jones points out that an advertisement appeared in the *Dublin Evening Mail* in October 1920 offering 'rubber goods, sprays, douches and enemas', together with a pamphlet detailing their use entitled 'The Manual of Wisdom'. Even after the Censorship Act of 1929 such advertisements still reached Irish men and women in some British newspapers distributed in Ireland.[283]

Of course there were women who could not have children, due to either their own medical problems or to their husbands', though the issue of male infertility was an absolute taboo. Women in rural areas, including those in arranged marriages, were prized above all else for their suitability to do hard work and their fertility, and when the problem was one of male infertility, women had a difficult task to cast off the assumption that it was somehow their fault. One woman in this situation who was on the receiving end of a lot of grief from her mother-in-law came up with her own effective solution: '... she got the doctor to write out a few lines to explain that it was the husband that was at fault. So she gave that to the old woman and that sorted that one, that finished that.'[284]

'All appliances and substances for contraception are to be definitely prohibited and no exceptions whatsoever are to be made'

It is also worth placing the ban on the importation and sale of contraceptives provided for by the 1935 Criminal Law Amendment Act (CLAA) in a broader international context. Discussion about birth control and the use of the term 'race suicide' in Ireland was a reflection of a European pro-natalist discourse. Although there was little discussion of eugenics (something that shaped the fascist demographic campaign) in Ireland, it was asserted that Ireland was going to learn from the mistakes of other European countries. In 1929, the Minister for Justice, Fitzgerald Kenney, lamented 'the decay of one of the greatest nations in the world. France cannot keep up its population ... That is an evil we are not going to have in this country.'[285]

In Italy, according to a 1928 census, over 14 per cent of families were described as 'large' (that is, containing at least 7 children); middle-class couples had an average of 3 children, while agricultural labouring couples had an average of 6.5. The practice of birth control was much more common in the more industrialised north; in the south, particularly under the archaic *Mezzadria* system of share-cropping, the family economy depended on the exploitation of female and child labour and there was less incentive to limit family size. In 1927, Mussolini launched his pro-natalist campaign, announcing that he 'wished above all else to correct these evolutionary errors which had made Italians such a dying and degenerate race' and insisting that it was 'absurd' to think a decreasing birth rate would improve the living standards of the Italian people. His declarations fell on deaf ears. Italian natality continued to decline until after the Second World War, though with 95.35 annual births for every 1000 women of child-bearing age in 1931, the Italian fertility rate was still very high compared to France (67.37 in 1930) and Britain, which had the lowest level of fertility of any western European nation at 56.43.[286]

There was ambivalence about debating the issue of contraception in Italy, and its birth control movement has been described as 'moderate'. Under the fascist regime, much of the support for larger families was cosmetic; 'great shows of public support' such as *Giornata della Madre e del Fanciullo* (Mother's and Child's Day), inaugurated in 1932 as a national holiday to be celebrated on 24 December, were preferred to more costly forms of social welfare.

Nor was the Irish interrelation of religion and politics unique. In the Netherlands, for example, both Catholic and Orthodox Calvinist groups wielded significant political power. The close connection between religious ideology and socio-political organisations, combined with the efforts of doctors, psychologists and educationalists, meant that control of sexuality 'through intervention in the nuclear family ... was considered crucial'. In particular, the confessional succeeded in imposing its moral ideology on the Catholic population, as evidenced by 'the exceptional demographic pattern of Dutch society from the late nineteenth century until 1965' – the decline in the Dutch birth rate was more gradual than elsewhere.[287] In France, the left-wing governments of the Popular Front attempted to stamp out the French neo-Malthusian birth control movement. In Germany and Austria, war and inflation intensified socioeconomic pressures to control fertility, which led to a belief that large numbers of children was synonymous with 'unmodern behaviour'; in the 1920s there was more marketing and advertising with regard to contraceptives.[288]

Many of these efforts were parcelled under the label 'moral hygiene', which involved defining 'normal' and 'deviant' sexual behaviour and 'frenzied attempts by the state to restrict the boundaries of sexuality'.[289] But there was ambivalence also about defining some of these boundaries, and in this sense Catholic Ireland may have been different from Catholic Italy. It was common for fascist penal codes to institute harsh penalties for abortion and infanticide, but in Italy child abuse was not recognised legally in the way that it was in Ireland. A charge of 'indecent behaviour' was often a cover in Italy for child abuse, 'but the accused seldom faced trial' in order for scandal to be avoided, or else legal technicalities were employed to avoid confronting the issue – acts of child abuse committed in private not being deemed 'impermissible' public offences.[290]

But the general European preoccupation with contraception was particularly strong in Ireland. The Criminal Law Amendment Act has often been described as an illustration of a repressive Catholic state, but significantly the initial legislative proposals concerning the prohibition of contraception did not contain the blanket ban that transpired. The committee examining this and other related issues in the aftermath of the Carrigan Committee Report was chaired by Fianna Fáil minister James Geoghegan (he was replaced as minister by P. J. Ruttledge in 1933, but remained chair of the committee), who felt a blanket ban would be 'unduly severe on persons who did not regard the use of such appliances as improper and who were advised by their doctors to employ them'. Geoghegan doubted whether it was wise to 'prohibit completely the importation and sale of such appliances', and there was a proposal that qualified medical practitioners should have the power to supply such appliances to their patients, imported under a licence granted by the Minister for Local Government and Public Health.

The minister with that responsibility, Seán T. O'Kelly, objected and, after he exerted pressure at cabinet level, Geoghegan was informed on St Valentine's Day 1934 that 'all appliances and substances for contraception are to be definitely prohibited and no exceptions whatsoever are to be made'. A year later that was the law, despite disagreements amongst the Geoghegan committee and the efforts of a minority of politicians, including Fianna Fáil's Senator Kathleen Clarke, who wanted something less drastic. Dublin TD Robert Rowlette argued that it should be left to a woman's own conscience, that 'it is questionable whether it is either feasible or just to try to enforce moral principles by statute', and that it would be likely to lead to an increase in criminal abortion and infanticide.[291]

'There are now four houses engaged in openly selling contraceptives'

Undoubtedly, some people did manage to get access to contraception. Tom Garvin observes that 'occasionally there were murmurings as to how it was that middle-class relatively well off people seemed to have relatively small families. They seemed to know something that the rest of us didn't.'[292] Others alluded to this during the 1930s and after. Father Richard Devane, in a letter to the Minister for Justice P. J. Ruttledge in 1933, insisted that in Dublin 'there are now four houses engaged in openly selling contraceptives – 3 in Fownes Street alone ... up to a few years ago there was only one shop dealing in these "goods". Several chemists – I am informed – have also engaged more or less furtively in this vile traffic.'[293] Ruttledge also sought information from the customs authorities, but the revenue commissioners struggled with his queries, because 'many of the articles in question are not included as such nor described as such in official customs documents'. The difficulty, it seems, was whether or not to classify contraceptives as 'drugs' or 'appliances'.[294]

When there was debate about repealing the CLAA in the late 1960s and early 1970s, some more information emerged about the clandestine selling of contraceptives in earlier decades. In June 1972 Taoiseach Jack Lynch asked his secretary to seek advice from the Attorney General after he received a letter from a man from Drimnagh, Dublin, who said he had been supplying contraceptives since 1929 ('this information is vital at the present moment, as the Hierarchy or the law have not got it').[295] The man followed up his letter in August with more details:

> In 1928 or '29 I became an assembler with a man by the name of T. Far-quaharson in the Sundries Dept. He and myself had sole charge of a press with a Yale lock. Nobody, not even the manager or director, had entry to this press. The reason: it was stocked with cigarettes, confections and razors and blades, also carried a stock consisting of 2 gross rubber pre-ventives ... we supplied I'd say about four or five Chemists occasionally in the city. Names I remember Blakes, Fownes Street and Liffey Street, Roseanthal Merrion Row, Hamilton Long, O'Connell St, Prices Clare St. The quantity: about 1 dozen.

He recalled that one-third of staff members was Protestant, and of those

> no one availed of contraceptives, with the exception of one Protestant occasionally. We would usually cover this up by putting through an order for a sponge ... on this subject I had a disgusting experience one Easter Sunday morning. I was proceeding to the John Redmond Society which was licensed for drink about 11.30 a.m., year 1948. Lo and behold two little girls about five or six and dressed beautifully, one of them picked one of those foul things off the ground fully loaded and blew it out for a balloon. I froze to ground and could not get near her.[296]

Following his initial correspondence, the Attorney General had decided 'nothing which Mr Adams might have to contribute would be of interest to the AG'.[297]

Some who were prosecuted under the CLAA were dealt with severely. Greta Jones observes that such prosecutions reveal a trade in contraceptives: the *Birth Control News* (which Marie Stopes began publishing in 1922 and which was written and edited almost entirely by Stopes herself) in 1936 reported on such prosecutions, including cases where fines of £250 were imposed along with six months' imprisonment with hard labour. There were also some cases of seizures at the ports, in which the chemists in their defence produced prescriptions from medical doctors. In 1937 John Busteed, Professor of Economics at University College Cork, told an academic audience in Dublin that 'it is a fact that during the past 2 years a remarkable distribution of the literature and knowledge of the subject ... has been quietly proceeding among the Irish middle classes'. His suggestion that this was exclusively through methods approved by the Catholic Church[298] seems far-fetched, although there were some who went over the border to Belfast to source contraceptives.

The lack of contraception undoubtedly led to the birth of more illegitimate children, but it would be a mistake to see this as the only factor. Had contraception been more readily available it would still have been the preserve of the more well off. In any case, there was the other issue of lack of sex education, and ignorance in this regard was not necessarily confined to the poor and uneducated. Seán O'Faoláin was twenty years old and midway through his studies at University College, Cork before he learned how childbirth happened, later bemoaning the fact that pious elders 'sent us naked to the wolf of life. I think chiefly it was over-protectiveness; as if they believed that if nobody mentioned sex organs we would not notice that we had them.'[299]

'His doctor attributed the man's mental breakdown to coitus interruptus'

In the UK, the first family planning clinic was opened in London in 1921. In 1933 during a House of Lords debate, Lord Dawson of Penn urged the responsible sale, display and advertising of contraceptives, and in 1934 Marie Stopes visited Belfast, after which a clinic organised by volunteers was started at Mountpottinger, Belfast, but which languished and closed down in 1947. In 1940 a clinic was established at the Royal Maternity hospital, which initially struggled but did survive.[300] There was no attempt to ban birth control in Northern Ireland during this period, though there was strong disapproval.

The opening in 1936 of the Mother's Clinic in Belfast, funded by the Marie Stopes Society for Constructive Birth Control, was prompted by the introduction of the CLAA in the south. Its establishment was made easier by the Anglican Lambeth Conference of 1930, which gave recognition to birth control under certain strict conditions.[301] There was also a belief in some quarters that, as well as facilitating those of the middle classes whose consciences allowed for the use of contraceptives, it could be used to alleviate the poverty of the working classes; indeed, Stopes aimed her clinics at poorer women, believing the middle classes would make private provision. (The Northern Ireland government had previously rejected all approaches to establish such clinics as was permitted under a British Ministry for Health directive in 1930, under which local authorities could establish clinics to provide birth control if there was a risk to the health of the mother.)

Clinic patients in the 1930s referred to homemade remedies such as sponges, condoms, *coitus interruptus* and abortion, and from her research of the surviving case notes (not all survived), Greta Jones suggests that 'it is clear that many women knew of, or practised, some form of fertility control prior to attending the Mother's Clinic'. The resident nurse, Catherine Armstrong, wrote to Stopes in 1940, 'You will see we had 3 pregnant mothers on Wednesday. They had all noticed our advertisement and came hoping to terminate an unwanted pregnancy, not understanding our work.'[302] Stopes ruled the clinics 'with a rod of iron', insisting that they were staffed by married women. In the absence of political support, the female doctors who travelled to London to be trained by Stopes were crucial.[303] The Catholic Church denounced the clinic, but Stopes was pleased it had a few Catholic patients. It was also clear from the cases the clinic dealt with that the issue of birth control placed considerable strain on marriages, with rows over abstinence, *coitus interruptus* and condoms. Visits were usually at the initiative of the woman, but 'in one case a woman was referred by her husband because his doctor attributed the man's mental breakdown to *coitus interruptus*'.[304]

Another factor relevant to this debate was the high level of maternal mortality in Belfast, which the chief medical superintendent had highlighted in 1935. At that time, infant mortality was also noted as 'appallingly high', at a rate of 101 per 1,000 births, compared to 66 for London. In 1930,

Northern Ireland also, at 140 per 1,000 births, had a higher death rate for illegitimate children than England and Wales (105), but only half that of the Free State (251).[305] Maternal mortality was attributed to poor nutrition, the high birth rate and the presence of unqualified midwives, which had been a concern for many years – in Belfast in 1901 a woman who attended mothers during childbirth went on trial for the killing of a woman who had given birth to twins, one of which had died, at Ravenhill Road in Belfast; it was stated that the woman was 'not a trained and certified midwife'.[306]

The Belfast medical superintendent also mentioned that one of the causes of maternal mortality was abortion; nine such deaths were recorded in his 1935 report.[307] These women may have tried their own methods to prevent a successful pregnancy. But women sought abortions for various reasons. The stigma of illegitimacy was perhaps the most common, but it was also an option explored by married women.

The playwright Seán O'Casey married the actress Eileen Reynolds in Chelsea in September 1927 and they spent their honeymoon in Dublin. 'Eileen was miserable at first, being unhappily pregnant and taking "all and sundry to get rid of it".' However, a gynaecologist recommended by a friend of Seán's 'persuaded her to keep the baby'.[308] Back in London, Eileen continued to work as an actress after the birth of their son, Breon, despite O'Casey's wish that she play the conventional role of housewife. Her absences made him long for her sexually, 'with a fervency which lights up the page' of his correspondence with her. But she commenced an affair which resulted in pregnancy, 'and the standard remedies having failed she was forced to tell Seán', who forgave her ('mostly it's my fault') and helped to secure a Harley Street specialist to perform an abortion. But tensions continued due to her involvement in the London theatre scene and, although they resolved their differences, her fear of pregnancy as a threat to her career remained a dilemma for them.[309]

Rita North, a 21-year-old dancer and girlfriend of the Irish writer and politician Darell Figgis, died of peritonitis in London in 1925 as a result of an infection following an attempt to self-abort in Dublin by injecting glycerine into her womb.[310] It was the second tragedy to affect Figgis; the previous year his wife Millie had shot herself with a revolver in the Dublin mountains, having never recovered from the injuries she suffered during an attack on them by Irish republicans at the outset of the civil war. When one of the doctors who had treated North informed Figgis about what she had done in order to cause a miscarriage (he was aware of the pregnancy) he 'looked very astonished, but said nothing and went away very excited'. Figgis said he had told North that he thought the right thing to do would be 'to marry at once', but his suggestion that they write to North's family to explain the situation 'terrified her'. Eight days after she died, Figgis committed suicide by filling his hotel room with gas.[311]

A few years later, in September 1929, an Irish emigrant from County Wexford who had been living in London for five years was found dead on the pavement outside 16 King's Place as a result of an abortion.[312] However, abortions were also being performed clandestinely in the Free State and Northern Ireland. In 1929, amidst concern about increased infanticide rates, the Catholic Bishop of Ossory referred to abortion in his Lenten Pastoral. The bishops were concerned that non-Catholic doctors might perform abortions and also about the issue of emergency abortions to save the lives of the mothers. In 1931 the Archbishop of Dublin, Edward Byrne, rejected the candidacy of Andrew Hone, a Catholic, for the mastership of Holles Street maternity hospital on the grounds that to accept a candidate trained at Trinity College would 'nullify my own Episcopal monition'.[313]

Mamie Cadden, who because of a high-profile court case in 1956 became the most notorious Irish abortionist (see chapter 3), was a native of Mayo who saw no future for herself in the family shop and so trained as a midwife, qualifying in 1926. She established a nursing home in Rathmines in Dublin and carried on her business there until 1939, when she was disqualified as a midwife after being convicted of abandoning an infant when one of her patients' babies was dumped at the side of the road in Dunshaughlin, County Meath.

After serving a year in Mountjoy jail for that crime, she again set up business, this time providing treatment for dandruff, constipation and skin problems, but also performing abortions.[314] A recent biography of Cadden by Ray Kavanagh portrays her as a liberated feminist, an exposer of hypocrisy, one who fought against a conspiracy to deny the fact that there were many Irish women who wanted abortions, a martyr who was ultimately consumed by the suffocating alliance of Church and state. Kavanagh further emphasised how professionally competent she was, having trained as a midwife; how sexy she was, with her blonde hair, fashionable clothes, insistence on lying about her age and, most importantly, her open-top MG sports car – such an unusual sight in Dublin in the 1930s.[315] But the truth was that Cadden was an incompetent abortionist whose botched operations led to the death of at least two pregnant women and caused physical pain for others.

The records of abortion cases that came before the courts often contain detailed information about the private lives of unmarried couples, including the roles played by men, who frequently encouraged the women to self-abort or bought them abortifacient drugs, and sometimes accompanied them to the abortionist, but whose involvement tends to be overlooked. Medical evidence at trials emphasised the mental disturbance caused to single girls who got pregnant; in the words of Dr Paul Carlton in 1931, such women 'go mad when they are pregnant' and are inclined to 'do anything'. The women who had undergone illegal abortions were often the main witnesses for the state and so were subject to lengthy questioning in court and were likely to be subjected to character assassination by the lawyers defending those charged with performing the operations.[316] One 1931 case revealed that a married man in Dublin had pressurised his pregnant mistress into having 'a second operation performed' after she became pregnant for a second time, but she refused to consent.[317] As noted by Cliona Rattigan, judges in these cases were scrupulous in reminding juries that they were required to separate legal fact from morality, and that the court in which an abortion case was heard was not a court of morals, though in his summing-up in a case in 1945, Judge McCarthy added, 'perhaps one often wishes that it were.'[318]

'Has had six pregnancies and so far nothing to show for it'

Bethel Solomons, a distinguished gynaecologist, who was master of the Rotunda hospital from 1926 to 1933, invited his close friend Signe Toksvig to watch him perform a caesarean section operation in 1932 on one of her many visits to the hospital (much of what she observed was incorporated into her 1937 book *Eve's Doctor*). He told the students attending that the woman he was operating on 'has had six pregnancies and so far nothing to show for it', mentioning that she had had three abortions and two caesarean sections after which her babies had not survived.[319] On another occasion he wrote case notes on a woman of 25 who, having attempted her own abortion, 'was admitted with a history of vomiting and of having taken a large quantity of abortifacients', but did not respond to treatment. Solomons admitted to 'warped judgement' in relation to this case. He also believed that women with heart disease 'should not marry, and if they do, they should not become pregnant or they will surely die'. These instances have been cited as proof of the conservative ethos of the medical profession, Jo Murphy Lawless claiming that the profession, 'unable to confront the image of unregulated female sexuality, was many years coming to terms with women's active practices compared with the passive formula of abstention and denial Solomons recommended'.[320]

That may be true, but at least Solomons acknowledged the connection between risk of illness and death through pregnancy. Halliday Sutherland, who practised as an obstetrician in the same hospital, argued in his 1922 book *Birth Control: A Statement of Christian Doctrine against the Neo-Malthusians* that the high birth rates in Ireland were evidence that 'in this matter at least the poorest Irish peasants are richer than the peasants of England' and that the neo-Malthusian argument for the prevention of expanding populations could be rejected. [321]

But Solomons was no conservative, nor was he seen as such by his contemporaries; indeed, Francis Hackett described him in his diary as 'a romantic, in some ways tender-minded and in some ways tender-skinned, Irish-Jewish man with a first-rate brain ... a combination of energy, social instinct and hard sense ... this isn't the usual Dublin ½ acre, with a picket fence of Catholicism around it. He thinks freely'.[322]

He also had a somewhat tortured love life and conducted an affair about which he regularly complained to Toksvig ('Quivering to be rid of her. Told me she forced herself on him'), who admired his healing and communication skills but frequently grew irritated by his 'ghastly puns, limericks and sex jokes ... he would whisper things like "that man who just came in is a virgin"'.[323] Solomons also complained of the rows with 'his lesbian matron' in the Rotunda, who, he maintained, had tried to go over his head about postgraduate courses for nurses: 'she has that clergyman's daughter mixture of sanctimoniousness and vice'.[324]

Solomon's wife Gertrude wondered if her husband's affair 'had been due to her own lack of interest in sex experience – "don't care if I have any" – and I think she hit on the right clue'.[325] Toksvig spent an extraordinary amount of time with the Solomons; indeed, she seems to have developed a certain erotic preoccupation with them and their son. She expressed her love for Gertrude and admired Beth's 'Greek' body at a bathing party ('odd how very natural partial nakedness seems').[326] Undoubtedly she found their company a pleasant and liberating antidote to that of all those she perceived as repressed Catholics. This was happening in the summer of 1932, at the time of the Eucharistic Congress, an event intended to deepen spiritual awareness through a greater understanding of the Eucharist. Organised to celebrate the fifteen-hundredth anniversary of the arrival of St Patrick to Ireland, the congress was an emphatic public assertion of Irish Catholicism. Regarded as an organisational triumph, the crowds assembled were vaster than for any gathering in the country until the visit of Pope John Paul II in 1979.

The ceremonies in 1932 included a procession from the Phoenix Park to O'Connell Street Bridge for the Solemn Benediction. Contemporary radio broadcasts mention that the procession included 20,000 priests, while the *Irish News,* the Catholic daily newspaper of Northern Ireland, refers to the congress as demonstrating 'the triumph of Catholic Ireland over 750 years of persecution such as even the early Romans or the Jews had not endured'.[327] The congress seemed to indicate that Ireland was a Catholic state for a Catholic people and undoubtedly contributed to a more pronounced sense of exclusion for non-Catholics. But it may also have stirred the passions of some Irish Catholics in ways that could not be repeated. When the fledgling current affairs magazine *Magill* conducted a survey of changing Irish sexual habits in 1978, it was told that a prominent Dublin publican who was asked when he had last had sexual relations with his wife paused and replied, 'I think it was the time of the Eucharistic Congress.'[328]

'It'll have what's far better. It'll have two mothers'

Although in the event of an unplanned pregnancy, marriage was regarded as the ideal solution, this was not always in the best interests of all those concerned, as the work of playwright Seán O'Casey would suggest. In *Juno and the Paycock* (1924), which follows the lives of the Boyle family who live in a Dublin tenement, the young Mary Boyle is impregnated by a schoolmaster and disowned by her long-standing boyfriend. This is followed by what she perceives as the cruellest blow of all: rejection by her father: 'my poor little child that'll have no father', to which her mother's response is: 'It'll have what's far better. It'll have two mothers.' According to Declan Kiberd, this was 'O'Casey's epitaph on the Irish male'.[329] O'Casey also had time to reflect on the difference between the two sexes when writing a short story in 1933, 'I Wanna Woman', which 'has a Joycean quality, inasmuch as it records a stream of consciousness much occupied with sexual appetite'. It was written for *Time And Tide* magazine and the editor wanted to publish it as a special supplement, but the printers refused to touch it. It tells the story of Jack, who fails to seduce the woman of his desire and picks up a fashionable

prostitute to whom he pays an extravagant fee. After waking up 'in the horrors of spiritual nausea', he leaves behind the expensive bracelet with which
he had earlier planned to seduce his lady friend, but cannot face her. It is
'essentially a moral tale in which the sadistic, misogynistic male is taught a
lesson'.

According to Christopher Murray, the 'sex in the head' of which he is
a walking emblem renders Jack ridiculous, whereas the prostitute emerges
as lively, natural and sensual. Years later, in 1952, O'Casey was to recast the
story as a highly regarded one-act play, *Bedtime Story*, in which the woman's
role eclipses the man's to the point of absurdity. But what 'I Wanna Woman'
reveals is O'Casey's expansion of the positive view of women: 'O'Casey was
gradually developing a characterisation of women beyond the stereotypical mother/nurturer and towards the liberated sexual superior of the over-
intellectualised (and perhaps hypocritical) male. He was simultaneously
dramatising his sexual desire for Eileen.'[330]

'Excommunicates the woman guilty of the crime'

Such dramatic liberation was far removed from the reality of the experiences
of Irish women deemed to have sexually transgressed. The development of
medical history has served to shine a light on the practice of the committal
of women to lunatic asylums and the extent to which their committal had
to do with sexual transgression. In truth, evidence of female 'madness' was
often scant; asylums sometimes served as another way of silencing and hiding women who did not conform, particularly when it came to sexuality.
Some were committed after they had been cast out by their families due
to illegitimate pregnancies. Between 1916 and 1925, 56 per cent of female
admissions to the Enniscorthy lunatic asylum in Wexford were single, and
'almost half the women in Enniscorthy whose admission forms or case
records make reference to childbirth or miscarriage were single'. By locking
them up their threat to the ideology of femininity was neutralised.[331] The
traditional rural 'match', or arranged marriage, is also deemed to have driven
some women mad, while others were suffering from physical ailments often
associated with menstruation and miscarriage.[332]

Other obvious places to send the mothers of illegitimate children were
the mother and baby homes, it having been recognised that 'unmarried
mothers should not remain for long in the county homes if their admission

cannot be obviated altogether by sending them direct to homes of a suitable type'.[333] In the view of the Department of Local Government and Public Health, 'special institutions are necessary where by appropriate training and example, self-respect is restored'. The approach to these women confirmed the veracity of an observation made by a Catholic priest in the United States who wrote a book in 1922 called *The Women of the Gael*, which is quoted by James Smith: 'In Ireland whenever a child is born out of wedlock, so shocked is the public sense by the very unusual occurrence, that it brands with an irreparable stigma, and, to a large extent, excommunicates the woman guilty of the crime.'[334]

Also worrying were the number of women who were dying in childbirth; the maternal mortality figures in the Free State (as well as in Northern Ireland, as noted earlier) gave cause for concern repeatedly in the 1920s and, although there was some improvement by the 1930s, it was scarcely dramatic. The statistical abstract of 1931–2 reveals that the numbers of deaths of women directly attributable to or associated with pregnancy or childbirth were 330 in 1924 and 294 in 1930, or 5.21 per 1,000 births in 1924 and 5.04 in 1930.[335] The maternal mortality per 100 births had averaged 4.88 from 1919 to 1928, and in 1929 was 4.10, but there were worrying regional variations. There were, for instance, 'appalling mortality' rates recorded in the rural districts in Laois (7.78), Kilkenny (6.89) and Leitrim (7.12), due to 'delay in appointing county medical officers of health'.[336]

These figures were also of relevance to the practice of midwifery. The Midwives (Ireland) Act of 1918 imposed on county councils the duty of supervising midwives practising in their areas. Evidence given to the committee on the relief of unemployment in 1927 and 1928 made it clear that 'the mortality among women from puerperal septic diseases and accidents of pregnancy or childbirth is disproportionately high'. E. P. McCarron, secretary to the Department of Local Government and Public Health, gave evidence of primitive sanitary conditions in many places, and the deficiency of water and sewerage services, not helped by the fact that nearly a quarter of the total population of Dublin city (78,934 people) were living in one-roomed tenements. One example quotes queues outside one toilet that catered for between 50 and 60 people as 'an intolerable state of affairs'.[337]

In the Department of Local Government and Public Health reports for the same year, 'attention was called to the high mortality connected with childbirth in County Kerry', with the suggestion that a medical officer for the control of midwives was needed. Department of Local Government and

Public Health files for the Free State also refer to the problem of unqualified midwives; the Kilkenny Board of Health, for example, in 1936 wrote of 'two handywomen [who] ... take on themselves the duties of midwives though not qualified or registered to do so'. It was difficult to police such a practice, despite the Notification of Births Act, which allowed for the prosecution of unregistered midwives. One of the women 'despite an undertaking which she had given not to take on any more cases ... still practises midwifery'. Legal proceedings were initiated, but what were needed were 'the names of persons who could prove that the midwife in question acted as such'. The County Medical Officer stated that 'both these women practise midwifery "ad lib" and quite "openly"'.[338]

Debates about the quality of medical care for women and children were often superseded by a preoccupation with religious control of the hospitals, as is clear from correspondence in the archive of John Charles McQuaid, who at that stage was headmaster of the boys' school Blackrock College. A file on medical matters from 1933 to 1934 refers to the management committee of the National Children's Hospital in Harcourt Street and other hospitals with a capital 'P' placed beside the names of all Protestants. It also included the annual report of the Women's National Health Association of Ireland, a group concerned with the sort of issues raised above, and therefore deemed suspicious by McQuaid.

It was observed that in relation to birth control 'medical psychology in the hands of non-Catholic practitioners presents very real dangers which have been, on the whole, unfortunately overlooked'.[339] McQuaid received reports from a nurse at the children's hospital which included complaints about the attitude of paediatrician Dr Robert Collis and an account of a Sister Pollard, who 'said she objected to the children being mixed on moral grounds – to which Dr Collis said that there was no such thing as immorality among children up to puberty'. The following year, Dr Lea Wilson, a medical practitioner at Harcourt Street, plaintively asked, 'Do we need any more proof of proselytism?' The message was clear; in their view there was a need for an exclusively Roman Catholic children's hospital.[340]

Such tensions were also a result of the desire of Kathleen Lynn, a Protestant political activist and doctor who was the highest ranking female officer during the 1916 Rising and who had established St Ultan's children's hospital in Dublin in 1919, for her hospital to amalgamate with the Harcourt Street hospital. As neither hospital was under Catholic management, the proposed merger 'aroused accusations of sterilisation and sex education'.[341]

The Archbishop of Dublin, Edward Byrne, was opposed on the grounds that children 'would not be safe' from the dangers of 'naturalistic and wrong teachings on sex instruction or adolescent problems'. It was also contended that 'contraceptive practices are recommended by many non-Catholic doctors', to which Lynn responded that she believed birth control was 'immoral'.[342] The proposed merger never materialised; a large Catholic children's hospital was eventually opened in Crumlin in Dublin a year after Lynn's death, in 1955.

'A flood of imported Anglo-Saxon vulgarity'

From the 1920s onwards, libraries were obvious targets in the battle to prevent people from reading about sex or instructing themselves on the facts of life. The first public library legislation in Ireland dated from 1853; a public libraries act was introduced in 1855 and amended in 1902 to extend provision to rural areas. The charitable foundation the Carnegie United Kingdom Trust, whose initial work involved the building of libraries in the UK and Ireland, was formed in 1913, while an act of 1925 established county councils as the library authorities. The writer Hubert Butler published an essay in 1949 on sex, religion and censorship in the context of the county libraries. Twenty years previously he had worked as a county librarian in Coleraine, Northern Ireland, where county library committee members paid occasional visits of inspection, not to read, but to supervise the reading of others. Butler observed that 'in the North at that time, the most censorious in regard to morals as well as politics in literature were Presbyterians'.[343]

He recalled the controversy in 1924, also recorded in the diaries of Lady Gregory, when Lennox Robinson published a short story entitled the 'Madonna of Slieve Dun' in *Tomorrow*, a new periodical edited by Francis Stuart. It was a story about a peasant girl who had been raped and thought she would give birth to another saviour. A shocked Father Thomas Finlay (Professor of Political Economy at University College Dublin) sent his resignation to the advisory committee of the Council of the County Libraries, while William Cosgrave, then President of the Executive Council (prime minister) even thought of suppressing *Tomorrow*, 'because the rumour went about that Robinson was trying to pervert the nation to a new conception of the origins of Christianity'.[344] It also offended the Provost of Trinity College, as did another story, 'Colour' ('One must speak plainly – it is about the intercourse of white women with black men'). The writer George Russell was also deeply offended; at a meeting of the Carnegie Trust only Thomas O'Donnell, an Irish-speaking Catholic from Kerry, defended the story.

Father Finlay sent a letter of resignation, as did the Provost, who felt that if a Catholic clergyman had resigned, 'he must go with him and see eye to eye with him'. Cosgrave wanted to have Robinson prosecuted, but Minister for Home Affairs (later Justice) Kevin O'Higgins refused, maintaining that such a prosecution 'would merely represent the moral attitude of certain people, at a certain place and a certain time'[345] – a further reminder that those in charge of the Department of Justice in the 1920s and 1930s were not hidebound reactionaries. Notwithstanding, the advisory committee was suspended and Lennox Robinson dismissed; the central committee in Dublin was abolished and the headquarters of the Irish County Libraries was transferred to Dunfermline. As Butler angrily recalled: 'That was the last meeting of the Committee. By their disputes about sex and their competitive pieties and other irrelevant arguments, they abolished themselves and destroyed the bright hopes of the libraries.'[346]

In Butler's view, the fading of those hopes led to a preponderance of English literary trash on Irish library shelves – 'a flood of imported Anglo-Saxon vulgarity' – to the detriment of Irish texts, and lack of support for serious Irish writers. Instead, public money was being spent on 'drivelling English fiction' as evidenced by the library catalogue of 1936 which included the statistics of books issued in an average year and which reflected the popularity of penny dreadfuls by the likes of Charlotte M. Brame and Effie A. Rowlands: 'These write about the sins of English Peeresses. For example, to quote 4 consecutive entries from the catalogue, we have *Lady Brazil's Ordeal, Lady Damer's Secret, Lady Ethel's Whim, Lady Evelyn's Folly*.'[347]

'Naked to the wolf of life'

The writer Frank O'Connor, who joined the library service in 1923, working as a librarian in Cork until 1928, and then spent ten years working in a library in Ballsbridge in Dublin, also recalled the controversy over Lennox Robinson's alleged blaspheming, suggesting it added to the problem of getting local sanction to establish libraries, as some of the priests would not allow libraries at all in their parishes. As the parish priest in Rathdrum put it, 'It was all very well for sophisticated people like ourselves to read the works of dear George [Moore] but could we really thrust them into the hands of simple Irish townsmen?'[348] Frank O'Connor's considerable charm, however, and his ability to speak Irish, won the day, and permission was given for a library, but only on condition that the curate 'satisfied himself of the innocuousness of the books we sent out'.

Some librarians endured years of frustration, exacerbated by the government's refusal in 1937 to accede to a request for a commission of inquiry into library services.[349] Frank O'Connor evolved into a writer of distinction and was determined to confront the fact that young lovers were scared, frustrated and troubled by their desires, and their relationship with their mothers in particular. He summed up the dilemma of young men and women struggling with their sexuality by describing them as being sent 'naked to the wolf of life' (a phrase also used by Seán O'Faoláin). He, too, was a relatively late starter when it came to women and did not have any relationships until he was in his thirties.[350] He addresses these issues in his 1932 novel *The Saint and Mary Kate*, in which the 'innocents' are constantly facing 'thunderings' against sex. In the novel, 15-year-old Mary Kate McCormick is going out with Phil Drinan, eight months her senior, who is obsessive about piety (and his mother – 'I'll never marry a woman that isn't like my own mother'), and preoccupied with 'the terrifying moment of the judging seat'. Mary, by contrast, wants love, 'a love that was natural and free and easy and unencumbered by the obsessive fealty to penitential excesses'. Ultimately, she makes 'the most dramatic advance of her life by announcing that she thought a lot of talk was made about nothing, and, personally, if he, for instance, wanted to kiss her she wouldn't mind'.[351] He rejects her.

Temptation was undoubtedly troubling for many, and even if they did let their imaginations and desires take flight, fear often brought them back to reality. In his poem 'The Straying Student', part of his 1938 collection *Night and Morning*, Austin Clarke, who attempted to respond openly to the challenge of sexuality, the conflict between body and soul and the perceived sinfulness of illicit sex, and to what in *Pilgrimage* (1929) he regarded as the fear of women, describes an encounter with a visionary woman with 'strong limbs':

> Long had she lived in Rome when Popes were bad
> The wealth of every age she makes her own
> Yet smiled on me in eager admiration
> And for a summer taught me all I know

Banishing shame with her great laugh that rang
As if a pillar caught it back alone.

But this is a student at Mass, and ultimately the pressures of religious and social orthodoxy begin to impinge on his thoughts:

And yet I tremble lest she may deceive me
And leave me in this land, where every woman's son
Must carry his own coffin and believe
In dread, all that the clergy teach the young.[352]

'Who can doubt that the moral tone of the island of saints and scholars will be raised to unprecedented heights'

Writers like Kate O'Brien and Mary Lavin, both victims of censorship, continued in their substantial output of novels and short stories to write about the hopes, fears, frustrations and pleasures of Irish women. O'Brien's novels, which began to cause a stir in the 1930s, include *The Ante-Room* (1934) and *Mary Lavelle* (1936), which was banned. Significantly, it is the desire of O'Brien's youthful characters that moves the narrative, with an emphasis on their right to sensuality and physicality. *Mary Lavelle* also confronts the issue of illicit love, adulterous love and even homosexual love, with another theme the refusal of society to accommodate women who choose to love the wrong man. It was not that O'Brien was offering solutions or resolution, but rather that she was seeking tolerance. As Mère Marie-Hélène, a character in *The Ante-Room*, says, be the judge of your own soul, 'but never for a second, I implore you, set up as judge of another'[353] – advice that was lost on the proponents of censorship and the Censorship Board. Set amongst Irish governesses in Spain in the 1920s, *Mary Lavelle* tells the story of Agatha Conlan, who confesses the secret of her 'absurd infatuation' with Mary Lavelle, after which, in the words of the novel, 'a certain relaxation, even an affectionate, unspoken peace' prevails between the two women. Emma Donoghue has suggested that O'Brien was ahead of her time 'in presenting Agatha's unrequited love so seriously and sympathetically, and in having Mary react without homophobic panic'.[354]

There was a lot of painstaking work put into policing reading, which led to much barbed comment. Denis Ireland, in his book *From the Irish*

Shore (1936), wrote of the Irish Sisters of Mercy policing a book passage about a married woman and man conversing between a dressing room and a bathroom, with the door unlocked:

> It was evident that the Sisters of Mercy had been doing a bit of concentrated sleuthing, since it was necessary to turn back several pages and collate several apparently unconnected passages in order to prove that the bathroom door was unlocked – so that the vigilance and sense of public duty of the Sisters of Mercy cannot be too highly commended. With such selfless devotion at work in our midst, lengthening night dresses, reading the writing on the walls of lavatories in order to erase it, removing the words 'privy' and 'water closet' from the pages of our national literature and providing locks for all bathroom and lavatory doors, who can doubt that the moral tone of the island of saints and scholars will be raised to unprecedented heights, to the greater honour and glory of God and the delight of the sellers of smutty second-hand novels.[355]

The difficulty for banned Irish authors was that their books were being classified as 'filthy' or 'indecent' when they were in fact purveyors of quality literature and their ostracisation was not only professionally but personally painful. Seán O'Faoláin, whose first book, *Midsummer Night's Madness*, was banned in 1932, recalled the impact of censorship in the context of his relationship with his mother:

> My career gave her no satisfaction, much worry and some pain. I went completely outside any pattern she could recognise or understand. I often wonder what she must have suffered when my first book of stories was banned in Ireland as 'indecent and obscene'. I am sure that one of my deepest reasons for hating the Irish Censorship Board was what it did to her.[356]

'Damsels (of undoubted beauty) holding bowls and arrayed in scanty garments!'

Books were not the only concern of censorious authorities; civil servants and ministers in Northern Ireland were also conscious of the ability of stage productions of dubious morality to corrupt the minds of the innocent. In 1930, the Women's League of Health and Beauty applied for entertainment tax exemption for its staging of 'modern health and beauty cultural exercises' performed in the Co-operative Hall in Belfast. On the grounds that the movement was an educational one, exemption was granted, so the organisers then sought a further exemption for their show in Bangor, but an official in the Department of Finance was not convinced. In a letter to his counterpart in the Department of Education he wonders about the appropriateness of sending a young policeman to assess whether or not the show was educational, gymnastics, or something else:

> I must confess I had some doubts whether it could be so regarded, especially as the demonstration was heralded by pictures in the local press of damsels (of undoubted beauty) holding bowls and arrayed in scanty garments! ... I am not sure whether the sight of some 60 or 70 maidens exercising in scanty garments (we are informed the uniform consists of white blouse and white knickers) is conducive to the education of a young constable, but perhaps you can advise me on this point ... I may mention that we are informed that one of the reasons for the admission of both sexes to this proposed display is that the Bangor Young Ladies would not be bothered to go to anything without their 'boy friends'. This appears to me to cast grave suspicion on the educational aspect.[357]

There was also a highly amusing section of the draft letter, crossed out and deleted from the final official version:

> In the event of some untoward incident or unforeseen repercussion on the constabulary, Home Affairs might seriously complain and in this unfortunate event we would like to be fortified with your opinion that the presence of the constable was not only part of his duty but also of his education.[358]

In another letter to a member of the London Board of Education, the Minister for Education suggested that the dancing of the scantily clad women 'will no doubt prove a considerable attraction to many of the unsophisticated inhabitants of Bangor', to which the Board of Education offered its view that the performances could not be classed as educational. Tax exemption was duly refused.[359] The published prospectus of the Women's League of

Health and Beauty claimed it promoted 'racial health and beauty by natural means', and that 'at present 80% of potential health and beauty, particularly that of women, lies dormant. Obviously since women are so potent, we must enthuse women on the subject of training their own bodies.'[360]

Notwithstanding concern to protect the unsophisticated Bangorites, active state intervention in Northern Ireland was much less pronounced than in the south, and more reliance was put on self-policing. British Sunday newspapers came under fire for their lurid reporting of divorce cases, but newspapers in Northern Ireland were more circumspect about such cases.[361] There were demands in Northern Ireland for similar censorship of publications as existed in the Free State, with the *Derry People* particularly vocal about the merits of the Free State legislation, while 'the Unionist press also printed criticism of modern writing without always calling explicitly for censorship'. Presbyterians instead drew attention to 'bad books' and recommended readers stick to 'wholesome literature'.[362]

'The Rumba is the most sexy thing that has wriggled its way into modern life from the lusts of the Jungle'

Film censorship also gathered pace during these years, as did the public appetite for cinema, with 18 million tickets sold in the Free State's 190 cinemas in 1934, the people of Dublin averaging 23 visits apiece. The following year it was estimated that 160 of these cinemas were equipped for sound.[363] In 1923, without much debate, the Censorship of Films Act established a film censor with powers to 'cut' films or refuse them a licence if he found them 'subversive of public morality'. There could have been many more people involved in this than a single film censor; when Minister for Home Affairs Kevin O'Higgins was told of the concerns of some groups about the influx of celluloid, he mentioned the names of nine individuals, including W. B. Yeats and Oliver St John Gogarty, whom he proposed to invite to act as commissioners of the Censorship of Films Appeal Board. His measure was never approved.

Instead, James Montgomery was appointed sole film censor in 1923, while in Belfast film censorship was carried out by the Police Committee of the Belfast Corporation. In some Northern Irish towns cinemas were closed on Sundays, but those voices advocating censorship were not as organised as they were in the Free State. Initially Montgomery 'still watched films in silence and struggled to spot inappropriate dialogue with the help of a script', but after several years of discussion an amendment to the Censorship of Films Act was passed in 1930 enabling him to censor sound films.[364] Montgomery refused to issue 'adults only' certificates; he had offered to issue such certificates if the cinemas in question would exclude children at all times, but this offer 'was not availed of'. He justified his decision on the basis that if he did issue such certificates there would have to be precautions taken to prevent children seeing the films, and it would 'stimulate morbid curiosity and possibly excite the precocious to evade the law'.[365]

The comments of Montgomery, as recorded in his reject book, in which he explains why he censored particular films, are colourful, at times scathing, sometimes bewildering and often very funny. Thankfully, from the historian's perspective, he gave the lie to his own comment in July 1935 that 'all that concerns the censorship is that it is "immoral" within the meaning of the cert';[366] he in fact elaborated on a lot more than that.

Some of the films rejected in the 1930s include *Buzzy Boop*, *The Lost Gangster*, *Lady Behave*, *Law of the Underworld*, *Land of Contentment* and *Lady Objects*.[367] Mongtgomery believed he had to be vigilant from a number of different perspectives, continually using the word 'tedium' to describe much of the fare. He frequently expressed annoyance at ridiculous plots, although his antennae were particularly atuned to 'indecent' dances and costumes, double-meaning songs and gags, divorce, adultery, films that might stir up political or labour trouble and, of course, sex. In May 1935, he rejected Paramount's *Rumba*, noting 'apart from the plot and the indecent costumes, the Rumba is the most sexy thing that has wriggled its way into modern life from the lusts of the Jungle'.[368]

Another Paramount film rejected in the same month was *Making the Rounds*, which Montgomery found to be 'grossly vulgar, suggestive and indecent'. Other films were rejected for containing nudity and references to illegitimacy, but Montgomery reserved his particular ire for the 'banality' of English directors and the English producers' idea of comedy, which he found to be 'slapstick and smut'.[369] American films fared little better in his view: in June 1935, in a comment on MGM's *Forsaking All Others,* he wrote that it was a depiction of 'the sort of drunken debauched hen-run "society" rubbish that almost justifies communism'.

There was also no sex in Ireland during the War of Independence, according to Montgomery; in June 1935 he rejected *The Informer*, the film version of Liam O'Flaherty's book of the same name, which amounted, in his view, to a 'sordid and brutal libel', depicting a 'brothel bully' who turns informer to bring a prostitute to the USA. Passing it, he continued, 'could be used as an advertisement of the Free State's approval of the truth of this picture'. An appeal against his decision was successful and the film passed for viewing in July 1935.[370] There was plenty more sizzling viewing for Montgomery that summer, though. In July he viewed and rejected Paramount's *Devil is a Woman*: 'The whole rubbish heap reeks with sex. Hollywood in the old deeply rutted groove of sex.' He was also occasionally frustrated that there was nudity in the scenes which were essential to the overall plot, 'so I can't cut'.[371]

In November of the same year, Montgomery rejected MGM's film version of Leo Tolstoy's *Anna Karenina*: 'It may be advanced that suicide is the price of jaded lust, and that the film is therefore moral – but that is not my view.'[372] In 1935, he rejected a total of forty-three films. Very busy up to his retirement from his post in 1943, the censor took many opportunities to vent his feelings on poor filmmaking. He frequently employed the word 'nauseating', but he also used the word 'sophisticated' in a pejorative sense, insisting such films merely represented an attempt to be deceptive. He rejected films in 1937, for example, that were 'far too sophisticated and cynical'; 'secretary', he knew, was 'a euphemism for a type of prostitute'.[373]

He continued to employ colourful language in dismissing the efforts of the major film corporations. Paramount's *Go West Young Man*, starring Mae West, was rejected in 1937 as 'the slyly salacious story of a nymphomaniac, whose amorous efforts are baffled just at the boiling point of each episode'.[374] Montgomery himself regularly reached boiling point, but channelled his exasperation into his alliterative and cutting dismissals. Columbia's *Theodore Goes Wild* was rejected in March 1937: 'Hollywood has slipped back – this is in the old tradition – decency is sneered at – and divorce once more resumes its former position on the screen as the happy commencement of probably a series of marriages.' In rejecting Paramount's *I Met Him in Paris* in July 1937, he again asked, 'Is Hollywood slipping back into the old suggestive, sophisticated, sexy, slime?'[375]

Montgomery viewed British filmmakers' attempts 'to convey a continental tone' with disdain, and in November 1937 rejected *Girl in a Taxi* as 'a sneer at virtue. This is an example of flat-footed floundering by an English cast through a French plot.'[376] But his main concern, as he himself said, was to detect material unfit for adolescents, 'who form the major part of all cinema audiences'.[377] He may indeed have ensured that what appeared on the screen was more wholesome than would otherwise have been the case, but, as the court archives indicate, a visit to the cinema could still serve to satisfy sexual lust, if the number of reported assaults and gropes that occurred when the lights were dimmed was anything to go by.

1940–60

'Since my boyhood, I have heard my elders fulminating about keeping company, night courting, dancing at the crossroads, V necks, silk stockings, late dances ...'

When he began editing his seminal journal *The Bell* in 1940, Seán O'Faoláin was determined that it would resist abstractions, discuss social issues 'clearly and faithfully' and 'have nothing to do with generalisations ... not capable of proof by concrete expression'.[1] This was particularly important in a country where, according to O'Faoláin, 'there could not be heard a frank public discussion of any three of the following subjects: birth control, Free Masonry, the Knights of Columbanus, unmarried mothers, illegitimacy, divorce, homosexuality, rhythm, lunacy, libel, euthanasia, prostitution, Venereal Disease or even Usury'.[2]

It is unsurprising that themes related to sexuality received such prominence in O'Faoláin's list; like Francis Hackett he identified the Irish as ostriches when it came to open discussion of sex, though it became evident during these decades that there were those who were prepared to challenge this muteness, through public discourse and private reflection. As Marjorie Howes has pointed out, by the late 1940s celibacy was being critically questioned in Ireland as something that may have encouraged emigration and damaged the social and sexual relations between the sexes. O'Faoláin

had many further opportunities to give vent to his frustration and his cynicism in this regard, including the contribution he made to a book edited by
Father John O'Brien of Notre Dame University in 1954, *The Vanishing Irish*,
which offered contributors a chance to reflect on contemporary Ireland in
the context of its dwindling population and startling emigration rates:

> Since my boyhood, I have heard my elders fulminating about keeping
> company, night courting, dancing at the crossroads, V necks, silk stock-
> ings, late dances, drinking at dances, mixed bathing, advertisements for
> feminine underwear, jitterbugging, girls who take part in immodest
> sports (such as jumping or hurdling), English and American books and
> magazines, short frocks, bikinis, cycling shorts and even waltzing, which
> I have heard elegantly described as 'belly to belly dancing'.[3]

O'Faoláin had clearly followed the advice John O'Brien had given to
contributors to the book, which, according to writer Bryan MacMahon,
was that they should give it 'straight from the shoulder'. MacMahon, like
O'Faoláin, duly complied, recounting stories of clerical denunciation of
'company keeping' and the tyranny of clerical control of dances and social
life. It was a particularly brave thing for MacMahon to do given his position as a national schoolteacher whose management was clerical. The articles from the book were subsequently serialised in a Sunday newspaper and
MacMahon recalled:

> I became the subject of much misunderstanding. How dare a national
> teacher, whose employer was the Parish Priest, utter such sentiments? I
> woke up one morning to find that I had been mentioned from at least 3
> pulpits in the locality ... this did not bother me in the least. I was con-
> scious of an inner sense of rectitude.[4]

But the refusal to honestly engage with the book's content did bother Mac-
Mahon. He regularly corresponded with a friend of his in San Francisco,
and in a number of these letters he mentioned the stir the book had caused
and his frustration with the denial evident in the reaction to its publication. When the *Irish Press* newspaper, for whom he wrote a weekly column,
refused to publish his column responding to 'a man [who] started spouting
off fantastic nonsense attacking the Vanishing Irish writers', it proved to be

the final straw and I bade the *Irish Press* a fond farewell. But the problem here in Ireland, you can take it from me, is pretty desperate and every-body seems to give it the good old 'hush hush'. All of my spare time is spent rambling here and there throughout Ireland and the whole coun-tryside is crawling with ancient spinsters and bachelors. Marriage and birth rates for the past quarter ... indicate a further decline. It's very depressing when one is denied the right of utterance. I don't care two hoots who gets up the following day and cuts me asunder but silence and atrophy spell death.[5]

For all the fulminating and denial, and whatever the overall high degree of celibacy, examples from the circuit court criminal books of the 1940s and 1950s suggest the problem of sexual crime remained paramount. On 11 January 1945, the court book for the city and county of Dublin contained 98 indictments, 7 of which were cases of sexual crime including attempted carnal knowledge, buggery (the person convicted was sentenced to 3 years), indecent assault on a male (10 months' imprisonment), and incest. During the sitting of 17 April, there were 74 indictments, of which 5 were sexual crime cases. During the sitting on 4 June 1952, there were 92 indictments, of which 4 were sexual crimes.[6] In the Dublin circuit court state book for 1956, the indictments listed for 16 January included indecent assault of a male, indecent assault of a female, buggery and unlawful carnal knowledge of a female under the age of 15.

An analysis of the circuit court files from the 1930s to the 1960s would suggest that this was a typical day's sitting of the circuit court in Dublin, and that between 5 and 8 per cent of all cases were to do with sexual crime.[7] In the circuit court record book for 1960, 13 out of the 157 indictments listed were for sexual crime, including attempted buggery, carnal knowledge of an 8-year-old girl, indecent assault of a male and rape.[8] The case books and the depositions for the cases document a consistently high level of sexual crime directed against young boys and girls. Some of these cases were being recorded in the media; as well as the national dailies, provincial newspa-pers reported extensively on district and circuit court hearings. In the event of sexual crimes the journalists were sometimes discreet ('pleaded guilty to an offence against a young girl')[9] or simply reported the outcome ('A Cork man was acquitted of incest in the city')[10], but some newspapers reported more detail on 'acts of indecency'.[11] Many parents (usually the instigators of prosecutions), Gardaí and members of the legal profession had extensive knowledge of the existence of these crimes, as did the doctors who supplied graphic and detailed depositions regarding the physical damage resulting from the assaults.

✳

'A positive conspiracy of silence exists in Holy Ireland to cloak the doings of the unholy from the eyes of the just'

An interesting article on crime in Dublin, published in *The Bell* in December 1942, suggests 'a positive conspiracy of silence exists in Holy Ireland to cloak the doings of the unholy from the eyes of the just'.[12] While recounting the campaign against the Monto district in Dublin city (see chapter 2), the anonymous reporter told of the existence of a few illicit shebeens in Dublin's inner city 'and a nice line in sex-indulgence, now displayed by "privateers"'. There were instances of soliciting and wallet-stealing, 'though not, now, on anything like the old scale', and it was observed that the bordellos tended to be found 'in the better class residential areas. The trend is all towards respectability.'

The reporter emphasised that Dublin was relatively crime-free. In comparison with other European cities, it was 'almost as clean as the Garden of Eden'; few 'vice cases are ever mentioned in the press'. But he did devote significant attention in his article to the issue of sexual crime. Quoting from the Department of Industry and Commerce's statistical abstract for 1941, he noted that of the total number of people proceeded against in 1937, '*more than half were charged with indecent assault and other sexual and unnatural offences*' (italics in original);[13] in 1938 it was under half; in 1939 it was between a third and a half, 'and that the next largest category is crime of violence, other than murder and manslaughter – these only totalled roughly half the sexual offences in 1937 and 1938', though in 1939 violence exceeded these offences.

> The following case is typical. An old man was convicted of an offence against a child in a public park at Dun Laoghaire last month. In imposing a six-month sentence, the District Justice saw fit to remark: 'No child is safe in the People's Park, Dun Laoghaire at present.' A Garda informed him that, 'What the Justice says is true of every public park in the city.'

The reporter also commented that, 'It may come as a surprise to readers to know that on the books of one Dublin organisation alone which has been investigating the problem of sex-perversion in the city there are already seven hundred names of persons addicted to homosexuality.'[14]

The previous year, the decision by the Censorship Board to ban Kate O'Brien's *Land of Spices* because it contained a reference to homosexuality was an indication that any open discussion of homosexuality was not remotely likely. In O'Brien's book, set in Brussels, where its heroine Helen lives with her father, homosexuality is invoked only obliquely. It was the following paragraph that prompted censorship of the book:

> She looked into the room. Two people were there. But neither saw her; neither felt her shadow as it froze across the sun. She turned and descended the stairs. She left the garden and went down the curve of Rue Saint Isidore. She had no objective and no knowledge of what she was doing. She did not see external things.
>
> She saw Etienne and her father, in the embrace of love.[15]

'For a second they pause and point across the river, then laugh ...
they walk on together, seeking some darker place'

Earlier that year, *The Bell* published an account by 'Unemployed' of a typical day living in a Dublin slum during the Emergency:

> Even at this late hour there are prostitutes leaning against the quay side. Their lighted cigarettes finger and question the darkness. Two men pass by arm in arm talking; for a second they pause and point across the river, then laugh. Their high-pitched voices are unreal in the heavy darkness, they walk on together, seeking some darker place.[16]

Historian Richard Cobb, in his book *A Classical Education* (1985), recalls a trip to Dublin in July 1938 when he was aged 20, where an acquaintance, Michael, arranged for him to meet an 18-year-old man who took him for a walk along the coast. The silences were awkward and Cobb could not understand why they had been thrown together:

> Then he took the plunge ... was I not a fairy too, he asked; Michael had said that I was, and had suggested that we two might have a good time

together, making his point only too clearly by adding that there were plenty of secluded spots a bit further on, hidden glades and green and yellow mossy floors where there was no risk of being disturbed; he had been this way many times before and knew all the nice spots.

Cobb told the man he was not 'a fairy' and gave him £5 to compensate for his disappointment, which he took 'without the slightest embarrassment'.[17]

The sort of sentences gay men seeking sexual encounters in Ireland could expect if caught are revealed in the criminal court case books, though securing conviction was not always possible. One man convicted of buggery at the circuit criminal court in Dublin in January 1945 was sentenced to three years' penal servitude; another convicted of indecent assault on a male person was given a ten-month sentence, four months of which were to be served in Mountjoy jail in Dublin, after which he was required to 'go to Tavistock Clinic, London [the noted centre for psychoanalytic therapy], for appropriate treatment for a period of 6 months at his own expense.'[18] When he had served his four months at Mountjoy, the man came before Judge McCarthy and entered into a bond of £500, whereupon it was ordered 'that he immediately go to Belfast Mental Hospital, Purdystown, Belfast for appropriate treatment for a period of 6 calendar months at his own expense'. These sentences display a recognition that the only places deemed suitable for the treatment of an Irish sexual offender were outside the state, but also the belief that this form of 'addiction' could be treated (though presumably at significant cost, suggesting the defendant in the above case was well off).

In April of that year, 1945, two men were found not guilty of attempted gross indecency, while another was found guilty of attempted buggery with a boy under 15 in the Phoenix Park and sentenced to six years' penal servitude. Another man convicted of an attempt to procure an act of gross indecency was sentenced to six months' hard labour. In June a man convicted of indecent assault on a male person was imprisoned for twelve months; another man convicted of attempted buggery was sentenced to eighteen months' hard labour, while in October of that year a man convicted of the indecent assault of an 11-year-old boy was bound over to keep the peace for two years.[19]

Collectively, these cases would suggest not only that homosexual offences were being pursued quite vigorously, but also that each case was being considered on its own merits. The man found guilty of attempting to procure an act of gross indecency with a 12-year-old boy and sentenced to six months' hard labour was arrested after a Garda had received a complaint

from the boy who had been approached by the accused outside the door
of the General Post Office in Dublin's O'Connell Street: 'This man offered
me sixpence to go up a lane with him and I refused. He then told me he'd
give me one and sixpence if I would go up with him and let him have a feel.'
The defendant claimed that the boy had been begging; it also emerged that
five weeks previously the defendant had asked the boy to go to the cinema.
'I wouldn't go with him because I knew what he meant,' claimed the boy. 'I
heard the young fellows talking about men saying that to them.'[20]

In the same year a man from Sean MacDermott Street with previous
convictions for vagrancy, gross indecency and indecent assault received one
of the most severe sentences for attempted buggery – six years – despite his
plea for leniency on the basis that he had had 'a very hard life' and could
not get a job or be accepted into the army. This was an unusual case because
found in his possession was an advertisement from the *Evening Mail* newspaper from March 1945 which advertised for 'Boy as Page: 14–15, evening
work; enclose reference, £1 weekly plus tips. Box H716'. The boy had replied
to the advertisement and was offered the 'job' at the end of December 1944.
The defendant met the boy with his mother outside Christchurch cathedral;
the defendant then took the boy to the Phoenix Park and attempted to rape
him. He had used a false name in the advertisement and admitted he had
done this before and that 'my purpose in putting the advertisement into the
Evening Mail was to enable me to contact boys for the purpose of committing sodomy with them'. He also testified that he had received 113 replies to
his advertisement, an indication of the scale of unemployment for teenage
boys in Dublin at that time. The defendant was calculating in his approach,
as revealed in his statement. He prioritised the respondents

> who appeared to have inferior education judging from the handwriting
> and style of reply in each case. My object was that this kind of person
> would be more suitable for the purpose which I had in mind, namely, for
> committing sodomy, I mean more suitable in the sense that the person
> would not understand what kind of offence sodomy was and also that
> they would be more impressed with the work which I intended to get
> for them.

Pretending to be a handyman of the housemaster who had advertised for
the page, he systematically went and met about ten different boys who had
replied, to assess them in the company of their parents.

I have seen the produced box of Vaseline (full); the candle, a full sized cork, a portion of a second cork, which were amongst the property found in my possession on 21st March 1946 ... these articles are my property and I procured them for the purpose of facilitating me to commit sodomy. I use the Vaseline on myself as well as on the person with whom I commit sodomy and the candle and corks I use on the person who is with me. The reason I have told all this in so much detail is that I am anxious to relate everything as fully as possible in order to get everything cleared up now. I do not want to be questioned again.[21]

On the same day, another man was found not guilty of gross indecency by direction of the judge. It had been alleged that he brought a Christian Brother's schoolboy from Glasnevin, under the age of 15, to a lane in Dawson Street, after he had met him at the Mansion House where the boy was selling tickets for the Medical Missionaries of Mary. In the lane, they urinated together before the man arranged to meet the boy the following week at the 'Fun Palace amusements', after which they walked together to North Great Georges Street. The boy stated:

I did not know what he meant when he said did you ever go with girls. He then asked me to bring down more boys with me to meet him at the Fun Palace ... he said he had a whole lot of boys clubs on Belvedere Road ... the last thing he said about girls was that fellows got 5/10d. for riding girls.

After the boy told his parents what had happened, the Gardaí were contacted and, when he went along to meet the man again at the amusements, the Gardaí and his stepfather (also a Garda) were watching ('we took up our position in a stationary bus opposite the Fun Palace'). They observed the man talking to boys and giving them money, but nothing else. According to the Gardaí's evidence, the defendant said 'that he knew a lot of police, guards and detectives'.[22]

Gay men continued to be pursued into the 1950s, though again conviction was not always the likely outcome. In June 1954 a prosecution was dropped against a man who, it was alleged, had attempted to procure the commission of an act of gross indecency in Mountjoy Square, Dublin. The man he approached, a married bricklayer, gave evidence to the effect that 'he spoke to me and asked me could I show him anywhere where he could relieve himself – where he could "have a puncture" were the words he used. I stood beside him to shelter him from passers by … we could do something, he said. That was all he said. He had his penis in his hand. He said, "We could do something with this." But the bricklayer pushed him away and telephoned the Guards. He maintained that while the defendant smelt of drink, he was not drunk and was walking 'at the normal pace of an elderly man'.[23]

In 1955, two other attempts to prosecute for homosexual offences were unsuccessful. Two men were found not guilty of an act of gross indecency together in a public telephone kiosk at Bolton Street between 1 and 2 a.m. one night in October. They were charged with 'in sight of and along which the public habitually pass as of right, commit[ting] an act in such a way as to offend modesty, cause scandal or injure the morals of the community'. A Garda gave evidence that 'I saw one of the men working his hands backwards and forwards … in or about the region of O'B.'s penis. O'B. had the receiver in his hand as if he were making a phone call.'[24] In a case transferred to the Central Criminal Court, a 42-year-old waiter was found not guilty of buggery with an Englishman who had approached the defendant for money and food; he alleged the accused then took him back to his house and 'after I had intercourse twice with C. he put his arms around me and said endearing things'.[25]

In October 1957, a 63-year-old man was accused of attempted buggery with a 15-year-old boy, whose mother had agreed he could go to live with him at Upper Rutland Street, 'on account of another sister coming home from England. F.'s mother agreed to pay me something a week for his keep as soon as he got a job.' It also emerged that the alleged victim had fallen out with his father 'because I could not find suitable employment', which suggests that the father was happy to have his son out of the house. According to the defendant, the boy slept in the same bed as him because there were other boys sleeping in the room. The Gardaí found four empty Vaseline tins; the man claimed he used Vaseline for repairing bicycles and that he sold Vaseline to wholesale firms, but the boy gave evidence of sexual encounters between the two: 'The same thing had happened to me about 40 times. The defendant used to tell me on these occasions not to tell on him, that's all he used to say.'[26] The man was convicted and given a suspended two-month sentence.[27]

During the 1950s, the Archbishop of Dublin, John Charles McQuaid, expressed an interest in finding out more about homosexual activity in his diocese. In October 1959 he received a letter from Chief Superintendent

H. O'Mara, who wrote that he was prepared to call on him to discuss the problem:

> I ask Your Grace's pardon for not having written to you sooner, in connection with your anxiety concerning homosexuality and your desire to preserve the youth. It was only recently that I had an opportunity of discussing the problem with Superintendent Tim O'Brien of Store Street in whose district the area is. He is prepared to give every assistance within his power.

There is no reference to any further developments or follow-up meetings.[28]

'The youth of healthy muscle and slim-wrought form is not the same as the powdered pansy'

In the same year the spectre of the homosexual Roger Casement (see chapter 1) came back to haunt the Irish government, when it appeared that the British government was considering handing over his infamous 'black diaries', but they were instead deposited at the Public Record Office in London. Maurice Moynihan, a senior Irish civil servant, told the new Taoiseach, Seán Lemass, he had three choices in the event of them being given to the Irish government: keep them, burn them, or publish them. 'Whatever happened, the onus would now be on the Irish government to either prove or disprove Roger Casement's homosexuality (a view de Valera also strongly held). Have nothing to do with them was his advice.'[29] Irish politicians and diplomats, when pursuing delicate questions about the return of his body from Pentonville prison, England, in the 1960s (his remains were returned in 1965 and reinterred following a state funeral) were determined to separate the issue of his diaries from his contribution to the 1916 Rising. In 1964, Paul Keating, an official at the Irish embassy in London, suggested the diaries were irrelevant, and that 'if genuine, showed a strange aberration which had little to do with the character of the man as he was known by his friends'. While there was anxiety to see Casement's body returned, the Irish government was happy for the diaries to remain in London.

Another Irish man with strong homosexual tendencies and a high profile in London in the 1950s was the talented and irascible playwright Brendan Behan. There was some controversy after his death when biographers explored his sexuality: Behan's brother maintained he took him to the Phoenix Park in 1947 to visit prostitutes. Behan had written about homosexual experiences relating to his time in a Borstal when he was aged 19:

> Our lads saw themselves as beautiful and had to do something about it ... not a pattern of life, only a prolonging of adolescence – it was as beautiful as that ... homosexuality (of our sort) is not a substitute for normal sex ... without women it could not be a pattern of life ... the youth of healthy muscle and slim-wrought form is not the same as the powdered pansy.[30]

Behan's 'The Wake', published in *Points* in Paris in 1950, dealt in a much more overt way with homoerotic attraction, as the protagonist becomes erotically entangled with a young married couple in Dublin, both aged 21. It was a story that also drew attention to the role of living conditions in awakening sexuality and defining sexual preferences. The two young men chat after a swim,

> our bare thighs touching ... we talked of the inconvenience of tenement living. He said he'd hated most of all sleeping with his brothers – so had I, I'd felt their touch incestuous – but most of all he hated sleeping with a man older than himself.
> 'I don't mind sleeping with a little child,' he said, 'the snug way they round themselves into you – and I don't mind a young fellow my own age.'
> 'The like of myself', and I laughed as if it meant nothing. It didn't apparently, to him.
> 'No, I wouldn't mind you and it'd be company for me, if she went to hospital or anything,' he said.

That was what his wife was preparing for and the protagonist 'opened the campaign in jovial earnest', by removing the taint of 'cissiness' from homosexuality and mentioning well-known gay men who were masculine army types or athletic male role models. After the wife's funeral the two are left alone and the bereaved young husband retires to bed: '"You must be nearly gone yourself," he said, "you might as well come in and get a bit of rest." He did, admiring 'the supple muscled thighs, the stomach flat as an altar boy's and noted the golden smoothness of the blond hair on every part of his firm, white flesh'.[31]

Frederick May, musical director at the Abbey Theatre, was a regular correspondent of Behan's and visited him in prison, and, according to a friend, they had limited sexual contact. Although such stories are difficult to verify, there seems enough anecdotal and literary evidence to suggest Behan had homosexual encounters on a number of occasions and boasted of his 'Herod' complex, or preference for younger boys, though he did not sexually interfere with young boys. Anthony Cronin also points out that he may have been boasting to shock and that there was 'an element of picaresque braggadocio which was meant to suggest cynicism and villainy on his part,'[32] (such as when he shouted 'Up sodomy!' at a ballet).

Behan's book *Confessions of an Irish Rebel* (1965) refers to homosexual encounters at the Catacombs, a warren of basement rooms beneath a Georgian house at 13 Fitzwilliam Place which was rented by English homosexual Dickie Wyeman and served as a useful hideaway for Dublin's artistic crew to indulge in late-night drinking, and more besides. According to Behan 'there would be men having women, men having men and women having women. A fair field and no favour. It was all highly entertaining.'[33]

Either way, it is fair to note that alcohol took precedence over Behan's sexuality; in Michael O'Sullivan's biography of Behan, for example, there are fifty-four entries in the index for the 'role of alcohol' and fifteen for 'sexuality'. The definition of an Irish 'queer', notes O'Sullivan, is supposed to be 'a man that prefers women to drink ... he certainly did not come into that category'. In 1981, ex-seaman and troubadour Peter Arthurs published his book *With Brendan Behan*, in which he recounts their sexual encounters. Again, it is not possible to verify these, though his depiction of Behan's confusion, immaturity and uncertainty in relation to his sexuality seems quite insightful; according to Arthurs, 'Behan's main problem was a kind of sexual hysteria that hung over him like a wet overcoat on a small hook.'[34]

The difficult social experiences of Irish gay men mirrored those of gay men in other countries in the period, when homosexuality was seen as particularly threatening to the post-war 'cult of family and domesticity'. In the US, the recreation of 'the traditional equation between sodomy, heresy and treachery' in the context of the Cold War was laden with homophobic rhetoric. Homosexuality and other 'aberrations' were presented as dangerous to national security and 'rife' in Washington. After Walter Jenkins, Lyndon B. Johnson's chief-of-staff, was charged with performing 'indecent gestures' in a rest room with another man, the 'liberal' *New York Times* in October 1964 described 'sexual perversion' as 'an emotional illness'.[35] Prosecution of gay men was also particularly pronounced in 1950s England, due to the persistence of the then-Director of Public Prosecutions, Sir Theobald Mathew. High-profile prosecutions included the actor John Gielgud and the mathematician Alan Turing. But there was no Irish case during this era in which high-profile politicians or government officials were shamed and prosecuted as a result of gay activity.

'A very small group who meet in the afternoons, when other people are working'

There also remained little public discussion of the sexual abuse of young girls, which continued to occur on a regular basis, with devastating consequences for the victims who were often deemed, it seemed, to share guilt. The state appeared to get much more exercised about 'immoral girls' than it did about child abusers; when contemplating amending the Children's Acts in 1947, the Department of Education was anxious to make provision for a class of children who were not accepted by industrial or reformatory schools because 'they might have an evil influence on the other children', they being 'young girls who have been associated with sexual immorality'. It was argued that there was a need for 'guidance schools' where girls could be kept until the age of 17 because 'some girls might not have overcome their unfortunate weakness at the age of 16'. One such school, St Anne's at Kilmacud in Dublin, was proposed.

In attempting to draft a bill to deal with this issue it was acknowledged in the Department that 'owing to the difficulty of framing legislation to deal directly with sexual immorality (including the definition of that term) it is not proposed in the draft bill to deal specifically with that matter'.[36] This file gives a good indication of the degree of ambiguity associated with defining sexual immorality and who was responsible for it. When a phrase like 'young girls who have been associated with sexual immorality' is used it can be taken that this was meant to imply those involved in prostitution, or those who had got pregnant outside of marriage. But it could also have been used to refer to entirely innocent girls who had been sexually abused and were then tainted with the tag of 'immorality' and hidden away in institutions. James Smith refers to a disturbing case in June 1941, where the Central Criminal Court decided the fate of a victim of child sex abuse. The court decided that the girl, who had been raped repeatedly by her father between the ages of 11

and 14, was 'living in circumstances calculated to cause or encourage ... prostitution or seduction' and, under the terms of the Children's Act of 1908, she
was removed from her home and committed to High Park convent, one of
the bigger Magdalen asylums. Industrial and reformatory schools would not
accept her, 'fearing her mere presence would contaminate her young peers'.
As pointed out by Smith, 'although the young girl was the victim of a crime,
the various authorities initially regarded her as a threatening embodiment
of sexual deviancy'.[37]

Few bodies were inquiring into the practice of admission to these
institutions, though the Joint Committee of Women's Societies and Social
Workers (JCWSSW) did inspect some of them, and reported back positively on them. In 1952, the Irish Association of Civil Liberty, when corresponding with the JCWSSW, expressed anxiety 'to find out whether any
restrictions were placed on the liberty of these women in the Magdalene
[sic] asylums'.[38] It was unsurprising that convicted prostitutes 'generally prefer to go to Gaol than to an institution – the time of confinement being
shorter in the former'.[39] Those seeking to ask questions about the welfare
of the vulnerable inevitably found themselves stepping on the toes of the
powerful Archbishop McQuaid. He was anxious to ensure complete control
of social work; when the head of the Family Welfare Section of the Catholic Social Welfare Bureau (CSWB) requested permission from McQuaid
to attend sociological society meetings in Trinity College in 1948, she was
refused because, according to McQuaid, 'it would be inadvisable and misleading'.[40] Those who were intent on raising difficult issues like the welfare of
young women were dismissed by McQuaid and his colleagues as interfering
busybodies who had too much time on their hands and were not of the True
Faith. Cecil Barrett of the CSWB dismissed the JCWSSW as 'run by a very
small group who meet in the afternoons, when other people are working'.[41]

'I went with her every Saturday night. That's the truth.
I suppose I am the father ...'

Some of those who were sexually abused inevitably became pregnant, and
many of those ended up in the mother and baby homes for the period of their
'confinement', such incarceration underlying the degree to which the victims
had to pay a heavy price, despite having been criminally wronged. But the
appearance of women in these institutions also provided an opportunity for

the Gardaí to question the girls and subsequently pursue men who had had underage sex with them, and a number of these cases came before the courts. Many were found not guilty, despite incontrovertible evidence of pregnancy (it was not always possible to prove that they were the fathers). A number of such cases became before the courts in Donegal, for example, in the late 1940s. Regarding the typical jury panels for these cases, it is worth noting that the jury panel for the circuit court held at Letterkenny on 10 January 1950 included 40 names, all men, of which 35 were farmers, 3 were merchants, 1 a builder and 1 a bus conductor, giving an indication of the typical class and social profile of rural juries at that time.[42]

At the district court area of Ballyshannon in May 1949, a 20-year-old hotel worker was returned for trial at Donegal circuit court charged with the unlawful carnal knowledge of a 16-year-old domestic servant employed in Bundoran. She had met the accused at dances in Bundoran for two weeks running. What was unusual about this case was the admission by the girl that intercourse had taken place with her consent:

> I danced with him and he asked to see me home. I agreed and we went to a field on the West End Road where he had connection with me with my full consent ... I have made no complaint to anybody about him. I gave birth to a baby girl on 23 February 1949. Defendant is not the father of my baby.[43]

The hotel worker was found not guilty on all charges.

Two months later, at Letterkenny circuit court, during the trial of a man accused of the unlawful carnal knowledge of a 14-year-old girl in August 1948, it was established that the defendant, who was known to the girl, had given her a lift in a lorry to Letterkenny and raped her in the back of the lorry:

> I was trying to roar but he got on top of me ... I did not feel any pain [this sentence is heavily underlined in her deposition] ... when I got to the railway station, I went into the waiting room and combed my hair. I returned home on the half past ten p.m. bus. I did not say anything to my stepmother. I was afraid and ashamed to tell her ... I never went with a boy in my life. No other boy ever did that to me.

When her stepmother brought the girl to the local medical officer in

January 1949 it was discovered she was four months pregnant. When the defendant was arrested he said 'I admit I was with her up the railway line and tried to have connection with her but did not succeed.' Significantly, the defendant was found not guilty of carnal knowledge but guilty of attempted carnal knowledge,[44] raising the obvious question of why the jury accepted his statement as true, given that the girl was pregnant – was this because they did not believe that she had had only one sexual encounter, or was it because she said she 'did not feel any pain'?

The state files for Donegal circuit court in 1955 contain details of 20 cases, of which 4 were unlawful carnal knowledge cases – a high proportion, suggesting that the Gardaí were actively pursuing those who had impregnated underage girls. But the criminal books for previous years in Donegal suggest the conviction rate was abysmal. On 12 June 1946, for example, there were 5 unlawful carnal knowledge cases listed; not guilty verdicts were returned in 2 of the cases and a *Nolle Prosequi* was entered in each of the remaining 3.[45] At Letterkenny circuit court between April and October 1947, the 7 unlawful carnal knowledge cases resulted in five not guilty verdicts, the jury disagreed in 1 case and the defendant found guilty in the remaining case was imprisoned for six months with hard labour.[46] At the same court in January 1955 a labourer was accused of the unlawful carnal knowledge of a 15-year-old girl, the daughter of a labourer. The alleged victim gave evidence that she had been walking the Derry Road with four friends:

> We were met on the road by W.B. ... W.B. stopped me and took me up in his arms and carried me into a field next to the hockey field at Magheraboy, Raphoe, County Donegal and left me down on straw that was in the field. He then lay down on top of me and held me down with one of his arms. He then pulled up my clothes and took down my knickers and had sexual intercourse with me. On 8th October 1954 I gave birth to a male child in my home at Townparks, Raphoe and the father of that child is W. B.

As was usual in these cases, the defendant was known to the victim – perhaps inevitable in such small districts – and silence followed, until silence was no longer feasible due to the advanced state of the pregnancy. The victim mentioned that she 'told no-one what had happened in the field', while her mother testified that 'I had an idea but I didn't say anything about it until August [the alleged rape occurred in January], that there was something wrong with my daughter.' In November, a month after the birth of her son, the girl met the defendant, who, according to her, acknowledged he was the father and promised he would pay maintenance: 'He said that if I was content with him allowing me so much a week and I said I would do that. I know W.B. well – since he was a boy at school.' The defendant was found not guilty.[47]

The same man was also charged with the unlawful carnal knowledge of another local girl who was only 12½ years old, in the hockey field behind her great-uncle's farm, and who also became pregnant. Again he was found not guilty, meaning he had been charged with the unlawful carnal knowledge of two local girls, both of whom went on to have babies.

In another case heard in June 1955 at Letterkenny circuit court yet another local man denied that he had ever had unlawful carnal knowledge of the same 12½-year-old alleged victim. Her mother was dead and she lived with her 87-year-old grandmother, while her father lived in a separate house. The victim cleaned a house after school every day, another indication that young girls being sent out to work due to their families' economic circumstances were vulnerable. The alleged assault happened in the garden of the house she cleaned, but she told no one of the assault. Her deposition includes the following account of being moved from institution to institution and of a traumatic birth:

> I know what periods are. I had them every month before I met F., since I was 11½ years. After that time at the Rocky Quay I had no periods. I stayed in my grandmothers after that until I went to hospital on 4 July 1954 – the Rock Hospital, Ballyshannon. I was there about 3 months and a fortnight. I then went to St John's Hospital in Sligo and then to the County Hospital. I had my operation on 24 January 1955. The operation was for the birth of a baby boy. It is still alive.

The defendant was found not guilty.[48]

At the same court in April of that year a similar case was heard. A 16-year-old girl had given birth in January and claimed the defendant was the father: 'The first time it happened was in the lane down below our house ... G.G. is a neighbour of mine. He used to visit our house nearly every Saturday night ... it happened around 20 times. It nearly always happened in the nighttime, outside my own house.' The defendant, who pleaded guilty and had glowing references from the parish priest and his employers, gave a frank statement to the Gardaí: 'I went with her every Saturday night. That's the truth. I suppose

I am the father of B.'s child when she said so. There's no use in denying it. I asked her to marry me, and I am willing to marry her any day. There is no use going behind the bush with it.' It was common in many of these cases that the mother was dead, or for parental absence to be a factor, which made it easier for clandestine sexual encounters (almost invariably outdoors) to occur close to the house. In this case the girl was from a family of six with a widower father, who also gave a statement. He knew the defendant

> for the past 12 or 13 years. He used to call to my house and he and a son
> of mine used to run to pictures and dances. I go to a neighbour's house
> almost every night to hear the news on the wireless. It has been a practice
> of mine for the past five years to do that.[49]

'I went up to the Cathedral then and I was in time for the devotions'

It was also the case that young girls forced to work in the fields of rural Ireland were targeted. In 1944 a man was accused of the unlawful carnal knowledge of a neighbouring girl who used to herd the cows after school until 9.30 p.m. She was assaulted on a mountainside near the defendant's house. The victim pointed out, 'I have known him as long as I can remember.' It had happened on many occasions and a neighbour eventually saw them. The defendant admitted courting the girl, but not having sex with her: 'I intended to marry her in a year or 2 and I can tell you she would be quite satisfied too.'[50]

As in the past, local festivals, carnivals and religious celebrations featured as a backdrop to quite a number of cases. A case before the circuit court in Donegal in 1948 involved the alleged unlawful carnal knowledge of a 14-year-old girl, the eldest of five children, by a drunken bog worker in a field after they had met at the Rathmullen regatta. The mother had allowed her daughter to go to the regatta and stay with a family acquaintance. A *Nolle Prosequi* was entered.[51]

In the same year, statements were taken from a 16-year-old girl at St Mary's home, Tuam, County Galway, in preparation for a case heard in the circuit court in Galway in 1955 (there were 11 cases heard in 1955, 4 relating to unlawful carnal knowledge), where a man was accused of the unlawful carnal knowledge of the girl at the time of the Tuam carnival in 1953. The alleged victim was 'on my way home from confession alone' when the first assault occurred. On another occasion,

On the Feast of Christ the King in 1953, I was on my way to devotions in the Cathedral. I was alone, at Cahill's shop in Vicar Street, Tuam. I met M.M. He stopped me and said, 'Go into the Shambles', that is the big open place behind the lavatories. I went into the Shambles by the big gate opposite the Circular Road. M.M. followed me, he caught up on me in the Shambles, he brought me to a shed, he brought me in, he put me lying on the floor.

He then had sex with her: 'I left the Shambles first after M.M. told me to go. I went up to the Cathedral then and I was in time for the Devotions'. The girl subsequently had a baby at the children's home in Tuam. The girl's mother (her father had died when she was 10 months old) said, 'I know him well. From the time M.T. told me about her alleged relations with M.M. I never contacted him with regard to the same.' There was also a statement from the nurse at the Tuam dispensary:

I asked her if there was a possibility of her being pregnant and if anybody had interfered with her. She said, 'Yes.' I then said, 'You should get married if you can. Is there any possibility of this?' and she said, 'No.' I asked her why and she said the man was married.

The defendant, when cautioned, replied, 'There is nothing I can say. I did not think I did anything that would leave her in that state.' He was found not guilty by direction.[52]

In July 1953, during the Salthill races in Galway, a man had unlawful carnal knowledge of a 15-year-old girl (whose father was working in England) in a field:

I was crying. He said, 'Don't be ashamed, I know everything.' There was blood on my clothes when he had finished. I asked him his name again. He did not want to tell me at first ... he promised me a chain and a cross from Knock ... he said to me, 'Supposing I was married?' I asked him was he. He just laughed and did not say whether he was or not.

They went to the cinema the following week: 'He gave me the cross and chain on the way to the picture house. He did not forget it.'

On the third occasion,

I would not let him do it, so he said, 'We're through' ... I did not give him
back his cross and chain. I kept it ... I said I had to go home because my
brother would beat me ... I was in the bed and my sister C. came up to
me and asked me would I go on my 2 knees and swear I had nothing to
do with boys. So I could not. I told her I had been in trouble.

The victim was examined by a doctor, who discovered she was pregnant. Subsequently, the defendant approached the victim's brother at the
garage where he worked and said, 'You know I'm out of a respectable family.
I can prove it by many people in Tuam ... this is going to look bad for everyone.' The two men went for a drink after work to discuss the issue, during
which the defendant blamed the pregnancy on a friend of his. According to
the brother's statement:

Wouldn't it be better if this case was quashed, he said. I said it would but
the guards told me her name would not be on the paper at all and he said
you can't be up to the trickery of the Guards. I can guarantee you it will
be in all the papers. The *Press*. *Independent*. The *Herald* and even a bit of
it will get into the English papers.

Blood tests from the Department of Bacteriology in Galway Central
hospital proved the defendant was the father, and he was found guilty on
two counts of unlawful carnal knowledge. This conviction was quashed on
appeal and a retrial ordered, at which he was found guilty of a single charge
of unlawful carnal knowledge and sentenced to nine months' hard labour.
This was also appealed and subsequently an acquittal ordered, indicating
that even the use of blood tests was not going to ensure convictions.[53]
    In 1950 another man – this one married – was found not guilty of the
unlawful carnal knowledge of a girl who had given birth and was 'at present
an inmate of St Mary's House, Tuam, Co. Galway'. Her father told the court
that 'before she went to Tuam she refused to tell me who was responsible for
her condition'. When the defendant had a conversation with the investigating Garda: 'He said there were rumours that M.McL. was in trouble and
that he was responsible. He asked if it could be arranged that he could go to
Tuam to see her. I told him it would be better to see his parish priest, that
I could not make arrangements.' He was found not guilty, even though a
neighbour had given evidence of having seen them having sex in the defendant's field.[54]

Another young mother, aged 16, who ended up in the home in Tuam was from Foxford, County Mayo. A friend of the 30-year-old defendant accused of impregnating her gave evidence to the effect that 'he often told me he had connection with M.O'D. and he made no secret of the fact that he kept her company for that reason alone'; the sex had occurred in barns and fields and the baby was born in September 1944 ('I didn't know I was going to have a baby until I visited the doctors in September'). A friend of the girl made a statement to the effect that 'we all knew she liked him. She was permanently talking about him and telling us how she liked him.' The defendant, a migratory worker, claimed he was never in her company. He was found not guilty.[55] In 1951 another Mayo man was accused of unlawful carnal knowledge that led to birth. He and the mother were neighbours; the defendant was found not guilty.[56] All these cases highlight that there was a high level of unlawful carnal knowledge cases in Mayo during this period, that the Gardaí were determined to track down the fathers of babies born to young girls in the Tuam home, but that it was extremely difficult to obtain convictions.

'She only saw that he was stripping off veil after veil of romance'

At the heart of most of the cases that resulted in the birth of children was fear and exploitation, and a general ignorance of the facts of life and basic physical anatomy. Education in this regard was something the Church was loathe to cede to civil or state authorities. Prayer was deemed to be the solution to any doubt about physical contact between the sexes. In Mary Lavin's short story 'Sunday Brings Sunday' (1944), the priest makes the choice clear: 'I ask you to turn over in your mind whether it is better to get down on your knees for 3 minutes or to spend an eternity in the dark pit of damnation, lit only by the flames of hell.'[57] The 16-year-old girl at the centre of the story wants more specifics: 'Why couldn't he say straight out what was wrong and what was not. Why couldn't he? If only he gave an idea; only an idea. They should give people some idea.'

Frank O'Connor continued to address the theme of the loneliness of a celibate life and the longing for companionship, which was bordered by ignorance and lack of guidance and instruction. In the words of Sussie in 'Don Juan's Temptation' (1948):

I sometimes think young people are the loneliest creatures on God's earth. You wake up from a nice, well-ordered explainable world and you find eternity stretching all around you, and no one, priest or scientist or anyone else, can tell you a damn thing about it. And there's this queer thing going on inside you and you don't know how to satisfy it.[58]

There were those who did attempt to satisfy it. One of O'Connor's most enjoyable short stories is 'News for the Church', first published in the *New Yorker* in 1945, in which a 19-year-old woman, a teacher in a convent school, shows little shame in telling a priest, Father Cassidy, that she had sex with her sister's former boyfriend the previous night:

'I had carnal intercourse with a man, father,' she said quietly and deliberately.

'And you do know that unless you can break yourself of this terrible vice once for all it'll go on like that 'till you're fifty?'

'I suppose so', she said doubtfully, but he saw that she didn't suppose anything of the kind.

The priest began to ask her more intimate questions.

She answered courageously and straightforwardly trying to suppress all signs of her embarrassment. He stole a furtive look at her and once more he couldn't withhold his admiration.

He grew graver and more personal. She didn't see his purpose. She only saw that he was stripping off veil after veil of romance, leaving her with nothing but a cold, sordid, cynical adventure, like a bit of greasy meat on a plate.[59]

Many, of course, were accustomed to confession, but not always terrified of it; as Dermot Healy recalled in his memoir *The Bend for Home* (1996), it was a convenient way of wiping the slate clean. After receiving absolution in confession he skipped outside, 'then with a giddy heart ... I stood on the steps of the Cathedral, ready to start all over from scratch again'.[60]

There was still no shortage of thunderous admonishments coming from the likes of the Redemptorists, but how effective they were and how seriously they were taken is open to question. As pointed out by Brendan McConvery, despite the sometimes-hysterical admonishments, these parish missions often brought a dash of colour to many a grey parish; they seem in particular to have caught the imagination of poets. Austin Clarke's 1967 poem 'The Redemptorist' depicts them as symbols of all that was oppressive in the Irish clerical world, while Patrick Kavanagh, in his novel *Tarry Flynn* (1948), describes a mission in his native parish given by two Redemptorists 'who were such specialists in sex sins'. As he saw it, their vociferous preaching seemed to inject a degree of life in the locality; when old men heard the missioners were on their way, they 'began to dream themselves violent young stallions who needed fasting and prayer to keep them on the narrow path'.[61]

In 1993, novelist John McGahern described his memories of the Redemptorist missionaries who came every few years to his parish like a band of strolling players and thundered hell and damnation for a whole week. There were stalls selling rosaries and medals and scapulars, and prayer books and Stations set up along the church wall for what McGahern described as 'the macabre carnival'. As he saw it, they were simply brought in to purify through terror, but in his experience

> they were never taken seriously, though who can vouch for the effect they might have had on the sensitive or disturbed. They were evaluated as performers and appreciated like horror novels. 'He'd raise the hair on your head,' I heard often remarked with deep satisfaction. Poorer performances were described as 'watery'. Some of the local priests were a match for these roaring boys, and while they were feared and accepted, I don't think they were liked by the people, though they'd have a small court of pious flunkies.[62]

'An answer calculated to confound humanists, atheists, agnostics'

The amount of abuse the Redemptorists identified and sermonised about is also a reminder of how prevalent fornication and excessive drinking were in Ireland. The Irish were good at paying lip service to pledges to improve their errant behaviour, but then, as soon as the enforcers had disappeared, reverted to their preferred ways. Denunciations of masturbation, for example, were inevitably in vain, as was apparent in Limerick in the 1940s when Frank McCourt and his classmates were subjected to a Redemptorist priest telling them that impurity was so grave a sin the Virgin Mary turned her face away and wept:

And why does she weep, boys? She weeps because of you and what you are doing to her Beloved Son. She weeps when she looks down the long dreary vista of time and beholds in horror the spectacle of Limerick boys defiling themselves, polluting themselves, interfering with themselves, abusing themselves, soiling their young bodies, which are the temples of the Holy Ghost. Our Lady weeps over those abominations knowing that every time you interfere with yourself you nail to the cross her Beloved Son, that once more you hammer into his dear head the crown of thorns, that you re-open those ghastly wounds.

McCourt's reaction was not going to gladden the heart of the Virgin Mary: 'I can't stop interfering with myself. I pray to the Virgin Mary and tell her I'm sorry I put her son back on the cross and I'll never do it again but I can't help myself and swear I'll go to confession and after that, surely after that, I'll never do it again.'[63]

When the Taoiseach John A. Costello corresponded with Bishop Staunton of Ferns in November 1950 concerning an extension of the state's involvement in mother and child welfare, he acknowledged that 'education in regard to motherhood may include instruction in sex relationship, chastity and marriage', but that there would be nothing objectionable from the Church's point of view, and that 'care will be taken to ensure that the regulations governing its operation will include nothing of an objectionable nature under their head'. In any case, as far as Costello was concerned, 'there is an adequate [number] of zealous clergy [who] will be quick to detect any practices contrary to Catholic teaching and to instruct its flock appropriately'.[64] This was in reply to Staunton's assertion that the Hierarchy 'regard with the greatest apprehension the proposal to give to local medical officers the right to tell Catholic girls and women how they should behave in regard to this sphere of conduct at once so delicate and sacred'; he even went so far as to suggest that it was providing 'a ready-made instrument for future totalitarian aggression'.[65]

Minister for Health Noël Browne, who had responsibility for introducing the scheme, was more concerned with ensuring the service was free, and attacked the snobbery of the doctors 'who know little of the misfortunes and the unhappiness of the poor and care less'. He broadcasted on radio to highlight the fact that Ireland's infant mortality rates were twice those of England, and that in 1947 the number of infants who died under the age of one was higher than the number who died from TB.[66] But Browne was not a champion of the provision of sex education at this stage of his career, despite being critical of the Catholic Hierarchy in his autobiography *Against The Tide* for being more interested in the spiritual than the physical well-being of its flock. In a Dáil debate in May 1948 he revealed he had conservative views on such issues and, as his biographer John Horgan has pointed out, made no bones about his view that sex education for young people was unnecessary 'in view of the moral integrity and strong family life which results from the moral and religious teaching so readily and widely available in this country'.[67]

That teaching did not involve any instruction in matters sexual; what it did involve was complicated and abstract notions with an inordinate amount of attention devoted to purgatory. Many teachers were required to use Butler's catechism, a pocket-sized volume containing 112 pages and 86 questions and answers, which every child was presumed to have learned by rote. Bryan MacMahon, who taught in the diocese of Kerry in the 1940s, recalled:

> Much of the knowledge we imparted in the Christian doctrine lesson was abstract. One of the things we had to explain to children who were scarcely ten years old was that when a person died and went to heaven his body joined his soul on the last day and was then endowed with attributes that it did not possess while on earth: agility, subtlety and brightness.
>
> Another answer purported to offer with absolute accuracy proof of the existence of purgatory: This stout information provided the child, possibly destined for the emigrant boat, with an answer calculated to confound humanists, atheists, agnostics or even H. G. Wells himself.'[68]

Anna Murphy, the struggling adolescent in Kate O'Brien's *Land of Spices* (1941), feels that when her childhood is over 'she was going out from it with no lessons learnt and no preparations made'.[69]

'Feared always that she was not being pure, demure'

A book published by Mercier Press in Cork in 1949 entitled *Sex and Innocence: A Handbook for Parents and Educators* implored adults not to ignore the subject of sex education because 'it will not solve itself and cannot be safely left alone ... before considering what is offered in the following pages it would be natural for you to ask by what authority I write. For answer, I am a priest and I do love all little children ... to the complete and satisfactory solution of this problem prayer is absolutely necessary ... today, difficulties and temptations with regard to sex are more likely to arise than in Grand-mother's day.'[70]

The author acknowledged that few children turned to their parents to seek advice on this subject and bemoaned the fact that they would seek it elsewhere, creating the possibility of a 'filthy attack' on the sanctity of marriage. It was also deemed best to avoid any 'detailed treatment of sex matters' before a class of small children because 'it gives a sort of tacit licence to the children to treat of these things amongst themselves'. Clearly, the parents' role was more paramount than that of 'the outsider' and it was maintained that 'an honest confession of ignorance' on the parents' part 'helps immensely to draw the child closer to that parent. The child comes to realise that it shares ignorance with the most important person in the world.' The book also included 'an emphatic statement that the Church has adopted no "new line".'[71] This assertion is significant, coming as it did at the end of the 1940s, suggesting there may have been some criticism of the traditional Church teaching at an earlier stage than is usually thought.

One of the justifications put forward by the Department of Education in 1953 for maintaining its ban on married female teachers, at a time when the department was resisting pressure for its removal (the ban was rescinded in 1958), was that 'there is bound to be comment and a degree of unhealthy curiosity in mixed schools of boys and girls and even in schools for girls only, during the later months of pregnancy of married women teachers'.[72] Introduced in 1934, the ban was not uniquely Irish – marriage bans operated in Austria, Australia and Canada, for example – but the Irish ban was introduced just as other countries around the world were relaxing theirs. In practice, married women teachers had been employed for decades but received no pension rights or holiday pay.

A reluctance to engage with such issues in a frank manner continued beyond the school room, however. Archbishop McQuaid had particular advice for those involved in the marriage counselling division of the family welfare section of the Catholic Social Welfare Bureau. His notes relating to instructions for those lecturing married couples warned them to be 'very careful ... dealing with a mixed audience concerning a very delicate subject'. Talks for married couples at the Little Sisters Convent in Camden Street in 1955 included 'Moral purity with regard to company keeping'.[73]

That preoccupation with purity had a profound impact on many people, creating conflicting emotions and bubbling resentment, and is a theme reflected in much of the contemporary literature. In Gerald Hanley's *Without Love* (1957), Una Brennan is a timid, mother-dominated daughter who 'feared always that she was not being pure, demure. She lived not far from the confessional box, always.' Yet she also developed feelings of annoyance with her Church: 'Why had she not been born a pagan? She could have gone to bed long ago with a man and satisfied this gnawing, burning itch which filled her.'[74] Diarmuid Devine, the 'hero' of Brian Moore's novel *A Moment of Love* (originally published as *The Feast of Lupercal* in 1957), is unable to perform sexually with a young Protestant girl and blames his failure on his Catholicism: 'If I had been a Protestant, this would never have happened, he thought. I would have had my fill of girls. I would never have had to worry about going to confession.'[75] Patrick Kavanagh's Tarry Flynn, even though he escapes from a restrictive environment, is unable to embrace sex or love, finding it impossible to balance his faith and his sexuality: 'some men could dabble in sin, but it doesn't fit into his life.'[76] More tragically, Stevie Golden, the central character in the Francis MacManus book *The Fire in the Dust* (1951), an English youth living in Ireland who intends to become a priest, is expelled from the ranks because of his belief that 'a bodily act could be holy'. He maintains that if he listened to fanatics in these matters long enough 'he'd almost hate God', but he eventually drowns, suggesting the impossibility of the survival of a healthy attitude to sex in the Ireland of his era.[77]

'She was afraid of touch. All the time I was growing up I craved to be touched'

Of equal importance in terms of its long-term effect on the ability of individuals to be comfortable with intimate physical contact was the lack of demonstrations of affection. Growing up in the 1950s, Tom Inglis subsequently spent much time contemplating the significance of the fact that his mother did not hug him as a child: 'She was afraid of touch. All the time I was growing up I craved to be touched. I knew I was loved, but I wanted to feel it. When I look back over my early adult life, I can see how this lack of physical affection manifested itself later.'[78] It may also have made some of those who were reared in the 1950s more determined as adults to prioritise physical affection as if to compensate for the barrenness of a youth devoid of hugs.

Inglis has used his personal experience as an introduction to the assertion that this absence of physical affection, along with an obsession with sex
and an emphasis on self-denial, 'has been central to what makes the Irish different'. But his oft-repeated assertion that a Victorian repressiveness lasted
much longer in Ireland than elsewhere is problematical: internationally in
the 1950s there was still much concern about open displays of affection with
an emphasis instead on the façade of the 'story-book ... happy families'.[79]
There was much attention given to the research findings of US sexologist
Alfred Kinsey, published as *Sexual Behaviour in the Human Male* in 1948,
but also a backlash against such research and the perceived permissiveness in
Britain and the US in the post-war period.

If it is true that in Ireland 'the body was a source of awkwardness, guilt,
shame and embarrassment', then it could also be asserted that the same attitudes pertained in Britain; the Cold War climate in the US also manifested
itself in an anti-physical pleasure ethos and a preoccupation with 'aberrations'.[80] Internationally, the construction of middle-class norms of the body
and sexual behaviour and 'codes of bourgeois morality' were widespread,
but caveats inevitably need to be added to assertions about national sexual
characteristics. In Ireland, for example, Conrad Arensberg and Solon Kimball qualified their characterisation of the conservatism of Irish attitudes to
sex with the observation of 'very hearty sometimes ribald attitudes, which
make their appearance in banter, jibe and repartee even between speakers of
different sex'.[81] In public, a formal segregation of the sexes was common, as
manifested by separate aisles for men and women in churches. The history of
Irish masculinity has yet to be written; in obvious contrast to some of their
continental counterparts, Irish men were not prone to formalised displays of
affection. Mary Daly has also cautioned against exaggerating sexual frigid-
ity, 'at least for those who married', highlighting data on Dublin births from
1943–5 indicating that almost 7 per cent of first babies were born to women
married for less than six months and 44–7 per cent to mothers married less
than a year.[82]

Harsh attitudes to perceived female misconduct persisted, but perhaps one indicator of change was the emergence of a more positive and
romantic discourse based on dancing. This was associated with increased
consumption and urbanisation, although, as Barbara O'Connor points
out, this was not 'unproblematic'. The discourse of romance and modernity
gained strength through the proliferation of commercial ballrooms, magazines and films. The original Ballroom of Romance (The Rainbow) was

established in Glenfarne, County Leitrim, in the 1930s; bigger and more modern ballrooms with resident bands and orchestras began to appear in the 1940s, including the National in Dublin in 1945 and Seapoint in Salthill, County Galway, in 1949. There were many others in provincial towns and rural areas, and increased mobility made them more accessible. Despite a new emphasis on style, dress, consumption and romance, strict gender divisions still often operated inside – men on one side, women on the other and no hands on hips. William Trevor's famous short story 'The Ballroom of Romance' (1972) uses one such hall to contextualise themes of loneliness, sexual frustration and emigration from 1950s Ireland. What is noticeable is the degree to which the comments of the men about the women are overtly sexual ('that's a great pair of braces', or 'Eenie Mackie is very kind of tight in herself tonight'), but also that their own lack of care for their appearance and hygiene repulses Bridie, who tells Bowser Egan, 'I don't like being kissed by you. I don't like the sweat on the sides of your face and the way your teeth stick into me. And I don't like the way you take a swig of a bottle every time you have a go at me.'[83] But women looking for companionship in these areas had little to choose from.

'The romping of sturdy children'

These instances of frustration, the bubbling resentments, the occasional defiance and the preponderance of sexual crime contrast strongly with the picture Irish society wanted to paint of itself and present to others. Éamon de Valera's most quoted broadcast, the 1943 St Patrick's Day 'Ireland that we dreamed of' speech, is often now seen as encapsulating a hopelessly unreal and romanticised articulation of an ideal, rural, family-centred existence. Its mention of 'cosy homesteads' and the 'laughter of comely maidens' has perhaps inevitably been the target of revisionism by a generation who paid the price for the failure of the Irish economy to be self-sufficient. But it also conjures up an image that every society needs to be healthy – 'the romping of sturdy children'.

Some years ago, the historian Joe Lee suggested that this speech was important in terms of its emphasis on the links between generations and the dependent ages in society – childhood, youth and old age – and because it stressed that rights in Irish society had to be balanced by responsibilities. He also suggested, no doubt accurately, that many family, social and community relationships bore a broad similarity to this ideal.[84] But re-examining that speech in the light of what has been revealed in recent years – the evidence before the Commission to Inquire into Child Abuse (CICA), established in 2000 to assess the extent of abuse in residential institutions and which reported in 2009, for example, or what has emerged in legal cases relating to sexual crime – it is now known many were failed by the contract between the dependent generations, had no rights recognised and were burdened with responsibilities which should not have been theirs, often as a result of institutionalisation and child abuse. There was also a casualness about the abuse, as recalled by Dermot Healy: 'When you stepped into Brother Felim's class with the roll-call book he brought you behind his desk and felt your mickey as you called out the names.'[85] Nor was child abuse just a problem for the Catholic Church; when Norman Ruddock, a retired Church of Ireland clergyman, published his memoirs in 2005, he revealed he had been sexually abused as a 12-year-old boy in 1947, and again as a student boarding in a Church of Ireland college that was 'a citadel of repressed sexuality and abuse'.[86]

Children romping sturdily while away from school were often targeted by paedophiles. Depositions for a circuit court case in Dublin in January 1949 refer to the alleged activities of a 48-year-old yacht owner in Dun Laoghaire who seems to have been wealthy, given that a chartered accountant in Monkstown stood him bail of £100. He had allegedly brought four girls aged 11 to 14 on to his yacht. The 11-year-old gave evidence of how the children had asked him for work: 'we all went aboard the yacht. He showed us how to open the presses and asked us were we dirty. We thought he meant do we curse, we said yes, he then put his hand up our clothes in turn ... we came down the next day that was Corpus Christi, after mass about 11 a.m.' She then detailed the sexual abuse the girls experienced during the next few visits, including graphic descriptions of his fetishes, which involved their being asked to insert objects into his body, urinate into his mouth and wear macintoshes, in return for which he offered money and sweets: 'when I was on the yacht with Mr W. he showed us pictures of naked women several times and he read us stories out of a book and told me he had made a will and left me £2000. Several times he got us to whip him with a cane.' The book exhibits included *The Best Laid Schemes* and *Sun Bathing Review*. The events on the yacht came to the attention of the girls' parents because they took £4 on their last visit, dividing it among themselves, and the defendant came looking for the money.[87] A bench warrant was issued for the man's arrest, but he appears to have fled the district, and the case was not proceeded with.[88]

But it was sexual abuse by family members and relations which contin- |
ued to predominate. At Castlebar circuit court in 1950, a man was accused
of the unlawful carnal knowledge of his cousin at the house where he lived
with the victim and her aunt. The assaults, which took place when the aunt
was out of the house, resulted in pregnancy; the girl, one of six children and
another example of children who were 'farmed out' due to large families and
little money, ended up in a nursing home in Leeson Street.

Domestic servants were also still vulnerable. In the Castlebar area in
Mayo in 1943 a pregnant domestic servant was admitted to the Tuam home;
a 25-year-old man was charged with unlawful carnal knowledge of her which
allegedly occurred on Christmas night after a dance in a local hall, up against
a fence: 'I did not try and stop him.' The defendant, who was found guilty
with a recommendation to leniency, admitted he kissed the girl but insisted
he did nothing more: 'I thought she was a good girl.'[89]

That last statement speaks volumes about the way victims in these
cases were perceived and why the odds were so often stacked against them.
Undoubtedly, there must have been the occasional case where the wrong
man was pursued, and even a deliberate attempt to do this for fear of the
identity of the real father being revealed, but it is difficult to avoid the conclusion that an undercurrent of feeling that the woman was to blame dominated many of these cases. The constant references to 'character' and what
was expected from girls is not explored in relation to the conduct of the
men. Most of the negative language was used in relation to the girls, all the
medical inspections were of girls, and the men are almost peripheral to the
character dissection that went on. Clearly, many girls were regarded as archi-
tects of their own 'trouble' and 'downfall'.

'She may be trying to cover her shame – though this excuse is less cogent today than formerly'

Given all these considerations, it is not surprising that infanticide was still
prevalent in Ireland in the 1940s (though in most cases criminal proceedings were not initiated) and that abortions were being performed illegally.
The Garda Commissioner's first annual report on crime, published in 1947,
refers to six cases of infanticide of babies under one year, with proceedings instituted in two cases, in one of which the accused was convicted and
sentenced to death, although the sentence was subsequently commuted to

penal servitude for life. In the second case the accused was found 'guilty but insane' and ordered to be 'kept in strict confinement during the pleasure of the government'. In a third case, a young married woman 'administered poison to her infant son and herself. Both died soon afterwards.'[90]

Some of the debate about the law on infanticide during these years evidently attracted the attention of Archbishop McQuaid; included in his files is a memorandum on the Infanticide Bill by Patrick Duggan, who offered McQuaid advice on legal and legislative matters and who argued that the death penalty should be retained even though it had not been carried out in Ireland or England for a hundred years. He justified this on the grounds that infanticide was murder ('a very important moral truth') and that legislation should be left as it was. There was some comment in this memorandum on the social context of infanticide:

> She may be trying to cover her shame – though this excuse is less cogent today than formerly. To my mind, the consideration that appeals most to the ordinary person is that the man responsible for her condition, and so often more guilty than she, so often gets away scot free, while she has to bear all the trouble and all the shame.

This was indeed true; there were also comments about the physical and mental state of the mothers involved. According to Duggan, 'it also seems strange to me that such a natural process as lactation should be considered as having an unbalancing effect on the mind of the mother'. Another unsigned memorandum reveals a similar lack of understanding of pregnancy on the part of male lawmakers in their attitudes to these distressed women: 'As I understand it no woman on giving birth to a child feels any maternal solicitude on its behalf. It is only after she has handled it and nourished it and realised its complete dependence upon her that her natural and powerful maternal instinct is aroused.'[91] What was seemingly also not recognised was that shame and the fear of ostracisation were powerful enough stimulants to outweigh the feeling of attachment to the baby in the immediate aftermath of the trauma of childbirth, though doctors and barristers did attempt to convey a sense of this fear and confusion.

In Northern Ireland, the cases coming before the Belfast Assizes revealed a decline in the number of infanticide cases in the 1940s and 1950s, with only one case recorded in 1940 and no prosecutions at all recorded in the years 1945, 1950 and 1955.[92] Doctors and nurses, who were often the first to discover infanticide after women who had given birth alone were forced to seek medical aid, frequently commented on the mental health of the women, which did influence verdicts and sentencing at the conclusion of criminal proceedings. On occasion, single women found their entry to county homes blocked, and Gardaí could also threaten to take suspected women to the doctors for a medical examination in order to seek the truth. Lung tests could establish if the baby had been born alive. Another notable feature of many of the infanticide cases tried at the Central Criminal Court was the poverty, lack of education and illiteracy of a lot of the women involved.

But most cases were tried at the circuit court under 'concealment of birth' charges. A typical case in 1945, for example, resulted in a woman who pleaded guilty being sentenced to twelve months at High Park convent, Drumcondra.[93] Between 1922 and 1949, twelve women were sentenced to death at the Central Criminal Court for the murder of their illegitimate infants. Three of those sentenced were females related to the birth mother; one was married and one was a widow. Few women served more than three years in prison. Recommendations of mercy were common and, with the passing of the Infanticide Act in 1949, it has been suggested by Sandra McAvoy that 'infanticide came to be seen as the act of a woman temporarily unbalanced by the trauma of childbirth',[94] though in reality this was something doctors had regularly suggested long before the new law reached the statute; some of these women would have also displayed suicidal tendencies. With the passing of the act in 1949 a woman charged with infanticide was not deemed to be fully responsible for her actions and it became a non-capital offence, though in reality the legislation may have made little difference to the women, because in practice such cases were nearly always treated differently from other categories of murder, and doctors and juries were often sympathetic.

'I didn't look in the bag. To tell you the truth I didn't have the courage to look in the bag'

One case of concealment of birth that occurred in the same year as the new act was unusual in that the accused was a married woman, and the father of the baby – who was not her husband – was involved in concealing the birth. It sheds light on many aspects of sex and society in mid twentieth-century Ireland, including extramarital liaisons, the difficulty of keeping a secret in heard?

'great silence'

a small community, the impact of emigration on sexual mores and frustration, the terror of shame brought by an illegitimate child, the close confines in which people lived, and the great silence about unwanted pregnancy. The details were laid bare before Castlebar circuit court in the district court area of Achill, where the man and woman were charged with concealment of birth and conspiracy, after an infant's body had been found eighty yards from the man's house wrapped in a pair of lady's knickers in a shopping bag. The woman, who was the mother of a young child and lived at Dugort on Achill island with her husband's family, was 28 years old; her husband was a migratory labourer who came home only for a month or five weeks each year. According to the husband's brother, 'there were ugly rumours afloat about her condition. She told me that there was no foundation for these rumours.' The woman eventually went to the doctor shortly before she was due to go into labour; she had planned to have the baby in Ballina and put it into care, but the baby arrived early. Her statement recounts the birth:

> In September 1948 I discovered that I was pregnant as a result of J. H. Dugort having intercourse with me – connection. I told him about it but he said nothing. What could he say. Things went on normally until May 1949 ... I had nobody to help me as I couldn't let on to the people in the house ... the cord came with the afterbirth and I left all aside and baptised the baby myself as I knew it was weak. It was then dead ... I didn't do anything that would cause the death of my baby and I knew when I saw it that it couldn't live ... I wouldn't have cloaked the birth at all only for my husband not being the father and to save the name of my own little child.

The father was a 32-year-old unmarried farmer living nearby with his parents and sister. He was anxious to know what was happening and came knocking on the woman's window at 2 a.m. She handed the shopping bag out the window and asked him to bury it. According to his statement:

> I didn't look in the bag. To tell you the truth I didn't have the courage to look in the bag. I brought the bag to my own house which is over two miles from Mrs McH.'s house. I cycled. When I cycled as far as my own house I got a spade and dug a hole and buried the bag just the way I got it. I have no doubt the child was dead in a normal way, otherwise I would not have anything to do with it. My reason for keeping it so

quiet was to save Mrs McH. troubles with her husband and as a result he might take the other child from her and I know that she is very much attached to that child. If she had got to her mother in Ballina as we had arranged everything would be all right and she would get proper attention. I know that she never told her people in law or anybody anything about her state. If I had any doubt that the baby met with foul play, I would have nothing to do with it.

The coroner gave evidence that the baby was born alive, and that the cause of death was due to 'want of proper attention at birth ... the inattention would be consistent with fear of her in laws'.[95] Both of the accused were found guilty, but were discharged by Judge Wyse Power, a further reminder that humanity was not lacking in the circuit courts.

This case was reported in the local newspaper, the *Mayo News*. The barrister for the male defendant 'did not propose to go into the gruesome details of the case' (it was simply acknowledged that the defendants 'had become intimate'), but he asked that the man 'be dealt with in humane understanding' as 'he was the victim of human frailty' and was 'to a certain degree led on', but did not want this taken into account 'as a mitigating factor at the expense of the other accused'. In relation to the woman, 'one fortunate outcome of the case was that her husband had made a home for her in England and when it would be over she would reunite with him permanently there ... the judge said he had been thinking of binding the accused to the peace for 12 months, but in view of the unusual circumstances of the case he would make no order against them and would discharge them.'[96]

Irish writer Frank O'Connor, using his real name Michael Donovan, caused controversy in the same year as this Achill case when he published an article on Ireland in the American magazine *Holiday* in December 1949. While it contained beautiful photographs of the landscape, he drew attention to slum tenements, lack of hygiene, poor education, a Church intent on suppressing innocent social activities and the shadowing by police of girls who walked with boys. He also contended that 'infanticide is appallingly ✳ common'. The article resulted in considerable protest from Irish-Americans for its 'unseemly attack on the virtue of Irish womanhood'. In retaliation, Conor Cruise O'Brien, then in the Department of External Affairs, published an article in *Ireland,* the weekly bulletin produced by his department, in which he maintained that 'infanticide statistics are nothing remarkable one way or the other', and suggested the editors had got O'Connor either to change the original article or to make it more dramatic and controversial because initially he had 'apparently failed to take the expected crack at the clergy'. O'Brien was correct in his assertion that the editors had asked O'Connor to make significant revisions to his initial draft, requesting that he made it more dramatic ('we feel that the poverty of Ireland and the Irish people could be considerably sharpened by a section pointing up this poverty with specific examples'), but they did not mention the clergy. They were, however, particularly happy with his 'use of anecdotes', including, presumably, the one about infanticide that had caused most offence.[97]

Wexford Corporation, in its response to the article, accused O'Connor of 'vilifying Ireland and the morals of the girls of Wexford'.[98] The article was in fact thoughtful, well-written and honest ('at any rate I am not tempted to live anywhere else. Dublin, where I spend my days, is a beautiful city'). He suggested loneliness was rare, as was suicide, and included some hyperbolic passages for dramatic effect. The two offending passages included one where he referred to infanticide as 'appallingly common, though almost from the moment a girl starts walking out with a boy she is kept under observation by the police; if she leaves the neighbourhood she is shadowed and if she has a baby in another area, the police return and spread the news throughout her own town. Yet, it never seems to have occurred to anybody that there is any other way of stopping the crime.'[99] Wexford natives were particularly aggrieved about O'Connor telling of an encounter he had with an old man in Wexford while he was looking for directions:

> 'Are you married?' asked the old man in the way old men in Ireland have of plunging off at a tangent.
>
> 'I am not,' I said with resignation.
>
> 'Don't ever marry a woman without feeling her first,' said the old man firmly. 'The parish priest will tell you differently, but priests have no experience. There was a man in a house near me that married a girl like that, and the first night they were together, whatever occasion he had of grabbing hold of her, he felt the child jump inside her. I would never marry a girl without feeling her first and I would never give information about a neighbour.'
>
> 'You're a man of high principles,' said I.[100]

O'Connor's contribution to this subject is particularly significant because of the international reputation and acclaim he enjoyed (and still does) in contrast to the animus that often existed towards him in Ireland in the 1940s and 1950s, when he suffered real financial hardship (at one stage he had to write in the *Sunday Independent* under an assumed name). The offending article seemed to confirm his status, as an *Irish Press* editorial put it, as an 'anti-Irish Irishman', and his wife Harriet O'Donovan Sheehy recalls how some people would cross the street to avoid meeting him. When O'Connor's 1945 translation of Brian Merriman's epic Gaelic poem *The Midnight Court* was banned, the chairman of the Censorship Board declared, 'I do not think there is a magistrate in Ireland who would allow this book to pass.'[101]

'In a lonely farm or crowded tenement an extra child may not come under the notice of the authorities'

O'Connor's piece is another reminder that the stigma of illegitimacy remained strong throughout these decades. A passionate and angry article appeared in Seán O'Faoláin's magazine *The Bell* in June 1941, written anonymously, on this subject. The author described a typical court scene in which a woman was before a court for begging with her infant child. Asked by the judge whether she would go back to her family, she replied: 'They don't know about the baby, sir, they wouldn't take me.'[102] The author suggested the Affiliation Act of 1930 was not working in practice because of the difficulty of establishing paternity due to men disappearing, emigration and lack of income. It was suggested that 'in 2 out of 200 cases before the courts over a certain period was paternity successfully established – and the man solvent'. In any case, the wording of the act ensured that the primary 'sinner' was still the woman ('nothing in this act shall operate to remove or diminish the liability of the mother of an illegitimate child to maintain such a child').

There was no adoption legally available in Ireland until 1952; in 1940, 2,349 children between the ages of 2 and 15 were boarded out to foster homes around the country. The report of the Commission for the Relief of the Poor had recommended in 1924 that women traditionally sent to the county homes should instead experience the 'blending of individual charity and sympathy in their treatment', but in 1940 seven counties continued to send women to the county homes. The real need identified was for social workers ('in this respect we remain in the Dark Ages'). For those girls who agreed to stay two years in one of the mother and baby homes (in effect 'imprisonment'), their child was boarded out at the expense of the local authority and the mother had to go and find work elsewhere; some women had to work to support their children through their wages, while the children were in homes they could rarely visit.

By 1940, these five homes contained '5,600 women and children at a given time', but not one could 'boast of a resident doctor', and no attempt was made to 'train the unmarried mother'. With regard to the hostels ('miserably comfortless') there was no follow-up work and the author wrote approvingly of the work of the British National Council for the Unmarried Mother, of which there was no Irish equivalent, and the development of British social services resulting in a 'more widely informed and constructive body of public opinion'.[103]

It was also suggested that official statistics on the illegitimate birth rate, which gave figures of an average 1,700–1,800 such births a year, 'cannot be accurate ... It is impossible to calculate the number of children registered as legitimate at the discretion of the nursing home or midwife and in a lonely farm or crowded tenement an extra child may not come under the notice of the authorities. England also, before the war, provided a means of avoiding scandal for those prepared to pay.'[104] The high death rate for illegitimate children, highlighted in the last chapter, had improved, but it was still much higher than in England: in Ireland in 1940, 26 per cent of illegitimate children born died (it had been 30 per cent in 1924); in England and Wales the figure in 1939 was 8 per cent. Meanwhile the rate of illegitimate births in Ireland increased to 3.93 per cent of all live births in 1945, which was the highest rate recorded between 1864 and 1977.[105] This rise may be attributable to the increased restrictions placed on travel during the Second World War, which made it harder for women to leave, and also because of the introduction of the Children's Allowance in 1944, which made it likely that more women would register births.[106]

But some Irish writers addressed the issue of illegitimacy in ways that suggest it was not always hell and damnation and suffocating judgement. Mary Lavin's short story 'Sarah', published in 1942 in the collection *Tales from Bective Bridge*, refers to the character of the title as a woman with 'a bit of a bad name' who has had three children out of wedlock by three different fathers. But because she so faithfully attends to her religious duties, her neighbours are protective of her, while at the same time 'charity was tempered with prudence and women with grown sons and women not long married took care not to hire her.'[107] There was also another 'solution' to the problem of illegitimate children, which was for them to be brought up as a sibling of the mother, or to be informally adopted by one of the mother's siblings, many never knowing the true story of their parentage while their parents were alive.

In 1950, Helen Cooke temporarily became the most famous woman in Ireland when she was at the centre of a political row over the appointment of a new sub-postmaster in the small village of Baltinglass in County Wicklow. Cooke had been running the post office for fourteen years due to the illness of her aunt and expected to succeed her when she resigned, but Labour Party minister James Everett appointed the son of one of his party's activists. There was uproar at the blatant political jobbery; high-profile protests and a boycott of the post office ensued, which ultimately resulted in Cooke getting her job back. Cooke retired in 1963 and went to live in Australia where she died in 1972. She was survived by a daughter who had been adopted by one of Cooke's sisters but did not know until years later that in fact her real mother was Cooke.[108]

'Hustled off, normally to London, Paris, Biarritz ...'

Given the obvious stigma usually associated with illegitimacy, it is unsurprising that some women opted to have abortions instead. There were no prosecutions in Ireland for illegal abortions between 1938 and 1942, suggesting the abortion trail to England began in the late 1930s, but as a result of the travel restrictions imposed during the war years there were 25 cases prosecuted in Ireland between 1942 and 1946, while after the war the number of prosecutions decreased, with only 12 cases between 1947 and 1956, though these figures only relate to abortions that went wrong or were found out.[109] In 1941 a contributor to *The Bell* suggested that some young pregnant women from well-off backgrounds were 'hustled off, normally to London, Paris, Biarritz, comes back without the baby and nobody is any the wiser'.[110]

Both Sandra McAvoy and Ray Kavanagh have revealed the extent of the abortion clinics in 1940s Ireland. There were a number of people convicted for performing abortions during this period and, after a clampdown in 1943–44 they were dealt with severely by the courts, receiving long prison sentences of penal servitude. Those convicted included Christopher Williams, a prominent chemist, Dr James Ashe, medical examiner to the matrimonial division of the High Court, and William Coleman, who ran an extensive abortion practice in Merrion Square and who received a fifteen-year sentence in 1944, reduced to seven years on appeal.[111] A list of the desperate remedies for unwanted pregnancies in the absence of safe abortion included hot baths, gin, knitting needles, pennyroyal, castor oil, quinine and household detergents.[112] Sandra McAvoy's overview of abortion and the experiences of women forced to give evidence in Dublin abortion prosecutions in the mid 1940s makes it clear that the 'back street' abortion option was the one most often taken because medical careers could be damaged by a failure to rigidly implement Catholic ethical standards and 'the fact that a pregnancy constituted a potential, rather than an immediate threat to a woman's life was not considered an ethical or legal ground for contraception or abortion'.

Two clients of Dublin abortionists Mary Molony and Christopher Williams had histories of haemorrhaging in childbirth.[113] Dr James Ashe admitted in 1944 that 'over the past four years [since the outbreak of the war] at least 30 women, married and single, from all parts of Ireland, have called on me to see if they were pregnant and if anything could be done for them'. The reason they sought him out was because Ashe, as a Protestant and former honorary president of the British Legion in Ireland, may have been perceived as influenced by a British rather than an Irish Catholic medical culture. In Britain at that time, while abortion was still illegal (and remained so until 1967), it was increasingly argued that it might be an ethical option when the health of a woman was threatened or where social and economic distress was involved. In 1938 the Bourne case established that abortion to protect the health of the woman was permissible, with the onus now on the Crown to prove a medical abortion had not been performed in good faith.[114] It was suggested that during the late 1930s an average of between 300 and 400 terminations were performed daily in England and Wales, 40 per cent of which were criminal abortions and, given the scale of emigration of Irish women to England, 'it is likely there was a high awareness of the possibility of obtaining back street abortions in England'.[115]

There was also a class element to some of the trials at home. In 1940 in Cork, a midwife 'of good reputation' was found not guilty of the murder of a 25-year-old woman allegedly from ergot and quinine poisoning: 'it seems likely that the state prosecutors had little stomach for winning a case in which a maternity nurse might face the death penalty'. The case was reported in the newspapers.[116]

The research done by Cliona Rattigan on those who were prosecuted for performing abortions between the 1920s and the 1950s is a reminder that many women who sought to terminate their pregnancies were not 'unfortunate victims'. Key determinants in any decision to have an abortion were the knowledge available to the women and whether they had access to money and contacts, as well as the attitude of their partners. Many who gave evidence in the trials were willing sexual partners, and a number had had previous abortions, while several had had more than one sexual partner, 'yet it was often assumed in Irish courtrooms that the decision to have a sexual relationship and to seek an abortion in the event of an unplanned pregnancy rested with the man'.[117]

'In my view she is quite amoral and in that sense I would consider her abnormal'

For a generation, perhaps two, the words 'Nurse Cadden' were regarded in Ireland as synonymous with evil. Despite having been disqualified as a midwife and serving a jail sentence after she was convicted of abandoning a patient's child. Marnie Cadden continued to flout the law by offering abortions. She performed a number of botched operations and became known nationally in 1956, when she was charged with the murder of Helen O'Reilly, a deserted mother of six who died from an embolism on Cadden's kitchen table in her bedsit in Hume Street, Dublin, as a result of the pumping of a mixture of air and disinfectant into the woman's body. Cadden was convicted of murder and sentenced to death by hanging, commuted to penal servitude for life, despite the flimsiness of the evidence against her. The ambiguity associated with the case is interesting. Former High Court Judge Kenneth Deale, who wrote an account of the trial, questioned whether it would have succeeded if Cadden 'had been a respectable midwife of good reputation', which also points to the suppression of a public discourse on abortion.[118] Cadden died in the Central Mental Hospital in 1959.

The reason for the murder charge was that under Section 58 of the 1861 Offences against the Person Act, a person who 'unlawfully' procured the miscarriage of a woman was considered to have committed a felony. A patient dying as a result of such a procedure was therefore not considered to have died during a medical operation, so a murder charge could be brought against whoever carried out the procedure. But this in itself was ambiguous. The act referred to those 'unlawfully' using instruments or administering drugs to procure abortion – did this imply that there were circumstances in which abortion might be lawful? And what was the implication of this legislation for the medical profession? No charges were ever brought against doctors or midwives for performing abortions for medical reasons, so the Irish courts never tested the application of the legislation in such cases.

The Cadden case, however, had a long history. The 1944 police clamp-down on abortion services in Dublin had once again brought her to the attention of the authorities, and in 1945 she had been sentenced to five years' penal servitude for procuring a miscarriage, after a trial in which the patient was the main prosecution witness. As an incompetent abortionist presiding over botched operations, Cadden's methods were to result in two deaths, the second being that of Helen O'Reilly. She also labelled the women who sought her services 'whores' and suggested in her statement to the police, after O'Reilly's death, that she considered the dead woman to have had 'the mouth of a prostitute'.[119] As Catriona Crowe points out, 'The fact that she was providing a much-needed service to desperate women who were denied access to contraception does not of itself make her a feminist heroine. She was well paid for her work, and insisted on money up front. Vera Drake she was not.' (This is a reference to the central character in Mike Leigh's 2004 film of the same name, in which a kind-hearted working-class woman in London in 1950, wanting to help young women in distress, performs abortions in a backroom and does not accept payment.)[120]

Why did the Cadden case create such a big stir in comparison with the other trials? Probably because prosecutions by this stage were so unusual: official Department of Justice figures reveal that the number of cases known or reported to the Gardaí in 1948 was 8, arising out of which there were 4 convictions (3 males and 1 female), whereas ten years later in 1958 there was only a single case known or reported and no prosecutions,[121] suggesting that the publicity attached to the Cadden case had made an impact.

The Cadden case reveals not so much that 'Ireland', as Ray Kavanagh exaggeratedly asserts, 'had returned to the savagery of a witch trial of the middle ages',[122] but more that there was a tendency to give more attention to the abortionist than to the victim. Those who were seeking the abortions were almost invisible. Helen O'Reilly was not a young girl in trouble: she was a 33-year-old mother of six who had been deserted by her husband, and whose children had been taken into care in various convents; she had already tried to induce a miscarriage through the use of abotifacient drugs. The dilemma of women with many children who desired no more, but lived in a country in which no contraception was available, was replicated all over Ireland. Cadden's first victim, Brigid Breslin, a 33-year-old dancer at the Olympia Theatre, also died after a botched operation on the Cadden kitchen table, in 1951, but she got away with that one.[123]

Cadden was completely dismissive of Catholicism (when told by the judge, 'May the Lord have mercy on your soul', she replied, 'I am not a Catholic. Take that').[124] The prison medical officer's report concluded that she was fully aware of the consequences of her action, but seemed to have 'absolutely no regard for the moral aspect of such an act. In my view she is quite amoral and in that sense I would consider her abnormal.'[125] This is significant, because, despite a contention that she was sane, Cadden ended up in Dundrum mental hospital. Her solicitor, when petitioning for the death sentence against her to be commuted, suggested she was not insane but 'of abnormal mentality'. The government agreed to commute her sentence in January 1957.[126] And what of Helen O'Reilly, her victim? There were nine days of evidence during this trial and eighty-eight witnesses for the prosecution. The police report, having detailed the gruesome discovery of her body on Hume Street, noted that 'it is necessary at this stage to state that enquiries regarding the deceased showed that she was a woman of loose morals who had been associating with different men'. O'Reilly had been spending a lot of time in public houses; her husband was not the father of her baby; and she was anxious 'to get rid of her pregnancy' before he was due to return home on leave from Nigeria.[127]

As far as the judge was concerned, in his charge to the jury concerning the private life of O'Reilly, 'it is proper you should have that evidence', though he did not explain why, and it was a significant comment given that it was Cadden who was on trial. The implication was clear: O'Reilly was also on trial due to her lifestyle.

The essayist Hubert Butler wrote a powerful essay on the subject of the Cadden trial, which was unpublished at the time, underlining the difficulty in trying to instigate public debate about sex-related issues in the 1950s. He noted that the *Irish Times* had been the only newspaper to report the case, suggesting

> the insufficiently explored danger zone of sexual mores ... the repugnance which the abortion trials inspired sprang, I believe, not only from the nature of the offence but also from the manner of its exposure. Two taboos, not one, had been violated. An unnatural act had been committed, and a more than unnatural searchlight focused on it. We revolted against looking in the direction in which the searchlight pointed.[128]

He argued that associating the welfare of the state with private morals was wrong and that, unlike the situation in Ireland, in countries where laws against abortion existed there had been debate about the consideration and modification of such laws. He provocatively queried whether the Irish sentiment of implacable opposition to abortion was truly genuine, wondering about a door in Merrion Square behind which some people knew abortions were being performed. He asked:

> Would we not have burst through it ourselves, had the law delayed intervention? Instead for years we have passed it by, laymen and professionals, with at most a disapproving shrug, a cynical observation. True feeling expresses itself otherwise.[129]

'Our people at home do not face the fact that there is original sin in Ireland as much as in any other part of the world'

Butler's questions in this regard may also have been prompted by the desire to confront the erroneous notion that such occurrences belonged elsewhere; that they were associated with the immorality of other countries and were inherently un-Irish. One of the overriding themes relating to sex and society in Ireland during this period was the preoccupation with the manner in which it was believed emigration would compromise the chastity and morality of the Irish by leading emigrants to immoral climates and environments that were the antithesis of what they had left behind. As Clair Wills points out, in 1946 Frank Carney's religious melodrama *The Righteous are Bold* ran for fourteen weeks at the Abbey theatre in Dublin, making it the most popular play of that period. Set in the kitchen of a small farmhouse in Mayo in 1945, it deals with the plight of Nora, who has been working in a factory in Lancashire but is sent home by the local priest because she has become 'satanically possessed by a modern, secular outlook' which causes her to have fits whenever she sees a crucifix or a picture of the Sacred Heart. During the exorcism scenes, 'England and its pleasures are literally beaten out of her.'[130]

This notion of foreign contamination was one of the greatest myths punctuating discussions about sex during this period. It was remarkably durable and potent, and in particular can be traced through the archives of

Archbishop McQuaid, due to his decision to establish an emigrant welfare bureau in 1942. This bureau had many concerns, but it is quite clear from the reports being sent back to McQuaid that sex was near the top of the list. He was not the only person who was worried about it; other religious figures, politicians and diplomats expressed the gravity of the 'moral dangers' associated with emigration. These fears were particularly notable when, as was the case between 1946 and 1951, it became apparent that more Irish women than men were emigrating; for every 1,000 men that emigrated from Ireland during those years, 1,365 women did so.

There was something of a role reversal going on here for a former colony. In his history of sex in twentieth-century Britain, Paul Ferris observes that in the early twentieth century 'the English were convinced their morals were better than those of the continent. The belief had little foundation. Illegitimacy rates were high; prostitution thrived; a decade earlier the VD rate in the army was among the highest in Europe. But moral discipline was the virtue that a powerful nation wished to assume before those it refused to see as equals.'[131] The Irish version of this mentality some forty years later was about a small, intensely publicly Catholic country believing it was the jewel in the Catholic empire's crown and that spiritually and morally it was far superior to both the UK and the continent, a version of the earlier belief in superiority beloved of the Edwardian English.

The view was continually expressed that Irish superior purity was under threat, not just as a result of the emigration of those who were uneducated but because of the risk of importation of external ideas that needed to be resisted by the educated. As McQuaid put it in a letter to the Minister for Health, Joseph Ryan, in January 1954, 'the fabric of our social life is being subtly and progressively undermined. I do not need to underline the effect on the educated sections of our society which such a fear of the unitary or socialistic state continues deeply to disturb.'[132] Francis Hackett, on turning a jaundiced eye on Ireland in the 1940s, was scathing about the attempt 'to lock up the Irish in their innocence and purity'.[133] Honor Tracy (the pseudonym of the British travel writer Lilbush Wingfield, a former staff member of *The Bell* who had a love/hate relationship with Ireland) published a book in America in 1953 in which she depicted what she regarded as 'that rancid Irish Puritanism, that fear and hatred of life … a bitterly wounding experience', and she lamented 'the terror, the moral paralysis that afflicts so many Irishmen in their dealings with the female sex'. But she may not have been entirely accurate in contending that 'there is no religious indifference, no large body of people vaguely agnostic and yet vaguely following the Christian ethic, as in England'.[134]

What some of the surveys of emigrant life held in the McQuaid archives reveal is that the existence of such a group of Irish people was in fact a serious problem as far as those policing the morals of emigrants and observing the impact of English life on those emigrants were concerned.

'An Irish girl who is foolish enough to seek to be as "modern" as her English compeers, renders herself open to grave abuse'

The preoccupations with women emigrating were evident in the reports sent to McQuaid by Henry Gray, the honorary secretary of the emigrant section of the Catholic Social Welfare Bureau. His report of June 1943 included the observation that

> an Irish girl who is foolish enough to seek to be as 'modern' as her English compeers, renders herself open to grave abuse ... many of them are innocent victims in that they have practically no knowledge of sex matters when they arrive in Britain. England's non-Catholic youth is, by contrast, saturated with unwholesome knowledge and it would seem to be essential that our Irish emigrant youth should be equipped to safe guard themselves by a Christian and normal understanding of sexual matters.[135]

Beside these two last words, McQuaid placed a disapproving, or perhaps curious 'x', which is not surprising – was this a frank call for Irish youth to be given sex education, or a contention that Irish youth did not have 'a Christian and normal understanding of sexual matters'?[136]

McQuaid remained very defensive about this portrayal of Irish emigrants for the next twenty years, complaining to the Archbishop of Westminster in 1960, 'that we must still endure the old misunderstandings is now evident'.[137] A year previously the Archdiocese of Westminster had asked the Newman Demographic Survey, a Catholic social survey group based in London, to prepare a report on the welfare of Irish immigrants in London and Wales. Irish clerics were critical of a section in the first draft of the report describing the characteristics of the Irish immigrants, which highlighted ignorance about sex and 'the general absence of sex education' as well as 'a view of clergy–laity relationships that polarises at either complete acceptance of priestly authority in all matters or equally complete rejection of any priestly authority'. In response, a furious Father Cecil Barrett, who oversaw the administration of the welfare bureau, prepared an alternative draft that suggested 'Irish children grow up in an atmosphere where purity and chastity are reverenced [and] without significant exposure to the naturalistic theories of sex education'.[138]

Such defensiveness was misplaced and disingenuous, especially as the reports prepared for McQuaid and Barrett provided ample evidence to support the assertions made in the Newman Report. The annual reports of the emigrants' section of the Catholic Social Welfare Bureau, which was officially opened in June 1942, give some idea of the scale of the work that was being attempted, most of it centred on 'rescuing' vulnerable emigrants. Between June and December of 1942, for example, the bureau received information regarding the emigration of 2,182 Irish Catholics, most of that information coming from the Legion of Mary. One hundred and fifty-three emigrants were placed in touch with Catholic societies or clergy in their adopted areas, 'and their welfare, both spiritual and temporal, is known to be assured, for the present at any rate'. Although the bureau highlighted anxieties about conditions of employment, it still maintained that 'the vast majority of our Irish emigrants are faithfully maintaining the practices of their faith'.[139] By 1943 it claimed to have provided for the welfare of 10,000 emigrants, and by the end of the war, claimed 37,000 had been surveyed, with a particular emphasis on the 'suitability of the contemplated employment' of first-time emigrants 'from the religious and moral standpoint'.

It was also concerned with tracking those who married outside the Catholic Church, and with the repatriation of those 'whose moral welfare would be better safeguarded at home', with one of the most common problems being the 'particular danger to the moral welfare of young girls'. In 1955, 12,000 cases were dealt with and the bureau reported a 'spectacular increase in the use of the Bureau's services', reflecting the increased emigration from Ireland.[140]

But it was during the war years that the alarm bells had started ringing about the damage emigration could potentially do to Irish moral standards. Henry Gray expressed particular concern about young Irish being 'more prone to adopt the "advanced" ideas of a considerably more sophisticated world'. Some indication of this tendency was perhaps reflected in the decision of Agnes O'Shea, a Catholic woman from Kerry who in 1942 emigrated to the north of England where she practised as a doctor, not to acknowledge the number of siblings she had. Her son, English author and poet Blake Morrison, only discovered after her death that she was the nineteenth of twenty children (thirteen of whom survived):

> Why the silence? Why not say she was one of twenty or at least one of thirteen? Perhaps the awkwardness was that such numbers advertised her Irishness. Many others in the Diaspora had likewise fudged their origins. Back then, in England at least, Irishness carried a taint – of peasant ignorance, poverty or gun-running – which emigrants did well to lose ... if my mother, making a career for herself among the English middle classes, had been reluctant to describe herself as the nineteenth child of twenty, that was surely understandable. She'd reinvented herself – and done it so thoroughly that she failed to set the record straight with her own children.

Morrison's discovery of his parents' wartime correspondence led to his memoir *Things My Mother Never Told Me* (2002), which reveals the frankness with which Agnes and her future husband, a Protestant, discussed their emotional feelings, religious mores (and differences) and family planning.[141]

Henry Gray, who maintained that his views were backed by 'informed opinion in England', expressed the belief that different standards were operating in England and there was a disturbance of the immigrants' 'reliance on standards which went unquestioned in their home environment'. He then outlined his views as to why this was the case:

> Public morals and conventions in Britain naturally depend for their standards on the degree of vitality animating the Church of England. English Protestantism was pre war tending more and more to degenerate into a simple cult of respectability. Many lead excellent lives but they are not imbued with any lively desire to see moral standards upheld generally. The absence of any religious incentive among the bulk of the population has brought the country to a state which can only be described as pagan. Standards of public morality have degenerated into a shamefaced and weak endeavour to 'preserve appearances'. This unfortunately applies especially to sex questions. The potential danger of such an atmosphere to the newcomer – no matter how high his or her own standards of morality may be – is obvious. It is a natural corollary to

the absence of moral standards that there are many 'wolves in sheep's clothing' whose delight it is to gain the friendship and confidence of the innocent newcomer by a profession of like ideals and interests and whose sole object is to undermine the religious or moral standards of their victims or alternately to commit them to the unwitting desertion of those standards.[142]

Gray's 1943 account was a good summary of the general attitude taken by the Catholic Church at that time – full of generalisations, sometimes alarmist, but also often frank, honest and gloomy. There was also a strong defensiveness at work in these reports, particularly in relation to what Gray believed was the prominence attached to the 'specious contention' that Irish Catholics were 'widely quoted as indicative of all that is bad and undesirable in human temperament'. He reiterated his belief that the bulk of Irish Catholics were attendant to their religious duties, but that there was a 'hopeless' minority who were 'anxious to escape from the restraints imposed upon their conduct by the conventions of Ireland'. This was a contention shared by others and repeated for many years; it was convenient in 1956 for the Garda Commissioner, in a letter to the Taoiseach, for example, to divide Irish emigrants into just two categories: those whose forebears were 'driven to the mountains and bogs by Cromwell and have been living on uneconomic holdings', and those 'who did not accept Irish institutions and laws, and preferred to live elsewhere'.[143]

In relation to declining standards of morality, much blame was placed by Gray on emigrants' accommodation, which meant they were forced to spend their leisure hours in locations other than the places in which they lived. He cited as an example an Irish hostel of 600 girls, 450 of whom were estimated to be attending Mass, but where there were problems of sexual immorality as a result of dance halls, clubs and time spent outside of lodgings. Gray suggested that 'the cry that many Irish Catholics in Great Britain are obsessed with sex is not a new one', but that such pronouncements were less sweeping than in the pre-war period, and that, in his view, 'it is still more a cause of joy that the real problem of grave sexual immorality among Irish people in Britain seems to have decreased at any rate so far as some areas are concerned'. He identified, none the less, 'grave cause for anxiety at the frequency of instances which Irish girls are found to be in trouble'. Equally significantly, 'It is also apparent that in most instances the men who are responsible are themselves Irish.'[144]

There was also the contention that girls who got into trouble were arriving in an advanced state of innocence and ignorance:

Girls are frequently victims of their own innocence or foolishness in allowing themselves to become intoxicated and hence leaving themselves at the mercy of their companions. It is not my intention to suggest that most or even a large proportion of Irish boys and girls lose their purity in Britain. But it is essential that it should be understood that a disturbingly large proportion do suffer in this respect.[145]

It was common for people in Gray's position to assume that English people were saturated with sex, though this may have been news to them. Paul Ferris's history of British sexuality suggests that the Second World War was 'less shocking' in its sexual aspects than the First World War, but that it is true that sexual matters were being dealt with more openly in relation to condoms and VD. War fiction magazines dealt matter-of-factly with physical relationships set against the backdrop of conflict; there was even a BBC radio programme aired called *Learning About Sex*, which was cautious enough but still allowed unorthodox suggestions about premarital sex to be made. However, in the context of censorship the assertions about sex saturation need to be highly qualified.[146]

Gray also detected a reluctance on the part of Irish girls to communicate with English priests due to the ingrained impression that 'a priest with an English accent is not a real priest at all', and furthermore that in London there was a lot of hostility to what was regarded as 'spiritual policemanship'. To his credit, Gray was honest about the dangers of making sweeping generalisations either way and he acknowledged that there were a variety of conflicting views and statements on all these matters and in relation to the morale of the emigrant Irish. He cited the example of an ordnance factory, seven miles outside Reading, which employed 1,000 Irish girls who were housed in a hostel where men and women moved freely ('the authorities maintain that they have no authority to limit the freedom of their employees while off duty'). He observed that out of this workforce there had been 'over 30 cases of pregnancy up to the present, all but three of which had originated in Ireland'. Contact by letter with the girls' parish priests proved relatively useless and 'the need is, of course, more pressing when there is the added complication of the existence of VD'.

Overall, McQuaid was satisfied that the observations contained in Gray's reports were 'sufficiently correct'.[147]

'I have do doubt that the wish of the Archbishop of Dublin would be treated by you as tantamount to a command'

VD began to be mentioned more frequently as a result of the war, during which there was a doubling of the rates of infection. J. C. Cleary of the VD clinic at Dr Steeven's hospital in Dublin warned in 1943 that VD constituted a greater public health problem 'than in any previously recorded period'.[148] It was something McQuaid was determined Irish hospital authorities should and would confront. In September 1944, Conor Ward, secretary to the Department of Local Government and Public Health, wrote to McQuaid to keep him informed of the department's intention to approve sending to Pennsylvania a doctor from Jervis Street hospital who would study methods of the treatment of VD and subsequently head up the VD clinic in the hospital. McQuaid was keen on this, but was opposed to the 1946 Health Bill which proposed to transfer to local authorities the power to deal with all infectious diseases including VD, which was originally dealt with by the sanitary authorities. McQuaid wrote to one adviser, Canon O'Keefe, expressing concern about the right of 'public authority to inspect the body; to inquire for or demand names of "contacts" in VD'.[149]

Conor Ward, who wrote regularly to McQuaid to keep him informed of developments and legislation affecting public health, was much more concerned with placating him than with taking on board the concerns of the opposition Fine Gael party, or, as he put it in a letter to McQuaid, 'If I am able to satisfy the Church on any points that may be causing uneasiness I shall not worry too much about the lay theologians', to which McQuaid responded by suggesting that public health 'seems to me to be on a level with national defence'.[150] As far as he was concerned this particularly applied to sexually transmitted diseases; during the war he had begun to correspond with the Dublin hospitals regarding the provisions they had in place for the treatment of VD. The Mother Superior of the Sisters of Mercy explained that the reason they did not treat VD patients at their Mater hospital as in-patients was 'the danger of infection to other patients and to the staff', and that if cases cropped up in outpatients they were treated in that department 'but in a private way, as the other patients would object, they have done so on previous occasions'. McQuaid rejected this reason for not providing more extensive treatment, stating clearly: 'It is my very keen desire that the several hospitals, under the control of religious sisters, in this city should treat venereal diseases, not only during the period of a war-time crisis, but also permanently in established departments.' Her reply was that 'we shall do our best to surmount all difficulties', to which he replied that he wanted an 'open-to-all clinic, with wards, male and female'.[151]

Clearly, progress was not being made quickly enough for McQuaid's liking and he had to resort to threats:

> It is to be presumed that when a person holding my office speaks and acts in regard to venereal diseases as I have spoken and acted, the policy outlined has been the subject of a careful decision. Unfortunately, I have to reckon with Catholics in my flock who maintain, in ignorance I must presume, a Protestant attitude towards my declared decisions. I hope that I shall never have to complain of such an attitude among any religious sisters in your congregation or in any other congregation in this diocese.[152]

The clinic was not operational at the Mater until March 1947, by which time there were four such clinics in Dublin. The Sisters of Charity, who ran St Vincent's hospital, endured correspondence with McQuaid on this subject also. In response to his demands, they replied that they did not have the accommodation, to which McQuaid replied, 'I am very pleased to learn that the reason for not treating VD at your hospital is not one of principle but is merely one of accommodation.'[153] But the following month he was angry at the medical board of St Vincent's for refusing to authorise a VD clinic, complaining that 'my Catholic people ... will have failed to receive the attention I had hoped they could receive' and that St Vincent's had 'failed in this, the first request I have made of it as Archbishop'.[154] He wrote again to the Superior General there: 'I have no doubt that the wish of the Archbishop of Dublin would be treated by you as tantamount to a command', and reminded her the following month that 'It might be presumed that the Archbishop of Dublin intervenes in medical questions only when spiritual issues are involved.'

McQuaid's determination to get the Dublin hospitals to treat VD during this period has been noted by Tom Garvin as being 'very honourable', as these were diseases that 'many Catholics tried to pretend did not exist, or, alternatively, if they were recognised as existing, were to be regarded as the (very just) wages of sin'.[155] McQuaid's correspondence on the subject is notable for its concern with medical treatment rather than casting moral or religious judgement. However considerable McQuaid's efforts in this regard (which are also an illustration that he did not always get his way), it seemed the rate of VD continued to cause alarm in the medical profession. In January 1945 Dr Desmond Reddin hand wrote a memorandum to McQuaid on the subject : 'I have written this memo as I did not wish my secretary to see its contents.' He expressed concerns about 'an alarming increase' in VD

> both in the city and the country generally which my rough survey convinces me has been largely brought about by people from outside countries returning infected rather than an increase of the indigenous cases. This causes an increase in the loss of child life due to abortions, miscarriages and stillbirths whether the parents are married or not. Amongst children born a high percentage particularly among the illegitimate class are mentally deficient epileptics, deaf and dumb or otherwise physically delicate due to these diseases.

He was concerned that unmarried mothers and people from poorer classes were only catered for 'in a small unsatisfactory way' at the maternity hospitals and Lock and Steeven's hospital. He believed 'all unmarried mothers should be blood tested as early as possible', as should 'all illegitimate children without exception' and warned of the potential 'for a further sharp rise' due to returning emigrants.[156]

'A few girls of doubtful virtue associate with sailors and sometimes go aboard their ships'

The Department of Local Government and Public Health had also noted in May 1943 that the incidence of VD was increasing 'to an alarming extent'. It acknowledged that it 'should be energetically dealt with at once', but suggested that before any publicity campaign was undertaken it would have to get the views of 'leaders of religious denominations', including Dr Barton, the Protestant Archbishop of Dublin. Three months later, the secretary of the department pointed out that VD schemes were now available in fifteen counties and four county boroughs, which was 'adequate', with 75 per cent of the cost of approved VD schemes borne by the state.[157] The Cork Port Sanitary Authority believed that the prevalence of VD had not altered significantly in 1940, with 12–15 people attending the local clinic, but acknowledged that 'it is known to the Gardaí and others that a few girls of doubtful virtue associate with sailors and sometimes go aboard their ships. If the Gardaí intervenes these girls and their sailor companions maintain that they are entitled to go aboard on invitation. The difficulty of proving prostitution in these circumstances will be appreciated.'[158]

At the Kildare turf camp (during the war it was essential to keep Ireland self-sufficient in fuel and in the region of 20,000 people were employed to work on the bogs), the medical officer compiled a report on VD the following summer. He wanted to send sufferers at the camps home to be referred to their county medical officers, but wondered 'if such men are sent home the local health authorities may say that "the turf camps are full of VD". Would this do the scheme harm?' It was decided that it would be necessary to discharge such men as medically unfit; but he was worried that if such men knew if they reported the condition they would be sent home, they might refrain from doing so, while the chief superintendent observed that 'there is a reluctance to report such a disease on the part of any man until it affects him to such an extent that he is positively ill'.[159] The possibility of setting up a 'prophylactic centre in each camp' was also mentioned, but there was a reluctance to make VD a notifiable disease due to the need for confidentiality.[160] It was also suggested in 1944 that emigrants returning from England should be screened on their return, but that 'it would be impossible to have it carried out without a general outcry'.[161]

The department also occasionally received confidential information from residents of a particular area informing it of 'a woman in the locality who is spreading the contagion'. One Clare resident called for the 'compulsory removal of such women' under the Emergency Powers Act 1940. He was told that this was not possible, although his complaints were examined seriously.[162]

In 1943, the total number of attendances at the outpatient clinic at Dr Steeven's hospital was 27,183.[163] The following year, the county medical officer for Wexford, Dr Michael Daly, spoke out publicly about a 'dangerous policy of "hush hush"' in relation to VD, and insisted propaganda would be 'a powerful weapon', along with a commission of inquiry to explore its prevalence. He noted that out of a county population of 93,800, 91 patients, or .09 per cent of the population, were under treatment for VD during the year; 13 were discharged or cured, but 44 had discontinued attendance for treatment; the difficulty of travel seems likely to have been one of the reasons. He argued that it should not be left up to individuals whether to seek treatment or not.[164] In private correspondence with the department he noted that 'returns cannot be relied upon for accuracy, because medical men as a rule do not keep records except when their position demands same'. He estimated that he was only seeing '1 in 5 or perhaps less of the actual number of cases occurring'.[165]

The reluctance of sufferers to seek treatment, as well as contrasts in the urgency with which medics in different areas highlighted the issue, might explain why there seemed to be such regional diversity. The county medical officer in Waterford considered its facilities adequate, reporting only 4 new cases in 1943, while those in charge of city health in Waterford reported a rise from 31 cases in 1938 to 89 in 1943, and the medical officer of health at the special clinic wanted to see 'compulsory segregation for infected persons, in particular infected females'.[166]

Thirteen cases were dealt with in Roscommon ('does not constitute a serious problem in this county'), while in Donegal the incidence of VD increased 'approximately four-fold'. The number of cases treated in Clare rose from 8 in 1938 to 34 in 1943, but the local authority was satisfied with the comprehensiveness of its scheme. Nearly all counties reported a rise in 1943 compared with 1938, but none of the figures are reliable, due to the small number of doctors who replied to requests for information, and discrepancies in form-filling. In Dublin, for example, 960 members of the medical profession in the city were circulated, but only 104 replied, who revealed that there had been 315 cases dealt with in 1938 and 672 cases in 1943. Again, given the absence of full information, these figures cannot be regarded as remotely approximating to the full picture. In the case of private doctors refusing to furnish information, a civil servant acknowledged that 'no action is open to the Department unless the defaulters are MOH [Medical Officers of Health] which appears unlikely'.[167]

In September 1944, a conference was held at the DLGPH concerning the increased incidence of VD, where it was suggested that there were not enough dispensary doctors qualified to treat it. The total number of VD cases treated in Dr Steeven's and Sir Patrick Dun's hospitals under VD schemes rose from 2,703 in 1935 to 4,188 in 1945, though these figures did not include local authority schemes and those being treated by private GPs. Overall, it is a scrappy picture, but it is clear men and women were viewed differently. In 1949 it was noted by the JCWSSW that there was only one clinic for women VD patients at Sir Patrick Dun's, 'where children also attend with the women', but it was not thought advisable that women should be treated at night in the hospital, as women ('never less than 30 and often more than 40') 'attending the outpatient department gave the impression of an ordinary hospital attendance'. It was also observed that 'all male clinics are held in the evening'.[168]

Lectures on VD were being given by army medical officers by 1945.[169] The previous year, the Wexford medical officer informed the department of details of a patient's history which had been sent to Ireland from Newfoundland – an 18-year-old girl, who had been infected by a Canadian navy man 'in a field' in Londonderry.[170] There was also correspondence regarding notifying the British War Office of an Irishman with VD returning to work in London in 1946. By 1948, Article 35 of the infectious diseases regulations obliged medical practitioners to furnish confidential notification to the chief medical officer of cases of VD (though it seems this was being done in some cases already), but it was suggested in Cork in 1952 that 'the full proposals do not seem to have been put into operation'. The numbers treated at the Cork district hospital clinic in the year ending March 1951 was 29, down from 52 in the year ending March 1949. The problem, according to the medical officer in Cork, was that the hospitals outside the city are 'not looked upon with any favour'.[171]

McQuaid continued to express opposition to the enforced treatment of people other than prostitutes for sexually transmitted diseases; in this matter Monsignor John Horgan, Professor of Metaphysics at University College Dublin, whom he already consulted on canon law issues, advised him. Horgan suggested that the state had a right to compel individuals to submit themselves or their children to treatment for VD to prevent the spread of disease, but 'at the same time it does not follow that ordinary state intervention would be the best method. This would be a field for voluntary and charitable organisations to educate and persuade ... the stigma attached to forced enclosure is so great that one would not care to see it adopted except as a desperate remedy.' McQuaid penned his own note in response to the letter: 'I agree. This has been my own view. We are in a quite different region when we treat ordinary persons who are not prostitutes, male or female. In such cases the state ought not to intervene or enclose with compulsion.'[172]

'Scare advertising has little effect as a preventative or as a deterrent'

Mention by the DLGPH of the usefulness of VD treatment propaganda during the war may have been made in full awareness of the fact that this was either being considered or implemented in other jurisdictions, though opinion on its merits was divided. In Northern Ireland, advertisements were placed in the *Northern Whig* and the *Irish News* in February 1943 highlighting that 'ignorance and secrecy are highly dangerous' and that there was a need for 'a plain and frank statement of the facts'. But within the Department of Health and Local Government there was doubt about advertising in the provincial as well as the Belfast papers: 'for political and other reasons it will be impossible to make any selection. This would only lead to endless trouble.'[173]

The following month, the Ministry for Home Affairs ordered material from the Central Council for Health Education in Britain on 'sex instruction'. The leaflets included such titles as 'Approach to Womanhood', 'From Boyhood to Manhood', 'Women in Wartime', 'Facts on Sex for Men' and 'What are Venereal Diseases?'[174] Their arrival was timely, given that the following month the Londonderry Temperance Council communicated with the chief medical officer at Stormont, expressing much concern about 'the moral conditions of this city' and the necessity to 'do something to educate the citizens to the dangers of illicit sexual intercourse'.[175] When the war ended, an official in the department expressed scepticism as to the value of media advertisements ('the newspapers are the only beneficiaries'), arguing that 'scare advertising has little effect as a preventative or as a deterrent but it may induce some parents to exercise a closer control over their children'.[176]

During the post-war period there was further concern about the incidence of sexually transmitted diseases in Northern Ireland and pressure was applied to replicate the British campaigns. It was noted that those with responsibility for implementing the scheme 'are much too engrossed in their other more lucrative appointments and private practices to devote the time and energy to VD work'. It was also recognised that Belfast 'presents the main problem', but it was decided not to do anything until 'if and when county medical officers of health are appointed',[177] an indication that Northern Ireland was behind the south in this regard.

But by the late 1950s there were nine clinics treating VD in Northern Ireland. The British Ministry of Health expressed concern about the increasing incidence of gonorrhoea, and in communication with Stormont referred to 'an increase of over 50% among women in 6 years', the suggestion being that 'a relatively small group of promiscuous infected women constitutes a most important factor in spreading the disease' as well as men 'who spend long periods away from home'.[178]

'One Yank and they're off!'

There were undoubtedly more sexual liaisons in Northern Ireland as a result of the Second World War, and the influx of troops. How this impacted on those from across the border seems to have worried some. Speaking at a confirmation service in Donegal in 1944, the Bishop of Derry mentioned the activities between women and American soldiers and commented, 'I wish I could take some of the people to see the conduct of their girls in Derry – girls from Donegal and Inishowen. It would be better for them to live on potatoes and salt.'[179]

The first American troops arrived in Northern Ireland in January 1942, their numbers peaking at 120,000 in December 1943, with a number of airbases serving as naval headquarters and the main US communications base in Europe during the war. Many soldiers were billeted in rural areas, and undoubtedly contributed, in the words of Leanne McCormick, to 'new patterns of female sexuality, and the techniques of parents, priests, religious organisations and local priests and doctors intended to control women's behaviour were, without a doubt, mightily challenged'.[180] 'One Yank and they're off' was the punchline of a popular wartime joke in Northern Ireland: 'Have you heard about the new utility knickers? One Yank and they're off!' Pleasure-seeking sexually active women in this regard were perceived as a threat to the imagined, unified, self-sacrificing community of the UK during the war years. McCormick has suggested this was not quite as clear cut in Northern Ireland, where ideas of national identity were more problematical and divisive, and support for the war was not wholesale. It was, however, still the case that across the religious and political divides, female virtue and chastity were prized. One magistrate in Derry, commenting on a woman who had been charged with indecent behaviour with a sailor, pronounced: 'We Irishmen are rather proud of the purity of our Irishwomen, just like the purity of our racehorses.'[181] The challenge to such purity was reflected in figures that revealed the number of illegitimate births rose in Northern Ireland between 1942 and 1945, and prosecutions for prostitution rose from 10 in 1941 to 185 in 1943.[182]

The cultural experiences of US soldiers were markedly different from the culture their new peers were reared in. The US military pocket guide to Northern Ireland explained that there was 'virtually no nightlife' and 'a woman's place is, to a considerable extent, still in the home'. P. S. Callaghan, who served during the war as a radio operator with the US air corps based in Belleek, County Fermanagh, and who later became a leading US scientist, recorded his reminiscences of this period. He enjoyed living close to the land and the people, made his way around on his bicycle, and recorded the typical stereotyped and desexualised version of the Irish woman in Northern Ireland. She

> represented the last of a disappearing type of European women, for which there is no comparable replacement in our modern world. She was faithful, hard-working and born to the land as if her body had been moulded and cut from the rocky Irish soil. In truth, her apparel, often smeared and dubbed with the black soot of the turf fire or her brogans covered with the manure and bits of heather from the pasture where she tended the cows, attested to her closeness to the land. During the late summer haying season, she could rake, stack and thatch the ricks of hay to the shame of any man.[183]

He also recounted the events of fair day and the local dance, where matchmaking 'was simple yet sophisticated beyond any modern folkways of matchmaking ... since all the girls were sitting on laps, no one girl could be considered forward'. But he also suggested that they were suspicious of the soldiers:

> people the world over simply do not want their daughters associating with strange men in uniform. If one of our 'yanks' should occupy a bench, it would take a considerable amount of courage for an Irish lass to perch herself in his lap. No one really likes to be different and this would certainly give her a reputation for being forward.[184]

'Any woman who has respect for herself isn't to be strolling the streets of derry at night'

Notwithstanding, troops from the US inevitably held a particular exotic and erotic appeal. American films were hugely popular in a cinema-addicted Northern Ireland, and these men in uniforms brandishing cigarettes and chocolate in a deprived and rationed state seemed straight off the silver screen, while many of the native women, employed as a result of the war, were living more independently.[185] In relation to this independence, Mary Muldowney's oral history of women during the war challenges the idea that women during these years were just watching, waiting and weeping while the men fought. They intervened to help the most vulnerable, they often controlled the household income, and some were given new employment opportunities. Many, like Olive, one of the women interviewed by Muldowney, chose to go to another country themselves, 'to sally off to the unknown over there'. Ethel, another interviewee, recalls being proud of her service in a British uniform, and says of a later reunion with her former colleagues: 'I wasn't anybody's wife or anybody's daughter or sister, I was me and it was really marvellous. It's nice to be yourself once in a while.'

Women did what they could to help in the delicate areas of sexually transmitted diseases. Another interviewee, Susan, who worked in the Rotunda hospital, summed up her position: 'It's not my job to condemn. I'm here to help.' She then moved to work in the VD clinic in the Royal Victoria hospital, where she dealt mostly with women:

> that was a very difficult job because I was the first social worker ever to work in the hospital ... I wasn't either a nurse or a doctor and the question of confidentiality was what was bothering them ... I remember the first morning when I went in, he [the senior doctor] called me into his private office and took me aside and read me the story from the Bible of the woman taken in adultery and he said, 'Now I don't want you to condemn anyone who comes in here.' I said I wouldn't do that, it's not my job to condemn, I'm here and it's completely outside my training to make any moral judgements.

Since syphilis and gonorrhoea were not notifiable, the Westminster government introduced Defence Regulation 33B, which stipulated that any person suspected of having infected two or more patients might be compelled to undergo treatment, and this was extended to Northern Ireland. As Muldowney points out, 'in theory Regulation 33B was supposed to be applied equally to both sexes but in practice, it was focused almost exclusively on women'.[186]

Irish homes were full of strong mothers who shouldered responsibility for their families' welfare during the most difficult of times, but many of their daughters grasped whatever opportunities the war brought their way, helping to erode some of the social barriers that then existed.[187] Before the war in Northern Ireland there were less than 300 women employed in engineering; this figure had risen to 12,300 by 1943. During the war women who moved from rural areas to the city to take up war-related jobs, were apt to socialise at night, something which worried groups like the Church of Ireland's Moral Welfare Association and other community leaders.[188]

Public criticism of the sexual behaviour of US troops was mute, but censored letters provide evidence of the complaints being made privately. The soldiers were perceived as too wealthy; they drank too much and caused tension by depriving local men and British soldiers of female companions. Some places were deemed off limits to them, including Amelia Street in Belfast, infamous for its prostitution. Some complaints of sexual assault were not taken seriously due to the 'questionable character' of the female complainants, and more blame was often placed on the women for 'throwing themselves at soldiers'. There was, in general, 'the re-directing of attention toward female sexual behaviour rather than the misbehaviour of American troops' or, as another Derry magistrate put it, 'any woman who has respect for herself isn't to be strolling the streets of Derry at night'.

Attempts to combat this problem in Belfast involved a 'women's patrol'. Even girls who abandoned jigs and reels in favour of 'jitterbugging' were frowned upon.[189] Some of those patrolling women were in for a sexual education of their own; Elizabeth McCullough, born in a middle-class suburb of Belfast in 1928, recalled that with the arrival of American troops, 'Mrs Toner formed a vigilante group that patrolled the grounds of Belfast city hall at night, torchlight in hand, spotlighting some of the intimate acts performed by the soldiers and their local pick-ups on the benches or the grass. I gathered it was possible to "do it" in quite a number of surprising positions.'[190]

Lower-class women were also regarded as more suspect, as were, with the arrival of African-American regiments, inter-racial unions, though the black soldiers found themselves to be held in particular demand by Irish girls. One American corporal suggested 'the people over here make absolutely no distinction between the races', but it was an issue for many white US soldiers. According to US anti-VD propaganda, women were assisting the enemy by infecting soldiers, but there was substantial opposition in Northern Ireland to the establishment of prophylactic stations at US bases there. Instead, they were labelled 'aid stations', but must have been well used, as a Home Office circular complained of the resultant littering: 'contraceptives are left in public places, private gardens, shop fronts, shelters, etc., where they cannot give but offence to decent people'.[191]

New romances also resulted in marriage, though such unions were actively discouraged and gaining permission was complicated. Pregnancy also led to marriage proposals due to fear of the stigma of an illegitimate child, and not just from the working classes; in April 1944 a pregnant woman from Derry begged Colonel Ladd at the naval base for permission to get married because 'through a slight mistake I have become pregnant ... my family have a very high reputation and owing to my father holding a government position I do not wish any scandal to be fallen on them'.[192]

'In Austria and Ireland whether it was allowed or forbidden, they did it if they wanted to'

Undoubtedly, sexual activity in the Twenty-six Counties was also affected by the war, partly because soldiers would have socialised and holidayed across the border and also because many women's husbands were working abroad; at least 60,000 southern Irish citizens served in the British forces during the war. In December 1946 a senior Garda told an interdepartmental ad hoc committee on the suppression of prostitution:

> During the Emergency years there developed a big increase in the number of loose women to be seen on the principal streets at night, attracted by visiting soldiers on leave and visitors from Northern Ireland and the provinces ... a number of these women are not previously convicted but are of the loose type of married women living apart from their husbands and young girls of the domestic servant type.[193]

In terms of military intelligence during the war, certain individuals became objects of fascination to the British and Irish authorities, not just because of their political affiliations but also because of their sex lives. The private lives of some of the Nazis and those who consorted with them in Dublin during the war were interesting in this regard. One of the drinking companions of Carl Petersen, who was appointed press attaché in the German legation shortly before the war broke out, was Alan Graves, a former British consular official with a German wife, and while he was emphatically pro-British, he was, 'in certain quarters ... regarded as "sex-mad" and has occasionally entertained certain theatrical ladies' in a flat he maintained for such liaisons. Eunan O'Halpin points out that sexual licence was a recurrent theme in some of the documents recorded by G2 informants (who also fed off the reports of British intelligence networks), particularly in relation to Petersen and his social circle. One woman who was investigated because she 'allegedly cohabits' with Petersen was found to be 'actually very respectable' and a weekly communicant, but she shared accommodation with Petersen's mistress.[194]

Another interesting outsider who found refuge in Ireland during the war, at the Dublin Institute of Advanced Studies, was the Austrian Nobel prize-winning physicist Erwin Schrödinger, discoverer of wave mechanics and author of *What Is Life?* His biographer, Walter Moore, notes that his 'unusual family did not cause much adverse comment in Dublin ... the official Puritanism was alleviated by an informed spirit of *laissez-faire*'. Schrödinger, who arrived in Dublin in October 1939, lived with both his wife and his mistress in Clontarf, County Dublin. Dublin, it seemed, 'was not a strait-laced city'. Schrödinger once commented himself, 'In Germany, if a thing was not allowed, it was forbidden. In England if a thing was not forbidden it was allowed. In Austria and Ireland, whether it was allowed or forbidden, they did it if they wanted to.'[195] Self-centred and sexually hungry, Schrödinger sought to put that theory into practice. He also became close to Monsignor Paddy Browne, Professor of Maths at St Patrick's College, Maynooth, described as 'a Rabelaisian priest, in the literal sense that he knew much of Rabelais practically by heart and also in the figurative sense that he had a great store of bawdy stories'.[196]

Browne may have chided Schrödinger about his 'Lolita Complex' (his attraction to adolescent girls), but it was his affair with actress Sheila May, the wife of renowned Celtic scholar David Greene, that came to consume Schrödinger from 1944, prompting an entry in his journal: 'What is life? I asked in 1943. In 1944, Sheila May told me. Glory be to God!' He rented a city centre apartment for their liaisons. Although she subsequently became pregnant, the relationship did not last, perhaps because this affair differed from his numerous other love affairs, in which he had been 'the supreme male, confident of his superiority over psychologically subservient women' – certainly not a description that could be applied to May.[197] Given his professional achievements, Schrödinger was indulged; as a fellow physicist Max Born pointed out, 'his private life seemed strange to bourgeois people like ourselves. But all this does not matter. He was a most loveable person ... and he had a most perfect and efficient brain.'[198]

'Irish girls who fall an easy prey to the
smooth-tongued well-dressed stranger'

In the post-war period, the Emigrant Welfare Bureau (EWB) had to deal with some of the problems created by the ending of the conflict and the inevitable dislocation it created. The bureau also spent time following up individual cases of either pregnant Irish girls who travelled to Britain or young girls who travelled with their babies. One such girl was deported from Birmingham in September 1944 to Dublin, but was 'upset and unwilling to return to her home in Cork with the child'. She was instead settled in the Legion of Mary hostel in Dublin. Another girl the following month was 'not willing to go to her home in Mayo'. An added complication was the closure of nurseries that had been used by Irish unmarried mothers in wartime employment.

But the Legion of Mary faced formidable obstacles in these large English cities, and the Irish government was not prepared to give the EWB personal details of intending emigrants; instead they had to rely on voluntary efforts to trace them.[199] Father Christopher Mangan, McQuaid's secretary, was informed by Henry Gray in December 1951 of the observation of the Legion of Mary that 'so small a proportion of Irish emigrants are known to us.'[200] In the 1950s, Gray (who, by 1967, had given twenty-five years of unbroken service to the bureau) was in regular correspondence with Father Mangan as he warned of the pitfalls of emigrating to various English cities, reminding him in March 1954: 'There are Irish girls who fall an easy prey to the smooth-tongued well-dressed stranger and it is inevitable that Liverpool would prove a happy hunting ground for some of these undesirables.' During 1953, the Liverpool Vigilance Association, which forwarded to the bureau the names and addresses of the Irish girls it encountered, sent 530 such names, mostly of girls aged 16 or 17 who arrived with nothing but 'a few shillings in their pockets'. Gray laid much of the blame on parents for not inculcating in their daughters an awareness of the dangers. He was not only concerned about the 'modern-dress white slaver', but also the idea that

> they run far greater danger from bad example in the cheap lodging houses into which they drift while looking for employment, encouragement to drink, petty theft and so on, all of which may soon produce a psychological state in which, save from the Grace of God, anything may happen. Incidentally, Liverpool itself because of its huge port traffic presents a

particularly ugly problem on this score, and I would say that quite a few
Irish girls who had reasonable home backgrounds in this country are to
be found living in the most degraded conditions in Liverpool lodgings
frequented by coloured seamen etc.[201]

The bureau was prepared to pay the fares home of girls if 'moral danger was
established'.[202] There was also an awareness that many a married woman was
anxious to travel to the English cities to join her husband due to 'anxiety in
regard to her husband's conduct'.[203]

McQuaid also remained preoccupied with the manner in which Irish
emigrants were portrayed and recorded officially, castigating the emphasis
on their 'nuisance-value', damaging reports since 1947 concerning loss of
faith, and a 'deterioration' of relations between the Irish and British hier-
archies. He clearly found these reports exaggerated, mentioned 'untoward
accounts that have been given of the emigrant situation on both the English and Irish side', and later noted that by 1954 the bureau had looked after
about 110,000 people.[204] But English charities had their own concerns about
the Irish girls, especially those who arrived pregnant. Over a 25-day period
in October 1948, for example, 48 pregnant Irish women had applied to the
English Catholic charity the Crusade of Rescue, many of them described as
'of the cheeky type', while at the Sacred Heart convent in west Hull, 85 of
the 89 children baptised between March and September 1948 were born to
Irish girls who were pregnant when they arrived.[205] Of the 3,291 women who
applied to the Westminster Crusade of Rescue between 1950 and 1953, more
than half (1,693) were Irish. Cardinal Griffin, the Archbishop of Westminster, suggested such girls had 'too great a fear' of the Irish clergy, and that
'too narrow a view' was taken of their 'offence' in Ireland.[206]

A three-part series in the *Manchester Guardian* in April 1955 also caused
a stir as it focused on destitute Irish girls ('these deplorable unsponsored
arrivals') who went 'on the streets within a week or so of their arrival'.[207]
Eight years later, it was suggested that one-sixth of the prostitutes coming
before the courts in London were Irish.[208]

Another important source of information on the fortunes of emigrants
was Hubert Daly of the Legion of Mary, whose reports are also preserved in
McQuaid's archives. He suggested that Irish parents seemed to be indifferent to the plight of their emigrant children and that 'they seem to compare
very unfavourably with parents in other countries in this respect'.[209] Daly
was frank about the prevailing view among priests and nuns in England that

Irish girls seemed to have little sense of commitment to their religion or country; 'one could sense an undertone of contempt for the whole set-up in Ireland which is producing so many young people who fail to live up to the ideals which they are supposed to be taught in Ireland'.

'The Irish have no real love for their priests – it is only a sort of superstitious fear'

That last observation is particularly significant; it suggests the degree to which many had been paying only lip service to the ideals of purity and chastity at home and calls into question the whole myth of the innocent Irish, which Daly was not shy about highlighting. Daly talked to Canon Fitzgerald in the East End of London, who highlighted excessive drinking and maintained 'a very great number, especially girls, misconduct themselves in the matter of purity and descend to a very low level': 'Irish girls are to be found in Brothels, living with coloured men, on the streets etc',[210] although he deemed nurses to be better behaved.

Daly stayed at the Irish Club, Eaton Square, in London from April to November 1954 at the request of McQuaid to assess the 'faith' of the Irish. Matters sexual inevitably appeared in his reports, as did class considerations – for instance, he reported on a woman who was attempting to get a hostel established for unmarried mothers, 'especially those who are what she called the better type, whom she wants to segregate and keep apart ... [from] types of girls who will have an evil influence on them'. The parish priest of Camden referred to 'an organised effort made at Euston Station to "capture" young Irish girls for prostitution'.[211] From Birmingham, Daly reported the view of an English priest that 'the Irish have no real love for their priests – it is only a sort of superstitious fear; they have no idea of the value of money and their only idea of an outlet when they need relaxation is over indulgence in drink and women'.[212]

Daly reported a high degree of criticism by English Catholics of Irish Catholicism (though significantly it was the priests rather than the emigrants he spoke to), particularly in its attitude towards pregnant women, which one priest believed was 'in direct contradiction to the Christian principles which we are supposed to profess so strongly in Ireland'. Canon Flint, in charge of rescue work in the Archdiocese of Birmingham, reported that in 1952 it dealt with 184 girls, of whom 102 were Irish and 52 were pregnant

before they arrived. Flint did not approve of Irish girls having to stay two
years 'doing penance' in an Irish mother and baby home. In September,
Daly concluded there was a distance between priests and Irish emigrants;
the problem of loss of faith was 'bigger than anyone seems to realise' and 'we
are producing a very weak kind of Catholic in Ireland at present'.[213]

Irish girls working in a motor factory who had stopped going to Mass
'told those who approached them to mind their own business'.[214] Father
Monaghan in Nottingham told of the difficulty of conversing with Irish
lads from the west of Ireland who 'went on the defensive immediately ...
they gave the impression that the only reason a priest ever has of speaking to
them is to reprimand them for something they have done wrong ... the usual
charge is that the priests have become too aloof from the people, show no
interest in them'. Another English priest said that 'Irish girls do not make
good housewives when they marry here, and that in his parish the dirtiest
homes are always the ones run by Irish women'.

J. Bradley, a probation officer in London, had similar home truths to
recount, arguing that

> there is too much fear in the average Irishman and it is consciously
> planted in him by many priests ... they feel they have escaped from what
> they believe to be a tyranny ... there is such an abhorrence of sin that the
> notion of sin goes right over to many things which are not sin but are very
> human. This is particularly true of anything relating to sex. 'Company
> keeping' is a euphemism which does more harm than anything and 2
> words which simply mean a straight forward natural affection have been
> given a meaning which Irishmen think is a sin and one would think the
> gravest sin in all Ireland. Perhaps there might be no harm in that were it
> not that the very going together of a boy and girl in the course of explor-
> ing a perfectly innocent world which leads to marriage itself comes to
> be damned as this other evil thing which ought to get its proper name
> as well as its condemnation. A consequence of all this is that the natural
> understanding of moral standards is confused.

By October 1954, McQuaid had heard enough and told Daly to return
to Ireland.[215] Undoubtedly he was uncomfortable with the fact that the
Irish emigrants and the English priests had provided a comprehensive and
accurate critique of the shortcomings of a faith that was too often based
on outward obedience, distance and fear. Father Cecil Barrett, head of the

Catholic Social Welfare Bureau and one of McQuaid's main advisers on social issues, was also concerned about the reports, telling Father Mangan, 'I must confess to some dissatisfaction at the way he tended to use the words "vast majority"!' He believed many of the priests interviewed had an anti-Irish bias.[216]

Another source of information was W. J. Stibbs, administrator of the Crusade of Rescue in Middlesex, who corresponded with Cecil Barrett concerning the work of the Legion of Mary, who reported in November 1954 that in the previous three and a half years it had dealt with 479 prostitutes in the Soho and Mayfair areas, 247 of whom were Catholics and 42 Irish. He did contend 'prostitution in London is not an Irish problem', but there were many areas such as Paddington, Edgware Road and Pimlico which they could not touch owing to a shortage of legionnaires. There were few Irish prostitutes in the East End, but he noted

> we have always felt that the Irish girls drift into an immoral life without malice, whereas others, especially the foreigners, are more deliberate about it. The area of the established prostitutes, Soho and the West End, has a comparatively small number of Irish. The Park [Hyde Park, where there were 195 prostitutes, 62 of whom were Irish], where the drifters are, has a higher proportion ... there are Irish dance halls here, of course, but they are the occasions of many falls, even though the organisers may be good people.[217]

'Secrecy is the unmarried mother's first and greatest need'

There was also consternation about the plight of the vulnerable and 'fallen' Irish. A particular concern was with what were believed to be 'seductive advertisements' for girls to work abroad – one of the issues raised by popular Irish journalist Aodh de Blacam when contributing to a government subcommittee on rural depopulation in 1947.[218] The following year a proposal to ban the emigration of women under the age of 21 (who accounted for about 35 per cent of those leaving) was considered on 'moral, social and demographic grounds'; an idea prompted by figures that showed the outflow of female workers had increased from 10,609 in 1945 to 19,205 in 1946, with a slight drop to 18,727 in 1947, about 70 per cent of whom were domestic servants.

The Department of External Affairs informed McQuaid that 'a great many of the young girls who emigrate to Britain become pregnant; many of the reports are tragic and alarming in the extreme'. The proposed ban, it was noted, 'would secure the warm approval of the Hierarchy.'[219] The JCWSSW also commented on this in 1953, mentioning the experiences of two girls, aged 15 and 17, who arrived in London without any references, their fares having been paid by a Brophy's Agency, which then looked for a refund. Such girls often did not find lasting employment: 'It was mentioned by members of the committee that frequently these girls going over are pregnant and their object is to prevent their condition being known.'[220] The advertisements for girls often included a commitment to 'time guaranteed to practise religious duties'.

Taoiseach Éamon de Valera also met Elizabeth Fitzgerald, president of the Westminster diocesan branch of the Catholic Women's League, which had compiled a memorandum on the problems of Irish girls in England. The main age groups causing worry were 14–18 and 18–20: 'they swell the ranks of the army of unmarried mothers'. In 1952 the Catholic Rescue and Protection Society had repatriated 85 mothers and their babies, but 'there were many times that number who refused to return to Ireland ... secrecy is the unmarried mother's first and greatest need'. It was also estimated that 80–90 of the 400 prisoners in Holloway Women's Prison were Irish Catholics. Mention was made of parents who were encouraging young girls to travel to find work, with the injunction to 'send home weekly 50% of their wages'; and there was a warning that parents needed to 'take at least elementary precautions about the safety of the very young people they send out'. De Valera requested of Mrs Fitzgerald that she keep his personal views on the situation confidential.[221]

Others expressed the opinion that, due to the 'poor results' being achieved by voluntary workers, welfare staff needed to be appointed to the Irish embassy in London.[222] F. H. Boland, the Irish ambassador, found the practice of getting 'simple girls from the country' to pay back booking fees from their wages 'scandalous' and 'most unconscionable'. The Minister for External Affairs was worried about the 'moral detriment' risked by young vulnerable girls going into domestic service in England,[223] though no such fears were expressed about those in domestic service at home in Ireland. F. H. Boland concluded mournfully that 'the word "welfare" in connection with the Irish population in Britain has an almost inexhaustibly wide connotation'. He also acknowledged 'the evil of moral lapsation which is commonly

said to be widespread among our people in this country' while the clergy
believed that 'anything which tends to keep the Irish together reduces the
risk of moral lapses'. Paradoxically, the clergy were also keen to organise
social activities 'to draw young Irish people here away from the commercial
dance halls run by Irish proprietors', though it was acknowledged that 'the
Irish here tend to hold aloof from social and recreational activities organised
under clerical auspices'.[224]

The consistent response from the Department of Finance was to reject
the funding of welfare officers on the grounds that it was not the function
of the state to assume responsibility for the moral welfare of Irish citizens
abroad; this would 'make emigration attractive by providing a form of insur-
ance against the hazards involved'.[225] Not all accepted the clamour of concern about the Irish being sexually exploited. Father Tom Fitzgerald, a native
of Tipperary and prison chaplain in some of the toughest parishes in the
East End of London, was reported in the *Standard* newspaper as insisting

> the self-righteousness of the Irish is the cause of the trouble. Our people
> at home do not face the fact that there is original sin in Ireland as much
> as in any other part of the world ... nine out of ten people who go wrong
> here were wrong before they ever set foot on England's shore ... a girl
> who goes wrong in England was restrained at home only by outward
> conventions, not by faith, not by anything deep within herself.[226]

The Hierarchy, for its part, preferred to stress the 'continuous drain on the
womanhood and future motherhood of the country as the result of the present wave of emigration'.[227]

'It's the only way a man can live nowadays'

The irony is that many of the 'evils' that were highlighted in relation to
moral decline on the part of emigrants were apparent at home. These
included prostitution, which in some cases could be a family affair. In 1942 a
man was accused at Dublin circuit court of getting his 19-year-old wife, 'not
being a common prostitute or of known immoral character, to have unlawful carnal knowledge with other persons'. He moved her around Merchant's
Quay, where she was observed in an air raid shelter. A plain clothes Garda
approached her husband, who was close by:

The prisoner looked into my face. I said to him who is this woman. It's my wife he said. I said to him what are you doing here. He said, she's earning a lot of money – it's the only way a man can live nowadays ... while I was talking to the prisoner his wife left the man and approached us, she then handed the prisoner 2/– at the same time saying 'that was all he would give me'. The prisoner attempted to put the money into his waistcoat pocket and I caught his hand.

The husband had been in the army but had been discharged for continually going absent without leave and the couple subsequently lived with the wife's father, whom she told she was going to earn money through 'immoral purposes'. According to the father, 'I told her she should not be carrying on that game. I told her to leave him.' The couple then moved into a lodging house. The defendant's statement made in June 1942 was disarmingly frank:

> About 12 months ago I started each night to take my wife out at about 11 p.m. to various places in the city, Capel Street, Halfpenny Bridge and the Quays where she used to solicit men. I was in the habit of keeping watch while she was going with the men. I always kept her within view and when she had finished with each man I took the money off her. I made about 6 shillings each night ... my reasons for making my wife go on the town are I wanted money to go home to Carlow to start a business. She objected to leading this life but I did not allow her to discontinue it. She went with 3 men tonight at Cork Street and Skipper's Alley. I was watching her while she was going with the men. She did not have connection with the men tonight, she only pulled them off. I was watching all the time. She gave me 2/– and then you came along.[228]

The government chose not to publish the report of its Interdepartmental Ad Hoc Committee on the Suppression of Prostitution (1947–8). Documents from the Department of Justice suggest that its main concern was with the treatment of VD, and the committee proposed the establishment of a treatment clinic in Mountjoy prison, rather than sending the prisoners out for treatment. The department also received correspondence during these years from concerned Catholic lay groups and business people, including Joseph Groome, of the well-known Groome's hotel in Dublin city, who in 1946 expressed alarm about 'the very undesirable situation which has arisen owing to the conduct at night of persons who frequent the lane adjoining the hotel [Rutland Place, at the corner of Parnell Square]'. This was particularly apparent on Friday and Saturday nights; 'the scenes on these nights are disgraceful and the language used is, to say the least, revolting'.[229]

Prostitution was an issue the JCWSSW continually addressed at its meetings in the 1940s and 1950s. In 1941 it received a letter from the National University Women's Graduate Association 'making suggestions and offering co-operation in any work undertaken in connection with prostitutes', it being argued that there was plenty of evidence of the need for female police in the vicinity of army barracks, an issue the JCWSSW continued to lobby on.[230] There was a particular concern with offering prostitutes homes where they could be taught some occupation.

The JCWSSW also sought the views of Justice Hanna, who was not prepared to publicly advocate for the recruitment of women police but did believe that 'in a city such as Dublin more might be hoped for an adequate system of probation than for any other method of dealing with offences'. His colleague Justice McCarthy believed 'trained social workers would be necessary' for the aftercare of prostitutes: 'suitable homes would provide the only solution for the remedying of this evil. Our present institutions do little to rehabilitate the prostitute. A system of segregation would be necessary and special homes should be provided for those girls who had first fallen.' Significantly, it was also suggested that 'many of the prostitutes came from institutions ... Mrs Clarke [NSPCC] thought that Mr McLaughlin [head of industrial schools] and Dr [Anna] McCabe [medical inspector of industrial schools] were trying to remedy this by having the girls taught the facts of life.' Developments in Liverpool were noted approvingly, because women police 'patrolled the docks and though they have no powers of arrest they were very effective'.[231]

Documents from the Royal Ulster Constabulary Museum in Belfast dating from the early 1940s indicate that female officers (who had been appointed since 1922 but did not patrol 'on the outlook of breaches of the law' in the same way as their male colleagues) were deemed to be especially suited to this kind of work. In March 1942, a letter regarding the employment of female police suggested there were about 45 prostitutes in Belfast. In a memorandum the same month it was maintained that women police should be employed to deal with cases of 'prostitution ... taking statements from women and children, particularly in cases dealing with sexual offences' and could be effectively employed in parks and railway stations.[232]

As mentioned previously, representatives from the JCWSSW regularly visited the Magdalen asylums, finding them 'well run' and the penitents 'happy and content', though not all of the religious orders who ran these institutions allowed them entry. Their surveys seem to have been superficial at best, but they were attempting to assess the conditions and effectiveness of these institutions and they noted the fact that former residents were often exploited on their release. Another group concerned about the institutions was the Irish Association of Civil Liberty, which in May 1952 wrote to the JCWSSW anxious to find out

> whether any restrictions were placed on the liberty of these women in the Magdalen asylums. A long discussion took place in the committee concerning conditions in these institutions and the treatment of unmarried mothers and women brought before the courts for soliciting on the streets. The chairman thought that we should again try to do something in these matters and it was suggested that members should again visit the courts and find out how cases of soliciting are now dealt with.[233]

It also expressed concern about the activities of men at Westland Row train station in Dublin who induced passengers coming off the train to go to 'bridging houses of a questionable character'.[234] Another area of concern was the perceived need for 'segregation of old from first time offenders' in places like the Regina Ceoli hostel, though Frank Duff insisted that this was not possible because it would require separate institutions. Duff had different priorities than others catering for these women: 'the idea of the hostel is to give the mother who desires it the opportunity to keep her child and bring it up. In practice after a few years the mother has generally settled herself sufficiently to live outside the hostel with the child.'[235]

At the end of 1945 the JCWSSW also noted an increase in the number of female prisoners at Mountjoy jail, from 50 to 87,

> mainly due to increased convictions for prostitution. Many of these were under 21 and a considerable number were infected with venereal disease … these prisoners only stay for 3 or 6 months and though they are treated while in prison, the course is not long enough to affect a cure. There is no evening clinic that they can attend after leaving prison.[236]

It was telling that, as was acknowledged at a meeting of the JCWSSW in November 1954, 'the prostitutes generally prefer to go to gaol than to an institution – the time of confinement being shorter in the former'.[237]

Mary Dooley, a probation officer, explained to the JCWSSW in 1953 that it was now necessary for two Gardaí to give evidence in the trials of prostitutes,

> and they must give evidence of having observed the accused over a period of time and of her having accosted men on various occasions. On the first occasion the usual sentence is a fine of 40/– and the case is usually referred to a probation officer, on whose report the fine may be reduced or remitted – subsequent appearances lead to six months in Mountjoy.[238]

'Shut up and say nothing, I will give you £5'

The JCWSSW also kept abreast of the sentencing of men convicted of sex crimes against young women in particular, and in 1941 wrote to Justice Price 'to congratulate him on the publicity given to a heavy sentence imposed by him on a man of 60 (3 years' hard labour) at Dungarvan when he committed a horrible crime on a girl of 16'.[239] This may well have been a rape case; there does not seem to have been much public discussion of such cases, despite the fact they occurred regularly – although not as often as cases of indecent assault.

In one case heard at the circuit court in Dublin, the evidence given suggests passers-by were reluctant to intervene. A woman walking away from the North Strand area was allegedly raped by four men, one of whom was 'in uniform'; all were intoxicated and had previous convictions for larceny. The man who eventually rescued the woman was also a soldier, but before he arrived, 'a couple of women passed ... the ladies heard me calling for help, because they stood and looked at me, but they were told to go on about their business. They went away then.'[240] One of the men was not arraigned because he was in a sanatorium; the Attorney General informed the court he would not be proceeding with the prosecution and the men were discharged.[241]

In contrast to that case, most victims of rape were likely to know their assailants, as happened in Galway in 1959 when a man who had been drunk at the time of the offence was found guilty of breaking and entering with intent to 'ravish' his neighbour near Tuam. The victim was 37 years old and living with her six children; her husband had been working in England for the previous three years, underlining the contribution emigration made to sexual violence at home (between 1951 and 1961, in the region of 500,000 people emigrated from Ireland). She was in bed with four of her children at the time of the assault. As she screamed and called for her children to turn on the light, her assailant responded, 'Shut up and say nothing, I will give you £5.' Her sister's deposition includes the observation that the victim 'felt a wet cold hand on her private in the bed and she thought it was one of the children's feet'.[242]

It was clear from other cases in the 1950s that women living without husbands were deliberately targeted. In 1950 at the district court in Ballina, County Mayo, a man was found not guilty of the attempted rape of a 30-year-old widow at Rathowen, Killala, despite evidence from the doctor who examined her that 'her injuries would be consistent with the story she told me'. The woman, who had two young children, had been widowed only three weeks previously, and the defendant had called by to offer his condolences as he had dealt with the woman's late husband over the sale of a bullock the previous year:

> He put one arm around my neck and the second one around my neck.
> He asked me back to the bedroom to have connection with me. He said,
> 'When we get to the bedroom we will go to bed together.' I struggled
> with him.[243]

The woman managed to escape.

When men were convicted of rape there seems in some cases to have been considerable leniency shown: two previously convicted men who conspired with others to commit a gang rape in Dublin were sentenced to fifteen and six months respectively at Dublin circuit court in October 1959.[244]

Women still played no part in jury proceedings. When lobbying for change in this regard, the JCWSSW was informed in 1958 by the Minister for Justice, Oscar Traynor, that 'he had no reason to think that public opinion disagrees with the 1927 Act', so the JCWSSW decided to get women to apply for service on jury panels instead. But progress was made on the issue of female police. In 1958 Traynor committed himself to a 'small division of women' (61 women applied for 18 vacancies) but the JCWSSW said it would not be satisfied until there was 'a fully trained women police force officered by women with specialised training for dealing with the problems of women and children'. Traynor refused to discuss with them the trainings and duties of female police.[245] A few years previously, Archbishop McQuaid, after he had been asked by Marie Gavan Duffy of the CSWB whether it could have

his permission to support female police officers, had suggested 'in my opinion women police can do a very great good in the city'.[246]

'He never interfered with me in an obvious sexual way, but he frequently massaged my belly and thighs'

As has been seen previously, throughout the first half of the twentieth century crowded living conditions made it more likely both that children would
have to witness crimes of a sexual nature, and that sexual crimes would be
committed against them. This is something that had been commented on
by many concerned parties over the years, and continued to be referred to in
the 1950s, this time in the context of emigration. A Jesuit priest in Manchester informed Henry Gray of the CSWB in Dublin that those with a house in
Ireland should not contemplate emigration to Manchester: 'Houses cannot
be obtained in this city. If they are fortunate they may obtain a room, but a
room for the family is bad, physically and morally for the family'.[247]

It was not unusual for adults and children to share beds, particularly
when accommodation was short, or in the case of one parent being widowed. In his memoir, John McGahern recalls that after his mother died in
1944 he slept in the same bed as his father while his five sisters and baby
brother slept in the other bedroom:

> When my father came into bed and enquired as he took off his clothes
> if I was awake, I nearly always feigned sleep. He never interfered with
> me in an obvious sexual way, but he frequently massaged my belly and
> thighs. As in all other things connected with the family, he asserted
> that he was doing this for my own good; it relaxed taut muscles, eased
> wind and helped bring on sleep. In those years, despite my increas-
> ing doctrinal knowledge of what was sinful, I had only the vaguest
> knowledge of sex or sexual functions and took him at his word; but
> as soon as it was safe to do so, I turned away on some pretext or other
> such as sudden sleepiness. Looking back, and remembering his tone
> of voice and the rhythmic movement of his hand, I suspect he was
> masturbating ...

The older he got, the more uncomfortable McGahern grew with this nocturnal routine and when the family housekeeper moved out of the house

he moved into the room she had stayed in: 'my younger brother was then moved to my place in our father's bed. He was six then, going on seven, and was delighted by the move, as my father presented it as a promotion within the ranks of the troops.'[248] McGahern's father's determination to have a young family member as sleeping companion was in stark contrast to his lack of desire for familial companionship during the day, when he dined alone at a separate table from his children. INSTITUTIONS

For those who did not own a house, including married couples, their living arrangements could become intolerable, which was precisely why many emigrated. In a memorandum submitted to the Commission on Emigration in June 1948, the Irish Housewives Association (IHA) drew attention to the fact that it was common for there to be 'young married couples living apart with their respective parents' due to lack of accommodation, though by 1952 it reported an improvement in this situation for newlyweds.[249] Many newlyweds were very young; until 1986 the minimum legal age for marriage was lower than the age of consent (in 1972, the minimum age of marriage for females was raised to 16 years, bringing it into line with that of males; prior to 1918 the permitted minimum age for marriage under the canon law of the Catholic Church was 12 years for girls and 14 years for boys, subsequently raised to 16 and 14).[250] Parental permission was required for those under the age of 21 who wished to marry, but the JCWSSW suggested in 1955 that reform of the law was needed in this area, reporting that: 'It is apparently easy for a couple under 21 years of age to get married in a registry office without their parent's consent. The production of a birth certificate is not compulsory, nor is written evidence of their parents' consent.' The Minister for Justice replied that it was not for him to get involved. The association raised the issue in the context of the UN's concern with it, noting that Ireland had no representation on the UN's Status of Women Committee. The JCWSSW wanted to know what had been done to bring civil law into line with the amended canon law of 1918.[251] – 16/14 ?

Women also found themselves burdened with husbands they had no desire for but, once again, there was no appetite for public discussion of this. In Maura Laverty's novel *Alone We Embark* (1943), banned in Ireland, the central character, Mary Sheehy, does not marry her true love, Denis Doran, but ends up married to a repulsive wealthy older man, Johnny Dunne, who bullies and blackmails her. She becomes pregnant with her true love's baby. Her articulation of her loneliness and disappointment at her marriage ('It cost me love, it cost me happiness') is dismissed out of hand by her repugnant husband who, above all else, and ironically given his lack of personal hygiene, is only concerned with outward appearances:

> 'Love! Happiness! A body would only have to hear the things you say to know the kind of a cracked flighty woman you are ... I've worked hard to make myself respected in this town and neither you nor Doran is going to pull me down.'[252]

Many women, such as those from the Dingle area of west Kerry, whose experiences were recorded in the book *Bibeanna* (an Irish word describing the aprons the women wore), continued to have arranged marriages in the 1950s; sometimes even the girl initiated the process. One recalled, 'My aunt made the match, because I chose my husband. I said no one else would satisfy me, and if I didn't get him, that I would go to America. In those days, a girl could send a man an offer just as easily as a man could send one to a woman. In any case, my match was made, and it was a good one.'[253] This observation echoes the assertion of the anthropologists Conrad Arensberg and Solon Kimball, who suggested matchmaking did not rule out 'some kind of sexual attraction ... matchmaking was, in fact, far from presenting a scene of "loveless" marriages. The match is a convention like any other. For those who are trained in it, it provides occasion for rousing sexual interest and marital aspirations in young couples in the manner of "falling in love" in communities where courtship is more immediately a matter of personal ambition.'[254]

Irish-language folklore, as recounted through numerous stories and folk anecdotes, was also important for the transmission of 'maternal wisdom' which was seldom recorded in written form. In the context of motherhood, such tales could question or reinforce certain social attitudes to motherhood and the family. A version of one popular folk anecdote, 'The Baby without a Mouth', was recorded by Peig Sayers of the Blasket islands. It deals with an encounter between two sisters; one poor with several children, the other rich and childless. When the rich sister criticises the other for bringing children into the world when she has no food to sustain them, the poor mother responds with the profession of faith, 'God never made a mouth but He created something to put in it.' The rich sister subsequently conceives but the baby is born with no mouth. In a related anecdote, a rich woman accuses a poor woman begging with her family of being like a sow with a litter of piglets. Subsequently, the rich woman bears a child with the head of a piglet. According to renowned Irish scholar Máirín Nic Eoin, these tales are examples of 'the manner in which, even in folk tradition, the female body can become the ground on which moral judgements are made. Fundamental to the discussion is the opposition between the mother and the non-mother, though one can also read in it a genuine societal concern regarding the relationship between fertility and social responsibility.'[255]

'A province in which many moral questions might arise for the church'

Although there was the occasional reference to the need for young people to be better educated about sex and reproduction, there were significant barriers in the way of this becoming widespread. Archbishop McQuaid, for example, found any public airing of issues to do with the female body and reproduction distasteful. In 1944 he contacted Conor Ward, secretary of the Department of Local Government and Public Health, to inform him of a meeting of the Irish Hierarchy at which 'I explained very fully the evidence concerning the use of internal sanitary tampons, in particular that called Tampax. On the medical evidence made available, the bishops very strongly disapproved of the use of these appliances, more particularly in the case of unmarried persons.' He also expressed gratitude to Ward 'for the assistance you have given and ... for the measures with which you propose to deal with the matter'.[256]

A few years previously, a correspondent of McQuaid's, J. Stafford, had sent him an issue of the *Catholic Medical Guardian* which contained the pronouncement of the English hierarchy on internal tamponage, but now, in 1944, he had an update: 'Tampax has been off the market here for over a year and a half. One of our Knight [of Columbanus] chemists has just rung me up to say it is about to be in stock once more but has not been delivered from the agent.' The agent in question was tackled by the chemist, who 'gave him a good talking to and pointed out the moral dangers. Apparently he made an impression. It looks as tho[ugh] we may be able to stop this business at source.'[257] As usual, McQuaid's enforcers were doing an effective job on the ground.

Doubtless, McQuaid was also conscious of there being a greater awareness of contraception, and kept a close eye on issues of maternal health, pregnancy and motherhood, as did others in the Catholic Church. This

manifested itself most obviously in the Mother and Child scheme controversy of 1951, which has been recounted in detail in a number of books. Dr
Daniel Cohalan, the Bishop of Cork, summed up the areas of impending
controversy as early as 1947 by expressing fear that the health authorities
would have control of 'education for women in motherhood and the health
of children, a province in which many moral questions might arise for the
church'.[258]

The following year, a health service for mothers and children was first
mentioned by the new inter-party government. The Minister for Health,
Noël Browne, was awaiting the deliberations of a council he had established
to advise him on matters relating to child health proposed by the previous
government. When a plan evolved to improve the health services available
to pregnant mothers and children it was opposed by the Irish Medical Association (IMA), which cited fears of 'socialised medicine'. But Browne, who
became preoccupied with his battle with the IMA, may not have anticipated
problems with the Catholic Hierarchy, which was concerned by the IMA's
contention that the proposals would amount to an undermining of private
GP practice and would threaten the 'moral well-being' of women and girls.

Echoing Dr Cohalan in 1947, though in more explicit terms, Dr James
Staunton, the Bishop of Ferns, expressed the Hierarchy's fear in 1950 that
education for motherhood under the plan would include instruction on 'sex
relations, chastity and marriage' which, in its view, was not the job of the
state.[259] A further fear was that such 'education', if provided by non-Catholic doctors, could pave the way to contraception and abortion. But the rest
of the government was not prepared to back Browne in a battle with the
Bishops and he resigned and, in an unprecedented move, made correspondence between the government and the Hierarchy available to the press.
The animosity between Browne and his party leader, Seán MacBride, who
saw himself as a Catholic first and a public representative second, and who
was, for a supposedly radical republican, embarrassingly fawning in his correspondence with Archbishop McQuaid, ensured the controversy was even
more embittered. Historians have spent decades raking over the ashes of the
personal animosity between these two.[260]

In the aftermath of the Mother and Child Scheme row and a change of
government, McQuaid seemed rather surprised by the views of the Tánaiste,
Fianna Fáil's Seán Lemass, who in the autumn of 1952 found himself nego-
tiating with the Bishops on what was to become the 1953 Health Bill. There
were a number of issues up for discussion, including another version of the

Mother and Child Scheme, compulsory detention of women suffering from VD, and the right of infected persons to marry. Lemass spoke of mother-hood as 'a "hazard", a burden recurring over about 15 years of married life. We pointed out that the state had no special right with regard to mother-hood.' The Minister for Health, Dr Ryan James, then made 'one of the most remarkable points of the whole discussion', pointing out that when partition was removed – and he hoped that it would be removed – 'one system of mother and infant welfare would be operating in the North and another in the Republic if the provisions of the White Paper were not accepted. The invalidity of such a merely political consideration was firmly pointed out.'[261]

These were the kind of views – pragmatic, ideological, political – that disturbed McQuaid, who regarded with distrust some of the once excommunicated politicians of Fianna Fáil and much preferred working with the conservative and, in his view, more obedient Catholics of Fine Gael. He enunciated these views in a letter to the Apostolic Nuncio in November 1952, making it clear he was annoyed that Fianna Fáil had been returned to power. It gives a direct insight into McQuaid's view of Irish politicians and contains cutting criticisms of de Valera personally, and Fianna Fáil generally:

> To deal with Mr Costello's Cabinet [the coalition government of 1948–51] was, with the exception of Dr Browne, Minister for Health, and Mr MacBride, Minister for External Affairs, a very pleasant experience; for one met with a premier who was not only an excellent Catholic, but also an educated Catholic, in immediate sympathy with the Church and the teaching of the Church. Nor was Mr Costello unduly worried about placating the Liberals and Freemasons of North and South. Neither was he anxious to remain in the position of being the political leader ... To deal with Mr De Valera and his Ministers is indeed a different matter.
>
> From Mr De Valera's re-assumption of political leadership, the chief element of note, as far as the Church is concerned, is a policy of distance. That policy is seen in the failure to consult any Bishop on the provisions of a Health Scheme. All the present difficulty results from that failure.
>
> It will be remembered that Mr De Valera had promised to give a Health Scheme based on 'the Constitution and Social Directives thereof'. It would not be in character for him to make any reference to the Hierarchy; such a reference would be felt to be inopportune in view of the Protestant support and the voting-power of the Liberal

Independents on whom he has been obliged to lean for a continuance in office. Further, any consultation of the Hierarchy would, if later discovered, bitterly antagonise the North of Ireland Protestants, whom Mr de Valera always considers, in the hope of being able to remove partition.[262]

There was a consciousness here that the welfare state that had been brought to Northern Ireland in the years after the war could facilitate the operation of a different culture of sexual morality, but the idea that Northern Ireland was intrinsically more liberal in these matters is open to question. There is a certain paranoia underpinning McQuaid's notes on the Health Act of 1953, but also a feeling that he had won the battle with secularists:

> Our Catholic people are aware that Catholic doctrine in regard to sex-relations, chastity and marriage is nowadays violently opposed; that gynaecological care in many countries means provision for birth control and abortion in so called health clinics and that health education often involves the claim to direct the child according to pernicious Freudian and materialistic principles. Yet the 1947 Act provided no safeguard that Catholic mothers and children would have the right to be treated or educated according to Catholic principles. We are glad that these sections of the act are to be repealed.[263]

It was to prove a pyrrhic victory, as many professional and middle-class families were already limiting the size of their families. In Dublin in 1955, 28 per cent of children born to unskilled labourers were the sixth or subsequent child, compared to 6.2 per cent of the children of higher professionals.[264]

'Amazingly, they were still risking sexual intercourse in the light of all that had gone before ...'

One issue that was not being addressed publicly was the question of women for whom pregnancy was life-threatening. Some of the most disturbing passages in John McGahern's memoir reveals how his parents continued to have full sexual relations despite the continuing risk that pregnancy posed to the recurrence of his mother's cancer. His mother's letters to his father frequently referred to whether or not her 'visitor' [period] has arrived; in the spring of 1943, 'in her letters to my father she states matter of factly that her "visitor" has not arrived, but by Easter she is certain she is pregnant'.[265] McGahern's father wrote to his mother's oncologist at the Mater hospital in Dublin and received a contradictory reply from him, with an unexpressed acknowledgement of the difficulties of lack of access to contraception, couched in archaic and ambiguous language:

> I can assure you, though I have advised against what has happened, I can readily appreciate the position and I see no reason why either of you should be worried ... It is a fact that if the possibilities of recurrence are present, that rapid progress [of the cancer] may be brought about by the present condition of affairs.

In November of that year, McGahern's mother gave birth to her seventh child, resisting her husband's desire for the child to be called Jude 'after the patron saint of lost causes because of her cancer'.

But it was indeed a lost cause. McGahern wrote about the situation early the following year: 'Amazingly, they were still risking sexual intercourse in the light of all that had gone before – fasting, novenas, Dr Corcoran's warnings. In a letter written that February, my mother reassures my father that he has no cause to worry further since her "visitor" had just arrived.'[266] She died that year, and McGahern's father refused to have any contact with her in the last months of her life, as if she was contaminated and had betrayed him.

'The reproduction of the species is controlled by vast and complex forces of which we know little'

Mary Daly has observed that, although completed family size fell in Ireland in the early years of the twentieth century (by approximately 20 per cent between 1911 and 1946), the rate of decline subsequently slowed, 'and may have been partly reversed among couples who married in the late 1940s', but that the fall resumed among couples married in the 1950s.[267] In 1946, 38 per cent of Irish children lived in families with five or more dependent children, while Irish couples who had been married for 30–34 years had an average of 4.94 children, compared to 6.77 for couples with marriages of similar duration in 1911. This meant that in 1946, Irish couples with marriages of twenty years' duration had twice as many children as their counterparts in Britain.

Large families were a factor in the late age of marriage in rural Ireland and statistics from the 1930s, which reveal low marriage and high marital fertility rates, suggest that such fertility was associated with low socioeconomic status. Of the 52,266 infants born between October 1937 and September 1938, almost one-third were the children of labourers, while higher professional households had the smallest families.

Other key issues when considering Irish demography in this period include housing and access to land: 'the nature of the Irish land market, the sanctified status of owner occupancy, and the importance attached to keeping land within the family meant that it was almost impossible for young people to acquire land other than by inheritance'. In 1926, more than one-third of married men in the Free State had three or more dependent children, almost double the proportion in England and Wales.[268] By the 1940s the consequences for those children, now adults, were often stark, given the size of families and the dependency rate, whereas in Britain, smaller families and improved welfare payments after 1945 relieved some of the pressure. It was hardly surprising so many Irishmen did not marry at all; according to the census of 1936, 44 per cent of men aged 35-44 were single. /celibate ?

The Commission on Emigration and Other Population Problems (1948–54) assigned responsibility for assembling the evidence on marriage and fertility to Cornelius Lucey, the Bishop of Cork, but 'the only evidence collected concerning pregnancy and childbirth was in relation to unmarried Irish women who gave birth in England', and Mary Daly notes that 'the failure to conduct a more comprehensive investigation of marriage and fertility is unlikely to have been accidental'.[269] Quite simply, the commission wanted to affirm the virtues of large families and the clergy wanted to prevent the discussion of birth control and remained hostile to the 'safe period' (even though in 1951 Pope Pius XII referred to it as 'a method open to all Christian couples'). Notwithstanding, many middle-class Catholic families were clearly deliberately limiting their family size by using abstinence and the 'safe period'.[270]

It was common in Europe from the 1920s to the 1940s for countries to introduce measures designed to boost births and marriages. The French, for example, had 'long been sensitive to the slightest shifts in fertility', and prided themselves on their commitment to the family, as evidenced by the preponderance of pro-natalist leagues and associations of large families in the 1920s (who acted like 'Christian storm troopers'), and the introduction of a family allowance act ('a measure which both the left and right could endorse'). Male and female celibates over the age of 30 paid more income tax, as did childless couples married for at least ten years, while in the 1930s marriage loans were provided to newlyweds if they agreed to stay in agriculture. The Vichy regime in the 1940s was quick to crack down on abortion and contraception and the influence of clerical pro-natalism was strong, while a pre-eminent role was assigned to fathers as *Chefs de famille* (heads of household). There were parallels with what was going on in Italy, where the focus was on paternity rights and masculinity and where women who practised birth control were regarded as a threat to national grandeur. By the 1950s, 'France could boast of being one of Europe's most generous providers of welfare directed at families'.[271]

Legislation for family allowances in Ireland was not introduced until 1943 (a delay explained by the comparatively high fertility rate of Irish marriages). When he introduced them, Minister for Industry and Commerce Seán Lemass explained that their purpose was to alleviate poverty in large families, rather than to have an impact on births.[272] There was widespread heated debate amongst politicians and clergy as to the merits of the allowances, and the desirability of state intervention in family affairs, during which Seán MacEntee presented his cabinet colleagues with excerpts from Halliday Sutherland's 1936 book *Laws of Life* (which was banned in Ireland because it mentioned the rhythm method of contraception) to demonstrate that 'the reproduction of the species is controlled by vast and complex forces of which we know little'. Four years later, keen to dismiss the relevance of the British welfare state to Ireland, he circulated his cabinet colleagues with an article from the English Catholic periodical *The Tablet*, which concluded, 'the bias against babies will not be beaten by Beveridge [the author of the report that formed the basis for the introduction of the Welfare State in Britain].'[273]

In 1955, an article on women and multi-pregnancies in the journal of the Irish Medical Association 'could still be written without a single reference to their need to regulate their fertility'.[274] Pregnancy was also still seen as something that required women to be cleansed in its aftermath, which involved the practice of 'churching'. Dinah Rooney, a midwife from Dublin's inner city, recalled that mothers who had recently given birth were required to light a candle, and the priest prayed over them: 'It seemed that woman was exposed delivering, she was exposed to a different man, and that you were classed as "the beast in the field" – now that was the meaning of being churched.'[275]

But Ireland did not remain immune from a concern with the health of mothers and there were doctors and other individuals who were privately seething at the consequences of multiple pregnancies. Dr Michael Solomons was Assistant Master of the Rotunda hospital when he first encountered the 'grand multiparas', a term attributed to Dr J. K. Feeney for women who had seven or more pregnancies; Dublin obstetricians 'became world experts on this medical phenomenon'. Medical texts did not necessarily discourage these women from having more children, though perhaps there was a certain ambiguity as to whether the term 'natural spacing' was sometimes being used as a euphemism for 'birth control'.[276] Solomons witnessed a 26-year-old woman on her sixth pregnancy go blind, only to return pregnant again the following year. In three years in the late 1940s, 23 women and 800 babies died at the hospital. As he recalled, for some of these women 'pregnancy was to be a death sentence'. A colleague of his attended the birth of a baby with the top of a Guinness bottle on his head: 'the mother had hoped it would act as a contraceptive'.[277] Of the 785 home deliveries Solomons attended while he was clinical clerk of the Rotunda in 1943, 93 (11.9 per cent) were of babies born to women pregnant for at least the tenth time.

Dr John O'Connell, who was a student at the Coombe maternity hospital in Dublin in the 1950s, 'was dealing as a matter of routine with mothers of ten children'.[278] The research of Brendan Walsh in the 1960s concluded that more than one-third of women who married between the ages of 20 and 24 in the period 1932–6 had at least seven live births; fertility, or 'desired family size', was higher than that of other Catholic countries and this persisted until the early 1960s. Of mothers giving birth in 1959, 32 per cent had given birth to four or more children already and almost one-third of births (30.9 per cent) were to women over the age of 35.[279]

Despite this, as Caitriona Clear has pointed out, the reports of the Commission on Emigration and Other Population Problems, published in 1954, referred to a downward trend in family size and suggested 'every effort should be made to arrest it'. At that stage, 23 per cent of Irish couples had five or more children. It was asserted in the majority report that 'it would be unreasonable to assume that our family pattern imposes an undue strain on mothers in general'. The commission could find 'no support for the view that, apart from the increased risk associated with child bearing, large families have a deleterious effect on the general health of mothers'. The Bishop of Cork, Cornelius Lucey, went further than this in his minority report by insisting that 'apart from the risk incidental to parturition itself, child-bearing seems to have no effect at all on the health of mothers; as to mental health, the effect seems to be salutary rather than deleterious', a view challenged by Dr Robert Collis, the well-known paediatrician and social activist, who warned of the danger of the 'large, unhappy, unhealthy family'.[280]

There was a widespread belief that breastfeeding, by delaying ovulation, offered some protection against pregnancy. A Mayo woman interviewed by Caitriona Clear recalled that "twas more or less a safety thing and there were a lot trying it'. What is missing to a large extent from the historical record is women's own descriptions of how they experienced the physical process of childbirth itself. Clear encountered 'an unwillingness to go into detail'.[281]

By the mid 1950s, Archbishop McQuaid was determined to introduce a more comprehensive overview of nurse and medical ethics as well as controlling the appointments in the teaching hospitals. In June 1955, the master of Holles Street, Dr Arthur Barry, wrote to McQuaid informing him that as part of medical training he wanted lectures on the ethical aspects of abortion, baptism, marriage guidance, ectopic pregnancy, professional secrecy, craniotomy, euthanasia, sterilisation and contraception.[282] McQuaid was withering in his dismissal of what thus far had been taught regarding ethics and psychology, suggesting in a letter to the Archbishop of Cashel that 'the previous course in Ethics was little more than a course in Hygiene'.[283]

Some indication of what was being taught at the medical schools and in the hospitals, and the extent to which they prioritised spiritual over physical matters, is provided by the recollections of Dr John O'Connell. When he went to a house to take care of a woman who had just had a miscarriage he discovered that 'on the windowsill was a condom. My immediate reaction was that the miscarriage served her right, because she had been flying in the face of God. I still had a great deal to learn.'[284] His anecdote is a reminder of how influential the medical profession was in the realm of female sexuality, particularly regarding training in the area of obstetrics and gynaecology.

Some women endured long-term physical pain and habitual incontinence because of symphysiotomy operations (which widened a woman's pelvis in difficult pregnancies), seen as a means of avoiding 'unwarranted' caesarean operations. At an international congress of Catholic doctors held in Dublin in 1954, Dr Arthur Barry revealed that he had performed over a hundred such operations from 1949 to 1954. He insisted that it was a natural procedure in accordance with the teachings of the Catholic Church and defended its use as an alternative to 'unwarranted and unnecessary' pregnant in wars / by foreign soldiers —

caesarean sections. He suggested it was 'unnecessary to stress to Catholic doctors that the practices of contraception, sterilisation and therapeutic abortion are contrary to the moral law ... but what we must all guard against ... is the unwarranted and unnecessary employment of caesarean section'. He maintained that the caesarean operation was the chief cause of 'the unethical procedure of sterilisation', and was frequently responsible for encouraging the laity 'in the improper prevention of pregnancy or in seeking termination'. Dr Barry dismissed the concerns expressed by another doctor about the danger of permanent disability among women following symphysiotomy operations. He also insisted that 'all the bogies and pitfalls' mentioned in medical textbooks against symphysiotomy were 'sheer flights of imagination on the part of inexperienced writers'. But they were not, and this harmful procedure was abandoned in the mid 1960s.[285]

'We can see now why you're so keen on your birth-control clinic'

Was it easier to find agreement on such matters in Northern Ireland? There were problems there too regarding maternity welfare. In the 1930s the Northern Ireland Cabinet had postponed a decision on improving provisions for maternity and child welfare and continued to reject any approaches concerning the opening of birth control clinics. The report of a House of Commons select committee regarding maternity and child welfare in Northern Ireland in 1945 found both antenatal and postnatal care 'wholly inadequate' and 'much below the standard of the rest of the UK'; 'a certain prejudice against' attendance at antenatal clinics was also highlighted. Most authorities relied on the local district nursing society rather than administering their own maternity and child welfare schemes, due to lack of government pressure or interest.[286]

The family planning clinic at the Royal Maternity hospital in Belfast was not openly recognised as a clinic and was entirely dependent on the voluntary effort of Olive Anderson, who gave advice on birth control but who 'received no recognition or financial payment from the hospital', although another one was opened in 1951.[287]

During the Second World War it was known that some women living in tenement blocks were giving birth to over twenty children,[288] which brought the issue of birth control into sharp focus for some, including Moya Woodside. In 1940 she had been recruited, along with hundreds of others in Northern Ireland, by the British Mass Observation organisation to keep a diary of everyday life, in an attempt to record national morale. One of Woodside's diary entries for April 1941, in the context of the ferocious bombing of Belfast and the evacuation of many people to surrounding districts, gives a good indication of the degree to which the issue of class was bound up with attitudes to contraception:

> The whole town is horrified by the filth of these evacuees and by their dirty habits and their take-it-for-granted attitude. Belfast slum dwellers are pretty far down and to those not used to seeing poverty and misery at close quarters, the effect is overwhelming. 'The smell is terrible,' says my sister-in-law. They don't even use the lavatory, they just do it on the floor, grown-ups and children. She ... was ashamed to have to ask decent working people with clean houses to take in such guests. I believe it is the same all over the countryside. At least it may do good in one way, if it makes people think about housing and homes in the slums. Complacency and/or ignorance has been rudely shattered these last few days. 'We can see now why you're so keen on your birth-control clinic,' my sister-in-law remarked. I felt quite cheered.

A few days later, Woodside recorded that 'it seems now that no less than 7 women gave birth to babies in police stations during the air raid'.[289]

As noted by Mary Muldowney, Moya Woodside was active in giving talks on birth control to women's groups, particularly in Protestant working-class districts of Belfast. Woodside observes in relation to one of them:

> Gave talk on birth control to co-op women's guild meeting ... response to my talk much as usual – older women (in the majority) inclined to repeat they had eight (or ten or twelve) children and were none the worse for it. One woman (60ish) enquired: 'Doesn't all this bother with birth control make you neurotic?' I told her how it soon became as automatic as your dentures, which amused the others greatly. Younger women are more receptive, although shy of asking questions in front of people. Although I have no children myself I find that at these meetings I am always made the recipient of intimate gynaecological and obstetrical histories, once the ice has been broken.[290]

She also arranged for the import of medical supplies for those who wanted to exercise some mechanical form of birth control.

Birth control and family planning clinics were not being discussed in such a manner in the South, and a determination to resist any such discussion and prevent the circulation of publications about contraception was evident, though it was not always possible to intercept such material being sent through the post. Despite censorship, information for women in the South was accessible through English newspapers or in Belfast. It was also suggested that the fact that 'the birth rate was lower and falling in Eire', where contraceptive information was illegal, 'falls pleasantly on Ulster Unionist ears'.

In 1959, Paddy Bourke, general manager of the Provincial Bank of Ireland, complained to the government about objectionable material sent through the post. In his letter he enclosed a small English published pamphlet he had received entitled *Heritage*, which trumpeted the dictum that 'planned parenthood is but a mark of advancing civilisation'. In response, Maurice Moynihan cited the 1929 Censorship Act, which banned the printing, publishing, distribution and sale of publications advocating contraception, although he acknowledged that it was 'in practice, very difficult to prevent such things from going through the post'.[291]

'We have done almost all we can – we are still storming heaven'

Censorship was given an added stringency due to the war. Between 1929 and 1946 over 1,800 books were banned, but significantly, in the year 1946–7, following the passing of legislation that established an appeal board, there were 124 appeals, of which 99 were successful. The Censorship of Publications Board experienced considerable difficulties in the 1950s culminating in the appointment of a new board in 1957. Up to that point, as was acknowledged by the Department of Justice in the 1960s, 'the members were, in general, extremely narrow in their outlook and were especially prone to ban books by Irish authors. Many of their worst decisions were upset by the appeal board.'[292]

Inevitably, it was another issue McQuaid kept a close eye on; in this he was ably assisted by Brian MacMahon of the Censorship of Publications Board, who in August 1947 offered sincere thanks for having brought the periodical *Modern Woman* to the notice of the Board and for the honour of your very kind personal letter ... It is very strange that none of the readers of this wretched publication, which I suspect has a wide circulation here, ever thought of reporting it and I feel ashamed of the fact that we have let it 'live' so long, even though it is not part of our duties or even within our powers to exercise supervision, officially, in the case of periodicals.[293]

McQuaid could also rely on the support of Stephen Roche, the secretary of the Department of Justice, who, whatever his private thoughts, was fawning in his personal correspondence with McQuaid ('there is no pleasanter privilege attached to my duties ... do please give me a summons over the telephone anytime you want me to call') regarding the banning of periodicals.[294]

But notes in McQuaid's archive suggest that the Censorship of Publications Board felt under considerable pressure in the 1950s from those 'concerned with evading prohibition by the well-planned spacing of objectionable issues' and, in an unsigned memo (perhaps from the chairman of the board), it was argued that 'since the inception of censorship a campaign of vilification has been maintained against the various boards by the civil liberties association, some disgruntled authors and others of the "arty-crafty" circles', with a suggestion such pressure reached its peak in 1955 and 1956. That year, two long-standing members of the board were lost, with the death of District Justice O'Sullivan and the resignation of Father Deery. They were replaced by two 'liberals', A. F. Comyn and R. F. Figgis.

There was a (justified) belief that the two newest members of the board were more interested in protecting authors than the public, and there was concern about public criticisms of censorship. Seán O'Faoláin and Denis Johnston spoke at a public meeting on censorship in April 1956 organised by the Irish Association of Civil Liberty (which had been established in 1948). O'Faoláin criticised the publishers of new editions of classic books such as *Roxana* by Daniel Defoe, on the basis of how they marketed them as pornography. As far as he was concerned, such publishers 'deserve nobody's sympathy', and were confusing the issue for all those who wanted to 'reconcile individual liberty with public taste'.[295] There was also an attempt to block the importation of the *Observer* newspaper in March and April 1956 when it ran a series of articles on sex, society and family planning. Despite the Irish Retailers, Newsagents, Booksellers and Stationers Association explaining to the *Observer*'s management about the pressure being exerted on its members by the Censorship of Publications Board, it 'insisted on for-warding the consignment, saying they would not be dictated to by anyone'. The importer went out to meet the consignment in the early hours of Easter Sunday morning, but he and the customs officer agreed 'it would not do to let them in'.[296]

In September 1957, McQuaid noted that J. J. Pigott, who along with Dermot O'Flynn and C. J. O'Reilly constituted the remaining members of the Censorship Board of Publications, told him that the 'situation ha[d] become impossible' due to the new appointments, but he demanded the chairman be fired rather than allowed to resign and he did not want to intervene directly with Taoiseach Éamon de Valera.[297] The difficulty for the more conservative members was that under the 1946 act, if one member objected to prohibition then the book could not be banned. Pigott refused to convene meetings of the board and demanded the resignation of Comyn and Figgis. The minister in turn requested Pigott's resignation and was duly obliged. O'Flynn and O'Reilly then resigned in sympathy with Pigott.

Paranoia, conspiracy and skulduggery all played their part as the Cen-sorship Board crisis unfolded, with Dermot O'Flynn requesting that his correspondence be 'type-copied and returned to me (the official typewriter could be traced)'.[298] It was argued that with the appointment of the two 'lib-erals', 'the flood of objectionable cheap novels reached an abnormal level', with revenue officials allowing the material in unchallenged. According to McQuaid, when addressing the annual conference of youth leaders attached to the girls club in his diocese, there was 'unquestionable evidence' that 'foul books' were on sale in Dublin: 'the only official reply was that not many individual members of the public had approached the Gardaí prepared to object and enter the public courts as a common informer'.[299]

But the real problem was deemed to be a 'go slow' policy by the two new members, who 'insisted on reading every book through instead of con-centrating on the marked pages'. Pigott acknowledged that in relation to books 'openly deriding chastity, the 2 recalcitrant members voted with us and banned them. Our real difficulty with them arose mostly with Freudian inspired novels where the obscenity was presented under the cloak of some social, political or military cause.'[300] Pigott pressed his case with the minister by showing him such books, but 'he showed not the least desire to examine the books himself'.

Meanwhile O'Flynn continued to write enraged letters to McQuaid suggesting both that customs officials were not doing enough and that deliberate 'hit and run' periodicals which published the occasional article on birth control or 'extreme sex article' should be dealt with on that one issue (instead of a number of them having to be collected for submission to the board). He declared that the former members of the board would continue to fight until 'we overthrow these satanic snares deliberately aimed at our growing boys and girls'.[301]

The government was increasingly dismissive of this tone of hysteria. In September 1957 the Taoiseach received a letter from the Irish League of Decency requesting an interview:

> This letter is written as a despairing cry from a frustrated body of Catholics to clean up on indecent books, picture-post cards, films etc. ... we have done almost all we can – we are still storming heaven – within the law to combat the imported press and film evils, but are being thwarted by the very law itself and so find ourselves foiled to remove sources of scandal from public display ... The Censorship of Publications Board is ludicrous – THREE MEETINGS IN FIFTEEN MONTHS AND IT IS YEARS SINCE THEY ISSUED AN ANNUAL REPORT ... where are we? Where do we go from here? We must and will carry on the fight ... Mr De Valera, for Our Dear Lady's sake at least grant us an interview that we may show you some of the stuff being sold in Catholic Ireland – it's even going the round in the classroom.

The government response was blunt and contemptuous. As a letter from the Department of Justice to the private secretary of the Taoiseach put it: 'The Minister [Oscar Traynor] is not prepared to receive a deputation from this body. It is apparent from communications received from their secretary over a number of years that the League have very exaggerated notions of what is indecent and any discussions with them could not fail to be embarrassing.'[302]

'Whether the tendency of the matter charged ... is to deprave and corrupt those whose minds are open to such immoral influences'

How did the operation of the Censorship of Publications Board work in practice before the appointment of the new liberals, and what was it like to be a member? Some indication is given in the notebooks of C. J. O'Reilly, who was a member of the board from 1951 to 1955. He taught Irish in St

Patrick's teacher training college in Dublin, where another member, J. Pigott, also worked, and he was a leading member of the Knights of Columbanus. Enthusiastic at the outset, he transcribed the objectionable passages of the first twenty-five books referred for his consideration,[303] but no doubt finding this overly laborious, he opted in most cases to simply indicate the objectionable text by page number, sometimes reinforcing his judgement with a pithy phrase to summarise. He also adopted the practice of underlining the page number – sometimes up to four times – as a personal guide to how improper he considered the text.

O'Reilly examined a total of 1,294 books from July 1951 to June 1955. The number of publications referred to the board reached an all-time high in 1955 of 1,217, up from 717 in 1951.[304] For O'Reilly, that meant examining 481 books; it was an onerous workload. But his notes give an indication of why the board's activities were coming under closer scrutiny, and why more liberals were being appointed. In the late 1940s the percentage of books banned as a proportion of the total never exceeded 55 per cent, but in 1951 this rose to 75 per cent and reached an astonishing 85 per cent by 1954; this pattern endured until 1957, when the percentage reverted to the levels of the late 1940s.[305]

As far as O'Reilly was concerned it was sufficient for a book to be 'indecent and vulgar' to recommend its prohibition, on the grounds that it was an incitement to immorality among the young, or the general public. More specifically, descriptions of or references to nudity, 'passionate scenes', sexual intercourse, masturbation, homosexuality, lesbianism, adultery and infidelity were deemed deserving of prohibition. The consequences of human sexual behaviour also prompted him to recommend a ban, evident from his discomfort with texts that featured illegitimacy, VD and prostitution, and he recommended that Rhys Davies' *Marianne* should be banned because it made 'very frequent reference to pregnancy' and included 'a minute description of [the] birth of a child'.[306]

Novels, autobiographies and works of non-fiction that described or promoted contraception, artificial insemination and abortion were judged to be objectionable. O'Reilly was also prepared to prohibit books deemed to misrepresent the Catholic Church or which contained criticism of the clergy. Those books he regarded as blasphemous, as well as those that challenged conventional gender roles, including Vera Brittain's *Lady into Woman* (1953), in which Brittain identifies fertility control as crucial to the woman who wants to 'choose her work and organise her future'.[307]

Of the 1,294 books examined by O'Reilly, 994 (76.8 per cent) were added to the register of prohibited books in Ireland, though he did not always get his way. He was overruled on a number of titles, including Iris Murdoch's *Under The Net* (1954), Graham Greene's *The Living Room* (1953) and Kate O'Brien's *Pray for the Wanderer* (1958). The authors he successfully recommended for prohibition include John Steinbeck, Doris Lessing, Truman Capote, Bertrand Russell, Samuel Beckett and F. Scott Fitzgerald, though these were exceeded numerically by authors of popular fiction, including Barbara Cartland, Rex Marlowe, Raymond Chandler, Ian Fleming and Leon Uris.

A note in the third of O'Reilly's notebooks indicates that he was guided by the criteria of Chief Justice Cockburn, Lord Chief Justice of England in 1859 – an indication of how reliant he was on Victorian sentiment. Cockburn had observed that the 'test of obscenity' was 'whether the tendency of the matter charged ... is to deprave and corrupt those whose minds are open to such immoral influences, and into whose hands a publication of this sort may fall'.[308] O'Reilly had a preference for archaic language, frequently finding descriptions of what he termed 'the act of sexualisation' objectionable; one such passage was enough to recommend a ban. Popular medical works were also deemed inappropriate if they engaged with issues of sex or contraception; he even wanted a history of penicillin removed from public libraries because it contained criticism of the attitude of the Church to artificial insemination, though he was overruled in this instance. He recommended no action in the case of George Bankoff's history of venereal diseases *The Shadow on the Path* (1949), because it was 'treated as a medical treatise in a restrained manner'.[309]

It is clear from his notebooks that no author was subject to automatic prohibition – some of the books of Graham Greene, Benedict Kiely and Kate O'Brien, for example, were banned and some were not, indicating that O'Reilly adhered to the practice of considering every book on its merits, although those he favoured form a much shorter list than those he wanted banned. Crucially, the mindset revealed by O'Reilly's notebooks also contributed to the undoing of the board as one dominated by absolutists.

*'It had always been one of the things she resented
most vehemently, the suggestion that a woman
should be regarded as in any way
ignorant of certain matters'*

Some Irish female authors were banned because their writing concentrated on the repressed energies of women – wives, mothers or single women – living in town and countryside. Like Kate O'Brien, Mary Lavin was honest about their frustrations, some of which were sexual, and born of a small-town morality. In Lavin's 1969 story 'The Lost Child' she confronts the contradiction that a Church so implacably opposed to abortion relegated unbaptised dead children to 'an equally ignominious fate. So if a woman has a miscarriage, her child is a lost soul.'[310] Angela Macnamara, who endured three miscarriages in the 1950s and later became the country's best-known agony aunt through her columns in the *Sunday Press*, also remembered that there was 'no real understanding of the aftermath of a miscarriage at that time'; she was engaged to be married at the age of twenty-one, but her middle-class mother had told her 'little or nothing about my developing body.'[311]

Lavin explores the difficulty of a 40-year-old celibate woman who fails to confront her own and her father's sexuality in *A Single Lady* (1951). The character's own sexual confusion is reflected in her indignation at her father's relationship with a servant:

> At his age! Why! If he had any inclinations of that sort he could have satisfied them long ago in a manner compatible with his position ... her father! – and a common servant! If she were even that! But a wretched little slut ... it had always been one of the things she resented most vehemently, the suggestion that a woman should be regarded as in any way ignorant of certain matters just because she was single ... she made a desperate effort to be tolerant ... all at once another aspect of her misery came over her. 'After all the sacrifices I made for him.'[312]

Kate O'Brien often dealt with characters comfortable with, but not completely controlled by, Catholicism. A short biography of her by Eibhear Walshe touches upon but does not elaborate on her probable lesbianism and the story that she may have had an illegitimate child brought up by her sister (the evidence, it seems, is inconclusive, but the probability is that this happened). Strong relationships between women are a regular theme in her work; or, as Walshe puts it, 'the web of interconnecting relationships in her life is the only reliable biographical material available for the evaluation of her sexuality'. Sexual orientation was another recurring theme of her work, but she did not make public her sexual preference. Walshe suggests that representations of sexual love in her work are 'always illicit, mostly outdoors and rarely pleasurable',[313] which could serve as shorthand for many of the sexual experiences of Irish people from the 1930s to the 1960s.

O'Brien was very successful, critically and financially, and it was interesting that it was in London in the 1920s that she found 'a sexual identity as a lesbian within the professional field of her London working life'.[314] In her 1958 work *As Music of Splendour* O'Brien explores the theme of conflict between moral teaching and the possibility of lesbian love and highlights 'the mania girls get for each other or for their teachers in school age'. Clare, the heroine of the story, in admitting her love for Luisa, regards herself as sinful and not in a state of grace as a practising Catholic: '"Well, anyway, at Mass I'm always sharply reminded that being happy isn't what we're here for!" She laughed and kissed Luisa's outstretched hand: "Much good that does me." "Thank God."'[315] But it is important to point out that Walshe's assertions, though probably true, are difficult to prove when it comes to O'Brien's lesbianism. Despite his focus on what he maintains is her 'clear' lesbianism, Catriona Crowe points out that 'it's precisely the mixed messages (mannish clothing; explicit lesbianism in some of the fiction; intense Catholicism; expressed dislike of homosexuality in some of the fiction) and lack of clarity that are interesting'.[316]

Another writer who dealt with sexual repression was the poet and novelist Patrick Kavanagh, though he was secretive in his published writings about romantic friendships and sex. He believed 'even to bandy the names of women friends in print would have been unseemly'. In his writings he tended to play the role of failed and unrequited lover or 'too poor to be a seducer'. In his youth he was so frustrated he resorted to groping his sisters. But, as Antoinette Quinn points out, the notion that he 'died longing' does not withstand scrutiny; he was a practising, highly sexed heterosexual who craved women's company. He talked to one woman, Peggy Gough, about his frustrations and she occasionally offered him an outlet for them. His epic poem 'The Great Hunger' (1942) depicts its main character Paddy Maguire as a lustful, sexually tormented man masturbating in the headland of a field, but he is too old and ignorant, his sexual inhibition a result of 'religion, the fields, the fear of the Lord and ignorance', while his sister has to endure 'the purgatory of middle-aged virginity'.

Quinn suggests that in the poem Kavanagh is preaching 'the gospel of the importance of human sexual fulfilment with all the zeal of the recently converted'. For Kavanagh sexuality and spirituality were interconnected. He also, Quinn suggests, unburdened himself of a guilty secret in the 1978 poem 'Lough Derg': 'The second subplot of a Franciscan monk's sexual intercourse with a young schoolgirl derives from Kavanagh's own first sexual experience with the gymslip-clad 15-year-old who confided that she had been sexually assaulted by a priest. The priest's paedophilia is not dwelt upon and the episode concludes laconically: "'Twas a failing otherwise, lost him his priestly faculties".'[317]

A book by James Plunkett, *The Trusting and the Maimed* (1955), deals with a girl 'getting into trouble', while Sean O'Casey's *The Bishop's Bonfire* (1955), through the character Foran, is an example 'of the more subtle kind of Irish Catholic Puritanism which makes chastity rather than charity the central ethic'.[318] It was a play that earned him the ire of Archbishop McQuaid, a reminder that theatre, though not subjected to the same kind of rigorous censorship as literature – indeed, it was relatively free from state censorship – was not immune from censure. In Athlone in 1946 the Little Theatre Group entered O'Casey's *Juno and the Paycock* for the Father Mathew Feis and it was rejected by the Capuchin fathers as 'not suitable', probably because of the part in which Juno's daughter is seduced by the crooked solicitor Bentham. The following year the same theatre group entered Gerard Healy's play *The Black Stranger* for the Feis and the organisers demanded that a whole scene be cut in which a woman sacrifices her virtue for a bag of meal. The actors and author refused to comply.[319] Frank McCourt, in his memoir *Angela's Ashes*, recalls how his mother ended up in a similar situation in Laman Griffin's house, forced to seek refuge after eviction:

> Mam tells us to go to bed, she'll be after us in a minute, as soon as she climbs to the loft with Laman's last mug of tea. We often fall asleep before she goes up, but there are nights when we hear them talking, grunting, moaning. There are nights when she never comes down and Michael and Alphie have the big bed to themselves. Malachy says she stays up there because it's too hard for her to climb down in the dark. He's only twelve

and he doesn't understand. I'm thirteen and I think they're at the excitement up there.[320]

In 1945 Frank O'Connor translated the Clare poet Brian Merriman's *Cuairt an Mheadhon Oidche* (*The Midnight Court*), a bawdy satire on peasant society and its priests, touching on themes of sex, marriage, inheritance and womens' rights. O'Connor was keen to contrast 'the sensuous eighteenth-century society evoked by Merriman' with the subsequent triumph of 'Puritanism', though the Censorship of Publications Board showed no such enthusiasm. Bryan Fanning makes the point that O'Connor felt certain restraints when translating the poem, seeking to evoke rather than directly translate Merriman's 'perfect crescendo of frustrated sexual passion', but that the 'tremendous physicality' of the poem was still evident in O'Connor's translation:

> Down with marriage! 'Tis out of date,
> It exhausts the stock and cripples the state.
> The priest has failed with whip and blinker,
> Now give a chance to Tom the Tinker,
> And mix and mash in nature's can
> The tinker and the gentleman;
> Let lovers in every lane extended,
> Follow their whim as God intended,
> And in their pleasure bring to birth
> The morning glory of the earth.[321]

'Upright citizens,
capable of spotting dirt at a hundred yards'

The following decade, in the most shameful episode of bullying in Irish theatre history, reputations, careers and a marriage were ruined by the decision to prosecute Alan Simpson, the director of the tiny Pike theatre in Dublin, for staging Tennessee Williams' 1952 play *The Rose Tattoo*. The myth that a condom featured on the stage endured for years afterwards; in fact there was no condom. The real reasons the production received such unwelcome attention was because of the battle between state and Church over who was seen to be doing the most in relation to the censorship of perceived unsuitable material. This was not about the play at all, the Minister for Justice apparently being pressured to close it before being called upon by Archbishop McQuaid to do so. A letter from the Attorney General's office in May 1957 states that the minister had been approached by a TD about the staging of this 'unquestionably indecent' play, 'that its production had been prohibited in several American cities', and that delays in closing it would result in the Archbishop intervening.

A civil servant advised the minister that he should not put himself in a position in which the impression was given that 'you act only at the dictation of the Archbishop or somebody else'.[322] Later in the month, two Gardaí attended the play and reported on 'lewd, vulgar and offensive' matters (despite the fact that 'a better class of audience attended', including well-known members of the political and legal establishment), such as 15-year-old Rossa Delle Rose dancing with an American soldier; she was 'close to her partner and sways with his rhythm'. Director Alan Simpson was eventually arrested; however, a district court judge refused to let the issue go to trial, and castigated the Garda case. The theatre never recovered, nor did Simpson's marriage to Carolyn Swift, who founded the theatre with him; she spent the last few years of her life working on a book about the case with co-author Gerald Whelan.[323]

This case was not about public indecency; it is no coincidence that it happened at the same time as the row over the Censorship of Publications Board described earlier. In the words of Fintan O'Toole, 'Simpson and Swift were simply picked up by the state, crumpled like pieces of used paper and tossed aside.'[324] Simpson used to joke that 'we died so that Irish theatre could be free'. There is an element of truth in that, and the price they paid was high.

Censorship had a continuing relevance for libraries, also. Dermot Foley, librarian in Ennis, County Clare, recalled that the suspicion created by the Censorship Board about public libraries meant that 'every two-bit prude or bigot could fancy himself or herself a moral policeman'. In one library the poetry of John Donne was locked up in a case with other books available on request only to 'readers of proven maturity of mind'. Foley also encountered 'a panel of spiritual vigilantes who would vet all books before they could be placed in the library'. These people were, he scoffed, 'a ragbag of 52 upright citizens, capable of spotting dirt at a hundred yards'; even the local priest found their list of suitable books ridiculous. Foley dryly recommended acceptance of one volume concerning male criminals in a penal settlement in Australia, on the grounds that there was 'not one female within a hundred miles of it'.[325]

State papers released in 2006 reveal that in December 1952 a civil servant contacted District Justice MacDonagh (the son of Thomas MacDonagh, one of the more free-thinking leaders of the 1916 Rising), who had anonymously written a favourable newspaper review of Austin Clarke's epic romance poem *The Sun Dances at Easter* (1952): 'I would add a nod and a wink in the direction of the nearest bookstore and make haste if you take my advice', the clear suggestion being that it was going to be banned. When contacted he admitted his authorship but defended it on the grounds that he had contributed in his capacity as a writer. The Minister for Justice was informed there was little he could do, as district justices were no more subject to the disciplinary control of the minister for their behaviour 'than they are to the man on the moon'.[326]

'There is no spectacle so ridiculous as the British public in one of its periodical fits of morality'

In time, some booksellers became more brazen. A bookshop in Fermoy, County Cork, was visited by two Gardaí in March 1957, where they discovered eight banned books, including Doris Lessing's *Retreat to Innocence* (1956), Brett Halliday's *She Woke to Darkness* (1954) and *Cancel All Our Vows* (1953) by John D. MacDonald. The Garda report concluded that Aileen Creedon, the bookseller, 'has an utter disregard for the censorship acts', though she claimed ignorance, and it emerged that there were two firms in Dublin who were supplying the prohibited books. It was a reader in Fermoy who had reported Creedon, having complained that 'everyone seems to know that they are being distributed freely, yet no one has done anything about it'.[327]

A case such as this would suggest that some of the tight control was showing signs of abating in the 1950s, but it was also the case that unlikely individuals still found themselves confronted by the law. In County Cavan in 1957 a copy of *Picture Post* was sold to a 52-year-old bachelor – this and six other copies were seized by a Garda sergeant on the small farm of the man who, the Garda reported, always took 'the fighting side in any discussion that might arise. He is of a contrary disposition.' The following year, a 75-year-old newsagent was told that he would be prosecuted for selling the bodybuilding magazine *Mr Universe*, which he claimed he did not know was banned; he was put on probation.[328] In May 1957, Florence Griffin of Foyles Libraries in O'Connell Street complained to the Gardaí that in the absence of an up-to-date alphabetical list of banned titles (she claimed librarians only received partial lists) it was difficult to keep track of all prohibited titles, particularly as 'we have roughly a stock of 50,000 books'. Her statement was in response to a complaint that she had issued Jack Mortimer Sheppard's *Harvest of the Wind* (1956), a novel based on the life of Simón Bolivar's mistress, Manuela Sáenz.[329]

There were also complaints about comics and 'still pictures', such as those being shown through a machine at the 'Funland' premises at Burgh Quay, in Dublin City, which depicted a woman in a state of semi-nudity. In 1949 the Garda Siochana Deputy Commissioner's office decided that showing these did not contravene the existing laws dealing with indecency, but the proprietor was persuaded to remove them. In December 1953 it was also decided that some picture postcards at Tyrrell's in Charlemont Street were vulgar and suggestive, but since they were on sale generally they 'did not contravene any of the existing laws'. The following year, Gardaí in the C District reported that 'publications relating to sex matters which were filthy in the extreme were found on the premises 14 Charlotte Street (shop). The proprietor James Birmingham was prosecuted on a charge of publishing an obscene libel and was sentenced to two years imprisonment.' 1950

Other successful prosecutions brought by the C District included one relating to the showing of indecent pictures in slot machines at the Pillar Café, Upper O'Connell Street. But the Gardaí were also at pains to insist that 'the interpretation of the terms "obscene" and "indecent" is too narrow and the powers to deal with objectionable matter are too restrictive' – it being pointed out that they could only act on complaints from the public; otherwise 'we do not exercise special supervision over premises'.[330]

There is also evidence that in relation to pornography and horror comics, civil servants on both sides of the border were privately cynical about censorship and the periodic fits of moral panic north and south. The humorous, affectionate and satirical correspondence between Thomas Coyne, secretary of the Department of Justice in Dublin, and A. Lynch Robinson, secretary to the Ministry of Home Affairs in Belfast, reveal their true feelings on these matters. They were dismissive of the idea that the state had any role to play in policing morals. Robinson, for example, believed 'the modern child is beyond any corrupting influence which the adult is capable of devising. However, mine not to reason why', to which Coyne responded, 'there is no spectacle so ridiculous as the British public in one of its periodical fits of morality'. This was his response to expressions of concern about the danger that unsuitable material being published in the Republic might find itself heading north: 'I confess I was somewhat shaken by the sight and sound of Mr Hanna whooping it up after the fashion of the Last of the Mohicans and brandishing tomahawk and scalping knife in the general direction of the unfortunate newsagents in the Six Counties.'[331]

'A base, sordid picture into which moral considerations of any kind do not even faintly enter'

The film censor also continued to be busy. Richard Hayes, who took up the post in 1940, was not as colourful in his language as his predecessor; he was more succinct and, during the war years, spent most of his time censoring material deemed unsuitable for the audience of a neutral country. But in the post-war years he devoted more attention to films such as Paramount's *The Affairs of Susan* (1946), detailing the amorous activities of a woman after her divorce, a film he felt included 'rather delicate situations and some dubious dialogue' – words and phrases he used repeatedly.[332] There were far too many films, it would seem, detailing the travails of married women; in reaction to *The Postman Always Rings Twice* (1946), he wrote: 'the usual triangle [i.e., wife, husband and lover] but in this case without a relieving feature ... it is a base, sordid picture into which moral considerations of any kind do not even faintly enter', nor was he keen on 'sensual scenes' or 'seductive situations'.[333]

He also found the cinematic depiction of blackmail, murder and gangsterism distasteful. In 1946 he got particularly fed up with 'a lascivious married woman with several lovers' who appeared in Columbia's *The Trespasser*.[334] That year forty-five films were censored; there was, at that stage, only one certificate in Ireland, so films suitable for adults but not children needed to be cut. Into the 1950s Hayes continued to bemoan 'the usual marital triangle' and was suspicious of the Italian film *Bambino* (1950), 'a typical French farce [sic]', with a story 'not a suitable one for this country, however suitable and unobjectionable it may be for France with its different traditional attitudes towards such subjects [as paternity]'.[335]

Accounts of pleasure were still, it seems, taboo, or not accepted as involving pleasure at all; with a cultural ambivalence about pleasure, and a silence on the issue often imposed by celibates, it was a 'tragic irony', as John O'Brien points out in *The Vanishing Irish* (1953), that there was such a reluctance to marry among 'a people who respect so highly the sanctity and indissolubility of Christian marriage and among whom artificial birth control is at a minimum'. The marriage rate per 1,000 population between 1936 and 1945 was 5.37 (in Northern Ireland in 1946 it was 7.4, and in England and Wales, 9). Ireland had 73 married women under 45 per 1,000 of population, compared to 145 in the USA:

> we are 25% lower in this figure than any other country in the world, the Northern Ireland figure, one of the lowest, being 97 per 1000, Scotland 105, England and Wales 123 ... in short 65% of Ireland's population is single, 6% widowed and 28% married. Moreover, 70% of its males and 63% of its female population, 15 to 44, is single. Seventy-nine per cent of Irishmen under 30 are not married ... the high esteem for the religious – priests and nuns – who are all celibates [has] been carried over to esteem for celibacy as a state of life ... in a nation where sexual morality is remarkably high it would be immensely better if priests were to devote their energies to promoting social acquaintance, courtship and marriage.[336]

'Business gent, 35, respectable, wishes to meet respectable girl'

These are quite startling statistics when placed in an international context, but some of O'Brien's conclusions and generalisations are highly questionable, particularly the idea that celibacy 'as a state of life' was cherished. Undoubtedly, behind such figures there lay considerable loneliness, and those seeking to counteract this rarely wanted to be seen as forward or assertive. In the *Dublin Evening Mail* lonely hearts columns in the 1950s, as pointed out by Mary Kenny, those seeking spouses would be termed mature and the most common self-description was 'respectable'. She cites examples such as 'Business gent, 35, Respectable, wishes to meet Respectable girl' and 'Working man, 36 years, steady job, good appearance, would like to meet respectable working girl, 30 years, with view to matrimony'.[337]

There was also a lonely hearts page in *Ireland's Own*, the widely read homely magazine with 'a high moral tone' whose survival into the twenty-first century, suggests historian and journalist Con Houlihan, is 'a romantic story in itself – and in every number you will find tales of men and women in the thralls of love'. *Ireland's Own* pages were a comforting lifeline for many, but to the cynical contemporary mind, some of those seeking love through its lonely hearts pages had a bigger eye on economic potential. The satirical magazine *Dublin Opinion* mocked the *Ireland's Own* lonely hearts service by composing its own version of an Irish bachelor's plea for companionship: 'Gentleman whose interests include singing, dancing, reading, hop scotch and playing the mouth organ, would like to meet lady with similar tastes who owns her own shop. Send photo of shop.' [338]

Angela Macnamara has painted an idyllic picture of middle-class dating in the late 1940s and early 1950s which is completely at odds with William Trevor's depiction of drunken lechery perpetrated by filthy bachelors in *The Ballroom of Romance*. According to Macnamara, there was no kissing on first dates: 'the subsequent hand holding felt like magic. We progressed slowly savouring all the little delicate advances ... the question of "what was a sinful kiss" became a problem for most of us.' She cited a journal entry she recorded when newly married: 'Today the Jesuit I went to consult told me, "If you cause your husband to lose seed without having sexual intercourse, it is a mortal sin."' [339]

In his provocative 1968 book *Is Ireland Dying?* Michael Sheehy preferred to use the phrase 'sex starvation' to describe what was afflicting the young, which set the scene for

> a chaotic form of sexual life which the clergy are never tired of condemn-
> ing and of which Synge wrote: "If I were to tell you ... all the sex horrors
> I have seen I could a tale unfold that would wither up your blood." [340]

How much had things changed in the intervening fifty years? As Sheehy saw it, the Irish were conditioned to see sex as ugly and there was not enough of a tradition of Irish humanism. He disputed O'Brien's contention in *The Vanishing Irish* that it was an admiration for celibacy that kept Irish men bachelors:

> If Irishmen choose to be bachelors, it is not usually with any inten-
> tion of depriving themselves of such sexual pleasures as may come their

way. An ideal of sexual purity, to be vital presupposes some faith in the essential goodness of the human mind. But Irishmen tend to lack this, and see in sexual excesses the more or less inevitable outcome of human corruption.

At the same time, they were continually being told, as Cardinal Conway (then Dr Conway, Bishop of Neve) put it in 1960, 'public opinion has been for the most part silent about the shameless exploitation of sex' in films and novels.[341]

'You wounded me! All of you wounded me! I don't forgive'

Some of those who grew up in the 1950s found it difficult to forgive their mentors and tormentors for instilling in them such a sense of shame and fear. Margaret MacCurtain notes that Irish women writing from the 1970s to the 1990s, when looking back to the Catholicism of their youth, did so 'to recall a lost innocence and to settle old scores with austere convent schools, whereas writers of previous generations critique the authoritarian patterns of family and social behaviour mediated by Church teaching, which relegated women to a passive and subservient station in life'.[342] In 1987, Gráinne O'Flynn recalled the socialisation strategies of a Catholic education in the 1940s that did not encourage women to engage with social or political life: 'some nuns at our school had told us that Our Lady wept when girls wore shorts or trousers', while parents' references to sex 'were usually about seeds and mysterious plantations'. Neither biology nor science was taught to the girls so they were 'quite vague about what arousal meant'. However, at the end of 'special' classes given to the senior girls, one thing was made very clear: 'we were potentially dangerous. The very female form was a source of evil. The best ways to rid ourselves of its encumbrances were to pray, be modest, adopt low vocal tones and become non-argumentative.'[343] In recalling her memories of nuns and her three years of boarding school in the 1950s, Nuala O'Faoláin found herself in the 1990s still wanting to cry out: 'You wounded me! All of you wounded me! I don't forgive. I know it was no one's fault, but I don't forgive. I feel I was got at.'[344]

As Seán O'Faoláin saw it in his book *The Irish* (1947), his compatriots did not succeed in integrating religion and life but opted for a dualism, or the simultaneous use of a double set of values. There is much merit in O'Faoláin's thesis, as expanded by Michael Sheehy, that there was public and private divergence from the ideals. Honor Tracy, who first published her impressions of Ireland in 1953, noted the cinemas in O'Connell Street with bills 'announcing films that glorified everything Ireland pretends to despise, where later on there would be long, patient, avid queues'.

Privately, maybe the sermons on sex and matrimony were not being taken as seriously as is sometimes thought; Tracy called to mind the words of one of the poet and writer Oliver Gogarty's characters, the mother of numerous children, who listens for a few moments to a Franciscan preaching about matrimony before remarking, 'I wish to God I knew as little about it as that one.' But Tracy also detected a 'rancid Irish Puritanism, that fear and hatred of life' and bemoaned 'the terror, the moral paralysis, that afflicts so many Irishmen in their dealings with the female sex', and their avoidance of it by joking: 'the Irish man replied jovially that down in the country they at least consoled themselves with the sheep'.[345] But underlying that joke was a reality for some.

Tracy had joined the staff of *The Bell* in 1945 and embarked on an affair with O'Faoláin, thirteen years her senior, who had previously had a relationship with the sexually liberated writer Elizabeth Bowen. Tracy's 'erotic expertise' continued to delight him, as did her extrovert rebellious character 'and what he saw as an amoral nature attracted his more cautious temperament'.[346] But Catholic guilt bothered O'Faoláin and he consulted a priest in Paris about the betrayal of his wife Eileen. He ended the relationship with Tracy (she subsequently had a nervous breakdown) but within six months was with another woman; his affair with wealthy New Yorker Arlene Erlanger was kept largely secret: 'Frank and outspoken about her feelings and sexual needs, Arlene was very different from any Irish women he had known.' There was, it seems, nothing unusual about Irish writers having extramarital affairs, indeed it would appear to have been part of the creative process: 'Liam O'Flaherty had run away with another man's wife, [Frank] O'Connor had a number of relationships as he [O'Faoláin] had had himself.'[347]

But by the late 1950s, some Irish women were becoming more assertive in their dealings with men. John McGahern wrote of such a relationship in his 1970 story 'My Love, My Umbrella', which charts the progression of a relationship in 1950s Dublin from the initial awkward, stilted encounter:

'Would you come with me for a drink?'
'Why?' She blushed as she looked me full in the face.
'Why not?'
'I said I'd be back for tea.'
'We can have sandwiches.'
'But why do you want me to?'
'I'd like very much if you come. Will you come?'
'All right I'll come, but I don't know why.'

The narrator's hope is that their bodies will draw closer than their speech, and so they do, but as the woman is living in lodgings, their sexual encounters are outdoors, under trees in an orchard. After numerous such encounters the man tires of their relationship and leaves, only to discover, 'I'd fallen more into the habit of her than I'd known.' But when he arrogantly attempts to rekindle the affair, it is the woman who ends their relationship because she does not want to be just a habit:

'I've thought about it and that our going out is a waste of time. It's a waste of your time and mine'
It was as if a bandage had been torn from an open wound.
'But why?'
'It will come to nothing.'
'You've got someone else then?'
'That's got nothing to do with it.'
'But why then?'
'I don't love you.'
'But we've had many happy evenings together.'
'Yes, but it's not enough.'[348]

But for many young girls, their transition to adulthood was marked by painful violation. A news story in 1996 about the trial of a murderer and the long-repressed aspects of his childhood was one factor that prompted the journalist Nuala O'Faoláin to write her 1996 memoir *Are You Somebody?* – in both sorrow and anger – recounting among other things, her experiences of a Dublin childhood in the 1950s. But she is able to dwell little on the child she was; there is a disconnection between girl and woman – a wider issue of the absence of Irish literary girlhood as identified by Jane Dougherty. The discovery of sexuality and the experience of sexual violence represents a break from O'Faoláin's childhood self. She writes that 'I was never afraid till I went to the Messiah in the Theatre Royal when I was eleven, and a man put his hand up my skirt and hurt me with his fingers.'[349] A similar scene occurs in Edna O'Brien's 1997 novel *Down by the River*, in which 'the trauma essentially brings her character Mary into being: sexual trauma is thus linked in that novel, as it is in O'Faoláin's memoir, with the creation of adult female subjectivity. In both texts, puberty represents the entrance of the female protagonist into the universe of patriarchal sexuality' and, to a certain extent, the erasure of childhood.[350]

Nor was O'Faoláin alone in this; she was deluged by correspondence from readers who had similar experiences. Angela Macnamara was an adult before she told her sister that, when she was 10, a family friend had exposed himself to her ('showing me what happens to men when aroused'); she also observed, 'I worked with children for years before any hint of this subject became more openly talked about.'[351]

'There is a grey area in between where we are not sure'

Many others were abused by a minority of those in religious life, but notably absent from the court files are members of the clergy, which would support the idea that their crimes were not reported to the civil authorities and that they had reason to be relieved they were not. This would explain some of the comments made during evidence given to the Commission to Inquire into Child Abuse, one of a range of measures introduced by the government to address the effects of abuse in childhood on the victims. Set up in April 2000, the commission had three primary functions: to listen to victims of childhood abuse who wanted to recount their experiences to a sympathetic forum; to fully investigate all allegations of abuse made to it, except where the victim did not wish for an investigation; and to publish a report on its findings to the general public. One Christian Brother quoted a contemporary internal comment about child abuse in the 1940s: 'The Lord has been very good to us in allowing the discovery [of child abuse] to have been made by the very prudent Dominican Fathers' – rather than the civil authorities.[352]

During other evidence given to the commission, reference was made to a 1941 visitation report concerning an alleged abuser and the response of his superior: 'so bad are the charges that I could not conscientiously allow him to remain with the boys any longer'.[353] This would suggest that senior Christian Brothers, like Gardaí and members of the legal and medical profession, were aware of the gravity of sexual abuse. However, the alleged abuser referred to above was moved to another institution rather than brought before the court.

The reports of the NSPCC from the 1940s and 1950s do not contain any detail on sexual crime. In the year 1944–5, the society dealt with 1,103 cases, the overwhelming majority of which were classed under the heading 'Neglect'. No cases were listed under the heading 'Criminal and indecent assault'. Eighteen people were prosecuted and the report indicated that 'of real and deliberate cruelty to children there has been practically none'.[354]

This was representative of the general tone of NSPCC reports mid century, but what the society often did do was graphically illustrate specific cases of neglect, squalor and parental irresponsibility, as well as calling for legal adoption, and strongly criticising the excessive use of industrial schools as an alternative to providing a new family life for the victims. 'It must be recognised', it reported in 1948–9, 'that the children are to a large extent deprived of home influences and it would be much better if we could avoid sending them to such institutions.'[355] INTERNAL EXILE

Its pleas went unheard and in 1956, when Archbishop McQuaid assumed control of the society, challenging and graphic case studies went and awkward questions posed about adoption and industrial schools were jettisoned in favour of quaint, superficial stories with happy endings. There was no context and no challenge. The exposure of the underbelly had ground to a halt. It was reiterated that the public 'have proven again that they are good guardians of the nation's conscience'; and the society's aim remained essentially conservative, focused on damage limitation –'the primary function of our society is to ensure that the life of every child in the state shall at least be endurable.'[356]

Endure many certainly did, despite the efforts of individuals such as Father Edward Flannagan, the Irish-American pioneer of a more humane system of institutionalised welfare.[357] In the same decades, no advances were made on the issue of adoption because, according to Gerry Boland, Minister for Justice in 1945 (the same man who had rebuked Flannagan for his criticisms of Irish residential institutions and prisons[358]) it had not proved possible to safeguard children against the potential danger to their religious faith.[359] Reading Boland's Dáil replies underlines the veracity of the testimony of Mary Norris, interviewed for Mary Raftery's 1999 book

Suffer Little Children: 'They didn't care about our bodies. Just as long as the little souls were safe.'[360] Likewise in his 1986 memoir *Against the Tide* Noël Browne castigates the actions of the clergy in blocking his proposed Mother and Child Scheme in 1951: 'I was left with a clear impression that the Church thrived on mass illiteracy and that the welfare of care in the bodily sense of the bulk of our people was a secondary consideration to the need to maintain the religious ethos in the health service.'[361] In his evidence to the commission, Brother David Gibson admitted that it was the spiritual as opposed to the emotional welfare of children that was the Christian Brothers' priority.[362]

In various memoirs, what it felt like to be a victim of class discrimination is given numerous powerful airings and, in this context, it is again worth noting the evidence of Brother Gibson to the commission, to the effect that the inmates of Letterfrack industrial school in Galway were 'almost exclusively from socially disadvantaged communities'.[363] In his evidence to the commission, Brother Michael Reynolds referred to the fact that 'At one stage in the 1940s, a letter appeared in one of the daily newspapers berating a judge for mentioning the fact that the boy in the sentencing had been in Artane [industrial school, Dublin] and telling him that if he had been in some high-class boarding school, that comment wouldn't be made.'[364] During the questioning of Brother Reynolds, a document was referred to in which there is an urgency about a particular case of sexual abuse: 'For a whole year he has been interfering in a homosexual way with two of these *very respectful boys* [author's emphasis] at Tramore Christian Brothers' School.'

The class background of inmates clearly affected the seriousness with which their complaints were taken. During the evidence given by Brother Gibson, reference was made to the complaints of sadism and vicious beatings as recounted by Peter Tyrrell, a former inmate of Letterfrack. A letter about this from the Christian Brothers to their solicitors makes a reference to a '"gentlemen" named Tyrrell ... I know you will know how to deal with him if he approaches.' The fact that the word gentlemen was put in inverted commas makes it clear that the author of the letter did not think that past inmates of an industrial school could be considered gentlemen.[365]

In the 1950s Tyrrell launched a campaign to highlight his abuse, but his letters were ignored. His written account of his abuse remained in the papers of Senator Owen Sheehy-Skeffington, who had encouraged him to record his experiences, until they were discovered in 2004. Tyrrell was of the belief that 'children were beaten and tortured for no other reason but lustful pleasure', but he also remembered the kind brothers and made it clear that non-teaching lay brothers also perpetuated some abuse – they had unsupervised access to boys in kitchens and on the farm. His searing memoir, wholly lacking in self-pity, *Founded on Fear*, was not published as intended in 1959.[366]

In 2006, the Christian Brothers apologised for abuse inflicted by some of their members – seven years after Taoiseach Bertie Ahern apologised on behalf of the state in an action that prompted more victims to come forward. Such apologies came over forty years too late for Tyrrell. In 1968 Scotland Yard asked Sheehy-Skeffington to identify a card addressed to him found next to the charred remains of a man who had burned himself alive on Hampstead Heath the previous year, which proved the only means of identifying Tyrrell.[367]

Tyrrell may have experienced more physical than sexual abuse, but he was correct to identify sexual violence and frustration as underpinning much of what he had experienced. There is now no doubt that from the 1930s the Church authorities were aware of sexual abuse and had canon law structures in place to deal with it.[368] In July 2004, Brother John O'Shea, the regional leader of the Brothers of Charity, referred to an 'authoritarian atmosphere in schools and institutions which made even credible people afraid to complain' and noted that 'they were seen as a group rather than as individuals in a group'. He suggested, accurately, that sexual abuse was seen as a moral issue with the emphasis on the spiritual, 'and a focus on the celibate life of the accused rather than on the abuse and hurt caused'.[369] This was a crucial distinction which permeated other aspects of sex and sexuality in Ireland during these decades.

Between 1930 and 1995, 650,000 children attended Christian Brother day schools and 10,000 were housed in their residential institutions; up to 2004, 791 complaints of abuse had been made against the Brothers. The Sisters of Mercy had 2,522 children in their care in 1941, but each convent was autonomous; from 1940 until the closure of their institutions, the Good Shepherd Sisters looked after 1,735 children. In 2004 they would not admit or deny abuse had occurred, but maintained 'there is a grey area in between where we are not sure'.[370]

chaplains?

> 'Lawmakers, jurists and the public of the period were
> in general well aware of the problem,
> even if there was little public comment' ×

A 1955 memorandum from the Department of Education suggested that cattle were being better looked after than the children in institutions. Both, though, were often being reared for export. Detailed inspections of the schools were carried out between 1939 and 1950 by Anna McCabe but, aside from that, 'the paper trail would suggest a very cursory inspection of the schools'. There were always more females than males within the industrial school system. Between the 1940s and 1950s, 5,500 children were committed, mostly through the courts, though there were many voluntary or health board admissions, and there were more in the twenty-six counties of the Republic than in all the UK combined. Religious congregations criticised the district courts for using the probation acts and tried to get the Department of Education to persuade the Department of Justice out of using them.

Between 1911 and 1960, half the children placed in these institutions were put there under the charge of destitution (which did not have to be proven), that is, of 'wandering and not having any home or settled place of abode'. Most disturbingly, five children were committed as a result of 'father convicted for a sexual offence against daughter', though it is important to emphasise that most of those committed to industrial schools were committed for reasons that had nothing to do with illegitimacy but more to do with parental poverty or neglect.[371]

In his memoir of growing up in 1950s Dublin, Gene Kerrigan notes that 'there were things that were not talked about back then, though they were no secret – for instance, there was a right way to be born and a wrong way, and those who came here the wrong way and their mothers were risking stone-faced rejection and years of misery'.[372] Bernadette Fahey, one of the many who came the 'wrong way', was also one of the victims who ultimately found her treatment so suffocating that she left the country. The most powerful passage in her 1999 book *Freedom of Angels* articulates the reasons why: *'coming the wrong way' → victim*

> I had left Ireland for several reasons, chief amongst which was the feeling that I didn't belong to anyone, anything or anywhere. I was also sick and tired of being asked where I came from and who I was. In common with

hundreds of others who were raised in orphanages, I was ashamed of
my past and did all in my power to hide it. England was a useful place
to evade these issues. It was less parochial. People were happy enough
to know which country you came from and leave it at that. For that
reason alone it became the safe haven of thousands of orphans who
couldn't bear the daily pressures that Irish society put on them. We
were constantly confronted with our lack of roots and identity. This
was extremely painful in a society that laid so much emphasis on one's
family pedigree, place of birth and religious persuasion. These were the
barometers by which individuals, families and groups were acceptable
or not.[373]

Bearing these observations in mind, it is no surprise that, according to
evidence given to the Commission to Inquire into Child Abuse, '40% of
former residents of the institutions were in Britain. Most had submerged
themselves in a British identity and many had not told spouses or children
of their background.'[374] It is also significant that support groups Survivors
of Child Abuse and One in Four were established in London in 1999.[375] It
is ironic that so many survivors of sexual abuse in Ireland chose to escape to
England to try and forget their abuse ordeals, given the frequent contention
that it was outside Ireland that sexual activity was more likely to occur, or
that the threat to Irish sexual morality was stronger.

In 1948, as observed by Eoin O'Sullivan in his evidence to the Commission, the Legion of Mary and members of the probation service highlighted
'ignorance of the facts of life' among industrial school children as one of
the reasons they were getting involved in prostitution,[376] and a consistent
connection was made between ignorance and immorality. In 1956, there
were 945 women in Magdalen asylums.[377] Concern about what happened
to those in institutions seems to have been a female prerogative, and 'males
were conspicuous in their absence of looking for change in this area'.[378] The
fact that men dominated the staffs of industrial schools and reformatories
caused occasional comment. In 1949, the Minister for Education, ecclesiastical authorities and school managers had, according to the minutes of the
JCWSSW, 'decided having regard among other things to the quasi adult age
and mentality of the boys and the need for constant supervision to maintain
order and discipline among such boys it would not be wise to employ women
in any capacity in the [industrial] school' at Daingean.[379] One-third of the
'street' girls dealt with at the Legion of Mary hostel in Harcourt Street were

ex-industrial school girls, according to a communication with the Department of Health in 1950 from Frank Duff, one of the few men who opposed
the use of these schools.[380]

In giving evidence to the Commission, Brother Gibson, when speaking
about Letterfrack industrial school, which operated from 1887 to 1974 and
about which there were 449 complaints up to 1994, maintained that abuse
was isolated, perpetrated by individual brothers and 'not concealed' when
known. He continued: 'sexual abuse in a period 60 years ago was seen more
as a moral failure than as a crime and that it was more the failure morally of
the person rather than the actual criminal dimension to the act'.[381]

Was this the case? And just how much awareness was there of sexual
abuse? The most common answer to those questions has been that the
suppression of information was part of a culture of containment, and that
through the actions of the Gardaí and the courts a 'moral order' was specifically shaped; that Catholic sensibilities guided official responses to sexual
immorality; and that there was no public awareness of child sexual abuse in
Ireland in the middle decades of the twentieth century.[382]

This is not true. Child sexual abuse simply was not prioritised as an area
worthy of immediate political and social action, as pointed out by Moira
Maguire: 'Far from being ignorant of the vulnerability of children to sexual
abuse in the first half of the twentieth century, lawmakers, jurists and the
public of the period were in general well aware of the problem, even if there
was little public comment ... in the government's response to sexual assaults
against children, the poor, disaffected, and marginalised were sacrificed
to the "greater good" – which in this case meant male sexual licence and
protecting the newly independent state's legitimacy and reputation in the
international arena. Finally, court cases from the 1920s to the 1950s reveal
fundamental flaws and misconceptions about sexual assaults against children presented by the witnesses who appeared before the Carrigan Committee. These flaws hindered the government's ability to act on the issue,
even if it had been so inclined.'[383]

Certainly, there was a distaste at the idea of Ireland's 'dirty laundry'
being aired in public and a preoccupation with controlling the flow of
information and pregnant women, but the court archive would suggest
there was also a belief that teenage girls were more responsible than their
male assailants for sexual assaults, concerns that the girls would blackmail
men, a regard 'for the reputation of innocent men', and more preoccupation with the 'character' of females than males. Despite the belief articulated

by Eoin O'Duffy that overcrowded urban housing facilitated sexual abuse, it has been pointed out that 'of the nearly 1500 sexual assault cases heard in circuit courts throughout the country in the period from 1924 to 1960 [and this does not represent all the cases because records are not complete for all counties] only a handful occurred under the kind of conditions he described. In fact, many sexual assaults against young girls occurred in isolated fields and laneways, in the homes of neighbours, and in their own rural cottages.'[384] There is truth in this assertion, but it still underestimates the urban dimension and the contribution of living conditions, as outlined earlier in this and other chapters.

Was it the case that governments and the Church focused on what they could control to divert attention from what they could not control?[385] Why was there virtually no discussion of the Infanticide Bill of 1949? Was the Church more concerned with dance halls than with the death of illegitimate children? For Church and state it was perhaps politically expedient not to address these gulfs in values. What cannot be denied is that the excessive focus on suppression and containment diverted attention from the fact that 'there was already substantial public and judicial awareness of sexual crimes against children. In many cases, knowledge of the danger of sexual assaults translated into fear and suspicion on the part of parents',[386] which would explain why many of them caught perpetrators in the act.

'Babies sold to US in secret'

The decision to cover up the scandal of foreign adoptions was taken for the same reasons that other issues had been repressed. Adoption legislation was eventually introduced in 1952, but only after foreign newspapers drew attention to what some termed the 'black market' in Irish babies. In March 1950 *The New York Times* printed a photograph of six Irish children departing Shannon airport for adoption by US couples: 'press coverage reached a crisis in 1951 when newspapers in the United States, Britain and Ireland documented how easy it was for the actress Jane Russell to adopt an Irish national who was living in London with his parents'. In 1945, Archbishop McQuaid had told Stephen Roche of the Department of Justice that 'no step be taken' until the Hierarchy was notified about any adoption legislation. But the JCWSSW was aware that, even then, 'there is far too much trading in babies at present amongst those who take them for a lump sum.

Sometimes the child is sent from one woman to another, the sum getting smaller and smaller at each transfer. It is difficult to trace some of these children and they may suffer much hardship.'[387] Even after adoption had been legalised, Cecil Barrett complained to McQuaid of a 'conspiracy' and a 'smear campaign' against Catholic adoption societies, a 'malicious campaign which must be fought and broken', with some suggesting that 'priests and nuns are getting rid of children and no one knows what is becoming of them'.[388]

Social workers and the NSPCC had made it clear this problem was urgent. In truth, what the critics were looking for was lay inspection, or at least local authority supervision, of the process. One of the organisations Barrett reserved his ire for was the JCWSSW, who pushed for the local authority amendment, as they were concerned that some children had been lost track of and that some who had been temporarily placed with a view to adoption were not then being brought forward for the whole adoption process. Since 1950 in Northern Ireland, legislation enforced notification to local authorities of all placements of children, even when placed by adoption societies. As far as Barrett was concerned, UN reports on adoption 'have no bearing on the conditions obtaining in Ireland'. In May he wrote simply to McQuaid, 'We have won our fight' – the amendment was dropped.[389]

As the newspaper stories referred to above suggest, some of the 'adopted' children were sent abroad, often without the genuine permission of their mothers, through a system in which the state colluded with Church agencies to allow foreign couples, mostly from the United States, to adopt them, in a system regulated by Archbishop McQuaid in conjunction with the Department of External Affairs, which referred in 1956 to 'this traffic in adoption children'.

According to Mike Milotte, 2,100 children were sent to America under this scheme between 1949 and the end of 1973. Of the 330 foreign adoption cases in 1952, 327 were illegitimate children and 3 were orphans.[390] There was no restriction on the entry of these children to the US, but the 'consent' of young and vulnerable Irish single mothers was in many cases no such thing. Undoubtedly, many of the children were afforded a quality of life in America unavailable in Ireland, but many grew to adulthood under assumed names and this 'created serious issues of confused identity when the truth was revealed or found out, as did the fact that the real mother's name was in some cases deleted from the record'.[391] In some cases babies were bought

– 'contributions' were made to the institutions that housed the babies, many of which were overcrowded at a time when births to unmarried mothers were on the increase – and for the prospective adopters the babies' removal was 'effortless acquisition', in contrast to Britain where adoption laws forbade such practices.

The primary concern remained the religious welfare of the children, though in time the practice created more embarrassing headlines ('Babies sold to US in secret') and some doubts were raised about the safeguards the Irish and American Churches had put in place. By the end of the 1950s the schemes were standardised. It was not until 1996 that the mothers were apologised to by the Irish government, though, owing to the constitutional right to privacy and archives legislation, mothers were still not permitted access to the files of such adoptions. The mothers had signed forms that included the wording: 'I hereby relinquish full claim forever to my child' and authorisation for the children to be taken out of the country. Some who had spent nearly two years caring for their children were distraught, yet were forbidden to question the procedure.[392]

The concern to ensure a greater deal of supervision over adoption was a well-placed one; in 2007 RTÉ television showed a documentary which recounted the harrowing experiences of Celine Roberts, who, abandoned by her biological parents, was 'sold' by her foster mother in 1957 when she was aged just seven and raped on the day of her first Holy Communion. She went on to endure rape and forced prostitution while her foster mother pocketed the money paid by 'an unknown number of faceless men, with forgettable names, in hidden places' in rural Kilkenny to abuse her daughter. Eventually, one local tipped off the authorities and Celine was placed in an industrial school, which by comparison with her experiences outside was 'like paradise'. She eventually tracked down her biological parents, who were married with nine children and wanted nothing to do with her.[393] Celine's story, though an extreme case, is just one of many that have emerged in recent years recounting lost, violated and traumatic childhoods in twentieth-century Ireland, many of them destroyed beyond repair by sexual violence.

The Report of the Commission to Inquire into Child Abuse, published in May 2009, contains the testimony of hundreds of such victims. A harrowing 3,000-page monument to those individuals, it vindicates those whose lives were so badly damaged and whose suffering had been compounded by a prolonged refusal to believe their stories. The conclusions of the report are unambiguous – thousands of children suffered systematic physical and sexual abuse between the 1930s and the 1970s and lived in a climate of fear in residential institutions funded by the state and run by religious orders. The report found that sexual abuse was endemic in boys' institutions, and more allegations were made against the Christian Brothers, the largest provider of residential care for boys in the state, than all other male orders combined. The Department of Education is sharply criticised for its deferential and submissive attitude to the religious congregations and its failure to carry out meaningful inspections.[394]

More than 1,700 men and women gave evidence of abuse to the Commission, chaired by Justice Seán Ryan, with over half reporting sexual abuse. The Commission's report details abuse in relation to 216 institutions, an extraordinary number for a country of Ireland's size. The vast majority of abuse was reported in industrial schools and reformatories. In presenting such an overwhelming body of evidence about what went on behind closed doors, the report provides a corrective to the atmosphere of secrecy and shame that surrounded these experiences for so many years.

The report also makes it clear that the extent of the sexual and physical assaults on children cannot be explained away by maintaining that the country was too poor and ignorant; there were much more calculated and sinister forces at work and a deliberate abdication of state responsibility. At a time when the industrial school system was being critically questioned and reformed in other countries, the increasing reliance on the system in Ireland suited far too many who were obsessed with the visibility of those whose behaviour or existence challenged the notion of the Irish as more chaste, pious and respectable than people elsewhere.

Souls, not bodies, were the intense preoccupation and this became overwhelming in a small Catholic country with little tradition of Church opposition and an exaggerated deference towards those deemed to be pillars of the community. There was a casual indifference to everyday violence that would not have been tolerated in other countries. The children enduring the thrashings were mostly poor and held in contempt, victims of an invidious Irish snobbery in a country that liked to pretend it was classless.

Many who supposedly had vocations for religious work clearly did not, and were the very last people who should have been put in charge of children. Forced celibacy, the young age of entry to religious training and single-sex environments compounded the problems and poisoned the atmosphere these men, women and children lived and operated in. Many

of the perpetrators of abuse were victims of another snobbery – the internal Church pecking order that deemed certain clerics to be more suited to
working in industrial schools. There is no doubt that the frustrations they
experienced had devastating consequences for the children and for themselves. They were products of a uniquely Irish mixture of large families,
thwarted ambitions, rigorous segregation of the sexes and lack of economic
opportunity, as were the children they took out their frustration on, often
in the most sadistic of ways.

souls not bodies '– ¹we?

purity derived from Virgin Mary?

– FOUR –

1960–70

'A rapid sex routine is effected as if his wife is some stray creature with whom he is sinning and hopes he may never see again'

The 1960s has been described as 'a watershed decade for Irish sexuality; it set in motion a number of changes which prepared the ground for the profound alterations of the 1970s and 1980s'.[1] There were many reasons for this, including more debate about contraception, the influence of external forces and the arrival in Ireland of television. At the personal level, many people were also challenging their religion and rejecting teaching they regarded as conditioning them to equate flesh with sin. This sense of defiance was captured in Michael Farrell's book *Thy Tears Might Cease* (1963), in which the character Martin Reilly, having been punished and humiliated by priests about his private feelings, decides to resist them 'and think what thoughts he chose in the solitude of his own heart'.[2]

If some anecdotes are to be believed, there was a certain lessening of severity: 'At Maynooth they laughed rather than fulminated at the story of a Galway priest who had noticed a young woman from his parish sprawled on a beach wearing a very brief bikini. The priest sent the woman a note, asking her to wear a one-piece bathing suit. She returned a quick reply: "Which piece do you want me to take off?"'[3]

But the degree of liberation should not be exaggerated. For many growing up in Ireland in the 1960s sex was still a taboo subject. Tom Inglis points out that Daniel Lord's pamphlet *M is for Marriage* (1962) does not mention sex, the implication being that it was not seen as having any bearing on the success of a marriage.[4] The Christian counsellor and agony aunt Angela Macnamara believed 80 per cent of the young girls who wrote to her would not even mention the word sex to their mothers.[5] Inglis also recalls that in the 1960s every time the subject of sex surfaced on radio or television, his father 'got up from his chair and walked out of the room'. He suggests there was a continuing ignorance about the facts of life, and 'an inability of husbands and wives to communicate their fears, needs and desires and consequently, to negotiate when and how they wanted to have sex'.[6] One Irish mother of nine children commented to Dorine Rohan, author of the book *Marriage: Irish Style* (1969), 'Whoever said you were supposed to enjoy sex? Sure, aren't we all here to suffer and the more we suffer in this life, the better it will be for us in the next.'[7] Rohan's book, a substantial part of which had first been published in the *Irish Times*, was described (after its launch, which the Taoiseach Jack Lynch and his wife attended) as 'provocative and probing', one that gave a frank overview of the internal dynamics of Irish marriage and was, in effect, 'a concise compilation of much that has been said over the past few years about marriage in Ireland'. It was also cited as significant that Rohan was neither a doctor, a sociologist nor a psychiatrist but a freelance journalist.[8]

Donald Connery's book *The Irish* (1968) painted the following portrait of the Irishman's view of his wife:

> ... a kingsize hot water bottle who also cooks his food and pays his bills and produces his heirs. In the intimate side of marriage he behaves as if he were slightly ashamed of having deserted his male friends and his bachelorhood. He takes what should be the happy, leisurely lovemaking of marriage like a silent connubial supper of cold rice pudding. A rapid sex routine is effected as if his wife is some stray creature with whom he is sinning and hopes he may never see again. Though many Irish wives are preconditioned to such behaviour, having seen its like in their own fathers and uncles, they resent it deeply.[9]

Within Connery's analysis lie some clues as to why things did change in the 1960s. More people were prepared to write about these subjects, and resentments that had been buried for many years surfaced and were aired. But this did not automatically generate greater personal liberation and the broader context is significant here also. The tale of international attitudes to sex and sexuality is 'not simply a story of inevitable progress'. Jeffrey Weeks, one of the pioneers in the writing of the history of sexuality, warned in 2000 about the necessity of avoiding 'an unthinking progressivism, a sexual whiggism' in charting sexual history.[10] While it is true John Updike's book *Couples* (1968) includes the exchange that seemed to define a new era of liberation – the female response to the man worried about contraception is – 'welcome ... to the post-pill paradise' – the Pill was only used by a minority of women in North America in the 1960s. In France in the 1970s, 18 per cent of French couples still relied on the withdrawal method, while only 6 per cent of French women were on the Pill in 1970. When John Ardagh (who turned his attention to Ireland in the 1990s) published his book *The New French Revolution* in 1968, he argued that the transformation of sexual attitudes in that country was more laboured than in England, and that while for women 'old-style anti-Catholicism may be receding fast in France', it left behind it 'a widespread legacy of semi-conscious guilt, superstition and prudery about sex'.[11]

Internationally, despite the preponderance of the baby boomers, 'male ideas changed very little in a purported age of sexual revolution',[12] with a preference for compliant female partners, while 'a strong anti-homosexual bias was obvious in much of the male push for sexual liberation'. Some have argued that 'the 1960s did not begin until about 1965',[13] in Ireland, it could legitimately be maintained that the 1960s did not begin until the 1970s. Jonathan Green has asserted that this is also true of Britain: 'The sixties, as widely celebrated, is chronology as pure myth. Everything in the myth pertains to sex ... the real revolution would not emerge until the seventies, a harder-edged phenomenon, shorn of the glossiness of the previous decade.'[14] Alan Bestic confidently asserted in 1972 that England had 'soared into the sexual stratosphere', but he also maintained that in some respects the English were more physically repressed than the Irish, that they compartmentalised sex and that they would not talk about it within marriage due to 'fear, guilt and ignorance'. They were coy about sex education in schools (only one-third of local educational authorities producing guides or handbooks for that purpose) and, overall, the terrain of the jungle of English sex life was 'tortuous, paradoxical, dangerous'.[15] In truth, if there was a sex revolution in 1960s England it was mostly urban and centred around London and the south-east. None the less, there was a discernible shift internationally in

middle-class female sexual behaviour. Betty Friedan's *The Feminine Mystique*
(1963) legitimised and encouraged the anger many women felt about their
enforced subjugation; meanwhile, Helen Gurley Brown, editor of *Cosmo-
politan* from 1965, spread the word that 'nice girls did it', and that freedom
could be equated with sexual pleasure. William Masters and Virginia Johnson's *Human Sexual Response* (1966) provided scientific justification for
women's demand for sexual pleasure.[16] In authoritarian Catholic Portugal,
despite the survival of António Salazar's regime until 1974, and the fact that
'all-concealing costumes' remained *de rigueur* for men and women, social
culture and the conservative traditions of the 'Grande Bourgeoisie' were
gradually erased 'after surviving both wars in Edwardian isolation and splendour'. The Portuguese government indicated a shift in tolerance by 'discon-
tinuing the registration of common bawds and by ending the public health
licensing of the parlours, complete with string quartets, in which young
ladies catered for the private sexual tastes of Salazarian High Society.'[17] In
Italy, 'where femininity had long been equated with maternity', fertility limitation led to an 'amazing transformation' in female autonomy.[18]

'There is probably a saner attitude to sex in this country than almost anywhere else'

By the 1960s, the Archbishop of Dublin, John Charles McQuaid, was over
twenty years at the helm, and though he detected the winds of change blow-
ing in the area of sexuality, he was determined to reiterate the belief that
Ireland was different from elsewhere when it came to sexual morality and
practice. His biographer John Cooney has been particularly vocal on what
he regards as the most interesting and, indeed, unattractive of McQuaid's
traits:

> Where things go off the rails a bit, I think, is that he's not just prepared
> to deal with the social issues, to make Ireland a better society. His
> weakness is that he's totally obsessed with sex, and it's the imposition
> of a very severe code of sexual conduct, the opposition to 'filthy' books
> and the opposition to the great writers, the snooping on people about
> their sexual mores, the obsession with purity, segregation of boys and
> girls, that girls have to be primarily trained in domestic education, to be
> housewives and so forth, the very fact that he's against mixed sports. His

whole attitude to Irish society becomes therefore about him being 'the spy in the cab': he's almost like Ceausescu [Romania's former dictator] or any of these Eastern European leaders – he's bringing Ireland more and more under a kind of spiritual terrorism that is austere, that is backward-looking and which is also pretty strict theologically. By the late 1950s, he's pretty well taken on everyone in the state ... When you look at his archive, you can see he's got priests and laity, even people like Frank Duff of the Legion of Mary are effectively his spies.[19] *Modern cm*

In contrast, Deirdre McMahon, in a perceptive overview of McQuaid's time as archbishop, published in 2000, warned against the 'crude caricatures of hidebound Catholic reaction with which McQuaid has become identified since his death in 1973'.[20] As McMahon points out, many benefited from his public and private charity, and she argues that his life and career 'cannot be understood without encompassing this context of change in the life of his *?* Church and his country'.[21]

In 2004, Tom Garvin returned to the fray with his assessment of McQuaid who, he wrote, was 'an odd mixture of the progressive, the reactionary, the creative and the authoritarian'.[22] Garvin cites his determination to destroy the careers of those who were perceived to have stepped out of line in the conduct of their personal lives, including short story writer Frank O'Connor and his partner 'who were deprived of state employment in Irish radio on the grounds that they were giving public scandal by living together. Years later, in 1965, he ensured the dismissal of John McGahern ... from his *✗* job in the teaching profession. In both cases, the obsessively sexual nature of the Archbishop's preoccupations was obvious.'[23]

Elsewhere in his work, Garvin draws attention to the changes of the 1960s and the fact that 'with the new freedoms (including the arrival of the *employment* contraceptive pill) came sexual openness and the end of the fear of powerful people' and he concludes that the collapse of clerical power in Ireland towards the very end of the twentieth century was directly related to the obsessional nature of the Catholic clergy's attitude towards people's sex- *✗* ual lives.[24] It is interesting to examine the extent to which the archive of McQuaid reflects these pressures and battles. Arguably, it is on the issue of *✗* sex that McQuaid was finally defeated in the 1960s, and it is possible, by delving deep into his archive, to get a sense of an archbishop and a/church *ʌ clerical* under a degree of siege.

McQuaid was, more often than not, preoccupied with controlling

RMhse

prevention of sexual activity, but not Abuse

discussion of religion. Sex was only one of the areas with which he was concerned and he was sometimes preoccupied with it precisely because he realised there was a growing resistance to traditional Catholic teaching in relation to sexual morality. The determination of many people to make their own decisions about their sexual activity and to seek out information about sex means that the labels applied to McQuaid by Cooney – 'ruler of Catholic Ireland' or 'undisputed champion of Catholic supremacy'[25] – actually rang somewhat hollow by the 1960s and the early 1970s, when he was 'brooding in his Victorian Gothic mansion in Killiney' having, it seems, been punished by Rome and deprived of the cardinal's hat for his failure to adapt to Vatican II reforms.

McQuaid won some of his political battles, but he also lost some, including, in the long run, the most celebrated of all: the issue of state intervention in the health services, and the war against social change and sexual liberalisation in the 1960s. Although it is apparent from his archive that increased sexual permissiveness was not his only preoccupation – he acted on new social problems such as drug addiction and juvenile crime, adapted well to the communications age by setting up the Catholic Communications Office, and encouraged training in television – he retained a deep distrust of social liberalisation. Contraception was only one challenging subject for him in the 1960s; others included the behaviour of Irish Catholics abroad, television, new perspectives on marriage, new publications with a sexual content, and the fact that the Church was being more closely scrutinised than ever before.

This ultimately led to a siege mentality, which was summed up in McQuaid's exasperated response to yet another query from the media. In March 1970 he wrote to Oscar (Ossie) Dowling, his faithful and often fawning press secretary: 'I am very tired of RTÉ's attention to Bishops and priests. I do not understand why they do not pay attention to the Army, the Law, Medicine and especially journalism; fruitful fields for investigators. They are not anxious to promote the Kingdom of God.'[26]

Herein lay the weakness of McQuaid in face of the changes of the 1960s: he was still refusing to accept the fact that sex sold, and one of the reasons why so many journalists wanted to ask so many questions was because the Church (and McQuaid) were struggling with sexual issues, if not delusional about them. In April 1965, journalist Tim Pat Coogan requested replies from McQuaid to a questionnaire he had asked him to fill in for a forthcoming book (subsequently published under the title *Ireland Since the Rising*).

[handwritten: 1 male celibates only voices]

McQuaid wrote to Dowling: 'I shall not meet Mr Coogan; the questions are impertinent intrusions with my personal life or tendentious misrepresentations in several cases. Only yesterday the Bishops warned me that this man is going to write a flaming book of criticism.'[27]

None the less, McQuaid did draft replies to the questions (which were never sent to Coogan), including the boldest one, which read: 'Is it fair to say that the Irish Church is obsessed with sex and fails to concern itself sufficiently with things like poverty, lack of equal educational opportunity for all, the level of widows and orphans pensions?'

McQuaid's draft reply was as follows:

> No. There is probably a saner attitude to sex in this country than almost anywhere else. Family life is stable, women are respected, and vocations are esteemed. Sex, in the sense used here – illicit sex – is a sin and is the concern of the Church. The other comparatives are not sins.[28]

[handwritten: NIL CELIBATE]

Coogan and others were well aware, of course, that this was a complete fallacy, and by the 1960s the myth that the Irish were the most sexually pure race on earth was beginning to wear thin. Coogan had even privately joked with Dowling that 'if His Grace doesn't like the questions I'll have to leave town!', a reflection of the intimidating reputation that McQuaid had created. But it was also a measure of the changing times that certain people were now prepared to employ a degree of brazenness in their dealings with the most powerful individual in the Irish Catholic Church. McQuaid's response, which endorses the idea that sex is intrinsically sinful (Coogan had not specified 'illicit sex'), reveals much about the degree to which the Church was struggling to cope with the great social changes of the era; the reiteration of its core messages about sexuality and sexual behaviour began to seem increasingly archaic as the decade progressed. In some respects it suited McQuaid to be depicted, and to depict himself, as the 'ogre in the den', heroically resisting the tides of change, maintaining the strict line on Church teaching while all sorts of sexual carnage and secularism went on outside. But it was not quite as straight forward as that.

[handwritten margin notes: NON–sexuality]

'In many respects it most definitely is, the most de-sexed nation on Earth'

McQuaid was in fact determined not to ignore the new debates and new media but, where possible, infiltrate and control them, and his determination that his priests should embrace the new medium of television is one example of that. As early as 1954, eight years before the first Irish television programme was aired, radio and future television broadcaster Eric Boden had provided McQuaid with a survey on the prospects for television in Ireland and the impact it might have. Boden informed him that it was 'clearly destined to become perhaps the most influential secular force in our land. I have deep interest and high hopes that we may be able to do better than others in our use of television, that we may direct it to offset the cinema's influence, and that we may be able to bring such thinking to bear in these formative "pre television" days.'[29]

It is clear from such exchanges that McQuaid was thinking about the impact of television before many others, and that he was particularly concerned to have television production inspired by the principles of Catholic morality. But ultimately McQuaid's tactics of strict control and domination, which had been relatively effective in the 1940s and 1950s, were not working as well for him in the 1960s, because the appetite for change and debate had become so overwhelming, particularly so in relation to sex in a country where debate on this subject had for so long been avoided or prevented. What was still held to by conservative Catholic opinion was the notion articulated in McQuaid's draft reply to Coogan's questionnaire: that there was a healthier attitude to sex in Ireland than elsewhere because of the country's reverence for Church teaching; and, parallel with this, a belief that what was going on outside Ireland's borders was an orgy of indulgence, fornication and secularisation.

This view was summed up succinctly by Father Eoin Sweeney, an Irish-born priest who worked in England in the 1960s, who suggested that Irish people under the age of 18 should be prevented from leaving the country to travel to England due to 'the obvious danger to faith in a country in which illicit sexual indulgence is glorified as a normal way of life through all the media of communication'.[30] Sweeney was quoted in Donald Connery's 1968 book *The Irish*, a publication that summed up contemporary attitudes to sex in Ireland by indulging in stereotypes and making sweeping generalisations – that sex in Ireland was 'more of a function than a passion – a case of procreation without recreation'; that marriage had been defined as 'permission to sin'; and that the country contained the 'greatest percentage of virgins in the English-speaking world'. Connery even went so far as to compare Ireland to the Soviet Union in its attitude to sex: 'at first exposure it is refreshing to experience after regular contact with the sex-drenched world of America and Western Europe ... it appears to be and in many respects it most definitely is, the most de-sexed nation on earth'.[31]

This was a cliché that was beginning to tire, as was the equally glib liberal notion of the artist as pariah at odds with a smug, philistine society. In 1965, Augustine Martin, critic and lecturer in English at University College Dublin, challenged such views, and the out-of-touch writers fighting the battles of yesteryear, suggesting that the key challenge for Irish writers was to grapple with actual changes in Irish society – and that included challenging the jaded notion that Ireland was 'ignorant of the facts of life, [and] overcome with a Jansenistic fear of sex and the body'. Provincial life, Martin insisted, was changing and developing, as reflected in the words of John Montague's 1963 poem 'The Siege of Mullingar':

> Puritan Ireland's dead and gone,
> a myth of O'Connor and O'Faoláin

while the new 'great ugly dance halls' disputed the charge of Jansenism.[32]

'I've an Adam Faith poster in my bedroom'
+ ROHAN ?

In the midst of such social stirrings, many fought a determined rearguard action, and there was no shortage of advice to youngsters as to how to maintain Irish sexual purity or to resist the invasion of foreign sex ideas. McQuaid's Catholic Social Welfare Bureau, for example, acted as an umbrella group for a variety of boys' and girls' clubs, including concert clubs, Legion of Mary clubs and the Girl Guides. Proposed training courses for these clubs in the early 1960s instructed leaders to 'recruit new blood from the best sources', and topics covered included 'present attitude of Dublin children to religion and religious practice – contrasted with the ideal' and 'moral problems in adolescence'. When McQuaid addressed a youth leadership congress at Clonliffe in Dublin in March 1962, he suggested that such groups had not fully attained their aim, but 'how little this city suspects the active good that is obscurely and unceasingly leavening the mass of youth, boys and girls'.[33]

But many 'youth' were more concerned with dating the opposite sex and this too prompted no shortage of advice and publications in the 1960s. Angela Macnamara, who wrote for the *Sunday Press* as Ireland's best-known agony aunt in the 1960s, recalls the typical questions she had to deal with. 'Is it a sin to allow long kisses?' 'Is cheek to cheek dancing a sin?' 'I've an Adam Faith poster in my bedroom. My mother said it was not nice and to take it down. Will I?'

At the outset of her period as adviser to struggling adolescents, according to Macnamara, there were 'certain no go areas ... what was published underwent careful scrutiny'. She did not originally discuss sexual intercourse, but gradually she did. She was also a keen advocate of prayer, which not everybody wanted to countenance in the 1960s, and also received many letters from lonely widowers and bachelors seeking marriage partners.[34]

In the realm of sexual passion, youngsters tempted by forbidden fruit in the 1960s and, indeed, those not so young, were constantly told by Macnamara that they had to abstain or live with the consequences. In 1963, she informed one reader that the best thing to do was to compare the appetite for sex with the appetite for food. Both, she wrote, 'were natural appetites'. If you felt hungry, you ate meat 'and a climax of pleasure is reached when you eat it'. If you were on a diet and were forbidden meat, you would be ill as a result of breaking your diet. If you decided not to eat it, you would experience the disappointment of a frustrated climax, but you would not be ill. The same, according to Angela, applied to sex. In the context of marriage, she elaborated on the woman's role in *Living and Loving* (1969):

> Woman wants to be the object of man's desire. She craves the affection and protection of a man. Initially she may not feel as strong an urge for physical contact as he feels. She wants to give affectionate love in a thousand and one little ways, and eventually her demonstrations of affection will in the lovemaking of marriage culminate in her total surrendering of herself to her husband.[35]

But not all were in a position to be so focused on their lovemaking; some had nowhere to indulge in the act. In 1967, Father Liam Ryan, in the first work to be commissioned by the sociological journal *Christus Rex*, wrote an article entitled 'Social Dynamite: A Study of Early School Leavers', which offered an analysis of class and urban educational inequalities based on qualitative research undertaken in 1965 and 1966 on a housing estate in Limerick. It was novel because of its frankness about 'social factors' and its identification of resentments against officialdom in all its forms, including housing waiting lists. One respondent said:

> At present you must have four children to qualify for a house. But how can they have children? They live with a relative for a while. Then they get thrown out and move into the City Home. He is put on one side, and she on another. Where are they supposed to have sex; is it in the street? These were young married people.[36]

It would be easy to quote selectively from Macnamara and others like her and to dismiss them as conservative killjoys but, to her credit, she was promoting the idea of education about sex. She spent years travelling to schools to talk about burgeoning sexuality and the facts of life, and was pushing out boundaries. The very fact that she was addressing these issues in the *Sunday Press* and in the schools, however tame her replies may seem now, was a new and brave departure, and she understood that teenage hormones were not to be scoffed at or ignored. When McQuaid placed more focus on marriage counselling, Macnamara wrote to 'thank you personally for the courageous step you have taken', and she later told *Hibernia* magazine that she would like to see 'a wealth of counselling services available which would … make me redundant'.[37]

'If kisses are frequent, enduring, and ardent there can be hardly be any just Reason for them'

As a mother of four children in her thirties, Macnamara justified her advisory role on the basis of first-hand experience. The same could not be said of priests, but they too sought to dispense advice to Irish dating teenagers in the 1960s, often congratulating themselves on how frank they were being. A Jesuit priest, Joseph McGloin, wrote a fictional narrative, published first in the US and then in Dublin in 1960, under the title *What Not to Do on a Date*, in which a priest, warning of the dangers of 'imitating the junk that comes out of Hollywood', discusses 'necking' and 'petting' with two girls and two boys. According to the priest, 'there is no such thing as a little innocent

necking ... necking is not wrong *in itself*. It is still not to be indulged in ... as
you perhaps know, necking can easily become a habit, and once that habit is
established, it is only a short step to sin because, for one thing, necking alone
will be pretty tame after a while. It is very hard, too, to believe that people
indulge in necking just to show affection.'

Girls, he insisted, 'get much better dates if they never even consider
the idea of necking' and he spelt out the FEAR rule: 'if kisses are Frequent,
Enduring, and Ardent there can be hardly any just Reason for them'.[38] Five
years later, Father Thomas Finnegan, a priest of the Diocese of Elphin, published a pamphlet with the Catholic Truth Society of Ireland entitled *Questions Young Women Ask,* and was unashamedly Jansenistic in his assessment
of how girls could know true love: 'St Paul tells us Love is not self-seeking.
True love is unselfish. To be unselfish is to suffer. Therefore to love is to suffer. Some of the pop songs say that as soon as love begins, suffering ceases. It
is the exact opposite. A person who will not suffer will not love. No matter
what he says.' He too offered sample questions from teenagers, including the
following: 'I feel that marriage is really a sort of permission to be immodest.
Is it wrong to be thinking that way?', the answer to which was: 'Modesty is
not a hard virtue to practise because God has implanted in each person an
instinct of shame and fear to protect the powers of sex and the holiness of
marriage ... because of original sin ... our bodily instincts are in revolt against
conscience.'

It was also asserted that the male response to female attractiveness
was physical, whereas women's attraction to men was psychological. As
Finnegan's analysis moved from its doomladen main section to its blunt
and negative conclusion that passionate kissing was 'mortally sinful' for the
unmarried, he came up with suggestions as to how the wholesome girl could
keep lustful thoughts at bay:

> Do not think about your 'bad thoughts'. Say quickly, 'Jesus save me –
> Mary help me' and then think of something else. If you are a domestic
> sort of girl, picture to yourself the little house that you and your future
> husband are going to live in and decide on the colour schemes for the
> various rooms ... or, if you are the athletic type of girl, pretend to yourself
> that an uncle has given you money to buy a car with. By the time you
> have decided between the relative merits of a Morris Minor and a Ford
> Anglia the bad thoughts will be forgotten.[39]

Such advice was not only offered to Catholic adolescents; in May 1963 a Church of Ireland synod speaker suggested 'men looking for wives are not husbands looking for soiled goods, a fact that young girls should keep in mind'.[40] In the more rarefied atmosphere of theological journals, as pointed out by Tony Farmar, sex was referred to as 'use of marriage', kisses were '*actus impudici- tiae*' and contraception was 'onanism'.[41]

'*In the privacy of a cinema with only a thousand people in it they forget exactly what it was the priest has said*'

The psychological effect of many years of this kind of instruction took its toll on some people, notably the novelist Edna O'Brien, who told Donald Connery, '"I don't think I have any pleasure in any part of my body, because my first and initial bad thoughts were blackened by the fear of sin and there- fore I think of my body as a vehicle for sin, a sort of tabernacle of sin." (This was several years ago. She tells me that she has since managed to move on beyond her fears.)'[42]

What is clear from the various advice and instruction pamphlets pro- duced in the 1960s are the different ways the enforcers sought to impose their influence, with the traditional stern approach sometimes modified in an attempt to communicate with younger people in a language they could understand, or a determination to frame traditional and strict teachings in a more informal manner. At least the 'youth' were being recognised as a group worthy of attention, but the focus was still very much on the notion that they were born sinners and that they always should be made aware of that fact. It was also clearly still a man's world; there were no fallen men in Ireland but many potential fallen young women who should know of the traps that lay around every corner.

In discussing *What is Love?* in 1964 Aidan Mackey, who wrote for the Catholic Truth Society of Ireland which published pamphlets on these sub- jects, warned such girls not to be hoodwinked by 'the sloppy nastiness and nonsense which fills some of our papers and magazines and even advertise- ments'. He was also at pains to point out that girls who cheapened them- selves were not admired or respected by boys, and that was still the true test of their chasteness and their social respectability:

You can judge that from the names which boys give to such girls. They call them 'second hand'. They call them 'shop soiled'. They call them 'fly-blown'. These things do not make pleasant reading, do they? They certainly don't make pleasant writing. But it is far, far better to know these things and to face them now, as you start the change from child to adult, than to hear them later – possibly applied to you yourself.[43]

Courtships that were kept on a 'high plane' were those that did not 'degenerate to the physical'; kisses 'if prolonged a trifle' could quickly spoil an evening – this warning ironically, came from Father John O'Brien, the man who bemoaned the vanishing Irish and the reluctance of Irish men and women to marry and repopulate a dying island.[44] M. B. Crowe, writing in 1965 on sex scandals in public life, including the 1963 Profumo affair in England (in which Secretary of State for War John Profumo resigned after the revelation of his relationship with London callgirl Christine Keeler, who was also involved with a Russian spy), suggested that there was only one such episode in the canon of Irish political history, the Parnell divorce scandal, and such adultery that has become public 'would not be regarded as severely in twentieth-century England as, say, in Victorian England or in Catholic Ireland of the present day'.[45]

Lee Dunne's *Goodbye to the Hill*, an account of his teenage sexual awakening in Dublin's inner city, published in 1965, caused quite a stir due to its sexual content. It was also written in prose dripping with sexism: one girl at his work was 'a right prick-teaser', while other girls in the office were 'just nice heads of cabbage with powder and lipstick on. Well-shaped vegetables that beat words out of typewriters', though his mother, of course, 'was kindness and she was love'. For all Dunne's ground-breaking frankness, he was apt to indulge in crude stereotypes, but he did highlight the fact that most young people did not learn about their sexuality from Catholic Truth Society pamphlets, but rather in the dark and sometimes dingy back seats of cinemas. In writing about the Stella cinema in Dublin on a Sunday afternoon, Dunne observed that 'there was always a load of mots [Dublin slang for young women] that were on the lookout for a good neck and a grope and it's no exaggeration to say that they rarely went home disappointed. And to look at them outside in the queue you wouldn't think butter would melt in their mouths.' Dunne also made the point that, under the dimmed lights, class differences were conveniently forgotten in the interests of sexual gratification, with girls from the more salubrious southside suburbs of Dublin not discriminating between potential gropers. Some of these were girls that wouldn't talk to you if they knew you came from a place like the Hill. But they didn't know, they didn't even know your name and they forgot their class consciousness anyway and opened their bras-sières for you in the darkness of the back row of the Stella. There are people in Dublin who wouldn't and couldn't and can't accept this. Apart from scruff from the slums, our girls are all virgins until they go to their wedding beds. They believe in the Commandments of God and they listen to their priests. Maybe they do, but in the privacy of a cinema with only a thousand people in it they forget exactly what it was the priest has said and they remember only that they want to touch and be touched and to get as much out of it as they can.[46]

Although Dunne's book was not banned, and a stage version became Ireland's longest-running play, the film version of it, *Paddy*, starring Irish actor Des Cave, was banned in 1970 and was not issued with a certificate by the Irish film censor until August 2006. A measure of the changed times is that in 2006 the film was given a 12A rating (meaning that it was deemed suitable for viewers aged 12 and upwards and that even children younger than 12 could watch it if accompanied by an adult) by the film censor John Kelleher: 'By today's standards, there is nothing shocking in it. It is charmingly old-fashioned. But you have to remember it was banned in a different era, a very different time.'[47]

The *Limerick Rural Survey*, published in 1964, was something of a milestone in the development of social sciences and sociological surveys in Ireland. It devoted some attention to social life, the increased mobility of young men and women when it came to entertainment, and the preponderance of a more individualistic urban approach to leisure, while also underlining the continuing relevance of class divisions as regards suitable romantic pairings and dancing partners. It also highlighted the preference of young people for attending dances away from their own parishes, presumably to avoid the watchful eyes of parents and neighbours who had traditionally supervised meetings of the opposite sexes indoors.[48]

The preponderance of the books, columns and pamphlets cited above also raises the question of whether enough was being done to educate young people about the basics of sexuality and reproduction, which is why the columns of Angela Macnamara in particular were so important. For many, they were the only way of getting information. As Donald Connery put it, 'the fact that such letters are printed at all and answered with frankness, is a major departure from the traditional Irish conspiracy about sex'.[49]

'My husband's mother was married at 14. She had 18 children'

Undoubtedly, many people in the 1960s were entering into marriage with only vague notions about sex and many were still very young. However, it is also apparent that women were having fewer children. Statistics on fertility in marriage were collected in 1946, but not again until 1961; during the intervening years the average number of children per 100 married women dropped from 367 in 1946 to 353 in 1961. There were some regional variations, the figures being highest in Galway (397) and lowest in Dublin city and county (316). But the biggest differences centred on religion and social groups: 'the average number of children per 100 Catholic families was 361 in 1961 compared with 229 for families of other religious denominations. Among the different social groups, the average number of children per 100 married women ranged from 294 in the higher professional group to 396 in the group "farmers, farmers' relatives and farm managers".'[50] Breaking the statistics down further, Mary Daly notes that the average number of children born per 100 women with marriages of 20–24 years' duration was 416 according to the census of 1961, compared to 449 in 1946. In the year 1945–6, only 41 per cent of grooms were aged less than 30; by 1965 the proportion had risen to 66 per cent and the proportion of women aged 25–9 who were single had fallen by two-thirds, from 57.5 per cent to 37.8 per cent.[51]

Some non-Catholics were also marrying very young. The journalist June Levine recalled that her Jewish parents married when her mother was 15 and her father 18: 'I can still get in touch with the feeling of their sexuality in the atmosphere when I was a child. I remember them, in my early years, behaving towards each other as you'd expect turned-on teenagers to behave, touching, smooching, whispering. Their relationship was pretty stormy and sexually vibrant.'[52] Levine was also part of a group of women which included fellow journalist Mary Kenny that was beginning to question the desirability or inevitability of marriage. But in the early 1960s these ideas had not yet quite permeated downwards, particularly to those who were being taught by nuns. Instead, according to Kenny, it simply was not addressed:

> Marriage was hardly ever mentioned as an aspiration, which is perhaps logical from consecrated virgins. Occasionally, we might be told that we were 'the mothers of tomorrow' but that was as far as it went. The idea, which was very much to the fore in American culture at this time – and so brilliantly attacked and exposed in Betty Friedan's *The Feminine*

Mystique (1963) – that women were defined by their sex roles, inside and outside of marriage, was not in play.[53]

For those seeking assistance in finding a marriage partner, a matrimonial introduction bureau had been established in Ely Place in Dublin in 1963, though its founder, Michael O'Beirne, discovered newspapers were reluctant to take his discreet advertisements, and the Catholic Welfare Bureau discouraged him from his enterprise. 'Life provides its own introductions,' he was told by a priest; 'buying a packet of cigarettes is an introduction to the girl behind the counter.'[54] The Knock Marriage Bureau in County Mayo established in 1968 and later renamed the Marriage Introductory Bureau is still in existence today. Its progress report issued in July 2006 lists 841 marriages achieved – 'and they're just the ones they know about.'[55]

For members of the travelling community, matchmaking had traditionally gone on at fairs and meeting places, but gradually this died out. One of its members, Mary Margaret McDonagh, when interviewed in 2006, was not sorry to witness its passing: 'If you were alone with a fella for an hour, you had to get married. Even if you'd just gone up the road, it was classed as running away. You were never allowed to be on your own. That was in my mother's time. You had babies having babies. My husband's mother was married at 14. She had 18 children. My mother was married at 20, she had 15.'[56]

'Should I tell you to go forth and fornicate properly?'

As Brian O'Rourke has observed, the picture of Catholic marriage that emerges in some Irish novels is very unflattering, highlighting in particular the absence of sexual fulfilment. John Broderick's *The Pilgrimage* (1961) deals with Julia Glynn's attempts at love after a disastrous marriage to a pious homosexual 'whose attempt to reform his nature ends in brutality.'[57] Kevin O'Kelly's *The Sinner's Bell* (1968) depicts the first year of marriage between two young Catholics; its consummation is loveless and there is infidelity within a year. The book's hero sees sexual sin as a way to express both his independence and his rejection of religion; in seducing a girl 'he kissed her with hate … he could damn her soul for all eternity; the emotion was stronger and more violent than lust had ever been.'[58]

Writers of non-fiction were also prepared to tackle the subject, most obviously Dorine Rohan in *Marriage: Irish Style* (1969), as noted earlier.

This amounted to a semi-sociological analysis of a wealth of sexual dysfunction, ignorance and inhibition which was notable for the attention Rohan devoted to the feelings and opinions of ordinary Irish Catholics about sex. She observed that 'personally, I have never heard an honest conversation on sex in Ireland'.[59] Much the same had been discovered by an American Jesuit, Father B. F. Biever, who during his research on Catholicism, culture and values for a thesis submitted to the University of Pennsylvania in 1965 was told that 'all we hear is that adultery and fornication and prostitution and illegitimate babies are bad, bad, bad! Nothing else seems to matter to them.'[60]

Rohan was disturbed that 'the extent of satisfaction for most couples appears to be of a rather negative quality: "I'm lucky, I don't mind it", or "He's very good, he doesn't want it very often" were remarks I heard frequently from women I spoke to.' But men were upset, too: 'She never seems to want it', or 'When I am making love to her she keeps telling me that she is bored and to hurry up.' One man said to Rohan with a shrug, 'We're all animals after all, aren't we? I don't believe in all this spirituality lark about sex.'[61]

John B. Keane also identified the tension suffered within marriage as a result of sexual dysfunction in his play *The Chastitute* (1980). As Fintan O'Toole sees it, in his plays Keane was 'wrestling with the great contradiction of sex in rural Ireland – without it, there is no incentive to marriage; with too much of it, there is tension, instability and no incentive to marriage. Behind all of J. B. Keane's plays dealing with sex and marriage there is a notion of a sexual gold mean which keeps society together.' The parish priest in *The Chastitute* sums up the problem. John Bosco McLaine, a virgin farmer in his fifties (which is what Keane meant by the Chastitute) is harangued by the priest in the confessional: 'There are no marriages, no births. The young girls have gone. The boys have gone after them. You and your equals are all that is left. What am I going to say to you, McLaine? Should I tell you to go forth and fornicate properly and then come back so that I can give you absolution for a worthwhile sin, or should I allow you to decay in your own barren chastitution – or what am I to do with you at all?'[62]

Other sexual tensions were explored in Keane's *Year of the Hiker* (1963), in which a 'frigid man-hater' and a sexually demanding woman are deemed equally threatening. '[I]n Keane these two types of women often become one and the same person. The man-hater Freda turns out to have wrecked the hiker's marriage because her own sexual demands have not been fulfilled. Big Maggie, Keane's most all-embracing female creation, is at once a hater of men and a powerfully sexual woman. And in *The Chastitute* John Bosco

McCaine's housekeeper Eva who announces that "I detest men for what they're after. I loathe and despise men. Every time I think of a man my stomach turns inside out" later reveals herself to be a seething volcano of sexual passion.'[63]

It was often the priests who were seen musing on relationships and offering advice, condemnations or solutions when it came to sexual frustration. What was not acknowledged until very recently was that they suffered from their fair share of that frustration. Pat Buckley, who studied theology at Clonliffe college in the 1960s, recalled Archbishop McQuaid dispensing sex instruction in his Drumcondra study, decrying the dangers of 'self-pollution', then 'he'd give you this cross and tell you that whenever you were tempted to do anything impure with yourself, you were to tightly grasp the cross rather than your body'. McQuaid had a particular preoccupation with temptation. John Cooney points out that he was aware that 'the drawings of women modelling underwear used in Irish press advertisements actually revealed a *mons veneris* if one employed a magnifying glass,'[64] which was true; the boy in John McGahern's *The Dark* (1965) used such ads for masturbation.

At Clonliffe college, Buckley, who ultimately became a dissident priest and rebel bishop, recalled a corner where those seminarians who had indulged in masturbation the previous night were sent: a small oratory off the campus chapel. Humiliated young men waited their turn to atone for their nocturnal indulgence, plainly visible, for it to be announced to the campus 'that you had fallen during the previous night'. Buckley also maintained that some seminarians were issued with small whips for self-flagellation from which a number learned to derive sexual pleasure; that it became their sexual outlet: 'That's also why you had and have so many priests and nuns who seem to derive so much relief from beating the tripe out of children in school. It's a form of perverted sexual release ... if the normal erotic world is denied to you, you start to look elsewhere for your erotica ... a repressed mind can be very resourceful.'[65]

One of Ireland's best known priests, Father Brian D'Arcy, as a 17-year-old Passionist novice in the early 1960s, was made to go to his room three nights a week and flagellate his own naked backside with a scourge of tightly knotted cord for as long as it took to say five Hail Marys, five Our Fathers and five Glorias. He recalled in his 2006 memoir that the sound of whipping echoed down the corridors of the Graan monastery in Enniskillen at night and that 'to do it in the privacy of your own room/cell was an advance. Even then it felt sick.'[66] This was the sort of practice that killed self-esteem, 'even though most of us hadn't much of it to kill', and which led to some life-long struggles with confidence and self-image. D'Arcy was also sexually abused by a priest at the age of 10, and again in the Graan soon after he entered; but he stuck with the regime because he did not want to return home as a 'spoiled priest'. This is an indication of the private torture at the heart of the life of a very public priest – for some the original 'Father Trendy' – who became renowned for his contacts with the show business community and his newspaper columns.

A Redemptorist priest, Father Tony Flannery, who was ordained in 1974, caused quite a stir when his book *From the Inside: A Priest's View of the Catholic Church* was published in 1999. He too, as a novice for 13 months, experienced self-flagellation, and wore a steel chain with sharp points sticking into his flesh (like D'Arcy, he had been sexually abused as a child). As he saw it, 'the mistake of our system of training was that it was trying to convert us before we had lived'. There was much 'psychological damage' done as a result of the determination to build 'layers of repression' in these young men; novices were also denied access to newspapers, television and radio. On moving to a seminary, Flannery discovered 'a bit more freedom of thought', but it was still an institution that was 'a ferment of suppressed emotion', where senior students took younger students (known as 'sugar babies') under their wings. The most damning indictment of the system of training for priests, according to Flannery, was that he spent the second half of his twenty-five years as a priest 'trying to unlearn aspects of the religious training of the first part'.[67]

One historian of Irish Catholicism, Louise Fuller, has observed that the training of seminarians was 'radically and fundamentally' reformed by the late 1960s, with a 'new' theology placing more emphasis on the 'broader emotional, spiritual and psychological formation of seminarians', and personal development and education in human relations taking on a 'huge significance' in the lives of the religious in the 1970s. This was evidenced by the content and tone of the articles in religious journals like the *Furrow* and *Doctrine and Life*. The changes were also encouraged by the steep decline in religious vocations from 1965 onwards.[68] Tony Flannery maintained that his generation turned 'the theology of celibacy on its head', supported by books with titles like *The Courage to be Intimate* and *The Sexual Celibate*, but he ultimately concluded that most of what they were reading was 'idealistic but naïve in the extreme'.[69]

*'The people at the time obviously didn't think it was abusive
otherwise they would not have done it'*

An influential book published in 1962, *The Priest and Mental Health*, had
named masturbation 'a sexual deviation' most common amongst youths
who bed-wetted or had learning problems, most of them the sons of
women who were 'possessive and protectionist'. According to the book's
editor E. F. O'Doherty, Catholic priest, Professor of Psychology at University College Dublin and a member of the UN Committee on Mental
Health, 'the more experience I have in psychiatry and the more cases of
sexual disorder that I see amongst priests, the more rigid I have become in
advising the rejection of any student who has any manifestation of sexual
disorder such as compulsive or habitual masturbation, or any suggestion
of homosexuality'.[70]

In truth, these were issues that were not confronted in any meaningful
sense; nor was the problem of the environment that facilitated the practice
of sexual abuse by priests. When the report into the abuse of children in the
diocese of Ferns in Wexford was presented to the Minister for Health in
2005, it recounted a harrowing tale of neglect and analysed complaints of
abuse by 21 priests dating back to 1966 (90 people alleging abuse attended
oral hearings and a further 57 submitted written statements). It also revealed
an attitude to abuse in the 1960s which depicted it as a moral failure. Its
criminal and psychiatric aspects were not identified, while the commonly
held view that abusers could be rehabilitated also, according to Catriona
Crowe, raises issues of whether the lay health and psychology professionals,
as well as the Church, deserve criticism.[71]

The Commission to Inquire into Child Abuse also had to deal with the
issue of societal attitudes as they existed in the 1960s; in 1965, for example,
a priest who made veiled allegations about abuse was dismissed as a 'crank',
a view accepted by the Department of Education.[72] The tendency to be so
dismissive was also underpinned by a belief that to acknowledge such complaints would be to bring publicity to the sordid underbelly of some of the
institutions in which children were housed. The absence of detailed documentation also made for a very frustrating experience for victims, many of
whom were convinced that information was being deliberately withheld.
The question of access to documentation also goes to the heart of the complaints by abuse survivors and, indeed, is a central issue for historians seeking to find the truth of what went on in these institutions.

Many of the assertions made at the public hearings of the Commission were based on the documentation made available by the religious orders, which at times, like many administrative records, was cursory and formulaic, as were many of the visitation reports compiled on behalf of the Department of Education. The tension between the officially documented versions of events in institutions and the recalled experiences of those who lived through them will probably never be fully resolved. It is also the case that the sense that information was being withheld added to the impression that there was a lot more in the archives than there actually was. Sometimes when archives are restricted, unreasonable expectations exist as to what might be contained within them.

In 2005, Father Michael Hughes, provincial archivist of the Oblates Order, in his evidence to the Commission regarding St Conleth's reformatory school in Daingean, stressed that at all times while the institution was in the ownership of the state, pupils were being sent there 'who should not have been sent there'. Questions about this were raised in the Dáil in May 1966. Oblate management files show 'two complaints of excessive corporal punishment in the lifetime of the school'. Reference was also made by Father Hughes to a document sent from the Department of Justice to the Department of Education in April 1970, in which it was maintained that to make any reference to naked beatings would cause 'grave public scandal'. Father Hughes observed that when questioning the older brothers about practices of the school he 'always got very vague responses', his contention being that 'the people at the time obviously didn't think it was abusive otherwise they would not have done it'.[73]

Archbishop McQuaid also had skeletons in his diocesan cupboard on the issue of sexual abuse. In 1960, Father Paul McGennis, a priest in his diocese, sent pornographic photographs of children to be developed in England. The laboratory contacted the Gardaí. They in turn contacted McQuaid, who arranged for the priest to have 'treatment', but the priest continued to prey on children, and was eventually convicted in 1997.[74] There is no doubt McQuaid and other bishops failed to protect children from paedophiles, but as the Ferns Report revealed, there was also a fundamental failure to act on the part of the civil authorities and completely inadequate social services.[75]

As noted earlier, it has been contended by a leading Christian Brother that sexual abuse was seen more 'as a moral failure than a crime'.[76] This may have been true inside the walls of the religious orders, but not outside, which is why people continued to be prosecuted for sexual abuse. In 1960, for example, the Dublin circuit court record book documents prosecutions and convictions for indecent assault on a girl under 15 (the defendant was sentenced to 6 months' imprisonment), carnal knowledge of an 8½-year-old girl (12 months' imprisonment), carnal knowledge of a girl under 15 (18 months' imprisonment), gross indecency and attempted buggery with a male under 12 (2 years' imprisonment), attempted buggery with two boys aged 10 years (6 months' suspended sentence), and the rape of two women (3 years' imprisonment). Another convicted rapist was sentenced to 4 years in prison, while a man convicted of acts of gross indecency with two other men was sentenced to 18 months.[77]

> *'I suppose you have heard of "motor hawks" –*
> *strange men picking up girls with their cars?'*

The incidence of these trials would suggest that in the region of 8 per cent of indictments related to sexual crime. Some cases were not prosecuted for a variety of reasons or resulted in not guilty verdicts, but it is clear that assaults on young girls and boys were still very common and that male homosexual adults were being severely punished for acts of consensual sex. Although rape cases involving adults were not numerous, one trial of a man accused of attempted rape in June 1965 gives some indication of how the context of such cases was changing, how difficult it was to secure a prosecution, and the manner in which alleged victims were cross-examined.

The alleged victim was a nurse at the children's hospital in Crumlin in Dublin who was due to make a house call to her boyfriend's sister; she alleged that she was given a lift by a man who took her to a house in Enniskerry where the assault took place. Her boyfriend's sister gave evidence that 'she told me that she started to cry and he asked her why she was crying, that it was safe and he showed her some gaggets [condoms] ... she went on to say that she never realised that things like this could happen unless a girl went to look for it'. The 21-year-old woman, when cross-examined, was asked why she had accepted the lift and changed her frock beforehand. It emerged that she had met the man in the hospital, but that he had picked her up in O'Connell Street. The prosecution counsel put it to her: 'Hadn't he talked to you, chatted you up – is that the modern expression for flirting? I suppose you have heard of "motor hawks" – strange men picking up girls with their cars? This was a pick-up on O'Connell Bridge, wasn't it?' The nurse was accused of inventing the story 'to try and keep [her] reputation' with her boyfriend. She responded, 'I didn't think it happened in real life.' The defendant was found not guilty.[78]

The following year, in September, an 18-year-old man had sex with an 8-year-old neighbour in a field in County Limerick. Charged and convicted on counts of rape and unlawful carnal knowledge, he was sentenced to seven years' penal servitude. When he appealed to the Court of Criminal Appeal, the court quashed the rape conviction on legal grounds but upheld the conviction of unlawful carnal knowledge and his sentence was reduced to three years. The following part of the court's judgment suggests the convicted man felt entitled to do what he did.

> The Court after a careful consideration of the transcript is of the opinion that there is more than a possibility that the applicant [the accused] knew of allegations of previous sexual interference, not amounting to sexual intercourse with the prosecutrix [the young girl] by other youths in the neighbourhood. Further, and even more important, that he was aware that no action had been taken against those youths arising out of that alleged incident and as a result of this knowledge that he was tempted to do what he, in fact, did do to the prosecutrix.[79]

The case illustrates the difficulties faced by those seeking to bring about changes in the context of support for victims, changes in the law, and changes in how such issues were viewed culturally.

Young women who were victims of unlawful carnal knowledge also faced the prospect of abandonment as a result of pregnancy. At Galway circuit court in January 1968, details were given of the case of a man who pleaded guilty to the unlawful carnal knowledge of the daughter of a man he was working for. He made a statement in July 1967:

> M.T. and I were alone in E.W.'s house one day about nine or ten months ago and we were courting in my bedroom in a bed ... human nature took its course and I had full connection with her. I always wanted to marry her and she wanted to marry me. About six months ago M.T. told me she was pregnant. She said, 'I think we are in trouble. I suppose you will go away now.' I told her I would not go and I suggested telling her father about it, and she said not to, that it would be better to wait until the

baby was born. I did not tell him. I am now aware that M.T. gave birth
to a baby boy last Sunday. I admit that I am the father of that child. I am
still anxious to marry M.T.

In October 1967 he pleaded guilty to unlawful carnal knowledge; the hear-
ing was adjourned for sentencing and the man was allowed out on bail until
January but he failed to turn up for sentencing. The judge in the case, John J.
Durcan, had prepared the following letter:

> To your credit you pleaded guilty here in court and now you are prepared
> to take the fair step of marrying the girl and she is prepared to marry
> you ... I must sentence you and I am giving you a much shorter sentence
> than I would otherwise impose because (a) of the attitude you adopted
> here in court and (b) you are prepared to marry the girl and her father is
> prepared to consent and the girl is willing. I will impose a sentence of six
> calendar months from today and I recommend that if in the next couple
> of weeks or months you wish to get married, that you will be facilitated.[80]

The accused was eventually apprehended in England in June 1968.

In June 1963, a soldier based in Collins barracks, Cork, who was serving
with the Irish army in the Congo was found not guilty by direction of the
unlawful carnal knowledge of a girl under the age of 15 in June 1962, when
the girl was 14 years and 8 months old. She subsequently gave birth at the
Sacred Heart home in Bessborough, County Cork. The girl, the daughter of
a labourer, having left school at 14, began to date the defendant and claimed
they had intercourse on four consecutive nights in June 1962. He subsequently went to the Congo in November 1962, while she gave birth in January
1963: 'I did not have my usual period. I made enquiries as to what that meant
and I was told.' The defendant denied he had ever dated her, but extracts from
letters he wrote to her in the spring of 1963 were exhibited in court:

> I am Right in to you be case I Roaght to you be Fore and I tought you
> Mitend get it ... well K. I was exptheng a letter From you All the long but
> you Mite be going with a nother boy and you mitend want to Right to
> me, well that is the way it gose ... I have to come to the end so good by
> and god Bless you, from your loven friend d.,
>   Right Soon
>   x.

He sent another letter to the girl after she had responded to him:

> 'I got your most Well Come Letter, I Hope you Had a good xams and a
> happy New Year the black women are know good out here ... I was going
> mad Wen I don't See you be Fore I left to give me the good by Kiss ... you
> said in the Letter Wat is the girls name I was going with I don't know her
> Name I don't like her Aney Way you were the onely one I ever like it I
> supos that is love ha ha I hope Your Mother dosent go on over me right
> in to you I supos she wont.[81]

'I think he was genuinely taken aback that we wanted 36 in one go.
And to be honest with you, I don't think we used them all ...'

'sexual'   EXILES   of Australia/us

Some people left Ireland due to sexual abuse and others departed due to
sexual frustration. The climate in England seemed more liberating in this
context. Others who ended up in England in the 1960s from economic
necessity found attitudes to sexual experience and practice different, especially when it came to birth control. In 2003, Catherine Dunne recounted
the stories of ten people who had left Ireland in the 1950s and 1960s to settle
in England. Kevin Casey, one of the men interviewed, suggested that many
of the men were frightened of marriage 'perhaps from what they'd seen at
home. Too many children – they'd had to get out of those houses, and now
there are so many single men, old men with nowhere to go anymore.'[82]

One of the women interviewed noted that with regard to contraception and the ability to leave a marriage, 'the fact that we lived here did give
us more control over our lives'. There were still those who had to lead double lives; children were born to Irish mothers and Afro-Caribbean fathers
in London and the mothers 'couldn't bring them home. [They] would go
home to Ireland for Christmas as usual, leaving their children behind. Mind
you, that didn't just happen with mixed-race children – many young women
had babies here their families back in Ireland knew nothing about ... and
sometimes the grandparents in Ireland went on not knowing for the rest
of their lives.'[83] Father Seamus Fullam, from Longford, who ministered to
the Irish in London, recalled that fathers of pregnant Irish girls could be
'extremely violent' when the pregnancy was discovered and that

some poor girls never went home. Somehow it was always their fault.

The men got away with it. I remember hearing a story from a Canon
at home. He had a very dry sense of humour. This young girl had been
sent away to have her baby and the mother told everyone she'd gone to
have her appendix out. The Canon told me afterwards he had seen the
young girl out for a walk one day and she was 'pushing the appendix in
a pram!'[84]

Some of those interviewed talked about the obsession with covering up
'the disgrace' of a baby born out of wedlock; of babies being handed quietly
and quickly to adoptive parents; and of the lengths people went to cover
the birth. Some of the young women were still inhabiting an Irish world
while embracing aspects of London life that were anathema to Irish Catholic teaching. Phyllis Izzard recalled that the day before her wedding at the
age of 19 she went to confession to be in a state of grace before she got married and then went to Oxford Street with her fiancé to buy Durex condoms:

> We stood outside the Chemist, going from one foot to the other, delib-
> erating as to how we were going to go in and ask for these 'things' which
> obviously neither of us had ever done before. We were trying to work
> out before we went in how many we'd need. And we said, well, we're
> going away for a fortnight, so that's 14 days multiplied by ... anyway, we
> suddenly arrived at 3 dozen. Don't ask me how we worked it out but
> we did. Larry plucked up the courage to ask for them in the first place
> but then we had to insist that we wanted *thirty-six*. I don't think he was
> winding us up. I think he was genuinely taken aback that we wanted 36
> in one go. And to be honest with you, I don't think we used them all,
> and we never bought anymore. We were petrified, sick at having to go in
> and ask for them, particularly as we had just come home from Confes-
> sion. Here we were now, flying in the face of God. Buying them was the
> worst, using them wasn't all that bad and though I was happy with the
> decision not to have a baby immediately, I'd have to say that it worried
> me in terms of my faith.'[85]

It has been argued, however, that in England it was the late 1960s
before the 'long Victorian era' could be said to be over. The Obscene Publications Act had been passed in 1959 and there were thirty-four prosecutions
under its terms in the first year.[86] It sought to strengthen the law concerning pornography and stipulated that a book could be deemed obscene if it

was judged to have the potential to 'deprave and corrupt' the reader. English medical opinion was divided on the issue of contraception (the Pill became generally available in 1961) and, while in 1963 there was a separate family planning centre for the unmarried and the introduction of a British standard for condoms in 1964, illegitimate births were increasing, particularly among teenagers. The single mother 'was still a stigmatised figure', and there was 'an upsurge of moral panic' due to the preponderance of sexually transmitted diseases. A survey of the sexual behaviour of young English people by Michael Schofield of the Central Council of Health Education found that, although promiscuity was not that common, knowledge about birth control was rudimentary. Another survey of sex and marriage in England, published in 1969 by Geoffrey Gorer, found that one-quarter of men and two-thirds of women were virgins at the time of their marriage and that 'England still appears to be a very chaste society'. Combined, these findings would suggest that the term 'permissive society' is one that 'exaggerates the degree of liberalisation in Britain in the mid 1960s'.[87] This is also a reminder that 'there is an obvious gap between the literature – be it descriptive or prescriptive – and actual behaviour'.[88]

'I never approve of any device and do not approve of this'

For those who remained in Ireland, there was to be no change in the law in relation to contraception during the 1960s. In 1963, Archbishop McQuaid received a complaint about a programme aired on RTÉ called 'People by the Billions', one of a four-part series entitled *The Earth and Mankind* 'in which we are told we will be shown why the population must be restricted. I make my protest to you as I feel the television authority would not pay much attention if I went direct to them.' Cathal McCarthy, the president of Holy Cross college, Clonliffe, informed McQuaid that he believed 'there was nothing in any way objectionable' about the programme.[89] Two years later there was also concern about an advertisement for CD Indicators, used by women to facilitate the rhythm method. *Women's Way* magazine had defied the Archbishop in running the advertisement, and claimed it was the only method of birth control that was approved by all the churches. McQuaid's response was unequivocal: 'I never approve of any device and do not approve of this.' The advertising sales manager of the *Irish Times*, Arthur Rhys Thomas, contacted Ossie Dowling, McQuaid's press secretary, to tell him that the newspaper had received a request to advertise the same product and Dowling informed McQuaid's secretary MacMahon that he had spoken to Thomas and that 'the *Irish Times* will not be carrying the advert. Arthur is an old friend of mine.'[90]

There were thirty selected counsellors working in Dublin for Archbishop McQuaid's diocesan marriage counselling service in 1966. In February of that year the Maternity Group of Medical Social Workers at the Rotunda hospital wrote to McQuaid pointing out that 'for some considerable time now' they had been worried about the number of people seeking help with marital difficulties, 'many of a serious and deep-rooted nature'. McQuaid's reply was that he had been conscious of such problems and planning a service for several years.[91] Newspapers made it clear that one of the problems was family planning; writing in the *Irish Press* in September 1966 Richard Grogan insisted family planning needed to be addressed in the context of marriage guidance because 'marriage guidance is scarce in Ireland. Scarce, that is, outside the doctor's surgery – and sometimes within also.'[92] Most of the counsellors appointed under McQuaid's scheme were from affluent south Dublin, and parents of between four and six children.

McQuaid commented pointedly and defensively two years later, lest people thought it was just a modern response to fertility issues, that 'It would be a serious error to think that the marriage advisory service has not been utilised until recently. Such assistance has been the normal work of the Church since the very beginning.'[93] (As he put it to Cecil Barrett in 1956, 'the idea of putting the marriage counselling into the Bureau as a separate section is excellent, if I may say it, because it was my idea.')[94] But as Father Peter Cunningham, a priest working in the marriage counselling centre, explained to him in 1967, 'During 1966, there were 6,559 marriages in the archdiocese and only 972 couples passed through our course. It is hoped that many more would be willing to take part in shorter, improved courses.'[95] Another priest involved in this work, Father Michael Browne, made it clear to McQuaid in April 1971:

In Dublin there are only a small number of doctors who are genuinely interested in the temperature method of family planning; a smaller number again recommend it to their patients and help them with it ... one has good reason to believe that the majority of doctors regard the method as too time consuming for them as well as being too complicated and too restrictive for the average person. In very many cases the easy way out for the doctor is to prescribe the Pill.[96]

'There was an unseemly, but understandable rush for the "easy man"'

Such correspondence became more likely in the aftermath of *Humanae Vitae*, the papal encyclical published in 1968 that reiterated the Vatican's opposition to artificial birth control. Like many others, Angela Macnamara, as a mother of four, admitted she was 'gobsmacked' by the encyclical, and within a few weeks the volume of correspondence she was receiving on the subject grew dramatically:

> There were women with selfish husbands; women whose own needs for intimacy were great; couples who had very little other pleasure in life; men whose demands of their wives after excessive alcohol were unreasonable; couples who argued and fought about the meaning of the Encyclical ... I contacted a few priests for advice as to how to deal with all such queries from a compassionate but moral point of view. I received a variety of responses from the tough line, the ultra conservative, to the line that said 'encourage them to do their best'. At first, my responses swung somewhere in between. Suggesting that couples speak to their own priest in the privacy of the confessional brought me to realise that 'shopping around' for an understanding priest had begun. There was an unseemly, but understandable rush for the 'easy man'. Even from the early stage, the public were not taking this 'lying down' (if I may pun on it).[97]

Garret FitzGerald has argued that the 'dam burst' coincided with *Humanae Vitae*. The encyclical, in his view, represented a position that was 'non-credible in rational terms ... and once the church took up a position which was non-credible in rational terms its authority over the whole sexual area disintegrated. At the worst moment for us, when pressure on the dam was great already, you suddenly put a hole in the dam ... everything fell.'[98] It is impossible to give exact figures for the number of women who were availing contraceptives in the Republic in the 1960s. In 1968, it was reported in the *Irish Times* that the previous year, according to a pharmaceutical source, an estimated 15,000 women were on the Pill, 25 per cent for medical reasons and 75 per cent for social reasons – 'either that or there's a great increase in menstrual difficulties', according to the firm's spokesman.

A simultaneous survey of Irish gynaecologists confirmed that three-quarters of them prescribed the Pill for 'social' reasons; there were ten different brands by 1968 and one pharmacist in Dublin said his orders for the Pill had tripled between 1965 and 1968. Around the same time Dr Karl Mullen, during an inter-hospital course for nurses, said that in his experience 'about 40 per cent of married couples in this country were practising methods of contraception other than rhythm'. In February 1968 the *Irish Medical Journal* made it clear that from its perspective 'the issue for doctors is not the morality of taking the Pill, but rather the morality of refusing it for patients who feel entitled in conscience to take it. It is our duty to treat patients; it is the patients who take the moral decisions.' Although the number of marriages was increasing in the 1960s, and the age of husbands and wives decreasing, between 1964 and 1968 the birth rate fell from 64,072 to 61,004.[99]

Some Irish gynaecologists became quite adept at satirising the situation, and it was more often than not men who were asked for quotes from inquisitive journalists and authors about this. Dr Raymond Cross, for example, a well-known Dublin gynaecologist, stated that 'If a woman has heavy or irregular periods, or painful periods or sometimes none, or if she has premenstrual tension or endometriosis, bleeding between periods, excessive hairiness or pimples (caused by an excess of androgenic hormones) or is excessively fat, or is approaching the change of life, her doctor is morally justified in prescribing any treatment he likes.' Alan Bestic, author of *The Importance of Being Irish* (1969), noted that Cross's colleagues pointed out that 'his list was sufficiently comprehensive to cover half the women in the world'. Bestic, who maintained that in 1968 20 per cent of Irish women were using the Pill compared to 10 per cent in Britain, revelled in trite generalisations such as the contention that the rhythm method was practised with 'spectacular lack of success in many cases because the Irish are very bad on dates'.[100]

There was no family planning clinic in the Republic until February 1969. When assistant master at Mercer's hospital in Dublin, Dr Michael Solomons, formerly of the Rotunda hospital, began advising patients on contraception with the support of the International Planned Parenthood Federation (IPPF), 'it was to his knowledge the first time Irish public patients had access to contraceptive advice'.[101] Solomons was also present at a meeting called by the GPs James Loughran and Joan Wilson that led to the establishment of the Republic's first family planning clinic and the beginnings of the Irish Family Planning Association. Other attendees included Yvonne Pim and Joan Wilson who had been giving sex education talks to Protestant secondary school pupils and had become known as the 'sex ladies', along with Robert Towers, editor of the *Irish Medical Times*, pathologist Dermot Hourihane, both of whom were Catholics, as was Máire Mullarney, a mother of eleven 'who experienced a conversion to family planning while visiting a clinic in Portugal'.

Mullarney was also influenced by her unsuccessful experiments with the rhythm method and a book published in the United States in 1964 which detailed the experiences of marriage of thirteen Catholic couples, unprecedented because it contained 'the opinions and comments of a group of articulate wives on marital sexuality'. She also recalled the thirst for information about contraception and the search for a 'wise moral theologian', as well as meetings with like-minded and similarly frustrated women, some of the discussions lasting 'until 2 in the morning'.[102] The most important aspect of this was that Irish Catholic women were determined to find a way of reconciling their Catholicism with their desire for contraception and information. Later, many of them would find themselves identifying with the themes explored in English writer David Lodge's novel *How Far Can You Go?* (1980), which looked at the dilemmas of Catholic couples in 1950s England, from courtship ('your conscience would tell you, no further than you wouldn't be ashamed to tell your mother') to the fear engendered by the unwanted pregnancy ('I'll just go away somewhere to a home for unmarried mothers and never trouble you again'), the consummation of marriage ('Dorothy knew almost nothing about how a marriage was consummated; Adrian turned on the bedside lamp, sat up in bed and lectured her on the facts of life') and the volume of pregnancies.[103]

The family planning group, advised by senior counsel Noel Peart, set up the Fertility Guidance Company with the help of the IPPF. As the company could not sell or advertise contraceptives, 'improvisation was the order of the day. There were discreetly packaged mail orders and "contraceptive couriers", friends and relations of the clinic staff who smuggled condoms, spermicides and diaphragms into the country – Dr Solomons' mother and mother-in-law, women in their late 70s, played their part. The clinic was never without supplies for long and, in an emergency, toothpaste was used as spermicide.'[104]

Hibernia magazine reported on these developments in April 1969, noting that 'a quiet start has been made to a scheme with considerable significance in the Irish legal, medical and social fields. A small, privately-operated family planning clinic has been opened at 10 Merrion Square, Dublin.' It was a limited company formed by five doctors and two 'housewives' (Máire

Mullarney, mentioned above, and Yvonne Pim, mother of two and a social scientist). It operated two evenings weekly and was aimed at 'all social groups'.[105]

The clinic sought to circumvent the legal ban on contraceptives by offering them free of charge, with clients making donations to the clinic. Family planners in other European countries in the 1960s had devised similarly pragmatic methods to stay on the right side of the law. In 1961, the first *Centre de Planning Familial* was established in France; as a way of getting around the law against contraceptive propaganda and in order to obtain information, clients had to become members of the organisation.[106] Contraception was not decriminalised in France until December 1967 and, although the Irish legal ban was rescinded at a much later stage, there are strong parallels between the two countries in terms of how change came about. In 1968, John Ardagh observed of France and contraception:

> First, an intolerable situation is allowed to build up without anyone taking action. Then a handful of pioneers set to work and progress slowly follows, haphazard, empirical, unauthorised, usually resisted by the strong social forces always at work to protect the harmony of the status quo against conflict. Then, finally, legal or structural reform is sanctioned, not so much to facilitate change as to regularise changes that have already taken place.[107]

'Move into another room, because as long as you're sleeping with him, you're the occasion of his sin'

There seems to have been no shortage of men lining up to proffer advice and comment on contraception, with many adding jocose comments; in practice, it was anything but funny for women. Father Michael Cleary, Ireland's best-known 'media priest' displayed such male arrogance in Peter Lennon's 1967 documentary *The Rocky Road to Dublin*. When Lennon had written to Archbishop McQuaid seeking his help with the film, McQuaid had accused him of previous 'gross misrepresentations', but his press officer Ossie Dowling encouraged McQuaid to help Lennon on the grounds that 'he, too, has a soul to save'. To Lennon's request to use Father Cleary, McQuaid tetchily responded, 'I shall pick the priest.'[108] But it was Father Cleary who appeared in the film, because of his comfort in front of the cameras and his childlike urge to please the audience. He was filmed as the ultimate 'Father Trendy', singing in a Dublin hospital while the female patients looked on embarrassedly, and dispensing advice to a young married couple about their future life together. As Lennon recalled, Cleary gave a perfect illustration of how the clergy operated: 'they were there to remind you, in the friendliest way, of your inherent tendency to evil and extol the virtues of celibacy'. Three decades later, Cleary's own double life, including his fathering of children, was revealed (see chapter 5).

Only one woman speaks at length in Lennon's documentary, but she does not appear on screen. She talks off camera of yearly pregnancies since her marriage at 21 followed by a 'miserable three-year effort at birth control' through the practice of *coitus interruptus*. She says simply, 'I felt all the time guilty, and I hated it.' She felt so guilty that she went to confession and told the priest about her efforts at birth control, to which the priest's response was, 'Go home like a good child and move into another room, because as long as you're sleeping with him, you're the occasion of his sin.' Her conclusion on this exchange was as stark as it was accurate: 'Anyway, they're always on the men's side in this country, and so are the doctors. They think women should grin and bear it and put up with it, because, you know, we're Catholics and we shouldn't be making it harder for the men.'[109]

Dr P. J. Leahy, who was district medical officer at Ballyfermot health centre in the heart of one of Dublin's largest housing estates, told Alan Bestic that he would be 'guilty of criminal negligence as a doctor' if he didn't prescribe the Pill.[110] Donald Connery mentioned in his book *The Irish* a television programme broadcast on RTÉ in October 1966, *Too Many Children*, which pointed out that one-fifth of all Irish mothers had seven or more children and in the region of 6,000 had twelve or more.[111]

In his memoir of his time working on the RTÉ religious programmes *Radharc*, which were made by a group of Dublin priests with the initial encouragement of Archbishop McQuaid, Father Joe Dunn recalls his frequent encounters with Irish missionaries. On one occasion he attempted to raise the issue of contraception:

> It was clear first of all that many of them would prefer not to be asked about it. But I met nobody who was prepared to tell every couple using artificial contraception that they were committing serious sin. A common answer was, 'I don't have problems any more about that.' But in this case it often seemed to me that they had decided not to have

any more problems, without actually resolving the issue in their own minds.[112]

'We have a strongly Calvinistic element to deal with,
to whom we appear as the Scarlet woman in person!'

In Northern Ireland, whilst religious scruples were still very much in evidence, the approach to the issue of family planning overall was less veiled, more humane and sensitive than in the South. By the 1960s services were organised in a more comprehensive way, largely due to the efforts of the Belfast Women's Welfare Clinic (BWWC) and later the Northern Ireland Family Planning Association (NIFPA). At the AGM of the BWWC on its tenth anniversary in May 1960, it was estimated that in the ten years of its existence 5,772 women had used its services, the main issue being 'the problem of bringing the needy woman to the clinic'.[113] In October of that year it was observed that several of the clinic's doctors felt many of the patients attending could afford to pay for their consultation, but that 'in no case did a doctor seek personal remuneration' as 'it was not possible to charge a consultation fee while the clinic was on hospital premises'.[114]

A meeting to consider the formation of a NIFPA was held at the Belfast city hospital clinic in February 1964. The NIFPA's first public meeting in November 1965 was addressed by the Quaker Sir Theodore Fox, medical director of the London Family Planning Association and director of the Family Planning Association of Great Britain – perhaps an indication of the hope that Northern Ireland was going to mirror what had happened in the UK. But there were local considerations and inhibitions. By this time there were four clinics in operation.[115] Joyce Neill, chair of the NIFPA, was informed in November 1965 by BBC Belfast that it was not permitted to include an announcement about meetings in relation to family planning clinics as it came under the category of 'open advocation of controversial causes'. Neill replied, 'I find it hard to believe that the BBC really considers that the subject of family planning is controversial today. The need for controlling the size of families is freely admitted by the RC [Roman Catholic] Church; the only difference of opinion is on methods approved – a difference which our association has publicly respected.'[116]

The honorary secretary of the association summed up its dilemma by emphasising, in correspondence with the British Family Planning

Association in February 1966, that it was experiencing pressure from both religious communities in Northern Ireland: 'The proportion of clinics per head of the population is ridiculously low here, but, as you may appreciate, it is an uphill battle. Not only does our government lean over backwards to appease our "oppressed" Roman Catholic minority, but we have a strongly Calvinistic element to deal with, to whom we appear as the Scarlet woman in person!'[117]

threa:
the:

Joyce Neill obtained the name of a female doctor in Dublin, Dr W, who was 'willing to give advice on oral contraceptives' and passed it on to the British Family Planning Association 'for anyone who takes up residence in the Irish Free State [sic]. At the same time, it is information that cannot, of course, be used in your clinic from your point of view, while from Dr W's point of view things might be made unpleasant for her in Dublin if public attention was drawn to her activities. I still feel, however, that you should know about her – our clinics in Northern Ireland are, of course, only too glad to help anyone from the Free State who comes to us, but the journey is often long and expensive, and I can imagine that, for some, Dr W might be the answer.'[118]

The previous month a BBC television programme called *Inquiry* had included a contributor from Northern Ireland who complained that family planning there 'has a nasty taste. People don't like to talk about it – correspondence from the clinics sometimes has to be sent to an accommodation address in a very plain envelope ... we seem to be playing our usual apathetic and inhibited part. In London the first clinic was opened in 1921 – the first in Northern Ireland was opened in Belfast in 1952 – only thirty years later.' There were now, in 1966, six clinics in Northern Ireland: two in Belfast and one each in Rathcoole, Bangor, Portadown and Coleraine. During the programme, reference was made to the 'Puritanism of both Catholic and Protestant here'; it also featured an English woman in Northern Ireland who encountered difficulty finding a clinic, a Catholic couple interviewed separately who disagreed about the issue, a Catholic man who maintained that 'all anyone needs is self-control', and a priest who said that the 'Church does not now encourage large families.'[119]

Those running the clinics did not avoid the issue of religious beliefs. In November 1966 a meeting of the secretaries of the clinics was told of the need for 'efficiency, sympathy and complete discretion'. In January the following year a letter from a mother of eight was published in the *Belfast News Letter* in which she averred that 'having tried every device of birth control

I have finally resorted to the Pill of which I disapprove'.[120] In this context, the NIFPA felt it had to tread carefully; it was particularly conscious of the need for discretion and 'maintenance of dialogue between different points of view, esp. acceptance of RC standpoint'.[121]

Between 1961 and 1966 the rate of increase of population in Northern Ireland was more than double that of the rest of the UK, rising by 4.2 per cent, from 1,430,000 to 1,480,000. The birth rate was also the highest in the UK, and when infant mortality rates were compared between larger UK cities in 1964, infant mortality per 1,000 live births stood at 31.1 in Belfast, compared with 28.8 in Manchester and 21.7 in Liverpool.[122] Legislation introduced in 1967 placed responsibility for family planning on local health committees, which gave grants 'after great battles in some cases'. In December 1967 the Ministry of Health and Social Services wrote to the secretaries of health authorities suggesting that the availability of family planning could 'make an important contribution to the prevention of ill health and to family welfare', particularly if 'there is an established physical or mental disease which makes it undesirable for a woman to become pregnant'. It suggested that family planning meant the avoidance of 'criminal abortion and death', and stressed 'its obvious benefits in promoting stable family life'.[123]

The NIFPA also declared as one of its aims 'the relief of poverty'; by 1970 its clinics were dealing with '5,000 new patients a year'.[124] The correspondence of the NIFPA gives a good overview of the progress of the association in the 1960s and the difficulties it sometimes faced. In August 1966, Joyce Neill wrote to Ronald Green, Minister for Health, inquiring as to why the NIFPA had been refused help (alone, it could only raise £300), arguing that it could save the department money in the long term in the areas of maternity care and education.[125] In the following few years some individual local authority health committees refused to countenance support of the establishment of clinics. In April 1968 Neill wrote to the *Belfast Telegraph*, complaining that the County Londonderry committee had repeatedly refused financial assistance for a family planning clinic at Belmont in Derry, and made the point that 'no-one visiting a family planning clinic is persuaded to use methods conflicting with her conscience. Finally, if Cllr Brown knew what effort is required to start even one family planning clinic, he need have no fears that family planning will ever be a serious rival to dancing at the crossroads.'[126]

The minute book of the executive committee of the NIFPA for the late 1960s chronicles the frustration experienced as a result of recalcitrant councils. In April 1968, for instance, it was recorded that County Armagh's local authority 'had maintained complete silence', while County Londonderry 'had not sent us any notification about anything'. The following month, in County Armagh, 'Dr Paisley ... expressed his strong personal support'.[127] By 1968 there were fifteen centres, but the annual report of 1969 noted that for the first time the number of new patients dropped, as 'The Troubles of the year resulted in noticeably low attendance during certain months ... the overall number of new patients in Greater Belfast seen by NIFPA and Local Health Authority Family Planning clinics was 2,324, of whom 649 were seen by the local health authorities ... despite these figures, the total number of attendances in our own clinics throughout the province has risen by 5,300 (1968: 12,600; 1969: 17,900).'[128]

Significantly, in June 1969 there was a long discussion about unmarried patients; while most clinics did not want to refuse them advice, as public money was now involved, the clinics 'did not want to risk jeopardising good relations with their local health committee'. It was asserted that the primary concern of NIFPA was with families and 'Dr Neill said it was obvious that large numbers of unmarried girls could not and should not be coped with by the NIFPA'. Independent clinics, it was decided, could adjudicate on this issue for themselves, but NIFPA clinics on local health authority premises and in receipt of local health authority grants would not give advice to the unmarried unless they were about to be married 'or unless they need such advice for social reasons'.[129]

'The morals of the community and especially of young people are constantly in danger'

The media in Northern Ireland also played a significant role in facilitating increased discussion about sexual issues in the 1960s, to the dismay of some. Nineteen sixty-five witnessed the emergence of the *Sunday News* by the publishers of the unionist *Belfast News Letter*. Both the *News Letter* and the Nationalist *Irish News* were, according to Michael Bromley, supportive of the idea of modernisation in the north, but also believed that a reckless abandonment of traditional values would cause tension.[130] This was particularly the case in relation to sexual content, where the scent of sexual revolution 'promised to subvert traditional, authoritarian and communitarian societies like that of Northern Ireland'. In 1966 the *Irish News* decried the impact of television and the 'snide remarks at religious and normal standards of morality'.

The *Sunday News* was successful, with 30 per cent of adult Protestants subscribing to it. In its first year it began to give prominent coverage to pornography and prostitution, as well as alcoholism and drug abuse. The *News Letter* referred to the existence of a 'new morality' as involving the work of the Devil and 'gambling, promiscuity and pornography which were the objects of a Church campaign in 1965 were typical targets for attacks by the morally outraged'.[131] There were also claims by the *News Letter* of a lack of 'absolute standards and values', and the paper began a clean up TV campaign, while in 1965 the *Irish News* wondered 'why does the government run away when the morals of the community and especially of young people are constantly in danger from pornographic literature in our midst?'

There were a number of interesting aspects to these campaigns; like the situation in the Republic in previous decades, such views on 'modern' society 'were largely predicated on a negative description of contemporary Britain as a Godless place' where 'the spread of Paganism was unchallenged'. It was even asserted that the bookstalls of the Republic were 'far cleaner'.[132] The British Abortion Act of 1967, which legalised abortion, was not extended to Northern Ireland; some of those involved in the Northern Ireland Civil Rights Association (NICRA), such as Kevin Boyle, a popular young lecturer at Queen's University, Belfast, included the legalisation of abortion as part of their list of civil rights demands,[133] but it was virtually impossible to create a space for it to be prioritised.

Many of the taboos that existed in the Republic were shared by Northern Ireland, including illegitimacy. In 2007 a west Belfast journalist, Tim Brannigan, who supposedly died at birth, told his story on BBC Radio 4's *It's My Story*. Brannigan's mother was married with three sons when she met his father, an African medical student, at a dance; he, too, was married with a family. When she gave birth, medical staff conspired in a lie that the child had been stillborn; her husband colluded in the deception and Tim was taken to a children's home in another part of the city where his mother visited him until 'adopting' him when he was a year old. He didn't know he was adopted until he was aged 19. From a staunch Republican family, Brannigan observed: 'People ask me where I'm from, and I say Beechmount [west Belfast]. They look at the colour of my skin and say, "Where are you really from?"'[134]

'Máire Mac an tSaoí had said naked on The Late Late Show!'

That fear of frivolous and deteriorating social values was continuing to gain currency in the Republic. One of its most obvious manifestations was believed to be RTÉ's *The Late Late Show*, which became the bane of upholders of 'traditional' values in relation to sexual morality. RTÉ's first broadcast, on New Year's Eve 1961, featured an address by the President of Ireland, Éamon de Valera, who maintained it had the potential to 'build up the character of the whole people, inducing a sturdiness and vigour and confidence. On the other hand, it can lead to demoralisation and decadence and disillusion.'[135]

Initially, the television service was largely confined to Leinster, but growth throughout all of Ireland followed rapidly and, by the end of 1965, it was estimated that there were 350,000 homes with televisions, representing more than half the households nationwide. There were a few television programmes that seemed to encourage the ventilation of problems that had long gone unmentioned, in public at least. So irate did one politician – the redoubtable Fine Gael TD, Oliver J. Flanagan – become that he famously complained that 'there was no sex in Ireland before television,'[136] the most hackneyed phrase to date about the history of sex in twentieth-century Ireland.

The Late Late Show will forever be associated with encouraging more frank and open discussion in this regard. What began as a summer filler show in 1962, hosted by Gay Byrne, went on to become the longest running chat show in the world. Various, often extravagant claims have been made about its impact. There is much truth in Byrne's own simple contention that 'we looked at new ways of entertaining and that was it;'[137] he certainly did not see himself as remotely socially radical. One of the strengths of the show was its format, to which Irish audiences responded very well: they could watch discussions and debates in a free-flowing manner, much as they might observe such talks at home or in the pub. Essentially what Byrne was doing was experimenting, by redeploying the American chat show format but with a native twist, or an element of seeming 'adhockery', in which all three elements were crucial: the presenter, the panel and the audience. But the seeming casualness belied the careful planning and co-ordination that went into the show. This was ultimately about show business, with the row or heated discussion coming at the end; it was also risky, in the sense that it was always a gamble to have an unedited live show.

In the midst of debate about the impact of his show, Byrne had consistently maintained that he was a facilitator rather than an innovator; that he could not impose a discussion on a society that was not ready for it. On the face of it this suggests generous self-deprecation on Byrne's part, but it could also have been defensive – Byrne always had to protect his various viewing constituencies, so the idea of him as 'host' and not 'instigator' was important. Rarely did his mask, or his professionalism, slip.

Most people born in Ireland from the 1950s onwards will remember their first opportunity to watch *The Late Late Show*. Novelist Colm Tóibín remembers growing up in Wexford in the 1960s, where the children of the house

were banned from watching it. I was born in 1955 and it was the one thing you were not allowed to see and it was the one thing you kept asking about. Despite all the cartoons, all the other things that were on, it was the thing you wanted most to see, because I think all the adults watched it in a very serious way. The door was closed and the children were sent to bed and as you got to a certain age you'd say, 'When I'm what age will I be able to watch *The Late Late Show*?' Which was a sort of rite of passage. The first time I was brought down from my bed to watch it was not when an enormous sort of cataclysm took place in Irish society, but when Lieutenant Gerard from *The Fugitive*, who'd been searching for the one-armed man all the time, when he appeared on *The Late Late Show*, it was felt he would be suitable for me. But once it was over you never knew, because they never announced in advance who was coming on next and it could be a nun who didn't believe in being a nun or it could be someone talking about sex and there had never been talk about sex in our house. I remember sometime, I must have been let watch it from the age of 11 or 12, but I remember one night when Conor Cruise O'Brien and Máire Mac an tSaoí came on together and Máire said that there were couples who had been married for many years who had never seen one another naked and I can tell you, the silence ... Now I'm talking about an extended family, not the nuclear family, but aunts, uncles, maybe even a visitor, 12-year-olds, 13-year-olds, all of us watched – 'Máire Mac an tSaoí had said naked on *The Late Late Show*!' There weren't headlines the next day, but it was that sort of silence that caused people really to worry. You couldn't turn it off – no one had a zapper – you could have run over to turn it off but that would have been considered square. So it began for me by being forbidden, and then became immensely interesting with great moments of pure embarrassment and, as I say, a great amount of Hollywood in it – any actor who was passing through town would be on it as well, so the show business and whatever things that were unsayable in Irish life were mixed together.

Any discussion of sex was, of course, as mesmerising to the audience as it was uncomfortable. There was a simple reason for this, maintained Tóibín. There were so many people 'who had never heard about sex'; indeed, he went as far as to suggest that there was a whole generation of people who would have lived and died in twentieth-century Ireland without ever having heard any discussion about sex if there had been no *Late Late Show*. To that extent, at least, perhaps Oliver J. Flanagan was accurate.[138]

'Not infrequently to my frustration, I cannot be the policeman of all I want'

Archbishop McQuaid and his footsoldiers were very conscious of the impact television could make, and kept tabs on the personal lives of RTÉ's personnel, partly through the efforts of Dermot O'Flynn, Supreme Knight of the lay order of Saint Columbanus. A report sent by O'Flynn to McQuaid in March 1962 reveals that of the sixteen RTÉ producers, only four were Catholics, including 'Miss Chloe Gibson, an English convert, but separated from her husband' and 'Shelah Richards – Producer of Religious Programmes! – a divorced actress who has been associated with numerous left-wing groups for many years'.[139] McQuaid courted the senior RTÉ Catholics, including the Director General, Edward Roth (who wrote in January 1962; 'May I say Your Grace's selection of cigars is excellent'),[140] and the chairman of the TV authority Eamonn Andrews.

McQuaid and others wanted to exploit the potential of television to spread the faith, but they were also suspicious of its perceived dangers. In June 1962, the report of the Catholic Television Committee made it clear that its aim was that 'religion may have a central and honoured place in Irish television from the outset'.[141] It saw few causes for complaint in the initial years and was very satisfied with the 'moral tone', hardly diminished by the 'occasional lapse', but believed 'direct teaching on TV is still the unsolved problem'.[142] *The Late Late Show*, however, led to change in perspective.

Inevitably, because of its determination to facilitate regular discussion of previously taboo subjects, the complaints came thick and fast. In November 1966, a letter to McQuaid summed it up by concluding that *The Late Late Show* 'seems to be taken up with sex, pornography and obscene films. These "frank discussions" never contain a single reference to any religion, much less the Ten Commandments ... as a direct result of this terrible state of affairs, it would be interesting to know the number of teenage "shot-gun" marriages in Dublin over the past five years.'[143]

But an interesting aspect of *The Late Late Show* controversies is that they reveal that McQuaid's power was waning. As an anonymous letter writer pointed out to him, '*The Late Late Show* has developed into a sex orgy. The fact is that you have all fallen down on your job and raising a family in a Christian atmosphere is an impossibility.' Then came the real sting in the tail: 'We are no better than all the other countries of the world. No longer Christian, just masquerading under the name. Over to you.'

In response to the first point, McQuaid suggested that viewers had to publicly protest, as television 'is sensitive to public criticism' and that 'I have my own way of reaching these offenders.'[144] But the truth was that he did not have as much power as he claimed. As Director General of RTÉ Kevin McCourt admitted to McQuaid in February 1966, 'Not infrequently to my frustration, I cannot be the policeman of all I want.'[145] Neither could McQuaid.

It should not be assumed that *The Late Late Show* was primarily concerned with sex – it was not – but sexual issues received enough of an airing for McQuaid's file on the show to expand quite significantly. In February 1966 McQuaid wrote to 'my dear Kevin' McCourt:

> I have just seen *The Late Late Show*. I am afraid that it was, in part, really unworthy. The Questions and Answers in the case of Mr and Mrs Fox [when the wife suggested she may not have worn anything on the night of her marriage] were vulgar, even coarse and suggestive. You have not been fairly treated; for this type of thing is quite unlike what you have been so warmly thanked for. And I think that Gay Byrne need not, for a second week, return to the Bunnies.

This was a reference to a show which featured Victor Lownes, of America Playboy fame, who had come to Dublin in search of fifty Irish 'beauties' to help staff London's first Bunny club. This had prompted the manager of a bank in Sligo to write to McCourt that Byrne was 'permitting obscenities that are unheard of in normal Irish society ... the time has come when the public should be assured that definite action has been taken to prevent the recurrence of such scandalous incidents and if that cannot be done there can be no option only to have the show withdrawn completely'.[146]

In truth, the real problem was the failure to agree on getting clerics to debate on television, which became more pronounced from the mid 1960s onwards. Some believed that protesting from the margins was counterproductive. As Father Joe Dunn, one of the priests McQuaid had sent to New York for training in television techniques, put it in a letter to McQuaid:

> It seems to me the greater of 2 evils for religious leaders to protest about this kind of programme [those with a sexual content] ... Of course, the 'clean up TV' campaign in England was laughed at a lot, but it seems clear that it had some effect. I wouldn't like to say that it has reached the situation here where such a campaign is called for, but if it has, I think it is important that there are no clerics involved in it. It must be remembered that because of the nature of television production one can't keep a close censorship over producers.

McQuaid's reply, as was so often the case, was succinct and withering. Dunn's letter, he maintained, 'seems to ask that a cleric as such is to apologise himself out of existence, or hide himself permanently'.[147]

Other media battles McQuaid and others lost included that against the popular *Woman's Way* magazine. On 21 December 1967, McQuaid's secretary, J. A. MacMahon, recorded a memo for McQuaid after Dr Michael Browne, Bishop of Galway, had called to see him to discuss the nature and trend of *Woman's Way*:

> In regard to the editorial staff of *Woman's Way*, Dr Browne instanced Mrs Caroline Mitchell, the wife of Charles Mitchell of Telifís Éireann. Mrs Mitchell is a Protestant ... some of the other members of the editorial staff may be lapsed Catholics ... Dr Browne understands that the magazine has a wide circulation, particularly among teenagers who read the magazines in hairdressers and factories. Often this is the only journal that they read. Angela MacNamara contributes weekly to this magazine. Apart from her articles the other articles dealing with matters of sex are very much astray morally. Dr Browne stated that some mothers are

very perturbed by the whole tone of these sex articles and have said that while they read the magazine themselves they would not like to see their daughters reading it.

Interestingly, MacMahon also introduced a note of caution in his comment attached to the letter:

> These magazines contain articles by some serious people like Angela Mac-Namara. They also contain regular features from such well-known personalities as Charles Mitchell and Terry Wogan ... these magazines are dealing with questions which are very widely discussed. They might well reply that they are catering for a demand. It is possible that an appeal to women to exercise caution and moral judgement in regard to women's magazines might be better than a condemnation of these magazines as such.

It is not clear what, if any, action McQuaid took. In truth, he was powerless to stop these articles, despite pressure exerted informally or in private.

'The opinions of the pro-birth control slum mothers'

Another (unsigned) memorandum circulating in the Archbishop's office in March 1967 argued that what was really needed was 'the rehabilitation of the moribund system' to counteract the 'gutter press' who published salacious photographs, but it also referred to the fact that there was no censorship of theatre ('the sky is the limit') and that an RTÉ programme, *Too Many Children*, which won a Jacobs award, included 'recordings of the opinions of the pro-birth control slum mothers'.[148]

That the female members of McQuaid's diocese could be referred to in such disparaging terms in a memorandum in his office was an indication of the accuracy of John McGahern's observation on the priorities of some priests who had been trained in the 1930s and 1940s. He wrote about the strut of the arrogant priest in a typical Irish parish: 'In those days it took considerable wealth to put a boy through Maynooth, and they looked and acted as if they came from a line of swaggering, confident men who dominated field and market and whose only culture was cunning, money and brute force. Though they could be violently generous and sentimental at times, in their hearts they despised their own people.'[149]

Undoubtedly, McQuaid could be very generous also, and he was well aware of the difficulties many of his parishioners were facing as a result of having a large number of children and little money. The Catholic Social Welfare Bureau included a family welfare section, which received many letters in the late 1960s and early 1970s from families outlining hardship stories and seeking assistance. Letters of distress from mothers with husbands imprisoned or unemployed were common, some facing eviction, many living on the eldest daughter's earnings, trying to rear as many as thirteen children on a pittance. It would be a simplification to reduce all these problems to the issue of contraception, but it is relevant. A typical letter written on behalf of a Raheny family of nine children ranging in age from sixteen to nine weeks stated: 'the birth of their ninth child [meant the mother] was in hospital for longer than usual. During this time the eldest girl, the only wage earner at present, was kept at home to run the house.'

The writers of these letters were not going to challenge McQuaid or his stance on contraception – they were, after all, essentially distressing begging letters, with the authors emphasising their impeccable Catholic credentials – but there is also the occasional hint of resentment that people were so resigned to their situations. In December 1968, the brother of a mother of ten children ranging in age from six months to sixteen years wrote to McQuaid on her behalf, after the family had been evicted from their home in Ballyfermot:

> My sister's devotion is such that when I touched the subject of her distress, she merely replied: 'Blessed Martin will not let us down and God is good.' She also said there are plenty of others just as badly off. Well, Your Lordship, while such remarks are very complimentary to the teaching of the Church, I think you'll agree that in this particular case, a slightly more realistic approach is called for on the part of my sister.[150]

A mother of twelve who was looking for the train fare to visit her husband in Portlaoise prison wrote: 'I have 12 children of which the eldest is in St Patrick's Institution. I have 2 backward and one who is very delicate. Father, I receive £6 per week home assistance benefit.'[151]

'A task for the priest, not for the policeman'

Another issue that continued to preoccupy McQuaid was censorship. He corresponded regularly with Thomas Coyne, secretary of the Department of Justice, outlining his dissatisfaction with what he regarded as a lack of state commitment to strict censorship. Enclosed in the correspondence between them in 1960 was an advertisement from the *Observer* newspaper of 3 April 1960, in which a proud mother and her daughter, wearing her new bra, beam at each other under the heading: 'Delightful news for the understanding mother: New bras and girdles specially designed for 11–16 year olds.' McQuaid was disappointed that the state was not doing more to prevent the circulation of such advertisements, and was not satisfied with Coyne's insistence that 'if the state is encouraged or even allowed to become an arbiter of morals, it may be tempted to usurp the functions of the Church'.

Coyne wrote about the variety of 'unwholesome trash' now in existence in Ireland 'which have a demoralising effect not merely on the weak-minded but on the weak-willed as well and are a greater menace because they are retailed at a price which is low enough to give them a relatively wide circulation'. But it was difficult to name and shame because of the 'practical impossibility of specifying all such publications and the risk that those left unspecified might be wrongfully presumed to have ecclesiastical approval'.

Coyne maintained that the onus was on the Church to 'check the false emphasis on sex ... the moral flabbiness and the false philosophies that are so much in vogue. This, as I see it, is a task for the priest, not for the policeman.' He then referred to the bra advertisement, which, although not obscene in the eyes of the law, 'shows quite plainly how small girls and their parents are being systematically indoctrinated with the idea that sex appeal (to use the jargon) consists in a provocative display of secondary sexual characteristics. This is the sort of thing that cannot possibly be suppressed by the State without the State's appearing to make itself ridiculous which the civil authority is always unwilling to do.'[152]

In the early 1960s McQuaid continued to boast of his prowess when it came to the prohibition of 'obscene' literature; he wrote to Dermot O'Flynn in July 1962 concerning Edna O'Brien's 1960 novel *The Country Girls*: 'I had the book banned.' The Knights of Columbanus had organised a letter-writing campaign against the O'Brien book, with the letters sent to publications where it had been favourably reviewed (copies were also sent to McQuaid). One of them contains the following:

When all literary judgement has been exhausted does there not remain a moral question? Is it not the constant teaching of the Church (a) that as a result of the fall our sexual instincts are easily removed from the control of our reason, (b) that erotic representations of sexual desire and fulfilment are one sure way of arousing inordinate passion, (c) that every Catholic in every activity has a moral responsibility not to lead others into occasions of sin? Would your reviewer agree or disagree with me, a Catholic parent, when I assert that this book would almost certainly be an occasion of sin to a young unmarried man? If so, has not the author violated the Divine precept on Scandal, and has not your reviewer failed in his Catholic responsibility of indicating such dangers in this particular book?[153]

Edna O'Brien continued to publish novels, including *Girl with Green Eyes* (1962), *Girls in Their Married Bliss* (1964) and *August is a Wicked Month* (1965), which depicted the lives of characters Kate Brady and Ellen Sage, both of whom were products of upbringings dominated by fear and suspicion of sex. Both waver in their Catholic faith, but retain enough guilt about sex to prevent any liberation. Although her characters, in the words of Marjorie Howes, 'are often volubly inarticulate about their sexuality, their directness constitutes a search for sexual freedom and self-knowledge, rather than its abandonment'.[154] In *The Lonely Girl* (1962), the character of Caithleen (Kate) tells of her efforts to overcome sexual shame in the quest to lose her virginity: 'I had been brought up to think of it as something unmentionable, which a woman had to pretend to like, to please a husband ... I knew that I was about to do something terrible.' While her whole body stiffens, the man she is with asks her, 'Are you filled with remorse ... Have you had some terrible traumatic experience?'[155]

In 1963 McQuaid referred to a film in which there was nudity: 'it got through in my absence. I have taken effective action against it.'[156] But he knew there were some battles he could not win. In a letter to a woman who complained about a play at the Gate theatre, he acknowledged that 'Mr Hilton Edwards [co-founder of the theatre] would not, I fear, pay much attention to what I would say ... we can trust the people to distinguish between what is hypocrisy and what is sincerity.'[157] When McQuaid and his spies were incapable of influence they maintained it was up to the public to police their own morals.

'No good reason why the Press of Sodom should be allowed in here,
brash and unabridged'

During his correspondence with McQuaid in March 1960 Thomas Coyne
referred to the magazines that were being eagerly embraced by young people:
'If there is one thing more than another about this day and age which I personally dislike it is the apotheosis of the so-called teenager and I believe
no good can come of it.'[158] Despite his personal views, Coyne was consistent in informing McQuaid that the state on its own could not provide 'a
wholly satisfactory solution', while Dermot O'Flynn continued to decry the
amount of 'no action' decisions by the Censorship of Publications Board.[159]

The Department of Posts and Telegraphs was still receiving complaints
about English firms distributing pamphlets on birth control. The practice
of the department was to write to the firms asking them to desist, which
usually had the desired effect, though some, such as the Allen Surgical
Hygienic Company of Brighton, persisted. In 1960 postal sorting staff were
told to 'be on the alert' for these postings.[160] One woman in Sandymount
was more concerned about Irish editions of British newspapers such as the
Empire News; everyone knew that there was much filth outside Ireland, she
maintained, but 'that is no good reason why the Press of Sodom should be
allowed in here, brash and unabridged'.[161]

What is perhaps more interesting is the willingness of some members
of the Irish Hierarchy, such as the Bishop of Cork, Dr Cornelius Lucey, to
acknowledge that there were inconsistencies in the censorship system, particularly in the practice of banning a book on the basis of the content of a
sentence or paragraph; the idea was growing that while there was a need to
protect the public from pornography, there was also a need for intellectual
freedom. At Bandon in May 1962 Lucey argued that 'our censorship is represented to the world at large by our liberals, anti-Catholics and pornographers as a censorship destroying all real freedom of expression ... in point of
fact, it is the Irish writers who have done most to attack pornography and
cheap literature'.[162]

It was also wondered in 1963 what the legal situation was regarding the
publication of banned books in serial form in newspapers. This question
arose in relation to Edna O'Brien's *The Country Girls*, which an article in
the *Sunday Press* in October 1963 maintained 'will keep the city girls happy
during the winter months'. In 1965 it was due to appear in the magazine
Creation and the Censorship of Publications Board decided in November

of that year 'that they had no function in the matter'. The Attorney General
offered the opinion that its publication in serial form would not amount to
an offence because it had been banned as a book and not a 'periodical publication', though the minister warned the magazine's publisher that he had
to be careful in the extracts he selected for publication, as certain extracts
'might, of themselves, constitute a ground for prohibiting a periodical publication in which they appear'.[163]

There was certainly more ridiculing of the perceived heavy handed-
ness of the approach to censorship. In 1966 the English novelist and essayist
Brigid Brophy, who had controversial views on sex and feminism, wrote in
her collection of essays *Don't Never Forget*: 'A year or two ago I stood, an
invisible woman (and author of banned books) in one of the finest book-
shops in Dublin and copied down the notice pinned to one of the book-
cases: "There are over 8,000 books banned in Ireland. If, by chance, we have
one on display, please inform us, and it will be destroyed."'[164]

'There are hundreds of thousands of Irish girls going around with their tongues out for a husband'

Another victim of censorship in Ireland was teacher John McGahern, whose
literary career had taken off with the publication of his novel *The Barracks* in
1963. In 1965 he went to Finland to marry the theatre director and translator
Annikki Laaksi, the year his second novel, *The Dark*, was published and fell
foul of the Censorship of Publications Board. On his return to Ireland, a letter from his school manager, Father Patrick Carton, informed him that his
services were no longer required. No reason was given, but it later became
obvious that McQuaid was involved in the sacking. The school wanted him
to 'go quietly away', but he refused.

The Irish National Teachers Organisation (INTO) refused to take up
McGahern's case. D. J. Kelleher, the general secretary of the INTO, subsequently met McGahern, having first braced himself with a whiskey:

> 'If it was just the auld book, maybe – maybe – we might have been able
> to do something for you, but with marrying this foreign woman you have
> turned yourself into a hopeless case entirely,' he said, 'and what anyway
> entered your head to go and marry this foreign woman when there are
> hundreds of thousands of Irish girls going around with their tongues out

for a husband,' he added memorably, especially since not many of them
had been pointed in my direction.[165]

McGahern decided not to contest the banning of *The Dark*; instead, he
maintained a public silence, discouraging protests on his behalf by other
writers, including Samuel Beckett: 'I was secretly ashamed. Not because
of the book, but because this was our country and we were making bloody
fools of ourselves.' To join the protest, he felt at the time, 'would do the
whole sorry business too much honour'.

Years afterwards, McGahern expressed the view that 'literary censorship is nearly always foolish, since it succeeds in attracting attention to what
it seeks to suppress. There is no taste so tantalising as that of forbidden fruit.'
But the banning of the book was also something of a turning point; it is no
coincidence that shortly afterwards the appetite to liberalise the censorship
laws gathered momentum.[166]

It was clear over the next few years that some politicians were not content to leave the old systems and the old personnel unchanged with regard
to the policing of morality. Brian Lenihan made it clear to McQuaid when
he was Minister for Justice in 1964, for example, that he was determined to
reconstitute the Censorship of Films Appeal Board: 'I am aware that some
of the members are very advanced in years, some hard of hearing, some evidently do not understand the import of some of the film scenes at all, some
have been noticed to doze during film-showing and finally, decisions have
been made with only a small number of members present at appeals.'[167] Two
years later Lenihan went on to plan a change in the censorship laws because
definitions of what constituted obscene had changed so dramatically.

Figures supplied by the Department of Justice reveal that in 1962–3, 631
books and 52 periodicals were examined; 37 as a result of formal complaints
from the public and 594 on referral from the customs authorities; there were
also 408 prohibition orders issued in respect of books and 43 in respect of
periodicals. Lenihan's predecessor, Charles Haughey, ever keen to placate
McQuaid and to whom he deferred in a much more craven and submissive way than Lenihan, made a number of old-style pronouncements about
the contemporary world being 'inundated with a great tide of pornographic
publications and indecent films ... the argument for some form of censorship is, in my opinion, unanswerable, though there may be some scope for
honest disagreement on the form it should take'.[168] What Haughey was not
proposing to change were definitions of what constituted indecency; the

relatively few books referred to the Censorship of Publications Board by the public was, in Haughey's view, an indication that its existence was 'in itself a protection from the worst effects of the entrepreneurs in pornography'.

'A number of reds, some parlour pinks and a few Catholics who wished to be considered as belonging among the "intelligentsia"'

But it was made clear to McQuaid in the early 1960s that while a newspaper such as the *News of the World* might be considered offensive and vulgar, it did not merit prohibition, as Peter Berry, appointed secretary of the Department of Justice in 1961, informed him in July 1962.[169] Writing in the *Guardian* newspaper in 1965, Peter Lennon considered the 'cowardice and indifference' of Irish politicians when it came to obstacles towards the emergence of a more mature attitude towards censorship. In relation to Michael Viney's articles on unmarried mothers for the *Irish Times* in 1964, Lennon suggested 'it was largely because he was trained outside Ireland and had a different set of nerves and conditional reflexes to Dublin Taboos' that he was able to be so frank.[170] But within a few years, many more voices were being raised in opposition to censorship, prompting a memorandum in 1967 (included in McQuaid's papers) that referred to 'a number of reds, some parlour Pinks and a few Catholics who wished to be considered as belonging among the "intelligentsia"', and who were manufacturing letters 'in the Palace Bar and the Pearl Bar' to the *Irish Times* on the subject of censorship reform.[171]

In liberalising the laws on censorship to allow banned books to be re-examined by the Censorship of Publications Board after twelve years, Brian Lenihan justified his decision in a number of memoranda which make clear what was not about to change: 'The question of whether a book advocates the unnatural prevention of conception etc. is one of fact and the problem of changing standards does not arise in the case of the banning of books in this category.'[172] Between 1946 and 1965 the total number of books banned was nearly 8,000; 314 decisions had been repealed and 220 were successful. Lenihan elaborated on his own reasoning for introducing his bill:

> Critics of the Board, and of the system of censorship generally, often point
> out that many books stand banned which are recognised the world over
> as being of considerable literary merit (some of them by Irish authors)

and defenders of the present system are embarrassed by the undoubted truth of these assertions. The fact is that, until an entirely new board was appointed in 1957, the members were, in general, extremely narrow in their outlook and were especially prone to ban books by Irish authors. Many of their worst decisions were upset by the Appeal Board but there are still a number of books banned for all time under the law as it stands whose presence on the register can only reflect discredit on the whole system of censorship. Apart from the particular problem associated with the membership of the Board, it is a fact, in the minister's opinion, that standards of propriety do change and have changed greatly since 1946 in this country and he considers that, for that reason alone, the finality of a ban on a book on the ground that it is 'indecent or obscene' is indefensible in principle.[173]

State papers released in 2006 give some indication of the unease Lenihan's actions caused in certain quarters. Cardinal William Conway, the Archbishop of Armagh, suggested that Lenihan was doing too much too quickly and that 'quite frankly all this does not appear to me to be adequate notice to the public at large on a matter of this kind',[174] which missed the point, as it was quite clear that 'the public at large' was showing little interest in complaining about books. Notes compiled by the Department of Justice in relation to why Lenihan had not gone further in liberalising the law suggest that 'any major changes would have to be preceded by consultation with church authorities and adequate soundings of public opinion'. But it was also noted that 'The Bill, on the other hand, has provided a stimulus to discussion and thought on the censorship question though indeed not quite as much as might have been expected.'

Another argument put forward in the Senate in June 1967 was that 'contraception has become such a live issue at the moment that the present law could lead to the situation where even official Church pronouncements would be banned by the Board'. What of the operations of the board? One of the questions put forward in 1967 was why was there no provision for a personal appeal by an author of a banned book before the board? To which a civil servant in the Department of Justice replied: 'It would be the easiest thing in the world for an author or publisher to take an offending book, line by line, and question the Board as to where is the indecency or obscenity; talking as to literary merit, the appellant can make any Board appear to be a lot of ignoramuses.' Lenihan's response to this was that by a curious co-incidence, Judge Conroy [a judge of the circuit criminal court] phoned me this afternoon and I put the question to him. He said that personal appearance before the Board would make the system unworkable and, as far as he is concerned, he would resign immediately. The judge pointed out that at present the Board or Appeal Board may hear the author or publisher if they so wish, but in no case do they do so. If an author or publisher is given a statutory right to appear before the Board to argue his case he must have the right to legal representation and, in effect, a public hearing. The judge says that the legislation would become quite unworkable.[175]

Lenihan also maintained in his speech to the Dáil that membership of the Censorship of Publications Board was 'one of the most difficult and unrewarding task of any voluntary body performing a public service'. But a note sent to the minister by a civil servant reveals that, in some respects, the wheel had turned full circle on this issue, in that it was the writers rather than the Bishops who were now being looked to for advice with regard to the censorship question: 'Seán O'Faoláin in today's papers recognises that the social conventions of 20 years ago and more which gave rise to the standards of prohibition of that time have changed radically. That is your justification.'[176]

Ultimately, that was the main justification Lenihan used, and O'Faoláin can be legitimately seen as one of the midwives of the new birth in 1967. In 1968, the censorship board examined 290 books; only 10 had been referred to it by members of the public.[177]

'One of Britain's loveliest nude models in this very artistic movie'

There was also a considerable relaxation when it came to film censorship. This was another area that McQuaid and his allies had kept close watch on. The Department of Justice estimates for 1962–3 reveal that the film censor had examined 1,362 films in 1961, of which 1,117 were passed (1 on appeal), 206 passed with cuts (2 following appeals against rejection) and 39 were rejected.[178]

It was not uncommon for McQuaid to get individuals to watch films with a view to assessing their morality. In March 1961 his secretary, James MacMahon, enclosed for McQuaid a report by Monsignor Richard

Glennon, parish priest of Finglas, and Father Joe Dunn on a film called *The Singer and Not the Song*: 'The film censor asked if it did happen that a girl could become enamoured of a priest, and whether such a theme could be shown on the screens. If it could, then he would undertake to cut out objectionable lines and scenes.' McQuaid responded, 'Indeed it could!'[179] (On a related theme, Richard Power's book *The Land of Youth* (1964) explores the consequences of a seminarian, Padraig, yielding to the attraction of a woman, though Barbara, the object of his affection, refuses to marry him and their relationship degenerates.)

McQuaid also made representations to the Department of Justice in 1965 about a company called Heritage Films who were advertising 8mm home movies, including one featuring Annette Johnson 'at her dreamiest best' in *Dream of Annette*: 'One of Britain's loveliest nude models in this very artistic movie, incorporating slow motion and excellent lighting effects.' Unusually, McQuaid contacted Thomas Coyne at home asking him if he could block the entry into Ireland of this type of material; a chemist had sent it on to McQuaid pointing out it had been sent to all chemists selling photographic material. Coyne informed McQuaid that the film itself would be stopped by Customs if they found it, but that 'the advertising material is more difficult to detect'.

Significantly, there was also a note from Coyne attached to this correspondence for the minister suggesting he was no longer a regular correspondent of McQuaid, probably because he had reiterated on so many occasions that the state's role in censorship was in his view quite limited: 'It is rather curious that His Grace should write to my home. This is my first contact with him in 1965. At one time he used to phone me and write to me about all sorts of problems.'[180]

By the late 1960s the succinct instruction 'P[ass] without cuts' was becoming much more common in the film censor's office. In July 1967 Christopher Macken jotted down notes in relation to the film *Barefoot in the Park*:

Fertility dance
Same sex
Slept with a tie
Blood tests
Divorce

In the opinion of the censor these were all permissible except 'same sex'; it was recommended that the film could be passed with an Over 18 certificate providing there was a 'provisional' cut of the 'same sex' scene.[181]

Other countries in which cinema had been subjected to censorship also experienced a relaxation, but there was a lack of consistency, and it was sometimes unclear as to what the censorship criteria were – a reminder of how centralised the Irish system was in comparison with others. In both Spain and Portugal, for example, the notion of a 'national' cinema had been about presenting the nation 'as it should be' and prompted a number of 'ardent, Catholic-inflected films', though sometimes the censorship was circumvented or state agencies failed to exercise control. In Spain 'the Church and several political factors within Francoism, together with the censor's personal tastes, all contributed to this confusion'. While every script had to be submitted to censorship committees, 'filmmakers never proposed narratives that could be deemed controversial ... and for a long time such self-censorship seemed to be enough'.[182] Luis María Delgado's *Diferente* (1961), which presents a 'for the time' neutral portrait of a homosexual, slipped past the censors and 'even received official rewards'.[183] Two years later the first clear censorship guidelines were issued, following the disappearance of strict censorship in the US, but 'even at that point these were disappointingly narrow in terms of what was allowed'.[184]

Filmmakers were also recognising the attractions of Ireland as a film-making destination by the end of the 1960s. The epic, Oscar-winning David Lean film *Ryan's Daughter*, starring Robert Mitchum, was filmed in County Kerry in 1969. Mitchum allegedly flew high-class prostitutes into Shannon; indeed, for decades after the filming the area remained awash with stories of Hollywood excess. Local girls were not, it seems, to Mitchum's taste: 'You rarely ever see a pretty girl ... Over there in Ireland they're classic beauties or nothing.' When his wife of thirty years, Dorothy, was out of the way, he reputedly had a constant stream of 'pretty girls' flown in.[185]

In the same year that *Ryan's Daughter* was being made, a film shot in Kilkenny city, *Lock up Your Daughters*, had its premiere as a highlight of the Kilkenny beer festival. In announcing the festival programme, chairman Peter Farrelly maintained that 'the dignity and decorum of today's teenager will be upheld in Kilkenny. Some may come to misuse or abuse our facilities for merriment – but to those we say in plain terms – stay away.'[186] Presented in some contemporary media reports as touching on themes of rape, seduction and homosexuality, *Lock up Your Daughters* received a cool response despite showcasing the city's stately buildings and charming streets: one viewer commented that 'There is no point to it at all. It is just one long jumble of sex.' Following the lead of the Bishop of Ossory, Dr Peter Birch, local clergy stayed away from the premiere, though one of the priests from the friary in the city did turn up to see himself in the film; 'he apparently got a part when he wandered along in his habit one day and someone thought he was a costumed extra. Father Timothy, however, was not to be drawn into giving an opinion of the film'.[187] Fergus Linehan, however, in reviewing the film for the *Irish Times*, showed no such reluctance. He described it as 'a mess', a film which set out 'to provide a merry piece of Restoration bawdry but it's so poorly put together that it ends up as no more than third-rate fancy dress slapstick ... we are left with a mishmash of lavatory–fornication–queer jokes which would belong more properly in the "Carry On" series.'[188]

'It's a fellow who prefers women to drink'

Despite these developments, homosexuality was not something that was regularly discussed or acknowledged publicly in the Republic in the 1960s, although the Roger Casement controversy was still very much a live issue. As pointed out by Brian Lewis, the writer Monk Gibbons, who accepted that Casement was gay, echoing the belief of his cousin W. B. Yeats ('If Casement were a homosexual, what matter!'), had in the *Irish Times* in 1956 raised the possibility of compatibility between homosexuality and patriotism: 'a man is a great patriot; at all costs it must not transpire', he wrote sardonically, 'that he was also a homosexual'.[189]

There were a number of books published in the 1950s and 1960s that peddled the forgery theory in relation to Casement's diaries, including Alfred Noyes in *The Accusing Ghost or Justice for Casement* (1957), Roger McHugh's *Casement: The Public Record Office Manuscripts* (1960) and Herbert Mackey's *Roger Casement: The Truth about the Forged Diaries* (1966). Significantly, none of the authors of these works disputed the equation of homosexuality with perversion. McHugh, for example, littered his account with terms like 'psychopathy', 'insanity' and 'degeneration'; the forger had created a 'moronic or sub-human type' and 'a dull degenerate who has reached the last stages of abnormality, who has no moral scruples and who is under ... a compulsive or obsessive neurosis'. For Mackey in the mid 1960s, 'it would be fantastic to suppose that any human being except a criminal lunatic would attempt the enormities there, let alone record them'.[190]

The pressures of being gay in Dublin in the 1960s have been recounted by David Norris, who recalls collapsing in a Dublin restaurant with a suspected heart attack; it was actually a panic attack brought on by the death of his mother and his fear of the criminal prosecution of homosexuals. After counselling, 'I was referred to a psychiatrist whose advice to me was to leave this country forever and find refuge in a jurisdiction where a more tolerant attitude towards homosexual men prevailed, specifically, the South of France. This well-meant advice I found deeply offensive.'[191] He ignored it and went on, over the course of three decades, to battle persistently – and eventually successfully – for the decriminalisation of homosexuality. When he arrived at Trinity College in 1963, 'he had still never to his knowledge met a homosexual' and was worried about the criminal law in relation to homosexual practice. Fearing blackmail, 'he made no contact whatever with any other homosexual people in the University or in Dublin at that stage', and people on the staff of Trinity who knew he was gay advised him 'to say nothing about it'.[192]

Nor were Norris's fears unfounded; according to the annual reports on prisons, between 1940 and 1978 an average of 6 men a year were jailed for 'indecency with males' and 7 for 'gross indecency'. Chrystel Hug also notes that between 1962 and 1972 there were 455 convictions of men for these crimes, 342 of whom were over the age of 21, and who would not have been prosecuted in Britain.[193] Lee Dunne's 1965 autobiographical novel *Goodbye to the Hill* makes it clear that there was a discourse of abuse centred on homosexuality, and that there were many derogatory terms to choose from. He recounts a conversation with Harry, who does not want to get married to a particular girl:

> 'Tell her you're a bum boy.'
> 'I will in my ballocks tell her I'm a queer.'
> 'Anyway after the number of times I sunk the long last night she'd never believe I was a brownie.'[194]

Alan Bestic confined himself to this definition of an Irish homosexual: 'It's a fellow who prefers women to drink.'[195]

But there were other gay men, more streetwise and experienced than David Norris, who felt their relative invisibility in Dublin in the 1960s allowed them a certain freedom. George Fullerton, who emigrated to London in 1968, recalls that

> In 1960s Dublin the [gay] scene basically consisted of 2 pubs – Rice's and Bartley Dunne's. I never experienced discrimination as such, probably because we were largely invisible. Cruising areas were popular and there were private houses where men could meet. Of course, sex at that time was comparatively safe. I never had a classic coming out as such. It wasn't really an option.

For Fullerton, like many gay men, the move to London was liberating on many levels. There was a much more obviously commercial gay scene, but it brought different problems: 'awareness was such that homophobia was noticeable. I lost my first job as a result of being seen in a gay bar.'[196]

The one place, it seemed, where homosexuality was publicly tolerated in Ireland was in the rarefied atmosphere of the Gate theatre, where two of the legendary figures of Irish theatre, Hilton Edwards and Micheál MacLiammóir, did much of their best work while living openly in Dublin as a gay couple. In the words of Hugh Leonard, they were 'two incorrigible Renaissance men'. They enjoyed camping it up at rehearsals in the early 1960s, Hilton shouting to Micheál, 'You can't wear those ridiculous tights!' To which Mac Liammóir roared back, 'I have the best legs in Dublin!' 'It isn't your legs I'm referring to – it's your derriere!' A row developed, spurred by the knowledge that there was a select invited audience in the dress circle.'

In October 1969 *The Late Late Show* devoted a whole show to celebrating MacLiammóir's seventieth birthday with Edwards also centre stage.[197]

But MacLiammóir was a lot more complex than the anecdotes about jocular verbal flirtations with Edwards indicate, and over the course of his career he 'accommodated himself within Irish culture by being less direct [and] circumspect ... never actually naming his own sexuality. Theatre was the domain that MacLiammóir inhabited and because of its high public visibility, there was a high degree of screening and self-editing.' This went on throughout his life; although born in England, he reinvented himself as a native of Cork, embraced Celticism and sought from a young age an acceptable persona 'within which to be both homosexual and at the same time visible'. Growing up in the aftermath of the Wilde trials, according to Eibhear Walshe, his reinvention was also about a 'refutation of the taint of

Wildeian aestheticism and decadence'.[198] The extent to which MacLiam-móir operated in a rarefied atmosphere, however, should not be exaggerated; a fluent Irish speaker, he was also a pillar of amateur dramatic festivals for over thirty years, which involved extensive contacts with local clergy and bishops.

'Conform or get out'

In 1962 *Christus Rex*, the journal for clerics, contained an anonymous review of a book, *Morality and the Homosexual*, and commended it to priests who were 'challenged to transfer what had hitherto been regarded as an unnatural vice to the category of permitted human association'.[199] McQuaid's press secretary, Osmond Dowling, wrote to him in 1967 concerning homosexuality:

> the subject first came up in the correspondence columns of the *Evening Press* when a mother told – as a warning to other parents – the story of how her teenage son was led astray by an older man and only after a long time and great difficulty brought back to normality by talking to a priest. I would not say the letters are part of a campaign, and those that I saw seem inspired by a genuine desire to warn parents of the dangers abroad today. Whether these dangers have increased of late is hard to say. I have a couple of good contacts who would be able to give me an accurate picture of the situation if you are interested.

McQuaid underlined the last sentence and wrote in response, 'Yes I am,' but it is not clear who Dowling's contacts were and there is no documented follow-up on this particular issue.[200]

John Broderick's *The Fugitives* (1962), which explores the opposition between self-assertion through sex and acceptance of authority and faith, includes a homosexual character who is asked why he will not leave the object of his affections alone, to which he responds, 'Have people ever left me alone? It's majority rule, isn't it? Conform or get out.'[201] Maurice Leitch wrote about gay male experience in *The Liberty Lad* (1965), a book that was banned. Observing sexual identities from the perspective of its main character Frank Glass, it examines his homoerotic relationship with his openly gay friend Terry: 'Just how *normal* was our relationship anyway? Most people,

I have discovered, although they don't talk about it, are terrified of even thinking of *that* subject.' Leitch was not unduly perturbed by the banning of his books (*Poor Lazarus*, published in 1969, was also banned); he was 'very pleased in a way. I think that makes my books much stronger in many ways. I think that means they were hard hitting and powerful and honest. It seemed terribly shocking that I would actually mention the fact that homosexuality existed.' In contrast, Edna O'Brien was appalled and angered by censorship, believing it was rooted in 'fear of knowledge, fear of communicating our desires, our secrets, our stream of consciousness'.[202]

O'Brien also tackled homosexuality, or 'lesbian encounters', in *The Mouth of the Cave* (1968), in which the narrator is ambivalent about her homosexuality. When observing a woman she asks: 'Why am I running, why am I trembling, why am I afraid? Because she is a woman and so am I. Because, because? I did not know. In my more optimistic moments I like to think that she waits there expecting me to come and search her out.'[203] In Janet McNeill's *The Maiden Dinosaur* (1964), centred on middle-class Protestant Belfast friends, Sarah, a sex-phobic middle-aged spinster, is in love with her friend Helen: 'Loving Helen is the only deliberate dishonesty I allow myself and I justify it because I admit I am being dishonest.'[204]

In September 1963, Italian tourists complained to the *Sunday Press* newspaper 'about the reaction when they held hands on the street or kissed in a public place'.[205] But repression of homosexuality was not unique to Ireland: Gaullists in France in the 1960s still referred to homosexuality as a social scourge, and the fines for homosexual indecency were higher than those for heterosexual indecency. Although there was a gay liberation movement from the 1950s, 'there remained a conspiracy of silence'. After 1968 it was no longer acceptable in France to refer to it as a 'perversion'.[206] What occurred earlier in other countries was the visibility of homosexuality, though there was disagreement about their political impact; Betty Friedan, for example, labelled lesbians in the feminist movement 'the lavender menace', suggesting they threatened the chances of moderate organisations to build political coalitions.[207]

'I will give no approval to the Irish Association of Social Workers'

Archbishop McQuaid's almost obsessive preoccupation with ensuring sexual issues were not discussed openly had particular implications for social workers. The belief persisted that problems relating to sex and unwanted pregnancies only applied to the Irish in England, and were not domestic issues. The annual reports of the Emigrant Welfare Bureau of the CSWB make it clear that the idea of the moral danger posed to emigrants was still paramount. The emigrant bureau dealt with 9,923 cases in 1963, and it was estimated that 31 per cent of males and 14 per cent of females had no accommodation arranged before they arrived in England. As well as criticising lack of parental responsibility, Cecil Barrett also referred to 'far too many who are unsuited for emigration on other grounds as well as that of immaturity'.[208]

The number of girls availing themselves of the services of the Catholic Rescue and Protection Society in Dublin (CRPS) – through which women were placed in mother and baby homes and adoption or temporary care was arranged for the babies within eight weeks of birth with 'absolute secrecy' guaranteed for each girl – was 185 in 1962, 196 in 1965 and 213 in 1966. The vast majority were repatriated from the London area; of the 136 repatriated in 1963, it was noted that 'not one of these 136 girls sought help in Ireland before leaving.'[209]

When the pop star Boy George's mother, Dinah O'Dowd, one of an impoverished family of ten, announced she was writing her memoirs, most expected a tale of support for her troubled son and his well-publicised drug problems; what they got, however, was a grim portrait of domestic abuse in a tale of her own struggles with a violent husband.[210] This was a journey that began in Dublin in the late 1950s when she became an unmarried mother at the age of 18. Like so many others, her boyfriend ran away when he discovered she was pregnant and, like many other unmarried mothers in Ireland, she moved to London to 'escape her shame', where she met Gerry O'Dowd, a young builder from an Irish family with whom she had six children. His mental and physical abuse of her began in 1962 when she was seven months pregnant with Boy George and continued for forty years until 2002, when she discovered he also had a mistress.

In 1967 the Department of External Affairs officially sanctioned a system whereby English rescue societies which bore the cost of repatriation could seek reimbursement from the Irish embassy in London.[211] But McQuaid and his colleagues remained concerned about the attention these subjects were receiving. Cecil Barrett paid a personal visit to the chairman of the independent newspapers to complain about what he considered inaccurate portrayal of the work of the emigrant bureau. He and McQuaid were also worried about an Austrian sociologist, Richard Hauser, who had arrived in Dublin to highlight what he felt was the neglect of Irish emigrants in London. This provoked McQuaid's anti-Semitism:

> I know him: a chancer ... he is an Austrian Jew and has been eight months studying the Irish question ... a good actor and appeals to the emotions. He goes in for shocking and paints the gloomiest of pictures.'[212]

Barrett successfully persuaded Fianna Fáil's Brian Lenihan not to share a platform with Hauser when he was in Dublin – 'a very good result', according to McQuaid.

Hostility to Hauser was also rooted in the fact that he wanted to highlight for the Irish Association of Social Workers the high participation of the Irish in crimes of violence and prostitution. He maintained that one-sixth of the prostitutes coming before the courts in London were Irish, but that no one cared 'a hoot about them'.[213] Barrett also informed McQuaid that 'it is important to know what is happening between him and Artane [industrial school]. McQuaid told Barrett to 'inquire discreetly at Artane ... Hauser's evident determination to educate and train us is as puzzling as it is unsought. But then he is a difficult bird and quite aggressive.'[214]

At the core of these manoeuvres and suspicions was a reluctance to lose control of social work and a refusal to embrace the idea of looking at issues like prostitution in a different way. In January 1964, Cecil Barrett dismissed the Irish Association of Social Workers as a group 'anxious to talk a lot of hot air and to set themselves up as an action group to get the government and everyone else moving'. The association was talking of possible change in institutions in relation to the emotional needs of children (hence the concern about Artane industrial school). McQuaid told Barrett that it was necessary to continue to spy on them 'lest we be put in the wrong in the genuine work by the group's talk and pressure. This technique is necessary with such elements as the Irish Housewives [Association] ... I will give no approval to the Irish Association of Social Workers.'[215]

In February 1964 Barrett dismissed the content of some articles in the *Evening Herald* on conditions at night in Dublin streets and concerns about the care of ex-industrial school inmates going to England; in a letter to McQuaid, he insisted that the need for hostels was 'not very urgent'.[216] A confidential report of a special investigation into St Patrick's Institution for young offenders in Dublin in 1963, after allegations of excessive violence and naked beatings, was a complete whitewash which rubbished all the credible claims of violence. Allegations of boys being stripped naked and violently beaten, it was maintained, 'are manifestly so hysterical as to be absurd'. Minister for Justice Charles Haughey accepted the report 'unreservedly' in December 1963. In truth, the testimony of Patrick Baitson, a former inmate of St Patrick's, which suggested that these beatings had a sexual element, was credible and it was brave of him to write his letter, which included information that 'the boy was nacked [sic] except for a pair of underpants and Mr Farrington then boxed him with his closed fists, lashed him with the leather strap and kicked him all over the body and almost beat the boy unconscious'.[217]

As with other institutions, visitors were presented with sanitised scenes. Although McQuaid got a hostel built for inmates of St Patrick's for after-treatment, he also ignored a frightening report from the chaplain at Artane industrial school on the conditions in which the boys were living. It was suppressed and was only released by the Dublin diocese in 2007 as a result of the relentless efforts of Jim Beresford, who accurately described himself as a 'former child prisoner' of Artane, where a number of children had been sexually abused for many years.[218] 'Not in Ireland' still seemed to be the message; the same mentality which prompted a group of priests to write to McQuaid in 1968 about sex and television and *The Late Late Show* asking for Gay Byrne to be prevented from 'providing a platform for the vermin of England, France, USA or anywhere such vermin can be picked up'.[219]

The main concern in all this was to dispute the notion that Ireland had any of these problems. This was also the case with abortion. When a journalist working for a German women's magazine in 1964 asked the Department of Justice if any assessment could be made of the number of illegal abortions in Ireland, it provided figures from 1945 to 1965. In five of those years there were no charges; in total there were only 8 convictions, 3 acquittals and 1 charge withdrawn, figures which would satisfy those who wanted to maintain that abortion was virtually an irrelevance in Ireland. After something of a crackdown in 1948, not a single charge was made between 1952 and 1957, or between 1959 and 1963.[220]

'Equal moral responsibility
and punishment'

The Joint Committee of Women's Societies and Social Workers continued to highlight the double standards that operated in relation to the sentencing of women and men for soliciting, and the disturbing tendency to give suspended sentences to some men convicted of indecent assault on young girls, as happened in Cork in November 1965.[221] In 1967 the committee demanded 'equal moral responsibility and punishment' in relation to soliciting; it also decried the lack of trained social workers and the treatment of children before the courts. It regarded the canon law banning illegitimate children from receiving holy orders as a 'grave injustice' and highlighted child abuse again in 1969, in this case regarding the postponement of a court case relating to child molestation in Limerick and the refusal of the defendant to submit to a medical examination.[222]

Hilda Tweedy and the Irish Housewives Association also prioritised the issue of soliciting, Tweedy arguing in the early 1960s that 'the law for sexual offences (soliciting) should be the same for both sexes'. What she wanted was a more pro-woman reform of the law; her memorandum on the subject stated firmly that 'men can also be said to solicit', whereas the existing situation only allowed for the woman to be prosecuted for soliciting. Tweedy also highlighted the need for 'a more serious consideration to be given to the rehabilitation of sexually disturbed young people. Segregation from family and community is not enough in itself. We would stress the need for professional treatment also.' She also argued that the minimum legal age for marrying should be 16 for both sexes, not the current 14 for a boy and 12 for a girl, because delinquent girls up to the age of 17 could be brought before the juvenile courts and men could be tried for the carnal knowledge of a girl under the age of 17.[223]

When RTÉ screened a *Radharc* programme on prostitution in Cork in December 1968, *Open Port*, the issue attracted considerable media coverage, partly because in 1966 quayside prostitution had resulted in a 'grim series of scandals involving the deaths of two young women'. But there were very divergent views as to its significance. It was referred to by one correspondent as 'this particular delinquency' and 'a matter of public disquiet in Cork' due to 'poor Cork's lonely sailors and wayward sisters'.[224]

In November 1968, journalist Mary Leland wrote a feature on the issue in the *Irish Times*. She found 'no brothels but a steady traffic along the docks', and estimated there were about fifty prostitutes working in the city, which was 'not a frightening statistic for a city of a population of over 120,000 people', and certainly not enough 'to justify the various outraged attitudes that are being publicly taken up on the subject'.[225] She maintained that 'surprisingly many' of the prostitutes ended up marrying the sailors who had availed themselves of their services. With the permission of their parents, six young girls discovered by the Gardaí to be involved in prostitution were committed to a convent; four were subsequently regarded as rehabilitated, while the other two resumed prostitution. Father Leo Lennon, the port chaplain, also attempted to counteract the problem by offering sailors alternative entertainment, including a venue that was dubbed an 'anti-whore club' by locals.

In truth, pragmatism ruled the day; Gardaí, for example,

> are well and prudently aware of the line to be drawn between the criminal law and the moral law and have no doubt about the role in prostitution of the age-old system of demand and supply. Their relationship with the women is usually one of mutually guarded respect and as a result the older women help them to find and discourage the younger girls who might be just about to begin a life on the streets. Even the port chaplain does not allow himself to forget the casual demands of human nature.[226]

For those women who either remained in the home or were employed outside it, there were organisations dedicated to improving their lives and highlighting their concerns. Linda Connolly's sociological survey of the women's movement in Ireland, published in 2002, argues that an undue concentration on women and nationalism has distorted the hybridity of the history of the Irish women's movement, as has the lack of attention given to numerous Protestant middle-class female reformers. She also challenges the simplistic assumption that a backward Irish women's movement suddenly modernised at the end of the 1960s; or, as Hilda Tweedy put it, 'so many people believe that the women's movement was born on some mystical date in 1970, like Aphrodite rising from the waves'.[227] Tweedy and her colleagues provided a crucial link between the female activists of the 1940s and the 1950s and the Irish Women's Liberation Movement (IWLM) of subsequent decades, a reminder of the inadequacy of a historical assessment of the women's movement that leaps straight from the suffrage campaign to the 'contraceptive train' in 1971 (see chapter 5).

The women who worked and argued for change faced deep-rooted cultural attitudes that were hostile to any sense of female autonomy. In theory, women 'of the home' were still obliged to love, honour and obey. In practice, the politics of Irish sexuality ensured that marriage was often a business transaction about land, power and strictly prescribed gender roles, themes explored by John B. Keane in his first play, *Sive* (1959). Until the passing of the Succession Act in 1965, women were not even entitled to an automatic share of the land if their husbands died intestate; a man could leave his estate to a male relative, making no provision for his widow. The Succession Act entitled the widow to at least a third of the estate. But even that was a step too far for some men, who thought it would destroy the balance of gender power in Ireland. Joseph Leneghan TD commented, as the matter was being debated, that it was 'perverted petticoat legislation'. During his contribution to the debate, Fine Gael's John A. Costello gave a good overview of the attitudes that existed:

> There was a man who had seven daughters and finally a son was born and the son was the apple of his eye. He explained as the boy grew up what he was going to do for him; he would send him to the best school and then to university and his attitude was summed up when he said, 'You would like to do the best you can for the one child you have.' The seven daughters were in the halfpenny place.[228]

'Senior clerics, smiling or solemn, knew all about it too, for there were complaints'

There seemed little appetite to tackle the issues raised by Tweedy and her colleagues; the preoccupation remained with what was seen and heard publicly, as opposed to what went on behind closed doors. In this sense, the controversy over John McGahern's *The Dark* is understandable. It included understated passages acknowledging the horrors experienced by those who were abused: 'His hand closed on your arm. You wanted to curse or wrench yourself free but you had to lie stiff as a board, stare straight ahead at the wall, afraid before anything of meeting the eyes you knew were searching your face.'

As pointed out by Fintan O'Toole just after McGahern died in 2006,

> By accurately describing the human interiors of Ireland, McGahern
> helped to alter Ireland's sense of reality. The starkest example of this is
> the issue of child sex abuse. When it hit the headlines in the 1990s, it was
> spoken of as a stunning and awful revelation, a secret that hardly anyone
> knew. Yet it is there in black and white in *The Dark*, thirty years before.
> The book opens with the young protagonist, Mahoney, being forced to
> strip naked and bend over a chair to be beaten by his father, who derives
> a sexual pleasure from the act. Shortly afterwards, the boy is sexually
> abused by his father. Later, he stays in a priest's house and the priest
> comes into his room at night. The description is eerily like something
> that would be spoken aloud in Ireland decades later in *States of Fear* or
> the Ferns Inquiry. Such awful privacies were unspoken and, in the case of
> *The Dark*, unspeakable. Officialdom had no place for them, and though
> most Irish people knew about them, they did not want to really know
> them. But McGahern's calm persistence, his unrelenting integrity, drove
> them into our collective heads. The very conservativeness of the surface,
> the avoidance of shrillness or stridency, made the act of insinuation all
> the more explosive.[229]

In October 2006, Father Tom Doyle, a US canon lawyer, claimed in
a *Panorama* documentary on the BBC, *Sex Crimes and the Vatican*, that a
1962 church directive, *Crimen Sollicitationis*, imposed an oath of secrecy
on the child victim, the priest and any witness in an abuse case, and that
breaking the oath could mean excommunication. He maintained that the
directive was 'indicative of a worldwide policy of absolute secrecy and control of all cases of sexual abuse by the clergy'. This was emphatically rejected
by Dr Michael Mullaney, an Irish canon lawyer who insisted the directive
was about the misuse of the confessional; if someone complained about the
inappropriate behaviour of a priest in a confessional, then the confessional
priest and those dealing with the complaint had to treat it in a confidential
manner because of the seal of confession, but this did not prevent the com-
plainant from bringing the complaint to the civil authorities if a crime was
suspected.

But there is little doubt that the 'seal of confession' was used in some
cases to prevent action being taken. The programme interviewed one abuse
victim, Aidan Doyle, who had been sexually assaulted by a priest at school.

When he told another priest about it, the priest applied the seal of confession to the conversation 'so that you will never talk about this and it will be kept secret.' The victim remembers: 'I was simply told: you don't talk about this again. It's over. You'll get over it. It will fade away in time.'[230]

As Angela Bourke has pointed out in relation to Peter Lennon's film *The Rocky Road to Dublin*: 'The children we see in *Rocky Road* may have been safe, but hundreds just like them were being raped and tortured by some of the most revered members of society; the access-all-areas men in black who systematically terrified them into keeping sick secrets. These men were a minority, but their poison still lives on. Senior clerics, smiling or solemn, knew all about it too, for there were complaints. The first recorded and acted upon in Ferns was in 1966; a priest was removed from his teaching post and sent to England for two years as a penance. He was later appointed principal of the same school and continued to abuse the boys in his care. Like the doctors and priests who were "always on the men's side" taking no account of grown women as striving, suffering adults, the Bishops had been apparently so exquisitely trained to see things from a particular, special, Irish angle that they could no longer recognise and react as human beings to what was staring them in the face.'[231]   *1966*

Many writers when describing Ireland also wanted to know if they could capture the essence of the 'special, Irish angle' referred to by Bourke, Michael Sheehy concluding robustly that 'the great barrier to Irish development in the twentieth century was not British imperialism but Irish Puritanism'.[232] This may be a neat and compelling argument, but it does little to unmask the various veils around Irish sexuality or lives as they were lived as opposed to how, in theory, they were supposed to be lived. This was a country that had, in 1961, 2,000 licensed dance halls, one for every 1,500 people, and yet, as was noted by the Department of Justice, 'scarcely a week passes that there are not court applications for licences for new halls, some in the most extraordinary places', and in some cases the dances went on until three or four in the morning.[233]

Alan Bestic insists that when Irish marriages went wrong, they did so for different reasons than elsewhere and that, due to sexual dysfunction, ignorant newlyweds 'blunder through its physical aspects ineptly and often unhappily, the shadow of their ignorance clouding the bedroom ... [there is] an element of furtiveness about their love-making and therefore it creates no bond between them ... complicated and devious ... they create a cycle of inter-related problems that are almost insoluble ... A hospital sister told me of one woman who learned the full facts only when she woke up too soon from the anaesthetic while having her third child.'[234]

This stage-Irish anecdote may make for colourful copy but it can hardly be trusted as genuinely representative of Irish sexuality. Donald Connery recounted some similar tales, and asserted that sex in Ireland was 'more of a function than a passion', but he also discovered that 'people were talking publicly about sex as never before'.[235] In reality, what these authors seem to have wanted to do was to depict a changing society while holding on to the endearing yarns and simplicities which had never, in any case, been convincing. That is not to insist that their books did not touch on the truth: Connery observed, for example, that 'the sexual attitudes of Irish youth today are more or less comparable to those in America or Britain a generation ago'. But was it true that 'it is unusual, except in some university circles, for a boy and a girl to simply seek out each other's company for reasons of mind and purity'?[236] Those who attended University College Dublin in the 1960s have contrasting memories as to the extent of physical relationships; one woman recalls 'a rich, innocent, platonic style of loving'; another that it was quite usual to be 'going steady' by the second term of the first year, that 'vast quantities of beer' were consumed, 'raging hormones' and many parties in the bedsits that the students rented.[237]

'Female anger,
subtle, veiled but there'

What was not acknowledged enough was the extent to which women in the 1960s began to challenge their status and to confront attitudes to sexuality. As June Levine recalled in her 1982 book *Sisters*, there was a growing sense of a 'female anger, subtle, veiled but there. It was an anger the cause of which was only partly recognised or understood. It was a hangover, an almighty international hangover. It was an anger which clearly said: "OK, the awful fifties are gone; things were going right for a change. Going right for the boys. But what about us?"'

Part of this female anger involved closely observing the previous generation of mothers and being determined not to repeat their mistakes. Nuala O'Faoláin's mother, who had to cope with thirteen pregnancies, according to O'Faoláin, 'did not want anything to do with child-rearing or housework. But she had to do it. Because she fell in love with my father and they married, she was condemned to spend her life as a mother and a homemaker. She was in the wrong job.' Not all, of course, would end up doing things differently in the supposedly swinging sixties. Edna O'Brien's *Girls in Their Married Bliss* contains a conversation between two women bemoaning 'that we'd die the way we were – enough to eat, married, dissatisfied'.[238]

People were, however, flocking to grotty ballrooms around the country. They may have been unsophisticated, but they were on the move and on the hunt. More importantly, from the perspective of McQuaid, theological and legal arguments that supplanted the personal testimony of women with regard to contraception were being critically challenged. In the Senate, Mary Robinson, first elected in 1969, who was to be central to the campaign to legalise contraceptives (see chapter 5), highlighted the dilemma of women with many children who desired no more, but lived in a country where no contraception was available. The previous year, Robinson had completed her legal studies at Harvard, and had witnessed the growing demand for civil rights in the United States. According to her official biographers, 'it was time to come home, time to join the battle and Mary says that by the summer of 1968 Harvard had prepared her for it'.[239]

In 1971, McQuaid's final pastoral as archbishop was on the issue of contraception, entitled *Contraception and Conscience*. Perhaps this was apt given the fact that so many women were now defying Church teaching and the encyclical *Humanae Vitae* (1968). People were looking for more information and for new outlets. In November 1968, McQuaid wrote to the principal of the Irish School of Administration objecting to a proposed debate with the motion that 'the people of Ireland should reject *Humanae Vitae*': 'While it is undeniable that for some persons this teaching will involve great difficulty, it is for me a matter for amazement that your school could, in such terms, propose to deal with an encyclical letter that is deliberately meant to safeguard the sanctity of marriage.' To add insult to injury, his press secretary, Ossie Dowling, had been asked to chair the meeting. This invitation McQuaid regarded as 'provocative and hurtful'.[240] But for McQuaid even to acknowledge that it would create difficulties for some people was unusual.

In 1971 McQuaid was informed that a group of activists in the Irish Women's Liberation Movement were planning to protest about contraception at the laying and blessing of the foundation stone for a new church in his diocese. McQuaid wrote defiantly in the margin, 'Let them all come!'[241] He may have been defiant, but the fact that the women were prepared to confront him publicly was yet another sign that both his domination and an unquestioned obedience to his Church's teaching was coming to an end. To a certain extent, McQuaid's Ireland was already dead and buried before he vacated his post in 1972.

1970–2005

'*You may, but you can't*'

In terms of public debate and comment, the issue of contraception dwarfed many other considerations of aspects of sexuality throughout the 1970s and 1980s. In 1977, a groundbreaking survey of social attitudes, *Prejudice and Tolerance in Ireland*, was published, based on a sample of 2,311 adults' responses to different categories of stimuli. It revealed that 57.6 per cent agreed that premarital sex is always wrong, while 38.5 per cent disagreed. But there were plenty of other responses to questions related to sexuality recorded by the survey which seemed to indicate that public attitudes were ahead of Church and state representatives when it came to greater liberalisation, including on the issue of contraception. These included answers to the question of: whether priests should be free to marry (46.7 per cent agreed, 44.5 per cent disagreed); whether homosexual behaviour between adults should not be a crime (45.2 per cent agreed, 39.9 per cent disagreed); that sex education is a human right (89.2 per cent agreed, 7.5 per cent disagreed); that prostitution should not be a prosecutable offence (38.1 per cent agreed, 51.7 per cent disagreed); and that it is always wrong to use artificial contraceptives (31.3 per cent agreed, 63 per cent disagreed).[1]

Correspondence within government departments on the subject of artificial contraceptives in the early 1970s was the culmination of nearly

ten years of debate. The situation regarding access was different depending
on personal circumstances. Contraceptives were more available to some –
the middle classes, those with friends or family in England, and those with
the time and money to travel to Belfast or access to a liberal doctor – than
others. There was also a rearguard action being fought by groups such as
the Association for the Protection of Irish Family Life, who suggested in
March 1971 that confusion was being spread by phrases such as 'planned or
responsible parenthood'. The association was not for turning: 'If by planned
is meant the spacing of births by contraception, then that use of marriage is
not in agreement with the law of God.' While reiterating 'the proneness of
our human nature to evil', what galled such organisations most was the idea
that the law ought to be brought into line with the outlook of other countries – 'one can conceive of no worse fate for Ireland'.[2] In 1972, the Taoiseach
Jack Lynch's private secretary responded to such communications by insisting, in a contention that many would have disputed:

> The attitude of the government in relation to the existing law on divorce
> and contraception is not determined by the official teaching of any
> religion. In considering any case made for a change in such laws the gov-
> ernment have to have regard to several factors, among them the claim
> that the state should not legislate in the field of private morality and, on
> the other hand, the social implications of any change in the law.[3]

How had this shift in attitude occurred? In April 1970, David Goldberg,
the legal correspondent of the *Irish Times*, referred to the law on contraception as 'a pathetic pretence' which damaged respect for justice, and suggested that, while spermicides were being stopped by customs, diaphragms
were not. There was no law which prevented a doctor prescribing them, but
they couldn't be imported, and he pointed out that at the 1969 Fianna Fáil
Ard Fheis Jack Lynch had suggested the issue was one of conscience and that
his government had no intention of interfering with that conscience, which
amounted to saying 'You may, but you can't.'[4]

When Garret FitzGerald raised this issue in the Dáil his question was
transferred from the Department of the Taoiseach to the Department of Justice, with an accompanying note suggesting, with considerable understate-
ment, that with regard to the law 'there does seem to be a genuine difficulty'.
FitzGerald put it to Lynch that he had said people could import contraceptives for their own use according to conscience; Lynch insisted that was a

misrepresentation.[5] In the same month, a 30-page memorandum was prepared for the government on the subject in response to a Senate bill on contraception being proposed. This memorandum argued that the government should reject the Senate bill, but should also 'suggest something', referring to the 'moderate and, at first sight, reasonable proposal that it should be lawful to import a reasonable quantity ... for personal use'. It suggested the real problem with regard to 'public morality' (a phrase used repeatedly) was that those most affected by all this would be 'the young and immature'.

It also referred to the growing media attention on the subject as 'a deliberate effort to manufacture a "Church–state" confrontation', and that television audiences were being bombarded with sex and those who defended 'Christian thinking' were being shouted down, creating an atmosphere that could damage 'mental health'.[6] Furthermore, it maintained that it would be 'out of the question' to seek to enforce the law with regard to Section 16 of the 1929 Censorship Act relating to 'advocacy' of contraception, a significant admission that this law was out of date and completely unrealistic. This document was no rant, but was rather a memorandum seeking to strike a balance between legal and moral issues, and which acknowledged the viewpoints of the pro-contraception lobby. However, there was also a certain tone of bewilderment and suspicion: 'It is impossible, even if it were desirable, to treat the contraception issue as a single, isolated one – the point has already been made that there is also a campaign for divorce and a growing use of arguments for contraception that, if accepted, would make divorce inevitable. But that is not all.' It went on to refer to the 'campaign' led by Senator John Horgan for a 'secular constitution', a further indication that 'there is the growth of what is usually called the permissive society. For instance, RTÉ on the night of Holy Thursday had a feature on "Pornography in Ireland".'

The television critic of the *Irish Times* was quoted in the memorandum describing this feature as opening with 'a film clip of an anonymous film starlet showing off her breasts and most of the rest of her anatomy to photographers in Cannes ... incredibly tasteless shots of some model girls prancing around St Stephen's Green in hot pants with the cameras zooming in around their thighs. This feature was shown within a week of another feature in which a chemist in Enniskillen was photographed giving a detailed explanation of the functioning of various types of contraceptives which he sells.'

Many people, the author of the memorandum further argued, 'and not only Bishops and Clergy', may well have seen in all this 'a positive public acceptance of the arrival here of the Post-Christian age ... a change in the law to make them available to single people might seem to some, if not as an endorsement of immorality, at least an acceptance of its inevitability on a very wide scale'.[7]

On 1 April 1971, Jack Lynch was quite frank about the need for reappraisal and placed this in the context of the desire for a united Ireland:

> I said in Dáil Éireann on 28th July last 'in so far as there are constitutional
> difficulties which are legitimately seen by people to be infringements of
> their civil rights, then their views are worthy of intensive examination
> and we should try and accommodate them in our constitution and in
> our laws'. I repeat that now. The constitution of a united Ireland requires
> to be a document in which no element of Sectarianism, even uncon-
> scious or unintended, should occur.[8]

A small group had established the Irish Family Planning Rights Asso-ciation (IFPRA) in October 1970 to increase pressure for a limited legalisa-tion of contraceptives but its submissions were ignored by politicians. This prompted the IFPRA to draft a bill amending the 1935 law which it confided to Senator Mary Robinson, who made seven attempts in 1971 to have the bill (which proposed the limited sale of contraceptives to be legalised along with publications about family planning) read in the Senate, with the support of Trevor West and John Horgan. It could not be printed and published without a first reading, and so was placed on the agenda of the Senate in July, but a majority of senators (25 to 14) opposed its reading. Labour Party TD's Noël Browne and John O'Connell, both doctors, attempted to get it read in the Dáil in February 1972 but were shouted down.[9]

A sense of 'inevitably, but not yet' was widely current at this time, as reflected in the internal governmental response to the bill. In May 1971, the Minister for Lands, Seán Flanagan, for example, wrote to Jack Lynch suggesting that the secularisation of the laws of Ireland 'should clearly be done, but our people are not ready for it yet and with so much irrelevance about, not even ready to examine fairly. It will have to wait.'[10] Significantly, the Department of Justice was also criticised by the Department of the Taoi-seach because it sought to 'maintain that this memorandum requires some sort of secret treatment, which precludes the usual consultation with the other ministers concerned. They have tended to adopt this approach in the past too readily and I think it would be well to get them on a proper footing with regard to cabinet procedure.'[11]

It was also noted that in Portugal, France, the Netherlands and Spain 'contraceptives are easily available' and the Hierarchy did not appear 'to have taken any position against'.[12] The following month, in an interview with the *Irish Press*, Jack Lynch acknowledged the importance of the issue, but also encapsulated in his answers the contradictory approach of the government: 'it was not the most pressing problem to be considered ... It was a problem and it was not going to go away by shelving it.' In July 1971 the proposal was withdrawn from the cabinet agenda until further notice. In effect, it was shelved.[13]

The government file relating to resolutions and miscellaneous correspondence concerning contraception, released to researchers in 2002, got bulkier each month and contained many Irish solutions to Irish problems, including the contention that 'I can see no injustice to anyone under the present system when no one is prosecuted for having or using contraceptives'.[14] Another maintained that there were many, including priests, 'who at this time are totally in rebellion against papal authority in this and other matters', while a member of the National Health Council, a doctor in Meath, assured Lynch that if he did legislate for contraceptives he would have the support 'of most medical men for this reform'.[15]

One observer, casting a cold eye on the fire and brimstone emanating from Oliver J. Flanagan, Fine Gael TD and arch conservative in matters of sexual morality, wrote pithily: 'Mr Oliver Flanagan says Christian Ireland is being ruined by drink, drugs and sex. I wonder if he would be in favour of closing all our pubs. Drink has done more to wreck family life than sex.'[16] Never a truer sentence was written. Four years later, Flanagan secretly and anonymously circulated a document in his constituency that damaged his party colleague Charlie McDonald by suggesting that McDonald had 'erred' by voting for his party's bill on family planning: 'Flanagan used the facilities of the Knights of Columbanus for this particularly dirty work.'[17]

Other members of the public warned Lynch to stand firm, one reminding him that any liberalisation would involve 'alienating good, decent republicans of the Tom Barry calibre by your complete sell-out to England'.[18] This note was written on a card printed in England (and Tom Barry had served in the British army during the First World War and was also childless). Another correspondent was probably not far from the truth, at least amongst educated middle-class opinion, when he asserted that, in supporting change, 'I feel I am part of a large, normally silent group who regard the present law on contraception as wrong, unjust and contrary to normal human rights.'[19] The same was maintained by the side opposing contraception: 'we are labelled the "silent majority", I believe'.[20]

'A brilliant but simple-minded young lady who is being used by a small group of misguided people'

Clearly, Jack Lynch's speech at the Ard Fheis had struck a chord, or nerve, depending on which side of the contraception debate people were on. It is also clear that those who compiled the 30-page memorandum on the subject were correct in their observation that there was a tendency to link contraception with other issues, judging by the amount of letters that maintained legalised contraception would be the thin end of a wedge leading to divorce, abortion and euthanasia. Most of the correspondents demanded retention of the status quo and predicted dire consequences for Fianna Fáil if it endorsed liberalisation. Some, who signed themselves '100 per cent Catholic Irish and proud', told the Taoiseach that '90 per cent of the people that cross O'Connell Bridge each day are affected by this dreadful Venereal Disease, so please spare the other 10 per cent'.[21]

One woman took the trouble to write to Mrs Lynch, instead of Jack, urging her to use her influence with her husband. The 'childless widow' felt sorry for Mary Robinson, 'a brilliant but simple-minded young lady who is being used by a small group of misguided people ... this is a matter of truth versus error, Christ versus Anti-Christ.'[22] Others addressed the Taoiseach man to man, including one who decried 'the total waste of the male seed' that would occur with contraception: 'You still have time, Jack, to stop the evil course that your government have set out upon, vicious laws, pornography, anti-clericalism and trying to destroy the influence of the Bishops. You register as an extremely evil man, Jack, with more and more Irish men and women, the more so because you fully know what you do.'[23] Others appealed to his sense of heritage and urged him to take his guidance from the Vatican: 'Some time ago, our Holy Father, the Pope, remarked feelingly that looking out over the universe, Ireland was the one bright spot to console him. You will not extinguish that light. Do not let your name go down in history as the one who signed away our glorious heritage.'[24]

Others believed that potential liberalistion of the contraception laws was a consequence of the Irish state being pushed into the EEC and that large families could only be a good thing, given that 'the one- or two-child family is usually bored, pampered, unhappy, selfish and jealous.'[25] This wariness of the impact EEC membership would have on supposedly 'Irish values' was reflected in a book by Brian Rothery, *What Europe Means to the Irish*, published in 1973, the year in which Ireland became a member after a referendum in which 83 per cent of the electorate voted in favour. Rothery insisted that Ireland had remained isolated from 'the manifestations of conventional sexuality that sweep across Europe', where things were very different: 'There is much vulgarity in Europe. Pornography is the most vulgar thing. Pornography is rampant in Holland, Germany and Denmark ... sex shops filled with phallic objects and bizarre devices and clothes, some of which are extremely ugly ... magazine covers and pictures depicting in close-up every kind of sexual activity and perversion; newspapers advocate every kind of sexual behaviour.' Rothery also suggested that the Catholic Church would inevitably be weakened by Ireland's entry to Europe: 'The Catholic faith is bolstered by fierce nationalism ... as immigrants into a new Europe we cannot take our Catholicism or our fierce nationalism into Europe. They will not give a damn about our Sunday morning mass in the Germany or France that we go to.'

Rothery queried the Department of Justice as to whether there would be an increase in the importation of sexually explicit literature and other 'devices' as a result of EEC membership and he was informed that the legal implications to be assumed by the country on accession to the EEC did not extend to, or affect, the laws relating to censorship or contraceptives. Rothery was unimpressed: 'all signs are that the dykes are about to break. Europe now threatens to expose us ... by making contraceptives available and by creating standards of living that allow divorce.'[26]

The message was clear – keep Ireland poor and it would retain the faith and avoid immorality. Those who expressed such fears were also satirised. An *Irish Times* article written by Donal Foley in 1972 entitled 'The Church Goes to Market' predicted that 'Massive redundancies will take place in the Roman Catholic Church in Ireland when Ireland enters the European Community in January, according to plans prepared by the most Reverend Dr Mansholt, Bishop of Brussels, at the request of the Irish Management Institute. Mansholt noted there are far too many Catholics in Ireland ... 100,000 Irish Catholic heads are expected to roll as a result of the Mansholt axe.'[27]

Patrick Cogan, a former TD, was also on hand to offer advice to Jack

Lynch. He suggested that an Irish solution to an Irish problem was required, a commission of inquiry, as '2 things have got to be avoided: 1. The Catholic Church must not appear to overrule the state. 2. The Catholic Church must not appear to be defeated.' As had been the case for so long in Ireland it was, suggested Cogan, preferable that 'these questions be discussed in a responsible way in private than that they should be kicked about in the mass media'.[28]

But this was not an issue that could be kept behind closed doors and the traditional approach was simply no longer an option. Brendan Walsh, chairman of the Irish Family Planning Rights Association, was adamant that 'at present the State does not attempt to control sexual relations between consenting adults over 17. In view of this fact, it would be inconsistent to attempt to control the use of contraceptives in sexual relations between consenting adults'.[29] The most powerful appeal for change, as recorded in the National Archives, came from an Irish father in London who had fourteen children: 'I am not going to bore you with the grim details of the 14 members of the Cadden family, the hunger, misery, poverty, suffering, or the premature death of a fine woman.'[30]

The ethics of contraception use was also discussed at Dublin's Catholic maternity hospitals; 'ethic committees' were established at the Rotunda hospital 'in order to satisfy all staff consciences'. At the same hospital in 1967 a clinical report detailed the case history of an expectant mother with a history of TB, on her twenty-first pregnancy: 'her twelve living children were all undernourished'. Five of the children had TB, one had a cardiac complaint and the family was beset by chronic financial difficulties.[31] During the 1970s there were tensions between staff and numerous complaints and interventions by senior Church figures over the ethics of performing sterilisations at Holles Street hospital. According to Tony Farmar, in practice the operation of the ethics committee 'largely amounted to the theologian being presented with issues for his response'.[32]

But discussion of the morality of contraceptives was not confined to Catholics. The Synod of the Presbyterian Church in Dublin passed a resolution in March 1971 arguing the case for the freedom to use contraceptives in marriage, though it did not approve of them being 'a means of avoiding parenthood altogether for purely selfish ends'.[33] The Synod of the Dublin District of the Methodist Church insisted the following month that 'liberty of conscience is being infringed by the present laws', while the Protestant Mothers Union of Ireland supported change, as did the Quakers.[34]

Opinion polls, which were a relatively new phenomenon in Irish life, were being put to use in an attempt to gauge the public mood on this issue. *This Week* published the results of an opinion poll on contraception in June 1971 after polling 1,600 people: 34 per cent were in favour of the sale of contraceptives by law, 63 per cent were against and 3 per cent had no opinion. In terms of the breakdown, 58 per cent of men in the 16–24 year age bracket were in favour, compared to only 41 per cent of women in that age group, while of those aged over 55, 30 per cent of men and only 18 per cent of women were in favour. In terms of class, 32 per cent of the working-class males polled were in favour, whereas 58 per cent of middle-class men were. The corresponding figure for working-class women was 20 per cent, while 42 per cent of middle-class women were in favour. *This Week* asserted that 'the Poll must surely show that Ireland is set for a change some time in the future in its moral laws'.[35]

This cleavage in class attitudes is interesting, given that some middle-class proponents of change justified their advocacy on the basis of the undue suffering caused to the working class as a result of large families. This may have been the case, but the parents of those families also expressed a clear opposition to liberalisation. Perhaps housing waiting lists were also a factor in this; in the diocese of Dublin, one woman informed a priest with the Catholic Social Welfare Bureau that, in relation to waiting for housing, 'I gather that as a family of 3 not much priority can be expected'.[36]

John Charles McQuaid and his colleagues spent much of their time in the early 1970s under siege in relation to the contraception issue because it was being discussed with such regularity over the airwaves. In April 1970, Cecil Barrett had written to McQuaid to tell him he had advised Father Michael Browne, who oversaw the Dublin Diocesan Family Planning Service, not to participate in RTÉ's current affairs television programme *Seven Days* on this subject:

> We could not agree to the avoidance of the moral issue or to discussions of the safety of the Pill by medical experts. We would be willing to co-operate in a programme devoted to our own work alone – this will prevent Seven Days saying that we refused their invitation.[37]

Their 'own work alone' included a weekly session on the temperature method of birth control at which 10–12 couples were instructed, but Father Browne expressed a degree of panic in April 1971 that their meetings were 'taxed beyond capacity' and that people in the suburbs wanted advice at local level in order to avoid travelling to the city centre:

Meetings in various places with young married people have helped to confirm what the priests have been saying, viz. that couples who need help to plan their families will not come, and should not be expected to come at considerable inconvenience, to Westland Row. Urgent help is needed locally and the Church must be seen to provide it in accordance with the teaching and support of *Humanae Vitae*. Otherwise it will be said again that we are merely 'laying down the law for people', but not giving the practical help to observe it ...

He also mentioned that they were now up against the 'new fertility clinics' whose 'financial backing is considerable'.[38]

'Shaving and cutting one's nails was also against the natural law'

That was the sort of honest assessment that was not going to reach the television audience for *Seven Days* on RTÉ. In November 1971, there was further bad news for McQuaid on this subject when he received confirmation that some priests were making up their own minds. He was sent a letter from a young couple in Crumlin, engaged to be married, who had attended lectures at the pre-marriage course in the college of industrial relations. The letter-writer's uncle had encouraged them to go; he was essentially, in a move McQuaid would have been proud of, using them as spies, he and his wife being members of the Right to Life and Nazareth Family movements.

A few comments from the lecturer, Father Reynolds, were recorded as follows: 'The Pope has not condemned the use of the Pill' and 'It was up to your own conscience ... Father Reynolds then made his reply by stating that a cardinal had given permission to nuns in the Congo to take the Pill as precaution against being raped, and he then continued to say that if a cardinal could give permission it was good enough for him.' But worse was to follow. They complained to another lecturer, Father Baggott, who asserted that *Humanae Vitae*

was only an opinion of the Pope which he did not agree with. We pointed out that this was against the natural law and Father Baggot then said that shaving and cutting one's nails was also against the natural law and he then went on to give an example of Philip II of Spain refusing to change the direction of a river for the betterment of the community because he considered this to be against the natural law. We then asked him was he intending to express his opinion to the class and he stated that he would give a balance, which in our opinion he had no right to do. We feel that it is a sad reflection in the Catholic city of Dublin that these personal opinions were being put forward at a pre-marriage course in this diocese.[39]

Different perspectives emerged on the significance of McQuaid's final pastoral, *Conscience and Contraception*. Historian and Dominican nun Margaret MacCurtain maintained 'he was too old at that stage even to grasp the significance of what he was issuing – that the subject of contraception had become so uncontainable that this final pastoral is almost lip-service'. John Cooney took a different view, surmising that, were it not for *Humanae Vitae*, McQuaid would have slipped from view already: 'I think the whole passage of *Humanae Vitae* in 1968 gives him a new lease of life. He thinks that Pope Paul VI is beginning to see sense again and that the Council's aberrations are now a thing of the past and that we can go back to the real uniformity. He's becoming a hard-hitter again – he stops any attempts by Mary Robinson, John Horgan and Trevor West in the Senate from mobilising Jack Lynch to bring in a full contraception bill.' MacCurtain, however, seems to have believed that the game was up at that stage; that a momentum had developed which McQuaid was not in a position to resist: 'But he's overtaken by history. In a sense, we're on the verge of European union ... and the whole tenure of the Commission on the Status of Women, parts one and two, had the effect of bringing Catholic and Protestant women together in a united stand. He was up against too much.'[40]

In her contributions to a Senate debate on the status of women, Mary Robinson acknowledged that contraception was regarded as 'a knotty issue ... I am also, I hope, trying to put an end to this bogey in relation to family planning – that there is a case before the courts [the McGee case – see below] so therefore we cannot have legislation. This is absolute nonsense, as the Taoiseach, who is a lawyer, will appreciate.'[41]

Noël Browne suggested in the same debate that

one of the commonest problems of the anxious mother in my working-class practice is the fear of the next pregnancy. Recently, in Britain, where there is family planning, a third of the children born were unplanned and half of that one-third were unwanted. Personally, I would put the figure of unwanted children in Ireland very much higher than that. The women fail, first of all, to make up their minds as to the role they wish to follow as women. A woman can follow any career she wishes but once a mother has a child she has a role. There is no other role more important.

This was a reaction to Mary Robinson's criticism that there was an undue emphasis on married women, and her highlighting of the need for day care. Browne was unimpressed, suggesting the preoccupation with the 'right to work' was as unhelpful as a preoccupation with 'women in the home'. Acknowledging that he sounded old-fashioned, he believed the role of the mother was greatly undervalued in terms of the 'process of personality formation and the process of the psycho-sexual development of the individual', and the obsession with day care was born of ignorance: 'Misunderstanding of the role of the mother to her children if she thinks that having a baby is just like a cow dropping a calf in a field and going away and leaving it for somebody else to rear.'[42]

Browne had initiated a debate in the Labour Party about contraception and some had wanted him expelled for that reason; most of the party wanted nothing to do with it and refused to allow him and Dr John O'Connell to introduce a family planning bill. It remained a constant source of worry within the party, so many members were relieved when Browne established the Socialist Labour Party as an alternative.[43] John Horgan suggests it was an embarrassment that the issue of family planning in Ireland 'in so far as it is affected by law ... is affected by the criminal law'.[44]

This was something Mary Robinson also felt strongly about; the bill she proposed in 1973 was a revised version of the 1971 bill and, significantly, this time it would be the Minister for Health rather than Justice who would be responsible for the application of the terms of the future law. There was also an importance attached to getting the bill debated in parliament, but between its first and second reading (November 1973 and February 1974) a decision of the Supreme Court prompted a change in the law.

Mary McGee, a Catholic 27-year-old mother of four with a history of toxaemia in pregnancy (a potentially fatal complication that can get worse with each ensuing pregnancy), took a legal challenge to the 1935 Act after her contraceptives, ordered from abroad, were seized by Customs. She argued, ultimately successfully, that the 1935 Act violated her right to marital privacy. Her case was supported by the Irish Family Planning Association, with Mary Robinson acting as counsel. After her case was rejected by the High

Court, the Supreme Court held on appeal that Mrs McGee had a right to marital privacy under the constitution; the judgment, delivered by Mr Justice Brian Walsh, also cited a number of American decisions.

Meanwhile, in the Senate, Mary Robinson had warned of the inappropriateness of the judiciary taking over the role of legislators: 'we must not abdicate to the judiciary the function of gradually finding our laws unconstitutional and therefore, in effect, legislating'.[45] After the ruling, Robinson attempted to introduce a private members bill to legislate for the post-McGee case situation, but the government rejected this. Perhaps she was also occasionally wary of being seen as too strident and of neglecting her 'home duties'. In August 1973 Robinson dropped a note to the Taoiseach, Liam Cosgrave, explaining why she had to rush from a debate on the status of Irish women: 'I regret very much that I have had to leave the debate at this stage and I hope you will excuse my absence. Unfortunately I have a long-standing arrangement to be hostess at a dinner involving a member of the diplomatic corps among others and my husband would undoubtedly divorce me if I left him on his own.'[46]

'I come from a part of the country where we have our own natural family planning methods and they have worked reasonably well up to now. I have 8 children ...'

When Fine Gael and Labour had formed its coalition government in 1973 to replace the Fianna Fáil government, it had taken no interest in tackling the contraceptive issue. In correspondence with one priest in Dublin, Taoiseach Liam Cosgrave mentioned the government had given it 'no consideration'. The priest in question maintained that, not only was Ireland in a unique position to withstand the propaganda of the pressure groups, but that 'this country could do with a population explosion. Thomas Davis the Patriot, and incidentally Protestant, is on record that Ireland could support 25,000,000 people. With our improved social conditions, what could that figure stand at today?'[47]

Such delusion, and the continual shelving of the issue at government level, was shattered by the decision of the Supreme Court in relation to McGee's constitutional challenge. The coalition, in power until 1977, was thus the first government that had to confront the issue of legislating for family planning and contraception. Proposed legislation in 1974, the Control of Importation, Sale and Manufacture of Contraceptive Bill 1974, was the result, during the vote on which Cosgrave voted against his own government, along with six of his colleagues, and the bill was defeated by 75 votes to 61.

In terms of the government's struggle with legislation, the most interesting correspondence was between the office of the Attorney General, Declan Costello (son of John A. Costello), and the Department of Justice, which suggested Costello and the civil servants in his office were adopting a very cautious and conservative stance. According to a memorandum prepared for the government on the issue, the Attorney General suggested 'the inclusion of a provision making it unlawful for any unmarried person, other than certain exempted persons, to be in possession of a contraceptive'. The response from the Department of Justice, headed by Patrick Cooney, was that 'such a provision would involve an excessive intrusion into privacy. It will not be an offence for an unmarried person to accept (otherwise than by purchase) a contraceptive. Under the existing law possession of a contraceptive is not an offence.'

Cooney presented another memorandum on the subject, suggesting the proposed legislation to 'allow certain categories of persons, namely pharmacists' to import contraceptives under licence, would enable married people to have 'reasonable availability of contraceptives'. But there would be no personal right to importation – his interpretation of the McGee case was that it did not cover individual importation. He also noted 'there will be no legal right of personal importation for tourists, travellers, etc., from abroad. Assuming reasonable attempts will be made to enforce the proposed prohibition of general importation, embarrassment may arise in relation to visitors bringing in contraceptives in their personal luggage.' He also argued that the proposed bill would please Northern Protestants, and would 'liberalise our laws sufficiently ... in relation to the laws to apply in a future united Ireland', but that 'it would clearly be impossible to secure any political support for a move to legalise abortion'.

The severity of Costello's (or his civil servants') proposals for inclusion in the bill is striking. He wanted, for example, the following to be inserted:

A member of the Garda Siochana who has reasonable grounds for suspecting that a person who is in possession of a contraceptive has committed or is committing an offence under this Act, may require the person to state if he is married, and in case that he states that he is married, the place where and the date on which the marriage took place. A person

... who refuses to comply ... or who, in purported compliance with the requirements, gives any information which he knows to be false in a material particular shall be guilty of an offence and shall be liable on summary conviction to a fine.

The Minister for Justice was unimpressed:

The Minister is against the inclusion of such a provision. It is, of itself, insufficient to enable a charge to be proved as there would still be the need to prove purchase of the contraceptive and the Gardaí could very rarely do that. Moreover, the provision, as far as it goes, could perhaps be criticised as (a) an unjustified invasion of privacy and (b) an attempt to transfer the onus of proof, which appears to be prohibited by the European Convention on Human Rights, and also an attempt to make a person who has contraceptives incriminate himself, contrary to the UN Universal Declaration of Human Rights ... even if possession were to be made an offence, this would not significantly reduce the problem of proof, since a power of search would normally be necessary to enable the Gardai to prove possession.[48]

Alongside cross-party demonstrations of extreme conservatism in relation to contraception – Erskine Childers of Fianna Fáil wondered if the Labour Party would be prepared to support a measure 'whereby a married couple could buy twelve condoms per month from a chemist' – public debate on the subject was also littered with patronising and often farcical male interventions. One such contributor, Senator Michael O'Toole, asserted: 'I come from a part of the country where we have our own natural family planning methods and they have worked reasonably well up to now. I have 8 children – I know something about the subject.'[49]

> *'The man behind the counter would cheerfully remark,*
> *"It's your time again" or "safe for another month anyway"'*

In the midst of the legislative problems, some of the surveys conducted would suggest that opinion on greater access to contraceptives remained divided in the mid 1970s. Analysis done by Irish Marketing Surveys for *Hibernia* magazine in February 1974 found that 54 per cent of those surveyed were in

favour of contraceptives being sold in chemists, while 43 per cent opposed
(of those in favour, 70 per cent were in the 16–24 age bracket). In the same
year, 32 per cent of new clients at the Merrion Square family planning clinic
were single.

Two years later, Emer Philbin Bowman completed an MA dissertation
in psychology at Trinity College which looked at the sexual behaviour and
contraceptive practice of a sample of single Irish women, based on fieldwork
carried out from January to June 1974. Placing her research findings in an
international context, Bowman found that 47 per cent of new patients at
the Merrion Square clinic were unmarried, and 19 per cent were not planning to get married. Bowman concluded that, unlike the situation in Britain
and the United States, fewer of the Irish had sex; those who were sexually
active started later, and displayed more independence because 'they have
had to go further in rejecting the values and mindset of the society than
would be necessary in a more permissive culture'.[50]

But in small rural towns it was much more difficult to protect privacy.
Nell McCafferty refers to the *Sunday World*:

> By the simple means of filling in a cut-out coupon and sending it to
> the recommended address, readers could obtain by return post as many
> condoms as they wished, no questions asked about age or marital status.
> It was entirely illegal but the government of the day turned a grate-
> fully blind eye. It was not always successful, because other moral police
> officers were at work in the person of the village postmistress or post-
> master. The package would sometimes arrive steamed open, clumsily
> resealed and empty, no questions asked, no response expected. It is diffi-
> cult in the confined closely-knit communities of rural Ireland to sustain
> an absolutely private life. A Kerry woman's explanation of her 19-year-
> old daughter's inhibitions about nature's bodily functions was illuminat-
> ing. When the daughter used to go to the crossroads store for sanitary
> towels the man behind the counter would cheerfully remark, 'It's your
> time again' or 'safe for another month anyway'.[51]

In 1976, the Supreme Court overruled the Censorship of Publications
Board, declaring that the Irish Family Planning Association's book *Family
Planning* (1971) should not be banned because it was neither indecent nor
obscene, the first such challenge brought under the censorship legislation in
fifty years. The two family planning clinics in Dublin saw 25,000 patients in

1978, the year before Minister for Health Charles Haughey's 1979 Family Planning Act, which made contraception available to married couples only if they had a prescription from their doctor. Haughey's legislation to give effect to the Supreme Court decision in the McGee case was, in his own words, not designed to open the 'floodgates', but sought to 'provide an Irish solution to an Irish problem. I have not regarded it as necessary that we should conform to the position obtaining in any other country.'[52]

Although Haughey had demonstrated a fawning deference to McQuaid in the past,[53] it is probably unfair to depict him as having been in the pocket of the Bishops when it came to the 1979 legislation. His solution, according to Gene Kerrigan, was 'not simply the hypocrisy of a politician wary of the Bishops. It was a genuine attempt to accommodate the old values and the new, an impossible task, breeding a piece of legislation ignored in practice and condemned on all sides.'[54]

The debate around the impending legislation in the spring of 1979 often revealed a frustration that, at a time when an estimated 70,000 people were using the nine family planning clinics nationwide, the Irish body politic was devoting far too much attention to this issue at the expense of others. Labour Party TD Eileen Desmond lamented that other issues such as hunger, poverty, violence and drunkenness were being relegated: 'Our Irish conscience has been conditioned to agonise most about sex and sex-related matters. Would that we felt so strongly about the other issues I have mentioned and that those who helped form our conscience did as good a job in those areas.' Her younger colleague, Ruairi Quinn, invoked the ghost of the Minister for Education who had introduced free secondary education in 1967: 'If Donogh O'Malley were alive today and if he were Minister for Health would we be debating this nonsense? Would we be talking here about *bona fide* family planning and all the other compromise phrases and bits and pieces to accommodate this group and that group?'

John Kelly, a Dublin Fine Gael TD, and the finest orator in the Dáil, was eloquently withering: 'I think it fantastic and something that one would find only in a country inhabited by Leprechauns whom life had spared from most of the world's decisions the rest of the world has had to face that a handful of ageing men could sit around here talking about moral decisions that would be right or wrong depending on whether something was right or wrong with a urine dipstick.'[55]

Some women sought to retain the focus on themselves and their health. In the spring of 1979 a women's health seminar was organised at a Dublin hotel by the Contraception Action Programme. One of the speakers was Angela Philips, co-editor of the British edition of *Our Bodies, Ourselves*, a groundbreaking book about women's health and sexuality, originally produced in 1973 by the Boston Women's Health Book Collective. 'She commented that men had long considered it perfectly normal that they should conquer nature with aircraft, electricity and telephones but women's attempts to control their fertility were regarded as "unnatural".'[56]

'Wait until Monday'

The restrictiveness of the new family planning act infuriated many of those at the forefront of the Irish family planning movement, including Andrew Rynne, who became well known as Ireland's first vasectomy doctor, and even better known after he was shot (but not seriously wounded) by a disgruntled vasectomy client in 1990. He had trained as a doctor in Canada in the late 1960s, where he performed his first vasectomies ('GPs were expected to be able to do that kind of thing there') but he returned to Ireland in 1974, when he began to conduct vasectomies at the IFPA's premises in Dublin, and later at the Synge Street family planning clinic. The average age of men who underwent the operation was 34.9, with an average of 3.8 children.

After he had performed 631 such procedures Rynne was asked by the *Irish Medical Journal* to write a paper on his experiences. Following its publication, the *Sunday World* seized on the article, announcing on its front page 'IRISH DOCTOR STERILISES 631 MEN IN DUBLIN CLINIC'. Rynne's father was furious with his son and asked the local parish priest to visit him; when he arrived the two men 'got stuck into a bottle of whiskey ... but it was a no win situation and both of us knew it'. They agreed to differ and 'in the fullness of time, everybody settled down, including my father', though another priest called to intimidate Rynne with 'his version of gratuitous moral guidance' but received short shrift. He went on to perform about 25,000 vasectomies.[57]

In the midst of all this drama, Rynne's reaction to the 1979 act was one of incredulity:

A doctor's prescription, or so I was always led to believe, was for serious medicines like antibiotics, addictive sedatives and analgesics like opiates and morphine and things that in the public interest need to be controlled.

But condoms are not medicines or drugs, they are made from inert latex, so what are they doing on a doctor's prescription? It was clear from the very beginning that this proposed new legislation was being foisted onto us in an awkward attempt to 'medicalise' our national neurosis about things sexual and to let the government off the hook.[58]

In 1982, Rynne got 260 doctors to sign a petition against the new legislation and, in an attempt to embarrass the government, deliberately sold contraceptives directly from his surgery over a weekend, in contravention of the 1979 legislation, on the grounds that his patient could not get access to pharmacies because they were closed. In June 1983, Rynne was fined £300 at the Naas district court; at the hearing Mr Justice Frank Roe suggested that if the pharmacies were closed at the weekend, those in the mood for sex should show some restraint and 'wait until Monday'.[59]

Whatever the conflicting emotions being expressed about the 1979 legislation, some argued that the debate on contraception (and later abortion) was 'the nearest this country has ever got to a long overdue discussion of sexuality and these subjects are merely symptoms of a very narrow interpretation of what sexuality is really about'.[60] John Kelly, the TD mentioned above, perceptively warned in 1983 that those campaigning to save the soul of traditional Catholic Ireland would unwittingly create a large secular body of opinion that would ultimately succeed in rejecting the idea that Church and state went hand in hand. What developed as a backlash to the divisive campaigns of the 1980s, and the failure of politicians to resist pressure groups, was a sufficiently robust resistance to the idea that Catholic teaching in relation to sexual mores could exist in abstraction from the reality of people's lives.

Politicians gradually came to reject, in the words of Barry Desmond, Minister for Health in the 1982–7 Fine Gael/Labour coalition government, the idea that 'the common good' was the same as 'the Catholic good'. It was Desmond who initiated a further liberalisation of the law in 1985, as a result of which individuals no longer had to be married to obtain contraception and they could purchase them without prescription from certain named outlets if they were over the age of 18. Students' unions demanded more availability, but had to wait until the 1990s. During the presidential election in 1990, a poster of Mary Robinson was placed defiantly above an illegal condom machine in University College Dublin. The following year the Virgin Megastore in Dublin city was fined £400 for selling condoms.

It appealed but the appeal judge increased the fine to £500, observing that he was letting Virgin off lightly. As the law stood, each further condom sale could lead to a £5,000 fine, with an additional fine of £250 for every day condoms remained on sale. In 1992, the sale of condoms was deregulated and health boards were legally obliged to provide family planning services.

By now there were two family planning clinics in Limerick, one each in Cork, Tralee, Navan, Galway and Wexford, and seven in the Dublin area. Irish liberals were entitled to allow themselves a mischievous smile when in 1996 Irish EU Commissioner Padraig Flynn – a former minister whose attack on Mary Robinson's 'new interest in her family, being a mother and all that kind of thing' had badly backfired during the 1990 presidential election campaign – seemed to have transformed into a 'new man' as Social Affairs Commissioner, and sent out 300,000 Valentine's Day cards with condoms inside to promote a safe sex message.[61] His 1990 verbal assault on Robinson made him one of the prime targets of satirists, particularly those on RTÉ radio's *Scrap Saturday* show, whose scriptwriters caricatured him as a Stone Age chauvinist, or 'Flynnstone'.

'A deep fault line'

By the end of the twentieth century, the availability of condoms did little to prevent a dramatic rise in sexually transmitted diseases, and this rise continued into the twenty-first century. In 2001, 9,703 sexually transmitted infections were notified. In 2002 the figure rose to 10,471. There was a further 5 per cent increase between 2002 and 2003. The dramatic increases had been evident since the mid 1990s – the figures jumped by 157 per cent between 1994 and 2002, and by 370 per cent between 1989 and 2002. In 2004, the Crisis Pregnancy Agency (CPA) published research revealing that a quarter of 18 to 25-year-olds did not always use contraception when they had sex. According to another study carried out for the CPA, 58 per cent of men and 38 per cent of women agreed that drinking alcohol had contributed to them having sex, and 45 per cent of men and 26 per cent of women agreed that drink had resulted in them having sex without contraception. Nor, it seems, was this solely about the reckless abandonment of youth: the incidence of STIs among the over 50s also increased, according to data collated by the Well Woman Centre.[62]

But wider availability of contraception did impact on family size: in the 1960s and 1970s, the average rate was consistently above 3 children; it declined quickly during the 1980s and hit a low of 1.85 in 1995, but began to rise in parallel with economic growth. But the traditional family unit continued to change: over 31 per cent of new births in 2003 were outside of marriage, compared to 19 per cent in 1993 and 2 per cent in the 1960s. Figures from the Central Statistics Office for 2003 reveal that Ireland had a fertility rate of 1.98 children per woman, compared to 1.89 for France, 1.76 for Denmark and Finland and 1.18 for the Czech Republic. Ireland still had the highest fertility rate in the EU, and was slightly behind the US, but the real driving force seems to have been the then-booming economy.[63] The birth rate in Ireland in 2007 was 1.99 children per woman, compared to France at 1.90, Sweden at 1.75, Germany at 1.37, Spain 1.32, the UK 1.74 and the US 2.09.

Sociologist Betty Hilliard, who interviewed mothers of infant children in a working-class housing estate in Cork in 1975, returned to the same mothers in 2000. She observed how much of the fear and ignorance associated with sex and contraception – some of the women who were aware of the Pill couldn't get access to it even if they had wanted to; one believed 'one would only get pregnant if one willed the pregnancy' – was replaced by some with an anger about the ignorance they had endured and a sense of betrayal about some clerical sex scandals because many of the women had defended and promoted the Church's teaching. On O'Connell bridge in 1992, vendors were selling t-shirts with Bishop Eamon Casey's face and the message 'Wear a Condom Just in Casey', after the revelation that he had fathered a child with his lover Annie Murphy (see below). But for many, it was no laughing matter. One of the women interviewed by Hilliard recalled her reaction to the Casey revelations and how they had undermined her position with her daughter as a result:

> I will never forget, until the day I die, the Bishop Casey saga. I was ironing out there and I thought I heard something on the radio. I came in and said to my husband I'm sure Bishop Casey is resigning, he must not be well and I continued with the ironing and lunch. Later on that night it came on again. The following day anyway, they talk about bereavement and things but shock was the initial thing. I can't describe to you what it did to me inside, it was like there was a hole there that could never be filled. The shock I got, personally, that day. The more I thought about it and the things that followed I can say it damaged my whole life. This was

a great opportunity for [her daughter] to have a go at me so she came in
to see me. Sit down there and we'll have a cup of coffee and she draws a
deep breath, well Mam she said what have you to say for yourself now?[64]

Along with an increasingly critical assessment of the Catholic Church's
stance on contraception, information that came to light in 1998 about the
activities of Dr Michael Neary raised many questions about the medical profession and the issues that some obstetricians had about women and their
fertility, the failure of hospital consultants to challenge their colleagues
about disturbing practices, and the appropriateness of doctors policing
themselves. Neary was a consultant gynaecologist-obstetrician appointed in
1974 to Our Lady of Lourdes hospital in Drogheda, where he worked for
over twenty years. He had studied medicine at University College Galway
and worked in a number of hospitals in the UK. Inspections of the maternity unit at the hospital in Drogheda by three different professional bodies
over several years did not uncover the high level of hysterectomies being
performed at the unit by Neary.

In 2003, Neary was struck off the medical register after he was found
guilty of professional misconduct over the unnecessary removal of the
wombs of ten women at the hospital. An inquiry found that of 188 patients
who underwent a hysterectomy within six weeks of giving birth at the maternity unit between 1974 and 1998, some 129 of them had operations carried
out by Dr Neary; 'most obstetricians carry out less than 10 in their careers'.[65]
The report of the inquiry, by Judge Maureen Harding Clarke, maintained
that Neary was a doctor 'with a deep fault line' which was recognised early
but never corrected owing to inadequate supervision (including during the
time he spent working in England) and because in Drogheda he had worked
in a unit 'which lacked leadership, peer review, audit and critical capacity'.

Neary, the report found, had a heightened sense of danger and a morbidity to haemorrhage when performing operations: 'It is highly probable
that fear of losing a patient approached phobic dimensions and led him to
practise defensive medicine in one of its most extreme forms and probably
explains why, from an early stage in his career, he expressed rather frequently
to patients that the hysterectomy had saved your life.'[66] Neary's confidence
in his own ability was profoundly misplaced; and his actions and the failure
to stop them highlighted the arrogance of some members of the medical
profession when it came to women and their fertility.

'A foul basis on which to attempt to construct the unity of our people'

The situation in Northern Ireland with regard to family planning was very different, and it is interesting that some of the debate in the Republic in the early 1970s had been prefaced by remarks about the need for laws that could accommodate those of different religions. This was an argument summarily dismissed by Archbishop McQuaid in his communications to the priests of his diocese in March 1971, when he maintained that

> Hitherto, we have endeavoured to legislate according to the established beliefs and standards of our own people. One can conceive no worse fate for Ireland than that it should, by the legislation of our elected representatives, be now made to conform to the patterns of sexual conduct in other countries. It is also being suggested that such uniformity of sexual outlook and practice can, in some obscure way, assist the reunification of our country. One must know little of the Northern People, if one can fail to realise the indignant ridicule with which good Northern people would treat such an argument. It would indeed be a foul basis on which to attempt to construct the unity of our people.[67]

Clearly, this was not a view shared by Taoiseach Jack Lynch, given his own contention in the same year that

> in so far as there are constitutional difficulties which are legitimately seen by people to be infringements of their civil rights, then their views are worthy of intensive examination and we should try and accommodate them in our constitution and in our laws. I repeat that now. The constitution of a united Ireland requires to be a document in which no element of Sectarianism, even unconscious or unintended, should occur.[68]

By 1970, the Northern Ireland Family Planning Association (NIFPA) was dealing with 5,000 new patients a year, it being noted in 1972 that 'local authorities are now thoroughly involved'.[69] By 1975 it was estimated that about eighty doctors in Northern Ireland held a family planning certificate.[70] The NIFPA had spent much of the early 1970s seeking recognition and funding and had often expressed frustration with the slowness of some to acknowledge its efforts. The minute book of the executive committee in March 1970, for example, noted that a surgeon in Portadown was willing to perform a vasectomy, but in June of that year 'Dr Patton commented that many GPs, particularly in country areas, were indifferent to, misinformed about or hostile to family planning in general, not just vasectomy. Mrs I. Irwin agreed but had noticed a marked improvement in the Dungannon area, where formerly hostile GPs were now sending patients to the FPC.'[71]

In May 1973, the chairwoman of the NIFPA, Denise Fulton, wrote to junior minister for Northern Ireland, William Van Straubenzee, arguing that, as in the mainland UK, where family planning supplies were available on prescription from 1 April 1974, the arguments

apply here to an even greater extent. It is, I think, generally acknowledged that unsatisfactory social conditions have contributed to Northern Ireland's present troubles and the misery caused by unwanted pregnancies, too large families and overburdened mothers has been a factor in these conditions ... with the help of grants from the Ministry of Health and Social Services we have been able in some measure to fill the gap caused by the reluctance of virtually every local health authority in Northern Ireland to take adequate steps in either education or training ... the patients who attend family planning clinics are drawn from all sections of the Northern Ireland population regardless of religion. We have no evidence to suggest that a clear announcement that Northern Ireland was following Gt Britain policy in this vital matter would be greeted by any significant opposition.[72]

The following year the director of the Family Planning Association of Great Britain made it clear that that it would do everything it could to co-operate with its Northern Irish counterparts 'and treat you as, if not one of us, at least our nearest relation'.[73] The absorption of family planning work into the NHS meant that a member of the NIFPA was able to write at the end of 1976: 'the NIFPA is possibly coming to the end of its days now that medical and nursing training is out of our hands. That is as it should be.'[74]

'We Go All the Way'

In his survey of Ireland published in 1969, Alan Bestic stated that there were

24,000 unmarried girls in Dublin and that the city 'was becoming much more tolerant about affairs and mistresses'. He also referred to the activities of 'kerbside crawlers' and the practice of prostitution around Fitzwilliam Square in Dublin, and the 'flagrant prostitution practised in the quays of Cork'.[75] In the early 1970s it became clear that there was a hunger for information about the underworld of Irish sex. Newspapers began to tap into this interest, which ultimately, according to Tom Inglis, led to an 'explosion of sexual discourse' in the media by the 1980s, including more reporting of sex crimes and court proceedings and the growth of an alternative discourse to that dictated by the Catholic Church.[76]

By the middle of the 1970s, the Irish media had 'just discovered the retail value of sleaze. Vice stories were the order of the day and the *Sunday World* was the country's most voracious diner. Its reporters spent many fruitful afternoons making their excuses and leaving a dizzying range of massage parlours, escort agencies and knocking shops.'[77] The newspaper decried and revelled in sleaze, but at the same time managed to expose some of the 'deeply unpleasant men who controlled the prostitution racket'. As Sam Smyth, one of the journalists who was central to this crusade, observed, they worked with the assistance of 'whistle blowers', usually disgruntled customers of brothels nursing grudges.[78] Launched in March 1973, the *Sunday World* thrived on sexual innuendo, was marketed under the slogan 'We Go All the Way' and was notable for its occasionally 'tough and fearless journalism'. It was a commercial success from the outset, with sales of more than 200,000 by December 1973.[79]

'Promiscuity' and 'permissive' were the new buzzwords, as Ireland seemed to undergo a delayed sexual revolution, experiencing in the 1970s what many other nations had reputedly discovered in the 1960s. In 1974, Emer O'Kelly, a young freelance journalist, published her book *The Permissive Society in Ireland*, noting that 'many who think that the whole idea is irrelevant to Ireland will be astonished by the number of case studies here'. She made a plea for a more 'permissive society' to emerge.[80] Those interviewed for her case studies included: a woman who had undergone an abortion; a girl raped by her father who had fled to England where her brothers 'didn't want to know' and who had drifted into prostitution; and a 28-year-old gay man living at home with his parents ('his mother is fond of telling her friends what a devil he is for the women') who, as a teacher, had to be particularly careful ('automatically, they'd think you were going to interfere with the kids'). Other interviewees included: a girl pregnant at 18 in working-class Dublin ('me father gave me a terrible hiding, even though me mother tried to stop him'); a womanising businessman ('for Christ's sake, it's the 1970s, no bird's a blushing rose'); a lesbian, her social life pervaded by 'this attitude of feeling safer on the exclusively gay scene'; and a 'conservative couple' who maintained that 'illegitimacy is not part of our Irish heritage.'[81]

O'Kelly's book was admirable in its frankness and the way it let individuals tell their stories in an honest way. It also exposed a fair share of Catholic guilt on the part of the interviewees and a sense of the stigma and loneliness that came with being in a minority. A psychologist who was interviewed suggested that 'an obsession' with sex was a worldwide phenomenon but that in Ireland there was 'so much leeway to be made up', particularly in the context of sex education, in training for mature relationships and in an overriding need to get rid of fear.

As a priest willing to talk openly about sex, Father Feargal O'Connor was also interviewed and maintained that 'the rejection by society at large of the people who have indulged in what is generally labelled sexual permissiveness is also symptomatic of our inability to create a system of sound values ... to my mind we can really judge the quality of our society by the superficiality of sexual relationships, which are a symptom of the other wrongs that are conveniently forgotten about.'[82]

Writer Michael O'Loughlin, who attended college in Dublin in the 1970s, recalls there was much that was grim, empty and grey about the city at that stage, with little cultural inspiration. But poetry and cinema were booming, 'and there was sex. In retrospect, there was a surprising amount of it about, despite the unheated rooms and the alleged illegality of contraception. Trinity had about 4,500 students, and it was often said that at least 2,000 were on the Pill for medical reasons.' Perhaps it was because of the unheated rooms. There was little multi-culturalism – 'a Spanish au pair girl was considered the height of exoticism'[83] – and there were still many taboos that remained to be broken. When the RTÉ television programme *The Spike* transmitted a nude scene there was something of a furore. In it, actress Madelyn Erskine played the part of a shy girl going to confidence-building classes at a college where an art teacher asks her to pose for the class. She has become more confident, so she agrees. Adding spice to the reaction, it was claimed that 'the founder of the League of Decency, Mr J. B. Murray, suffered a heart attack, attributed to the stress caused by the sight of the naked female body on the television screen. His wife told the papers that the family had tried to stop him watching it but he insisted on doing so. He got very worked up over the nude scene and was phoning the newspapers to complain when he came to grief ...'[84]

'Dublin was ready for the body-rub boom'

When a new current affairs magazine, *Magill*, was launched in 1977, its contributors were determined to shed new light on many previously neglected or unreported aspects of Irish society. It was not long before sex dominated its front page. In April 1978, under the title 'The Sexual Explosion', it revealed the results of a survey conducted by the Market Research Bureau of Ireland, based on interviews with 400 women. It reported that 57 per cent of 18 to 34-year-old women in the Dublin and Dun Laoghaire areas believed that sex outside marriage was permissible in certain circumstances, while 68 per cent of them believed that 'sex outside marriage is now very much more common than five years ago'.[85]

It was estimated that 20,000 people were affected by marriage breakdown and 60,000 were cohabiting without being married. In relation to illegitimate births, the figure cited for 1974 was 2,309, rising to 2,578 in 1976 (this figure did not include pregnant brides), while 2,183 women were estimated to have had an abortion in 1977, a 21 per cent increase on the previous year, and up from 1,400 in 1974 and 600 in 1971 (statistics for the number of abortions were first recorded in Britain in 1970). The journalists analysing the data acknowledged that some of the statistics were crude, but that 'aggregating the 2,578 illegitimate births, the estimated 6,000 pregnant marriages and the 2,183 abortions, there are about 11,000 cases of pregnancy in Ireland each year resulting from pre-marital sexual intercourse'.[86] In 1975 there had been an 8 per cent increase in the incidence of VD in the Eastern Health Board Region over the previous year, with a total of 13,536 cases, of which 13,028 were male and 508 were female, it being estimated that this represented only half the cases in the country. The drug company Schering Ltd estimated that in 1977 there were 60,862 women on the contraceptive pill in Ireland, which, when aggregated with other forms of contraceptive, suggested there were over 100,000 Irish people using some form of contraceptive.

Many in the 'flatlands of Ranelagh, Rathmines and Terenure', it was maintained, were engaging in casual sex, while there were six massage parlours operating in Dublin before the *Sunday World* blew their cover. Some had been started by wealthy immigrants who had seen them operating in Britain and decided 'Dublin was ready for the body-rub boom'. It was observed that 'legally, they operate with impunity ... a lot of the parlours are of course brothels, but the Gardaí seem to have no stomach for employing the tactics used by the RUC in Belfast'. *Magill* was keen to emphasise not only that all these figures represented 'a sexual revolution', but also the casualness that seemed to underline much of it: 'a story associated with a wife-swapping Dublin suburb is of a man cutting his hedge and enquiring of his neighbour how the wife was. The neighbour responded: "Fine, how's mine?" '[87]

But such breeziness and casualness was by no means the norm. In 1978, Rosita Sweetman's book *On Our Backs: Sexual Attitudes in a Changing Ireland* was published. Despite the frankness with which some people were prepared to speak about their preferences, fears and conquests (one male middle-class interviewee suggested women all over the country were 'a bloody good lay ... they're walkovers'),[88] and space being devoted to gay rights activist David Norris, there was much more in it that underlined the sordidness and violence associated with some Irish sexual behaviour, most notably the preponderance of rape, wife-beating and general violence against women, with precious few references to pleasure.[89] Twenty pages were devoted to prostitution and massage parlours, while lesbians were only mentioned in the context of the women's movement. One lesbian reviewer of the book concluded that 'overwhelming evidence is presented of the hopelessness of heterosexual sex ever being healthy, joyous, liberating'.[90]

✝ 'Irishmen all want sex before marriage, but they want to marry virgins'

While some men boasted of the new sexual mobility, young unmarried women remained in fear of pregnancy. The registration of births from 1964 to 1970 show that the number of non-marital births as a proportion of total births remained virtually unchanged, but a steady increase in births outside marriage began in 1970, when 2.6 per cent of all births were to unmarried mothers; that figure had increased to 22.2 per cent by 1995.[91] There was a lingering sexism, if not misogyny, which was very apparent in relation to unmarried women becoming pregnant. In 1979 Maura Richards wrote the novel *Two to Tango*. Published in 1981, it is an angry, cathartic account of being left pregnant and abandoned in Ireland in 1970. Richards noted caustically that 'Irishmen all want sex before marriage, but they want to marry virgins'. The heroine finds herself unmarried, deserted by her lover, clinging desperately to her job and trying to hide: she could have adopted or aborted the baby 'but by keeping it, it is going to be a living proof that I broke the eleventh commandment: Thou shalt not be found out.'

But she was hardly the only one that 'for as long as I could remember the worst thing that could happen to anyone's daughter in Ireland was to have a baby and not be married'. The manner in which women were seen as the problem was blatantly obvious as her sister rounded on her for bringing shock and shame on the family, 'that it was well my parents were dead, because if they weren't they'd die of shame, that her own life was ruined and she'd never recover from the shock – she never mentioned that a baby was to be born, that being pregnant might be frightening, that I might be worried living in the caravan on my own'. The father, who turned out to be married, 'had humiliated me beyond endurance ... how was it that my doctor and this solicitor spoke as if married men making women other than their wives pregnant was an everyday occurrence and as if I was the only fool who didn't understand what was going on all around me?'[92]

Until the introduction of an allowance for unmarried mothers in 1973, there was no state support for women like Maura, who noted that 'The only people I can find to help me are called the Catholic Protection and Rescue Society'.[93] Data by the Federation of Services for Unmarried Parents from the late 1970s indicate that just over 40 per cent of putative fathers responded in a supportive way when initially informed of a pregnancy but fewer than one-third sustained their support during the pregnancy while 6 per cent denied paternity. Twelve per cent of respondents received financial help from the putative fathers through a maintenance order and 15 per cent received voluntary financial support, although 'many women hesitated at attempts to impose this because they might then be required to concede access to the children'.[94]

'They never said what we were to take care of'.

In November 1973, RTÉ Radio broadcast a two-part programme on children in care which highlighted the lack of sex education in residential institutions. Former residents spoke of their fear in relation to sex and their ignorance about the facts of life. One rape victim 'thought the man was going to the toilet', while another former resident commented, 'I'm married but still think I'm doing wrong – I mustn't love too much!' Other contributors to the programmes suggested that a concern existed in the early 1970s about the effect of institutions on the future sexual lives of the residents because in many cases the children were starved of affectionate relationships (and the public 'don't give a damn what goes on behind those walls'), as a result of which some subsequently 'quickly got involved in the sex act'. Some nuns told girls in orphanages in the 1950s to 'take care' but 'they never said what we were to take care of'.

One young woman who spoke, Maria, allowed herself to be interviewed because she said she did not want 'to be party to the shame and secrecy that surrounds the single parent and her child'. When one resident of her orphanage got a present of a teenage doll the girls were mesmerised:

> It was so pretty we just couldn't stop looking. It had bosoms and we were fascinated by these. We hadn't a clue what they were. We took off her clothes to get a better look and then the nuns came in. They went berserk. They grabbed the girl who owned the doll and made one of us hold her legs and the other hold her arms while they beat her black and blue. We were holding her and crying with fright at the same time. We never asked anything about sex after that. Six years later, when I left the place the teenage doll would have been as much of a mystery to me.

Three years later, Maria had her own baby. She gives an interesting insight into why some teenage girls who had grown up in orphanages because of their own illegitimacy themselves became unmarried mothes:

> I knew about sex, but I never thought I would get pregnant. It was just something friendly – something to look forward to. I never heard anything about contraception. If you asked me about pills I'd think you were talking about aspirin. When I was having the baby, it was horrible – all the pain! But I was thinking: Twenty years ago my mother had a daughter – me! Now I'm having a baby and I've no husband either. But things will be different for D [Maria's daughter]. I'll never leave her.

When she discovered she was pregnant, Maria's first impulse was to throw herself down the stairs to kill her baby and hopefully herself, too. 'Then I got

'illegitimacy' → orphanages → 'illegitimacy'

this thought: If I killed it, it would be because of what other people think. Other people don't care about me, but the baby will be mine. Someone just for me.'[95]

In March 1973, a social science student at University College Dublin wrote to the Taoiseach Liam Cosgrave to inform him that there was a need for

> adequate benefits for those mothers who cannot work or feel it is better to be with their children in the home. At present, no benefit is available specifically for unmarried mothers who wish to keep their babies. The figures are revealing: In Ireland approximately 95 per cent of illegitimate babies are given up for adoption whereas in Denmark only 5 per cent are given up. The fact is that unmarried mothers in this country are not given a real choice regarding their child's future and are, in the vast majority of cases, forced to give up their rights to motherhood because of the lack of state aid.[96]

1973

On some levels, by the 1970s there was more of a willingness on the part of the Catholic Church and the medical profession to be less judgmental in their approach to young women and their pregnancies. Dr Peter Birch, the Bishop of Ossory, when interviewed, suggested that ultimately the unmarried mother and her child were 'the product of our society and it is clear that we ourselves, because we have lacked the social, perhaps the moral responsibility, to ensure that the illegitimate children from previous generations have been brought up in suitable environments, that they, lacking any warmth and love as children, become the unmarried mothers of the present day'. In a similar vein, and even more frankly, Dr Declan Meagher, master of the maternity hospital in Holles Street, Dublin, admitted that 'there is an over-representation of girls who have themselves been illegitimate and who have grown up in the emotionally sterile unisexual atmosphere of an institution, and are thrown at an early age into a world of whose complexities and subtleties they have learned little'.[97]

female AND male

feminisms / comments

In this context the introduction of a state allowance for unmarried mothers in 1973 was important in reducing the stigma; it had been a key recommendation of the Commission on the Status of Women and, according to Finola Kennedy, 'In ideological terms the provision of a State allowance for the unmarried mother was like stepping on to a new planet. Henceforth the unmarried mother would be a visible, recognised member of Irish society.' The number of recipients rose from 2,000 mothers in 1974 to over 11,000 in 1985 and 37,215 in 1996.[98]

When *Prejudice and Tolerance in Ireland* was published in 1977, it was confidently asserted that 'the stigma of illegitimacy has been broken', because 98.6 per cent of respondents were in favour of the same treatment for children born out of wedlock as those born to a married couple. Added to this was a practically unanimous rejection of the idea that 'the unmarried mother should pay for their sins', though over 20 per cent indicated they would not welcome unmarried mothers or deserted wives into their homes.[99] Many traditions with regard to Irish illegitimacy (a term not legally abolished until 1987) continued. In his autobiographical novel *Nothing to Say*, published in 1983, Mannix Flynn recalls his unwed sister's pregnancy and the practice of Irish mothers rearing their grandchildren: 'I remember the time she got pregnant. The house was in uproar; the shame of it, the pain of it and what in the name of Jaysus are we going to do about it? My mother kept the child and reared it.'[100]

100,000 Welcomes

'Where do you have it? Do you have it in a car?'

In the 1970s there was also a growing acknowledgement of the issue of marriage breakdown, though it was still difficult for women to leave their marriages, and divorce was not even remotely on the horizon. Some women who sought to have their marriages annulled were humiliated in what was another men's club, the marriage tribunal. One woman who married at the age of 18 was abandoned by her husband and sought an annulment in the late 1970s, recounted to journalist Michael Farrell how she was interviewed by five priests, who also interviewed her mother and contacted witnesses including her doctor and former teachers: 'You had intercourse with your husband before you were married; how many other people did you have intercourse with before that? When was the first time you had intercourse? Are you going with someone now? Do you have intercourse with him? Where do you have it? Do you have it in a car?'

The woman in question eventually got the annulment seven years after she first applied for it and then received a bill from the tribunal for her trouble. Subsequently, the formal 'hearings' before five priests were done away with. From 1977 to 1984, 10,000 people were involved in applications to the Catholic marriage tribunals, but the success rate was not high, with only about 500 decrees of nullity issued. In 1984, over 600 couples a year were still lodging applications.[101]

Family law and the law relating to sexual offences still discriminated against women, 'relics of a system of law which viewed women in terms of property'.[102] A woman was still regarded in Irish law as her husband's 'chattel', his 'to the extent that he can sue for damages any man with whom she has sexual intercourse'. In one such case in 1972, a husband was awarded £12,000 'despite evidence of his own promiscuity'. Stanley Roche, the director of Roche's Stores, one of the country's best-known chain stores, began an affair with a decorating consultant, Heide Braun, after he had separated from his wife. Braun's husband, Werner Braun, learned of the affair and sued Roche in the High Court under the law of 'criminal conversation', which (until 1981) gave a man the right to take action against another man for having sexual intercourse with his wife.

Braun alleged that the 'acts' between his wife and Roche took place over a period of seven months between 1971 and 1972 at numerous locations; indeed, 'the evidence given during the court case revealed a group of people who were impressively in touch with the sexual side of their personalities'. In her evidence, Heide Braun estimated that her husband had committed adultery with 'approximately five' women, and that she had even been 'present in the room when my husband committed adultery'. For his part, Roche maintained, 'I am not sorry or ashamed.' Justice Butler informed the members of the jury, 'In this country a wife was regarded as a chattel, just as a thoroughbred mare or cow' and that they should be concerned 'merely with compensating Werner for the value of the loss of his wife and the damages to his feelings'. Roche and Braun subsequently married and lived together until his death in 2008.[103]

A man was also entitled to sue any person who gave his wife refuge 'and who thereby makes it possible for her to absent herself from the matrimonial home'. In relation to rape, 'the husband cannot be guilty of a rape committed by himself upon his lawful wife for by their mutual matrimonial consent and contract the wife hath given up herself in this kind unto her husband which she cannot retract'. In the 1950s, one judge explained, 'If the wife is adamant in her refusal the husband may choose between letting the wife's will prevail, thereby wrecking the marriage, and acting without her consent. It would be intolerable if he were to be conditioned in the course of action by the threat of criminal proceedings ... it is indeed permissible to wish some gentle violence had been employed.' The law of evidence in the context of rape also allowed evidence to be adduced concerning the sexual history of the prosecutrix.[104]

'More interested in avoiding pregnancy than achieving orgasm'

not e.g. Vatican 2

early 1970s

By the early 1970s the Irish women's movement had placed the issue of women and sexuality in the public realm but still had to fight hard to change minds and the law. Those who became involved in these battles have been identified as 'second-wave' feminists. They were not united or coherent in their campaigning and the relatively speedy rise and demise of the Irish Women's Liberation Movement (IWLM) was partly because it developed, in Linda Connolly's words, in an 'erratic, disorganised and chaotic fashion in 1970–72',[105] but also because of the emergence of ideological debates and tensions within Irish feminism during the 1970s. Derry socialist and feminist Nell McCafferty, for example, described herself as giving off the whiff of 'whiskey and petrol fumes' in contrast to *Irish Press* journalist Mary Kenny, who smelt of 'champagne and perfume'.[106]

None the less, the extent to which these women succeeded in bringing to the fore issues that had been considered private and taboo is striking, and they played a crucial role in informing and politicising a generation of women who achieved much in terms of changing both attitudes and the law, though innovation came more slowly than they would have wished. An ad hoc committee formed in 1968 from such diverse organisations as the Association of Business and Professional Women and the National Association of Widows had to wait a year for the government's response to its demands for a commission on the status of women.[107] In November 1969, Taoiseach Jack Lynch announced the establishment of such a commission at the annual dinner of the Soroptimists' Club in Cork. On 4 April 1970, the terms of reference of the commission were published. It was required to: 'Examine and report on the status of women in Irish society, to make recommendations on the steps necessary to ensure the participation of women on equal terms and conditions with men in the political, social and cultural and economic life of the country, and to indicate the implications generally – including the estimated cost – of such recommendations.'

religions?

The actual report was published in 1972, 'and its moderate tone made it widely acceptable'.[108] It contained forty-nine recommendations, of which seventeen related to equal pay and women's working conditions. It outlined the need for training facilities, an end to sex discrimination in employment and the provision of twelve weeks' maternity leave. Inequities that existed for women under the social welfare system, the law, taxation and the educational system were also highlighted, while women in political life, their right to sit on juries, and family planning were also covered. To oversee the commission's findings, the Council for the Status of Women (CSW) was established, which became an umbrella group for over thirty organisations. Eventually, two statutory bodies grew out of the council: the Women's Representative Committee in 1974 and the Employment Equality Agency in 1977.

In tandem with the commission's deliberations, the IWLM 'began over cups of coffee' in Bewley's café on Westmoreland Street, Dublin, and included in its ranks journalists, Labour Party activists, teachers, broadcasters, writers and other professionals who would often also meet at Gaj's restaurant in Baggot Street, owned by Margaret Gaj, a Scottish feminist.[109] There was disagreement from the outset as to how liberation could or should be achieved by this combination of left-wing activists and middle-class women, though they agreed an outline of their demands, published as the pamphlet *Chains or Change?* in 1971. The key changes they demanded were: equal pay; equality before the law; equality in education; justice for deserted wives, unmarried mothers and widows; and one family, one house. According to Nell McCafferty, 'It is a measure of our utter innocence that we did not include divorce. It just did not occur to us that marriage could or should be legally terminated.'[110]

In the same year, the IWLM was offered a slot on RTÉ's *The Late Late Show* to publicise its aims, though when the audience joined in, according to June Levine, 'the whole strategy of the IWLM fell apart'. The intention had been to present itself as a moderate group, but the anger mounted, a slanging match ensued, the women passionately vented their grievances and the publicity garnered was massive. A number of events were then organised, including the picketing of the residence of the Archbishop of Dublin, John Charles McQuaid, in protest at the Catholic Church's continued opposition to contraception, and a public meeting at the Mansion House, attended by 1,000 people. A trip to Belfast on World Communications Day in May 1971 to buy contraceptives in defiance of the Criminal Law Amendment Act on what became known as the 'Condom Train' attracted considerable controversy. According to McCafferty, the IWLM was 'more interested in avoiding pregnancy than achieving orgasm'.[111] A picket at the General Post

Office over the paying of children's allowances to fathers was also organised, as was a picket of the Four Courts to protest against women not being included in juries, and a picket of Leinster House when Mary Robinson's family planning bill failed to get a reading in the Senate in 1971.

Divisions within the IWLM were also apparent from the early stages due to disagreement as to what constituted issues that affected women. As Levine recalled, 'The Forcible Entry and Occupation Bill of 1971 distracted the attention of many of the women from purely feminist issues and emphasised the divergence between socialists and other members of the group. The socialists argued that women were the primary victims of the Bill, which was directed against the homeless.'[112]

After the initial enthusiasm, these divisions ensured the movement became fractured; as pointed out by Pat Brennan, 'a mass movement cannot be built on euphoria and then restructured into a highly autocratic organisation'. Brennan depicted the movement as one that had been riven by conflict, with an inability to develop operational organisational structures.[113]

But neither had its efforts been in vain. One group that emerged from the IWLM was Action Information Motivation (AIM). Formed by Nuala Fennell and others, it was instrumental in achieving the passing of the Social Welfare Act of 1974 through which payment of the children's allowance was transferred from fathers to mothers, the Maintenance Orders Act of 1974, and the Family Law Act of 1976 which gave protective directives for non-maintained families. The Save the Equal Pay Act Committee was another group that exerted considerable pressure, in order to persuade the government to enforce the Anti-Discrimination Pay Act of 1974. In relation to all-male juries, in 1976 judgment was delivered in favour of Máirín de Burca, who had challenged the constitutionality of the 1927 Juries Act (under which women were not obliged to serve on juries), maintaining it discriminated against women on grounds of sex and property. One of the judges asserted that all-male juries 'fall short of minimum constitutional standards'.[114]

'Upset the biological balance of a man and then claim they were raped'

Many in the women's movement in the 1970s also focused on the issues of marital breakdown and separation, rape and violence against women.

Women's Aid was an offshoot of AIM which opened its first home for battered wives in 1974; within its first year of existence, as pointed out by Susan
McKay, the Women's Aid Refuge had sheltered 117 women and children in a
four-bedroomed house.[115] Another group that emerged was the Committee
Against Rape (CAR) and one of its first actions was to object to the exclusion of women from the jury that was to try a man for the rape and murder
of a young Mayo woman. It had been argued that the facts in the case were
too emotionally disturbing for women and might result in a bias against the
defendant. 'What a comment on our society,' wrote Anne O'Donnell and
Evelyn Conlon. 'Should not such horrific facts be as disturbing to men as
they are to women?'[116]

In October 1978, thousands of women attended an anti-rape protest in
Dublin city, marching under the banner 'Women against Violence against
Women', which led ultimately to the establishment of the Dublin Rape
Crisis Centre (DRCC) in 1979. The march occurred after eight young men
had raped a 16-year-old girl and left her badly injured in an inner Dublin
basement. Pat Brennan later referred to the march as the last unified act of
the radical women's movement of the 1970s. There was a furore over Nell
McCafferty's reported comments when speaking at the march: 'The streets
are ours. We are not looking for jail for men; we are not looking for cas-
tration for men. We are not looking for men at all.' Other accounts suggest that McCafferty also said, 'There were no men on this march tonight
and that is why nobody was raped', which led to accusations of extremism.
McCafferty's own account of her involvement makes the point that contemporary news reports omitted her last comment – 'We are looking for fresh
air' – and that its omission made her remarks sound harsher than she had
intended.[117] Some women continued their march on to the Grand Canal to
show solidarity with prostitutes working there, leading to fury on the part of
the prostitutes because the marchers were 'queering up business'.[118]

On the subject of rape, those advocating change suggested that facilities for rape victims be available in every hospital, that half the jurors in rape
trials should be women and that the offender should be brought to trial
within three months of committing the crime. Susan McKay's history of the
DRCC centre points out that it was a militant and campaigning organisation; some Catholic extremists wanted the centre shut down, victims were
often blamed, and there was 'great ignorance on the issue'.[119]

When Gemma Hussey demanded in the Senate that the law on rape be
radically changed, one senator said that many women 'upset the biological

balance of a man and then claim they were raped'. The DRCC demanded
law reform, proper services for victims and treatment programmes to stop
rapists re-offending. Anne O'Donnell suggested the centre 'broke the taboo
on talking about rape and incest. Set up by women for women, when male
victims came looking for support, they were welcomed. It warned us about
clerical abuse before we heard of Father Brendan Smyth [the Norbertine
priest imprisoned in 1993 for twelve years after pleading guilty to seventy-
four charges of indecent and sexual assault on children over a 35-year
period].' Seventy women contacted the DRCC in its first year; twenty-five
years later, in 2004, over 15,000 people called its 24-hour helpline. It also
took on international work, running programmes for the victims of rape as
a war crime in Bosnia and Kosovo.

1978   ✱   Campaigners did succeed in getting the law changed. In 1978, when the
women marched, it was not a crime for a man to rape his wife; marital rape
1990   was criminalised in 1990, although many victims still remained hidden. The
discussion of sexual violence as a social and legal problem was also helped
by the publication in the early 1970s of influential US studies of rape, such
as Susan Brownmiller's *Against Our Will: Men, Women and Rape* (1975). In
Ireland there was discontent with the 'narrow range of behaviour encom-
passed by the definition of the offence'. Until 1987, the maximum sentence
for indecent assault was five years, after 1987 it increased to ten. After 1990,
immunity from rape convictions accorded to husbands and those under
the age of 14 no longer applied and also in 1990, complainants could no
longer be questioned about previous sexual experience. Overall, 'the level
of sentencing for rape in Ireland [was] quite severe', as pointed out by Tom
O'Malley in 1993, with prison sentences of 8–9 years on average.[120] But a
new focus on the rights of the victim did not transform the approach of
women to the issue of reporting the crime. In the early twenty-first century
up to 70 per cent of victims of sexual crimes were still not reporting them
to the Gardaí and between 1998 and 2001, Ireland had the lowest conviction rate for sexual crime of twenty-one EU countries, at just 1 per cent.[121]
Having researched this issue in depth, Susan McKay concluded starkly that
'no place is sacred. A girl was raped on Yeats's grave. It is hard not to feel
helpless and overwhelmed by the sheer extent of sexual violence in this
Catholic ✝ country.'[122]

    Other radical groups emerging in the 1970s included Irish Women
United, formed in 1975, which demanded women's centres and self-
determined sexuality, but it fell apart at the beginning of 1977. At a seminar

to discuss the general election of that year, tensions came to a head 'with socialist women arguing that working-class men were more oppressed than middle-class women'.[123] Roy Foster points out that the same year, the Women's Political Association (WPA), which evolved from the Women's Representative Association, sent a questionnaire on women's issues to serving TDs. The reply of Fianna Fáil TD Tim O'Connor encapsulated the hostility that existed to women participating in politics: 'In my own county the women are doing a great job of work in keeping their homes going and bringing up their families. This I think is just what Almighty God intended them to do.'[124]

'Great psychological damage to literally thousands in Irish government care'

Anne O'Donnell's reference to becoming aware of child abuse was also significant and raises the question of how much knowledge there was of this subject in the 1970s and the 1980s before the flood of revelations in the 1990s. There was much recognition by the early 1970s, especially in light of the report of the Kennedy Commission, issued in November 1970, about a need to change the approach to the care of deprived children. By 1973 there were a million children under the age of 16 in Ireland, 10,000 of whom were in public care at any one time. The organisation CARE, which launched a campaign for the care of deprived children, argued that the 1908 Children's Act was 'over 60 years out of date ... stigmatising, overbearing and unhelpful to the children who come within its scope'. It also called for a single government department to deal with children instead of responsibility being spread over the departments of justice, health and education.[125]

In 2007, at an inquest into the death of a baby in Dublin in 1973, allegations of serious abuse, incestuous rape, girls being hired out as sexual playthings and casually dismissed miscarriages emerged. The inquest was the only forum left for 45-year-old Cynthia Owen, previously Murphy, in her decades-long attempt to uncover the truth about the newborn baby girl found stabbed to death in a laneway in Dun Laoghaire in April 1973, which she had conceived when she was 11 years old and which had been killed with a knitting needle in the family home. The suggestions as to what had happened divided the family but Owen was vindicated, as the coroner, who had persisted in reopening the inquest, asked her if she had given the baby a name, and hoped the baby would finally 'rest in peace'.[126] Amidst all the claims and counterclaims of Owen's large family it was clear that of the six girls reared at home, five alleged they had been the subject of sexual abuse there. And who noticed? As Kathy Sheridan asked, 'Did no one notice what was happening to Cynthia Murphy, pregnant at 11, in fifth class of a convent school?'[127]

Barry Desmond also suggested that the public was becoming more critical of the lack of a co-ordinated and unified system of child care, and told Taoiseach Liam Cosgrave in the summer of 1974 of a 'very strong reaction from all sections of the community' concerning the case of a 10-year-old boy who was sent to Clonmel special school by a judge 'arising out of a charge against him of indecent assault'.[128]

The stigma that resulted from institutionalisation and illegitimacy had done untold damage, and was the focus of angry correspondence to some government departments. In 1972, a former inmate of Artane industrial school now living in London sent a number of letters to the Taoiseach Jack Lynch about his own experiences which are indicative of the anger that was felt by many who went into the system because of their illegitimacy. In November 1972, he wrote:

> It is now eight years since I left the Republic a free individual. Unfortunately for me, I can never forget one day of my 16 years in your country ... Being born illegitimate in the Republic of Ireland was no fun for me at all. Your governments have declared illegal the use of contraceptives within the Republic of Ireland. Your governments have also made miserable the lives of thousands of unwanted babies within the Republic. I was admitted to an orphanage at the age of two years; at the age of ten I was transferred to a borstal school where I was to stay another six years. I do not intend to put in writing at this very moment the treatment to which helpless children are subject to while in the care of the Irish Catholic authorities. I do not know if it could be possible, but I sure wish I had the opportunity to speak with you personally.[129]

He sent two follow-up letters that were passed on to the Department of Health:

> the problem of the upbringing of unwanted children in the care of government sponsored authorities must be looked at once again ... I do believe that if I had a chance to tell my story to members of your

government a great deal of good could be done. I am quite sure that the Irish government is a humane one and I've no idea how the Irish people would take it, if they knew what horror lay behind the Irish law on the use of contraceptives. I myself am still suffering from the terrifying effects of my upbringing in Irish government care.

He also referred to 'great psychological damage to literally thousands in Irish government care ... subject to a life of fear and hatred ... in the claws of the Irish Christian brothers ... the Irish people must know the psychological damage they had subjected these children to.'[130]

There is no explicit mention of sexual abuse in these letters, and it is still difficult to know the level of awareness of this issue outside of medical, legal and Church circles, and the degree to which hints or outright complaints were taken seriously. There were allegations of ill treatment of inmates at St Patrick's Institution for young offenders. In 1971, the chaplain McQuaid had appointed to St Patrick's, Father Raymond Freld, referred critically to food deprivation and solitary confinement at the institution and had to apologise to McQuaid for a letter he sent to the *Irish Times* on the subject. McQuaid told him to 'just keep quiet' – an indication that, whatever his private concerns, he did not want publicity given to the allegations.[131] The same approach undoubtedly prevailed when it came to allegations of sexual abuse.

'Just messing'

It was not until the formal investigations of the early twenty-first century that many of the secret histories of sexual abuse were publicised, as happened when the Ferns Report that investigated the sexual abuse of children in Wexford was published in October 2005. The Ferns inquiry was established after a BBC documentary, *Suing the Pope*, was aired in March 2002 which highlighted the activities of Father Seán Fortune ('a new grotesque image of the Catholic priesthood') and the suicide of a young man who had been abused by Fortune. Ninety people alleging abuse attended oral hearings and a further fifty-seven submitted written statements. The commission analysed complaints of abuse by twenty-one priests dating back to 1966. The report was notable for its lack of information on alleged abusers ('roughly half of those accused or convicted of child abuse did not co-operate') and 'a failure to situate the Ferns abuse in a wider context'.[132]

The 1908 Children's Act did not confer any power of intervention in child abuse cases perpetrated by anyone other than a parent or a carer. A Department of Health report in 1976–7 on non-accidental injury to children made no mention of sex abuse, and guidelines eventually drawn up in 1987 only related to abuse carried out by a family member or carer. It was therefore legitimate to ask why, given that the Archbishop of Dublin raised concerns about the legal liability of dioceses for claims of sexual abuse in 1986, guidelines were not drawn up then, as 'this was a pivotal moment when consistent information on their legal responsibilities and potential liability was made known to all Irish bishops'. Guidelines were established in 1996, but they were not given a 'recognitio' by the Vatican. An unavoidable conclusion to be drawn from the Ferns Report is that neither health professionals nor legislators did enough. In the words of Catriona Crowe, the report

does not reveal why Irish state agencies that employed professionals in the field of child protection took so long to deal with an issue 'recognised as a worldwide problem' since 1975 at the latest. A regime of appropriate state-sponsored education, information and guidelines about child sexual abuse, with the legislative powers and personnel to support it, would surely have made a great deal of difference to the victims mentioned in the report and forced the Church authorities to conform to civil law and practice rather than canon law. As it was, the Church did not formally acknowledge its proper obligations to civil and criminal law until 1996. The expert group which advised the inquiry team on these matters told them that perspectives on treatment for alleged offenders have changed dramatically over the last twenty years. Until the late 1990s, psychiatrists believed that a sexual propensity for children could be controlled through medication and therapy, and were prepared to recommend that such offenders be returned to ministry, with certain restrictions imposed. Current thinking is more pessimistic, holding that not even very good treatment can eliminate the risk of re-offence. From the late 1970s, the report reveals, priests with behavioural problems, including child sexual abuse, were sent for assessment and treatment to reputable psychologists and psychiatrists in Ireland and to a treatment centre in Stroud in England, but these professionals often were not aware of the allegations against the priests and their conclusions were often ignored.[133]

The report highlighted the extent to which St Peter's college, the Wexford seminary with a boarding school attached where priests were trained for the diocese of Ferns, 'provided an alarmingly high number of alleged and convicted abusers'. These included the principal of the college from 1988 to 1991, Father Donal Collins, who had taught there since 1964. It was also evident that screening of candidates for the priesthood was non-existent until the early 1980s.[134]

Meanwhile, at Maynooth college, Father Gerard McGinnity was forced to resign as a senior dean after acting on complaints of sexual abuse in 1984. His own bishop came to him and said, 'There are bishops gunning for you ... I can't go back to them without your resignation. Write it down, write it on anything. It doesn't matter.' He was humiliated and demoted as if he himself had done something wrong, while the man against whom allegations were made, Father Michael Ledwith, became president of the college, only to resign in 1994 when allegations of sexual abuse were made against him again; he denied both claims and moved to California.[135] All of this highlights the obsession with 'avoiding scandal' rather than moral responsibility. And was celibacy a contributing factor? The unanimous view of six therapists consulted by the Ferns inquiry was that the vow of celibacy contributed to the problem of sexual abuse in the Church. Garret FitzGerald suggested that 'whatever about celibacy for priests, one cannot help feeling that, if most bishops were married and had families, the Church's attitude towards child abuse might have been very different'.[136]

By the time of his ordination in 1979, Father Fortune, about whom twenty-six complainants gave evidence to the Ferns inquiry, had been the subject of at least two allegations of sexual abuse. But he described his behaviour to psychiatrists as 'just messing' and was unrepentant. The attitude to another priest who was sent away due to allegations of abuse and returned two years later was summed up by Bishop Herlihy of Ferns: 'Hasn't he done his penance?' Through their actions or lack of actions, the Bishops 'enabled avoidable appalling damage to young lives'.

What the report did succeed in doing was to vindicate the abused child, and set abused children at the centre of its deliberations, providing a new knowledge of the depth and force of the complaints. The account of graphic abuse, in the words of Crowe, 'while gruesome to read, is a necessary corrective to the atmosphere of secrecy and shame that has surrounded these experiences for so many years'.[137] Public groping, violent rapes and genital examinations abounded and the long-term consequences

– suicide, depression, marriage breakdown, self-doubt and loathing – are
as stark.

Fortune's manipulation was unrelenting: he told one victim that
'because he was a priest and was not married, what he was doing was not
wrong'. He also used to 'hunt them down' and, on occasion, rape a particular
male student he would catch. A consistent and recurring action of Fortune's
was to threaten that he would tell the victim's parents what had happened.
One victim noted that that 'frightened him more than what Fortune did'.
The violent rape of another boy 'left him in a mess on the floor, bleeding
heavily'. Fortune was also a blackmailer and, for most victims, 'the abuse had
the effect of alienating them from the Catholic Church and from organised
religion in general'.[138]

Fortune's predatory behaviour was not stopped until almost twenty
years after it started. But there were also inadequate social services, and fear
in a small community, as well as denial, disbelief and anger – one mother
'dismissed the suggestion outright and physically attacked' her son, the victim.[139] The report also reveals that after the alleged abuse of ten young girls
in 1988 by a priest, a divisive event for the community, 'the South Eastern
Health Board, which had vindicated their complaints, was unable to offer
counselling to them because of lack of resources; there were only 4 social
workers serving all of County Wexford'.[140]

There was also the problem of children and adults not being equipped
with the language to talk about the issue of sexual abuse. In reacting to the
Ferns Report, Olivia O'Leary maintained, 'Of course children were slow to
talk about it. They didn't have the language. Even women who suffered from
breast cancer didn't talk about it because you couldn't talk about breasts.'[141]
Experts in the field have pointed out that 'the relationship between professional social work, philanthropy and the statutory sector was a very complex
one in Ireland, only partially explained by ... the absorption of philanthropic
practices of child welfare into the realm of the state. In Ireland, the authority
to intervene with children and families, up to the 1970s, lay mostly with the
authority of the church (socio-spiritual) rather than the statutory legislation
(socio-legal).'[142]

It was not until the 1970s that social workers were accepted as the most
appropriate professionals to take on child welfare responsibilities. Tellingly,
they were not even mentioned in the first draft of the proposed new structures leading to the development of the health boards under the Health
Act of 1970. Most crucially, the role of social workers within the newly

formed community care structures, 'apart from the specific responsibilities, remained unclear throughout the 1970s and 1980s'.[143] Clerical politics at Ireland's largest third-level institution, University College Dublin, also played a part in stymieing the emergence of more autonomy and a secular approach to the education of social workers until the late 1960s. In 1998, Tom Garvin pointed out that 'McQuaid effectively controlled from a distance five academic chairs, all funded at the taxpayer's expense, in what might be termed the moral or social sciences: Ethics and Politics, Logic and Psychology, Education, Sociology and Metaphysics. All these chairs were occupied by Catholic priests, essentially nominated by McQuaid.' Such control led to an intellectual environment of 'ingrowness and cultural incest' and there was a particular vigilance about the possible infiltration 'of all kinds of terrible people and in particular by the ideas of those two brilliant Jews, Karl Marx and Sigmund Freud'.[144]

'One in four Irish girls may be sexually abused before the age of 18'

By the 1980s, some startling information and statistics were emerging in relation to sexual abuse in Ireland that underlined not that the scale of such abuse was unique when compared to other countries, but that the profile of the abusers was somewhat different. In July 1986, *Magill* magazine announced on its front cover that 'One in four Irish girls may be sexually abused before the age of 18'.[145] It referred to an unpublished report from the Department of Health that revealed 'the secret horrors behind the façade of the Irish family'. The report suggested that, as was the case in Britain and the United States, one in four girls and one in ten boys 'have been sexually assaulted by an adult before the age of 18', and it was a problem being ignored because 'most cases take place within the family and the vast majority go unreported'. This was a reference to a report drawn up by the Irish Council for Civil Liberties (ICCL) working party on child sexual abuse, which seemed to suggest that 'official' figures – as appeared in the annual crime reports – were a gross underestimation of the problem. For example, in the annual crime report for 1984, 17 cases of 'defilement of girls' under the age of 17 were reported, along with 8 cases of incest. Health boards reported just 33 cases of sexual assault; the sexual assault unit of the Rotunda hospital dealt with 150 cases of sexual assault on children, 'while the Dublin Rape Crisis Centre received 268 inquiries about possible child sexual abuse in the first ten months of 1985'. Significantly, doctors who responded to the ICCL working party dealt with 86 cases of abuse between them, 'but only 11 of them had reported to their health boards.'[146]

There was no legal requirement on anyone to take action if they suspected abuse and a lot of uncertainty as to the law, partly because there was no comprehensive legal definition of what constituted child sexual abuse. Eighty-six per cent of victims interviewed had not reported their cases to the police. It was also suggested that priests sometimes reinforced the victims' sense of guilt. One was reported as accepting the denials of the father of one of the victims and 'then made the girl kneel down to ask for forgiveness from her father'. This is an account that is very similar to the experiences of the victims of abuse in Wexford as detailed by the Ferns Report; when one girl threatened to tell her parents the priest slapped her and 'said he would pray for her'.[147]

There was little in the way of treatment for offenders, and familial abuse posed a particularly horrendous dilemma for mothers as 'the evidence suggests that it is extraordinarily difficult for mothers to believe that their husband is not merely being sexually disloyal, but that he is being disloyal with the very person whom he should be protecting from assault'. It was estimated that 75–80 per cent of abuse was by family members, friends or close relations, and 25 per cent by brothers, which, perhaps due to the large size of families and significant age gaps between siblings, was 'a figure much higher than that for other countries'. There were also more adolescents abusing children than in other countries. Most fathers involved would not accept it was harmful, which was not just a sexual issue 'but a problem of the power that some men have over their families'. *Magill* announced that the report was being redrafted following its rejection by the Department of Health.[148]

Journalist Pat Brennan made the point in 1982 that the law in relation to child abuse was inadequate and that there seemed to be no will to change it. At that stage there were 112 social workers in the Eastern Health Board area: 'It is not unusual for one social worker to have a case load of 40 or 50 families, of which 8 might be serious child-at-risk cases.' Social workers had not been employed in any numbers until the mid 1970s and they remained the 'poor relations' of the health boards.[149]

In the same year Brennan's article was published the Department of Education secretly decided to allow a paedophile teacher, Donal Dunne, to remain in his job. In the late 1990s, he was eventually convicted of indecent assault against six boys between 1965 and 1969 at a primary school in County

Offaly. The decision to ignore the allegations that surfaced against him in 1982 – he was a pillar of the community, well connected politically and involved in his local GAA teams – was made by a small group of civil servants, enabling the man to remain in the school system until his retirement.

Information about Dunne, who had been sexually abusing children since the 1940s, had been given to the Department of Education, members of the Oireachtas, the Irish National Teachers Organisation and the Church, but it had been 'ignored by every institution in the state charged with the protection of young people'. For the victims, when the Garda file was opened on him, it brought many memories flooding back, including one of not just physical abuse but also emotional seduction. He had put his arms around one victim 'and asked him if he loved him. The small, timid 10-year-old answered that he did.' As a 27-year-old, this victim talked to bishops and priests who said they did not want to drag up the past, as the abuser had since married, and this would, they believed, 'straighten out the "kink" he had'. The same victim also approached politicians and complained to the Department of Education in 1982. Wanting to contain the issue within the department, officials made no attempt to contact the source of the allegations. The conclusion reached by a civil servant was: 'If Mr Dunne has served as a secondary teacher – in girls schools – for the last 13 years without coming under notice, is it correct to rake up the past now? I have not attempted to trace any report re: NT [National Teacher] service.'[150]

> *'One contributing factor may be the fact that*
> *the victims didn't say anything ... '*

Other high-profile cases of child abuse unmasked the propensity of some priests to inflict horrific abuse on children, most notoriously Father Brendan Smyth, who in 1993 was convicted on numerous counts of the sexual abuse of children going back more than thirty-five years. The clerical authorities had known about his activities for many years and just kept moving him around, north and south of the border. His activities were eventually exposed by Chris Moore, a reporter with Ulster TV's *Counterpoint* programme (it was striking that it was often documentary makers and television stations from outside the Republic who explored these issues). A request by the RUC for Smyth's extradition to Northern Ireland which remained in the Republic's Attorney General's office for seven months caused a political storm that brought down the government, with accusations that ministers had misled the Dáil about their knowledge of such cases in the Attorney General's office. Another high-profile case was the Kilkenny incest case of 1993, which prompted an inquiry as to why the local health board had failed to stop a man raping his daughter for years, despite the fact that the girl had more than 100 contacts with social workers. The report of inquiry into the affair, by Judge Catherine McGuinness, called for a constitutional amendment on children's rights, which was not acted on.

Sophia McColgan's story, published in 1998, was another tragedy; she and her family had endured years of torture and rape in Sligo at the hands of their father. She showed extraordinary courage in both giving evidence against her father, who was jailed for life, and then taking the state to court for failing to protect the family from his excesses, resulting in compensation for her and her siblings. In allowing her story to be written, Sophia wanted to challenge readers about their own attitudes. Some people who followed the McColgan court cases blamed her mother for not saving her children. However, the bleak truth, according to Sophia, was that 'she could not protect us – she was one of us'; that it was social workers, Gardaí, doctors, priests, teachers and neighbours who had maintained the silence that had trapped her family for twenty years, and that it was the love shown to her by her grandparents that had saved her.[151]

But it was the abuse by priests that became the focus of most media attention, with the phrase 'paedophile priest' becoming so commonly used that, as Harry Ferguson has pointed out, a distorted impression was given of child abuse in Ireland: 'the most common single occupational group represented in these cases has in fact been farmers. Yet we have not begun to talk routinely about "paedophile farmers". Ferguson suggested that attention was being deflected from the fact that men from all social backgrounds were involved:

> What we are witnessing here in the emergence of the notion of the 'Paedophile Priest' is the selective construction of symbols of danger which serve certain social ends. There has been a conspicuous lack of attention in public debates to the causes of the abuse of children and women within the Irish family by married active heterosexual men. Children are most often sexually abused by known men within the context of the family, such as fathers and male relatives' – this had been clearly exposed in a

book published in 1993 on Child Sexual Abuse in the Eastern Health Board Region of Ireland in 1988.[152]

In 1988 the Eastern Health Board dealt with 990 cases of alleged child abuse. At the end of the year 15 per cent of those were found not to be cases of sexual abuse, while 40 per cent 'had still to be confirmed', which left 512 cases of confirmed sexual abuse. On that basis, the known rate of child sexual abuse in the region in 1988 was 1.2 per 1,000 children (there were 1.1 million children under the age of 15 in Ireland in 1990).[153]

Ferguson also drew attention to the language that was being used within the legal system in relation to both the perpetrators and the abuse victims. In March 1995 the Court of Criminal Appeal reduced the sentence of a rapist. This case involved a 14-year-old rape victim (identified only as X to protect her identity) who had been prevented from leaving the country for an abortion, though the decision was overturned by the Supreme Court. As she was suicidal it was deemed that the constitutional amendment on abortion with its phrase 'with due regard to the right of the mother' could not prevent the girl from travelling. Her rapist's sentence was reduced from 14 to 4 years, and Justice Hugh O'Flaherty characterised the convicted sex offender not in terms of his sexuality but as a 'hard-working, good family man' who had not committed 'out and out rape', which seemed to 'cloud issues of consent and implicitly draw attention to the behaviour of the child as somehow being complicit in her victimisation. At its worst, responsibility for the problem of sex crimes is shifted to the victims; the idea that somehow the desexualised man was led on by the sexualised child.' Furthermore, Ferguson argued that the construction of the paedophile priest 'serves to rehabilitate mainstream heterosexual masculinity and the "good family man".'[154]

Echoing Ferguson's arguments in more trenchant terms in 1999, journalist and author Kevin Myers suggested 'since the Brendan Smyth affair, we have seen a steady decline in the quality of public discourse about sexual and psychiatric disorders, almost to the point of medieval simplicity, as if the psychiatric advances since Freud had been totally forgotten.'[155]

But the Church did itself no favours when at times displaying hypocrisy, disingenuousness and insensitivity in how it talked about and responded to the revelations of the 1990s. In 1995 journalist Olivia O'Leary conducted an interview with Bishop Larry Ryan of Kildare and Leighlin ('a gentle and decent man') in which he claimed that 'it never dawned on anybody that the victim was going to suffer as a result of sexual abuse ... one contributing

factor may be the fact that the victims didn't say anything ... I think the
indications are it didn't dawn on people that it would have life-long effects',
to which an incredulous O'Leary responded, 'And this from a Church
obsessed with sexual sins as the greatest sins of all?' She suggested the explanation that was closer to the truth lay in the 'belief by an all-male Hierarchy
that priests are more important than the rest of us; the belief that anything
which might damage the power and reputation of the institutional Church
must be pushed aside; the belief that the Church is more important than
God's Justice'.[156]

'My own hatred had been turned inwards'

Colm O'Gorman, a victim of Father Fortune, who broke the silence and
subsequently set up the charity One in Four to assist victims of abuse, made
the point that he felt it necessary to disengage from the Church as a result
of its response. He also powerfully articulated the impact on the victim. He
was told to 'get the hell out of the country' when he came forward at the age
of 29:

> After years of believing I was awful, I remember the moment that I
> realised I wasn't ... I had to face the shadow aspect of humanity, because
> of what happened to me. My own hatred had been turned inwards,
> against myself, and also acted out on other people. One of the things I
> regret in my life is I spent a lot of it not relating to anyone on an honest,
> or real, or human level. I was too frightened to. I thought I was this
> awful, appalling, evil person. None of this was conscious. Until I was 29
> I didn't live below the neck, my body wasn't part of me. That was the age
> I had to do something, not for myself, but for what might be happening
> to someone else, right now, as a result of my silence in relation to the man
> who had abused me. It was the only way that I could engage with what
> had happened.[157]

In this sense, by the early twenty-first century there was a lot more
sophisticated analysis of the problem of child abuse than there had ever
been in previous years, but there was still the legacy of the failure to accept
its full extent in previous years. In 1990, for example, Nuala O'Faoláin had
pointed to a refusal to face the facts of child abuse by highlighting that in

narratives - Foster?

1989

1989 Childline received a total of 18,353 calls, of which 4,717 were from children 'who wanted to say to someone that they were being sexually abused'. Why, she wondered, were these figures being allowed to 'slide by'? Why was there a perception that 'the whole problem has been blown out of proportion by hysterical women'? And if it was true that there was ignorance about such things in the past, 'it does not make any sense to use our ignorance of child abuse then to block out knowledge of child abuse now'.[158]

Through her autobiographical writing, most notably *Are You Somebody?*, published in 1996, O'Faoláin highlighted the sexual trauma that was experienced by many. She wrote that 'something was dislodged in me' by the evidence given at the trial of triple-murderer Brendan O'Donnell in 1996, and the long-buried revelations about his childhood, which partly prompted O'Faoláin to begin to tell her own story. O'Donnell, who killed a woman, her child and a priest, did not get the psychiatric help that he needed as a child, was turned away from institutions, endured neglect, starvation and child abuse by a priest 'who fondled Brendan in public'. He killed himself at the age of 23.[159]

How or whether to write about sexual abuse became a difficult question for some writers. Should it have remained the preserve of those who had direct experience of it? There was controversy when Irish language poet Àine Ní Ghlinn published her collection *Deora Nár Caoineadh* (*Unshed Tears*) in 1996, which included a sequence of powerful poems on child sexual abuse. The poems were based on research she had conducted about particular instances of abuse, but some felt she was colonising others' experiences. The collection includes the poem '*Èalú*' ('Escape'):

> *Ní rachadh sí chun na sochraide*
> *Ach chuaigh sí dhon tórramh*
> *is leag a lámh ar a chlár éadain*
> *rinne gáire is lena súil*
> *do lean sí líne a shróine*
> *síos thar bheola nach n-éalódh*
> *teanga ramallach arís tríothu*
> *ná pislíní liobránta*
> *ná garbh-bholadh anála*
> *Síos arís thar choróin na maighdine*
> *is faoi bhráillíní bána an bháis*
> *samhlaíodh di a bhall beag chun gneiss*

ball nach meallfaí go deo arís
chun seasta ná chun preabarnaíle
ina pluaisín dorcha

Rinne comhbhrón
le baintreach
is le clan an tí
is d'éalaigh sí
amach an doras
síos an bother
siar i dtreo na coille
D'aimsigh sí
An leabha fhuar
Inar sháraigh sé
Ar dtús í
Is d'éalaigh uaithi
An liú uafáis
A bhí gafa ina scornach
Le breis is fiche bliain

(She would not attend the funeral
but went to the wake
and laid her hand on his forehead
She smiled and with her eye
traced the line of his nose
down over lips closed forever now
on his slimy tounge
his blubbering spits
his foul-smelling breath
Down again over his rosaried hands
and under the white sheet of death
she visualised the small sex organ
that would never again pulsate
in her small dark cave

She offered her condolences
to his widow
his children

and escaped
out the door
down the road
down towards the wood
She found
the cold bed
where he first
raped her
and screamed
the scream of horror
that had been stuck in her throat
for more than twenty years)[160]

'Their main concern was whether the figures would be believed'

The Sexual Abuse and Violence in Ireland Report (*SAVI*), initiated by the
Dublin Rape Crisis Centre, funded by Atlantic Philanthropies with additional funding from the Irish government and published in March 2002,
revealed a huge volume of child abuse in Ireland. Over 1 in 20 women (5.6
per cent, representing nearly 80,000 women) reported being raped in childhood; over 1 in 50 men (2.7 per cent, representing nearly 47,000 men)
reported being raped in childhood, while 30.4 per cent of women reported
some form of sexual abuse in childhood, as did 23.6 per cent of men. These
are astonishing figures. Hannah McGee, the lead author of the report, said
that at the time of its publication 'their main concern was whether the figures would be believed' and the report was particularly significant because,
prior to this, sexual abuse figures available in Ireland were based only on the
numbers seeking counselling or reporting sexual abuse to Gardaí. Of those
abused, only a tiny fraction were abused by members of the Catholic clergy.

The report made many recommendations. But although guidelines
on the handling of child sexual abuse were introduced across state and voluntary agencies, and impressive research into abuse was completed by the
Economic and Social Research Institute and the National Crime Council,
it was pointed out in 2005 that 'there has been little follow through on the
auditing of the extent and effectiveness of their implementation'. Most significantly, the urgent recommendation that a 'comprehensive public awareness campaign on sexual violence' be undertaken did not happen.[161]

There were still obvious gaps in child protection legislation and concerns about lack of powers for intervention in non-familial abuse, as also highlighted by the Ferns Report. Contrary to popular belief, fathers were not the main abusers; uncles were more likely to abuse and neighbours and authority figures were the abusers in 40 per cent of cases. Within the 'authority figures' category, babysitters were the most prevalent abusers.[162] The Department of Education and Science suggested 82 per cent of schools were teaching on an ongoing systematic basis the Stay Safe programme – a programme introduced in 1991 and designed to give children the ability to articulate concerns they may have about abuse or its potential. Fintan O'Toole made the observation in 2005 that while the institutional Church failed to meet its responsibility to protect children, it was also the case that when the issue of child abuse began to receive more attention in the 1980s, it was lay Catholic organisations who made 'the most aggressive attacks on attempts to acknowledge the problem and do something about it'. Parents against Stay Safe, for instance, did their utmost to prevent the programme being introduced; its Tralee chairman insisted that the programme invaded the privacy of the family, would lead to the break-up of families and was based on 'grossly exaggerated claims' about the extent of abuse.[163]

The focus on the Church sometimes obscured the extent to which this was a much bigger issue, and in that context, 'If *SAVI* shows one thing, it is that the present vilification of the Church, merited as it is, can be a smoke-screen that obscures other relevant factors', which included the sanction of the state for Church authority.[164] In 2008, it was asserted that 42 per cent of women in Ireland had experienced sexual violence, an extraordinarily high figure.[165] One hundred and two priests from the Catholic Archdiocese of Dublin were accused of child sex abuse between 1940 and 2006. By 2006, approximately 350 victims had been identified, with a further 40 yet to be identified or traced. Criminal convictions had been brought against 8 priests, while 105 civil actions had been brought against 32 priests. Settlements of the 65 civil cases involved payments totalling 5.8 million Euros, while from 2003 to 2006 the archdiocese invested 2.5 million Euros in child-protection services.[166] By 2006, 400 members of industrial schools and orphanages had given evidence to the investigation committee of the Commission to Inquire into Child Abuse, while more than 1,100 former residents of the institutions spoke to the commission's confidential committee about their experiences.[167] There were also complaints from some priests about 'over strict' interpretations by the Bishops of Church guidelines on dealing with those accused of child abuse, the idea being that too often priests were stood aside from ministry – 'and their reputations irreparably damaged' – upon the basis of flimsy allegations.[168]

The extent of abuse also posed particular challenges to psychiatrists and psychotherapists. In his memoir *Music and Madness* (2008), Ivor Browne, who served as Professor of Psychiatry at University College Dublin and was chief psychiatrist with the Eastern Health Board, observed how the silence of Irish victims was a result of them freezing their traumatic experiences and then dissociating from those events, as a result of which 'they usually knew little or nothing of what had happened to them'.[169] But the extent of the revelations of the 1990s and the breaking of the silences also provoked false memories. This was the result of 'hypnosis, or peer pressure in fundamentalist therapeutic groups, [in which] highly suggestible subjects complied with the production of pseudo-memories'. In unblocking actual abuse, or the activation of frozen experiences, Browne discovered for some patients who thought there had been only one incident of sexual abuse 'an extensive, rather sadistic history of physical and sexual abuse by the same person'.[170]

Was the scale or the practice of child abuse in Ireland unique? Such a question cannot be answered with any confidence in the absence of detailed comparative analysis and statistics, particularly regarding abuse within families and abuse perpetrated by clerics. Internationally, there was much more awareness of child abuse by the 1990s. Revelations in many countries made it clear that what had happened in Ireland reflected a much wider phenomenon, and few countries escaped exposure. In August 1996, the opening of a conference of the International Society for the Prevention of Child Abuse and Neglect in Dublin was overshadowed by news of the murder of sexually abused children by Belgian paedophiles. In the same month, an English computer analyst was jailed in the Philippines for seventeen years after having molested two boys aged 8 and 4 over a period of time. An Australian man in his sixties was also given a hefty jail sentence following his conviction for child abuse in the same year. While simultaneously a senior Australian diplomat on child sex charges contested the powers of an Australian court to punish him for activities alleged to have been carried out while he was representing his country in Cambodia.[171]

In 2001, British police claimed to have smashed the world's largest known paedophile ring, an exclusive internet operation known as the Wonderland Club. It was the largest ever international operation to be co-ordinated by the National Crime Squad in London. Simultaneous raids took place around the world in September 1998, with over 100 arrests being made in the UK, Australia, Austria, Belgium, Finland, France, Germany, Italy, Norway, Portugal, Sweden and the United States.[172] The memoirs of well-known personalities in other Catholic countries also exposed child abuse secrets from earlier decades. Italian film director Franco Zeffirelli revealed in his autobiography that he was sexually assaulted by a priest while attending a Roman Catholic school in Florence as a child; the priest had begged his forgiveness afterwards.[173]

Child abuse by clerics also did untold damage to the Catholic Church in the United States (where there were in the region of 60 million Catholics by the end of the twentieth century). By 2008 it had cost the US Church more than $2 billion in damages and had bankrupted six dioceses. The previous year, the Los Angeles archdiocese announced the largest church settlement of sexual abuse lawsuits to date, when it agreed to pay some 500 alleged victims a total of $660 million.

The scandal originally exploded in 2003 when Boston's archbishop, Cardinal Bernard Law, resigned after documents showed 'his cavalier response to allegations of the most horrifying abuse by his priests', and the 'Voice of the Faithful' campaign in the city ensured prominent leadership was displayed by those seeking to bring the abusers to justice. Many blamed priestly celibacy for the scandals.[174] The parallels with the situation in the Irish Catholic Church, particularly in terms of initial response to abuse, are obvious. Perhaps Catholic Ireland also exported this problem abroad along with its 'spiritual empire'. AUSTRALIA/ CANADA ?

'There is very little thinking amongst ordinary women'

In 2003, Mary Kenny, who came to prominence in the women's movement in the 1970s as a journalist and activist, suggested that in some respects women looking for change in the Republic were simplifying what was a complex issue:

> The Vatican was right to treat the introduction of the Pill as a crisis. It was. This is still not an easy question to resolve. Women are entitled to some control over their fertility. But the mechanistic view that prevails among the population lobbies and the birth control gurus occludes not only moral considerations but at the deepest level female sensibilities. It was

June Levine who said to me in 2002, 'They [the mechanistic birth con-
trollers] don't seem to understand that the baby is part of the sexuality.'
The fruit of the womb is not, after all, so easily separated from the transmission of life ... looking back on those years, almost all our own lives were
tempestuous in some way. Liberation was not as easy as it looked. Raising
children was not as easy as it looked. Deciding not to have children was
not as easy as it looked. 'Lifestyle choices', whether these be cohabitation,
marriage, divorce or homosexuality, all brought their own sorrows.[175]

Aside from the crassness of referring to homosexuality as 'a lifestyle
choice', Kenny's assessment overlooks the misogyny that was continually
directed towards women during the 1970s and even more so in the 1980s.
Though there were distinctive Irish impulses behind these developments,
they also reflected an international backlash against feminism, and in a sense
mirrored some of the 'moral panics' of a century earlier, when, in relation
to Victorian sexual attitudes, the possibility that human libido and passion
could be reduced by cultural and political mechanisms 'was an empirical
claim which was invoked quite readily in support of anti-sensual attitudes'.[176]
In Britain and North America in the 1970s and 1980s there was also a reaction, one which often divided feminists and sexual minorities on the issue of
'identity' politics. Some labelled it a 'new Puritanism' of the 'fundamentalist
Right'.[177] Internationally, the language and labels being used in relation to
sexuality also became more charged, as seen in the tendency in America in
the 1970s to refer to the 'explosion' in teenage pregnancies and the eagerness
to lay blame and pathologise individual conduct.[178]

Given his preoccupation with the various forces that shaped and regulated sexual lives, and recognition that the contemporary discourse on sexuality was part of modern society's quest for a means of control over the
individual, the work of French philosopher Michel Foucault is relevant here,
not just because of his association of the control of sexuality with power –
and the history of sexuality in Ireland in the 1980s raises many questions on
the subject – but also because of his fascination with the theme of sexuality as transgression. There was a certain ambiguity in his six-volume *History
of Sexuality* (1976) which, for some, leaves open the possibility that there
might be a 'need' for the 'repression' of sexuality. Developments in the 1980s
are a reminder of the accuracy of Foucault's critique of any simple notion of
sexual 'liberation'.[179]

There were a number of Irish groups whose campaigns to halt the tide of liberalisation involved invective and wild and unsubstantiated allegations being made against and about women. Ann Marie Hourihane recalls:

> It was like living in Franco's Spain ... I would have been much more involved than most people because I was a member of the women's right to choose group and our slogan was 'every bishop a wanted bishop'. But to say that we were in a tiny minority is to understate the case. I worked counselling women who were going to Britain for abortions, so I was much more closely associated with the subject than most people, most of my friends and so forth. But I also worked in family planning clinics and women were in an appalling position at that time. If you think about it – the 1979 Family Planning Act is what was on the books, which said you had to be married and you had to have a prescription in order to obtain condoms. Imagine the patronising result of that to women and men. Now the abortion issue was not discussed, it really wasn't. Even though women were going in a steady stream to Britain for abortions, as of course they still are today. But there was no divorce, homosexuality was illegal ... women came into family planning clinics in secret, it was unusual if their partners came with them frankly – they travelled enormous distances to come to Dublin, because their doctor or their local pharmacist – they literally didn't want to go there. So that's actually a very difficult thing even to remember with accuracy, let alone to imagine if you haven't personally witnessed it.[180]

One woman, Mary Kennedy, representing the Irish Family League, maintained in a radio programme broadcast in 1980 that if a woman uses contraceptives 'she realises that she can have sex with the milkman or anyone else who comes her way'. In 1980, a branch of the Responsible Society –established in Britain in 1971 by Valerie Richards, a medical social worker, 'in response to the exploitation of children through sex education' and in opposition to artificial contraception and abortion – was established in Ireland by Bernadette Bonar. The Irish branch even targeted a group called Sexual Problems of the Disabled on the grounds that the 'ultra-permissive can fasten on to what appears to be a compassionate or charitable cause'. In 1981 the Responsible Society fought against the renewal of the government grant to the Rape Crisis Centre, declaring unambiguously: 'It is our belief that in funding the Rape Crisis Centre, the state is funding and lending respectability to promoters of abortion.'

Other active groups included the Council of Social Concern, the League of Decency and the Irish Family League, many of these uniting under the Pro-Life Amendment Campaign umbrella in 1983 to support a proposal to have a 'pro-life' amendment inserted into the constitution (see below).[181] There is a tendency to regard some of the individuals leading such groups as almost comic. Roy Foster's remark on Mrs Dunne's Christmas Day Anti-Contraception Fast in 1979 –'she might just as well have enjoyed her turkey' – suggests the inevitability of their defeat, but it should not be underestimated how well connected and determined they were, with people like John O'Reilly orchestrating many of the campaigns in the background while never speaking directly to the media himself. Nor was it the case that their liberal opponents were particularly well united or effective, Emily O'Reilly labelling some of their efforts 'shambolic'.[182]

Contraception, inevitably, was presented as the first domino that would bring the others – divorce, abortion, euthanasia – crashing down, and the phrase 'ultrapermissive' was used to add urgency to the cause, even though, initially at least, legislative change came slowly. Charles Haughey's legislation in 1979 prompted groups like the Knights of Columbanus to go public in their opposition as well as quietly pressurising TDs with mail and circulars. Opus Dei, another semi-secret Catholic group, wrote a position paper which asserted that 'there is very little thinking amongst ordinary women. They mostly express a rehash of something they have heard or read or seen on television. They're very much swayed by their own emotions.'[183]

'The state acknowledges the right to life of the unborn and,
with due regard to the equal right to the life of the mother ... '

What some pregnant Irish women shared, north and south, was the dilemma of unplanned or unwanted pregnancies in states where abortion was not an option. The 1967 act legalising abortion passed in Great Britain was not applied to Northern Ireland, while in the Republic abortion was illegal under the 1861 Offences against the Persons Act. On 7 September 1983, the Irish electorate was asked to decide the fate of the proposed eighth amendment to the constitution, in what was otherwise known as the 'abortion referendum'. There were a few public references to abortion in Ireland during the previous decade, but the huge debate in the United States on abortion after the Roe *v.* Wade decision of the US Supreme Court in 1973 greatly influenced Irish pro-life groups. In this case the court struck down a state ban on abortion, delivering its judgment in favour of a poor 23-year-old Texas woman, Norma McCovery, who, when her own doctor refused to assist her in procuring an abortion, became Jane Roe, the plaintiff in the first constitutional challenge to anti-abortion laws. The Supreme Court's justice Harry Blackman declared on behalf of the 7–2 majority that the US constitution's Fourteenth Amendment implied a concept of privacy or personal liberty 'broad enough to encompass a woman's decision whether or not to terminate her pregnancy'. Blackman also asserted that judges could not decide the question of when life began, but that 'the word "person" as used in the Fourteenth Amendment, does not include the unborn'.

In February 1974, Noël Browne became the first member of the Oireachtas to advocate publicly the provision of therapeutic legal abortion in the Irish state, during a contribution to a Senate debate: 'I do not believe that we have any right at all to deny any minority within our society. For this reason I have interested myself in homosexuality, in therapeutic legal abortion and in contraception.' Acknowledging that abortion was 'very distressing', he insisted it should be legal in certain situations and that would reduce the number of women going to the UK. He said he made deliberate use of the word therapeutic 'because it is going to help the lady from the point of view of her health'.[184]

In 1975, Dr Dermot Walsh reported that 88 per cent of the Irish women getting an abortion in Britain in 1971–2 had invoked the ground of 'mental or psychiatric troubles' in order to obtain the go-ahead that two doctors had to give before the operation could take place.[185] In 1990, Ruth Riddick recalled counselling a working-class woman with a crisis pregnancy in the 1970s:

> At 22 years of age, she was already the glorious widow of a Republican martyr. She was Roman Catholic, abortion is murder and she was not to be permitted in her widowhood to have a sexual relationship, much less to produce incontrovertible evidence of her 'betrayal'. This unlovely story is but one from the largely unwritten and unspoken annals of the Irish abortion reality, north and south ... in the 23 years of the British abortion act only 3 Irish women have publicly named themselves as women who have had abortions. In this silence, in these statistics, real women live.

Riddick was one of those women; she spoke at a public meeting of a woman's right to choose group at Liberty Hall in Dublin and was later offered a position with the Irish Pregnancy Counselling Centre, but the group subsequently split internally. The meeting had been chaired by Mary McAleese, a future president of Ireland, who later claimed to have misunderstood the nature of the meeting, though she did maintain that 'I would see the failure to provide abortion as a human rights issue'.[186]

Female journalists, particularly powerful writers such as Nell McCafferty, Mary Holland – who wrote publicly of her own experience of having an abortion – and Nuala O'Faoláin, also influenced the way society looked at issues of relevance to women, including the manner in which the law and the legal system affected them. In 2004, Ivana Bacik, Reid Professor of Law at Trinity College Dublin, recalled:

> My first introduction to Nell McCafferty was through her radical writing. In 1985, Trinity College law lecturer (now President) Mary McAleese told her first year class to read *In the Eyes of the Law*, a collection of McCafferty's columns in the *Irish Times* observing proceedings in the Dublin district courts over previous years. These insightful, often poignant descriptions of the humdrum reality of law in action had a huge effect on us teenaged school-leavers – and remain relevant today. The book is still on the first year criminal law reading list in Trinity.[187]

The female journalists often broke new ground and continued to ask difficult questions. The editor of the *Irish Times*, Geraldine Kennedy, when she spoke at Mary Holland's funeral in 2004, summed this up by saying of Holland that 'she interfered with our comfort zones and challenged all of us'.[188]

One of the reasons these female journalists wrote so powerfully and often so angrily was because of the hostility that was continually directed towards women and their sexuality in the 1980s. This became strikingly manifest during the abortion referendum. At the time of the amendment campaign, 3,600 women annually who sought abortions in Britain were giving Irish addresses.[189] The text of the amendment, originally introduced by Dr Michael Woods, Fianna Fáil Minister for Health, read: 'The state acknowledges the right to life of the unborn and, with due regard to the equal right to the life of the mother, guarantees in its laws to respect, and, as far as is practicable, by its laws to defend and vindicate that right.'

In the event, the amendment was endorsed by 66.45 per cent of those who voted. 'Bitter' and 'divisive' have been the two words most frequently used to describe the referendum campaign. It has also been referred to as a watershed in Irish politics, and 'the second partitioning of Ireland'.[190] It was, according to Nell McCafferty, 'the weight of the pig ignorant slurry of woman-hating that did us temporarily down'. In contrast, William Binchy of the Pro-Life Amendment Campaign (PLAC) insisted the amendment was 'desperately necessary'.[191] Given the emotiveness of such language, and the obvious passions the campaign engendered, it is surprising that only 55.6 per cent of the electorate actually voted.

Under section 58 of the 1861 Offences against the Persons Act, anyone who 'unlawfully' procured the miscarriage of a woman was considered to have committed a felony. A patient dying as a result of such a procedure was not considered to have died during a medical operation, so a murder charge could be brought against the person who carried out that procedure. But this in itself was ambiguous. The act referred to those 'unlawfully' using instruments or administering drugs to procure abortion. Did this imply that there were circumstances in which abortion might be lawful? And what was the implication of this legislation for the medical profession? No charges were ever brought against doctors or midwives for performing abortions for medical reasons, so the Irish courts never tested the application of the legislation in such cases. It may have been the case that by the 1980s there was a fear that the law relating to abortion might be interpreted in a way that legalised abortion, prompting a small group to exert pressure on politicians to give a commitment to a referendum, which both Fianna Fàil and Fine Gael did in the early 1980s.

An obvious question that arose was, given that since 1861 it was illegal to procure or to have an abortion in Ireland, why was it necessary to have a referendum? Alex White, a barrister who campaigned against the amendment (and who was elected a Labour Party senator in 2007), explained that

what the Pro-Life Amendment Campaign said at the time was that the way the Irish constitution was being interpreted by the judges and by the Supreme Court led them to believe or to suspect or I suppose to fear that, in due course or in time, the constitution would be interpreted in a particular way by the Supreme Court so as to allow abortion. The privacy provisions in the constitution would be interpreted in a particular way by the Supreme Court which would 'allow abortion in' and that was a phrase I remember very much at the time. That was certainly something that William Binchy said and his colleagues said, that we would have abortion, and I also remember the phrase (and I'm not saying Binchy used it) that we would have 'abortion in the back door', which was the suggestion it would come through Europe and all that, so the 1861 act was the act that was the law, but the PLAC campaign suggested we needed to be sure that (a) the Supreme Court doesn't change it in some way by interpreting the constitution in a particular way or (b) politicians and the Oireachtas wouldn't introduce legislation or do something inside in the Dàil or the Senate which would change things that the people wouldn't have control over. So that's why they said we need to lock it in to the constitution – this is the way the argument was put – a 'pure form ban' in the constitution that has the effect of banning for all time, abortion, or any abortion law in Ireland.[192]

The issue had in fact been far removed from the centre of political debate and the lobby group involved was 'tiny' and 'the significance of the commitments [given to private meetings at a time of great political instability] enormous'.[193] The Pro-Life Amendment Campaign, launched in 1981, was initially headed by Dr Julia Vaughan, assistant master at Holles Street maternity hospital and a former nun. She exemplified a small but eminent section of the medical community who were worried about sexual permissiveness and what they regarded as the ethical decline experienced in other countries which might contaminate Ireland.

It has also been suggested that one of the sparks that lit the fuse came about when Galway medical student Maria Stack said at the Fine Gael Ard Fheis in April 1981 that she favoured abortion in certain circumstances – she had just been elected vice president of Fine Gael.[194] A number of small groups were galvanised such as the Society for the Protection of the Unborn Child (SPUC), the Responsible Society, the League of Decency, Youth Alert and the Council for Social Concern. Professor John Bonnar, a gynaecologist and advocate of natural family planning methods, was another influential figure. Initially the PLAC seemed to be more interested in a signature campaign, but instead went direct to the politicians, probably due to the political instability that existed at that time (as a result of which politicians were perhaps overly eager to make promises that would secure votes from anti-abortion activists), and there was undoubtedly fear among staff at the maternity hospitals that speaking against the proposal would affect promotion prospects.[195]

'I said in the senate that I gave thanks to God that
I was (a) not heterosexual (b) not a woman'

In his in-depth analysis of the referendum campaign in September 1983, *Magill* journalist Gene Kerrigan accurately described it as 'the Moral Civil War'.[196] He began to look back at the evolution of such groups as the Council of Social Concern, which had told the *Catholic Standard* as far back as 1978 about 'certain undesirable developments in Ireland in recent years'. The same year, the League of Decency had sent pictures of foetuses to TDs, who also received a letter from a Redemptorist priest, Father John Francis Corbett, demanding a referendum which would bring about 'a pre-McGee situation'.

Professor John Bonnar, in an address to the Knights of Columbanus at their headquarters in Ely Place, Dublin, announced that 'Ireland stands alone in her fight to defend the Judeo-Christian moral code of sexual behaviour and the sanctity of life'. In contrast, in February 1980 a small number of Irish feminists publicly protested about the absence of abortion facilities and the resultant reliance on Britain by Irish women wanting abortions, and a women's right to choose movement soon followed. Not long after, SPUC appeared with posters, garish anti-abortion films and a slide show, suggesting that a narrative that places the pro-life group as emerging out of the blue is skewed. Kerrigan pithily summarised the situation of SPUC at that stage: 'the problem was that it was all dressed up, in its Sunday best, with nowhere to go. Abortion was already illegal.'[197]

In the Senate, Mary Robinson pointed out in May 1983 that when she asked social workers about what the view or discussion was in their areas of work, their response was 'What discussion? What amendment? It never comes up.'[198] What was not expected, perhaps, was 'the size and strength' of the opposition to the amendment. The PLAC's proposed wording in April 1981 recognised the 'absolute right of life of every unborn child from conception', but there was no mention of the mother. In relation to this, David Norris recalled that 'I said in the Senate that I gave thanks to God that I was (a) not heterosexual (b) not a woman and (c) not married to any of the Fianna Fáil hypocrites. I would not like to be told, after thirty years of marriage and ten children that I was valued at the same intensity as an embryo the size of the head of a match.'[199]

Intimidation was rife during this referendum campaign. Dr Michael Solomons, when asked what he thought inspired the amendment, replied, 'With the ability to control their fertility, women came out of the house and many men didn't like losing their authority.' He saw the amendment not only as sectarian but as a possible means of outlawing contraception; as a result, he feared vigilantism 'could become rampant in Irish hospitals'.[200] PLAC members who were also members of the Council of Social Concern wrote to the employers of Sally Keogh, a member of the National Social Services Council who had been involved in family planning groups, in an attempt to engineer her dismissal from her job. There were also 'the rabid accusations, the political speeches from the pulpit, the poison pen letters, the threatening phone calls, the attacks on the media, the bomb threats to RTÉ'.[201] Dr Andrew Rynne, chairman of the IFPA, spoke against the idea of conferring human rights on a fertilised ovum as it would 'interfere with established methods of contraception and treatment for rape victims [the morning after pill]'.

Those who spoke against the amendment as dangerous because of the attempt to enshrine the religious views of one section into the constitution, including the Capuchin priest Father Brian O'Mahony, were told by the PLAC that this was not a religious but a human rights issue. Twenty years after the referendum, Goretti Horgan, national organiser of the Anti-Amendment Campaign, acknowledged that her campaign made the 'tactical mistake to have concentrated so much on stopping the referendum. That, and the fact that we had a whole range of sometimes complicated arguments against the amendment, weakened us ... we could and should have been more audacious.' But she also insisted that the anti-amendment activists made a difference and 'kept the door open for the more tolerant Ireland we live in today'.[202]

One of the 'successes' of the pro-life campaign was in reducing the issue to a simplistic 'pro' versus 'anti' life stance, which began to supersede more sophisticated approaches in the past. In 1980, for example, one of Ireland's most accomplished broadcasters, Marian Finucane, won the Prix Italia for a documentary on abortion: 'she had interviewed a woman who was about to have an abortion, had travelled with her to England, been with her in the hospital and talked to her afterwards. The programme offered no opinions as to whether abortion was right or wrong. The woman herself didn't know. The listener, any listener, was made to sense that this was a very complex matter.'[203]

In contrast, because an artificial line had been drawn in the sand, three years later, Fred O'Donovan, the chairman of the RTÉ Authority, prevented Gay Byrne from hosting a *Late Late Show* on the issue because of O'Donovan's own anti-abortion views and the fear it would be a 'trivial' and

'emotional' show. He quoted Dr Bernard Nathanson to justify the censorship: 'we succeeded [in breaking down the laws on abortion in the USA]
because the time was right and the news media co-operated'.[204]

Despite the accusations, those on the anti-amendment side, including Ann Marie Hourihane, were able, twenty years after the event, to be
measured and dignified: 'it is correct to emphasise the sincerity, indeed the
goodness of most of the people who were in the pro-life movement and
voted pro-life. But the fact of the matter was – and *both* sides let this slip
– that the argument became so arcane, so obscure that it alienated most vot-
ers.'[205] It also served to underline the differences between Dublin and the
rest of the country and demonstrated that the urban–rural divide was still
very pronounced. There was more opposition to the amendment in urban
than in rural areas; the battle for votes was more intense in Dublin than
anywhere else and it was also in Dublin that the anti-amendment campaign
was most effective. All five of the constituencies that returned majorities
against the amendment were in Dublin.[206] But it is important to point out
that hypocrisy abounded during this era in relation to the so-called 'sanctity
of life'. In May 1982, at a meeting in a hotel in County Wexford to discuss the
setting up of a family planning centre, Father Seán Fortune, later unmasked
as a serial child rapist, sanctimoniously criticised two Fine Gael TDs who
were present in support of the meeting: 'He said that he now knew that the
two TDs were not pro-life.'[207]

'The wording should read "Get All the Protestants Out"'

Writer Hubert Butler, who had previously written of the hypocrisy and
denial that existed about abortion in Ireland during the Nurse Cadden trial
in the 1950s (see chapter 3), tackled the issue again in 1983 when addressing an anti-amendment campaign meeting in Kilkenny. Abortion, he maintained, was 'always an evil, but best seen as a symptom of a far greater evil,
the total uncaringness of our society'. He insisted the amendment would do
nothing to solve the human dilemmas. Nor was it just a moral issue, it was
also a practical one; if more unwanted children were born: 'Are we going to
shoulder our responsibility towards them? ... Stop and think! What have we
done in the past years for an unmarried mother or an unwanted child? ... the
world in which the unwanted child is born today is a very cruel one.'[208] Butler
raised the questions that few others seemed to want to address. If some had

had their way, as a Protestant, he would have been chased out of Ireland. One fervent anti-abortionist, Irish-language activist and critic of the perceived liberalism of post-Vatican II Catholicism, Mina Bean Uí Chribín, arrived at a meeting in the Mansion House to disrupt an anti-amendment campaign meeting attended by Eamon McCann (who pointed out that abortion 'is as Irish as the green little shamrock'). She addressed Mary Robinson – 'you've the morals of a tom cat' – and RTÉ journalist Anne Daly –'That's the tramp who presents *Women Today*.' She insisted 'pregnancy never ensues from rape' and wrapped up her poisonous contributions with the suggestion that 'the wording should read: 'Get All the Protestants Out.'[209] Nearly twenty-five years later, in 2006, she still maintained that what was at work here was the 'deliberate destruction of the Irish Catholic Church' by a small band of liberal forces.[210]

The PLAC had, in fact, little reason to be bombastic about getting the amendment inserted, given the very poor turn-out, which should also have worried the Catholic Church in light of its extensive exhortations to vote yes.[211] Another overriding question was ignored until the time of the X case in 1992 when the pregnant 14-year-old victim of rape was prevented from travelling to the UK for an abortion, until the decision was overturned by the Supreme Court. Mary Harney, the first female leader of an Irish Political Party, also directly addressed a fundamental question: 'If it is morally right in London, I can't seen why it is morally wrong in Dublin.'[212] That question, avoided and fudged by others, remains unanswered.

In the eighteen years after 1983 there were four referenda on the subject (including one prompted by the X case mentioned above) and thousands of Irish women continued to travel outside the state to have abortions. One, sometimes overlooked impact of the original 1983 referendum was the cynicism it engendered about the capacity of Irish politicians to deal honestly and effectively with issues that directly affected women. Ann Marie Hourihane suggested in 2003:

> To me, one of the biggest results of the amendment was that parliamentary politics lost its thrust. Ever since, social change has come from outside the Dáil and the politicians have been running after the public. I think that's one of the big changes. The Dáil never got to grips with this – it disgraced itself. The momentum moved outside the Dáil to the courts, the tribunals ... But of course, the one set of people it didn't make any difference to were the women who were going to England for

abortions. And all those figures were always underestimated. So it made
no difference. No one gave a curse about them and the politicians still
don't. [213]

The abortion law exemplified both moral and legal ambiguities and a
lack of courage on the part of legislators. In 1992, Justice Niall McCarthy of
the Supreme Court, referring to the 1983 constitutional amendment and the
X case, insisted 'the failure by the legislature to enact the appropriate legislation is no longer unfortunate, it is inexcusable. What are pregnant women
to do? What are the parents of a pregnant girl under age to do? What are
the medical profession to do?' Jennifer Spreng, an American academic, suggested in a 2004 book on divorce and abortion law in Ireland that the current inertia may have arisen 'more from uncertainty about what to do than
from any real satisfaction with the current state of the law'.[214] But this was
better, she seemed to imply, than the situation in the US, where, due to the
liberalisation of the 1960s and attempts to rescind that, absolutists on both
sides were allowed to dominate the debate.

LISTENING

The voices of women who had had abortions were rarely heard in
Ireland. In 2000, for example, after a green paper on abortion appeared,
organisations and individuals were invited to address an all-party Oireachtas committee. The churches and the doctors duly made their submissions,
but the views of women with direct experience were not heard. Medb Ruane
concluded, 'Theological and legal arguments supplant the personal testimony of women.'[215]

But a younger generation of feminists did not appear as willing to take
the issue up. Mary Holland made this plea in March 1995 in the midst of
more bitter words about abortion and the right of Irish women to obtain
information on the subject in Ireland: 'It would be an enormous relief if
some younger woman or women were to start writing about the issue of
abortion from personal experience and leave me to the relatively easy task of
analysing the peace process. Please.'[216] In the same year, during a Dáil debate,
Fine Gael TD Michael Noonan made an impassioned plea for parliamentar-
ians to learn from their previous mistakes:

I call on all deputies to reject the pressure put on them by various inter-
locking organisations, both overt and covert, which constitute the
pro-life movement. I call on all deputies tonight to reject those who
would reach back into the mists of history and try to pressure us with

the ghastly weapons of bell, book and candle ... I call on all Fianna Fáil deputies to stand for the primacy of Dáil Eireann.[217]

One notable feature of the abortion question was the increase in the number of teenagers seeking abortions in Britain between 1975, when 230 travelled, and 2001 when about 900 travelled, though this had dropped to about 650 in 2005, according to the Crisis Pregnancy Agency. The rate of teenage fertility (the number of live births per 1,000 females aged 15 to 19) remained stable; it increased from 16.3 in 1970 to a peak of 23 in 1980; declined through the 1980s but from the mid 1990s rose again, increasing to 20.2 in 1999, and decreased to 16.8 in 2005. The teenage fertility rate was higher than the EU average, but much lower than the UK and the US. Overall, the teenage pregnancy rate (births and abortions) remained 'relatively stable' between 1995 and 2005.[218] In 2006, 5,042 women gave Irish addresses at British abortion clinics.[219]

'There has never been a homosexual republican'

As with abortion, the laws criminalising homosexual acts between men dated from 1861. Many Irish men and women who wanted to live an openly homosexual life found it was better to leave the Republic, and the 1967 legislation legalising homosexuality in England and Wales was not applied to Northern Ireland. The 'Save Ulster from Sodomy' campaign of the late 1970s was a reaction to the bravery of Jeffrey Dudgeon of the Northern Ireland Gay Rights Association (NIGRA), who took the British government to the European Court of Human Rights on the basis that the failure to apply to Northern Ireland the 1967 legislation discriminated against gay people's right to privacy. Dudgeon, who went on to become a civil servant, blazed the trail that was later followed by David Norris in the Republic. This was a remarkable feat given the exceptional homophobia that existed in Northern Ireland and the difficulties that presented for gay people, who were likely to come from very religious backgrounds, Catholic and Protestant. Given the full-scale religious and political conflict that afflicted Northern Ireland, the task Dudgeon set himself was formidable.

Dudgeon faced diehard opposition to his campaign, and not just from the followers of Ian Paisley of the Democratic Unionist Party (DUP) and followers of Free Presbyterianism. From 1972 to 1976 the Northern Ireland

Office ignored pleas for reform that came from the Gay Liberation Movement that had first taken root in 1972. It sent circulars to members of the ill-fated power-sharing assembly in 1974; 63 members did not reply, and of the 14 that did, only 2 Alliance members appeared mildly sympathetic but said that they felt 'unqualified to act'.[220] A Sinn Féin spokesman asserted, 'There has never been a homosexual republican.'[221] In the same year, *Gay News*, Europe's largest circulation newspaper for homosexuals, pictured on its front page six men at Stormont in Belfast, the seat of the Northern Ireland parliament, shortly after they handed in a protest letter demanding a change in Northern Ireland's 'barbaric sex laws. Pushed into the background is the statue of Sir Edward Carson, the man who led the prosecution against Oscar Wilde ... appropriately enough he stood watching the motorcade drive past with 2 bronze fingers raised at the delegation. The seats surrounding the monument are supported by pairs of bronze male nudes, kneeling with bended backs. The sculptor appears to have had a wry sense of humour.' The paper also criticised the belief that the Northern Ireland Civil Rights Association 'threatens to kiss the whole thing to death through apathy'.[222]

The Cara (the Irish word for friend) Group, established in October 1974 as an information and befriending organisation for gay people, was faced with 'direct refusals by most of the Northern Ireland newspapers to accept our advertisements'. In the region of 800 people were contacting it every year; one quarter were or had been married, and 90 per cent were male. Between 1974 and 1978, 2,380 people contacted Cara, 47 per cent of them in their twenties. Of all of these, only one in seven had established contact with gay people. Things did begin to improve, though, and Dudgeon was able to write that it was 'heartening that in a province where religious differences divide most of the community, the gay scene has never been sectarian ... the bond of a common sexuality is far stronger than adherence to sectarian differences. Heterosexual society in Ulster could well take a lesson from the homosexual minority in its midst'.[223] The NIGRA wrote in April 1976 of the irony in the fact that the organisation Cara 'which could quite easily be accused of corrupting public morals under Northern Ireland law ... gets £750 p.a. from the Department of Health and Social Services.'[224]

The Secretary of State for Northern Ireland, Merlyn Rees, justified taking no action regarding the legality of homosexuality on the basis that he was only standing in for a devolved legislature and therefore he could not act, even to guarantee the basic human freedoms that had been granted to the gay community in England and Wales. Meanwhile, prosecutions continued. In 1976 a trial judge in Coleraine, before sentencing two men aged 20 and 24 to suspended terms of imprisonment for consensual sex in private, reminded them that 'they were lucky not to be executed as happened in the recent past'.[225] In the same year a letter writer to the *Sunday News* was 'afflicted with the notion that homosexuality is a peculiarity of the English upper class and a cult to which the inadequate are easily attracted'.[226] For Dudgeon and others there was some success in terms of providing information, social events and solidarity, but they failed to get *Gay News* stocked in Belfast Central Library, 'as it would encourage illegal acts', or to extract any promise from the Director of Public Prosecutions (DPP) not to prosecute gays for acts legal in England, as in Scotland the Lord Advocate had done.[227]

In the same year, Dudgeon lodged his case with the European Commission of Human Rights on the grounds that male homosexuals were denied the right of respect for private life guaranteed in Article 8 of the European Convention of Human Rights. He also claimed they were discriminated against on the grounds of residence, because citizens of the same state living in Liverpool could not be jailed for acts that were liable to bring life imprisonment in Belfast, under the late nineteenth-century laws that still operated in respect of homosexuality. Dudgeon also argued that homosexual men faced further discrimination since lesbian women were not singled out for prosecution.[228]

In 1976, Mervyn Rees admitted in parliament that law reform should be considered, but at the same time a squad of four RUC officers was established to target gay men and over a six-month period it arrested twenty-two, including every male committee member of NIGRA. The 'Gay Squad' included a detective inspector, a top CID sergeant and a drug squad constable who knew how to 'mingle with deviants'. Dudgeon recalled, 'Every scrap of paper relating to gay matters was seized and held for over twelve months. Questioning was sordid and humiliating – diaries and personal letters were read back to the authors. Threats, of exposure to parents and employers, and forcible medical examinations, were freely made. Several individuals were taken for questioning in front of their unsuspecting parents, leading to traumatic relationship problems on release.'

It took six months for the DPP to prepare cases against four of the men and there was nothing but silence from the political parties in the North, although Liberal MPs tabled questions in the House of Commons. In April 1976, Dudgeon, in his role as chairperson of the committee for homosexual law reform, wrote to Sam Silkin, the Attorney General, concerning the RUC activities: 'It goes without saying that many people here are now extremely frightened and have been forced to adopt extreme measures such as destroying many of their papers, especially as the investigation has become open-ended. As you know, all gay males here are potentially criminal and liable to investigation.'[229]

The Attorney General eventually told the DPP not to proceed with the charges, though NIGRA's complaint against the RUC for not producing search warrants was turned down. There were some suggestions from Liberal MPs in the House of Commons that the 1967 act should be applied to Northern Ireland, and the Northern Ireland Office asked the Standing Advisory Commission on Human Rights to assess public opinion on law reform. It suggested extending the 1967 act to Northern Ireland, but there was further delay when new Secretary of State for Northern Ireland Roy Mason's administration made implicit deals with the Unionist MPs to hold off on reform in return for their abstention in critical Westminster votes.

There is no doubt that prejudice was also exacerbated by some of the churches (though support was given by the Church of Ireland) and there were divisions within the gay rights movement, partly due to the external pressures under which it operated during fierce sectarian violence. In December 1977, the NIGRA newspaper reported that the SDLP passed a motion at their conference from the Queen's University branch supporting reform, the first party to do so. It was also observed that a member of the SDLP's executive, Alban Maguinness, regarded gay rights as civil and human rights, in contrast to his party colleague Paddy Rowan, who opposed them on the grounds that homosexuality 'was a perversion, a deeply frustrating experience and led to deep neurosis and psychosis'. NIGRA was vocal about 'the hypocrisy of the DUP, who one moment are clamouring for the same rights and democratic institutions as Britain and the next are campaigning to stop the implementation of British laws here'.[230] An opinion poll conducted for Ulster Television in January 1978 suggested that society in Northern Ireland was split down the middle when it came to law reform in this area. Responding to the question 'Are you in favour of divorce and homosexual law reform?', 42 per cent of adults responded favourably and 42 per cent against, with 15 per cent undecided.[231]

'Save Ulster from Sodomy'

The oppressive social and political climate that existed in Northern Ireland in the 1970s made it easier for the advent of the DUP's 'Save Ulster from Sodomy' campaign, which attracted 70,000 signatures (5 per cent of the population), though as Dudgeon wryly recalled, 'this diversion did not express itself in any greater hostility to gays as queer bashers tend not to be great church goers anyway'. A supporter of Dudgeon wrote to him in May 1979: 'Ought I to write again as an individual to the Northern Ireland Office to object to the Save Ulster from Sodomy list being interpreted as a plebiscite?'[232] The DUP literature during this protest stressed: 'our protest is not against homosexuals, it is against the social and legal acceptance of homosexuality as "normal". Homosexuality demands not acceptance but a cure. The legalising of homosexuality would open the floodgates of immorality with countless other vices demanding acceptance. The consequences of such a deluge would be grim.'[233]

The DUP was apt to quote from the *Universal Evangeliser*: 'You were not born that way and there is very little evidence that these traits are inherited, it is more a habit pattern you have built over a period of time. It is not just "natural", nor is it a chemical imbalance in the glands. It can however be a result of spiritual imbalance.' A local election candidate from the DUP, targeting the gay rights campaign in the late 1970s, also published outright lies, maintaining that homosexuals posed a particular risk to children: 'the grave danger to children is shown to be all the more real when one considers that at a recent conference of the campaign for homosexual equality over one-third of the delegates present expressed a homosexual interest in children, while the Paedophile Information Exchange is presently conducting an insidious campaign to have sex with children legalised'.[234]

In 1978 the Belfast *Sunday News* reported that in Belfast 'the secretary of NIGRA was assaulted by RUC officers while picketing a newsagent's shop in protest at its refusal to stock *Gay News*. KM was dragged into the back of a police Land Rover, hit twice in the face and left blood splattered and bleeding from the nose.' The following year, Anthony McCleave was found dead in one of the city's best-known 'cruising areas'. Although police maintained they were confident his death was accidental, as a result of a fall, the man's family and NIGRA rejected this: 'They are convinced that the nature of the injuries inflicted and the surrounding circumstances show him to have been the victim of a "queer bashing" gang. An acquaintance of the family had been chased by a gang of youths only 45 minutes before McCleave's death in the same area. In the previous week other gay men had been beaten up in the same street – one of whom had earlier been to the same gay club where McCleave had last been seen alive, 90 minutes before his body was found. In the previous five years two other gay men, Frederick Davis and Thomas MacKenzie, had been murdered in the same area.'[235]

Between May 1977 and May 1980, 250 incidents of attacks on gay people in Great Britain and Northern Ireland were reported, 15 per cent of which resulted in death or disablement. In relation to the McCleave case, 'most disturbing of all was the evidence which emerged at the inquest, when the police themselves revealed that they had taken statements from firemen at a local fire station, who had heard a disturbance a few minutes before the time of the death. The inquest returned an open verdict.'[236]

In 1979, one activist queried the Attorney General about the possibility of Irish gay people becoming refugees in England, given that they were 'liable to prosecution in their own states for crimes that lack victims ... we ask therefore if the UK government accepts the political nature of gay liberation and sexual orientation and would grant political asylum in such instances?'[237]

Dudgeon's arguments were declared admissible for a hearing in Strasbourg in July 1979, with the onus of proof that 'interference by public authority with the exercise of the right to an unhindered private homosexual life is necessary in a democratic society' resting with the respondent government.[238] Dudgeon's papers (held in the Public Record Office of Northern Ireland) also contain notes from the court hearing statements by the lawyer for the British government. He maintained there was no support from the North's politicians, that a 'different moral ethos obtains in Northern Ireland', that there was a desire for 'a unified conservative Christianity' in Northern Ireland and that there existed a 'strong streak of independence in NI character.'[239]

An important part of Dudgeon's case was that the British government was acting inconsistently by partly funding the group Cara, thereby authorising expenditure on services which encouraged homosexuals to associate with other homosexuals, while at the same time maintaining that restrictions were necessary in criminal law on the grounds of public morals. The European Court of Human Rights accepted 'the change in moral climate towards homosexual conduct throughout Europe' and that homosexuality was not a disease,[240] though in a dissenting judgment, Irish judge Brian

Walsh wrote that 'a distinction must be drawn between homosexuals who are such because of some kind of innate instinct or pathological constitution judged to be incurable, and those whose tendency comes from a lack of normal sexual development or from habit or from experience of other similar causes but whose tendency is not incurable. So far as the incurable category is concerned, the activity must be regarded as abnormalities or even handicaps and treated with compassion and tolerance which is required to prevent those persons from being victimised.'[241]

In 1981, Dudgeon won his case when the European Court held that the legislation criminalising male homosexual acts violated the European Convention on Human Rights. In the same year he observed of the policy advisory committee on sexual offences in London which submitted a report to the court that it appeared 'irrational and contradictory' for the UK government to submit this report which unanimously supported the view that its citizens had a right to a homosexual private life from the age of 18, when the same government was arguing that 'no man in Northern Ireland should have this right at any age.'[242] Even after he had won his case, Dudgeon suffered discrimination when he applied for a job in the civil service.[243]

Dudgeon's story was often forgotten in the midst of the Troubles in Northern Ireland. His successful legal action also represented a rare defeat for Ian Paisley, as 'the pink hand slapped him across the face'.[244] Dudgeon was also honest about the divisions that existed in the gay community, pointing out that 'most Lesbians in Belfast are simply apolitical – a fact which surely must be blamed in part on the failure of "political gays" to communicate their ideas and to demonstrate their relevance'.[245]

'Filthy, lewd and perverted'

Despite Jeffrey Dudgeon's legal victory, the climate in Northern Ireland remained very cold when it came to tolerance of sexual diversity in the late twentieth century. In 1995, Marie Mullholland described herself as someone who 'has been out as a dyke and a Republican for 17 years. These two influences ensure that she never becomes complacent.'[246] A Gay IRA member who spent seventeen years in prison wrote a letter on the subject of homosexuality from H Block 5 in 1995 pointing out that it was only in 1980, a full six years after the emergence of a gay and lesbian movement in Ireland, that Sinn Féin adopted a (one-line) motion at its Ard Fheis in relation to

homosexuality. In 1991 an article appeared in *Glór Gafa* ('Prisoner's Voice')
a quarterly magazine written exclusively by Republican prisoners, entitled
'Hidden Comrades: Gays and Lesbians in the Struggle'. It was the first time
that a Republican, and a prisoner to boot, had come out publicly as gay and
argued that 'national liberation by its very nature incorporates gay/lesbian
liberation'. The article received a mixed reaction and it was eighteen months
before Sinn Féin agreed to pass a new motion in relation to homosexual
rights.[247]

In 1979, Margo Gorman had argued that the struggle for lesbians in
Northern Ireland should not be about 'accepting paltry reforms granted by
the British government', suggesting gay women could help to 'undermine
the ideologies of both reactionary camps' and challenge any political analysis 'which sees these issues as diversionary'.[248] The 'dirty protest' by female
Republican prisoners the following year had raised the issue of the male
treatment of young female prisoners from Armagh who were 'socialised in
a strict Catholic morality that strongly emphasised modesty. The handling
of women prisoners' bodies by male officers was deeply distressing.' The subsequent dirty protest was, in that sense, one of reclamation and resistance;
Nell McCafferty did her best to highlight that 'there is menstrual blood on
the walls of Armagh prison in Northern Ireland'.[249]

The first Belfast Pride festival was organised in 1991 at a time when a
Protestant minister referred to the gay community as 'worse than dogs'.[250]
Such rhetoric was commonplace in Northern Ireland for many years. As
outlined above, members of the DUP had never made any secret of their
personal distaste for homosexual practice, but in 2005 the Parades Commission rejected claims by the Free Presbyterian Church and the Stop the Parade
Coalition that the Gay Pride march was 'filthy, lewd and perverted'[251] and so
should be banned. In the same year, James Knox became the first openly gay
man to be appointed a member of the Equality Commission for Northern
Ireland. Greater tolerance was facilitated by Section 75 of the 1998 Northern
Ireland Act, which stipulated that more than 200 government agencies des-
ignated under it have to communicate with all groups, including gay rights
groups, when they consult on policy.

But in no sense was homophobia eradicated in Northern Ireland;
there were an estimated five homophobic murders between 1999 and 2005,
including one in south Belfast, in which a 31-year-old civil servant was
stabbed and battered to death with a wheel brace by two teenage boys out
on what a judge called a 'queer-bashing expedition'. Between 2004 and 2005

homophobic incidents reported to police doubled to almost 200; according to Belfast's Institute for Conflict Research, homophobia was still seen as a 'respectable and acceptable prejudice' and its research found that only 27 per cent of gay, lesbian or bisexual people in Northern Ireland felt safe walking down the street at night. In Derry, reports of homophobic incidents increased by 300 per cent between mid 2004 and mid 2005: there was an increase in the ferocity of the attacks but clearly the gay community's confidence had grown in reporting abuse to the police.

One man stabbed outside a gay nightclub with a screwdriver indicated the confused nature of the province's hate crimes and the legacy of the sectarian conflict. The gay Protestant victim, subjected to the taunt of 'Die, you Fenian bastard!', 'was not sure whether to report the attack as sectarian or homophobic'. In 2005, police clearance rates for homophobic crime stood at 22.5 per cent.[252] A measure of the change in attitudes over forty years was evident in July 2007 when the iconic Free Derry Wall in the Bogside of Derry was painted pink for the Gay and Lesbian Foyle Pride Festival, the theme of which was 'Free to be Me'. The festival organiser, David McCartney, pointed out that the climate had improved greatly for gay people in the North in the previous few years. In 2002, the last time the festival had been held in Derry, there had been 93 homophobic attacks in the city; in 2007 there were two.

Veteran British-based gay rights activist Peter Tatchell maintained in 2008 that 'homophobia still runs deep' in Northern Ireland. He also claimed that William of Orange, so revered in the Unionist tradition, was gay, as reflected in the political satires and poems about his homosexuality during his reign and the political elevation of his male lovers. Most historians do not accept there is definitive proof of King William's homosexuality, although Brian Lacey insists, 'One thing is definitely clear: there is as much – if not more – circumstantial evidence that William was homosexual as that he was heterosexual',[253] – but Tatchell asserted that the truth about his sexuality had been censored and there was a 'great deal of hypocrisy' among Unionist politicians in the North, some of whom publicly spoke of homosexuality as a disease. The previous year, a survey found that 36 per cent of people in Northern Ireland would not want a gay person as a neighbour.[254]

*'If there's one thing Catholic and Protestant reactionaries
in the North can unite on, it's that young people
mustn't be allowed to enjoy sex'*

Attitudes to sexuality generally in Northern Ireland have undoubtedly been
affected by fundamentalism across the board; to those who shared the mindset of Ian Paisley, Catholicism was viewed, not just as a false religion, but
also as the source of social vice. Steve Bruce draws attention to the beliefs
espoused by Protestant extremists: the notion that, while Ulster Protestants
were 'self-reliant, hard-working, diligent, honest, loyal, responsible and tem-
perate', Catholics, 'discouraged from thinking for themselves by priests who
wish to keep their people in a state of dependency ... are slothful, dishonest and untrustworthy, are sexually irresponsible, use confession to wipe
the state clean, while priestly celibacy encourages sexual perversion'. Paisley thrived on shouting such assertions.[255] Issues of sexual morality loomed
large in Free Presbyterianism; the Church's General Presbytery cautioned
against new trends such as line-dancing, which was deemed to be 'as sinful
as any other type of dancing, with its sexual gestures and touchings. It is
sensual, and not a crucifying of lust, but an excitement to lust.' This warning
gave rise to a joke in Belfast: 'Why do Free Presbyterians not have sex standing up?' 'Because it could lead to line-dancing.'[256]

The incidence and legacy of child abuse, within institutions and families, also haunted certain individuals and families in Northern Ireland. In the
summer of 1977, an 11-year-old girl was raped by her father, a high-ranking
prison officer, beginning a catalogue of sexual abuse. Eleven years later she
went to the police but dropped the allegations after her father begged her
to, citing her mother's fragile health. In 2002 he was charged and the following year sentenced to nine years in prison (there was a 50 per cent remission
rule for sexual offenders). His daughter then had to fight a compensation
battle as the law from 1978 to 1983 stated that a child was not entitled to
compensation if raped by a member of the same household. The law was
subsequently changed but it did not apply to victims whose abuse dated
from those years.[257]

Ministry of Defence information officer Colin Wallace, an Ulster-born
ex-soldier who frequently briefed the media and allegedly spread black propaganda on behalf of his MoD masters, was sacked in 1975; he claimed it
was for threatening to expose a homosexual ring at the Kincora boys' home
in east Belfast, which was run by extreme Loyalist William McGrath. The

allegation that Ian Paisley failed to act on allegations about McGrath's pae-dophilial inclinations was dismissed by followers of Paisley as yet another perfidious plot against him. But, as has been pointed out by Ed Moloney, 'the incidental fact that McGrath was a fellow fundamentalist and head of a bizarre Loyalist paramilitary group, Tara, with which some DUP figures were associated, was conveniently overlooked'.[258]

In 1980, the Kincora affair was exposed and three men were subse-quently convicted of sexual abuse. Wallace was then charged with the mur-der of his best friend, Jonathan Lewis, who was found floating in the river Arun at Arundel, West Sussex. He protested his innocence but was found guilty of manslaughter in 1981 and jailed for ten years, serving six years of the sentence before being released on parole. While in prison he sent a dossier to the British Prime Minister Margaret Thatcher alleging a dirty tricks cam-paign in Northern Ireland in the early 1970s. But after his allegations were repeatedly raised by MPs – Ken Livingstone, then a backbench Labour MP, was particularly vocal – it was admitted in 1990 that such a dirty tricks cam-paign had indeed been in operation. After an investigation into his sacking, Wallace was awarded £30,000 compensation for wrongful dismissal and in 1996 the British Court of Appeal overturned his manslaughter conviction.[259]

Another disturbing case was disclosed in the family division of the Bel-fast High Court during a health and social services trust application for a care order for the victims in January 2006. The judge referred to 'a haunting picture of a household subsumed in an atmosphere of sexual malevolence', with multiple child rape by a father and older brother. What was also shock-ing, as Suzanne Breen has pointed out, was that 'the youngsters came to the attention of various agencies and professionals on numerous occasions over the two years before they were taken into care'. Significantly more children per head of population were on the child protection register in Northern Ireland (1,593 in 2006) compared to England and Scotland; 15 per cent of them were deemed to be at risk of sexual abuse.[260] A bisexual ex-IRA pris-oner from north Belfast was cleared in 2006 of 28 accounts of indecent assault on three boys after a jury failed to reach a verdict, but he found there was a reluctance within the Republican movement to acknowledge him or the verdict: 'I wasn't the only bisexual in the movement,' he insisted. He wrote a book on the issue, *Republican Outcast*.[261]

The peace process and the continuing preoccupation of paramilitary groups with drugs and hedonism prompted a kiss-and-tell memoir from Jackie Robinson, mistress of the Shankill UDA commander Johnny Adair.

Suzanne Breen notes that the book opened the door 'on a sordid world of sex and sectarianism, where morality had been extinguished. There is no Republican equivalent.'[262]

Kevin Myers, when reflecting on his time in Belfast as an RTÉ journalist in the early 1970s, during some of the worst of the violence, very confidently recalled his own sexual conquests – 'occasional one-night stands: an artist, a woman the week before she got married – a final fling – and a married woman for whom I was her first extra-marital affair' – in considerable and often colourful detail ('I opened her bra, and out fell her vast, stunning breasts, upon which would have feasted an entire consistory of homosexual cardinals, yodelling with joy').[263] He recounted such encounters and drew attention to 'resolutely casual' sex, because 'this book is also about a naïve young man in pursuit of the adrenaline of war and that cocktail of hormones accompanying love and sex. During the 1970s I behaved like young men have always wanted to, and always will.' Given the number of journalists reporting on the conflict, there were also opportunities for prostitutes to make a living from servicing them.[264]

In relation to young people in Northern Ireland and their attitude to sex, one survey, which involved 1,013 respondents in the 14 to 25-year-old age bracket, reported that 53.3 per cent had had sex, of which 27.4 per cent said they had not used contraception. Most wanted to see more sex education in school and the majority 'regarded friends as their most important source of sex education'. Despite the sectarian divides, 'religious differences accounted for few and mostly insignificant differences in sexual attitudes and lifestyles of young people in Northern Ireland'.[265] In 1991, an unusual coalition of the Free Presbyterian Church, the Society for the Protection of the Unborn Child (SPUC), the Orange Order, the DUP, the Knights of Columbanus, the Official Unionist Party and Opus Dei opposed the establishment of a Brook Advisory Centre clinic in Belfast, at a time when the Brook organisation was already operating in seventeen centres in Britain. Its clinics offered free, confidential advice to young people on all aspects of sexuality, including options in the event of unwanted pregnancy. The Eastern Health Board had promised to part fund the clinic. Eamonn McCann noted the constant mention of contraception 'as a danger' from which young people must be protected, and what he regarded as the sleight of hand involved in linking the issues of contraception and abortion. This was evident in the words of Kathleen McQuaid, the Northern secretary of SPUC, who referred to 'the disastrous consequences of contraception and abortion'. McCann wrote acidly: 'If there's one thing Catholic and Protestant reactionaries in the North can unite on, it's that young people mustn't be allowed to enjoy sex.'[266] But there was more tolerance in other respects: few people seemed to rush to condemn the PSNI boss Hugh Orde in 2007 when he admitted his decision to have a child with his divorced mistress of three years while still married to his wife of twenty-two years.[267]

'Homosexuals Are Revolting'

Sociologist Paul Ryan has argued that there was a 'uniquely Irish coming-out experience' for homosexual men in the Republic and that the process cannot be 'adequately explained within a modernisation perspective so frequently used to explain social change in Ireland'. Based on interviews with four gay men reared in Ireland in the 1970s, he argues that it was within families, Christian Brothers' schools and Gaelic playing grounds that 'a unique sense of sexual confusion, anxiety and ultimately identity was produced'. He further maintains that boys did have sexual encounters with other boys but remained free of sexual categorisation at a time when there was no language to describe such encounters; that schools in fact 'multiplied the number of discourses in which sex could be spoken', even if the discussion of sexuality 'centred upon a categorical condemnation of masturbation'.[268]

Notwithstanding this, the evidence of the detailed documentation to be found in the Irish Queer Archive, which charts the struggle of the Irish gay rights movement to achieve equality for gay Irish men and women in the Republic from the 1970s to the early twenty-first century, and which was donated to the National Library of Ireland in 2008, contains plenty of evidence of the fear, anxiety and isolation that was experienced by Irish homosexuals. For many, the challenge was to seek out people experiencing the same feelings and, for those who were politically active, to confront the fact that they were seen as being in a different category from those demanding civil rights during an era of widespread protest. In 1971, Joycean scholar and Trinity College Dublin lecturer David Norris attended a meeting of the Southern Ireland Civil Rights Association which was convened to discuss the plight of minorities: 'he wondered when they were going to discuss homosexual minorities but none of them did'; he then informed them that 'there were more homosexuals in the Republic than there were Protestants.'[269]

The archive also underlines the considerable social, political and administrative achievements of a number of dedicated individuals and small organisations devoted to the welfare of the gay community and to the repeal of the 1861 law criminalising homosexual acts between men, which was eventually decriminalised in 1993. Established initially by young men, the Irish gay rights movement became an impressive lobbying group and its attention to detail was exceptional, as was its resilience. The archive also indicates that those involved kept abreast of relevant developments in the international gay community by amassing a huge quantity of foreign publications devoted to gay issues: almost 200 international titles dating from 1976, as well as the International Lesbian and Gay Association (ILGA) bulletin, are contained in the archive. The ILGA, established in England in 1978, included representatives from over thirty countries; there were also Irish representatives at the conferences of the International Gay Association. At its third annual conference Ireland had four member groups: the National Gay Federation (NGA), the Cork Gay Collective, the Campaign for Homosexual Law Reform and the Irish Gay Rights Movement (IGRM). In contrast, Italy, Norway, Finland and Greece each had only a single member group.[270]

The gay rights battle in Ireland was hard fought, and there were numerous tensions within the movement, particularly between those who wanted to prioritise law reform in as loud a manner as possible and those who preferred to concentrate quietly on creating a social space for the gay community. The NGF and the IGRM fought publicly on the international gay stage about which group was best placed to represent Irish homosexuals.[271]

In 1974, the year of the first Gay Pride March in Britain, the Irish Gay Rights Movement was established and a handful of people marched from the British embassy in Ballsbridge to the Department of Justice carrying banners, including one that announced, 'Homosexuals Are Revolting'. When they were outside the department, a van delivering a carpet stopped, one of the two men got out to have a look and shouted back to his colleague in the driving seat, 'Jesus, it's fucking queers!' The driver responded, 'Wohrra bowra sure I don't give a bollicks, a picket's a fucking picket!', and with that 'an even larger and more muscular lorry driver jumped out of the cab and joined in the picket for a quarter of an hour, leaving the minister's carpet stranded on the pavement'[272] – perhaps an early indication that the campaigners would attract support from what they would have regarded as some unlikely quarters.

'It's a completely unnatural performance'

Within a few years there was a concerted effort to establish a network of gay activists who sought to do a lot more than stage public protests but, given the laws against the practice of male homosexuality, they faced formidable obstacles. Nell McCafferty's influential 'In the Eyes of the Law' columns for the *Irish Times* included an account from September 1975 of two men brought to trial after a sexual encounter in a public toilet. What was illuminating was the manner in which the men were 'pathologised, represented as immature, recommended for medical treatment and publicly humiliated'. A priest referred one of the defendants to a psychiatrist; the other was deemed to be suffering from depression. They were bound to keep the peace for a year, the judge commenting, 'It's a completely unnatural performance.'[273]

Other gay men were forced to undergo humiliating treatment. In 1996, one such victim from Waterford wrote to Stephen Meyler, the features editor of the *Gay Community News* newspaper, informing him of the aversion therapy he underwent: 'I ... had a bad time of it myself in 1975 and it was unbelievable what they got away with.'[274] In the mid 1970s another man informed his GP he was gay: 'He nearly fell off his chair, said he knew nothing about the subject and told me to ring St Brendan's hospital for an appointment.'[275] Of the 180 callers to the Samaritans in 1978 whose problem was homosexuality, 20 per cent were classified as suicidal.[276]

In September 1975, the IGRM announced 'with confidence' the opening of a new disco called the Phoenix Club at Parnell Square, which was accessed from the basement.[277] In the context of the emergence of the IGRM, David Norris, who said he had feared being taken in for police questioning, consulted a Garda superintendent in Dublin 'whose response had been humane and sympathetic ... at that level they were ignored'.[278] But Norris also recalled that during the 1970s there was a 'considerable number' of cases of men being arrested in compromising positions and the 'humiliation' that followed even when they were acquitted. In particular, he recalled one case in which a young man in the Dublin district court was forced to recount the sex act he had performed with another man in the Phoenix Park: 'the judge amused himself by making comic remarks ... to the huge enjoyment of those in the body of the court and to the understandable human distress of the accused'.[279] Norris recounted district court cases at which he would turn up as a character witness in which men were fined, given suspended sentences or ordered to see a psychiatrist: 'I would be wearing a three-piece suit, a Trinity tie, a briefcase, look terribly respectable and give character evidence. The Gardaí were used to people coming in a state of collapse saying I'm guilty, I'm terribly sorry, please don't ... when we started defending and we had a string of successes, they realised it was not worth their while.'[280]

According to figures used by Norris in his legal case in Europe (see below), between 1979 and 1987 the following number of men were prosecuted for indecency with males or gross indecency: 13 in 1979; 33 in 1980; 41 in 1982; 19 in 1983; 52 in 1984; 33 in 1985; and 25 in 1986. Norris also focused in particular on 1973 and 1974 – of the 23 men sentenced in 1973, 18 (78 per cent) were over the age of 21 (the age of homosexual consent in Britain). While it was true that the number of prosecutions was small, that in itself indicated, according to Norris, 'the existence of fundamentally bad law, which is in general inoperable, and where random attempts at enforcement are made, arbitrary and unjust in the extreme.'[281]

'The schismatic tendency of the Irish temperament should always be borne in mind'

Profiles of the candidates seeking election to the national executive of the IGRM in May 1977 included references to the fact that 'the recent problems within the IGRM have caused a lot of energy to be directed towards solving internal matters.'[282] Other problems identified included the isolation of gay people in rural areas, a sense that 'the organisation is in danger of being seen as too Dublin-oriented', and concern about 'those unfortunate people who for one reason or another cannot find an opportunity to travel to Dublin'. There were also references to a 'gay discussion group' run by the Legion of Mary and educational meetings with 'a large group of Maynooth seminarians'.

Edmund Lynch, a founder member of the IGRM who organised the first symposium on gay rights in Ireland at Trinity College in 1974, was employed by RTÉ, which 'helped the movement to obtain interviews and programmes on gay issues'. This was a reference to a half-hour programme, *Challenge*, broadcast in early 1977, in which David Norris challenged a studio audience on why the laws on homosexuality should be changed.[283] Perhaps ironically, given his flamboyance, fluency and the larger-than-life personality that so many Irish people were subsequently to become familiar with – and the fact that he became the most recognised gay man in Ireland

– Norris, in seeking election to the executive of the IGRM, declared he was against 'the promotion of personalities rather than issues'.[284]

Nor were all the experiences referred to negative: one candidate who had spent nine years in England returned to Ireland for a holiday in 1976 'and liked the scene here so much that I decided to stay'. Tom Shine observed that on his return to Dublin from abroad in 1975 he was 'more than surprised, albeit pleasantly, to find a gay liberation movement in Ireland'. Positive mention was also made of Father Michael Cleary, who, it was maintained, had 'come out in favour of gay rights', and the fact that RTÉ radio was tackling the issue.[285] But there was no unanimity on the direction the IGRM should take: a minority of the more politicised members moved to create the Campaign for Homosexual Law Reform, while dissent within the ranks of the IGRM ultimately led to the formation of the National Gay Federation (NGF), which opened the Hirschfeld Centre in Fownes Street, Dublin city, as a gay and lesbian community centre in 1979.

The same year, the NGF launched its in-house journal *In Touch*, one of a number of short-lived publications for the gay community. This contained details of the operation of the Hirschfeld Centre (named after Magnus Hirschfeld, the early twentieth-century German sexologist and gay rights advocate), designed to 'establish a network of community services for gay people ... run largely by volunteers but to the standards usually associated with a commercial enterprise'. Norris maintained that the Gardaí welcomed its existence as it kept homosexuals off the streets and out of their orbit. The truth, suggests Colm Tóibín, was that the Gardaí did not want to enforce the laws against homosexuals, but neither did anybody want to see a change in those laws: 'police and politicians just want homosexuals to go away.'[286]

The Hirschfeld Centre, with a nightclub, cinema and boardroom, provided a haven for many but was subjected to frequent internal criticism in the early 1980s, as was the structure of the administrative council of the NGF and its subcommittees. One discussion paper maintained: 'The present structure is a hierarchy. It is rigid, business-like, efficient and ideally suited to the administration of a businessmen's club. It is not suited, in fact it militates against, open discussion on gay political issues. Too many council meetings deal with minutes, matters arising, correspondence and perhaps one or two items out of a list of nine or ten. Items dealing with the administration of the centre itself seem to outweigh all others, i.e. social activities outweigh political.'[287]

This tension between the 'social' and the 'political' (which some believed was 'a false distinction')[288] remained divisive, but what is clear from the archive is that the very existence of the Hirschfeld Centre, particularly for those in isolated rural areas prepared to travel to Dublin, was liberating. Notwithstanding, concerns were expressed about the perceived caution of the gay organisations. In 1982, Tonie Walsh, president of the NGF, received a letter from a 19-year-old Sligo man seeking a pen friend who said he had contacted the IGRM, but because of his youth 'they said they were very sorry to hear about my problem; they said they would like to help but they said I could get them into trouble ... If they only knew how lonely I am and depressed and am on the verge of a breakdown so will you please help me ... If I could write to somebody and share my problem it would be a great help.'[289]

Another 19-year-old Sligo man told Walsh two years later, 'I visited the centre recently when I was in Dublin ... I was amazed at the amount of people there'. The same man had also been looking for pen friends: 'I would like to make new friends in Dublin, but anywhere in the country or in the world would be great'.[290] The NGF had identified the problem of lonely young gay men in 1979 with a detailed 60-page discussion document by Bernard Keogh, which underlined the need for information, support and contact with people of a similar age. A National Youth Group was established in the same year.[291] Tonie Walsh, who was only 23 at the time, recalls how the befriending and counselling service, tel-a-friend, and the Hirschfeld Centre provided a 'haven' after many years of agonising about his homosexuality, his difficulty with the language of deviance used by the Church about homosexuality and his regular prayer at his local church in Clonmel when he was a teenager: 'Please God don't let me be a homosexual.'[292]

But rows continued about the structure and activities of the centre and the NGF. John Grundy informed members of the NGF of the fear that too few people had a monopoly on policy making and, in seeking election to its executive, he promised to 'reform the relationship between the NGF and the private limited company known as Hirschfeld Enterprises Ltd, which has the gravest implications for democracy'. In June 1980, Norris referred to tensions between the original IGRM (dubbed the 'Provisionals' by the NGF) and the 1,300-member NGF, by suggesting the choice was 'between teeney parties with the 'Provisionals' or gay liberation with the NGF'.[293] But two years later, Norris used a different language when addressing the third annual general meeting of the NGF in his capacity as political co-ordinator: 'the bitter, sometimes tragically frustrating experience of the past has been to show us how difficult and yet how necessary it is to keep the two twin functions – social and political – running in harmonious tandem rather than pulling against each other ... the schismatic tendency of the Irish temperament should always be borne in mind.'[294] He also maintained that getting involved in other issues such as contraception and abortion campaigns would be 'a serious tactical error on our part'. It was also argued that there was a need for a 'lavender flying column' to saturate correspondence columns (which Bernard Keogh, the general secretary of the NGF, did very effectively), fill the airwaves and influence professional groups to counteract the claims of 'these crypto-fascist groups in Ireland who have always claimed that the decriminalisation of homosexual acts is the thin end of the wedge'.[295]

But others were critical of such a strident tone, including John Grundy, who opposed the notion of a 'gay identity' on the grounds that it meant only 10 per cent of the population could be identified with. Grundy lambasted the internal power politics of the Irish gay rights groups, in particular the 'small number of crusading ideologues with a gargantuan Messianic complex' and those who believed they knew 'what every person of homosexual orientation is thinking or feeling'. There are many gay people, he insisted, 'who feel helpless against the glib verbal fluency of the gay liberation dialecticians' and there was a tendency to exaggerate the prejudice that existed against the gay community.[296]

In this sense, how did the Irish gay community fare in comparison with its international peers? There are numerous references in the Irish Queer Archive to sympathetic Gardaí, but the second edition of *In Touch* magazine also felt it necessary to include an article on the danger of gay men being blackmailed. In April 1981, Oliver Cogan, a Cork gay rights activist who wrote to Bernard Keogh, maintained that 'unfortunately, developments within the gay situation in other countries tend to put us in Ireland somewhat in the shade'.[297]

Notwithstanding, there was no shortage of stories from abroad about the persecution of homosexuals in the 1980s, as reflected in the international publications being read by the Irish gay community. Dr Robert Runcie, the Archbishop of Canterbury, suggested in 1981 that homosexuals should be treated as 'handicapped'.[298] Scottish laws were similar to their Irish equivalents regarding homosexual acts and the International Gay Association Bulletin in 1985 referred to homophobia in Britain, 'increased political activities against us [and] sensationalism about AIDS'. There were stories of the court-martialing of Spanish soldiers who under the Spanish military penal code could be imprisoned for 'indecent' acts with individuals of the same sex. One gay soldier was imprisoned for three years in the early 1980s 'for those sexual relations and for being the victim of the rape'.[299] In Greece, there were prosecutions for the publication of gay material, while under the Soviet penal code of 1960, sex between men was punishable by up to five years in prison, and in 1985 it was reported: 'Situation in Leningrad chaotic. One can't speak of an active group any more and the mutual conflicts and accusations of co-operation with the KGB are an everyday event.'[300] In the early 1980s, the secretariat of the International Gay Association (IGA) was based in Dublin, and its secretary, Edmund Lynch, wrote to US president Jimmy Carter to express 'concern and sadness that we learn that the US in its deeds and actions appears to be returning to the early 1950s and the McCarthy era especially in relation to gay people' as a result of the congressional mandate to exclude gay people from entering the US.[301] Lynch also wrote to the Attorney General of Canada regarding the imposition of censorship on the gay media there, the 'kind of action we usually associate with totalitarian states'.[302]

'The place, it seems, is crawling with them'

The emergence of gay rights groups also prompted some external reflection on the status of the homosexual in Irish society. In *Furrow* magazine in September 1979, Ralph Gallagher, a Redemptorist priest lecturing on moral theology, noted how confused the debates on homosexuality had become and how many such debates 'reveal prejudice, fear and unsupported statements rather than the elements of reason and freedom which, theoretically, are the basis of ethical analysis'. His article also highlighted the 'ignorance and prejudice of professed Christians ... the homosexual question is bedevilled by a facile use of terms which owes much more to prejudice than dispassionate knowledge'. He maintained there was homosexuality in everyone; that there were between 100,000 and 200,000 homosexuals in Ireland; that some were married, were from all classes and were not a danger to children; and that there was enough evidence to suggest that people were born gay. Six years previously, the American Psychiatric Association had deleted homosexuality from its official list of mental disorders.

Gallagher also suggested that homosexuality only became immoral when 'after an analysis of the significance of the action itself, the motivation, the circumstances and the consequences, a person has not made a serious effort to live the ideal that is practical in the circumstances of his life'. He also criticised the Catholic Church in Ireland as being too slow to accept 'the need for special pastoral care for homosexuals', with the exception of the Legion of Mary, which, for over twenty years, had 'done extraordinary work among the homosexual community in a quiet and discerning way'.[303] The official Church line the following year was that it did not blame or condemn people because they were gay and that they 'need and are entitled to friendship, acceptance and affection' but that 'gay acts' were immoral.[304] This was the same year in which Father Michael Cleary, in his column in the *Sunday Independent*, expressed sympathy for homosexuals: 'As a Catholic priest I cannot condone extra-marital sexual indulgence by anyone but I must understand it and have compassion on those who have difficulties in coping'.[305] It was also reported in the *Irish Press* in 1980 that 'over the last few years, there have been many meetings, discussions and liturgical celebrations organised specifically for those of the homosexual community'.[306] Reach, an organisation for gay Christians that met monthly in Cork and Dublin, had been founded by the Legion of Mary but by 1990 was 'self-directed'.[307]

Both tolerance and prejudice were on display in the limited public debate about homosexuality in the 1980s. In October and November 1980 the *Longford Leader*, the largest selling weekly newspaper in the midlands, published columns and letters on the subject after being given a circular by the Longford Branch of the IGRM. The correspondence dealt with psychiatry, the labels used to describe gay people, the degree to which homosexuality was compatible with Christianity, the fear of discrimination and the issue of anonymity, after which, one letter writer responded: 'So we thought there were no homosexuals in Longford. The place, it seems, is crawling with them.'[308] Despite some of the juvenile jibes that were made, the IGRM was happy that the issue of gay rights was receiving publicity and with a 'very moderate editorial conclusion', which was perhaps helped by the fact that Clause 14 of the National Union of Journalists code of work practice included a prohibition of discrimination on sexual grounds.[309] There was, however, anger in the gay community in 1980 when an agony aunt in the *Sunday World* newspaper told a 22-year-old gay man that 'the hormones can be unbalanced until a man is at least 26' and that 'some sort of hormonal therapy' might be of valuable 'help' to him. The alternative was a life of celibacy, which would 'at least save you from loneliness'. It was this 'primeval drivel' that 'naturally infuriated David Norris'.[310]

*'That affected braggadocio which is said by some
to distinguish a gay from a mere homosexual'*

Norris's High Court case challenging the constitutionality of the laws against male homosexual acts was heard in June 1980. When the *Irish Independent* newspaper referred to Norris as 'a self-confessed homosexual', Norris responded by arguing that in the public mind 'the law suggested that automatically somebody who was homosexual by orientation was regarded as being criminal'.[311] Norris had decided to pursue the case at a time when he admitted there was no 'definite groundswell of opinion for a change in the law'.[312] In 2007, Colm Tóibín talked about Norris's High Court case in an address to the Burren Law School:

> Norris was, in my opinion, both the best and the worst person to bring such a case. He was the best in that, as a lecturer in Trinity College and a person of immense independence of mind, he was in no danger of losing his job or having his position made impossible as a result of the case. But he was the worst in that he seems, on the face of it, not to have been greatly damaged by the laws in question; he had not served a prison sentence, or suffered directly at the hands of the law. To any fair-minded person, he seemed to be a happy, well-balanced person living a life of ease and privilege in Ireland ... a courtroom, with its adversarial traditions, did not seem the best place to explain that being gay in a repressive society affects every moment of your life, every time you look, think, remember, imagine – all these things are clouded by what is forbidden and secretive.[313]

A liberal priest giving evidence in favour of Norris suggested ways of interpreting the Bible and the Gospels which did not prevent a country from having laws against homosexuality declared unconstitutional:

> In one moment, under fire, the priest used the word 'we' referring to homosexuals. The senior counsel, acting for the state, was a well-known figure at the Bar. He stopped, left silence, and then said quietly: 'Father, did you say "we"?' A chilly wind blew through the court, making clear to all of us how brave David Norris was to bring this case, and how brave this priest was now as he attempted still to make his argument. For days afterwards, the question in all its insinuation, in the ease with which

it could be asked, stayed in my mind. I was not surprised when David Norris lost his case in the High Court.[314]

Two of the five judges dissented from the majority judgment. In his judgment Mr Justice McWilliams suggested it was 'reasonably clear that current Christian morality in this country does not approve of buggery or of any sexual activity between persons of the same sex', a reference to the judgment of Mr Justice Brian Walsh in the McGee case in 1973, in which he said that rights under Article 40 (which reads 'the state guarantees in its laws to respect and, as far as is practicable, by its laws to defend and vindicate the personal rights of its citizens') 'are to be related to the laws of God as understood by Christians'.

Norris, represented by Mary Robinson, appealed to the Supreme Court, which also rejected his case in 1983, Mr Justice O'Higgins maintaining that 'a right to privacy or, as it has been put, a right "to be left alone" can never be absolute. There are many acts done in private which the state is entitled to condemn, whether such be done by an individual on his own or with another. The law has always condemned abortion, incest, suicide attempts, suicide pacts, euthanasia or mercy killing.' Much harm could be done, he also suggested, because homosexual conduct, 'although carried on with full consent, may lead a mildly homosexually oriented person into a way of life from which he may never recover'. He also argued that male homosexual behaviour in other countries contributed to the spread of venereal diseases, could lead to despair and suicide, was inimical to marriage, and in any case 'I regard the state as having an interest in the general moral wellbeing of the community and as being entitled, where it is practicable to do so, to discourage conduct which is morally wrong and harmful to a way of life and to values which the state wished to protect'.[315]

Tóibín suggested that this was a judgment that a younger generation would find 'totally irrelevant and absurd', because freedom to express sexuality was happening anyway despite the law.[316] The dissenting judgments have not received the same attention, but included observations by Mr Justice Henchy condemning the 'shame, ridicule and harassment' homosexual men were subjected to and the 'insidiously intrusive and wounding ways he [Norris] has been restricted' from engaging in activities heterosexuals take for granted as an 'involuntary, chronic and irreversible male homosexual'. Henchy then made the 'idiotic' observation that 'Norris's subsequent public espousal of the cause of male homosexuals in this State may be thought to be tinged with a degree of that affected braggadocio which is said by some to distinguish a gay from a mere homosexual'.

As Tóibín acidly commented in 2007: 'But we must not blame Mr Justice Henchy. Such remarks belong congenitally to judges, being also involuntary, chronic and irreversible, especially when their lordships are in the dissenting position.'[317] Henchy, however, did imply that O'Higgins's remarks were not derived from any evidence given to court, were private prejudices and did not belong in a written judgment.

The other dissenting judgment came from Judge McCarthy, whose response included the following:

> If a man wishes to masturbate alone and in private, he may do so. If he and another male adult wish to do so in private, may they not do so? No, each commits an offence under Section 11 of the Act of 1885. If a woman wishes to masturbate in private she does not commit an offence. If two women wish to do so in private, neither of them commits an offence. If a man and a woman wish to do so in private, not being married to each other, neither of them commits an offence. In such latter circumstances, the act committed by the woman upon the man may be identical with that which another man would commit upon him, save that his partner is a woman. In my opinion, a very great burden lies upon those who would question personal rights in order to justify state interference of a most grievous kind (the policeman in the bedroom) in a claim to the right to perform sexual acts or to give expression to sexual desires or needs in private between consenting adults, male or female.[318]

Tóibín's observations of the court cases and sometimes struggling judges undoubtedly provided him with much material for his novel *The Heather Blazing*, published in 1992, which dwelt on a society in which cherished ideals were coming under pressure, as he interrogated the 'disjunctive, problematic relationship between Republican ideology, constitutional discourse and social reality in modern Ireland ... Through his central character, Eamon Redmond, a Dublin High Court judge, Tóibín dramatises the personal and societal consequences of cleaving too rigidly to institutional and constitutional imperatives rather than responding reflectively to the evolving rights and demands of a diverse citizenry'; the constitution is seen as a 'sacred text' of Irish nationhood, but its authority becomes undermined by cases that expose its inconsistencies and ambiguities, forcing Redmond ultimately to read the constitution as 'social process rather than immutable truth'. The particular case that perplexes Redmond is that of a pregnant schoolgirl challenging the decision of the Catholic school authorities to expel her; or, as he encapsulates it, 'the right of an ethos to prevail over the right of an individual'.[319]

This was also the central issue for Irish homosexuals, and it was no theoretical problem. The year before the Supreme Court ruling, Charles Self, a gay man, was murdered in his home in Dublin; gay organisations called for co-operation with the Gardaí, whom they maintained were used to exploit and harass them. During the investigation 'some 1,500 homosexuals were interrogated, photographed and put on file, as if some of the questions asked had the objective of compiling a base of information on the Dublin gay community'.[320] In the same year as the Supreme Court rejected Norris's case, another Dublin man, Declan Flynn, was murdered in Fairview Park by young men who had grown up playing in the same park. Journalist Maggie O'Kane subsequently talked to the killers: 'The night they killed Declan Flynn the girls had gone home. The girls always went home when they went queer bashing or bashing people they thought were queer. Sometimes it didn't really matter if they were or not but it was better if they were because queers used to molest young kids and stuff like that in the park ... one of the lads thought it would be a good way of getting a few bob – robbing a few queers ... Steamers, they called them.'[321]

The teenagers who killed Flynn – blood pumped out of his mouth as they attacked him just ten yards from the gate he sought to escape through – were expecting to be sent to prison for about seven years. They received five-year suspended sentences. One of the 16-year-old peers of the killers thought 'they went too far' with Flynn, 'but he's not against bashing queers. But that's pervert queers, not ordinary gay people who go to their friends' houses, but perverts, fellas that molest little boys, are different ... a pervert is a person who has a mental disorder and you can't fix mental disorders, you have to do something physical to them.'[322] Those convicted held a 'victory march' in Fairview Park, while a news story contained in the Irish Queer Archive tells the story of a man who went to the Garda station complaining about queer bashing, months before the Flynn killing: 'he was jeered and laughed out of the station.'[323]

*'There were no votes to be won in pursuing fairer treatment
for this country's homosexuals'*

Norris, represented again by Mary Robinson, took his case to the European
Court of Human Rights where a judgment in his favour was delivered in
1988. The previous year, he had been elected to the Irish Senate by the electorate of Trinity College Dublin. He regarded this development as illustra-
tive of the tolerance of the Irish who were not, he maintained, conservative
on the issue of sexual diversity: 'I was the first person in the world elected
to a national parliament having always campaigned as an openly gay candidate.'[324] He remained the only one in Ireland; as Katie Hannon observed in
2004 regarding Norris and his openness, 'that breath of fresh air did little to
blow open any more closets in the houses of the Oireachtas. It remains resolutely firm-wristed. On the face of it, a heterosexuals-only house.'[325] In 1990
one of his fellow senators referred to Norris as 'a pervert' and was rebuked
by other senators.[326] In contrast, by 1998, there were nine openly gay and
lesbian MPs at Westminster.[327]

But politicians were slow to legislate in line with the European decision in favour of Norris, even though some had been embarrassed by the
Irish law for many years. Cleverly, gay activists initiated an award in 1982,
named after Magnus Hirschfeld, for services to the gay community, and the
first two awards went to Irish politician Noël Browne and former Labour
MEP Brendan Halligan.[328] The 'lavender flying columns' busied themselves
cajoling and embarrassing politicians throughout the 1980s and early 1990s,
inviting them to events and launches, demanding that they state their parties' positions on homosexual law reform and seeking evidence of consistency or lack of it.

In November 1980, Tonie Walsh, in his capacity as president of the
NGF, wrote to Fine Gael TD Michael Keating reminding him that in 1979
his party passed a motion calling for the reform of the laws but subsequently,
in May 1980, criticised the Dutch parliament's second chamber's motion
calling for reform in Ireland. The Fine Gael motion had been initiated by
Young Fine Gael's Roy Dooney. In April 1979 he had maintained in a press
release that 'just as heterosexuality is a state of mind, so too is homosexuality ... I want to dispense with the myth about homosexuals, particularly as
teachers and their preferences for "small boys" ... there is a higher incidence
of sexual activity between heterosexual teachers and their pupils than homosexual ones.'

Dooney also quoted sociologist and Jesuit priest Micheál MacGréil (author of *Prejudice and Tolerance in Ireland* (1977)), who 'believes that a change from Dáil Éireann would cause none of the fury that I know so many TDs here today fear ... before speaking on this motion today many people told me not to bother on the grounds that there were no votes to be won in pursuing fairer treatment for this country's homosexuals. I believe that they may be right, but I utterly reject the thinking behind their arguments.'[329]

In July 1981, Tonie Walsh prepared a questionnaire for Irish political parties modelled on one drawn up by a Scottish homosexual rights group. In its response, the Communist Party of Ireland kicked to touch: 'The party has no immediate plans for taking further action in gay rights and is generally happy to leave work of that type to rights organisations such as the Irish Council for Civil Liberties.'[330] The National H Block Committee wrote to David Norris in appreciation of his support for the H Block protests and wished him 'every success in your struggle against imperialism', but pointed out that 'we campaign on a single issue only'.[331] The attempt to link the gay struggle with the 'fight against imperialism' in the early 1980s led to the formation of a short-lived group, Belfast Gays against Imperialism, which at a meeting in December 1981 insisted 'only through national liberation can genuine liberation be achieved', and wanted to be involved in Republican and Marxist groups.[332] Making an impact was never going to be easy; to mark the tenth anniversary of Bloody Sunday in 1982, there were only two people to carry the 'Gays against Imperialism' banner. One of them got tired halfway through, which presented something of a dilemma as 'she asked a few of the comrades' from People's Democracy to help her, 'but they made their excuses and refused'.[333]

But most of the replies the NGF received were positive, with Fine Gael in particular determined that there would be a centralised approach, Peter Barry informing David Norris that all such questionnaires should be sent to Garret FitzGerald's office as 'we can't have every candidate giving possibly a different reply'.[334] Fianna Fáil remained mute on this issue and Bernard Keogh of the NGF also challenged the Irish Labour Party to follow the lead given by the British Labour Party and Scottish Trades Union Congress in calling for recognition of the rights of homosexuals.[335] The previous year, Keogh had expressed the belief that 'because public debate on the whole question is still in its infancy', Ireland needed a commission of inquiry on the nature and incidence of homosexuality in Ireland and the need for law reform, like the Wolfenden Report in England of 1957 that preceded the decriminalisation of homosexuality there. Six months later the Labour Party referred the issue to its 'policy committee.'[336] Jim Kemmy, president of the Democratic Socialist Party, referred to the laws against homosexuality as 'backward'.[337]

Even prior to Norris's European case, politicians seemed to accept the law was going to change, but they were cautious about publicly identifying with the gay rights campaigners. In May 1985, Fine Gael TD George Birmingham, Minister of State at the Department of Labour, informed Tonie Walsh of the difficulties of holding a reception for the Gay Youth Congress in Dublin: 'While I accept that there are very cogent arguments for changing that law I feel that as long as it remains in the statute books it would not be appropriate for me to host a reception of the sort suggested.'[338]

In the aftermath of the Norris European decision, and in the context of proposed legislation outlawing incitement to hatred, Tonie Walsh wrote to Anne Colley, the Progressive Democrats' spokesperson on justice, in the hope that 'as we reach the end of the 1980s, it does not need to be argued that gay men and women are entitled to be treated as equal citizens in a civilised society'. Colley's reply expressed the belief that the Norris judgment 'has turned the corner on changing our attitudes in Ireland', but that the proposed legislation was designed to protect ethnic groups and was 'not the appropriate vehicle' for protecting gay rights.[339]

Conscious of previous divisions amongst the gay community, in waiting for the 1988 Norris judgment, activists were keen to stress the need for 'a united response' to the pending verdict and to be 'clear and united in their demands for law reform.' At a seminar on lesbian and gay reform in September 1988 Norris expressed the concern that, if he won his case, the Irish government might just 'slavishly follow the British law'. Kieran Rose, reflecting the continual focus on coherent strategy but also the frankness with which gay activists assessed their own mistakes, acknowledged that while 'we have become a more confident and mature voice embedded in Irish society ... we have failed in so far as we have never really succeeded in our lobbying ... our successes have been facilitated by the advancements gained by the women's movement over the years ... as part of our strategy we should tap into the positive side of Irish society and the concern for justice and fair play. We should also involve the many gays living abroad and thus return to them a sense of being Irish ... we must divide the opposition and isolate the bigots.'[340]

Universities were slow to facilitate the organisation of homosexuals. In

1989, University College Cork was the first constituent National University of Ireland college to officially recognise a lesbian or gay college group; University College Dublin's academic council refused to do likewise.[341] Perhaps this also reflected the distinct development of the gay and lesbian civil rights movement in Cork in the 1980s (it hosted the National Gay Conference in 1981) when connections were also made with the Women's Collective, the Anti-Nuclear Group and Labour Youth and trade unionist Kieran Rose (mentioned above) also had a high profile.[342]

'We know that achieving success is not simply a matter of providing information'

In 1990, the Irish Council for Civil Liberties published a study calling for the decriminalisation of homosexuality in the Republic, while the conservative Family Solidarity group published *The Homosexual Challenge: Analysis and Response*, in which it highlighted the existence of 'men-only saunas that are openly advertised in city magazines' and rent rooms that 'can be booked into for willing sexual partners'.[343] This publication also referred to Norris as a 'propagandist', castigated the use of the word 'homophobia' as 'an ideological concept which can easily confuse people into silence and acquiescence', and called homosexuality itself an 'ideology [that] lacks objectivity and scientific support'. In 1990, the Catholic Church, through the Congregation for the Doctrine of the Faith, labelled homosexuality 'an objective disorder'.[344] But it was also the case that the Catholic Church's position on AIDS and condoms – in arguing that celibacy was the only solution it insisted 'the Church offers a 100 per cent effective way to avoid AIDS and must rest its case there' – created an avalanche of criticism, while the Church of Ireland supported the government's AIDS programme for second level schools.[345]

In 1992, a memorandum from Monsignor Robert Lynch to the Irish Bishops referred to the Congregation for the Doctrine of the Faith's description of homosexuality as an 'objective disorder' and included some 'considerations' concerning the Catholic response to legislative proposals on non-discrimination against gay people: 'There are areas in which it is not unjust discrimination to take sexual orientation into account, for example, in the consignment of children to adoption or foster care, in employment of teachers or coaches, and in military recruitment.' Beside this section, a member of the NGF wrote '90 per cent of all paedophiles heterosexual.'[346]

Most strikingly, in passages the DUP would have been proud of, Family Solidarity commended with satisfaction the 'considerable foresight' of Justice O'Higgins, who had spoken of homosexuality 'as a danger to the health of society'. It then quoted Department of Health figures for February 1990 which suggested that 914 people in the Republic were HIV positive, 128 had AIDS and 60 had died.[347] The first four cases of AIDS in Ireland were identified in 1983 and, according to the National Disease Surveillance Centre in Dublin, all were from the gay community.[348] In 1985 the country's first AIDS group, Gay Health Action (GHA) was established; it observed that the three clinics dealing with STDs in Ireland offered a diagnostic service under archaic conditions that had changed little since the 1950s, and the gay community faced further marginalisation.

The GHA not only began to take the initiative in providing information but also secured government funding and in 1987 there was praise for the government's information on AIDS and warning posters in second and third level educational institutions from the Joint Committee of Women's Societies and Social Workers.[349] In 1988, 45 people were diagnosed with AIDS, 22 from the gay community, and for the next six years the numbers continued to climb, but by 1989 the number of drug users with AIDS had surpassed the number of gay men with the disease. In the same year, the Aids Alliance Forum was established comprising a number of groups working in both the voluntary and statutory sectors.[350] John Ardagh, in his book *Ireland and the Irish*, observed that 'an AIDS video produced in 1991 by the Department of Health for schools and clubs devoted almost all of its 37 minutes to arguing that no sex (outside of marriage) is the only safe sex and spent just one minute on condoms as a protection'.[351]

In May 1987, Nuala O'Faoláin argued that the gay information campaign on AIDS should receive more funding, 'if only because it is gay communities which offer the only example of people actually changing their sexual behaviour in each other's interests. But then, self-declared homosexuals are by definition candid about their sexuality in a way no other group in this country is.'[352] But it is also the case that by 1989 the National AIDS Strategy Committee was expanded to include the voluntary sector. The Gay Men's Health Project emerged in 1992, as statutory body established by the health board, which probably would not have happened but for the efforts of the voluntary groups in the gay community. Towards the end of the 1990s there was also concern that 'with all the concentration and concern centred on HIV many people have forgot[ten] or were never informed about other

STDs', but it was also lamented that 'after years of producing safer sex information we know that achieving success is not simply a matter of providing
information'.[353]

In 1989, *Magill* magazine began publishing extracts from the diary
of a 32-year-old middle-class gay Dublin man with full-blown AIDS who
was diagnosed in June 1988 and told he could expect to live for 3–5 years.
The diary gave not only an insight into dealing with the illness but also an
account of the man's life in Ireland in the 1970s and 1980s, and the guilt,
frustration and anger he felt about his condition: 'Not everything about
me is unique. I did not have sex on my own.' He had conflicting feelings
about the campaign of the Irish Haemophilia Society, which was demanding special compensation for haemophiliacs who were afflicted by AIDS, as
in the eyes of some 'they are innocent victims (which of course they are) and
gay sufferers are not. The silence of voluntary organisations, gay leaders and
spokespersons for the disadvantaged on this issue leaves us with feelings of
being even more abandoned than we had previously felt.'[354]

In 1987, an Irish AIDS sufferer in London maintained he could get 'far
better treatment than in Ireland and people are far less judgemental. Here,
they seem to regard me as unclean.' It was also maintained that 'some hospitals would refuse to treat HIV positive patients, or staff would abuse them.'[355]
In 1988, Patrick Barrett, a 28-year-old London-based Dubliner with AIDS,
appeared on the RTÉ television current affairs programme *Today Tonight*
to speak about the disease at a time when it was shrouded in fear 'and, in
some quarters at least, loathing'.[356] By the summer of 1991, it was reported
that 47,381 people had taken part in the country's AIDS-testing system of
whom 1,086 had been found to have contracted the HIV virus. Of those,
203 had gone on to develop full-blown AIDS. So far 83 had died of whom
homosexual or bisexual men accounted for 29, 23 were intravenous drug
users, 5 were heterosexuals and 10 were haemophiliacs.[357] In 1998, a report of
developments in the Gay Men's Health Project (which was supported by the
Eastern Health Board), reflecting on its first full year of service, noted that
1,757 medical consultations had been carried out.[358]

Colm Tóibín's 1999 novel *The Blackwater Lightship* dealt with AIDS in
an Irish context, as the victim Declan spends his last days in an atmosphere
of claustrophobia with his family and gay friends, Larry and Paul, who get
to tell their stories and outline their histories with all the characters, gay
and straight, getting their chance to explain, elaborate and excuse their
actions with highly personal narratives.[359] The story is set in 1993, the year

of decriminalisation, and, while it brought an Irish AIDS narrative 'into mainstream Irish cultural discourse', Declan does not dominate the narrative; there is instead a preoccupation with the manner in which his plight affects and redeems the (heterosexual) family unit. In 2003, Tóibín pointed out that characters in more recent gay fiction have a much easier time, but that 'I'm just slightly too old [he was born in 1955] to have experienced that liberation so that it fundamentally entered my spirit'.[360]

One of the most high profile victims of AIDS was popular disc jockey and presenter of the first television show in Europe dedicated entirely to showing music videos, Vincent Hanley, whose friend and producer Bill Hughes recalled that Hanley, even when filming in New York, was constantly in denial about his condition – he had 'absolutely no acceptance about what was going on'. Hanley, who died in April 1987, insisted on filming even when he was unable to stand. Hughes recalled, 'I would open out a cardboard box and place it on the street. Then I'd kneel on it and Vincent would sit on my back and do his piece to camera.'[361]

In the aftermath of the Norris judgment and into the early 1990s there was a growing confidence within the gay rights movement (homosexuals in countries such as Brazil even began to look for 'guidance' from the Irish Gay and Lesbian Equality Network, GLEN)[362]. This also reflected the positive cumulative impact of the space and voice the activists had created, ten years after one young gay rights activist who had spent some time in Dublin before returning to Brixton had wearily written to his friends in Ireland: 'I sometimes think these days that "advanced consciousness" must be synonymous with paranoia which in itself induces a strange mixture of freneticism plus lethargy. A lot of rushing around takes place, but not much gets done.'[363] The intervening ten years had proven that much could be done, but also that much could be frustrated; the Hirschfeld Centre, for example, was burnt to the ground in 1988, and the government declined to fund its rebuilding.[364]

'A necessary development of human rights'

1993

Homosexuality was finally decriminalised in Ireland in June 1993, and the business diaries of Kieran Rose of GLEN reflect the extent of the media interest.[365] In introducing the reform, Máire Geoghegan Quinn had been heavily influenced by meeting the mother of a young gay man who had underlined the need for equality. She had received a number of requests from gay and lesbian organisations campaigning for reform and agreed to meet them. 'The first group included gays and lesbians but also a middle-aged woman: I found her presence puzzling ... She was the last to make her case. "My son came home and told me he was gay." The woman said her first reaction was that he would grow out of it. Then she brought him to a priest, a doctor, a psychologist and a psychiatrist. It was one mother talking to another mother; she said she loved every bone in his body and wasn't going to stop loving him. But now she had discovered that the Government had decided he as a homosexual was a criminal.' This woman had a profound effect on the minister: 'I found myself wondering what if it were one of my sons.'[366]

As Minister for Justice, Geoghegan Quinn faced potentially strong opposition from within her party for decriminalising homosexuality, but there was nothing inevitable about her status in Irish gay rights history: 'I had no views about it all,' she recalled in 1996; ' I was looking at outstanding business in the law division, and the decriminalisation of homosexuality was on the list of outstanding legislation. I asked about the David Norris case and realised here is a man who could take us to Europe – again.'

The legislation was justified as 'a necessary development of human rights ... we are in an era in which values are being examined and questioned ... it is no more than our duty as legislators to show that we appreciate what is happening.' It granted parity before the law to homosexual citizens and introduced a common age of consent of 17 years for both heterosexual and homosexual relations. It was passed without a division. In its aftermath, Suzy Byrne, a member of GLEN who was in the Dáil when the legislation was passed, wrote a celebratory letter to a gay colleague in Illinois, despite suffering from 'total exhaustion and gay community overkill'. Her letter was, however, tinged with some reservations about the extent to which public opinion was in favour of the new legislation: 'After working 7 a.m. to 2 a.m. for the previous four days I was exhausted but woke up when I saw Maire Geoghegan Quinn smile up at us.' It helped, she maintained, that the female Fine Gael TDs were 'determined' not to allow their colleague Gay Mitchell 'to suggest an amendment of 18 years for consent'. Labour Party TDs then took members of GLEN to the Dáil bar: 'David Norris was kissing the men in the bar upon greeting them. The others were not impressed.' Byrne summed up her elation: 'Words written or spoken cannot describe how I feel; I know I have been part of history, of liberation and for me, one year out, it has been a great release.'[367]

But seasoned activists like Kieran Rose were well aware that there were further struggles ahead: 'the issues which are of relevance to us include: recognition of partnerships, custody/adoption, protection in employment, equal status legislation.'[368] In the following years he and others strove to warn about the dangers of 'a narrow definition of family' and kept a close eye on developments in countries like England and Canada in the context of gay marriage, transgender, transsexual rights and adoption.[369] Some of their opponents, including Justice Rory O'Hanlon, continued to articulate the belief that homosexuality was a 'lifestyle' that was 'as harmful as drug addiction.'[370] The traditional problem of the isolation of young gay people continued: in October 1998, a report of the Dublin Gay and Lesbian youth group pilot project OutYouth (which had been operating for fifteen years) revealed that 45 per cent of 6,000 calls received by the gay switchboard in 1997 were from those under the age of 25, and 10 per cent were from under 17s. The OutYouth group was 'effective but struggling' and needed more resources.[371]

'An in-your-face gay aesthetic'

By the very end of the twentieth century 'an in-your-face gay aesthetic' emerged, including literature with explicit scenes of sexuality, while political campaigns 'produced both coming-out narratives and human rights based arguments.'[372] In Tom Lennon's 1993 novel *When Love Comes to Town*, one of the characters is paranoid about his dress, behaviour and speech and rings an RTÉ radio show to reassure a bigot that 'it's not a glamorous lifestyle. In fact it's quite the opposite.' Inevitably, the novel also features gay bashing: 'a thump in the ribs. A kick. Searing pain. Taste blood ... on the ground. Faggot! Queer! Spewing hatred. Please stop. Faggot! Fuckin Queer!'[373] The character is accepted as a homosexual but not as a practising homosexual; his interpretation of his parents' words of 'support' is that 'we'll love you, providing you hide your love away.'[374]

Gerry Stembridge, in *The Gay Detective* (1996), looks at state surveillance of gay men, and the propensity for blackmail engendered by secrecy. He also makes it clear that homosexuals are at the centre of Irish society and its institutions and not marginal figures; the gay detective is told by a senior officer that if he wants promotion he will need to be discreet: 'even though we mightn't enforce it, it's still the law isn't it?'[375] Keith Ridgeway, in *The Long Falling* (1998), depicts the activities of gay men involved in the 'bath house' (sauna) scene and an alienated, promiscuous, drug-using urban gay experience of the type found in novels set in London, New York or San Francisco.[376] What could have been straight out of a novel, but was in fact real, was a news story from 1994, recalled by Colm Tóibín: 'In a gay sauna in Dublin in the early hours of the morning a priest will die, but there will be two other priests there – dressed in civilian clothes, or "civvies" as it were – who will be able to administer the last rites to him.'[377]

In the Irish language, Cathal O'Searchaigh's love poems challenged 'the perceived conservatism of modern Gaelic culture' and revived possible homoerotic traditions in Gaelic poetry, although O'Searchaigh was more attracted to Buddhism than Catholicism because it was less dogmatic: '"Thou shalt not" is replaced by "It would be better for you". It doesn't scream at you.'[378] But his attraction to the eastern world also became controversial when the extent of his sexual relationships with young men in Nepal emerged in 2007.

Within academia, Eibhear Walshe and others did much to develop 'queer theory' – essays on literary criticism from a gay perspective – which was deemed to be particularly appropriate to a post-colonial country like Ireland: 'a distrust of the "unmanly homosexual" resulted in a complete obliteration of the homoerotic from within nationalist discourse ... the tenuous nature of national identity necessitated a denial of difference with its incipient threat of dissidence'.[379]

'Darling, I was never in!'

In April 2007, it was reported that research conducted in twenty-four countries between 1999 and 2002 suggested Ireland was one of the most homophobic countries in the western world, with almost one-third of its people having problems with the idea of living next to gay neighbours (only Northern Ireland and Greece were found to be more homophobic).[380] In 2006, a study by researchers at Dublin City University of 364 teachers found that 80 per cent of them were aware of instances of verbal bullying where homophobic terms were used, and 16 per cent reported physical bullying of students labelled homosexual by their peers. It was also the case that if a teacher was gay, he or she could be fired from Catholic schools, which were exempt from Ireland's employment equality legislation.[381] Alongside this, gay rights groups pointed to the overall strength of Irish anti-discrimination legislation, which included prohibition of incitement to hatred and equal status and unfair dismissals legislation, which outlawed discrimination on grounds of sexual orientation.

But violent attacks on gay men had not been eradicated; indeed, the level of street violence against gay men in the early twenty-first century was still high, prompting the Gardaí to appoint gay liaison officers. One of the victims of such violence was Dermod Moore, a psychotherapist who in 1993, at the age of 30, began writing (anonymously) a column for the influential pop cultural magazine *Hot Press*. Moore found the environment in Dublin in stark contrast to London, where he had spent twelve years 'with never a hint of violence'. He referred to the 'calculated pack decision' of groups of young men who targeted attacks on gay men coming out of Dublin's best-known gay pub, The George. According to Quentin Fottrell, homophobic attacks in Ireland were also a result of the increased visibility and acceptance of gayness in a traditionally homophobic society, with violent people being distressed by their own powerlessness and looking for scapegoats over whom to wield power.[382]

Moore's columns ('Journeys of a Man-lovin' Man' or 'Stories from the Silence') were just one example of the contribution *Hot Press* made to providing a forum for open discussion about homosexuality (and indeed, young people's sexuality generally). An absorbing, talented writer, Moore did not shirk the difficult questions facing the gay community, including drink, therapy and psychoanalysis, as well as positive developments such as the impact of the internet and its significance for correspondence between gay men.[383] He also detailed his thoughts on the London gay scene, the virtues of celibacy, his experience of anonymous sex, the importance of safe sex in the contest of AIDS and HIV and the wider social and cultural context of homosexuality.

But not all gay Irish men had as positive an experience of London as Moore. In a reminder of the longevity of certain myths and stereotypes, some openly gay Irish men in London in the early 1990s were told by their Irish friends it was 'an English phase' they were going through; when one man came out to his London-based peers 'they just said I was becoming like the English'.[384] Middle-class Irish gay men in England were more likely to have positive experiences than working-class Irish men, one of whom commented, 'On the gay scene here you're still a thick Paddy,' underlining the idea that, in terms of how they were perceived, ethnicity overrode sexuality.

Dermod Moore also commented on the extent of secret gay lives: 'I'm allergic to the Closet; it hurts too much to be placed in situations where I feel I have to be "discreet" – for "discreet" read "ashamed".'[385] But some of the new generation of young gay men were keen to demonstrate that, in their view, such discretion belonged to the twentieth century. In July 2007, the *Gay Community News* was edited by a group of gay teenagers who graced the cover with the headline 'Out, Proud and Loaded'. Tonie Walsh, who became the archivist of the gay rights movement, commented on the changing times and the lack of role models in the 1980s in comparison to the twenty-first century: he asked an 18-year-old when he had 'come out'. The reply he received was, 'Darling, I was never in!'[386]

'No one declaring themselves lesbian or speaking about it'

There was some sympathy for the idea that Irish lesbians needed to keep a firm distinction between themselves and gay men as, whatever the prejudices against them, gay men could still benefit from the power and privilege of masculinity, while the lesbian movement was somewhat fractured because of its energies being divided between gay rights and women's liberation issues.[387] Notwithstanding, it was strongly argued in 2001 that 'marginalisation from heterosexual and gay male communities has not lessened their resolve or their strength', though it is fair to assert that lesbians were expected to keep their sexuality relatively private within the women's movement for fear of alienating potential supporters. When the Women's Centre opened in Dublin City in 1981, though lesbians were numerically strong in the running of the centre, it was made clear that 'nothing that might alarm straight women' should appear on the notice board.[388]

Although some fleeting references were made to lesbians in some 'learned' court judgments, they had little visibility in Ireland. The writer Mary Dorcey recalls going to a meeting of the IWLM in the early 1970s: 'I met wonderful women, but, to my surprise, no one declaring themselves lesbian or speaking about it. Then one dark wet November night my girlfriend and I were walking past Trinity College and we saw a poster which amazed and excited us: "The Sexual Liberation Movement meets tonight at 8 o'clock."'[389] The meeting was addressed by English activist Babs Todd who also appeared on *The Late Late Show*, making her the first overt lesbian to be seen on Irish television. This and subsequent public appearances by lesbians empowered women, 'many of whom had never heard the word lesbian, let alone used it in reference to themselves on to a path of self-recognition.'[390]

Some remained reluctant to use the word, including Derry writer and feminist activist Nell McCafferty, as recounted in her deeply absorbing 2004 memoir, *Nell*. In public, laughing, defiant and bold; in private she was lonely, sometimes feeling betrayed and fearful because of her complicated relationship with fellow writer Nuala O'Faoláin. They were partners for fifteen years, staying together too long 'because we both feared a return to the separate worlds we had so gladly abandoned. She feared loneliness and that worm in the heart of feminism which she called loving a man. I feared a return to the lesbian ghetto, and the social exclusion that came from engaging as a Northerner with the South in which I lived ... This book might take the fear of that word "lesbian" out of me.'[391]

In 1979, Joni Sheeran suggested that the Irish gay rights movement had a membership of '300 men and 3 women'. She also made the point that the tendency to identify homosexuality as a 'male problem' worked to the advantage of gay women because there was no law criminalising lesbian acts in Ireland, 'but it also means that many isolated Irish lesbians see no way out of their isolation'.[392] In 1975 the Irish Women United group offered a platform for lesbians by calling for the 'right of all women to a self-determined sexuality', but made no explicit reference to lesbian rights.

In November 1976, Gay Sweatshop, a London-based lesbian and gay theatre company, brought a show consisting of two short plays to the Project Arts Centre in Dublin for a two-week run, as a result of which Dublin Corporation threatened to withdraw the £6,000 grant allocated to the arts centre. Contemporary headlines included: 'Obscene Plays at the Project Arts Centre'; 'Fighting Pornography'; and 'No Grants for Vice'. But the initiative also had its supporters. In 1977, a women's disco was started in the Tailor's Hall, then moved to the Pembroke Inn, which attracted about 40 women weekly. In 1978, approximately 85 people attended a gay women's conference that led to the formation of Lesbian Line, and in September of that year the group Liberation for Irish Lesbians was formed with a membership of about 20. It rented out J. J. Smyth's pub in Dublin for women-only events twice weekly, which was regarded as a major achievement for Irish lesbians in the 1980s, as was 'the monumental act of making Thursday nights women's night at the Hirschfeld Centre'.[393]

In June 1980, on International Women's Day, another women's disco was launched with a membership of 40; an accompanying press release maintained 'as women and lesbians we experience double oppression in this society. The NGF recognises the special position of women in its organisation and respects the right of women to organise separately.'[394]

'She listened, said nothing, and was afraid for me'

In private, individual lesbians were also confronting the difficulties of accepting their sexuality. On Christmas Eve 1980, Nell McCafferty walked in the door of her family home in Derry, 'sat down beside my mother on the sofa, said, "Mammy, I am a lesbian" and burst into tears ... it was the day after Christmas that I said to my mother, "Think of me as one of God's freaks." "You're no freak," she said. I went to see Sister Agatha again. She listened, said nothing, and was afraid for me.'[395]

That year, the lesbian activist Jodi Crone appeared on *The Late Late Show* and, though this validated the identity of many lesbians in Ireland, it also 'brought harassment and family problems'. As an activist she found it easier to go abroad.[396] The NGF had a large administrative council on which there were seats reserved for women, largely through the efforts of the autonomous group Liberation for Irish Lesbians, but it was not until 1990 that it finally renamed itself the National Lesbian and Gay Federation (NLGF).

In the same year, journalist Brighid McLaughlin highlighted the absence of a lesbian voice when it came to controversies such as the Church's stance on homosexuality – 'why is there never a lesbian representative available to speak out? – and suggested that lesbians were carrying more burdens than gay men because many of them had children and less money at a time when 'the economy is now realising the spending potential of single gay men'.[397] This was true even in the 1980s; while the Hirschfeld Centre was still operational, a leaflet was produced asking businesses and advertisers, 'Are you tapping the pink economy?'[398]

In 1990, the *Sunday World* trumpeted the 'coming out' of Hazel Robinson, a 23-year-old Limerick woman who talked to Gay Byrne on his RTÉ radio show, urging other lesbians to 'come out'; the show also received calls from married women who had discovered they were gay. Another Irish woman, artist Sorcha Ní Ríáin (this was a pseudonym she used in Ireland), came out on the BBC Radio 4 programme *Telling Lies*, revealing she had had secret affairs with other women while married in Ireland. Living in

Munster, she had felt great pressure socially to get married and pregnant, but used to travel to the Hirschfeld Centre. She eventually lost custody of her children and became 'estranged from her parents in Ireland who regard lesbianism as some kind of sinister cult.'[399]

In the 1980s lesbian activists were involved in campaigns against the pro-life amendment and in anti-nuclear campaigns. A strong lesbian movement also took root in Cork, while its visibility was increased as a result of the 1983 march against queer bashing and the pride marches of 1983 and of 1984, at which a car was driven into the marchers. At the following year's parade there were only twenty people, and no further parades until 1992, though what also complicated matters was the 'general overcommitment of activists to other struggles.'[400]

Maura Richard's *Interlude*, published in 1982, was, arguably, the first explicitly lesbian novel set in Ireland; "'You will burn in hell, you are not women at all", the local sheep farmer, with only his dog to love, spat in disgust when he realised his two female neighbours were living together as a couple.'[401] In 1985, ex-nuns Rosemary Curb and Nancy Manahan caused a storm when they appeared on *The Late Late Show* to promote their book of interviews with lesbian-identified nuns. Mary Dorcey became bolder still; at a women's week in University College Dublin she described heterosexuality as sado-masochism and declared, 'If feminism is the theory, lesbianism is the practice', adding later that in making such a declaration, 'I just about escaped with my life.'[402]

In the 1970s and 1980s it was suggested that radical Irish lesbians felt they had more in common with radical feminists than with homosexual men, but in the 1990s it was argued that it was possible to identify as a lesbian without acknowledging any allegiance to feminism. None the less, Irish lesbians still felt compelled to satirise Pat Robertson, the US politician who maintained in 1992 that 'feminism encourages women to leave their husbands, kill their children, practice witchcraft, destroy capitalism and become lesbians'.[403]

'We don't have that many role models'

Lesbians Operating Together (LOT), established as an umbrella organisation in 1991, opened an office in Dublin in 1993, from which it made submissions to the Department of Equality and Law Reform, and ensured coverage for lesbians in *Gay Community News* and that attention was focused on gay health issues. It was Ireland's best-known feminist, Mary Robinson, who, as president in 1992, invited members of LOT to Áras an Uachtaráin, the official residence of the Irish president, but 'none of the representatives who attended ... released their names to the press'.[404] In the same year, at the St Patrick's Day parade in Cork, the float of the Munster gay and lesbian collective was warmly applauded by the crowd and then given a prize. This prompted Mary Holland to suggest that 'it is beginning to seem that almost all of the laws which affect the majority of people at the most intimate levels of personal morality are held in open contempt ... if the laws relating to marriage, homosexuality, abortion are so out of touch with the needs of society that the state allows them to be broken with impunity, how can it hope to encourage quite different attitudes of civic responsibilities towards laws designed to stop people evading tax, or defrauding semi-state companies, or ripping off the welfare system?'[405]

The following year, five months after male homosexual acts had been decriminalised, Emma Donoghue's play *I Know My Own Heart* was staged in Dublin; it included scenes of sexual intimacy between women and 'probed the choices of a woman trying to understand and express herself in a society based on rules and silences'. Donoghue also reworked traditional fairy tales from an overtly lesbian perspective. In 1990, angered by the constant references to the 'unhappiness' of homosexuals, Donoghue had asked, 'When will Irish people wake up to the fact that the only cause of homosexual unhappiness is homophobia?'[406] In an interview with *Hot Press* magazine in 1994, Donoghue talked frankly about lesbian sexual practices and desires and the prospect of long-term relationships: 'we don't have that many role models'.[407] Meanwhile, another group of Irish women were 'on the boat to England', travelling not to have abortions, but to get pregnant – lesbian couples who were denied access to donor insemination in Ireland.[408]

University College Dublin academic Ailbhe Smyth has written for many years about her experiences as an Irish lesbian. She came out in 1985, but recalled:

> I didn't really come out at all; many of my family and straight friends did not want to know. In an ironic return of my 1970s 'non-marital' situation, everything was alright (except for me), provided I didn't talk about it. Since then, I have been warned many times – usually indirectly but rarely with any subtlety – that it would be 'better' (for whom?) not to

draw attention to the fact that I am a lesbian. But I do, because my sexuality is a central part of me, complexly intertwined with other aspects of my identity and because it is a politically significant act in a culture deeply resistant to lesbian existence'.[409]

In contrast, Ide O'Carroll referred to 'a wonderful lesbian community in Cork in the 1980s', and by the 1990s, 'while certain American-Irish continue to refuse to admit Irish-born lesbians and gays to the St Patrick's Day parade in New York city, lesbians and gays received an award as the "best new entry" in the Cork parade in 1992'.[410] Mary Dorcey, in prose and poetry, continued to write powerfully and lyrically about erotic lesbian relationships, without in any sense avoiding painful realities:

Although we had talked all night
About rejection, hurt
And the bitterness of those
We had once trusted,
Lying in your arms, in a warm bed,
Rummaging through our injuries,
Like two old drunken women on a bench,
It no longer mattered at all
– None of it.
Breast against breast
Desiring nothing more than sleep,
Loss was a once sharp blade
That had cut me loose
For this friendship.[411]

The Women's Education Research and Resource Centre (WERRC) at University College Dublin also facilitated public and academic discussion about lesbianism in a national and international context, organising annual Lesbian Lives Conferences from the early 1990.[412] But there remained, for some, a sense that the 'vibrancy' of modern Ireland did not include lesbians and that they still had to focus on making Ireland a tolerable place in which to live. The woman who ran Open House in Westmeath, a network for lesbians in rural Ireland, maintained that loneliness was still an issue: 'we are important for the rural community and the gay community in Ireland as a whole. By making us content in our own environment we won't have to emigrate.'[413]

Developments abroad ensured there was considerable attention devoted to the issue of same-sex marriage in the opening years of the twenty-first century, along with debate as to whether or not male and female gay couples should have access to the same adoption and tax laws, as evidenced by the legal case taken by two academics, Katherine Zappone and Ann-Louise Gilligan, who married in Canada in 2003. They saw no reason to be exempt from the same tax allowances as married heterosexual couples and made their case to the Revenue Commissioners, who rejected it in July 2004. An unsuccessful High Court case followed, with the court also refusing to accept that they had brought their case in the public interest (which meant costs were awarded against them). Gilligan asked the question: 'I really need to know why. Our love hasn't indented the common good. It hasn't added any depravity to this society. So what are people's fears?'[414]

'Nowhere else in the world do pimps live with their wives while living off another woman'

Some of the TDs who contributed to a debate in the Dáil in October 2007 on the introduction of the Criminal Law (Human Trafficking) Bill, while decrying the exploitation of vulnerable women, got very nostalgic for the old days. Fianna Fáil TD Mary O'Rourke insisted, 'We may not be open about the subject, but it is a question of men paying money to get women and of the debasement of women ... the Ireland of which we speak and to which women are being trafficked is no longer the land of comely maidens and youthful swains who are seeking to meet, talk and walk with one another. Rather, it is a land of sleazy brothels where seedy acts are carried out for money.'[415]

The idea that such exploitation was new was nonsense. The Joint Committee of Women's Societies and Social Workers had repeatedly raised the issue of the exploitation of prostitutes in the early 1970s, it being felt that 'propaganda should be directed to parents in the country' and that male clients should be prosecuted as well as female prostitutes. The Irish Housewives Association was also 'adamant that the law must be changed'. In June 1972 the JCWSSW also highlighted the fears of the homeless charity Simon in Cork concerning 'the use of children as contacts between pimps and prostitutes.'[416] In October 1972, the society discussed an article on the career of a prostitute which had appeared in *Woman's Way* magazine, it being worried 'young people could be badly influenced by the information given in the article'. The Garda crime squad maintained that 'four pimps were caught and Mespil and Burlington Roads cleared of prostitutes', while the Minister for Justice pointed out to the society, after it complained about the targeting of women, that 'proceedings can be and have been taken against prowling men who approach women in the streets'.[417]

Many Irish prostitutes were working on English streets; in September 1970 an Irishman then living in Victoria, central London, complained to the Department of the Taoiseach that 'a very high proportion of the prostitutes are Irish ... It is amazing how it is accepted over here for Irish girls to go into prostitution.'[418] A Cork-born, convent-educated prostitute was central to the downfall of British minister Lord Lambton in 1973; pictures of the Under Secretary of Defence smoking cannabis in bed with 26-year-old Norma Levy and another prostitute finished his political career. Ostensibly, Levy worked as a 'hostess' at the private members' Eve Club in Regent Street; in fact she was one of a number of call girls run by Jean Horn, 'a high-class strictly word of mouth madam'. One of the personal cheques Lambton used to pay Levy later became public evidence of his activities. Levy was quoted as saying, 'This life is like a drug. I love hotels and fine clothes and travel and can have them by just spending an hour or so with a kinky lord who is daft enough to pay by cheque. How can I stop?'[419]

In the 1970s, there were turf wars in Dublin between English and Irish pimps after the English pimps began to place prostitutes on Fitzwilliam Square, and the *Sunday World* began to expose the underworld associated with prostitution. The drug epidemic in Dublin in the 1980s changed the prostitution scene, which prior to that had been controlled by older prostitutes 'largely without the aid of pimps'. One prostitute, Lyn Madden, came to prominence after she gave evidence in 1983 against her lover and pimp, John Cullen, who murdered another prostitute, Dolores Lynch, by throwing a firebomb into her house. Lynch's mother and aunt were also killed during the blaze. In November 1983 the High Court barred publication of the story in *Magill* magazine, as John Cullen was appealing against his conviction for murder, but on appeal the Supreme Court allowed it to be published. It was an exceptional piece of writing by June Levine 'and a frightening account of the life of a prostitute and a violent pimp in the Dublin we all inhabited'.[420]

Giving evidence was a brave thing for Madden to do, given the potential for Dublin's violent underworld to exact revenge, and the fact that she had spent many of her forty years fleeing to the next brute to protect her from the previous one. As well as being a murderer, John Cullen was a serial rapist ('I will kill every whore down there. I fuckin' hate prostitutes'). As Madden recounted, 'I've lived in gangland for twenty years ... and I know what "grass" means.' She was helped and protected by June Levine, who subsequently wrote about Madden's life in *Lyn: A Story of Prostitution*, which detailed the abuse Madden had suffered throughout her life, following her mother's abandonment of her in Cork as a child. She ended up in various institutions, served time in prison in England, and was exploited and abused by pimps, whom she described as 'vicious, slave-owning blood-suckers. It's not the clients who destroy women. It's the pimps.'[421]

It was also clear that there had been a good deal of money to be made from wealthy clients in the 1960s and 1970s; that women like Madden and Dolores Lynch saw prostitution as a business and wanted it to be treated as such, seeking meetings with the Minister for Justice and becoming more politicised on behalf of prostitutes, with Dolores known as the 'women's libber' among the prostitutes. But ultimately, they were beaten and terrorised into submission by the pimps, 'the ones unique to Ireland who support their wives and families off the women on the canal. Nowhere else in the world do pimps live with their wives while living off another woman.'[422]

In 2007, Madden published an account of her life after the Cullen trial. She lived under Garda protection during the trial, but when it came to an end and Cullen was convicted of murder, Madden was put on the boat to England. That was the end of the story as far as the Irish establishment was concerned. There was no support offered afterwards, no system in place to ensure her future safety and quality of life, and no co-operation between the two jurisdictions to protect her from more exploitation or to guarantee her any quality of life. Her 2007 book, *Lyn's Escape*, is ironically titled, as due to the lack of back-up she was forever looking over her shoulder. She experienced more encounters with violent men, fretted about her own damaged children and struggled in low-paid jobs. There is no happy ending, but she emerges as a strong, brave, witty and self-aware person who has had to rely on herself and nobody else to survive.[423] Her story is also a reminder that it was one thing to identify the women being exploited and remove them from the cause of immediate danger; it is quite another to ensure they have some chance of a better quality of life.

The Criminal Law Sexual Offences Act of 1993, which made soliciting an offence for both men and women, also led to an increase in the popularity of brothels established by entrepreneurs 'who saw a gap in the criminal market' – though by 1999 there were high levels of media interest in their operations and frequent Garda crackdowns.[424] In trying to estimate the number of women working as prostitutes in 2003, Paul Reynolds observed that data from charities and health boards put the number at between 600 and 750 in Dublin alone, 'but these figures represent only those women who are known and are in touch with services. It could easily be twice or three times that amount.'[425]

Increased prostitution was also connected with human trafficking in Ireland. The Oireachtas Joint Committee on European Affairs was informed in October 2005 that 'hundreds' of women were being sent to Ireland to work as prostitutes. Ruhama, an organisation that works with prostitutes, came across its first victim of sex trafficking in 2000. For the next two years the organisation worked with thirty-three such women and was aware of another seventy in a similar position, figures regarded as 'the tip of the iceberg'. Most of the women were aged between 18 and 25, though some were minors; their main countries of origin were Nigeria, Albania and Romania, and most had suffered sexual and psychological abuse.[426]

Sister Breege Keenan of Dublin's Vincentian Refugee Centre highlighted the fact that foreign national women were being lured to Ireland by the promise of jobs and ended up working 'against their will' in the sex industry, and in 2006 complained that Ireland was not a party to the European Convention Against Trafficking.[427] In 2007, when the Criminal Law (Human Trafficking) Bill of that year, which created a specific criminal offence of trafficking persons for the purpose of their sexual exploitation, was being debated, the Minister for Justice told the Dáil that at least seventy-six women had been trafficked into Ireland between 2000 and 2007 for sexual exploitation, though it was rightly pointed out by other politicians that this represented 'only the tip of the iceberg' because of the 'invisibility of the sex industry'.[428] Outside of Ireland, Dublin-born priest Father Shay Cullen led a long campaign against child abuse in the Philippines, where it was clear Irish men were one of the leading nationalities paying to have sex with children.[429]

There was also a lot more money to be made from prostitution in Celtic Tiger Ireland, and prostitutes working in Dublin were believed to be earning significantly more than was possible in most other European cities (some eastern European prostitutes were said to be charging up to 400 Euros an hour). A senior Garda suggested lawmakers should consider legalising the business. Prosecutions for brothel keeping and organising prostitution became more frequent, but it was the organisers rather than the prostitutes that were targeted; the prostitutes were not breaking the law because they were not soliciting on the streets.[430]

There was also a disturbing demand for images of sex with children, as was made clear from the scale of the Garda operation, Amethyst, which investigated people downloading child pornography from the internet. In 1997 an Eastern Health Board study found that fifty-seven boys and girls were working as prostitutes.[431] In 2000, Evanna Kearins described male prostitutes as 'a marginalised, disenfranchised, criminalised and misunderstood section of Irish society'; most of them were unemployed, with little education beyond primary level, and had suffered early emotional deprivation and had difficult family lives. A measure of the difficulty in assessing their numbers was the assertion that there was anywhere between 100 and 600 male prostitutes in Dublin, in different categories (rent boys, masseurs and escorts). In June 1998, 12 per cent of homeless people in Dublin were under the age of 18 and 77 per cent were male. One rent boy interviewed by Kearins said of his clients, 'Most of them I know are married.'[432]

In the 1990s there was also 'a hidden modern Ireland of sadomasochism' exposed in a brothel known as the Kasbah in a basement in Mountjoy Square, which came to light in 1991 when it was alleged that it was a regular haunt of politicians, Church figures, businessmen and stalwarts of the legal profession. These allegations led to a three-day criminal trial in 1993, during which the 'madam' of the girls working there, who was given a six-month suspended sentence for running a brothel, asked outside the doors of the court, 'Why are we always the fucking underdogs? What about the clients? These powerful bastards who are never charged or identified.'[433] Those 'powerful bastards' included politicians, whose sex lives were generally not intruded on, the Irish tabloid media being much more restrained in this regard than their English counterparts in the 1990s.

'They could not unearth a single incident when the politician had defended family values'

When female political journalists such as Olivia O'Leary and Geraldine Kennedy began to make an impact in the early 1980s, some politicians seemed to regard them as legitimate targets for seduction. In 1981, a senior Irish politician invited Kennedy, then a journalist with the *Sunday Tribune,* for a Christmas drink. He quickly moved from talk of politics to his declared longing for Ms Kennedy, professing she alone, of the women he knew, had the intellect and the beauty which he found irresistible. He wanted to know when their affair would begin. Geraldine dispensed with his overtures with a curtness normally associated with the male species. It was not the first time this person had pressed his attentions on the political correspondent of the *Sunday Tribune*. On a previous occasion he did so even to the point of applying mild physical force. Incidentally, this politician is married and professes concern for the stability of Irish marriages being threatened by the prospect of divorce.[434]

In March 1994, Emmet Stagg, a Labour Party politician, was questioned by the Gardaí about why he had been sitting in a car with a man he had just met 'in the part of the park known to me as a place where gay men meet'. As political journalist Katie Hannon noted, 'the incident was treated as a personal crisis that need never be referred to again in political circles. When Labour's national vote plunged in the following general election in 1997, Stagg's vote held up better than most'.[435] Had he been a politician in Britain, he almost certainly would have had to resign. The relationship between the most controversial politician of his era, Charles Haughey, and a married female journalist, Terry Keane, was widely known. She wrote about it regularly in her gossip column in the *Sunday Independent*, in which she constantly referred to him as 'Sweetie', though when she spoke in 1999 on Irish television of the 27-year affair there was anger at her public betrayal and she was widely characterised as isolated and greedy.[436]

In 1999, photographers staked out a high-profile married male politician with a woman who was not his wife in a car up the Dublin mountains and got the pictures they wanted. But for the editor of the newspaper who wanted to publish them there was a problem: 'Despite an extensive trawl of the cuttings files, they could not unearth a single incident when the politician had defended family values. Unable to justify running the story on the grounds of exposing the politician's hypocrisy, an editorial decision was taken to pull the sensational spread' (though it subsequently appeared in a tabloid newspaper).[437]

In the long run, the long silence and denial about marriage breakdown in Irish society helped Taoiseach Bertie Ahern (in office from 1997 to 2008), whose own marriage broke down, to 'in effect, make a woman not his wife the first lady'. After bruising public debates and rows about private and public morality in previous decades, and the excesses of expressions of righteous indignation in the 1980s, most Irish people seemed to believe Ahern's personal arrangements were his and his partner Celia Larkin's business alone.[438] Given the manner in which British Foreign Secretary Robin Cook was pressurised into marrying his mistress in 1998, the contrast between Britain and Ireland in this regard is quite striking.

Significantly, it was the *Church of Ireland Gazette* that criticised Bertie Ahern's situation in December 1998 and took the Catholic Church to task for staying silent, particularly when, in 1997, for the first time, Larkin's name appeared alongside Ahern's on a state invitation and in November 1998 when both were toasted by Tony and Cherie Blair at a state dinner. David Quinn, a journalist and family values campaigner, suggested in this context 'it is at least arguable that this is a matter of public concern and that it is adversely affecting public perceptions of marriage'.[439] The truth is that few cared, and if they did they stayed largely silent; what constituted the definition of a marriage and family was something that had changed hugely in Ireland and, given the revelations of the 1990s, the Catholic Church was in no position to throw stones.

'The most relentless assault which has ever been presented to a mass audience on the accepted version of reality'

That was just one indication of a change in attitudes. There were many others, and particular events that caused people to question assumptions, challenge taboos and critically question the manner in which the law had been, and was, applied. The questions that schoolchildren were asking Angela Macnamara, for example, changed dramatically in the 1990s; in contrast to questions such as, 'Is it a sin to allow long kisses?' or 'Is cheek to cheek dancing a sin?' that were asked in the 1960s, the 1990s equivalent included, 'What exactly is a homo?', 'What's a test tube baby?' and 'My mam and dad were married last Christmas and I was a bridesmaid. Is that OK?'[440]

The changes in the various dimensions of Irish family life amounted to a social revolution within an economic revolution, as Ireland, for so long the exception to normal European demographic trends, began to mirror the trends of its European neighbours. By the end of the century, births to unmarried mothers stood at 30 per cent of the total, rising from 1,600 in 1921 to over 15,000 in 1998. In 1921 the rate of maternal mortality was 4.8 per 1,000; by 1994 Ireland had the lowest rate of maternal mortality in the world. The infant mortality rate fell from 99 to 6 per 1,000 live births between 1900 and 1995. In 1991, 80 per cent of homes were owner occupied, compared to 53 per cent in 1946, and 40 per cent of married women were in the workforce by the end of the century, compared to only 5 per cent in 1966. Between 1975 and 1995 the probability of female marriage declined by one-third, from 90 per cent to 60 per cent, while 32 per cent of those attending clinics for sexually transmitted diseases at the end of the century were teenagers.[441]

1974

1987

| The status of 'illegitimate' was legally abolished in 1987, largely as a result of the efforts of Mary Robinson, who first tabled a motion on the rights of illegitimate children in 1974. In the 1980s, despite legal change, there was a hostility towards single mothers that seemed to be rooted, not just in concerns about sexual morality, but in 'economic concerns about the drain of resources on the welfare state in spite of a plethora of studies indicating that lone parent families are over-represented in poverty statistics. In addition to economic concerns, disquiet also began to be expressed in the media about the decline in the family and the role of fathers.'[442]

sacraments?
sex?

But what the 1980s and 1990s made clear was that illegitimacy, abortion, rape, sexual abuse and sexual exploitation were emphatically already a part of the 'Irish heritage' and the more events that received publicity, the more people were prepared to unburden themselves in relation to their own experiences. In this regard, serious questions were also being raised about attitudes to women. Four particular issues 'dominated the public imagination' between 1983 and 1985: the abortion amendment discussed earlier, the sacking of Eileen Flynn from a post as a school teacher by local nuns because she was pregnant and unmarried and living with a married man (her legal challenge to the sacking failed), the death of 15-year-old Ann Lovett and her child in Granard, County Longford, and the Kerry Babies Case.

no one to
speak to?
listen?

Lovett was found on a bitterly cold January day in 1984 by three boys who noticed her red schoolbag lying at the entrance to the grotto of the Blessed Virgin on a small hill outside Granard, with a pair of scissors she had brought with her to cut the umbilical cord of her newborn baby. The baby boy, who everyone claimed not to know she was carrying, was lying on a moss-covered stone beneath the statue. She died shortly afterwards in hospital from irreversible shock brought on by haemorrhaging and exposure. The case was reported on by Emily O'Reilly in the *Sunday Tribune* and, in response, Gay Byrne's radio show solicited letters from listeners telling their stories. One of the researchers on the show suggested the letters received could have filled a book; it was decided instead to devote three programmes to just reading the letters. What resulted 'was the most relentless assault which has ever been presented to a mass audience on the accepted version of reality in this country'.[443] The stories were of 'clandestine childbirth, clumsy self-abortion, brutal husbands or incestuous fathers'.[444]

According to Fintan O'Toole, the Lovett tragedy 'struck most of us like the lash of a bull-hide whip ... say the words "Ann Lovett" to most Irish people over 35 now [in 2002] and they know what you mean. Hers is the name we give to lies and hypocrisy, to the reality behind the official veneer of Holy Ireland. The version of Ireland that most of us carry in our heads changed for good. It is not that Ann Lovett's awful death stayed at the forefront of our collective consciousness, but it did take up residency in the back of our minds'.[445] In the words of Medb Ruane, Lovett's death 'made Granard the whipping boy for the guilt of a whole nation. The people suffered, comforted her family, and tried to move on'.[446] It also inspired a powerful poem by Paula Meehan, 'The Statue of the Virgin at Granard Speaks', in which the Virgin Mary is made to castigate human hypocrisy and divine impotence:

On a night like this I remember the child
Who came with fifteen summers to her name,
And she lay down alone at my feet.
Without midwife or doctor or friend to hold her hand.
And she pushed her secret out into the night,
Far from the town tucked up in little scandals
Bargains struck, words broken, prayers, promises
And though she cried out to me in extremis
I did not move,
I didn't lift a finger to help her,
I didn't intercede with heaven,
Nor whisper the charmed word in God's ear.[447]

*'A succession of professional men, including this married man,
came forward to strip her character'*

The focus remained on girls and women; in the early 1990s, Siobhán Kilfeather suggested that 'scandals around female sexuality and reproduction in recent years have produced sympathy for the women involved precisely in so far as these women ... have not sought to publicise themselves but have been dragged unwillingly into public view. Their sexualities have been repurified by their representation as victims not only of patriarchal violence but also of public inspection.'[448] This certainly seemed true for Joanne Hayes, whose story brought a common problem historically and one that was rarely discussed – infanticide – into the open in 1984, after the body of a baby with multiple stab wounds was washed up at a beach in Cahirciveen, County Kerry.

A Garda investigation to trace the mother led to a confession by Hayes, a single mother, to its murder, but the discovery of the body of a second baby on the farm on which Hayes lived in Abbeydorney raised doubts about her confession – a confession she subsequently retracted. The Gardaí claimed that Hayes was the mother of both babies until scientific tests proved that she was not the mother of the Cahirciveen baby. The murder charge against her was dropped, though some continued with the idiotic insistence that she had given birth to twins conceived by two different men. The mother of the Cahirciveen baby has never been identified.

An inconclusive internal inquiry into Garda treatment of Hayes and her family led to a public tribunal of inquiry that lasted eighty-two days, attracted considerable public interest and generated much public sympathy and support for Hayes and her family, who, the report concluded, had perjured themselves. The report also rejected the family's allegations of ill treatment by the Gardaí. What became known as the Kerry Babies Case revealed many things, including alleged Garda intimidation, perjury, infanticide and the sexual mores of a hidden Ireland. When the Gardaí originally descended on the town of Cahirciveen to conduct their inquiries, they circulated a questionnaire and began what amounted to a sexual profile of the town, which had a population of 1,428: 'The collated information profiled an Irish town where such features are not normally given public recognition. Families were named where incest was suspected; a married woman was having an affair with a young woman; the female partners in broken romances were checked out; women who had to get married because of pregnancy were reported.'[449]

It was one of the most emotive episodes of modern Irish history, evoking sympathy and anger about the dissection of a woman's private life by an all-male inquiry, and there were many questions left unanswered as well as instances of hypocrisy in public and behind the scenes. As Nell McCafferty recalls:

In the opening days of the 'Kerry Babies' tribunal a married man went to bed in a Tralee hotel with a woman who was not his wife. He was one of the forty-three male officials – judge, fifteen lawyers, three police super-intendents and twenty-four policemen – engaged in a public probe of the private life of Joanne Hayes. When this particular married man was privately confronted with his own behaviour he at first denied it. Then he crumpled into tears and asked not to be exposed. He had so much to lose, he said. 'My wife ... my job ... my reputation ...' He was assured of discretion. No such discretion was assured to Joanne Hayes, as a succes-sion of professional men, including this married man, came forward to strip her character.[450]

As pointed out by Tom Inglis, the case also revealed how the state 'symbolically dominates society through maintaining a monopoly over the means of producing the truth'.[451] It raised the question as to whether the treatment of Hayes, who was accused of no crime, was a paradigm for Irish male attitudes to women, and to single mothers, though in truth Hayes was not 'the classic Irish single mother'. She did not hide, or give up her baby, she was 'a bold and transgressive figure'; indeed, the case illustrates how 'sexually transgressive' women became isolated, marginalised and oppressed.[452]

It was also an important time for the media, as without them the fam-ily's allegations of ill treatment would not have come to light. The presiding judge castigated the 'raucous, ignorant urban dwellers', as he described the women's groups who were protesting outside the tribunal. Nor did the tri-bunal answer the most obvious question: How did detailed statements from the Hayes family, identical in details known to be false, come to be taken? It was no wonder the Hayes family preferred to call it the 'Kerry Garda Case', and Hayes pointed out that when the report was published in 1985, it 'was made public with the same indifference to our feelings that we experienced throughout all our relations with the law'.[453] When, in 2005, Judge Morris issued his second report into Garda corruption in Donegal in the 1990s, he referred to 'the ability of hatred to transform myth into facts'.[454] It seems that was at play in Kerry in the 1980s also.

'What's wrong with tradition?
That's the way it's always been up to now'

This case also came at a time when the Church was active in reasserting

itself as the arbiter of sexual morality, reflected in the words of the Bishop
of Kerry, Kevin McNamara, in 1983: 'It is necessary to call things once again
by their true names – fornication, adultery, lustful desires, immoral displays
in cinemas.'[455] He phrased this as if liberal advances had been made and the
tide needed to be turned back to the 1920s; but it was clear less than ten
years later that this was not going to happen. In the early 1990s, when John
Ardagh was researching his book *Ireland and the Irish*, he interviewed the
Bishop of Limerick, Jeremiah Newman, who maintained: 'Of course, the
Church *must* be authoritarian ... what's wrong with tradition? That's the
way it's always been up to now, and I just don't understand why it's all gone
wrong. Why are the media so vitriolic against us? Why?'[456] Some of the
other individuals he interviewed provided the answer to Newman's question, including Father Peter McVerry, a well-known campaigner on behalf
of homeless young men, who suggested the Church should concentrate on
social issues such as poverty 'and shut up about the sexual issues. Priests are
simply not trained to understand these things.'

In March 1992 Ardagh had lunch with the Bishop of Galway, Eamon
Casey, who denounced the rise in sexual activity and spoke of his work with
unmarried teenage pregnant girls: 'One cannot pick and choose with the
Church's teaching.'[457] This was the same bishop whose private life became
full public knowledge two months later when the fact that he had a son as
a result of his relationship with an American woman, Annie Murphy, was
dramatically announced on RTÉ's *Morning Ireland* programme and broken
in the print media by Conor O'Clery, then US correspondent of the *Irish
Times*.

Throughout his career Casey wore many hats: entertainer, political and
social activist, often champion of the dispossessed, but he was also a man
who lived life to the full, ate and drank well and drove fast cars, and all of this
while being one of Ireland's favourite bishops, first of Kerry, where he was
appointed in 1969, and later of Galway and Kilmacduagh. He managed to
stay out of the limelight after his dramatic resignation in 1992, travelling to
South America. To some, this was a case of Casey fleeing and leaving his fellow bishops to 'pick up the pieces';[458] to others, it seemed this was the appropriate course of action, given the disgrace and humiliation he had brought
on himself, particularly when it emerged he had dipped into diocesan funds
in order to finance his son's education (the funds were subsequently repaid).

Casey's wide interests had been reflected in the various commissions
of the Bishops' conferences that he served on, including mass media, social

welfare and the Third World. He was critical of the government in relation to their paltry response to Third World development and, indeed, American foreign policy. He was also prominent in the right to life debate in 1983, rejecting the assertion that the referendum on abortion was sectarian, arguing that the right to life was 'antecedent to all churches. It is there before there was ever a church.'[459] Ten years earlier, as revealed by Annie Murphy, he had been consumed by another thing that was there before there was ever a church – sexual passion: 'There stood the Bishop, my love, without clerical collar or crucifix or ring, without covering of any kind. The great showman had unwrapped himself. Christmas of all Christmases. This was for me more of a wonder than all the mountains, lark song and heather scents of Ireland. He stood before me, his only uniform the common flesh of humanity ... he looked forlorn, almost like a child lost in a dark wood ... I witnessed a great hunger. This was an Irish famine of the flesh.'[460]

But this scandal was about more than salacious passages such as this. In the words of Catriona Crowe:

at the heart of the story, what we have is a really harrowing account of a woman having a baby and being pressurised by her lover and many other people to give the child up for adoption which raises huge issues about Irish society at that time. We also have the first and only account of what it was like to be in St Patrick's home on the Navan Road [the mother and baby home where Annie Murphy was sent] and it is incredibly moving and very anger-making to read what happened her. We can't judge people, and one wouldn't want to, but I think some important issues came out of this very old-fashioned scandal as it turned out to be ... Peter Murphy was not the first child of someone sworn to celibacy, but it raised issues, for example about absentee fathers in situations where women are raising children on their own – what that does to the child; what it does to the mother. In terms of the Church itself, it raised the issue of the loss of good authority; Eamon Casey would have been seen as someone who wielded good authority within an institution that needed to change, and then of course the huge identity issue which became in the 1990s one of the main issues in Ireland crystallising around subjects like the foreign adoption issue that uncovered itself and institutional care – children, now adults, searching for information about their identity and looking to repair broken and fragmented relationships. Now, Peter Murphy is different in the sense that he knew who his father was, but he wasn't recognised by him until very late in the day, so a lot of issues come up from this that I think are still obsessing us in Irish society.[461]

Margaret MacCurtain also suggested 'in a way, by remaining Eamon Casey the Bishop he acts really as the weakest link and he acts as a kind of a shield for the Hierarchy in the 1990s because they have become embroiled in stalling strategies around the issue of child abuse. Were Bishop Casey in a sense more respected, more vibrant, he could have acted as a kind of mediator between the issue of married clergy in the Church – which is a very important issue for the future.'[462]

'We give the Maker's instructions and we can't bend them – they're not ours to bend'

The situation regarding the private life of Ireland's best-known priest, Father Michael Cleary, and revealed after his death in 1993, was even more disturbing. He lived with his housekeeper, Phyllis Hamilton, with whom he had two children, one of whom had been adopted out, while the other, Ross, lived with them. In September 2007, RTÉ broadcast the programme *At Home with the Clearys*, which was a potent reminder of the megalomania of Cleary, a man who was always happy to be in the limelight as long as he was telling other people what to do. When confronted with his personal issues and domestic situation, however, he was cowardly.

It was an absorbing documentary, partly because of its exposure of the misogyny, bullying and manipulation that formed the spine of Cleary's career. He was a fraud, far more interested in his own profile and feeding his ego than in showing any humanity towards the people he wounded, despite his image as a man of the people. He could not resist a microphone and an audience, whether it was with young schoolgirls whom he 'advised' about dating and sex, lapping up their titters while he took them through the steps of light and heavy petting, telling them to use condoms, or joked with Catholic congregations about a woman who was pregnant with the next-door neighbour's child. He also indulged in self-congratulation about his ability to take troubled married couples into his confidence in order to dispense wisdom on modern relationships.

When Bishop Eamon Casey's secret was discovered in 1992, Cleary fumed that Casey – 'that bastard', he called him – had not disclosed his secret to him, feeling betrayed because Cleary had told Casey about his own situation. Even at that stage, all that consumed him was his sense of himself and of what he was entitled to. To some, it was still Hamilton's fault, as the destroyer of a good man, just as Gay Byrne, in his most disgraceful interview as host of *The Late Late Show*, blamed Annie Murphy for the downfall of Bishop Eamon Casey after she gave birth to their son Peter. Byrne said to Annie: 'He would say, Annie, he didn't have faith in your capacity as a mother ... if Peter is half the man his father is, he'll be doing well.' Murphy replied, 'I'm not so bad myself,' and stormed off set as the interview concluded.

Cleary cherished celibacy and the priestly role in public, while taking advantage of a vulnerable young woman in private. He revelled in his status as 'Ireland's most famous Catholic priest' and defender of Catholic traditional values, most especially in the sexual realm. He wrote a regular column for the *Sunday Independent*, followed by another column in the *Star* newspaper, and presented a phone-in radio show on 98FM that ran for an hour five nights a week for four years. His son Ross was sometimes by his side in studio as he reiterated the teaching of the Church on matters sexual. A typical declaration from Cleary was as follows: 'The Church can alter certain regulations and laws that it makes itself, but it can't change the laws of God. We give the Maker's instructions and we can't bend them – they're not ours to bend.'[463]

These cases also highlighted the degree of ambivalence in Irish society about physical pleasure and how they could be balanced with duties and responsibilities, and, as Tom Inglis points out, 'these ambiguities were not resolved in the silence about sex imposed by celibates.'[464] When the Archbishop of Dublin, Kevin McNamara, gave his first major print interview to *Magill* magazine in 1986 he complained that the Bishops' statements on issues other than sexuality – justice and nuclear war, for example – were ignored. He expressed certainty that 'from my meetings with many young people today, that they reject the slavery of sexual indulgence as they would the slavery of drugs ... purity sets young people free from a truly person-centred lifestyle'. It was appropriate for celibate priests to advise on matters of sexuality, he maintained, because 'one doesn't need to have an illness in order to cure it'. He also maintained that natural family planning methods when faithfully followed 'are no less effective' than artificial methods. He criticised the manner in which the principle of censorship was abused in the past ('one now looks back on this with embarrassment'), but maintained there was the contemporary challenge of 'the insidious aggression of pornography', while homosexuals needed to be treated with compassion and 'competent counsellors'.[465]

McNamara's successor as archbishop, former university lecturer in philosophy Dr Desmond Connell, struggled under the weight of the revelations of the 1990s. He was appointed Archbishop of Dublin at a time when he was the last person the Church needed, precisely because he was inflexible and driven by his belief in absolute truths. Shortly after his appointment in 1988, Fintan O'Toole wrote a profile of Connell in *Magill* magazine, which pointed out that in one of the first articles he wrote, in 1957 in *Studies*, a journal published by the Jesuits to give space to Catholic debate on literature, philosophy and science, Connell complained about unqualified people talking about religion on the radio. According to O'Toole this article reflected 'an impatience with the modern world in which mass communications gives all sorts of people the right to be heard on subjects he believes they know nothing about'.[466]

Connell remained consistent in his views on that issue, and his approach was in stark contrast to his successor, Dr Diarmuid Martin. As soon as he was appointed in 2004, Martin made a number of media appearances to promise the issue of child sexual abuse by the clergy would be dealt with in a transparent manner, however difficult that might be for the Catholic Church. It would have been unimaginable for Connell to go on television and be surrounded by lay people who, as he would have seen it, were not qualified to talk about what the Church should and should not do. While Martin knew that if the Church was to survive, it had to adapt as a matter of urgency, for Connell, the notion of the Church adapting to a changed environment was anathema. Just as he did not want modern philosophy in University College Dublin, he did not want the Church to change with the times.

Connell never courted popularity because he did not believe that to be his job. He did and said what he thought was correct, based on what he regarded as principle and truth, and followed that truth and its consequences with vigorous logic. He and his fellow Thomists (the followers of ideas based on the writings of Aquinas) saw no room for doctrinal debate and individual conscience and regarded a metaphysics based on the writings of Aquinas as an absolute science. Connell argued that virginity is of a higher order than sexuality, and that the highest possessor of this virginity is 'the consecrated virgin' – the male priest. Unfortunately for him, he

presided over the diocese of Dublin at a time when some of these 'consecrated virgins' were inflicting great pain and damage on children, and his
time as archbishop will be remembered both for that issue and for his inability to cope with a changing world and the Church's role within it.[467]

On the issue of celibacy the Catholic Church did not adapt; instead,
many priests left, finding the burden and responsibility of celibacy too much
to bear. In 1995, in a decade during which the Irish Catholic Church was
humiliated and its credibility eroded on issues of sexual morality, the Bishop
of Ferns, Brendan Comiskey, suggested the compulsory celibacy requirement for priests should be relaxed. He was admonished and summoned
to Rome to explain himself at a time when among the Catholic laity and
some clerics there was 'a growing consensus that compulsory celibacy is an
inhumane imposition'. Three years later, Comiskey again called for a debate
on the matter, pointing out that there were already married priests in the
Catholic Church – converted Anglicans in the diocese of Westminster.[468]
This was not just an Irish Catholic dilemma. In 1996, Cardinal Basil Hume,
Archbishop of Westminster, expressed similar reservations about compulsory celibacy; while from the 1960s to the 1990s an estimated 20,000 left
the active priesthood in America, most to marry. It was maintained in 1996
that 'at any one time, 20 per cent of priests in good standing are involved
in sexual relationships with women'. In the same year, one-third of European parishes were without a resident priest and a mere eighteen students
entered the seminary at Maynooth college, the lowest intake in its 200-year
history.[469] In 1995, Father Colm Kilcoyne, Irish religious affairs columnist
with the *Sunday Press*, wrote starkly, 'In seven years in Maynooth I never had
a minute's advice on how to live in celibacy and still stay normal and warm.
In thirty-five years as a priest I have never been at a local conference in our
diocese when we talked openly and honestly about celibacy.'[470]

*'The most pro pornography, pro violence, pro child sex agency
in the history of the state'*

From the 1970s to the 1990s, many Irish people looked in a variety of new
directions for erotica, and the increase in the availability of pornography
attracted considerable concern. In a Dáil debate in June 1970, the new Minister for Justice, Des O'Malley, referred to cheap paperbacks with lewd covers: 'I glanced at some that were shown to me and I do not mind saying

that my reaction was one of disgust.'[471] There was also concern about this type of material in Britain in 1970 when the Committee for the Reform of the Obscene Publications Acts (CROPA) was active, prompting a similar organisation in Ireland, the Society to Outlaw Pornography (STOP), who by the late 1970s were assured by senior Gardaí that 'owners of pornographic film would be prosecuted'. Others were unsure whether the censorship board was still in existence and, if it was not, wanted it 'reactivated'.[472]

Later, in the 1980s, with the arrival of video, groups like the JCWSSW and the Children's Protection Society drew a direct link between pornographic videos and an increase in sexual attacks, highlighting newspaper reports about 'vicious sex attacks' by English schoolboys in the early 1980s. In 1986 the *Irish Times* reported on a man who had a collection of video porn films convicted of the 'monstrous' murder of a 9-year-old girl. The previous year, the director of Dublin's sex assault treatment unit said pornography was responsible for 'a lot of the increase in child sexual abuse'.[473]

Even when child sex abusers were convicted, the JCWSSW was 'very perturbed' about sentencing in these cases and supported a call for 'specific judges with training in this area'.[474] The Children's Protection Society did not want the film censor's office to have responsibility for monitoring pornographic videos, as it was 'the most pro pornography, pro violence, pro child sex agency in the history of the state ... the then film censor told our secretary that he personally connected sexual assault with the "soft" porn passed by his office in 1978 ... in 1982 the then film censor contributed to and made a personal endorsement of a porn magazine published in Dublin. Almost simultaneously, a man aged 61 pleaded guilty to assault in the circuit criminal court. He had shown this magazine and others to four girls aged under 15, who then spent the night with him.'[475]

In 1984, it was claimed in the *Irish Press* that 'racketeers' controlled 50 per cent of the country's videotape industry. In 1986, in advance of the Video Recording Bill of 1987, the secretary to the Department of Justice informed the JCWSSW that 'the showing of a pornographic video film could be held to be an indecent exhibition contrary to common law. A person was fined £1000 in the circuit court in 1984 for exhibiting a pornographic video film on a television set in his licensed premises.'[476]

There was also concern about inconsistency in sentencing for sexual assaults and rapes; when her boyfriend of six months who raped her on New Year's Eve 1991 was given a suspended sentence, Lavinia Kerwick publicly identified herself as a rape victim, the first woman to do so in Ireland. She subsequently became gravely ill with anorexia nervosa. A book about her case also broke new ground by including a detailed account of the rape; she had been prevented for legal reasons from giving her account in court.[477] By the middle of the 1990s there was an upsurge in criticism of judicial decisions in this regard. The Court of Criminal Appeal noted that in the fifty cases of unlawful carnal knowledge dealt with between the years of 1987 and 1993, all but three of the convicted were sentenced to less than seven years.[478] There was also the issue of the gender distribution of the judiciary; in reaction to the case of the man convicted of raping the girl in the X case, who had his sentence reduced from fourteen years to four because he was a 'hard-working family man', Nuala O'Faoláin wrote: 'No one up there seems to recognise the burning, choking anger that women especially, but women-understanding men too, feel at the way sentencing seems sensitive to everything about the man, but insensitive – dead – to the value we place on being able to live in our bodies (and our children in their bodies) with health and joy and confidence in our sexuality.'[479]

'You've forgotten half your skirt'

Joy and confidence in sexuality was also being undermined by the increasing sexualisation of young people. According to John Ardagh, there was a sense that by the 1990s 'the Irish are in the thick of a kind of sexual revolution, in a muddled sort of way'.[480] As Tom Inglis explained, 'Many young people have torn up the Catholic guide to living a good life and turned to an ancient Greek notion that it is up to each individual to construct an ethical life based around duties, responsibilities and pleasures. For the ancient Greeks, not paying attention to one's pleasures was as unethical as not fulfilling one's duties and responsibilities.'[481]

In 1996, a Utopia sex shop was opened in Limerick, while in 1999 an Ann Summers shop was opened on O'Connell Street, Dublin's main thoroughfare. Some saw this as representing the normalisation of sexuality by its being transformed into a commodity, though this development was also presented as a threat to collective and individual well being.[482] In 1999, the ban imposed on *In Dublin* magazine for advertising 'massage parlours' was a reminder that the Censorship of Publications Board had remained active and publishers outside Ireland were hardly going to appeal against bans on publications such as *Butchboys, The Best of Asian Babes* and *Stories for Men*

Who Need It Bad. In Dublin was seen as mainstream but was banned for advertising 'health clubs', massage parlours and advertisements seeking staff for such establishments. It was banned for six months; while at the same time plenty of publications with sexually explicit material remained on the shelves. Madonna's book *Sex* was banned in 1992 but, between its import and the ban, 2,500 copies had been sold and 'that was probably all that was going to buy it anyway'.[483]

Concern was also expressed at the manner in which young girls were prematurely sexualised in Celtic Tiger Ireland. Ann Marie Hourihane described some of them at the POD, a Dublin nightclub, in 2000: 'One girl is wearing a crochet miniskirt, pink cowboy boots, a crochet bra on her tiny breasts. She looks young and old at the same time, like a page-three girl.' Another girl, a 'tall tanned girl with blond hair, a micro-mini with a lilac leather belt, a green cut-off top and a pale jeans jacket', is told sarcastically, 'You've forgotten half your skirt'.[484]

Another consequence of this increased sexualisation was a dramatic rise in sexually transmitted diseases. Similar to patterns elsewhere in the world, sexual health research garnered much academic and public interest, because nationally reported rates of STDs other than HIV and AIDS were on the increase, and there seemed to be a new complacency about safe sex. But the increase may also have been due to increased surveillance rather than their actual levels in society; the JCWSSW had pointed out in 1974, for example, that in relation to venereal disease 'at the moment there are four clinics in Dublin but few know where they are situated'.[485]

As Tom Inglis noted, by the early twenty-first century self-indulgence had replaced self-denial, but that too had its downside: 'In a strange twist of fate, however, the rapid movement from a culture of self-denial to one of self-indulgence may have led to people not being able to cope with greater money and freedom and that this has led to uncontrolled over-indulgence, which, in turn, leads to a form of self-elimination.'[486] As elsewhere, the internet played an important role in this, as it expanded sexual horizons and facilitated the search for the forbidden, 'from pornographers and paedophiles ... to infertility clinics ... to the lonely and the hopeful seeking "Love Bytes".'[487]

Some, most notably the renowned psychiatrist Anthony Clare, also identified a crisis of masculinity, arguing that 'phallic man, authoritative, dominant, assertive – man in control not merely of himself but of woman – is starting to die'. In response, it was wryly suggested by journalist Sheila O'Flanagan that 'men's emotional well-being has been a popular topic of discussion ever since women became financially independent of them'.[488] Some Irish fiction writing made it clear that 'if women were once the ones that cried ... now it's the men'; Molly McCloskey, in her 2002 short story 'A Nuclear Adam and Eve', identified an obvious 'emasculation of modern man'.[489]

To what extent was the new gender role conflict related to sexuality? Clare suggested that, because men have always feared women and sought to dominate and control them, they were struggling in the face of challenges to patriarchy by the end of the twentieth century, but given their repudiation of the feminine they denied their own vulnerability and need for intimacy, leading to an incompetence in dealing with their own emotional distress: 'Might the fear and contempt [for women] be related to a deeper fear, a more profound anxiety about male sexuality itself?' he asked.

> clergy?
>
> Given the extent to which control is for many men the defining mark of their masculinity, any suggestion or threat of being out of control challenges the very essence of what being a male is all about ... men fall because women tempt them. This remains *the* explanation of male sexual behaviour most favoured by men. Rather than expose to a genuinely rigorous analysis the nature of male sexuality and its relationship to power, social status, aggression and control, most male commentators retreat into a self-pitying and ultimately depressing moan about the difficulty of being a full-bloodedly sexual man in a dynamic relationship with a woman in the new post-feminist world of gender equality.

Clare underlined the reality of how violent men still are to women and children but also the threat to fatherhood as a result of the rise of reproductive technologies. He stressed the importance of an active fathering role 'as a key civilising influence on men' along with the need for men to 'become more capable of expressing the vulnerability and the tenderness and the affection we feel'.[490] Some got second chances, like Jimmy Rabitte, in Roddy Doyle's novel *The Snapper* (1990), who discovers the significance of fatherhood, not through fathering his six children, but by educating himself about his unmarried daughter's pregnancy: 'There was Veronica, his wife and his children. Some of his own sperms had gone into making them so, fuck it, he was responsible for them. But, by Jaysis he'd made one poxy job of it so far ... but from now on it was going to be different.'[491]

Doyle, along with Dermot Bolger, author of *The Journey Home* (1990),

'Holy Father'

wrote grittily and powerfully about life in working-class Dublin in the 1980s and 1990s, detailing the corrupt and criminal side of that life as well as alluding to sexual dishonesties, sexual violence and challenges to the ideology of the family. Doyle's *The Woman Who Walks into Doors* (1997) describes the troubled life of Paula Spencer, 'a sucker for romance', who grew up in an environment where 'anything could get you called a slut', marries for protection and is stuck with a violent drunk who makes her life hell. Patrick McCabe's novel *Breakfast with Pluto* (1998) describes the experiences of Patrick Braden, the illegitimate child of an Irish priest who evolves into a transvestite prostitute; 'in real life love has gone sour, has been degraded into mere sex'. Recurring themes of McCabe's work are 'emotional malnourishment and social transgression', with betrayal, mindlessness and murder the consequences.[492] Jennifer Johnson also confronted difficult, traditionally taboo subjects; in *The Invisible Worm* (1991), the protagonist's discovery of a capacity to love requires not only facing a failed marriage but confronting her incestuous past.[493]

'These findings do not present a picture of a population
where the majority are having daily or even weekly sex'

The extent and consequences of sexual indulgence were considered in a plethora of reports and statistics in the early twenty-first century. In 2006, for example, a report entitled *Women and Sexually Transmitted Infections: A Gendered Analysis* from the Women's Health Council, an advisory body to the Minister for Health, referred to a 'staggering' increase of 173.8 per cent in notified STDs in the Republic of Ireland in the decade from 1994 to 2003. While it suggested the rise was partly due to increased awareness and screening, more sensitive diagnostic methods and improved notification systems, 'it still points to a significant upsurge in risky sexual behaviour'. It suggested the statistics were a 'huge underestimate' of the real incidence of STDs because of the lack of a comprehensive system of surveillance; similar increases had been documented throughout the EU. In Ireland there was no national strategy for the screening of chlamydia (linked to infertility in both men and women) even though there was a 1,044 per cent increase in cases reported to the Health Protection Surveillance Centre between 1995 and 2004.[494]

Despite all the focus on the age of consent, there were those who argued that such debates were 'irrelevant to today's reckless and rudderless young teenagers ... when their sexual reference points are being defined by a bizarrely erotic popular culture that rewards ... damaging promiscuous experimentation at the expense of a healthy journey to sexual maturity ... we have given so much freedom to children and young teenagers and expected confidence in return, yet all we have got is confusion.'[495] A *Sunday Tribune/ Millward Brown IMS* opinion poll, published in 2005, reported that 77 per cent of adults thought that sex before marriage was acceptable, 79 per cent would live with a partner before marriage, and 25 per cent thought it acceptable to have more than one sexual partner; 23 per cent were 'not at all concerned' about STDs, while 21 per cent were 'very concerned'. Psychosexual problems were also becoming much more common and people, it appeared, had unrealistic expectations of sex, as well as more interest in sexual experimentation and fetishes.[496]

A Durex survey of 2005 also suggested Irish people were sexually promiscuous – it ranked Ireland tenth highest of 41 nationalities for the number of sexual partners, revealing that the average Irish person had 11 sexual partners in their lifetime, compared to a global average of 9. Sixty-two per cent of Irish people said they had experienced a one-night stand, while 58 per cent admitted to having unprotected sex without knowing their partner's sexual history.[497] A dating website for people with sexually transmitted diseases had a very positive response from Irish sufferers when it was launched in Ireland and the UK in September 2006, with 500 signed-up members in Ireland after a few weeks.[498]

In 2006, a survey conducted by the Economic and Social Research Institute (ESRI) and the Royal College of Surgeons in Ireland also revealed dramatic changes in the behaviour of Irish people in the previous twenty years, with an increased trend among young people towards paying for sex, and the incidence of STDs having increased by 243 per cent between 1998 and 2003. It also found attitudes towards abortion 'have undergone immense change since the early 1980s', with 64 per cent of those surveyed now expressing the view that abortion was acceptable in at least some circumstances. It found that just 6 per cent of people believed premarital sex was always wrong, compared to 71 per cent in 1973; more than 90 per cent believed emergency contraception should be available in Ireland, with 52 per cent of men and 42 per cent of women believing it should be available without prescription.

This research also revealed that the age at which people first had sex was falling. Over the previous forty years the age of first sexual experience had dropped by five years for men and six for women, with the median age at which young people first had sex found to be 17 years. This survey was funded by the government, something that the reports' authors, Richard Layte and Hannah McGee, suggested was unlikely to have been done ten years previously. They concluded: 'the good news is that overall, young people are now more likely to use contraception and protection the first time, but earlier sex is also strongly associated with a lower likelihood of using contraception'. Notwithstanding, 'social inequalities in sexual health also emerged from the study as a concern', with regard to sex education and likeliness to use contraception. Almost 50 per cent of those surveyed said they got no sex education at all.[499] Nor was sex that frequent, it seemed, among adults: 58 per cent of them 'have sex less than once a week and a quarter less than once a month ... these findings do not present a picture of a population where the majority are having daily or even weekly sex.'[500] While acknowledging that this survey revealed a great deal about sexual attitudes and practices, Tom Inglis cautioned that 'it does not tell us the extent to which sex has become written into the Irish body. It reveals little about the degree to which everyday life and the sense of self have been colonised by an obsession with the body and being sexually attractive.'[501]

Dr Susan Clarke, Ireland's leading expert in infectious diseases, suggested in 2006 that as many as 15 per cent of teenagers under the age of 18 who had been screened in Ireland had been found to have an STD. Another problem was testing, with waiting times of up to nine weeks for a STD screen in public hospitals – there were just two walk-in STD clinics in Ireland, in Dublin's St James's hospital and Galway University hospital, but still no guarantee of being seen at either due to the high number of people presenting. The Irish Family Planning Association set up two private STD clinics in Dublin in 2006, but there was a sense that more GP training was necessary to take the pressure off over-burdened clinics and there was much fear about the level of undetected STDs.[502]

Clarke also referred to the problem of dealing with teenagers under the age of consent with STDs as a 'legal nightmare', as legally, such people presenting themselves at clinics should have been reported to the Gardaí. The context for this was newly introduced emergency legislation which deemed a 17-year-old boy to be guilty of statutory rape if he had consensual sex with a girl under that age, although she was exempt from prosecution.[503]

'What is commonly believed to be the reality of sexual activity among teenage boys and girls'

There was something of a dilemma for legislators anxious for the age of consent to be brought into line 'with what is commonly believed to be the reality of sexual activity among teenage boys and girls'. But an Oireachtas committee on child protection was also conscious of the volume of submissions in favour of retaining it at 17 after the Supreme Court struck down the law on statutory rape. The Rape Crisis Centre also wanted the age to remain at 17.[504] The real surprise about the exposure of the ambiguity relating to the law of consent in Ireland was that it took so long to happen. Section 1 of the 1935 Criminal Law Amendment Act had been used to deal with men accused of sexual relations with a child, which provided for a maximum sentence of penal servitude for life if convicted of sex with a girl under 15. In theory, the law also prevented sex between consenting teenagers. But this was bad law in practice, as was revealed in 2006 when a male who genuinely believed a girl was older – much more likely as teenagers became more sexually active by the end of the twentieth century – found he had no defence.

This had been seen as questionable as far back as the 1980s and was referred to the Law Reform Commission in 1990, which remarked on the 'combination of prosecutorial and judicial discretion' that was preventing the law from being exposed for the unfair legislation it was. It was only a matter of time before it was struck down in the Supreme Court on the grounds that a defendant who genuinely believed that, for example, a 14-year-old was 16, was deprived of a defence, but politicians were reluctant to confront its unfairness because the same law was being used to jail adult abusers. Once it was struck down, older men convicted of having carnal knowledge of children could claim their freedom, as the law was now defunct. The response was to rush through another law, and the Supreme Court sent back to prison a man released although it had ruled that the law that convicted him no longer existed.[505]

The new law made sex with children an offence but allowed for a defence of 'honest belief' on a girl's age. It made sex with a child under the age of 15 punishable by up to life imprisonment, and sex with a child between 15 and 17 punishable with five years in prison. There followed widespread calls to reinstate the offence of statutory rape of a minor, which was abolished by the Supreme Court, or introduce an amendment to the constitution that covered the right of children not to be sexually exploited. The original case that began this crisis emerged in 2001 when a man (Mr 'C') faced four challenges of unlawful carnal knowledge with the same 15-year-old girl. He pleaded not guilty on the basis he believed she was 16. This was still an offence, but deemed less serious than if the girl had been under 15.[506]

In other respects, traditional attitudes and gender divides remained deep rooted in Ireland. A study from University College Dublin published in the *Journal of Sexual Health* in 2008 suggested young Irish men judge whether a woman is likely to have a sexual disease by the way she dresses and by local rumours about her past. One of the authors of the report, Dr Abbey Hyde, highlighted the frequency with which young men were prepared to use the term 'slut', not just for women who were deemed to have had sex with multiple partners: 'the term could also arise out of the style of dress of a woman, her perceived behaviour or simply rumour or gossip'. Male sexual behaviour was rarely subjected to the same level of criticism, the author concluding 'sexual double standards continue to be a feature of young people's culture' and, though men were accepted to be engaging in more sex than women, women were seen as 'the bearers' of sexual disease.[507]

There were, however, those who took alternative routes sexually, by deciding to remain celibate until marriage, some of whom were involved in Youth 2000, a Catholic youth group with about 700 members in Ireland in 2006. Another, non-denominational Christian group, Authentic Youth, travelled to schools and organised retreats.[508] While it is clear that the highlighting of the premature sexualisation of young people was important, as was the highlighting of ignorance about STDs and contraception, it was not the case that these were battles between traditional Catholics and liberals; perhaps neither group was homogenous.

There was also much sensationalist and titillating reporting of underage sex, as if it was a late twentieth-century invention, written with a determination to 'lift the lid' on what young people were 'getting up to', unknown to their parents. Young people were presented as 'other', in tones that transmitted a sense of loss, alarm and dismay. In February 1998, for example, the *Sunday World* suggested as 'fact' that 'one in ten of every child of secondary school age (13–17) had experience of sexual intercourse'. Voyeuristic photographs taken from above of groping teenagers often accompanied such reports, with strident assertions that young people's sexual behaviour was a problem, 'with scarcely any substantiation or analysis' to justify such assertions.[509] In July 1999, following a court case in which a young man was acquitted of the rape and sexual assault of a young woman (he was 17 and she was 15 at the time), an *Irish Times* article posed the question: 'Is it commonplace for girls as young as fifteen to be performing oral sex on boys they have known for only a few minutes?'

As Maurice Devlin has observed, the interesting thing about such questions is that they underline the extent to which it was the behaviour of young females that was highlighted as deviant; the idea being that the reputation of young women is at stake in a way that does not apply to men.[510] Historically, this represents continuity rather than change, a reminder that, despite the extent to which Irish sexuality has become less restricted by the demands made by family, religion, society and economy, a narrative of Irish sexual history that moves seamlessly from repression to liberation is incomplete and simplistic.[511]

This is why Irish agony aunts and psychologists found that, while they were dealing with different issues in the early twenty-first century, there was still much pain being caused by sexuality. Patricia Redlich noted that when she was studying psychology in the late 1960s, the main issue in therapy was tackling guilt as a result of repression, whereas thirty-five years on, the real problem was freedom and lack of taboos and boundaries. Ultimately, she argued, they both had the same consequences:

> wives pursue their work colleagues with frustrated ferocity, leaving husbands simmering offside. Married stalwarts of the community find themselves addicted to high-risk homosexual encounters. Lonely young men visit prostitutes instead of engaging with girls. Mistresses are devastated when their married lovers won't leave home. Wives simply surrender when their husbands say they are going. Parents feel powerless. Young women put it out, indiscriminately and often while under the influence. Cross-dressing is considered a personal choice. Virtual infidelity is the norm in chat rooms, addiction to porn so commonplace it seems almost silly to comment.[512]

The continuing rise in sexually transmitted diseases in the early twenty-first century – also a problem 100 years previously – prompted the contention that 'there has been much mythology about the Irish sexual culture in relation to its conservatism and sexual morality'.[513] The sexual history of modern Ireland proves that emphatically.

One hundred years after the controversy over J. M. Synge's *Playboy of the Western World*, and the image of 'chosen females' standing in their underwear, a succession of developments, including the availability of contraception, a lessening of censorship, the decriminalisation of homo-sexuality, revelations about the extent of paedophilia, and 'the right freely to dispose of one's body according to one's own needs and desires'[514] have ensured that the *Playboy* row now seems almost quaint.

By the early twenty-first century, the boundaries of what is and is not acceptable to publish in the realm of Irish sexuality have changed beyond recognition. There is a high premium placed on the value of personal testi-mony, a dominance of the memoir as a literary genre, a confessional culture and the personalisation of debate, which have all combined to expose the myth of exceptional Irish sexual purity. Alongside this, 'it is because of the interest that various governments of Ireland have taken in regulating sexu-ality, promoting some kinds of reproduction and discouraging others that many intellectuals have insisted that there needs to be a debate about sexual-ity in Ireland'.[515]

But sexual liberalisation and advanced secularism have not necessarily resulted in an all-encompassing freedom. As Tony Judt has pointed out in *Postwar*, his far-reaching history of post-war Europe, for example, the sexual revolution of the 1960s was 'almost certainly a mirage for the overwhelming majority of people, young and old alike. So far as we can know, the sexual interests and practices of most young Europeans did not change nearly as rapidly as contemporaries liked to claim'.[516] The phrase Judt uses, 'so far as we can know', is a reminder of the difficulties of researching sexual history. Few are fortunate enough, like the writer Blake Morrison, to 'stumble into the archive of my parents' courtship'. The correspondence between his Irish mother and English father in the 1940s reveals a frankness about sexual matters and 'the ideas they had; the emotions they felt'. For him, 'to see my parents cooing and billing like this was strangely comforting'.[517] Notwith-standing, he also suggested that to read voluminous intimate correspon-dence not intended for his eyes was 'transgressive' and 'a shit's trick'. This underlines the sensitivities and ethical dilemmas associated with the use of such material, an issue that also arises in relation to the personal testimo-nies prepared for court cases concerning sexual crime which need to be used carefully and placed in a broad context.

As has been demonstrated in this book, there are many other routes to travel in the search for an understanding of Irish sexual culture. A perusal of books by Irish authors reveals a lot about sex, but during much of the twentieth century their writing was often guarded, making it necessary to

read between the lines. Some writers just avoided or deleted the subject altogether because it was not deemed to be worth the controversy that would
ensue. Even Flann O'Brien (Brian O'Nolan), a man who suffered few fools,
and was one of the most skilful satirists and novelists of the twentieth century, did not put up a fight. When the Irish publishers of his 1941 book *An
Beál Bocht* (*The Poor Mouth*) expressed concern about an initial draft that
contained marital infidelity, he responded, 'I have cut out completely all references to sexual matters and made every other change necessary to render
the text completely aseptic and harmless ... I am satisfied that the thing is
now safe from any Puritanical objection.'[518]

The variety of sources used in this book support the notion expressed
elsewhere that sexual identity and preferences are 'more fluid and nuanced
than they have been traditionally considered', as a result of which 'one sees
historical and fictional characters, their behaviour and relationships (both
the historical and the imaginary) in a different light than before'.[519] There
were also continuities throughout the period this book is concerned with:
a concern with outward conventions, a decidedly middle-class discourse
about sexuality, deep strains of homophobia and misogyny that cannot be
regarded as only belonging to the first half of the twentieth century.

There is little doubt that increased prosperity in the western world
undermined much traditional censoriousness in relation to sexuality and
that such a relaxation came to Ireland later than to some other European
countries. The resultant changes gave rise to a challenging of the perception
that sexuality could only serve as a means of reproduction. It could now also
be a route to pleasure, forging a certain 'sexual consumerism' that, arguably,
has 'defeated sexual Utopianism', with sexual desire being constructed in a
different way.[520] But an evident confidence (some would say crassness) in
sexual expression does not mean that conflict, guilt, uncertainty and anger
over sexuality, marriage, chastity, feminism, masculine identity, censorship,
sex education and public health policy ceased to exist. The preoccupation
with what is sexually acceptable is still of relevance in modern Ireland.

It is clear that in Ireland, as in Europe generally, during times of social
crises, anxiety about sexual behaviour has tended to erupt but that even
though authorities – lay and clerical – have consistently tried to manage
sexual desire, they have frequently failed.[521] There has also been considerable disagreement about what is desirable or feasible for the state to do in
the field of sexuality. On a personal level, many Irish people have indulged
in 'twilight moments', a concept introduced by Anna Clark in her 2008

*book *Desire*, the most recent history of European sexuality. Activities seen as shameful or dishonourable have none the less been indulged in, and even sometimes tolerated when 'concealed by shadows'.[522] Nor have all those who have engaged in forbidden sexual acts been 'stigmatised with deviant identities' – men who frequent prostitutes, or make young unmarried women pregnant being obvious examples in Ireland. For five decades, the juries that passed judgment on sexual crimes in Ireland were exclusively male, which had significant implications for the way in which the judicial system viewed men and women in relation to sexual crime. Despite the best efforts of those who sought justice for women who had been violated, there was a frequent, sometimes blatant discrimination against such women.

Delusions about Irish sexual purity proved to be quite durable. In the late 1980s, when in Galway to give a lecture on the general theme of prostitution, historian Maria Luddy discovered that some shops refused to display an advertisement for her presentation 'because the words prostitution and Ireland appeared together in the same space'. Others 'thanked God the British had gone as there had been no prostitution in Ireland since'.[523] For much of the twentieth century, the contention that public debate on sexual morality was inappropriate stood alongside public sermonising and a preoccupation with what was seen, not what was suffered. As the sociologist Mark Finnane has argued, 'an obsession with the visibility of sex (in dance halls, on country lanes, or imagined in the motor vehicles parked along the roads) avoided a more considered attention to the contexts and harm of serious sexual offending'.[524] During an Irish century when there was an avowedly Catholic ethos, oppression and watchfulness, there was also no shortage of clandestine and illicit sexual behaviour. The challenge that various authorities set themselves was to keep uncomfortable truths behind closed doors. They often contended that the most important thing was to keep souls, not bodies, safe – a stance that did considerable damage and was increasingly challenged by a variety of activists and the Irish women's movement in particular.

It is important that the history of sexual exploitation, vulnerability and abuse be highlighted, but also the considerable courage shown in relation to sexual matters in twentieth-century Ireland and the significant battles won by advocates of change, greater tolerance and choice.

GUIDE TO ACRONYMS

Main Archives

NAI National Archives of Ireland
PRONI Public Record Office of Northern Ireland
DDA Dublin Diocesan Archives
UCDA University College Dublin Archives, School of History and Archives
JJBL John J. Burns Library, Boston College, Massachusetts
SPCDA St Patrick's College Drumcondra Archives, Dublin

Individual Archives

BMH Bureau of Military History
IQA Irish Queer Archive

Government Departments, Committees and Offices

CEL Committee on Evil Literature
CICA Commission to Inquire into Child Abuse
FCO Film Censor's Office
DCAB Cabinet Secretariat (Northern Ireland)
DF Department of Finance (Northern Ireland)

DH Department of Health
DHA Department of Home Affairs (Northern Ireland)
DJ Department of Justice
DLGPH Department of Local Government and Public Health
DT Department of the Taoiseach
HO Home Office (Northern Ireland)

Legal Transcripts

CBA Crown Books at Assizes
CFA Crown Files at Assizes
CBQS Crown Books at Quarter Sessions
CFQS Crown Files at Quarter Sessions
SBCCC State Books at Central Criminal Court
SFCCC State Files at Central Criminal Court
SBCircCC State Books at Circuit Criminal Court
SFCircCC State Files at Circuit Criminal Court

Non-Government Organisations

BCSW Belfast Council of Social Welfare
BWWC Belfast Women's Welfare Clinic
CPRSI Catholic Protection and Rescue Society of Ireland
CSWB Catholic Social Welfare Bureau
GLEN Gay and Lesbian Equality Network
ICGPS International Catholic Girls Protection Society
IHA Irish Housewives Association
JCWSSW Joint Committee of Women's Societies and Social Workers
NIFPA Northern Ireland Family Planning Association
NIGRA Northern Ireland Gay Rights Association
NLGF National Lesbian and Gay Federation
NSPCC National Society for the Prevention of Cruelty to Children

NOTES

Introduction

1. *Sex and Sensibility*, broadcast on RTÉ One, 26 June 2008.
2. Fergal Tobin, *The Best of Decades: Ireland in the 1960s* (Dublin, 1984), p. 68.
3. See Diarmaid Ferriter, *What If? Alternative Views of Twentieth-century Ireland* (Dublin, 2006), p. 47.
4. Anthony Copley, *Sexual Moralities in France, 1780–1980* (London, 1992).
5. David Evans, *Sexual Citizenship: The Material Construction of Sexualities* (London, 1993), p. 2.
6. Michel Foucault, *The Use of Pleasure* (London, 1988), p. 10.
7. George L. Mosse, *Nationalism and Sexuality: Respectability and Abnormal Sexuality in Modern Europe* (New York, 1985), pp. 9–10.
8. Tom Inglis, 'Foucault, Bourdieu and the Field of Irish Sexuality', *Irish Journal of Sociology*, vol. 7, 1997, pp. 5–28.
9. Tom Inglis, 'The Constitution of Sexual Subjects in Irish Religious and Moral Discourse', paper presented to Theory, Culture and Society Conference, Berlin, August 1995, UCD Library photocopy 13743.
10. Tom Inglis, *Global Ireland: Same Difference* (London, 2008), p. 122.
11. ibid., p. 249.
12. Inglis, 'Foucault, Bourdieu', pp. 5–28.
13. NAI, DJ, H247/41A, memorandum of Eoin O'Duffy for the Carrigan Committee, October 1930.
14. NAI, DT, S5998, *Report of the Committee on the Criminal Law Amendment Acts (1880–1885) and Juvenile Prostitution* (Dublin, 1930), pp. 12–15.

15. Marjorie Howes, 'Public Discourse, Private Reflection: 1916–1970', in Angela Bourke *et al.*, (eds.), *The Field Day Anthology of Irish Writing, Vol. 4* (Cork, 2002), p. 925.

16. C. B. Murphy, 'Sex, Censorship and the Church', *The Bell*, vol. 2, no. 6, September 1941, pp. 65–76.

17. Unemployed, 'Neutral Night', *The Bell*, vol. 4, no. 1, April 1942, pp. 37–40.

18. Angela Bourke, 'Rocks in the Road', *Dublin Review*, no. 21, Winter 2005–6, pp. 102–12.

19. NAI, DJ, H247/41/B, 19 November 1932.

20. *The Standard*, 11 December 1953.

21. NAI, DT, S11582E, Irish Labour Emigration, memorandum by F. H. Boland, 15 July 1953.

22. NAI, DT, S4183, 'Venereal Disease in the Irish Free State: Committee of Inquiry', memorandum by Dr McDonnell, 7 May 1927.

23. NAI, DJ, H247/41/B, Daniel Keane to James Geoghegan, 20 January 1933.

24. NAI, DT, S16210, 'Appointment of Women Police, General', 6 July 1938.

25. NAI, DT, 2002/8/459, Patrick Cogan to Jack Lynch, 3 April 1971.

26. *Cork Examiner*, 18 January 1936.

27. NAI, V4B/23/12, SFCirCC, Galway, 25 June 1954.

28. Mark Finnane, 'Irish Psychiatry Part 1: The Formation of a Profession', in German E. Berrios and Hugh Freeman (eds.), *150 Years of British Psychiatry* (London, 1991), pp. 306–13.

29. Ivor Browne, *Music and Madness* (Dublin, 2008), p. 300.

30. NAI, DT, S5553D, Committee on Relief of Unemployment, 4 February 1928.

31. Sandra McAvoy, 'Sex and the Single Girl: Ireland 1922–49', in Chichi Ania Golu (ed.), *In from the Shadows: The University of Limerick Women's Studies Collection*, vol. 3, 1997, pp. 55–67.

32. Francis Hackett, 'De Valera's Ireland', *American Mercury*, January 1945, vol. 60, no. 253, pp. 29–39.

33. NAI, DT, S14716, 19 December 1949.

34. Tom Inglis, 'Pleasure Pursuits', in Mary P. Corcoran and Michael Peillon (eds.), *Ireland Unbound: A Turn of the Century Chronicle* (Dublin, 2002), pp. 25–35.

35. Paul Ferris, *Sex and the British: A Twentieth-century History* (London, 1993), p. 1.

36. Ralph Gallagher, 'Understanding the Homosexual', *Furrow*, vol. 30, no. 9, September 1979, pp. 559–68.

37. Chrystel Hug, *The Politics of Sexual Morality in Ireland* (Basingstoke, 1999), p. 234.

38. Anthony Bradley and Maryann Gialanella Valiulis (eds.), *Gender and Sexuality in Modern Ireland* (Amherst, MA, 1997) pp. 6–7.

39. Quoted in Patricia Craig (ed.), *The Oxford Book of Ireland* (Oxford, 1998), p. 411.

40. Inglis, *Global Ireland*, p. 186.

– ONE –
1845–1922

1. Christopher Morash, 'All Playboys Now: *The Playboy of the Western World* and the Audience', in Nicholas Grene (ed.), *J. M. Synge and Irish Theatre* (Dublin, 2000), pp. 131–51.

2. Ibid.

3. Declan Kiberd, 'Synge's Opening Night to Remember', *Irish Times*, 26 January 2007.

4. Ibid.

5. Róisín Ní Ghairbhí, 'The Use of Hiberno-English as a Mouthpiece for Irish Identity in the Irish Theatre: Synge's *The Playboy of the Western World* and the Drama of Martin McDonagh', in Eoin Flannery and Angus Mitchell (eds.), *Enemies of Empire: New Perspectives on Imperialism, Literature and Historiography* (Dublin, 2007), pp. 142–60.

6. Morash, 'All Playboys now', pp. 131–51.

7. Ann Saddlemyer (ed.), *The Collected Letters of John Millington Synge, Vol. 1, 1871–1907* (Oxford, 1993), p. 74, letter to Stephen McKenna, 28 January 1904.

8. Declan Kiberd, *Inventing Ireland* (London, 1995), p. 67, and Colm Tóibín, *Lady Gregory's Toothbrush* (Dublin, 2002), pp. 58–68.

9. Saddlemyer (ed.), *Collected Letters, Vol. 1*, pp. 90–91, letter to Frank Fay, 1 July 1904.

10. J. M. Synge (edited by Robert Skelton), *The Aran Islands* (Oxford, 1979; first published 1907), p. 84.

11. Ibid., p. 31.

12. Ibid., pp. 114–17 and p. 122.

13. Máirtín O'Direáin with Declan Collinge, 'J. M. Synge', *Irish Review*, no. 6, Spring 1989, pp. 63–4.

14. John McGahern, 'An tOileanach', *Irish Review*, no. 6, Spring 1989, pp. 55–63.

15. Anne Enright, 'Bad at History', in Colm Tóibín (ed.), *Synge: A Celebration* (Dublin, 2005), pp. 115–25.

16. Stephen Tifft, 'The Parricidal Phantasm: Irish Nationalism and the Playboy Riots', in Andrew Parker *et al.* (eds.), *Nationalisms and Sexualities* (London, 1992), pp. 313–35.

17. Mark Finnane, 'The Carrigan Committee of 1930–31 and the "Moral Condition" of the Saorstát', *Irish Historical Studies*, vol. 32, no. 128, November 2001, pp. 519–36.

18. *Irish Times*, 30 January 1907.

19. Kiberd, *Inventing Ireland*, p. 67ff.

20. Frances Finnegan, *Do Penance or Perish* (Kilkenny, 2001), p. 114.

21. James M. Smith, *Ireland's Magdalen Laundries and the Nation's Architecture of Containment* (Notre Dame, ID, 2007), p. 211.

22. John O'Brien (ed.), *The Vanishing Irish: The Enigma of the Modern World* (London, 1954), pp. 6–7.

23. Art Cosgrove (ed.), *Marriage in Ireland* (Dublin, 1985), p. 3.

24. Mary E. Daly, *The Slow Failure: Population Decline and Independent Ireland* (Madison, WI, 2006), p. 76.

25. Ibid., p. 94, and Cormac Ò'Gráda, *Ireland Before and After the Famine* (Manchester, 1993), pp. 152–97.

26. Liam Kennedy, 'Bastardy and the Great Famine: Ireland 1845–50', in Carla King (ed.), *Famine Land and Culture in Ireland* (Dublin, 2000), pp. 6–29.

27. Maria Sophia Quine, *Population Politics in Twentieth-century Europe* (London, 1996), p. 4.

28. Ibid., pp. 7–9.

29. Tom Inglis, 'Foucault, Bourdieu and the Field of Irish Sexuality', *Irish Journal of Sociology*, vol. 7, 1997, pp. 5–28.

30. Ibid.

31. Tom Inglis, 'The Constitution of Sexual Subjects in Irish Religious and Moral Discourse', paper presented to Theory, Culture and Society Conference, Berlin, August 1995, UCD Library photocopy 13743, and Inglis, 'Foucault, Bourdieu', pp. 5–28.

32. Joe Lee, *The Modernisation of Irish Society, 1848–1918* (Dublin, 1992; first published 1973), p. 6.

33. Inglis, 'The Constitution of Sexual Subjects'.

34. Lee, *Modernisation*, pp. 5–6.

35. K. H. Connell, *Irish Peasant Society: Four Historical Essays* (Oxford, 1968), p. 113.

36. David Fitzpatrick, 'Marriage in Post-Famine Ireland', in Art Cosgrove (ed.), *Marriage in Ireland*, p. 117.

37. Daly, *The Slow Failure*, p. 5.

38. Ibid., pp. 125–8.

39. Ibid., p. 129.

40. Both quoted in Tony Farmar, *Ordinary Lives: Three Generations of Irish Middle-Class Experience, 1907, 1932, 1963* (Dublin, 1991), p. 35.
41. Connell, *Irish Peasant Society*, p. 119.
42. Paul Gray and Liam Kennedy, 'A Sexual Revolution in the West of Ireland?', *History Ireland*, vol. 14, no. 6, November/December 2006, pp. 19–22.
43. S. J. Connelly, 'Illegitimacy and Pre-Nuptial Pregnancy in Ireland before 1864: The Evidence of Some Catholic Parish Registers', *Journal of Irish Economic and Social History*, vol. 6, 1979, pp. 5–23.
44. Ibid., p. 22.
45. NAI, DT, S5931, memorandum from Department of Justice on Illegitimate Children (Affiliation Orders) Bill 1929, 11 June 1930.
46. Rosita Sweetman, 'The Blanket of Silence', in Mark Patrick Hederman and Richard Kearney (eds.), *The Crane Bag Book of Irish Studies* (Dublin, 1982), pp. 765–9.
47. Quoted in Siobhán Kilfeather, 'Sexuality, 1685–2001', in A. Bourke *et al.*, *The Field Day Anthology of Irish Writing, Vol. 4* (Cork, 2002), p. 755.
48. Tom Inglis, 'Origins and Legacies of Irish Prudery: Sexuality and Social Control in Modern Ireland', *Éire–Ireland*, vol. 40, nos. 3 and 4, Fall/Winter 2005, pp. 9–38.
49. Franz Eder, Lesley Hall and Gert Hekma (eds.), *Sexual Cultures in Europe: National Histories* (Manchester, 1999), p. 20, and Tony Fahey, 'Religion and Sexual Culture in Ireland', in Eder *et al.*, (eds.), *Sexual Cultures in Europe*, pp. 53–70.
50. Kilfeather, 'Sexuality, 1685–2001', p. 756.
51. Ibid.
52. Inglis, *Global Ireland*, p. 3, and Inglis, 'The Constitution of Sexual Subjects'.
53. Inglis, 'The Constitution of Sexual Subjects'.
54. Kilfeather, 'Sexuality, 1685–2001', pp. 757–8.
55. Inglis, 'Origins and Legacies of Irish Prudery'.
56. Joe Lee, 'Women and the Church Since the Famine', in Margaret MacCurtain and Donncha O'Corráin (eds.), *Women in Irish Society: The Historical Dimension* (Dublin, 1978), pp. 37–46.
57. Jeffrey Weeks, *Sex, Politics and Society: The Regulation of Sexuality Since 1800* (London, 1981).
58. Copely, *Sexual Moralities in France*, p. 79.
59. Inglis, 'Origins and Legacies of Irish Prudery', pp. 9–38.
60. NAI, IC 28 7, CBQS, Dublin, June 1891–June 1894.
61. Angela Bourke, *The Burning of Bridget Cleary* (Dublin, 1999), pp. 85–6 and p. 205 ff.

62. Siobhán Kilfeather, 'Sexual Expression and Genre, 1801–1917', in Bourke *et al.* (eds.), *The Field Day. Anthology of Irish Writing, Vol. 4* (Cork, 2002), p. 868.

63. Ibid.

64. Maria Luddy, 'The Army and Prostitution in Nineteenth-century Ireland: The Case of the Wrens of the Curragh', *Bullán*, vol. 6, no. 1, Summer/Fall 2001, pp. 67–85.

65. Ibid.

66. Maria Luddy, *Women and Philanthropy in Nineteenth-century Ireland* (Cambridge, 1995), p. 98.

67. David Fitzpatrick, 'Militarism in Ireland, 1900–1922', in Tom Bartlett and Keith Jeffery (eds.), *A Military History of Ireland* (Cambridge, 1996), pp. 381 and 406.

68. Con Costello, 'The Curragh Army Camp: "A Goodish Place, Sort of, in Dry Weather"', *History Ireland*, vol. 6, no. 3, Autumn 1998, p. 37.

69. Ibid.

70. Thomas W. Grimshaw (ed.), *Manual of Public Health for Ireland* (Dublin, 1875), pp. 185–9.

71. Elizabeth Malcolm, 'Troops of Largely Diseased Women: VD, the Contagious Diseases Acts and Moral Policing in Late Nineteenth-century Ireland', *Journal of Irish Economic and Social History*, vol. 26, 1999, pp. 1–15.

72. Ibid.

73. Maria Luddy, *Prostitution and Irish Society* (Cambridge, 2007), pp. 150–52.

74. Kilfeather, 'Sexual Expression and Genre, 1801–1917', p. 876.

75. Luddy, 'The Army and Prostitution', pp. 67–85.

76. Luddy, *Women and Philanthropy*, pp. 118–48.

77. Frank Duff, *Miracles on Tap* (Dublin, 1978), pp. 1–5.

78. Brian Lalor (general ed.), *The Encyclopaedia of Ireland* (Dublin, 2003), p. 736.

79. Paul Rouse, 'Law and Order', text of the NAI, Dublin 1911 Census Project, www.nationalarchives.ie/census. See entry for the Royal Military Infirmary, 94720.

80. Maria Jolas, 'The Joyce I Knew and the Women around Him', *Crane Bag*, vol. 4, 1980, pp. 82–8.

81. Frank Millar, 'Erotic Joyce Letter Sold by Sotheby's for £240, 800', *Irish Times*, 9 July 2004.

82. David Cotter, *James Joyce and the Perverse Ideal* (New York, 2003), pp. 1–7.

83. Bruce Bradley SJ, '"You Ought to Allude to Me as a Jesuit", Joyce Once Remarked', *Irish Times*, 14 June 2004.

84. Cotter, *James Joyce*, p. 9. See also Richard Brown, *James Joyce and Sexuality* (Cambridge, 1985).

85. Suzette A. Henke, *James Joyce and the Politics of Desire* (London, 1990), p. 4.

86. Quoted in Maria Luddy, 'Magdalen Asylums, 1765–1992', in Bourke *et al.*, *The Field Day Anthology of Irish Writing, Vol. 5* (Cork, 2002), pp. 745–7.

87. Smith, *Ireland's Magdalen Laundries.*

88. Ibid., and Inglis, 'Origins and Legacies of Irish Prudery', pp. 9–38.

89. Dympna McLoughlin, 'Women and Sexuality in Nineteenth-century Ireland', *Irish Journal of Psychology*, vol. 15, nos. 2 & 3, 1994, pp. 266–75.

90. Ibid.

91. Connell, *Irish Peasant Society*, p. 86.

92. Quoted in Michael Sheehy, *Is Ireland Dying? Culture and the Church in Modern Ireland* (London, 1968), p. 79.

93. George Moore, 'A Letter to Rome', in *The Untilled Field* (London, 1976; first published 1903), pp. 131–50.

94. Sheehy, *Is Ireland Dying?* pp. 82–3.

95. Tom Garvin, *Nationalist Revolutionaries in Ireland, 1858–1928* (Oxford, 1987), p. 61.

96. Quoted in Aongus Collins, *A History of Sex and Morals in Ireland* (Cork, 2001), p. 32.

97. Horace Plunkett, *Ireland in the New Century* (New York, 1908; first published 1904), pp 299–331.

98. Kilfeather, 'Sexual Expression and Genre, 1801–1917', pp. 825–6.

99. Patrick M. Geoghegan, 'Setting the Liberator Free', *Irish Times* Weekend Review, 10 May 2008, p. 9.

100. Paul Bew, *Charles Stewart Parnell* (Dublin, 1980), p. 112.

101. F. S. L. Lyons, *Charles Stewart Parnell* (Dublin, 1977), pp. 640–41.

102. Elisabeth Keohe, *Ireland's Misfortune: The Turbulent Life of Kitty O'Shea* (London, 2008).

103. Mary Rose Callaghan, 'Katherine O'Shea and C. S. Parnell', in Donal McCartney (ed.), *Parnell: The Politics of Power* (Dublin, 1991), pp. 137–48.

104. Anne Dolan, ' Uncrowned Queen Stuck in History's Shadows', *Irish Times* Weekend Review, 3 May 2008.

105. Maria Luddy, 'Unwitting Architect of Parnell's Downfall', *Sunday Business Post* Agenda Magazine, 15 June 2008, p. 26.

106. Kilfeather, 'Sexual Expression and Genre, 1801–1917', p. 826.

107. Barbara O'Connor, 'Ruin and Romance: Heterosexual Discourses on Irish Popular Dance, 1920–60', *Irish Journal of Sociology*, vol. 12, no. 2, 2003, p. 50.

108. Eoin O'Sullivan, '"This Otherwise Delicate Subject": Child Sexual Abuse in Early Twentieth-century Ireland,' in Paul O'Mahony (ed.), *Criminal Justice in Ireland* (Dublin, 2002), pp. 172–202.

109. Ibid., pp. 175–6.

110. Ibid., p. 182.

111. Thomas O'Malley, *Sexual Offences: Law, Policy and Punishment* (Dublin, 1996), p. 1.

112. Ibid., p. 4.

113. Eder *et al.* (eds.), *Sexual Cultures in Europe*, pp. 15–20.

114. Ibid., p. 15.

115. Ibid., p. 33.

116. *Magill*, May 1979, p. 40.

117. Paul Ferris, *Sex and the British: A Twentieth-century History* (London, 1993), pp. 4–5.

118. Diarmaid Ferriter, *The Transformation of Ireland* (London, 2004), p. 106.

119. Dean Rapp, 'The Early Discovery of Freud by the British General Public, 1912–1919', *Journal of the Social History of Medicine*, vol. 3, no. 2, August 1990, pp. 217–45.

120. Eder *et al.* (eds.), *Sexual Cultures in Europe*, p. 96.

121. Maria Sophia Quine, *Population Politics in Twentieth-century Europe* (London, 1996), p. 15.

122. Eder *et al.* (eds.), *Sexual Cultures in Europe*, p. 85ff.

123. Fahey, 'Religion and Sexual Culture in Ireland', p. 55.

124. Eder *et al.* (eds.), *Sexual Cultures in Europe*, p. 90.

125. Sandra McAvoy, 'Sexual Crime and Irish Women's Campaign for a Criminal Law Amendment Act 1912–35', in Maryann Gialanella Valiulis (ed.) *Gender and Power in Irish History* (Dublin, 2008), pp. 84–100.

126. See, for example, NAI, IC 71 83, CFQS, Dublin, 8 October 1918.

127. McAvoy, 'Sexual Crime and Irish Women's Campaign', pp. 84–100.

128. Ibid., p. 87.

129. Ibid.

130. Margaret Jackson, *The Real Facts of Life: Feminism and the Politics of Sexuality, c.1850–1940* (London, 1994), p. 3.

131. Ibid., pp. 2–4.

132. NAI, IC 78/66, CBQS, Dublin, August 1917–April 1924.

133. McAvoy, 'Sexual Crime and Irish Women's Campaign', p. 88.

134. Conor Reidy, 'Borstal Boys: The Institution at Clonmel: 1906–1914, *History Studies* (University of Limerick), vol. 6, 2005, pp. 64–78.

135. NAI, IC 13 15, CFQS, Dublin, 1 August 1900.

136. PRONI, 1/1/2/46/6, CFA, Belfast, 1 July 1914.

137. Quoted in NLI, *NSPCC 22nd Annual Report, 1910–11* (Dublin, 1911), p. 21.

138. O'Malley, *Sexual Offences*, p. 10ff.

139. NLI, *NSPCC 20th Annual Report, 1908–9* (Dublin, 1909).

140. Eimear Burke, 'The Treatment of Working-class Children in Dublin by Statutory and Voluntary Organisations, 1889–1922' (MA thesis, UCD, 1990).

141. See Diarmaid Ferriter, 'Suffer Little Children? The Historical Validity of Memoirs of Irish Childhood', in Joseph Dunne and James Kelly (eds.), *Childhood and Its Discontents* (Dublin, 2002), pp. 69–107.

142. Finola Kennedy, *Cottage to Crèche: Family Change in Ireland* (Dublin, 2001), p. 147.

143. NLI, *NSPCC Dublin Aid Committee Reports 1889–1918, Annual Report, 1904–5* (Dublin, 1905), p. 19.

144. NLI, *NSPCC 18th Annual Report, 1906–7* (Dublin, 1907), p. 19.

145. NLI, *NSPCC 21st Annual Report, 1909–10* (Dublin, 1910), p. 24.

146. NLI, *NSPCC 25th Annual Report, 1913–14* (Dublin, 1914), p. 21.

147. Ibid., p. 19.

148. *NSPCC 22nd Annual Report, 1910–11* (Dublin, 1911), p. 21.

149. Mary Raftery and Eoin O'Sullivan, *Suffer the Little Children: The Inside Story of Ireland's Industrial Schools* (Dublin, 1999).

150. NLI, *NSPCC 18th Annual Report, 1906–7* (Dublin, 1907), p. 24.

151. *Northern Whig*, 30 May 1910. See PRONI, D 3757, Ulster Children's Aid Society.

152. L. A. Jackson, *Child Sexual Abuse in Victorian England* (London, 2000), p. 2.

153. PRONI, BELF/1/1/2/1/13, CFA, Belfast, Spring Assizes 1900. Case relates to 19 January 1900.

154. NAI, IC 13 15, CFQS, Dublin, indictment no. 8, 1 August 1900.

155. NAI, IC 13 18, CFQS, Dublin, indictment no. 7, 3 June 1902.

156. Mary E. Daly, *Dublin: The Deposed Capital: A Social and Economic History, 1860–1914* (Cork, 1984), pp. 279–308.

157. NAI, IC 13 18, CFQS, Dublin, indictment no. 19, 4 February 1903.

158. NAI, IC 28 8, CBQS, Dublin, bill no. 28, 6 August 1901–11 June 1904.

159. NAI, IC 13 20, CFQS, Dublin, indictment nos. 1 & 2, 3 February 1903.

160. Ibid., indictment no. 15, 4 February 1903.

161. NAI, IC 28 95, CBQS, Dublin, indictment no. 25, 4 August 1908; IC 28 10, CBQS, Dublin, June 1907–June 1909, p. 307.

162. NAI, ID 65 26, CFQS, Cork, 25 June 1908.

163. Crown Book detailing sentence imposed is unavailable.

164. NAI, IC 42 64, CFQS, Dublin, 18 May 1911.

165. NAI, IC 42 64, CFQS, Dublin, 20 March 1911, and IC 40 35, CBQS, Dublin, August 1909–October 1911, p. 410.

166. NAI, IC 71 85, CFQS, Dublin, indictment no.7, 9 July 1919.

167. NAI, IC 71 85, CFQS, Dublin, indictment no. 16, 17 November 1919.

168. NAI, IC 78 66, CBQS, Dublin, pp. 176 and 202.

169. Kevin Kearns, *Dublin Tenement Life: An Oral History* (Dublin, 1994), p. 42.

170. Quoted in Connell, *Irish Peasant Society* p. 136.

171. Moore, 'Home Sickness', in *The Untilled Field*, p. 65.

172. Ibid., 'Julia Hill's Curse', pp. 165–73.

173. David Fitzpatrick, 'Marriage in Post-Famine Ireland', in Art Cosgrove (ed.), *Marriage in Ireland* (Dublin, 1985), p. 122.

174. Patrick Maume, 'Between Fleet Street and Mayo: P. D. Kenny and the Culture Wars of Edwardian Ireland, *Bullán*, vol. 6, no. 2, Winter/Spring 2002, pp. 21–43.

175. Quoted in William Lawson, 'The Amendment of the Law in Ireland as to the Maintenance of Illegitimate Children', *Journal of the Social and Statistical Inquiry Society of Ireland*, Dec. 1914, p. 182–207.

176. NAI, DT, S5931, Illegitimate Children (Affiliation Orders) Bill, 1929, memorandum from the Department of Justice, 1 June 1930.

177. Connell, *Irish Peasant Society*, p. 51.

178. Ibid., p. 136.

179. Saint Vincent de Paul Society, *Social Workers Handbook: For Catholic Social Workers in Dublin* (Dublin, 1942), p. 72.

180. Lawson, 'The Amendment of the Law in Ireland', p. 188.

181. Ibid.

182. Ibid.

183. NLI, *First Annual Report of the Bureau of the International Catholic Girls Protection Society* (Dublin, 1913).

184. NLI, CPRSI, *Report for the Year 1914* (Dublin, 1914).

185. Ibid.

186. NLI, CPRSI, *Report for the Year 1915* (Dublin, 1915), p. 13.

187. Quine, *Population Politics*, p. 23.

188. Cath Quinn, 'Images and Impulses: Representations of Puerperal Insanity and Infanticide in Late Victorian England', in Mark Jackson (ed.), *Infanticide: Historical Perspectives on Child Murder and Concealment, 1550–2000* (Aldershot, 2002), p. 202.

189. PRONI, ARM/1/2D/2, CFA, Armagh 1890–1928.

190. PRONI, DOW1/1B, CFA, Down 1900–1940.

191. PRONI, BELF/1/1/2/15/8, CFA, Belfast, Winter 1904, relating to events of 18 July 1904.

192. NAI, IC 71 82, CFQS, Dublin, indictment no. 12, 22 February 1918.

193. NAI, IC 13 15, CFQS, Dublin, 3 December 1900.

194. NAI, IC 51 76, CFQS, Dublin, 4 February 1914.

195. Luddy, *Prostitution and Irish Society*, p. 184.

196. J. V. O'Brien, *Dear Dirty Dublin* (Dublin, 1978), pp. 116–17.

197. Luddy, *Prostitution and Irish Society*, pp. 167–8.

198. Ibid., p. 4.

199. Eder *et al.* (eds.), *Sexual Cultures in Europe*, p. 41.

200. Luddy, *Prostitution and Irish Society*, p. 185.
201. NAI, DT, S4183, 'VD in the Irish Free State: Committee of Inquiry', *Report of the Interdepartmental Committee of Inquiry Regarding VD*, p. 11.
202. Ibid.
203. Eder *et al.* (eds.), *Sexual Cultures in Europe*, p. 41.
204. Richard Ellmann, *Oscar Wilde* (London, 1987), pp. 448–9.
205. Lisa Z. Sigel, *Governing Pleasures: Pornography and Social Change in England, 1815–1914* (New Jersey, 2002), p. 115.
206. Ellmann, *Wilde*, pp. 448–9.
207. J. B. Lyons, 'Oscar Wilde's Final Illness', *Irish Studies Review*, no. 14, Spring 1996, pp. 24–7.
208. Declan Kiberd's review of C. George Sandulescu (ed.), *Rediscovering Oscar Wilde* (London, 1994), in *Irish Studies Review*, no. 14, Spring 1996, p. 56.
209. Eibhear Walshe, 'The First Gay Irishman? Ireland and the Wilde Trials', *Éire–Ireland*, vol. 40, Fall/Winter 2005, pp. 38–58.
210. Richard Dellamora, *Masculine Desire: The Sexual Politics of Victorian Aestheticism* (North Carolina, 1990) pp. 193–201. See also Jeffrey Weeks, *Coming Out: Homosexual Politics in Britain from the Nineteenth Century to the Present* (London, 1977).
211. Walshe, 'The First Gay Irishman?', p. 39.
212. Ibid.
213. Walshe, 'The First Gay Irishman?', pp. 38–58.
214. Ibid.
215. Myles Dungan, *The Stealing of the Irish Crown Jewels: An Unsolved Crime* (Dublin, 2003), p. 93.
216. John Cafferky and Kevin Hannafin, *Scandal and Betrayal: Shackleton and the Irish Crown Jewels* (Cork, 2002), p. 219.
217. Dungan, *The Stealing of the Irish Crown Jewels*, p. 93.
218. Ibid., p. 182.
219. Kilfeather, 'Sexual Expression and Genre, 1801–1917', p. 890.
220. See Tim O'Sullivan's letter on 'Pearse's Passions', *Sunday Business Post*, 30 March 2008.
221. See Ferriter, *Transformation of Ireland*, p. 147.
222. Ruth Dudley Edwards, *Patrick Pearse: The Triumph of Failure* (Dublin, 1977), pp. 52–4 and 126–7.
223. Madeleine Humphreys, *The Life and Times of Edward Martyn: An Aristocratic Bohemian* (Dublin, 2007), p. xiii.
224. Ibid., p. 204.
225. Ibid., p. xiii.
226. Eder *et al.* (eds.), *Sexual Cultures in Europe*, p. 96.
227. Ibid.

228. Brian Lewis, 'The Queer Life and Afterlife of Roger Casement', *Journal of the History of Sexuality*, vol. 14, no. 4, 2005, p. 367.

229. Lewis, 'The Queer Life and Afterlife of Roger Casement', pp. 363–82.

230. Séamas O Síocháin, *Roger Casement: Imperialist, Rebel, Revolutionary* (Dublin, 2008), pp. 477–95.

231. Jeff Dudgeon, 'Mapping 100 (and One) Years of Belfast Gay Life', published electronically at www.//upstartpublishing.com/2007/05/25/mapping-100-years-of-Belfast-gay-life.

232. Lewis, 'The Queer Life and Afterlife of Roger Casement', p. 369.

233. Ibid., p. 373.

234. NAI, IC 13 20, CFQS, Dublin, February and April 1903, Wednesday 1 April.

235. NAI, IC 13 20, CFQS, Dublin, indictments nos. 5 and 6, February and April 1903.

236. NAI, IC 13 14, CFQS, Dublin, February, April and June 1900, 3 April 1900.

237. NAI, IC 13 24, CFQS, Dublin, August, October and December 1904, indictment no. 7, 1 December 1904, and NAI, IC 40 36, CFQS, Dublin, June 1903–April 1910, p. 111.

238. NAI, IC 42 61, CFQS, Dublin, 19 May 1910, indictment no. 30 Crown Book containing sentences imposed is unavailable.

239. NAI, IC 42 61, CFQS, Dublin, indictment nos. 30 and 31, 19 May 1910.

240. NAI, IC 42 61, CFQS, Dublin, indictment no. 34, 19 May 1910.

241. NAI, IC 28 106, CFQS, Dublin, indictment no. 3, 1 November 1909.

242. NAI, IC 40 35, CBQS, Dublin, August 1909–October 1911, p. 410.

243. NAI, IC 51 81, CFQS, Dublin, 8 December 1915.

244. Paul Ryan, 'Coming Out, Fitting In: The Personal Narratives of Some Irish Gay Men', *Irish Journal of Sociology*, vol. 12, no. 2, 2003, pp. 68–86.

245. Emma Donoghue, 'Lesbian Encounters', in Bourke *et al.* (eds.), *The Field Day Anthology of Irish Writing, Vol. 4* (Cork, 2002), p. 1090.

246. Ibid.

247. Ibid.

248. Marie Mulholland, *The Politics and Relationships of Kathleen Lynn* (Dublin, 2002), p. 7.

249. Ibid, p. 16.

250. Described in Lalor (ed.), *Encyclopaedia of Ireland*, p. 624, as belonging to 'a network of Lesbians living in Dublin'.

251. Mulholland, *Kathleen Lynn*, p. 9.

252. Ibid., p. 10.

253. NAI, *Census of Ireland 1911*, return for Henrietta Street, 78496.

254. Paul Rouse, 'Poverty and Health', text of the NAI, Dublin 1911 Census Project, www.nationalarchives.ie/census.

255. Grimshaw (ed.), *Manual of Public Health for Ireland*, p. 185.

256. Marjorie Howes, 'Public Discourse, Private Reflection, 1916–1970', in Bourke *et al.* (eds.), *The Field Day Anthology of Irish Writing, Vol. 4* (Cork, 2002), p. 953.

257. NAI, DT S5553D, Committee on the Relief of Unemployment, Minutes of Evidence, 4 February 1928.

258. NAI, IC 14, CFQS, 3 April 1900. Crown Book detailing sentence is unavailable.

259. NAI, IC 13 14, CFQS, Dublin, June 1900.

260. NAI, IC 28 95, CFQS, Dublin, indictment no. 20, 4 August 1908, and IC 28 10, CBQS, Dublin, June 1907–June 1909.

261. NAI, IC 71 86, CFQS, Dublin, 17 November 1919, Crown Book detailing sentence imposed is unavailable.

262. PRONI, BELF/1/1/2/45/6, Ulster Winter Assizes 1914, relating to events on 15 August 1914.

263. Connell, *Irish Peasant Society*, p. 53.

264. Mona Hearn, 'Life for Domestic Servants in Dublin', in Maria Luddy and Cliona Murphy (eds.), *Women Surviving* (Dublin, 1989), pp. 148–80.

265. NAI, IC 13 14, CFQS, Dublin, indictment no. 2, 3 April 1900. Crown Book detailing sentence imposed is unavailable.

266. NAI, IC 13 14, CFQS, Dublin, indictments nos. 3 and 4, 3 April 1900.

267. NAI, ID 65 32, CFQS, Cork, 18 December 1919. Crown Book with details of sentencing is unavailable.

268. NAI, IC 44 78, CFQS, Dublin, indictment no. 22, 2 April 1914. Crown Book detailing sentence imposed is unavailable.

269. NAI, IC 13 27, CFQS, Dublin, 7 February 1906, and IC 28, 9, CBQS, Dublin, August 1904–April 1907, p. 268.

270. NAI, IC 71 83, CFQS, Dublin, 18 November 1918.

271. *Irish Times*, 20 November 1918; Crown Book detailing sentence imposed is unavailable.

272. NAI, IC 13 18, CFQS, Dublin, 3 April 1902. Trial postponed from February 1902.

273. PRONI, BELF/1/1/1/27, CBA, Belfast, Summer 1914, pp. 37 and 41.

274. Ibid.

275. PRONI, LON1/2A/1/3, CBA, Londonderry, 1908–26.

276. Tóibín, *Lady Gregory's Toothbrush*, p. 81.

277. Catherine Candy, 'Margaret Cousins 1878–1954', in Maria Luddy and Mary Cullen (eds.), *Female Activists: Irish Women and Change 1900–1960* (Dublin, 2001), pp. 113–41

278. Michael Mason, *The Making of Victorian Sexual Attitudes* (Oxford, 1994), p. 3.

279. R. F. Foster, *W. B. Yeats: A Life: 1. The Apprentice Mage, 1865–1914* (Oxford, 1997), pp. 151–76, 201–31 and 301–30.

280. Ibid., pp. 174–82.

281. Risteárd Mulcahy, *Richard Mulcahy (1886–1971): A Family Memoir* (Dublin, 1999), p. 301.

282. *Irish Times*, 11 December 2000.

283. *Irish Times*, 25 November 2000, and Diarmaid Ferriter, *Judging Dev: A Reassessment of the Life and Legacy of Éamon de Valera* (Dublin, 2007), pp. 327–8.

284. John A. Murphy, 'Human Side to a Demonised Dev', *Sunday Independent*, 21 October 2007.

285. NAI, BMH, Witness Statement 856, Elizabeth M. Colbert, 8 June 1953.

286. Seán O'Tuama (ed.), *The Gaelic League Idea* (Cork, 1972), p. 30.

287. David Fitzpatrick, *Harry Boland's Irish Revolution* (Cork, 2003), p. 73.

288. Ibid.

289. Fitzpatrick, *Harry Boland*, pp. 250–51.

290. Ibid, pp. 162–3.

291. NAI, BMH, Witness Statement 1280, Colonel Eamon Broy, pp. 87–8.

292. Mulcahy, *Richard Mulcahy*, p. 94.

293. *Freeman's Journal*, 3 March 1922.

294. Louise Ryan, '"Drunken Tans": Representation of Sex and Violence in the Anglo-Irish War, 1919–21', *Feminist Review*, no. 66, Autumn 2000, pp. 73–95.

295. Ibid.

296. Ibid.

297. Fitzpatrick, *Harry Boland*, p. 227.

298. Peter Hart, *Mick: The Real Michael Collins* (New York, 2006), pp. 342–8.

299. Fitzpatrick, *Harry Boland*, pp. 251–9.

300. Deirdre McMahon, 'Collins for the Celtic Tiger Clubs', *Irish Times*, 22 October 2005.

301. Melissa Llewelyn Davis, 'The Women in Collins's Life', *Irish Times*, 5 May 2007.

302. Ryan, '"Drunken Tans"', pp. 73–95.

303. C. S. Andrews, *Man of No Property* (Cork, 1982), p. 25.

304. JJBL, Manuscript 86–8, Papers of Seán O'Faoláin, Box 2, Correspondence, C. S. Andrews to O'Faoláin, 5 May 1965.

305. NAI, DT, S4183, *Report of the Interdepartmental Committee of Inquiry Regarding Venereal Disease*, p. 29.

306. Seán O'Faoláin, 'The Small Lady', in *Midsummer Night's Madness* (London, 1932), pp. 117–79.

307. Lis Pihl (ed.), *Signe Toksvig's Irish Diaries 1926–37* (Dublin, 1994), p. 182, entry for 20 May 1932.

308. *The Killings at Coolacrease*, RTÉ One Hidden History, broadcast 23 October 2007.

309. Brian Hanley, 'Fear and Loathing at Coolacrease', *History Ireland*, vol. 16, no. 1, January/February 2008, pp. 5–7.

310. Pat Muldowney, letter to the *Irish Times*, 17 November 2007.

311. UCDA, Papers of Desmond Ryan, LA10/J, copy book 1917, entry for 30 May 1917.

312. Ibid. and 24–30 June 1917 and 25–27 July 1917.

313. Ibid., 25–27 July 1917, pp. 47–57.

314. Ibid.

- TWO -
1922–40

1. Maria Luddy, 'Sex and the Single Girl in 1920s and 1930s Ireland', *Irish Review*, no. 35, Summer 2007, pp. 79–92.

2. Ibid.

3. Quoted in Maryann Valiulis, 'Virtuous Mothers and Dutiful Wives: The Politics of Sexuality in the Irish Free State', in Maryann Gialanella Valiulis (ed.), *Gender and Power in Irish History* (Dublin, 2008), pp. 100–115.

4. Angus McLaren, *Twentieth-century Sexuality: A History* (Oxford, 1999), p. 45.

5. Ibid., p. 21.

6. Luddy, 'Sex and the Single Girl', pp. 79–92.

7. Marjorie Howes, 'Public Discourse, Private Reflection: 1916–70', in Angela Bourke *et al.* (ed.), *The Field Day Anthology of Irish Writing, Vol. 4*, p. 924.

8. Luddy, 'Sex and the Single Girl', p. 79.

9. McLaren, *Twentieth-century Sexuality*, pp. 85–123.

10. Mary E. Daly, *The Slow Failure: Population Decline and Independent Ireland* (Madison, WI, 2006), p. 76.

11. Ibid.

12. Howes, 'Public Discourse, Private Reflection', p. 925.

13. Daly, *The Slow Failure*, p. 26.

14. Conrad M. Arensberg and Solon T. Kimball, *Family and Community in Ireland* (Cambridge, MA, 1968), pp. 99–103 and 222–3.

15. Howes, 'Public Discourse, Private Reflection', p. 926.

16. NLI, MS 32, 582/53–59 papers of Rosamund Jacob, Diary 12 September 1926.

17. Ibid., 10 and 31 October 1926.

18. Ibid., 15 November 1926.

19. Ibid., 5 April 1927.

20. Ibid., 31 December 1928.

21. Ibid., 18 July 1928.

22. Ibid., 31 December 1929.

23. Ibid., 31 December 1932, 31 December 1933 and 31 December 1934.

24. Senia Pašeta, *Modern Ireland: A Very Short Introduction* (Oxford, 2003), p. 100.

25. Franz Eder, Lesley Hall and Gert Hekma (eds.), *Sexual Cultures in Europe: National Histories* (Manchester, 1999), pp. 38–127.

26. Ibid., pp. 186–92.

27. Norberto Bobbio, *Ideological Profile of Twentieth-century Italy*, trans. Lydia G. Cochrane (New Jersey, 1995), pp. 15–31.

28. Lis Pihl (ed.), *Signe Toksvig's Irish Diaries, 1926–37* (Dublin, 1994), entry for 17 December 1930, p. 91.

29. Ibid., 6 February 1932.

30. Francis Hackett, 'De Valera's Ireland', *American Mercury*, vol. 60, no. 253, January 1945.

31. Pihl (ed.), *Signe Toksvig's Irish Diaries*, p. 92.

32. Ibid., entry for 29 October 1931, p. 136.

33. Ibid., p. 413, Francis Hackett's diary entries for 8 and 12 March 1932.

34. Sinéad McCoole, *Hazel: A Life of Lady Lavery, 1880–1935* (Dublin, 1996), p. 118.

35. Ibid.

36. John P. McCarthy, *Kevin O'Higgins: Builder of the Irish State* (Dublin, 2006) pp. 246–8.

37. Moira Maguire, 'The Carrigan Committee and child Sexual Abuse in Twentieth-century Ireland', *New Hibernia Review*, vol. 11, no. 2, Summer 2007, pp. 79–101.

38. See, for example, *Mayo News*, 29 October 1949, *Mayo News*, 9 July 1932, *Dublin Evening Mail*, 6 July 1942.

39. *Cork Examiner*, 17 January 1936.

40. *Cork Examiner*, 18 January 1936.

41. NAI, IC 94 15, SBCirCC, Dublin, 18 October 1927–10 December 1929.

42. NAI, IC 94 15, CBQS, Dublin, 17 January 1928 and 16 October 1928.

43. Finola Kennedy, *Cottage to Crèche: Family Change in Ireland* (Dublin, 2001), p. 158.

44. NAI, ID 60 79, SFCirCC, Dublin, 14 January 1938.

45. NAI, IC 78 65, SBCCC, Dublin, 4 April 1922.

46. NAI, ID 15 63, SBCirCC, Galway, 11 October 1927–2 June 1930.

47. NAI, ID 60 79, January 1938, Circuit Court Borstal reports.

48. NAI, IC 94 15, SBCirCC, Dublin, 17 January 1928–16 October 1928.

49. Ibid., calendar of prisoners for trial at Dublin circuit court commencing 14 January 1938.

50. PRONI, DOW1/1B, CFA, Down, and BELF1/1/2/1–90, CFA, Belfast, 1920.

51. PRONI, LON1/2A/3, CBA, Londonderry, 1908–26.

52. PRONI, BELF1/1/2/65/10, CFA, Belfast, 10 May 1921.

53. Maryann Gialanella Valiulis, 'Engendering Citizenship: Women's Relationship to the State in Ireland & the United States in the Post-Suffrage Period', in Maryann Gialanella Valiulis and Mary O'Dowd (eds.), *Women and Irish History* (Dublin, 1997), pp. 159–73.

54. *Official Reports of the Debates of Dáil Éireann, 1922–2003*, 15 February 1927, col. 469.

55. Ibid., col. 480.

56. Ibid., col. 478.

57. NAI, IC 78 69, CBQS and SFCirCC, 1913–24, p. 350, 22 March 1922.

58. See Brendan O'Cathaoir, 'An Irishman's Diary', *Irish Times*, 27 December 2001.

59. Jean Grigel and Tim Rees, *Franco's Spain* (London, 1997), p. 28.

60. Ibid., p. 134ff.

61. John Hooper, *The New Spaniards* (London, 1986) pp. 152–3.

62. *Cork Examiner*, 15 June 1936.

63. NAI, ID 60 80, SFCirCC, Dublin, indictment no. 29, 14 January 1938.

64. NAI, ID 61 2, SBCirCC, Dublin, 5 April 1937–14 October 1938.

65. NAI, IC 90 8, SFCCC, Galway, 1925–28, 21 April 1925. State Book detailing sentence imposed is unavailable.

66. NAI, ID 65 48, SFCirCC, Cork, 19 June 1935. State Book detailing sentence imposed is unavailable.

67. NAI, ID 42 2, SFCirCC, Limerick, 28 October 1927.

68. NAI, ID 42 27, SBCirCC, Limerick, 1927, p. 41.

69. NAI, IC 94 15, SBCirCC, Dublin, 18 October 1927. See also NAI, DT, S7788A.

70. PRONI, ARM/1/2D/2, CBA, Armagh, Summer and Winter Assizes 1928, and DOW1/1B, CBA, Down, 1920.

71. PRONI, LON/1/2A/1/3, CFA, Londonderry, 6 February 1925.

72. PRONI, LON/1/2A/1/3, CBA, Londonderry, 1908–26, 6 February 1925.

73. Louise Ryan, 'The Massacre of Innocence: Infanticide in the Irish Free State', *Irish Studies Review* no. 14, Spring 1996, pp. 17–21. See also Louise Ryan, *Gender, Identity and the Irish Press, 1922–37: Embodying the Nation* (New York, 2001).

74. NAI, DT, S13311A, 'Insanity as a Defence to Criminal Charges', 1943–4.

75. Ryan, 'The Massacre of Innocence', pp. 17–21.

76. NAI, DT, S7777, death sentence on Elizabeth and Rose Edwards, 15 May 1935.

77. NAI, DT, S5886, death sentence on Deborah Sullivan, February 1929.

78. NAI, DT, S5195, death sentence on Mary Kiernan, 28 October 1926.

79. NAI, DT, S11040, death sentence on Mary Somerville, 8 December 1938.

80. Ibid.

81. Ibid.

82. NAI, DJ 8/451, 'Sexual Crime and Juvenile Offenders', memorandum by Intelligence Division in connection with Judge Hanna's speech, March 1936.

83. Ibid.

84. Ibid.

85. Maria Luddy, *Prostitution and Irish Society* (Cambridge, 2007), p. 198.

86. NAI, DT, S8345, *Department of Local Government and Public Health Report 1929–30*, p. 34.

87. Ibid., report for 1930–31.

88. James M. Smith, *Ireland's Magdalen Laundries and the Nation's Architecture of Containment* (Notre Dame, ID, 2007), pp. 48–50.

89. Ibid., pp. 63–5.

90. Ibid., pp. 52–5.

91. NAI, DT S8345, *Department of Local Government and Public Health Report 1930–31*, p. 130.

92. Lindsey Earner Byrne, '"Moral Repatriation": The Response to Irish Unmarried Mothers in Britain, 1920s–1960s', in Patrick J. Duffy (ed.), *To and From Ireland: Planned Migration Schemes c.1600–2000* (Dublin, 2004), pp. 155–97.

93. Ibid.

94. Norah Hoult, *Bridget Kiernan* (London, 1928), quoted in Howes, 'Public Discourse, Private Reflection', p. 933.

95. Pihl (ed.), *Signe Toksvig's Irish Diaries*, p. 152.

96. Margaret Kelleher and Philip O'Leary (eds.), *The Cambridge History of Irish Literature, Vol.2, 1890–2000* (Cambridge, 2006), p. 254.

97. Pádraig Ua Maoileoin, *Macadúna* (Dublin, 2001). Thanks to Máirín Nic Eoin for this information.

98. 'Former Garda Who Had Writing in His Blood', *Irish Times*, 26 October 2002.

99. C. B. Murphy, 'Sex, Censorship and the Church', *The Bell*, vol. 2, no. 6, September 1941, pp. 65–76.

100. NAI, ID 8 66, SFCirCC, Kerry, 1937–9, 22 June 1939.

101. NAI, ID 53 30, SFCirCC, Mayo, 1936, 4 February 1936.

102. NAI, DT, S5931, Illegitimate Children (Affiliation Orders) Bill, 1929.
103. NAI, IC 90 36, SFCirCC, Dublin, indictment no. 51, 18 October 1927.
104. Luddy, *Prostitution and Irish Society*, p. 228.
105. NAI, DJ, H/171/39, 2 November 1923, and Eric Drummond to Department of External Affairs, 26 June 1926.
106. NAI, DJ, H/171/39, Irish Women Citizens' Association to Attorney General's office, 11 January 1924.
107. NAI, DJ, H/171/39, Criminal Law Amendment Act: Indecent Assaults, November 1924.
108. NAI, DJ, H/171/39, J. McKean to Department of Justice, 22 November 1926.
109. NAI, DJ, H/171/39, Secretary of Department of Justice to F. Morrow, Fitzwilliam Place, 30 May 1930.
110. NAI, DJ, H/171/39, Minister for Justice to William Carrigan 30 May 1930.
111. James M. Smith, 'The Politics of Sexual Knowledge: The Origins of Ireland's Containment Culture and the Carrigan Report (1931)', in *Journal of the History of Sexuality*, vol. 13, no. 2, April 2004, pp. 208–33.
112. Ibid., p. 211.
113. Ibid., pp. 208–33.
114. NAI, DJ, H/171/39, 20 January 1933.
115. NAI, DJ, H247/41A, memorandum handed in by Eoin O'Duffy when giving evidence on 30 October 1930.
116. NAI, DT, S5998, Report of the Committee on the Criminal Law Amendments Acts (1880–1885) and Juvenile Prostitution (Dublin, 1931) p. 26.
117. Luddy, *Prostitution and Irish Society*, p. 231.
118. Ibid., p. 234.
119. NAI, DJ, H247/41A, 30 October 1930.
120. Mark Finnane, ' The Carrigan Committee of 1930–31 and the "Moral Condition" of the Saorstát', Irish Historical Studies, vol. 32, no. 128, November 2001, pp. 519–36, 532.
121. Ibid.
122. Ibid.
123. Cited in Smith, *Ireland's Magdalen Laundries*, p. 11.
124. NAI, DJ, H247/41A, evidence of Eoin O'Duffy, 30 October 1930.
125. Smith, *Ireland's Magdalen Laundries*, p. 225.
126. Ibid., p. 229.
127. Ibid., p. 229.
128. NAI, DJ, H247/41/B, 13 November 1932.
129. NAI, DJ, H247/41/A, evidence of Eoin O'Duffy, 30 October 1930.
130. Ibid.

131. Ibid.

132. NAI, DJ, H247/41C, 30 November 1932, Department of Justice memorandum, also a copy in NAI, DT, S5998, Criminal Law: Committee of Inquiry, 1930–31.

133. NAI, DJ, H247/41/B, M. J.Browne to James Geoghegan, Minister for Justice, 13 November 1932.

134. Ibid.

135. NAI, DJ, H247/41/B, Revd J. Canavan to James Geoghegan, 19 November 1932.

136. NAI, DT, 5998, 27 October 1932.

137. Ibid.

138. Ibid.

139. NAI, DJ, H247 41/B, Daniel Keane to James Geoghegan, 25 November 1932.

140. Ibid., Geoghegan to Keane, 16 December 1932.

141. Finola Kennedy, 'The Suppression of the Carrigan Report', *Studies*, vol. 89, no. 356, Winter 2000, p. 362.

142. Smith, *Ireland's Magdalen Laundries*, p. 216.

143. Women's Library, London Metropolitan University, papers of the Association of Moral and Social Hygiene, 3AMS/D14, Eire, 1934–49, R. S. Devane to Alison Neilans, 9 August 1934.

144. Ibid., notes by Alison Neilans, in response to a letter from Father Richard Devane, 9 August 1934.

145. NAI, 98/14/5/1, JCWSSW Minute Books 1935–9, 12 March 1935.

146. Ibid., 24 September 1935.

147. Ibid., 30 October 1935.

148. NAI, DT, S16210, 'Appointment of Women Police: General', 23 November 1939, S. A. Roche to Department of the Taoiseach, 23 November 1939.

149. NAI, DT, S16210, S. A. Roche to Garda Commissioner, 6 July 1938.

150. NAI, 98/14/5/1, JCWSSW Minute Book, 27 February 1936.

151. Ibid., 29 May 1936.

152. Ibid., 27 April 1939.

153. NAI, 98/14/5/1, JCWSSW Minute Books 1939–48, 5 June 1941.

154. Luddy, *Prostitution and Irish Society*, p. 195.

155. Ibid., pp. 210–211.

156. Ibid.

157. NAI, DH, B/135/11, 'VD, Miscellaneous Papers 1930–53', Sean Murphy to Secretary of the Department of Local Government and Public Health, 15 August 1935.

158. Anne Enright, 'Bad at History', in Colm Tóibín (ed.), *Synge: A Celebration* (Dublin, 2005), pp. 115–25.

159. Frank Duff, *Miracles on Tap* (Dublin, 1978), p. 12ff.

160. Luddy, *Prostitution and Irish Society*, p. 216.

161. Diarmaid Ferriter, *What If? Alternative Views of Twentieth-century Ireland* (Dublin, 2006) p. 174.

162. Finola Kennedy, 'Inspirational Layman Who Brought Life to the Hostels', *Irish Times* 7 November 2005.

163. NAI, DT, S4183, 'Venereal Disease in the Irish Free State: Committee of Inquiry', 2 January 1925. Frank Duff describes the work of the rescue society at 76 Harcourt Street.

164. Terry Fagan and the North Inner City Folklore Project, *Monto: Madams, Murder and Black Coddle* (Dublin, 2002) p. 24.

165. Ibid., pp. 34–43.

166. Kevin Kearns, *Dublin Tenement Life: An Oral History* (Dublin, 1994), pp. 85–6.

167. Luddy, *Prostitution and Irish Society*, pp. 238–9.

168. Kennedy, 'The Suppression of the Carrigan Report', p. 362. See also Colman Cassidy's 'An Irishman's Diary', *Irish Times*, 10 January 2001.

169. Enright, 'Bad at History', pp. 115–25.

170. NAI, DJ, H247 41E, 10 November 1933.

171. NAI, DJ, H171/39, Memorandum from Attorney General's office, 25 November 1924.

172. Ibid., Secretary of the Department of Education to secretary of the Department of Justice, 15 January 1925.

173. PRONI, HA, 5/1488, 'Complaint re. Conduct of Immorality of Police in Dunamanagh, Co. Tyrone', 15 April 1925, 10 September 1926, 22 September 1926 and 26 October 1927.

174. Cronin, *Samuel Beckett*, pp. 170–71.

175. Ibid., p. 280.

176. NAI, DT, S4183, *Report of the Interdepartmental Committee of Inquiry Regarding VD*, February 1926, and NAI, DT, 2007/56/021, Interdepartmental Committee of Inquiry Regarding VD.

177. Ibid.

178. Ibid.

179. Tom Garvin, *Preventing the Future: Why was Ireland So Poor for So Long?* (Dublin, 2005), p. 71.

180. NAI, DT, S4183, secretary of the Department of Defence, to secretary of the Department of Local Government and Public Health, 19 May 1933.

181. NAI, DT, S4183, VD report, pp. 22–3.

182. NAI, DJ, H247/41A, O'Duffy's evidence to Carrigan Committee, October 1930.

183. NAI, DT, S3963, 'VD among Seamen: International Agreement', memorandum of 18 June 1930.

184. NAI, DT, S4183, 19 March 1926.

185. Ibid., 7 May 1927.

186. ibid., Dr McDonnell's report of his interview with Archbishop Byrne, 7 May 1927.

187. Philip Howell, 'Venereal Disease and the Politics of Prostitution in the Irish Free State', *Irish Historical Studies*, vol. 33, no. 131, May 2003, pp. 320–34.

188. Susannah Riordan, 'Venereal Disease in the Irish Free State: The Politics of Public Health', *Irish Historical Studies*, vol. 35, no. 139, May 2007, pp. 345–65.

189. Ibid.

190. Ibid.

191. NAI, DT, S4183, VD report, pp. 13–14.

192. NAI, DH, B/135/11, Venereal Disease, Miscellaneous Papers 1920–53, *Report as to the Incidence of VD in West Mayo*, 31 May 1926.

193. NAI, DH, B/135/11, Miss B. B. to Secretary, DLGPH, 2 May 1932.

194. Ibid., E. J. Banks to DLGPH, 17 February 1930.

195. Ibid., 18 June 1934.

196. Ibid., 12 March 1934.

197. Ibid., 13 March 1934.

198. Ibid., registrar of St Patrick Dunn's to Secretary, DLGPH, 13 June 1939.

199. NAI, DH, B17/27, Limerick VD scheme, 10 November 1927, 12 November 1930 and memorandum by Dr McPolin, May 1931.

200. NAI, DH, B/135/11 Estelle Candell to Secretary, DLGPH, 19 March 1938.

201. NAI, DJ, H247/41A, Submission of Eoin O'Duffy, 30 October 1930.

202. Ibid., p. 18.

203. Ibid.

204. Chrystel Hug, *The Politics of Sexual Morality in Ireland* (Basingstoke, 1999), p. 207.

205. Thomas O'Malley, *Sexual Offences: Law, Policy and Punishment* (Dublin, 1996), p. 6.

206. Fearghal McGarry, *Eoin O'Duffy: Self-made Hero* (Oxford, 2005) pp. 163–9.

207. Maria Sophia Quine, *Population Politics in Twentieth-century Europe* (London, 1996), p. 46.

208. McGarry, *Eoin O'Duffy*, p. 163ff.

209. Emma Donoghue, 'Lesbian Encounters: 1745–1997' in Bourke *et al.*, (eds.), *The Field Day Anthology of Irish Writing, Vol. 4*, pp. 1109–11.

210. NAI, IC 71 79, CFQS, Dublin, indictment no. 204, April 1922.

211. NAI, IC 78 66, CBQS and SBCirCC, August 1917–April 1924.

212. NAI, IC, 90 36 SFCirCC, Dublin, indictment no. 48, 18 October 1927.

213. Ibid., indictment no. 50.

214. Ibid., indictment no. 53.

215. NAI, IC 90 36, SFCirCC, Dublin, indictment no. 67, 12 October 1927.

216. NAI, IC 90 39, SFCirCC, Dublin, 1928, indictment no. 18, and SBCirCC, Dublin, 17 April 1928.

217. NAI, IC 90 39, SFCirCC, Dublin, 17 April 1928.

218. NAI, ID 65 48, SFCirCC, Cork, 16 January 1935.

219. Ibid., 16 January 1936.

220. NAI, V15 4 50, SBCirCC, Cork city, 1930–37, p. 330.

221. *Cork Examiner*, 18 January 1936.

222. Ibid.

223. NAI, ID 65 48, SFCirCC, Cork city, 15 January 1936.

224. NAI, DT, S16210, 6 July 1938.

225. NAI, DT, S16210, Appointment of Women Police, S. A. Roche to Department of Finance, 6 July 1938.

226. Ibid., Report of Henry McCarthy, 21 June 1938.

227. Ibid.

228. Ibid., response of J. J. Hanigan, 3 August 1938.

229. Seán O'Faoláin, *An Irish Journey* (London, 1940), pp. 72–92.

230. Hazel Lyder, 'Silence and Secrecy: Exploring Female Sexuality during Childhood in 1930s and 1940s Dublin', *Irish Journal of Feminist Studies*, vol. 5, nos. 1&2, 2003, pp. 77–88.

231. Ibid.

232. DDA, Papers of John Charles McQuaid (McQuaid Papers), AB8/A/II–III, 24–38, Mixed Athletics, February 1934.

233. Ibid., J. P. Noonan to McQuaid, 9 February 1934, and Joseph Walsh to McQuaid, 12 February 1934.

234. NAI, IC 90 8, SFCirCC, Galway, 30 June 1924.

235. NAI, IC 90 36, SFCirCC, Dublin, 19 July 1927.

236. NAI, ID 65 48, SFCirCC, Cork, 14 January 1935. State Book unavailable.

237. NAI, ID 65 48, SFCirCC, Cork, 2 January 1936.

238. *Cork Examiner*, 18 January 1936.

239. NAI, ID 65 48, SFCirCC, Cork, 16 January 1936, and *Cork Examiner*, 17 January 1936.

240. NAI, ID 8 66, SFCirCC, Kerry, 17 June 1936.

241. Evidence of Brother David Gibson, given to the Commission to Inquire into Child Abuse (CICA), Dublin, day 99, 16 June 2004. See www.childabusecommission.ie.

242. Frank O'Connor, *The Saint and Mary Kate* (London, 1932) p. 47; see also Maurice Wohlgelerntner, *Frank O'Connor: An Introduction* (New York, 1977).

243. Brendan McConvery, 'Hell Fire and Poitín: Redemptorist Missions in the Irish Free State (1922–36), *History Ireland*, vol. 8. no. 3, Autumn 2000, pp. 18–23.

244. Ibid.

245. James Smyth, 'Dancing, Depravity and All That Jazz: The Public Dance Halls Act of 1935', *History Ireland*, vol. 1, no. 2, Summer 1993, pp. 51–5.

246. Barbara O'Connor, 'Ruin and Romance: Heterosexual Discourses on Irish Popular Dance, 1920–60', *Irish Journal of Sociology*, vol. 12, no. 2, 2003, p. 57.

247. Brendan Grimes, 'Carnegie Libraries in Ireland', in Library Commission of Ireland, *The University of the People: Celebrating Irish Public Libraries* (Dublin, 2003), pp. 31–43.

248. DDA, McQuaid Papers, AB8/A/II–III, 1939 file: Statutes of Maynooth National Synod (1927).

249. Smyth, 'Dancing, Depravity and All That Jazz', pp. 51–5.

250. NAI, DT, S5998, 'Criminal Law, Committee of Inquiry 1930–31', memorandum from Department of Justice, 30 November 1932. Also a copy in NAI, DJ, H247/4/C.

251. Ibid.

252. NAI, ID 42 4, SFCirCC, Limerick, 28 October 1927.

253. NAI, ID 8 66, SFCirCC, Kerry, 15 October 1937.

254. Ibid., 16 January 1937.

255. NAI, ID 53 30, SFCirCC, Mayo, 17 February 1936.

256. NAI, ID 49 173, SFCirCC, Mayo, 6 July 1932.

257. *Mayo News*, 9 July 1932.

258. NAI, ID 65 48, SFCirCC, Cork, 25 March 1935.

259. John H. Whyte, *Church and State in Modern Ireland, 1923–70* (Dublin, 1971), p. 47.

260. Michael O'Sullivan, *Brendan Behan: A Life* (Dublin, 1997), p. 137.

261. Kearns, *Dublin Tenement Life*, pp. 43–8.

262. See for example, NAI, IC 13 18, CFQS, Dublin, April, June and July 1902, where several such prosecutions are recorded.

263. Smyth, 'Dancing, Depravity and All That Jazz', pp. 51–5.

264. NAI, IC 91 142, SFCirCC, Galway, 28 May 1935.

265. NAI, ID 15 64, SBCirCC, Galway, p. 329.

266. Pihl (ed.), *Signe Toksvig's Irish Diaries*, entry for 17 December 1930, p. 92.

267. Eder *et al.* (eds.), *Sexual Cultures in Europe*, p. 102.

268. Ibid., pp. 125–6.

269. Peter Martin, *Censorship in the Two Irelands, 1922–39* (Dublin, 2006), p. 87.

270. Howes, 'Public Discourse, Private Reflection', p. 928.

271. Martin, *Censorship*, p. 61.

272. Ibid.

273. NAI, DJ, 7/1/2, CEL, Secretary's Papers, 12 February–12 May 1926.

274. Ibid.

275. NAI, DJ, 7/2/7, Submission of Christian Brothers, April 1926.

276. Ibid., Eamon Coogan to Eamon O'Frighil, 17 May 1926.

277. NAI, DJ, 7/2/9, Collection of Evidence: Richard Devane to Revd. J. Dempsey, 21 April 1926.

278. Nicholas Allen, *George Russell and the New Ireland, 1905–30* (Dublin, 2003), pp. 213–18.

279. NAI, DT, *Censorship of Publications Act, 1929*.

280. NAI, IC 90 39, SFCirCC, Dublin, indictment no. 25, 17 April 1928, and SBCirCC, Dublin, 18 October 1927–10 December 1929.

281. NAI, DT, S10241, Censorship of Publications Act 1929: Proposed Amendments, F. O'Reilly to Department of Justice, and reply, 10 November 1938.

282. Ibid., memorandum of interview between Censorship Board and Minister for Justice, 1 August 1940.

283. Greta Jones, 'Marie Stopes in Ireland: The Mother's Clinic in Belfast, 1936–1947', *Social History of Medicine*, vol. 5, no. 2, April 1992, pp. 255–77.

284. Sarah MacEvilly, '"A Match Made in Heaven?" A Woman's Perspective on Arranged Marriage in Ireland in the 1930s', in Chichi Ania Golu (ed.), *In from the Shadows: The University of Limerick Women's Studies Collection*, vol. 3, 1997, p. 91.

285. Valiulis, 'Virtuous Mothers and Dutiful Wives', p. 108.

286. Quine, *Population Politics*, p. 15.

287. Eder *et al.* (eds.), *Sexual Cultures in Europe*, p. 75.

288. Ibid., pp. 151–2.

289. Quine, *Population Politics*, p. 46.

290. Ibid.

291. Kennedy, *Cottage to Créche*, pp. 159–61.

292. Garvin, *Preventing the Future*, p. 71ff.

293. NAI, DJ, H247/41/E, Criminal Law Amendment Act Committee, 20 May 1933.

294. Ibid., 9 March 1934.

295. NAI, DT, 2003/16/453, Keith Joseph Adams to Jack Lynch, 10 June 1972.

296. Ibid.

297. Ibid., 13 July 1972.

298. Jones, 'Marie Stopes in Ireland', pp. 255–77.

299. Quoted in Donald S. Connery, *The Irish* (London, 1968) p. 174.

300. PRONI, D3543, NIFPA, 3543/2/1, notes on the history of family planning in Northern Ireland, n.d.

301. Jones, 'Marie Stopes in Ireland, pp. 255–77.

302. Ibid.

303. Ibid.

304. Ibid.

305. Kennedy, *Cottage to Crèche*, p. 37.

306. PRONI, BELF/1/1/2/4/6, CFA, Belfast, Spring Assizes 1901.

307. Jones, 'Marie Stopes in Ireland', pp. 255–77.

308. Christopher Murray, *Seán O'Casey: Writer at Work* (Dublin, 2004), p. 196.

309. Ibid., pp. 215–20.

310. Cliona Rattigan, '"Crimes of Passion of the Worst Character": Abortion Cases and Gender in Ireland, 1925–50', in Valiulis (ed.), *Gender and Power in Irish History*, pp. 115–40.

311. Richard Pine, *2RN and the Origins of Irish Radio* (Dublin, 2002), pp. 189–99, and Rattigan, '"Crimes of Passion"', p. 132.

312. Rattigan, '"Crimes of Passion"', pp. 115–140.

313. Sandra McAvoy, 'Before Cadden: Abortion in Mid-twentieth-century Ireland', in Dermot Keogh,, Finbarr O'Shea and Carmel Quinlan (eds.), *The Lost Decade: Ireland in the 1950s* (Cork, 2004), pp. 147–64.

314. Ray Kavanagh, *Mamie Cadden: Backstreet Abortionist* (Cork, 2005), pp. 39–66.

315. Ibid., pp. 157–209.

316. Rattigan, '"Crimes of Passion"', p. 119.

317. Ibid., p. 134.

318. Ibid.

319. Pihl (ed.), *Signe Toksvig's Irish diaries*, entry for 6 July 1932, pp. 194–5.

320. Jo Murphy Lawless (ed.), 'Childbirth 1742–1955', in Bourke *et al.* (eds.), *The Field Day Anthology Vol. 4*, pp. 896–913.

321. Ibid., p. 896.

322. Pihl (ed.), *Signe Toksvig's Irish Diaries*, p. 152.

323. Ibid., p. 186, entry for 12 June 1932.

324. Ibid., p. 197, entry for 12 July 1932.

325. Ibid., p. 192, entry for 25 June 1932.

326. Ibid., p. 190, entry for 12 June 1932.

327. Marianne Elliott, *The Catholics of Ulster: A History* (London, 2000), pp. 447–8.

328. *Magill*, April 1978, pp. 10–14.

329. Declan Kiberd, *The Irish Writer and the World* (Cambridge, 2005), p. 180.

330. Murray, *Seán O'Casey*, p. 222.

331. Áine McCarthy, 'Hearts, Bodies and Minds: Gender Ideology and Women's Committal to Enniscorthy Lunatic Asylum 1916–25', in Diane Urquhart and Alan Hayes (eds.), *The Irish Women's History Reader* (London, 2002), p. 102.

332. Ibid.

333. NAI, DT, S8345, *Department of Local Government and Public Health Report, 1930–31*, pp. 129–31.

334. Quoted in Smith, 'The Politics of Sexual Knowledge', p. 208.

335. NAI, DT, S6209A, Statistical Abstract 1931–2, compiled by the statistics branch of the Department of Industry and Commerce, Table 11.

336. NAI, DT, S8345, *Department of Local Government and Public Health Report, 1928–9*, p. 47.

337. NAI, DT, S5553D, Committee on Relief of Unemployment: Minutes of Evidence and Relevant Documents, 29 December 1927 and 7 January 1928.

338. NAI, DH, A14/38, 'Unqualified Midwives', 17 August 1936.

339. DDA, McQuaid Papers, AB8/A/IV, 34–46: Medical Matters: Dr Lea-Wilson, 1933–4.

340. DDA, McQuaid Papers, AB8/A/IV, 34–46, Dr Lea Wilson to McQuaid, 16 February 1936.

341. Margaret Ò hÒgartaigh, *Kathleen Lynn: Irishwoman, Patriot, Doctor* (Dublin, 2006), pp. 95–103.

342. Ibid., pp. 101–3.

343. 'The County Libraries: Sex, Religion and Censorship' (1949), in Hubert Butler, *Grandmother and Wolfe Tone* (Dublin, 1990), pp. 50–64.

344. Ibid.

345. Ibid., p. 52.

346. Ibid.

347. Ibid., p. 58.

348. Library Council of Ireland, *The University of the People: Celebrating Ireland's Public Libraries* (Dublin, 2003), p. 25.

349. Ibid., p. 37.

350. Jim McKeon, *Frank O'Connor: A Life* (London, 1998), p. 72.

351. O'Connor, *The Saint and Mary Kate*, p. 129.

352. Austin Clarke, 'The Straying Student', in Thomas Kinsella (ed.), *Austin Clarke: Selected Poems* (Dublin, 1976), pp. 21–2.

353. Rose Quiello, 'Borderline Women: The Heroines of Kate O'Brien's Novels', *Irish Studies Review*, no. 3, Spring 1993, pp. 8–10.

354. Donoghue, 'Lesbian Encounters', p. 1111ff.

355. Quoted in Patricia Craig (ed.), *The Oxford Book of Ireland* (Oxford, 1998), p. 406.

356. Seán O'Faoláin, *Vive Moi!* (Dublin, 1993, first edn 1963), pp. 83–4.

357. PRONI, DF, 18/10/128, G. C. Duggan to N. Bonparte Wyse, 21 November 1930.

358. Ibid.

359. Ibid., PRONI, DF, 22 November 1930 and 16 December 1930.

360. Ibid.

361. Martin, *Censorship in the Two Irelands*, p. 32.
362. Ibid., pp. 94–6.
363. Ibid., p. 149.
364. Ibid., p. 147.
365. Ibid., p. 153.
366. NAI, FCO, 98/29/4, 29 July 1935.
367. NAI, FCO, 98/26/3, Register of Films Censored 1938–50.
368. NAI, FCO, 98/29/4, Reject Book 1935–53, 10 May 1935.
369. Ibid., 21 May 1935, 28 May 1935 and 29 May 1935.
370. Ibid., 11 June 1935, 28 June 1935 and 9 July 1935.
371. Ibid., 10 July 1935, 20 October 1935.
372. Ibid., 1 November 1935.
373. Ibid., 6 July 1937, 13 May 1937.
374. Ibid., 5 March 1937.
375. Ibid., 18 March 1937 and 27 July 1937.
376. Ibid., 12 November 1937.
377. Ibid., 6 July 1937.

– THREE –
1940–60

1. Seán O'Faoláin, 'Answer to a Criticism', *The Bell*, vol. 1, no. 3, December 1940, pp. 5–7. See also Bill Kirwin, 'The Social Policy of The Bell', *Administration*, vol. 37, 1989, pp. 99–119.
2. Seán O'Faoláin, 'The Mart of Ideas', *The Bell*, vol. 4, no. 3, June 1942, pp. 153–8 .
3. Cited in Marjorie Howes, 'Public Discourse, Private Reflection: 1916–1970', in Bourke *et al.* (eds.), *The Field Day Anthology of Irish Writing, Vol. 4* (Cook, 2002), p. 923.
4. Bryan MacMahon, *The Master* (Dublin, 1992), p. 25.
5. JJBL, MS 03–18, Papers of Bryan MacMahon, correspondence with John O'Reilly, San Francisco. MacMahon to O'Reilly, 1 November 1954.
6. NAI, ID 27 2, SBCirCC, Dublin, 1945.
7. NAI, V14 821, SBCirCC, Dublin, 1956.
8. NAI, IC 17 89, SBCirCC, Dublin, 1959–60.
9. See, for example, *Donegal Vindicator*, 23 October 1948.
10. See, for example, *Cork Examiner*, 15 June 1936.
11. See, for example, *Mayo News*, 9 July 1932.

12. 'Crime Reporter', 'Crime in Dublin', *The Bell*, vol. 5, no. 3, December 1942, pp. 173–83.

13. Ibid., p. 181.

14. Ibid.

15. Quoted in Siobhán Kilfeather and Eibhear Walshe, 'Contesting Ireland: The Erosion of Heterosexual Consensus, 1940–2001', in Bourke *et al.* (eds.), *The Field Day Anthology of Irish Writing, Vol. 4* (Cork, 2002), p. 1040.

16. 'Unemployed', 'Neutral Night', *The Bell*, vol. 4, no. 1, April 1942, pp. 37–40.

17. Richard Cobb, *A Classical Education* (London, 1985), pp. 136–41.

18. NAI, ID 27 2, SBCirCC, Dublin, 11 January 1945.

19. NAI, ID 27 2, SBCirCC, Dublin, 17 April 1945, 4 June 1945 and 12 October 1945.

20. NAI, ID 27 12, SFCirCC, Dublin, 17 April 1945.

21. Ibid., indictment no. 68.

22. Ibid., indictment no. 52.

23. NAI, V 15 14 38, SFCirCC, Dublin, indictment no. 25, 21 June 1954.

24. NAI, V 14, 8, 8, SFCirCC, Dublin, 4 October 1955.

25. Ibid., indictment no. 7.

26. NAI, IC 17 83, SFCirCC, Dublin, 10 October 1957.

27. NAI, IC 17 87, SBCirCC, Dublin, indictment no. 25, p. 87.

28. DDA, McQuaid Papers, AB8/B, Government Box 3, DJ, 12 October 1959.

29. Deirdre McMahon, 'Maurice Moynihan (1902–1999): Irish Civil Servant', *Studies*, vol. 89, no. 353, Spring 2000, pp. 71–7.

30. Michael O'Sullivan, *Brendan Behan: A Life* (Dublin, 1997), p. 69.

31. Quoted in Kilfeather and Walshe (eds.), 'Contesting Ireland', pp. 1044–6.

32. Anthony Cronin, *Dead as Doornails* (Dublin, 1976), p. 8.

33. O'Sullivan, *Brendan Behan*, p. 135.

34. Peter Arthurs, *With Brendan Behan* (New York, 1981), pp. 24–38.

35. Andrew Parker *et al.* (eds.), *Nationalisms and Sexualities* (London, 1992), p. 263.

36. NAI, DT, S14101A, Children's Acts 1908–1941, Amending Legislation 1947, memorandum from Department of Education, 1 July 1947.

37. James M. Smith, 'The Politics of Sexual Knowledge: The Origins of Ireland's Containment Culture and the Carrigan Report (1931)', in *Journal of the History of Sexuality*, vol. 13, no. 2, April 2004, p. 232.

38. NAI, 98/14/5/3, JCWSSW Minute Book 1948–56, 27 May 1952.

39. Ibid., 12 November 1954.

40. DDA, McQuaid Papers, AB/8/B/xix, CSWB, Box 4, Family Welfare Section, Gavan Duffy to McQuaid, 18 February 1948.

41. DDA, McQuaid Papers, AB8/B, Government Box 3, DJ, Adoption Legislation 1957–71, Cecil Barrett to McQuaid, 16 December 1958.

42. NAI, ID 32 109, SFCirCC, Donegal, 10 January 1950.

43. Ibid., 24 May 1949.

44. NAI, SBCirCC, Letterkenny, 5 April 1949.

45. NAI, V15 2 22, SBCirCC, Donegal, 12 June 1946.

46. NAI, SBCirCC, Letterkenny, 15 April 1947–15 October 1947.

47. NAI, V15 14 56, SFCirCC and SBCirCC, Letterkenny, 11 January 1955.

48. NAI, SFCirCC and SBCirCC, Letterkenny, 21 June 1955.

49. NAI, SFCirCC, Letterkenny, 19 April 1955. State Book detailing verdict and sentence unavailable.

50. NAI, ID 16 152, SFCirCC, Castlebar, 31 October 1944. State Book detailing sentence imposed is unavailable.

51. NAI, ID 32 109, SFCirCC, Letterkenny, 18 October 1948.

52. NAI, V4B 23 12, SFCirCC, Galway, 25 June 1954.

53. NAI, V4B, 23 12, SFCirCC, Galway, 12 January 1955.

54. NAI, V15 2 6, SFCirCC, Castelbar, 17 June 1950.

55. NAI, ID 16 152, SFCirCC, Castlebar, 31 October 1944.

56. NAI, SBCirCC, Castlebar, 13 January 1951.

57. Leah Levenson, *The Four Seasons of Mary Lavin* (Dublin, 1998), p. 154, and Mary Lavin, 'Sunday Brings Sunday', in *The Long Ago and Other Stories* (London, 1944), pp. 114–42.

58. Frank O'Connor, 'Don Juan's Temptation', in *The Common Chord: Stories and Tales* (London, 1947), p. 276.

59. Frank O'Connor, 'News for the Church', in *The Collar: Stories of Irish Priests* (Belfast, 1993), pp. 23–34.

60. Dermot Healy, *The Bend for Home* (London, 1996), p. 103.

61. Brendan McConvery, 'Hell Fire and Poitín': Redemptorist Missions in the Irish Free State (1922–36)', *History Ireland*, vol. 8, no. 3, Autumn 2000, pp. 18–23.

62. John McGahern, 'The Church and Its Spire', in Colm Tóibín (ed.) *Soho Square 6* (London, 1993), pp. 16–30.

63. Frank McCourt, *Angela's Ashes: Memoir of a Childhood* (London, 1996), p. 292.

64. NAI, DT, S14997A, 'Mother and Child Scheme', John A. Costello to Bishop Staunton, 24 March 1950.

65. Ibid., Staunton to Costello, 10 October 1950.

66. Ibid., Noël Browne to Costello, 16 December 1950, and *Irish Independent*, 9 March 1951.

67. John Horgan, *Nöel Browne: Passionate Outsider* (Dublin, 2000), p. 72.

68. MacMahon, *The Master*, p. 90.

69. Quoted in Kilfeather and Walshe, 'Contesting Ireland', p. 1043.

70. Jerome O'Hea, *Sex and Innocence: A Handbook for Parents and Educators* (Cork, 1949), pp. 2–3.

71. Ibid., p. 48.

72. NAI, DT, S6731B, 'Women National Teachers: Question of Compulsory Retirement', memorandum from the Department of Education, 14 February 1953.

73. DDA, McQuaid Papers, AB/8/B/xix, CSWB Box 5, Family Welfare Section, Marriage Section 1955–71, 7 September 1955.

74. Brian O'Rourke, *The Conscience of the Race: Sex and Religion in Irish and French Novels, 1941–73* (Dublin, 1980), pp. 13–14.

75. Ibid.

76. Ibid.

77. Ibid., p. 20.

78. Tom Inglis, *Global Ireland: Same Difference* (London, 2008), p. 1.

79. Angus McLaren, *Twentieth-century Sexuality: A History* (Oxford, 1999), p. 8.

80. Inglis, *Global Ireland*, p. 259, and Alan Bestic, *Sex and the Singular English* (London, 1972), p. vii. See also Parker *et al.* (eds.), *Nationalisms and Sexualities*, p. 263.

81. Conrad M. Arensberg and Solon T. Kimball, *Family and Community in Ireland* (Cambridge, MA, 1968), p. 199.

82. Mary E. Daly, *The Slow Failure: Population Decline and Independent Ireland* (Madison, WI, 2006), p. 134.

83. Quoted in Barbara O'Connor, 'Ruin and Romance: Heterosexual Discourses on Irish Popular Dance, 1920–60', *Irish Journal of Sociology*, vol. 12, no. 2, 2003, p. 62.

84. Quoted in Harry Bohan and Gerard Kennedy, *Are We Forgetting Something?* (Dublin, 1999), pp. 30–34.

85. Healy, *The Bend for Home*, p. 102.

86. Norman Ruddock, *The Rambling Rector* (Dublin, 2005), pp. 35–41.

87. NAI, ID 28 102, SFCirCC, Dublin, indictment nos. 12–17, 11 January 1949.

88. NAI, ID 28 102, SBCirCC, Dublin, 11 January 1949.

89. NAI, V 15 2 6, SFCirCC, Castlebar, 12 June 1950. State Book detailing sentence imposed unavailable. And NAI, ID 16 152 SFCirCC, Castlebar, 2 November 1943.

90. NAI, DT, 1471A, *Report of Commissioner of Garda Síochána on Crime, 1947*, p. 6.

91. DDA, McQuaid Papers, AB8/B Government Box 3: DJ, memorandum by Patrick Duggan, 24 February 1949, and unsigned observations.

92. PRONI, BELF/1/1/2/122 1940, BELF/1/1/2/137 1945, BELF/1/1/2/153 1950, BELF/1/1/2/170 1955, CFA, Belfast, 1940, 1945, 1950, 1955.

93. NAI, ID 27 2, SBCirCC, Dublin, 17 April 1945.

94. Sandra McAvoy, 'Aspects of the State and Female Sexuality in the Irish Free State, 1922–49', University College Cork, PhD thesis (1998), p. 276.

95. NAI, V15 2 6, SFCirCC, Castlebar, 25 October 1949.

96. *Mayo News*, 29 October 1949.

97. JJBL, MS 03–22, Papers of Frank O'Connor, letter from Harry Sions to Don Congdon (O'Connor's agent), 17 January 1949.

98. NAI, DT, S14716, article on Ireland in *Holiday*, December 1949, *Irish Press*, 19 December 1949; *Irish Times*, 6 January 1950.

99. NAI, DT, S14716, *Holiday*, December 1949, p. 40.

100. Ibid., p. 58.

101. Harriet O'Donovan Sheehy, 'Memories', in Hilary Lennon (ed.), *Frank O'Connor: Critical Essays* (Dublin, 2007), pp. 156–66.

102. 'MPRH', 'Illegitimate', *The Bell*, vol. 2, no. 3, June 1941, pp. 78–88.

103. Ibid.

104. Ibid.

105. Chrystel Hug, *The Politics of Sexual Morality in Ireland* (Basingstoke, 1999) p. 161.

106. Clair Wills, *That Neutral Island: A Cultural History of Ireland During the Second World War* (London, 2007) pp. 325–7.

107. Levenson, *The Four Seasons of Mary Lavin*, p. 150.

108. 'An Irishman's Diary', *Irish Times*, 15 March 2007.

109. Hug, *The Politics of Sexual Morality*, p. 161.

110. 'MPRH' 'Illegitimate', pp. 78–88.

111. Sandra McAvoy, 'Before Cadden: Abortion in Mid-twentieth-century Ireland', in Dermot Keogh *et al.* (eds.), *The Lost Decade: Ireland in the 1950s* (Cork, 2004), pp. 147–64, and Ray Kavanagh, *Mamie Cadden: Backstreet Abortionist* (Cork, 2005), 87–101.

112. McAvoy, 'Before Cadden', pp. 147–50.

113. Ibid., p. 151.

114. Ibid., p. 153.

115. Ibid., p. 154.

116. Ibid., p. 158.

117. Cliona Rattigan, 'Crimes of Passion of the Worst Character': Abortion Cases and Gender in Ireland, 1925–50', in Maryann Valiulis (ed.), *Gender and Power in Irish History* (Dublin, 2008), p. 136.

118. Kavanagh, *Mamie Cadden*, pp. 157–200.

119. Ibid.

120. Catriona Crowe, review of Ray Kavanagh's *Mamie Cadden, Irish Times*, 19 February 2005.

121. NAI, DJ, 2004/46/7, Inquiries *re*.: Abortion and Euthanasia, 17 December 1963.

122. Kavanagh, *Mamie Cadden*, pp. 157–200.

123. Ibid.

124. NAI, DT S16116, Mary Anne Cadden: Death Sentence, 18 December 1956, and *Irish Times*, 2 November 1956.

125. NAI, DT, S16116, Prison Medical Officer's report, 27 December 1956.

126. NAI, DT, S16116, 4 January 1957.

127. NAI, DT, S16116, Police Report, 27 December 1956.

128. Hubert Butler, 'Abortion', in *Grandmother and Wolfe Tone* (Dublin, 1990), pp. 69–79.

129. Ibid., p. 73.

130. Wills, *That Neutral Island*, pp. 322–5.

131. Paul Ferris, *Sex and the British: A Twentieth-century History* (London, 1993), p. 2.

132. DDA, McQuaid Papers, AB8/B, Government Box 4, Health, Local Government and Censorship: Correspondence with Department of Health 1948–70, McQuaid to Joseph Ryan, 26 January 1954.

133. Francis Hackett, 'De Valera's Ireland', *American Mercury*, vol. 60, no. 253, January 1945, pp. 29–39.

134. Honor Tracy, *Mind You, I've Said Nothing! Forays in the Irish Republic* (Washington, 1968; first published 1953), pp. 71–126.

135. DDA,McQuaid Papers, AB8/B/xix, CSWB, Box 2, Emigrants Secton, Henry Gray to McQuaid, 12 June 1942.

136. Ibid., report of Henry Gray, pp. 22–5.

137. Ibid., Box 3, McQuaid to William Godfrey, 12 May 1960.

138. Daly, *The Slow Failure*, pp. 304–5.

139. DDA, McQuaid Papers, AB8/B/xix, CSWB, Box 2, Statistical Review of the Bureau's Attempts to Secure the Welfare of Emigrants, 17 June 1942–31 December 1942.

140. Ibid., reports for years 1949, 1953 and 1955.

141. Blake Morrison, *Things My Mother Never Told Me* (London, 2002), pp. 21–7 and 87–124.

142. DDA, McQuaid Papers, AB8/B/xix, Box 2, Henry Gray's report and letter to McQuaid, 14 June 1943.

143. NAI, DT, S11582G, Garda Commissioner to John A. Costello, 23 October 1956.

144. DDA, McQuaid Papers, AB8/B/xix, CSWB, Box 2, Gray's Report p. 10*ff.*

145. Ibid.

146. Ferris, *Sex and the British*, p. 142.

147. DDA, McQuaid Papers, AB8/B/xix, Box 2, McQuaid's response to Gray's report, 9 December 1943.

148. Wills, *That Neutral Island*, pp. 321–5.

149. DDA, McQuaid Papers, AB8/B, Government Box 4, Department of Local Government and Public Health 1941–6, McQuaid to Canon O'Keefe, 4 February 1946.

150. Ibid., Conor Ward to McQuaid, 5 February 1946 and McQuaid's reply, 6 February 1946.

151. DDA, McQuaid Papers, Box L/2D/26/1–10, Hospitals: Mater: VD Clinic, M. Madeleine Sophie to McQuaid, 24 November 1943, and McQuaid's reply, 25 November 1943, and a further two letters, 26 and 29 November 1943.

152. Ibid., McQuaid to M. Madeleine Sophie, 28 June 1944.

153. Ibid., Hospitals: St Vincent's Elm Park VD Clinic, McQuaid to M. Bernard Carew, Superior General, 23 November 1943.

154. Ibid., McQuaid to Francis Morrow, Hon. Sec. Medical Board, St Vincents hospital, 28 December 1943.

155. Tom Garvin, *Preventing the Future: Why was Ireland So Poor for So Long?* (Dublin, 2005), p. 71.

156. DDA, McQuaid Papers, Box L/2D/26/1, Dr Desmond Reddin to McQuaid, 25 January 1945.

157. NAI, DH, B/135/11, Venereal Disease, misc. papers 1930–53, 6 May 1943 and 7 August 1943.

158. NAI, DH, Extracts from Minutes of the Proceedings of the Cork Port Sanitary Authority, 30 November 1940.

159. Ibid., Medical Report on VD in the Kildare Turf Camp Scheme, 7 June 1944.

160. Ibid., memorandum from secretary of DLGPH, 30 June 1944.

161. Ibid., 1 August 1944.

162. Ibid., 'CH', 1 resident of Newmarket on Fergus to Conor Ward, 19 February 1945.

163. NAI, DH, B/135/12, VD, Return of Cases in 1938 and 1943.

164. *Irish Times*, 23 November 1944.

165. NAI, DH, B/135/12, Return of VD Cases 1943 and Dr Michael Daly to DLGPH, 9 June 1944.

166. NAI, DH, B/135/12, Return of VD Cases 1943, 15 June 1944.

167. Ibid., 19 August 1944.

168. NAI, 98/14/53, JCWSSW Minute Book 1948–56, 24 February 1949.

169. NAI, DH, 1 B/135/12, secretary of Department of Defence to secretary, DLGPH, 16 May 1945.

170. Ibid., M. J. Daly to Dr Ward, 20 July 1944.

171. NAI, DH, B4/50, Cork, VD, 7 February 1953.

172. DDA, McQuaid Papers, AB8/B, Government Box 5, Health, Health Bill 1952, John D. Horgan to McQuaid, 6 October 1952.

173. PRONI, D, HLG, 1/2/2, Venereal Disease: Publicity and Propaganda, 25 February 1943.

174. Ibid., 20 March 1943.

175. Ibid., 28 April 1943.

176. Ibid., 16 April 1945.

177. Ibid., VD: Incidence in Northern Ireland, 19 June 1946.

178. Ibid., 27 April 1959.

179. Wills, *That Neutral Island*, p. 320ff.

180. Leanne McCormick, '"One Yank and They're Off": Interaction between US Troops and Northern Irish Women, 1942–1945', *Journal of the History of Sexuality*, vol. 15, no. 2, 2006, pp. 228–57.

181. Ibid., p. 230.

182. Wills, *That Neutral Island*, p. 320ff.

183. PRONI, T/3566/1, Reminiscences of P. S. Callaghan, Part II, p. 3.

184. Ibid., p. 15.

185. McCormick, '"One Yank"', p. 234.

186. Mary Muldowney, *The Second World War and Irish Women: An Oral History* (Dublin, 2007), pp. 162–6.

187. Ibid.

188. McCormick, '"One Yank"', p. 235.

189. Ibid., pp. 238–42.

190. Elizabeth McCullough, *A Square Peg: An Ulster Childhood* (Dublin, 1997), pp. 114–15.

191. McCormick, '"One Yank"', p. 257.

192. Ibid.

193. Wills, *That Neutral Island*, pp. 322–5.

194. Eunan O'Halpin, *Spying on Ireland: British Intelligence and Irish Neutrality During the Second World War* (Oxford, 2008), p. 115.

195. Walter Moore, *A Life of Erwin Schrödinger* (Cambridge, 1994), p. 257.

196. Ibid.

197. Ibid., pp. 261–88.

198. Ibid., p. 6.

199. Daly, *The Slow Failure*, p. 279.

200. DDA, McQuaid Papers, AB8/B/xix, CSWB, Box 2, Henry Gray to Christopher Mangan, 5 December 1951.

201. Ibid., 30 March 1954.

202. Ibid., 23 October 1952.

203. Ibid., Minutes of the 79th Meeting of the Committee of Management of the Emigrants' Section, 27 April 1950.

204. DDA, McQuaid Papers, AB8/B/xix, CSWB, Box 3, Report on emigrants by McQuaid, 21 June 1960; McQuaid to William Godfrey, Archbishop of Westminster, 5 June 1960; and McQuaid to Father Barrett, 28 November 1959.

205. Daly, *The Slow Failure*, p. 288.

206. Ibid.

207. DDA, McQuaid Papers, AB8/B/xix, CSWB, Box 2, Survey of Irish Emigrant Cases 1959.

208. Ibid., 18 November 1963.

209. Ibid., Correspondence *re*. Liaison with Legion of Mary, Hubert Daly to Frank Duff, 17 July 1954.

210. Ibid.

211. Ibid., Hubert Daly to McQuaid, 5 August 1954.

212. Ibid., 16 August 1954.

213. Ibid., 9 September 1954.

214. Ibid., 18 September 1954.

215. Ibid., 28 September 1954 and McQuaid to Hubert Daly, 8 October 1954.

216. Ibid., Cecil Barrett to Father Mangan, 22 November 1954, concerning Daly's reports.

217. Ibid, W. J. Stibbs to Cecil Barrett, 4 November 1954.

218. NAI, DT, 97/9/780, Aodh de Blacam, Rural Depopulation: Report, 1 September 1947.

219. DDA, McQuaid Papers, AB8/B, DJ, Government Box 3, Proposed Ban on Emigration of Women: 1948, memorandum from Department of External Affairs, 30 September 1948, and McQuaid's comments.

220. NAI, 98/14/5/3, JCWSSW Minute Book 1948–56, 26 March 1953.

221. NAI, DT, S11582, memorandum by Elizabeth Fitzgerald, sent to Éamon de Valera, 25 August 1953, and de Valera to Fitzgerald, 13 October 1953.

222. NAI, DT, S11582, Irish Labour Emigration, 22 August 1953, and memorandum handed to Department of External Affairs in London in 1952 by Miss Mary V. Byrne.

223. Ibid., memorandum by Bill Fay, secretary, Department of External Affairs, 16 October 1952.

224. Ibid., memorandum by F. H. Boland, 15 July 1953.

225. Ibid., memorandum from Department of Finance, 15 July 1953.

226. Ibid., *Standard*, 11 December 1953.

227. NAI, DT, S14997A, Resolution of the Irish Hierarchy on Emigration, 10 October 1950.

228. NAI, ID 20 110, SFCirCC, Dublin, indictment no. 40, 6 July 1942. State Book detailing sentence imposed is unavailable.

229. NAI, DJ, 72/94A, File Relating to Prostitution, 1946–8, Joseph Groome to Department of Justice, 9 April 1946.

230. NAI, 98/14/5/2, JCWSSW Minute Book 1939–48, 5 June 1941.

231. NAI, 98/14/5/2, JCWSSW Minute Book 1939–48, 25 September 1941 and 25 October 1941.

232. NAI, Directory of Sources for Women's History in Ireland, RUC Museum, Belfast, 31 March 1942, and memorandum on areas where women should be employed, 30 March 1942.

233. NAI, 98/14/5/3, JCWSSW Minute Book 1948–56, 27 May 1952.

234. Ibid., 17 December 1941, 26 November 1942 and 24 January 1943.

235. Ibid., 30 November 1944, account of conversation with Frank Duff.

236. Ibid., 29 November 1945.

237. Ibid., 12 November 1954.

238. Ibid., 29 January 1953.

239. NAI, 98/14/5/2, JCWSSW Minute Book 1939–48, 27 November 1941.

240. NAI, ID 27 6, SFCirCC, Dublin, 11 January 1945, indictment no. 21.

241. NAI, ID 27 2, SBCirCC, 12 January 1945.

242. NAI, IC 90 99, SFCirCC, Galway, 7 October 1959. State Book detailing sentence imposed is unavailable.

243. NAI, V15 2 6, SFCirCC, Castlebar, 24 October 1950.

244. NAI, IC 17 89, SBCirCC, Dublin, indictment no. 28, 7 October 1959.

245. NAI, 98/14/5/4, JCWSSW Minute Book 1956–64, 15 August 1958 and 20 November 1958.

246. DDA, McQuaid Papers, AB8/B/xix, CSWB, Box 4, Activities 1954/5, McQuaid to Marie Gavan Duffy, 21 January 1954.

247. Ibid., W. D. Abdrin to Henry Gray, 29 December 1950.

248. John McGahern, *Memoir* (London, 2005), pp. 188–90.

249. NAI, 98/17/5/3/13, Papers of the IHA, memorandum submitted to the Commission on Emigration, June 1948, p. 3, and 98/17/5/3/19, memorandum on housing, 30 September 1952.

250. Finola Kennedy, *Cottage to Crèche: Family Change in Ireland* (Dublin, 2001), pp. 141–2.

251. NAI, 98/14/5/3, JCWSSW Minute Book 1948–56, 30 June 1955 and 25 July 1957.

252. Quoted in Howes, 'Public Discourse, Private Reflection', p. 971.

253. Brenda Ní Shúilleabháin, *Bibeanna: Memories from a Corner of Ireland* (Cork, 2007). See also reminiscences of Cait Firtéar in 'The Doyens of Dingle', *Irish Times*, 14 July 2007.

254. Arensberg and Kimball, *Family and Community in Ireland*, p. 137.

255. Máirín Nic Eoin, 'Maternal Wisdom: Some Irish Perspectives', *Irish Journal of Feminist Studies*, vol. 4, no. 2, 2002, pp. 1–16.

256. DDA, McQuaid Papers, AB8/xviii, Government Box 4, Health, DLGPH, 1941–6, McQuaid to Conor Ward, 24 April 1944.

257. Ibid., J. Stafford to McQuaid, 25 January 1944.

258. Ibid., Health Act 1947, n.d, Dr Daniel Cohalan to McQuaid.

259. NAI, DT, 14997A, Mother and Child Scheme, Dr James Staunton to John A. Costello, 10 October 1950.

260. Elizabeth Keane, *Seán MacBride: A Life* (Dublin, 2007), pp. 186–207.

261. DDA, McQuaid Papers, AB8/B, Government Box 5, Health: Mother and Child Scheme, Health Bill 1952, 10 December 1952, notes of a meeting between Seán Lemass, James Ryan and the Hierarchy.

262. DDA, McQuaid Papers, AB/8/B, Government Box 5, Health Bill 1952, McQuaid to Revd Gerald P. O'Hara, 7 November 1952.

263. Ibid., McQuaid's notes on Health Bill.

264. Daly, *The Slow Failure*, p. 130.

265. McGahern, *Memoir*, pp. 76–7.

266. Ibid., p. 94.

267. Daly, *The Slow Failure*, p. 130.

268. Ibid., p. 116.

269. Ibid., p. 121.

270. Ibid., p. 130.

271. Maria Sophia Quine, *Population Politics in Twentieth-century Europe* (London, 1996), p. 32.

272. Ibid., p. 98.

273. Ibid., p. 106.

274. Mary Jo Lawless (ed.), 'Childbirth 1742–1955', in Bourke *et al.* (eds.), *The Field Day Anthology of Irish Writing, Vol. 4* (Cork, 2002), p. 913.

275. Margaret MacCurtain, 'Recollections of Catholicism, 1906–1960', in Bourke *et al.* (eds.), *The Field Day Anthology of Irish Writing, Vol. 4* (Cork, 2002), p. 599.

276. Caitriona Clear, *Women of the House: Women's Household Work in Ireland 1922–1961* (Dublin, 2000), p. 123.

277. Obituary of Dr Michael Solomons, *Irish Times*, 1 December 2007.

278. Clear, *Women of the House*, p. 124.

279. Ibid., p. 122.

280. Ibid., p. 58.

281. Ibid., p. 97 and p. 139.

282. DDA, McQuaid Papers, LII, Hospitals, Nurses: Ethics and Psychology, Dr Barry to McQuaid, 22 June 1955.

283. Ibid., McQuaid to Dr Kinnane, Archbishop of Cashel, 27 January 1956.

284. Quoted in Tony Farmar, *Patients, Potions and Physicians: A Social History of Medicine in Ireland, 1654–2004* (Dublin, 2004), pp. 161–2.

285. John Cooney, 'Catholic Church Did Urge Doctors to Use Symphysiotomy Operation', *Irish Times*, 19 September 2003.

286. PRONI, DCAB, 4/252, 18 March 1930, and HLG 1/1/2, Maternity and Child Welfare: General Policy, 12 September 1945.

287. Greta Jones, 'Maries Stopes in Ireland: The Mother's Clinic in Belfast, 1936–1947', *Social History of Medicine*, vol. 5, no. 2, April 1992, pp. 255–77.

288. Muldowney, *The Second World War and Irish Women*, pp. 160–72.

289. PRONI, T/3808/1, diary of Moya Woodside, 20 April 1941 and 25 April 1941.

290. Muldowney, *The Second World War and Irish Women*, pp. 160–62.

291. NAI, DT, S2321 c/94, Maurice Moynihan to Paddy Bourke, 19 December 1959, and Moynihan to T. J. Coyne, secretary of the Department of Justice, 21 December 1959.

292. NAI, DT 97/6/561, Censorship of Publications Act 1967, Memorandum for the government, September 1966.

293. DDA, McQuaid Papers, AB8/B/xviii, Government Box 4, Brian MacMahon to McQuaid, 6 August 1947.

294. Ibid., S. A. Roche to McQuaid, 22 May 1945.

295. Ibid., AB8/B, Health, Local Government and Censorship: Censorship Board, and *Irish Times*, 23 December 1957.

296. DDA, McQuaid Papers, AB8/B, memorandum of secretary of Censorship of Publications Board, 12 April 1956.

297. Ibid., McQuaid's notes, 3 September 1957.

298. Ibid., Dermot O'Flynn to McQuaid, 12 April 1958.

299. Ibid., memorandum on Censorship of Publications Board *c.* December 1957.

300. Ibid., J. J. Pigott's memorandum, *c.* January 1958 .

301. Ibid., Dermot O'Flynn to McQuaid, 19 May 1958.

302. NAI, DT, S2321A, circa September 1957.

303. SPCDA, A/1/23, Papers of Christopher O'Reilly, Censorship Notebooks.

304. Michael Adams, *Censorship: The Irish Experience* (Alabama, 1968), p. 119.

305. See James Kelly, 'The Operation of the Censorship of Publications Board: The Notebooks of C. J. O'Reilly, 1951–55', *Analectia Hibernica*, no. 40, 2004, pp. 223–369.

306. Ibid., and SPCDA, A/1/23, O'Reilly Papers, Censorship Notebooks, entry no. 84 (references are to the numbers in his notebooks).

307. Ibid., no. 734.

308. Ibid., no. 3, back flyleaf.

309. Ibid., no. 644.

310. See Julie Anne Stevens, 'Mary Lavin (1912–1996): A Tribute', *Irish Journal of Feminist Studies*, vol. 1, no. 2, Winter 1996, pp. 25–36: Mary Lavin, *Happiness and Other Stories* (Boston, 1970), pp. 101–52.

311. Angela Macnamara, *Yours Sincerely* (Dublin, 2003) p. 51.

312. Howes, 'Public Discourse, Private Reflection', p. 990.

313. Eibhear Walshe, *Kate O'Brien: A Writing Life* (Dublin, 2006), pp. 65–6 and 129–31.

314. Ibid.

315. Quoted in MacCurtain, 'Recollections of Catholicism', p. 585.

316. Catriona Crowe, review of Eibhear Walshe's *Kate O'Brien: A Writing Life*, *Irish Review*, nos. 36–7, Winter 2007, pp. 158–60.

317. Antoinette Quinn, *Patrick Kavanagh: A Biography* (Dublin, 2001), pp. 138–204.

318. Michael Sheehy, *Is Ireland Dying? Culture and the Church in Modern Ireland* (London, 1968), p. 133.

319. Roger McHugh, 'Too Immoral for Any Stage', *The Bell*, vol. 15, no. 2, November 1947, pp. 60–64.

320. McCourt, *Angela's Ashes*, p. 291.

321. Quoted in Bryan Fanning, *The Quest for Modern Ireland: The Battle of Ideas 1912–1986* (Dublin, 2008), p. 57.

322. Kitty Holland, 'Minister Advised to Close Dublin Run of Rose Tattoo', *Irish Times*, 4 January 2000.

323. Carolyn Swift and Gerard Whelan, *Spiked: Church–State Intrigue and the Rose Tattoo* (Dublin, 2002).

324. Fintan O'Toole, 'In a Cold Climate, A Heroic Stand', *Irish Times*, 19 November 2002.

325. Library Council of Ireland, *The University of the People: Celebrating Irish Public Libraries* (Dublin, 2003), pp. 83–4.

326. NAI, DJ, 2006/148/7, Censorship of Publications Act 1929: General Inquiries, Informal Complaints, 10 December 1952.

327. Ibid., 15 February 1957 and 28 March 1957.

328. Ibid., 14 January 1957 and 24 February 1958.

329. Ibid., 7 May 1957 and 7 June 1958.

330. NAI, DJ, 2006/148/13, Censorship of Publications: Complaints about Comics, Garda Commissioner's Office, 29 September 1955.

331. Ibid., 27 November 1954, and A. Lynch Robinson to Thomas Coyne, 25 November 1954 and reply.

332. NAI, FCO, 98/26/3, Register of Films Censored 1938–50, and 98/29/4, Reject Book 1935–53, 9 January 1946.

333. Ibid., 1 May 1946 and 12 June 1946.

334. Ibid., 7 August 1946.

335. Ibid., 5 August 1952 and 13 August 1952.

336. John O'Brien (ed.), *The Vanishing Irish: The Enigma of the Modern World* (London, 1954), pp. 6–17.

337. Mary Kenny, 'Forty Years On', *Studies*, vol. 92, no. 365, Spring 2003, pp. 7–13.

338. Con Houlihan, 'One of Our Own', *Evening Herald*, 9 July 2008, p. 35.

339. Macnamara, *Yours Sincerely*, pp. 22–43.

340. Sheehy, *Is Ireland Dying?* p. 204.

341. Ibid., p. 203.

342. MacCurtain, 'Recollections of Catholicism', p. 570.

343. Ibid., p. 593.

344. Ibid.

345. Tracy, *Mind You, I've Said Nothing*, p. 55.

346. Maurice Harmon, *Séan O'Faoláin: A Life* (London, 1994).

347. Ibid., pp. 197–9.

348. John McGahern, *The Collected Stories* (London, 1992), pp. 165–75.

349. Nuala O'Faoláin, *Are You Somebody?* (Dublin, 1996), p. 20, and Jane Elizabeth Dougherty, 'Nuala O'Faoláin and the Unwritten Irish Girlhood', *New Hibernia Review*, vol. 11, no. 2, Summer 2007, pp. 50–66.

350. Ibid.

351. Macnamara, *Yours Sincerely*, p. 22.

352. CICA, evidence of Brother David Gibson, 16 June 2005. See www.childabusecommission.ie.

353. Ibid.

354. NLI, *NSPCC Annual Report 1944–5* (Dublin, 1945).

355. NLI, *NSPCC Annual Report 1948–9*.

356. NLI, *NSPCC Annual Reports 1963–8*.

357. See also Eoin O'Sullivan and Mary Raftery, *Suffer the Little Children: The Inside Story of Ireland's Industrial Schools* (Dublin, 1999), p. 30ff.

358. Ibid.

359. See Diarmaid Ferriter, 'Suffer Little Children? The Historical Validity of Memoirs of Irish Childhood', in Joseph Dunne and James Kelly (eds.), *Childhood and Its Discontents* (Dublin, 2002), pp. 69–107.

360. O'Sullivan and Raftery, *Suffer the Little Children*, p. 30.

361. Noël Browne, *Against the Tide* (Dublin, 1986), pp. 198–201.

362. CICA, evidence of Brother David Gibson.

363. Ibid.

364. Ibid., evidence of Brother Reynolds, 15 September 2005.

365. Ibid.

366. Peter Tyrrell, *Founded on Fear: Letterfrack Industrial School, War and Exile* (Dublin, 2006).

367. *Irish Times*, 18 October 2006.

368. *Irish Times*, 22 July 2004.

369. *Irish Times*, 15 July 2004.

370. CICA, evidence of Sister Clare O'Sullivan, as reported in the *Irish Times*, 2 July 2004.

371. Moira Maguire, 'The Carrigan Committee and Child Sexual Abuse in Twentieth-century Ireland', *New Hibernia Review*, vol. 11, no. 2, Summer 2007, pp. 179–201.

372. Gene Kerrigan, *Another Country, Growing Up in '50s Ireland* (Dublin, 1998), p. 205.

373. Bernadette Fahey, *Freedom of Angels: Surviving Goldenbridge Orphanage* (Dublin, 1999), p. 194.

374. CICA, evidence of Sally Mulready of the London Women's Group, 23 July 2004.

375. CICA, evidence of Colm O'Gorman and Mick Waters, 21 July 2004.

376. CICA, evidence of Dr Eoin O'Sullivan, 21 June 2004.

377. Ibid., pp. 25ff.

378. Ibid.

379. NAI, 98/14/5/3, JCWSSW Minute Book 1948–56, 24 February 1949.

380. CICA, evidence of Eoin O'Sullivan.

381. CICA, evidence of Brother David Gibson.

382. Maguire, 'The Carrigan Committee and Child Sexual Abuse', pp. 79–100.

383. Ibid.

384. Ibid.

385. Ibid.

386. Ibid

387. DDA, McQuaid Papers, AB8/B/xviii, Government Box 3, Adoption, McQuaid to S. A. Roche, 13 March 1945 and notes by JCWSSW and request for interview with McQuaid, 2 December 1947.

388. DDA, McQuaid Papers, AB8/B/xviii, Government Box 3, DJ, Adoption legislation 1957–71, Cecil Barrett to McQuaid, 16 December 1958.

389. Ibid., Cecil Barrett to McQuaid, 5 May 1959.

390. Mike Milotte, *Banished Babies: The Secret History of Ireland's Baby Export Business* (Dublin, 1997).

391. Diarmaid Ferriter, *The Transformation of Ireland, 1900–2000* (London, 2004), p. 515.

392. Milotte, *Banished Babies*, p. 153.

393. *Sunday Independent*, 18 March 2007, and 'Flesh and Blood', programme broadcast on RTÉ One, 22 March 2007.

394. *Report of the Commission to Inquire into Child Abuse* (Dublin, 2009), and *Irish Times*, 21 May 2009.

– FOUR –
1960–70

1. Marjorie Howes, 'Public Discourse, Private Reflection: 1916–1970', in Bourke *et al.* (eds.), *The Field Day Anthology of Irish Writing, Vol. 4* (Cork, 2002), p. 929.

2. Quoted in Brian O'Rourke, *The Conscience of the Race: Sex and Religion in Irish and French Novels, 1941–73* (Dublin, 1980) pp. 20ff.

3. Quoted in Tony Farmar, *Ordinary Lives: Three Generations of Irish Middle-class Experience, 1907, 1932, 1963* (Dublin, 1991), p. 192.

4. Tom Inglis, 'The Constitution of Sexual Subjects in Irish Religious and Moral Discourse', paper presented to Theory, Culture and Society Conference, Berlin, August 1995, UCD Library photocopy 13743.

5. Farmar, *Ordinary Lives*, p. 195.

6. Tom Inglis, *Lessons in Irish Sexuality* (Dublin, 1998), p. 37.

7. Dorine Rohan, *Marriage: Irish Style* (Cork, 1969), p. 67.

8. *Irish Times*, 1 May 1969.

9. Donald S. Connery, *The Irish* (London, 1968), p. 200.

10. Jeffrey Weeks, *Making Sexual History* (Cambridge, 2000), p. 12.

11. John Ardagh, *The New French Revolution* (London, 1968), pp. 257–8.

12. Angus McLaren, *Twentieth-century Sexuality: A History* (Oxford, 1999), pp. 166–74.

13. Ibid., p. 163.

14. Jonathan Green, *IT: Sex Since the Sixties* (London, 1993), p. 9.

15. Alan Bestic, *Sex and the Singular English* (London, 1972), pp. 23–134.

16. Ibid., p. 174.

17. David Birmingham, *A Concise History of Portugal* (Cambridge, 2003), pp. 175–6.

18. McLaren, *Twentieth-century Sexuality*, p. 192.

19. Diarmaid Ferriter, *What If? Alternative Views of Twentieth-century Ireland* (Dublin, 2006), pp. 40–52 .

20. Deirdre McMahon, 'John Charles McQuaid: Archbishop of Dublin, 1940–1972', in James Kelly and Daire Keogh (eds.), *A History of the Catholic Diocese of Dublin* (Dublin, 2000), pp. 331–44.

21. Ibid., p. 333.

22. Tom Garvin, *Preventing the Future: Why was Ireland So Poor for So Long?* (Dublin, 2005), p. 56.

23. Ibid., p. 57.

24. Ibid., p. 160.

25. John Cooney, 'McQuaid Has been Betrayed by His Own Voluminous Archive', *Irish Times*, 7 April 2003, and John Cooney, *John Charles McQuaid: Ruler of Catholic Ireland* (Dublin, 1999).

26. DDA, McQuaid Papers, AB8/B/xxxx/ic, Diocesan Press Office, McQuaid to Oscar Dowling, 6 March 1970.

27. Ibid., McQuaid to Dowling, 27 April 1965.

28. Ibid, draft reply to questionnaire of Tim Pat Coogan, 19 April 1965.

29. DDA, McQuaid Papers, AB8/B/xxvi/a–b, Communications: Radio Éireann 1952–61, Eric Boden to McQuaid, 28 September 1954.

30. Connery, *The Irish*, p. 93.

31. Ibid., p. 160.

32. Bryan Fanning, *The Quest for Modern Ireland: The Battle of Ideas 1912–1986* (Dublin, 2008), p. 170.

33. DDA, McQuaid Papers, AB8/B/xix, CSWB, Box 7, Youth Welfare Section, copy of McQuaid's address to youth leadership congress at Clonliffe, 3 March 1962.

34. Angela Macnamara, *Yours Sincerely* (Dublin, 2003), pp. 62–7.

35. See Diarmaid Ferriter, 'Women and Political Change Since 1960', *Éire-Ireland*, vol. 43, nos. 1&2, 2008, pp. 179–205.

36. Quoted in Fanning, *The Quest for Modern Ireland*, p. 128.

37. DDA, McQuaid Papers, DDA AB8/B/xix, CSWB, Box 7, Marriage Counselling Service 1966–71, Angela Macnamara to McQuaid, 4 March 1968, and *Hibernia* magazine, 28 February 1969.

38. Joseph McGloin, *What Not to Do on a Date* (Dublin, 1960), pp. 7–13.

39. Thomas Finnegan, *Questions Young Girls Ask* (Dublin, 1965), pp. 1–16.

40. Farmar, *Ordinary Lives*, p. 195.

41. Ibid.

42. Connery, *The Irish*, p. 173.

43. Aidan Mackey, *What is Love?* (Dublin, 1964), pp. 7–13.

44. John O'Brien, *A Chaste Courtship* (Notre Dame, 1965), pp. 7–31.

45. M. B. Crowe, *Private Morals and Public Life* (Dublin, 1965), p. 37.

46. Lee Dunne, *Goodbye to the Hill* (London, 1965), pp. 71–2.

47. 'Film Banned for 35 Years Coming to a Screen Soon', *Sunday Independent*, 13 August 2006.

48. Jeremiah Newman (ed.), *The Limerick Rural Survey, 1958–64* (Tipperary, 1964). See also Mary E. Daly, 'Two Centuries of Irish Social Life', in National Gallery of Ireland, *A Time and a Place: Two Centuries of Irish Social Life* (Dublin, 2006), p. 9.

49. Connery, *The Irish*, p. 174.

50. NAI, DT, 96/6/344, Census of Population 1961 Reports, memorandum for government from Central Statistics Office, January 1965.

51. Mary E. Daly, *The Slow Failure: Population Decline and Modern Ireland* (Madison, WI, 2006), p. 136.

52. June Levine, *Sisters* (Dublin, 1982), pp. 12–13.

53. Mary Kenny, 'Forty Years On', *Studies*, vol. 92, no. 365, Spring 2003, pp. 7–13.

54. Farmar, *Ordinary Lives*, chapter 5.

55. Ann Marie Hourihane, 'They Travel to Knock to Hail Mary', *Sunday Tribune*, 13 August 2006.

56. Ibid.

57. O'Rourke, *The Conscience of the Race*, p. 49.

58. Ibid., p. 53.

59. Quoted in Howes, 'Public Discourse, Private Reflection', p. 1017.

60. Bruce Francis Biever, *Religion, Culture and Values: A Cross-cultural Analysis of Motivational Factors in Native Irish and American Catholicism* (New York, 1976).

61. Rohan, *Marriage: Irish Style*, pp. 67–85.

62. Fintan O'Toole, 'The Sexual Politics of John B. Keane', *Magill*, February 1985, pp. 51–2.

63. Ibid.

64. Cooney, *John Charles McQuaid*, p. 282.

65. Liam Fay, *Beyond Belief* (Dublin, 1997), pp. 217–20.

66. See Brian D'Arcy, *A Different Journey* (Dublin, 2006).

67. Tony Flannery, *From the Inside: A Priest's View of the Catholic Church* (Cork, 1999), pp. 52–74.

68. Louise Fuller, *Irish Catholicism Since 1950: The Undoing of a Culture* (Dublin, 2002), pp. 166–7.

69. Flannery, *From the Inside*, p. 77.

70. E. F. O'Doherty, 'Sexual Deviations', in E. F. O'Doherty and S. Desmond McGrath (eds.), *The Priest and Mental Health* (New York, 1963), pp. 124–35.

71. Catriona Crowe, 'On the Ferns Report', *Dublin Review*, no. 22, Spring 2006, pp. 5–26.

72. *Irish Times*, 25 June 2004.

73. CICA, evidence of Father Michael Hughes, 9 May 2005. See www.childabusecommission.ie.

74. See *Irish Times*, 26 November 1999.

75. Crowe, 'On the Ferns Report', pp. 5–26.

76. CICA, Evidence of Brother David Gibson, 16 June 2005.

77. NAI, IC 17 89, SBCirCC, Dublin, 12 January 1960, 25 April 1960, 5 October 1960.

78. NAI, ID 3, 175, SFCirCC, Dublin, indictment no. 24, 17 June 1965.

79. Quoted in Tom O'Malley, 'Perceptions of Sexual Violence', in Byrne *et al.* (eds.), *University College Galway Women's Studies Review*, vol. 11, 1993, pp. 131–47.

80. NAI, VB4 8 23, SFCirCC, Galway, 9 January 1968.

81. NAI, VB4 6 10, SFCirCC, Cork City, 18 June 1963.

82. Catherine Dunne, *An Unconsidered People: The Irish in London* (Dublin, 2003), p. 61.

83. Ibid., p. 18.

84. Ibid., p. 140.

85. Ibid., pp. 46–7.

86. Lesley A. Hall, *Sex, Gender and Social Change in Britain Since 1880* (London, 2000), p. 171.

87. Ibid.

88. McLaren, *Twentieth-century Sexuality*, p. 6.

89. DDA, McQuaid Papers, AB/8/B/xxvi, Communications: Television RTÉ 1963, Sean Holohan to McQuaid, 8 April 1963, and Cathal McCarthy to McQuaid, 9 April 1963.

90. DDA, McQuaid Papers, AB/8/B/xxxxic, Diocesan Press Office, Osmond Dowling to MacMahon, 12 July 1965.

91. DDA, AB/8/B/xix, CSWB, Box 6, Marriage Counselling Service 1966–71, Maternity Group of Medical Social Workers to McQuaid, 7 February 1966, and reply, 8 February 1966.

92. *Irish Press*, 9 September 1966.

93. DDA, McQuaid Papers, AB/8/B/xix, CSWB, Box 6, Marriage Counselling Service 1966–71, McQuaid Address to Our Lady's School Templeogue, 3 March 1968.

94. DDA, McQuaid Papers, AB/8/B/xix, CSWB, Box 6, Marriage Section 1955–71, 5 October 1956.

95. Ibid., 2 November 1967.

96. Ibid., memorandum by Father Michael Browne, 19 April 1970.

97. Macnamara, *Yours Sincerely*, p. 69.

98. Finola Kennedy, *Cottage to Crèche: Family Change in Ireland* (Dublin, 2001), p. 164.

99. Chrystel Hug, *The Politics of Sexual Morality in Ireland* (Basingstoke, 1999), pp. 86–7.

100. Alan Bestic, *The Importance of Being Irish* (London, 1969), pp. 112–15.

101. Obituary of Dr Michael Solomons, *Irish Times*, 1 December 2007.

102. Máire Mullarney, *What About Me?* (Dublin, 1992) pp. 160–61.

103. David Lodge, *How Far Can You Go?* (London, 1980), pp. 4–57.

104. *Irish Times*, 1 December 2007.

105. *Hibernia*, 24 April 1969.

106. McLaren, *Twentieth-century Sexuality*, p. 169.

107. Ardagh, *The New French Revolution*, p. 200.

108. DDA, McQuaid Papers, AB8/B/xxxx, Diocesan Press Office, 8 August 1967.

109. Angela Bourke, 'Rocks in the Road', *Dublin Review*, no. 21, Winter 2005–6, pp. 102–12.

110. Bestic, *The Importance of Being Irish*, p. 114.

111. Connery, *The Irish*, pp. 170–71.

112. Joe Dunn, *No Tigers in Africa* (Dublin, 1986), p. 104.

113. PRONI, D3691/1, BWWC, Executive Committee Minutes 1960–66, 30 May 1960.

114. Ibid., 26 October 1960.

115. PRONI, D3543, NIFPA, 3543/2/1, 20 April 1964 and 12 November 1965.

116. PRONI, D3543, NIFPA, Duncan Hearle, BBC Belfast, to Joyce Neill, 12 November 1965, and reply, 23 November 1965.

117. PRONI, D3543, NIFPA, D. J. Unwin to Mrs Pullen, 4 February 1966.

118. PRONI, D3543, NIFPA, Joyce Neill to Mrs Pullen, 5 February 1966.

119. PRONI, D3543, NIFPA, notes on *Inquiry*, broadcast 14 January 1966.

120. PRONI, D3543, NIFPA, 8 November 1966 and *Belfast News Letter*, 5 January 1967.

121. PRONI, D3543, notes on establishment of NIFPA, n.d.

122. Ibid., notes on establishment of NIFPA, n.d.

123. Ibid., D3543/3/1, correspondence 1965–7, letter from Ministry of Health and Social Services to secretary of health authorities, 4 December 1967.

124. Ibid., notes on Belfast Women's Welfare Clinic, Belfast City Hospital (Family Planning), n.d.

125. Ibid., Joyce Neill to Ronal Green, 27 August 1966.

126. Ibid., Joyce Neill to editor of *Belfast Telegraph*, 19 April 1968.

127. PRONI, D3543/2/2, Minutes of the Executive Committee of the NIFPA, 2 April 1968 and 7 May 1968.

128. PRONI, D3543/2/2, Annual Report, 1969.

129. PRONI, D3543/2/2, Minutes of the Executive Committee of the NIFPA, 12 June 1964.

130. Michael Bromley, 'Sex, Sunday Papers and the Swinging Sixties: Cultural Consensus in Northern Ireland Before the Troubles', in Yonah Alexander and Alan O'Day (eds.), *The Irish Terrorism Experience* (Dartmouth, Aldershot, 1991), pp. 57–81.

131. Ibid., p. 66.

132. Ibid..

133. Simon Prince, *Northern Ireland's '68* (Dublin, 2007), p. 197.

134. *It's My Story*, BBC Radio 4, broadcast on 16 August 2007. 'Black Belfast Catholic "Adopted" by His Mother Reunites with Father', *Irish Times*, 15 August 2007.

135. *Irish Times,* 1 January 1962.

136. Fergal Tobin, *The Best of Decades: Ireland in the 1960s* (Dublin, 1984), p. 63.

137. Ferriter, *What If?*, pp. 1–14.

138. Ibid.

139. DDA,McQuaid Papers, AB/8/B/xxvi, Communications: Television, RTÉ, 1960–62, Dermot O'Flynn to McQuaid, 7 March 1962.

140. Ibid., Edward Roth to McQuaid, 20 January 1962.

141. Ibid., AB/8/B/xxxx 1 q, Report of the Catholic Television Interim Committee, June 1962.

142. Ibid., Report of June 1965.

143. Ibid., Gearoid Kelly to McQuaid, 21 November 1966.

144. Ibid., McQuaid's reply, 30 November 1966.

145. Ibid., Kevin McCourt to McQuaid, 15 February 1966.

146. Ibid., McQuaid to Kevin McCourt, 12 February 1966, and Sean Foran to McCourt, copy to McQuaid, 31 March 1966.

147. DDA, McQuaid Papers, AB/8/B/xxxx/q, Communications: Radharc, 1963–9, Joe Dunn to McQuaid, 26 July 1968, and his reply, 31 July 1968.

148. DDA, McQuaid Papers, AB/8/xviii/13, Censorship Reform 1964–67, memorandum on Censorship March 1967, and J. A. MacMahon to Roland Burke-Savage, 31 March 1967.

149. John McGahern, 'The Church and Its Spire', in Colm Tóibín (ed.), *Soho Square 6* (London, 1993), pp. 16–30.

150. DDA, McQuaid Papers, AB/8/B/xix, Box 5, CSWB, Family Welfare Section, 3 December 1968.

151. Ibid., M. A. to McQuaid, 1 October 1968.

152. DDA, McQuaid Papers, AB/8/xviii/13, Evil Literature 1956–61, Thomas Coyne to McQuaid, 5 April 1960.

153. DDA , McQuaid Papers, AB8/B/xxxxic, letter of Diarmuid Moore, *c.* July 1962.

154. Howes, 'Public Discourse, Private Reflection', p. 929.

155. Siobhán Kilfeather and Eibhear Walshe, 'Contesting Ireland: The Erosion of Heterosexual Consensus, 1940–2001', in Bourke *et al.* (eds.), *The Field Day Anthology of Irish Writing*, Vol. 4, p. 1047.

156. DDA, McQuaid Papers, AB/8/B/xxxx ic, McQuaid to Dermot O'Flynn and McQuaid to R. J. Glennon, 11 January 1963.

157. Ibid., McQuaid to Miss Gleeson, 13 July 1963.

158. DDA, McQuaid Papers, AB/8/xviii/13, Evil Literature 1956–61, Thomas Coyne to McQuaid, 28 March 1960.

159. Ibid., Dermot O'Flynn to McQuaid, 1 March 1960.
160. NAI, DT, S2321 c/94, Department of Posts and Telegraphs, 16 January 1960.
161. Ibid., 30 May 1960.
162. *Irish Times* report of Dr Lucey's comments on censorship, 8 May 1962.
163. NAI, DJ, 2006/148/16, Publication in Newspapers of Banned Books in Serial Form, 2–4 November 1965.
164. Brigid Brophy, *Don't Never Forget: Collected Views and Reviews* (New York, 1967).
165. John McGahern, *Memoir* (London, 2005) pp. 250–51.
166. Ibid, p. 250ff.
167. DDA, McQuaid Papers, AB/8/xviii/10, Government Box 3, DJ, 10 December 1964.
168. Ibid, Department of Justice Estimates 1962–3: Censorship of Books.
169. Ibid., Civil Censorship 1959–65, Peter Berry to McQuaid, 6 July 1962.
170. *Guardian*, 20 January 1965 and 19 January 1965.
171. DDA, McQuaid Papers, AB/8/xviii/10, memorandum on censorship, *c.* 1967.
172. NAI, DT, 97/6/561, Censorship of Publications Act 1967, memorandum for government, September 1966.
173. Ibid.
174. NAI, DT, 2006/140/123, William Conway to Brian Lenihan, 16 June 1967.
175. Ibid., 8 June 1967.
176. Ibid., note to Minister, 28 April 1967.
177. NAI, DJ, 2006/148/10, figures supplied for meeting between Des O'Malley and the Irish Countrywomen's Association to discuss pornography, April 1972.
178. DDA, McQuaid Papers, AB/8/B/xix, Government Box 3, DJ, Estimates 1962–3.
179. DDA, McQuaid Papers, AB/8/B/xxxic, Civil Censorship 1959–65, James MacMahon to McQuaid, 1 March 1961.
180. NAI, DJ, 2006/148/15, 'Pornographic Films: Representations from Archbishop of Dublin', McQuaid to Thomas Coyne, 12 July 1965.
181. NAI, FCO, 98/26/3, FCOI6, 98/31/1 Censor's notebook 1966–67, 27 July 1967.
182. Alberti Mira (ed.), *The Cinema of Spain and Portugal* (London, 2003), p. 3.
183. Ibid.
184. Ibid.
185. See Michael Tanner, *Troubled Epic* (Dublin, 2007), and 'Drink, Drugs and Debauchery: Raising Hell with Ryan's Daughter', *Sunday Independent*, 29 April 2007.
186. *Irish Times*, 18 April 1969.

187. *Evening Press*, 27 May 1969.

188. *Irish Times*, 16 June 1969.

189. Brian Lewis, 'The Queer Life and Afterlife of Roger Casement', *Journal of the History of Sexuality*, vol. 14, no. 4, October 2005, pp. 363–82.

190. Ibid.

191. Ide O'Carroll and Eoin Collins (eds.), *Lesbian and Gay Visions of Ireland: Towards the 21st Century* (London, 1995), pp. 18–21.

192. *Irish Times* and *Irish Independent*, 25 June 1980.

193. Hug, *The Politics of Sexual Morality*, pp. 207–11.

194. Dunne, *Goodbye to the Hill*, p. 176.

195. Bestic, *The Importance of Being Irish*, p. 114.

196. Stephen Robinson, 'Bringing It All Back Home', *Gay Community News*, March 1998, p. 18.

197. Christopher Fitz-Simon, *The Boys* (London, 1994), p. 260.

198. Eibhear Walshe (ed.), *Sex, Nation and Dissent in Irish Writing* (Cork, 1997), pp. 11–12.

199. Fanning, *The Quest for Modern Ireland*, p. 116.

200. DDA, McQuaid Papers, AB/8/B/xxxx, Diocesan Press Office, July–December 1967, Osmond Dowling to MacMahon, 22 November 1967.

201. Quoted in O'Rourke, *The Conscience of the Race*, p. 28.

202. Julia Carlson, *Banned in Ireland: Censorship and the Irish Writer* (Georgia, 1990), pp. 69–109.

203. Emma Donoghue, 'Lesbian Encounters', in *The Field Day Anthology of Irish Writing, Vol. 4* (Cork, 2002), p. 1114.

204. Kilfeather and Walshe, 'Contesting Ireland', p. 1052.

205. Farmar, *Ordinary Lives*, p. 198.

206. Anthony Copley, *Sexual Moralities in France, 1780–1980* (London, 1992), p. 222.

207. McLaren, *Twentieth-century Sexuality*, p. 186.

208. DDA, McQuaid Papers, AB/8/B/xix/12g, Box 2, CSWB, Emigrant section, Annual report for 1963.

209. DDA, McQuaid Papers, AB/8/B/xix, Box 2, CSWB, Catholic Rescue and Protection Society, Report of 1963.

210. *Guardian*, 16 January 2007. See also Dinah O'Dowd, *Cry Salt Tears* (London, 2007).

211. DDA, McQuaid Papers, AB/8/B/xix, CSWB, Box 2, Report of Repatriation Work of the CRPS 1959–66.

212. Ibid., McQuaid to Cecil Barrett, 12 November 1963, and notes of a phone conversation, 18 November 1963.

213. *Irish Times*, 18 November 1963.

214. DDA, McQuaid Papers, AB/8/B/xix, CSWB, Government Box 3, Cecil Barrett to McQuaid and McQuaid's reply, 23 March 1964.

215. Ibid., Cecil Barrett to James MacMahon, 23 January 1964; McQuaid to Cecil Barrett, 27 January 1964 and 3 March 1964.

216. Ibid., Cecil Barrett to McQuaid, 7 March 1964

217. DDA, McQuaid Papers, AB/8/B/xviii/10, Government Box 3, DJ, Confidential Report of Special Investigation into St Patrick's Institute, 3 December 1963, Charles Haughey to McQuaid, 31 December 1963, and copy of the letter of Patrick Baitson.

218. See Paul Cullen, 'Brothers Criticise Archbishop', *Irish Times*, 25 August 2007.

219. DDA, McQuaid Papers, AB/8/B/xxxx, Communications: Television, RTÉ, 1968–9, 'A Group of Priests' to McQuaid, 13 May 1968.

220. NAI, DJ, 2004/46/7, Inquiries re: Abortion and Euthanasia, 21 September 1964.

221. NAI, 98/14/5/5, JCWSSW Minute Book, 1964–72, 18 November 1965.

222. Ibid., 20 November 1969.

223. NAI, 98/17/5/3/6 and 98/17/5/3/33, Hilda Tweedy Papers, 'Programmes of Law Reform in the early 1960s', *c.* 1964.

224. *Irish Times*, 12 December 1968.

225. Mary Leland, 'Prostitution in Cork', *Irish Times*, 28 November 1968.

226. Ibid.

227. Linda Connolly, *The Irish Women's Movement: From Revolution to Devolution* (Basingstoke, 2002), pp. 71–2.

228. Kennedy, *Cottage to Crèche,* p. 225.

229. Fintan O'Toole, 'Picking the Lock of Family Secrets', *Irish Times*, 1 April 2006.

230. Alison Healy, 'Canon Lawyer Denies Code Silenced Sex Abuse Victims', *Irish Times*, 2 October 2006.

231. Bourke, 'Rocks in the Road', pp. 102–12.

232. Michael Sheehy, *Is Ireland Dying? Culture and the Church in Modern Ireland* (London, 1968), p. 242.

233. NAI, DJ, 2006/148/5, Dance Halls: Miscellaneous Inquiries and Reports, 4 February 1961.

234. Bestic, *Importance of Being Irish*, p. 109.

235. Connery, *The Irish*, p. 171.

236. Ibid., p. 179.

237. Anne Macdona, (ed.), *From Newman to New Woman: UCD Women Remember* (Dublin, 2001), p. 144ff.

238. See Ferriter, 'Women and Political Change Since 1960', pp. 179–205.

239. Olivia O'Leary and Helen Burke, *Mary Robinson: The Authorised Biography* (London, 1998) pp. 45–52.

240. DDA, McQuaid Papers, AB/8/B/xxxxic, Diocesan Press Office 1968–1970, 22 November 1968.

241. Ibid., Osmond Dowling to McQuaid, 23 January 1971.

- FIVE -

1970–2005

1. Mícheál MacGreil, *Prejudice and Tolerance in Ireland* (Dublin, 1977), pp. 410–14.

2. NAI, DT, 2003/16/453, 'Contraceptives: Resolutions and Miscellaneous Correspondence Relating to Laws re.', 22 March 1971.

3. Ibid., 5 April 1972.

4. *Irish Times*, 16 April 1970.

5. NAI, DT, 2003/16/34, Criminal Law Amendment Act 1935, extracts from Dáil debate, 21 April 1970.

6. Ibid., Memorandum for Government on Controversy about Contraception, 19 April 1971.

7. Ibid.

8. Ibid., Jack Lynch to Bernadette Cullen, 1 April 1971.

9. Chrystel Hug, *The Politics of Sexual Morality in Ireland* (Basingstoke, 1999), pp. 91–5.

10. NAI, DT, 2003/16/453, Seán Flanagan to Jack Lynch, 21 May 1971.

11. Ibid., note from DT, 21 April 1971.

12. Ibid., Supplementary Note for the Government, 26 July 1971.

13. Ibid., *Irish Press*, 22 May 1971, and cabinet minutes, 6 July 1971.

14. NAI, DT, 2002/8/458, Resolutions and Miscellaneous Correspondence Relating to Laws Re. Contraceptives, C. T. Ennis to DT, 7 March 1971.

15. Ibid., letters of F. O'Meara and Dr D. Waldron, 10 March 1971 and 7 March 1971.

16. Ibid., letter of Ann Doyle, 15 March 1970.

17. *Magill,* May 1983, p. 7.

18. NAI, DT, 2002/8/458, unsigned letter, 15 March 1971.

19. Ibid., letter of Padraig Flaherty, 16 March 1971.

20. Ibid., letter of Bernadette Cullen, 26 March 1971.

21. Ibid., unsigned letter, 24 March 1971.

22. Ibid., Brigid O'Malley to Mrs Lynch, 12 March 1971.

23. Ibid., letter of F. J. O'Meara, 31 March 1971.

24. Ibid., letter of Father Michael Le Mhuire, 24 March 1971.

25. Ibid., letter of N. Finlay, 29 March 1971.

26. Brian Rothery, *What Europe Means to the Irish* (London, 1973), pp. 93 and 54–5.

27. Quoted in Fintan O'Toole, *The Irish Times Book of the Century* (Dublin, 1999), p. 234.

28. NAI, DT, 2002/8/458, Patrick Cogan to Jack Lynch, 3 April 1971.

29. Ibid., Brendan Walsh to Jack Lynch, 13 April 1971.

30. Ibid., letter of Bob Cadden, 30 April 1971.

31. Alan Browne (ed.), *Masters, Midwives and Ladies in Waiting: The Rotunda Hospital, 1745–1995* (Dublin, 1995), p. 47.

32. Tony Farmar, *Holles Street, 1894–1994* (Dublin, 1994), p. 176.

33. NAI, DT, 2002/8/458, 16 March 1971.

34. Ibid., 30 April 1971, 13 May 1971 and 18 May 1971.

35. *This Week*, vol. 2, no. 35, 25 June 1971.

36. DDA, McQuaid Papers, AB/8/B/xix, CSWB, Box 6, Family Welfare Section, Ursula Hurley to Father Williams, 30 October 1970.

37. Ibid., Cecil Barrett to McQuaid, 30 April 1970.

38. Ibid., Memorandum on Marriage Counselling Services by Fr Michael Browne, 27 April 1971.

39. Ibid., Joan Devitt and Bernard Duff to McQuaid, 30 November 1971.

40. Diarmaid Ferriter, *What If? Alternative Views of Twentieth-century Ireland* (Dublin, 2006), pp. 40–52.

41. NAI, DT, 2004/21/24, *Seanad Debates,* 25 July 1973.

42. Ibid.

43. John Horgan, *Noël Browne: Passionate Outsider* (Dublin, 2000), p. 238.

44. Ibid.

45. Hug, *The Politics of Sexual Morality*, p. 98.

46. NAI, DT, 2004/21/24, Mary Robinson to Liam Cosgrave, 3 August 1973.

47. Ibid., Liam Cosgrave to Father Dick Mulcahy, 17 April 1973, in response to Mulcahy's memorandum.

48. NAI, DJ, 2005/341, Memorandum on Family Planning Bill, including Attorney General's Suggested Amendments, 12 March 1974.

49. Barry Desmond, *Finally and in Conclusion* (Dublin, 2000), p. 247.

50. Quoted in Hug, *The Politics of Sexual Morality*, p. 105.

51. Nell McCafferty, *A Woman to Blame: The Kerry Babies Case* (Dublin, 1985), p. 33.

52. R. F. Foster, *Luck and the Irish: A Brief History of Change, 1970–2000* (London, 2007), p. 43.

53. DDA, McQuaid Papers, AB/8/B, Government Box 3, DJ, Charles Haughey's telegram to McQuaid, 27 December 1961, and his letters to McQuaid, 15 January 1963 and 3 September 1963.

54. *Magill*, September 1983.

55. *Magill*, May 1979, p. 12.

56. Ibid., p.40

57. Andrew Rynne, *The Vasectomy Doctor: A Memoir* (Dublin, 2005), pp. 114–23.

58. Ibid., p. 133.

59. Ibid., p. 141.

60. Ethna Viney, *Ancient Wars: Sexuality and Oppression* (Attic Press, 1989), p. 11.

61. *Irish Times,* 27 January 1999.

62. *Village*, 26 February 2005.

63. *Irish Times*, 22 December 2005.

64. Betty Hilliard, 'The Catholic Church and Married Women's Sexuality: Habits Change in Late Twentieth-century Ireland', *Irish Journal of Sociology*, vol. 12, no. 2, 2003, p. 42.

65. *Irish Times*, 27 February 2006.

66. Martin Wall, 'Doctor with "Deep Fault Line" Which was Never Corrected', *Irish Times*, 1 March 2006.

67. NAI, DT, 2003/16/453, reprinted for the Association for the Protection of Irish Family Life, 22 March 1971.

68. Ibid., Jack Lynch to Bernadette Cullen, 1 April 1971.

69. PRONI, D3543, NIFPA, notes on Belfast Women's Welfare Clinic, n. d.

70. PRONI, D3543/3/1, correspondence, Brenda Shimeld to D. McCauslaid, 31 January 1975.

71. PRONI, D3543/2/2, executive committee of the NIFPA, minute book, 12 March 1970 and 11 June 1970.

72. PRONI, D3543, Denise Fulton to William Van Straubenzee, 23 May 1973.

73. PRONI, D3543, Caspar Brock to Dr Joyce Neill, 10 April 1976.

74. PRONI, D3543, unsigned letter to Dr Joan Wilson, 15 November 1976.

75. Alan Bestic, *The Importance of Being Irish* (London, 1969), p. 112.

76. Tom Inglis, 'The Constitution of Sexual Subjects in Irish Religious and Moral Discourse', paper presented to Theory, Culture and Society Conference, Berlin, August 1995, UCD Library photocopy 13743.

77. *Magill*, February 1999, p. 62.

78. Ibid.

79. John Horgan, *Irish Media: A Critical History Since 1922* (London, 2001), pp. 108–9.

80. Emer O'Kelly, *The Permissive Society in Ireland* (Cork, 1974).

81. Ibid., pp. 18–64.

82. Ibid., p. 66.

83. Michael O'Loughlin, 'Those Glorious Seventies', *Sunday Independent,* 27 August 2006.

84. Ciara Dwyer, 'The Heart of a Scandal', *Sunday Independent* Living Section, p. 3, 15 July 2007.

85. *Magill,* April 1978, pp. 10–14.

86. Ibid.

87. Ibid., p. 14.

88. Rosita Sweetman, *On Our Backs: Sexual Attitudes in a Changing Ireland* (Dublin, 1979), pp. 191–6.

89. Ibid., pp. 43–50.

90. *Irish Times,* 14 March 1980.

91. Abbey Hyde, 'Marriage and Motherhood: The Contradictory Position of Single Mothers', *Irish Journal of Feminist Studies,* vol. 2, no. 1, July 1997, pp. 22–37.

92. Maura Richards, *Two to Tango* (London, 1981), pp. 87–121.

93. Ibid., p. 63.

94. Hyde, 'Marriage and Motherhood', pp. 22–37.

95. NAI, DT, 2005/7/94, collection of extracts from media programmes and interviews about children in care, compiled by J. E. Algeo and sent to Department of Taoiseach, *c.*1974.

96. NAI, DT, 2005/7/94, Children: General: Kennedy Report and Care Proposals, Erica Mason to Liam Cosgrave, 24 March 1973.

97. O'Kelly, *The Permissive Society in Ireland.*

98. Finola Kennedy, *Cottage to Crèche: Family Change in Ireland* (Dublin, 2001), p. 219.

99. MacGreil, *Prejudice and Tolerance in Ireland,* p. 40.

100. Mannix Flynn, *Nothing to Say* (Dublin, 1983), p. 30.

101. Michael Farrell, 'Inside the Marriage Tribunal', *Magill,* February 1984, p. 34.

102. Mary Hederman, 'Irish Women and Irish Law', *Crane Bag,* Vol. 4, no. 1, 1980, pp. 55–9.

103. Ibid. and John O'Keefe, 'Case That Woke Us All Up to Sexual Scandal', *Sunday Independent,* 13 July 2008.

104. Hederman, 'Irish Women and Irish Law', p. 58.

105. Linda Connolly, *The Irish Women's Movement: From Revolution to Devolution* (Basingstoke, 2002), p. 129.

106. Nell McCafferty, *Nell* (Dublin, 2004), pp. 147–50.

107. Diarmaid Ferriter, 'Women and Political Change Since 1960', *Éire-Ireland,* vol. 43, nos. 1 & 2, 2008, pp. 179–205.

108. June Levine, 'The Women's Movement in the Republic, 1968–80', in Bourke et al. (eds.), *The Field Day Anthology of Irish Writing, Vol. 5,* (Cork, 2002), p. 178.

109. Ibid., p. 181.

110. McCafferty, *Nell*, p. 201.

111. Ibid., p. 235.

112. Levine, 'The Women's Movement in the Republic, 1968–80', p. 182.

113. Pat Brennan, 'The Women's Movement in Ireland', *Magill*, April 1979, pp. 40–46.

114. Diarmaid Ferriter, *The Transformation of Ireland, 1900–2000* (London, 2004), p. 571.

115. Susan McKay, *Without Fear: 25 Years of the Dublin Rape Crisis Centre* (Dublin, 2005), pp. 11–17.

116. Ibid.

117. McCafferty, *Nell*, p. 319.

118. Ibid.

119. McKay, *Without Fear*, p. ix.

120. Tom O'Malley, 'Perceptions of Sexual Violence', in Byrne *et al.* (eds.), *University College Galway Women's Studies Review*, vol. ii, 1993, pp. 131–47.

121. *Irish Times*, 8 March 2008 and McKay, *Without Fear*, p. ix.

122. Ibid.

123. Brennan, 'The Women's Movement in Ireland', p. 46.

124. Foster, *Luck and the Irish*, p. 41.

125. NAI, DT, 2005/7/94, CARE campaign for the care of deprived children, 13 February 1973.

126. Kathy Sheridan, 'Cynthia's Day of Vindication', *Irish Times*, 17 February 2007.

127. Ibid.

128. NAI, DT, 2005/7/94, Barry Desmond to Liam Cosgrave, 6 August 1974.

129. NAI, DT, 2003/16/453, Contraceptives: Resolutions and Miscellaneous Correspondence Relating to Laws Re., A. J. Wallace to Jack Lynch, 17 November 1972.

130. Ibid., 29 November 1972.

131. DDA, McQuaid Papers, AB/8/B, Government Box 3, DJ, 2 August 1971.

132. Catriona Crowe, 'On the Ferns Report', *Dublin Review*, no. 22, Spring 2006, pp. 5–26.

133. Ibid.

134. Ibid.

135. Sarah McInerney, 'Banished: Fr McGinnity's 20-Year Punishment for Speaking Out', *Sunday Tribune*, 30 October 2005.

136. Garret FitzGerald, 'Would Married Bishops Have Acted on Abuse?' *Irish Times*, 29 October 2005.

137. Crowe, 'On the Ferns Report', pp. 5–26.

138. *The Ferns Report: Presented to the Minister for Health and Children* (2005), pp. 82, 92, 94, 96, 100 and 74.

139. Ibid., p. 93.

140. Crowe, 'On the Ferns Report', pp. 5–26.

141. Olivia O'Leary, *Party Animals* (O'Brien Press, 2006), p. 228.

142. Caroline Skehill, 'Child Protection and Welfare Social Work in the Republic of Ireland', in Noreen Kearney and Caroline Skehill (eds.), *Social Work in Ireland: Historical Perspectives* (Dublin, 2005), pp. 127–46.

143. Ibid., p. 140.

144. Tom Garvin, 'The Strange Death of Clerical Politics in University College, Dublin', *Irish University Review*, vol. 28, no. 2, Autumn/Winter 1998, pp. 308–15.

145. *Magill*, July 1986.

146. Ibid.

147. *The Ferns Report*, p. 82.

148. *Magill*, July 1986.

149. *Magill*, January 1982, p. 46.

150. *Magill*, April 1999, pp. 24–8.

151. See Susan McKay, *Sophia's Story* (Dublin, 1988).

152. Harry Ferguson, 'The Paedophile Priest: A Deconstruction', *Studies*, vol. 84, no. 334, pp. 247–57.

153. *Irish Times*, 19 March 1990.

154. Ferguson, 'The Paedophile Priest', p. 254.

155. *Irish Times*, 13 August 1999.

156. O'Leary, *Party Animals*, pp. 229–30.

157. Interview with Colm O'Gorman by Suzanne Power, *Sunday Tribune*, 7 May 2006.

158. Nuala O'Faoláin, 'Failing to Face the Facts of Child Abuse', *Irish Times*, 19 March 1990.

159. Tony and J. J. Muggivan, *A Tragedy Waiting to Happen: The Chaotic Life of Brendan O'Donnell* (Dublin, 2006).

160. Àine Ní Ghlinn, *Unshed Tears: Deora Nár Caoineadh* (Dublin, 1996), p. 13. Translated by Pádraig Ò Snodaigh. Thanks to Máirín Nic Eoin for this reference.

161. Emma Browne, Sara Burke and Vincent Browne, 'Child Rape Crisis', *Village*, 3–7 November 2005, p. 13.

162. Ibid.

163. Fintan O'Toole, 'A Culture That Failed to See Evil', *Irish Times*, 1 November 2005.

164. John Lalor, 'Vilification of Church Obscures Our Role in Ignoring Child Abuse', *Sunday Independent*, 6 November 2005.

165. *Irish Times,* 8 March 2008.

166. *Irish Times,* 8 March 2006.

167. Ibid.

168. *Irish Times,* 9 March 2006.

169. Ivor Browne, *Music and Madness* (Dublin, 2008), p. 300.

170. Ibid., p. 303.

171. *Irish Times,* 21 and 23 August 1996.

172. Ibid., 11 January 2001.

173. Ibid., 21 November 2006.

174. *Irish Times,* 19 April 2008.

175. Mary Kenny, 'Forty Years On', *Studies,* vol. 92, no. 365, Spring 2003, pp. 7–13.

176. Michael Mason, *The Making of Victorian Sexual Attitudes* (Oxford, 1994), p. 225.

177. McLaren, *Twentieth-century Sexuality*, p. 8; Jonathan Green, *IT: Sex Since the Sixties* (London, 1993), p. 327.

178. McLaren, *Twentieth-century Sexuality*, p. 3.

179. Jeffrey Weeks, 'Foucault for Historians', *History Workshop*, no. 14, Autumn 1982, pp. 106–20.

180. Ferriter, *What If?*, pp. 14–27.

181. *Magill*, May 1986, p. 3.

182. Foster, *Luck and the Irish*, p. 39; *Magill*, May 1986, p. 3; and Emily O'Reilly, *Masterminds of the Right* (Dublin, 1992).

183. Brian Trench, 'The Contraception Backlash', *Magill*, January 1979, p. 17.

184. Horgan, *Noël Browne*, p. 254.

185. Hug, *The Politics of Sexual Morality*, p. 161ff.

186. Ruth Riddick, *The Right to Choose: Questions of Feminist Morality* (Dublin, 1990), pp. 4–9.

187. Ivana Bacik, 'Tales of an Outspoken Woman', *Irish Times*, 27 November 2004.

188. Mary Holland, *How Far We Have Travelled: The Voice of Mary Holland* (Dublin, 2004), p. x.

189. *Irish Times*, 3 September 2003.

190. Thomas H. Hesketh, *The Second Partitioning of Ireland? The Abortion Referendum of 1983* (Dublin, 1990).

191. Nell McCafferty, *The Best of Nell* (Dublin, 1984), pp. 58–63.

192. Ferriter, *What If?*, pp. 14–27.

193. *Magill*, July 1982, p. 4.

194. *Magill*, May 1983, p. 7.

195. Ibid., p. 22.

196. *Magill*, September 1983, p. 7.

197. Ibid.
198. Quoted in Hug, *The Politics of Sexual Morality*, p. 149.
199. Quoted in John Ardagh, *Ireland and the Irish* (London, 1994), p. 184.
200. Obituary of Dr Michael Solomons, *Irish Times*, 1 December 2007.
201. *Magill*, January 1983.
202. Goretti Horgan, 'Pro-Choice Lobby Served Important Purpose', *Irish Times*, 8 September 2003.
203. *Magill*, January 1983, p. 11.
204. Ibid.
205. Ferriter, *What If?*, pp. 14–27.
206. Hesketh, *The Second Partitioning of Ireland*, pp. 368–7.
207. Ibid.
208. Hubert Butler, *Grandmother and Wolfe Tone* (Dublin, 1990), p. 77.
209. *Magill*, February 1983, pp. 18–19.
210. *Magill*, November 2006, p. 92.
211. Hug, *The Politics of Sexual Morality*, p. 156.
212. Ibid., p. 171.
213. Ferriter, *What If?*, p. 26.
214. Jennifer Spreng, *Abortion and Divorce Law in Ireland* (London, 2004), p. iii.
215. Medb Ruane, *The Irish Journey: Women's Stories of Abortion* (Dublin, 2000), p. ii.
216. Holland, *How Far We Have Travelled*, pp. 147–51, *Irish Times*, 2 March 1995.
217. *Dáil Debates*, 8 March 1995, quoted in Hug, *The Politics of Sexual Morality*, p. 195.
218. *Irish Times*, 23 January 2007.
219. *Irish Times*, 8 March 2008.
220. *Belfast Telegraph*, 19 May 1976.
221. PRONI, D/3762/1/3/8, NIGRA, *Gay News*, no. 51, 18–31 July.
222. Ibid.
223. PRONI, D/3762/1/1/11, NIGRA, Jeffery Dudgeon, 'Gay Rights in Northern Ireland', n.d.
224. Ibid., D/3762/1/8/10, NIGRA, NIGRA to Trevor Phillips, University of London Union, 28 April 1976.
225. PRONI, D/3762/1/1/11, NIGRA, Dudgeon, 'Gay Rights in Northern Ireland'.
226. *Sunday News*, 2 May 1976.
227. PRONI, D/3762/1/1/11, NIGRA, Dudgeon, 'Gay Rights in Northern Ireland'.
228. Ibid.
229. PRONI, D/3762/1/8/9, NIGRA, Jeffrey Dudgeon to Sam Silkin, 21 April 1976.

230. Ibid., *NIGRA News*, December 1977, vol. 2, no. 5.

231. Ibid., D/3762/1/8/10, 3–15 January 1978.

232. PRONI, D/3762/1/8/15, NIGRA, Letters of Support to Dudgeon, R. B. to Jeffrey Dudgeon, 9 May 1979.

233. PRONI, D/3762/1/11/5, NIGRA, Anti-Gay Literature (Various), The Gay Rights Campaign Answered, *c.* 1979.

234. Ibid.

235. PRONI, D/3762/1/1/10, NIGRA, Attacks on Gay People, Draft Reports in Confidence, and Belfast *Sunday News*, 30 April 1978, and *Belfast Telegraph*, 3 July 1979, and *Attacks on Gay People: A Report of the Commission on Discrimination*, 2nd ed., May 1977–May 1980 (London, 1980).

236. Ibid., p. 30.

237. PRONI, D/3762/1/8/9, Richard Kennedy to Michael Havers, 25 May 1979.

238. PRONI, D/3762/2/1/3, April 1977, observations by the applicant on the observations of the government of the UK on the admissibility of application no. 7525/76 lodged by Jeffery Dudgeon.

239. PRONI, D/3762/2/1/21, NIGRA, notes to Keenan Boyle, notes from court hearing statements by NI Counsel B. Kerr.

240. Ibid., p. 10.

241. Colm Tóibín, 'A Brush with the Law', *Dublin Review*, no. 28, Autumn 2007, pp. 11–34.

242. PRONI, D/3762/2/1/12, NIGRA, Observations of the Applicant on the Report of the Policy Advisory Committee on Sexual Offences (London, 1981), p. 8.

243. PRONI, D/3762/2/1/17, NIGRA, 'Applicant's Comments on the UK Government's Proposal for a Friendly Settlement', 24 February 1982.

244. Susan McKay, 'The "City for Everyone" Goes Back on Its Word', *Irish Times*, 7 July 2005.

245. PRONI, D/3762/1/1/11, NIGRA, Dudgeon, 'Gay Rights in Northern Ireland'.

246. Ide O'Carroll and Eoin Collins (eds.), *Lesbian and Gay Visions of Ireland: Towards the Twenty-first Century* (London, 1995), notes on contributors.

247. Brendí McClenaghan, 'Letter from a Gay Republican', in O'Carroll and Collins (eds.), *Lesbian and Gay Visions of Ireland*, pp. 122–31.

248. Siobhán Kilfeather and Eibhear Walshe, 'Contesting Ireland: The Erosion of Heterosexual Consensus, 1940–2001', in Bourke *et al.* (eds.), *The Field Day Anthology of Irish Writing*, Vol. 4 (Cork, 2002), p. 1056.

249. Ferriter, *The Transformation of Ireland*, p. 657.

250. McKay, 'The "City for Everyone"'.

251. Ibid.

252. Angelique Chrisafis, 'Gays and Lesbians under Siege as Violence and Harassment Soar in Northern Ireland', *Guardian*, 6 June 2005.

253. Brian Lacey, 'Billy's Boys, or an Orangeman's Dilemma', *History Ireland*, vol. 16, no. 5, September/October 2008, pp. 18–19.

254. Kitty Holland, 'Many Unionists Bigoted against Gays, Says Leading Activist', *Irish Times*, 29 July 2008.

255. Steve Bruce, *Paisley: Religion and Politics in Northern Ireland* (Oxford, 2007), pp. 209–67.

256. Fiona Meredith, 'Dissenters Want Paisley Gone', *Village*, July 2007, p. 14.

257. *Sunday Tribune*, 30 July 2006.

258. Ed Moloney, *Paisley: From Demagogue to Democrat* (Dublin, 2008), p. 243.

259. *Irish Times*, 18 September 2002.

260. Suzanne Breen, 'The House of Horrors', *Sunday Tribune*, 9 July 2006.

261. *Sunday Tribune*, 6 August 2006.

262. Suzanne Breen, 'Sex and Death with Mad Dog', *Sunday Tribune*, 29 October 2006.

263. Kevin Myers, *Watching the Door: A Memoir, 1971–1978* (Dublin, 2006), pp. 39 and 213.

264. Ibid., pp. viii, 41 and 243.

265. See *Irish Journal of Sociology*, vol. 12, no. 2, 2003, p. 13.

266. Eamonn McCann, *War and Peace in Northern Ireland* (Dublin, 1998), column of 5 September 1991.

267. *Sunday Tribune*, 18 February 2007.

268. Paul Ryan, 'Coming Out, Fitting In: The Personal Narratives of Some Irish Gay Men', *Irish Journal of Sociology*, vol. 12, no. 2, 2003, p. 68.

269. NLI, IQA, Box 173, Newsclippings: 1980s, *Irish Times*, 25 June 1980.

270. NLI, IQA, Box 19, Report of Third Annual Conference of the International Gay Association.

271. Ibid., p. 7.

272. Quentin Fottrell, 'Having a Gay Old Time', *Sunday Tribune* Review, 25 November 2007.

273. Nell McCafferty, *In the Eyes of the Law* (Dublin, 1981).

274. NLI, IQA, Box 130, letter from T. B. to Stephen Meyler, 30 December 1996.

275. NLI, IQA, Box 228, National Lesbian and Gay Federation (NLGF), *Irish Times*, 28 September 1984.

276. NLI, IQA, Box 173, Newsclippings: 1980s, *Evening Herald*, 25 June 1980.

277. NLI, IQA, Box 143, *Gay Community News*, November 1998.

278. NLI, IQA, Box 173, Newsclippings: 1980s, *Irish Times*, 25 June 1980.

279. O'Carroll and Collins (eds.), *Lesbian and Gay Visions of Ireland*, p. 21ff.

280. Hug, *The Politics of Sexual Morality*, p. 211.

281. Ibid., pp. 208–9.

282. PRONI, D/3762/1/1/6, NIGRA, Profiles of Candidates Seeking Election to the National Executive of the IGRM in May 1977.

283. Ibid., profile of Edmund Lynch.

284. Ibid., profile of David Norris.

285. Ibid., profiles of Thomas A. Kelly and Tom Shine.

286. *Magill*, May 1983, p. 4.

287. NLI, IQA, Box 187, 'Hirschfeld Enterprises Limited, The Structure of the NGF Administrative Council: A Discussion Paper', presented by Joni Crone.

288. Ibid.

289. NLI, IQA, Box 228, NLGF, J. M. to Tonie Walsh, 27 May 1982.

290. Ibid., M. McM. to Tonie Walsh, 7 January 1983 and 17 May 1984.

291. NLI, IQA, Box 202, 'National Gay Federation: Discussion Document: A Youth Group for Gay Adolescents', September 1979.

292. NLI, IQA, Box 228, NLGF, *Irish Times*, 28 September 1984.

293. NLI, IQA, Box 173, *Irish Times*, 2 June 1980.

294. NLI, IQA, Box 228, NLGF, 'Report of Political Co-ordinator David Norris to the Third Annual General Meeting of the National Gay Federation (NGF), Liberty Hall Dublin', 18 September 1982.

295. Ibid.

296. NLI, IQA, Box 175, John Francis Grundy, 'Irrepressible: Gay Liberation in Ireland', January 1982.

297. NLI, IQA, Box 228, NGLF, Oliver Cogan to Bernard Keogh, 3 April 1981.

298. *Irish Times*, 28 February 1981.

299. NLI, IQA, Box 19, IGA Bulletins, 1/1985, 3/1984.

300. Ibid., 6/1985.

301. NLI, IQA, Box 19, Edmund Lynch to Jimmy Carter, 29 January 1980.

302. Ibid., Edmund Lynch to Roy McMurtry, 29 January 1980.

303. Ralph Gallagher, 'Understanding the Homosexual', *Furrow*, September 1979, vol. 30, no. 9, pp. 559–68.

304. NLI, IQA, Box 173, Newsclippings: 1980s, *Irish Times*, 26 March 1980.

305. Ibid., *Sunday Independent*, 19 October 1980.

306. NLI, IQA, Box 173, *Irish Press*, 4 December 1980.

307. NLI, IQA, Box 235, *Irish Times*, 6 April 1990.

308. PRONI, D/3762/1/1/12, NIGRA, extracts from *Longford Leader*, October and November 1980, and circular by the Longford Branch of the Irish Gay Rights Movement by General Secretary Sean Connolly, *c.* 1980.

309. PRONI, D/3762/1/1/12, NIGRA, letter of Stephen Heron of Northumberland Road, n.d.

310. NLI, IQA, Box 173, Newsclippings: 1980s, *Hibernia*, 19 June 1980.

311. NLI, IQA, Box 173, Newsclippings: 1980s, *Irish Independent*, 25 June 1980; *Evening Press*, 25 June 1980.

312. Ibid., *Irish Times*, 28 June 1980.

313. Tóibín, 'A Brush with the Law', pp. 11–34.

314. Ibid.

315. Ibid.

316. *Magill*, May 1983, p. 4.

317. Tóibín, 'A Brush with the Law'.

318. Ibid.

319. Liam Harte, 'History, Text and Society in Colm Tóibín's *The Heather Blazing*', *New Hibernia Review*, vol. 6, no. 4, Winter 2002, pp. 55–68.

320. Hug, *The Politics of Sexual Morality*, p. 213.

321. Maggie O'Kane, 'The Fairview Killers', *Magill*, April 1983, p. 10.

322. Ibid., p. 16.

323. *Sunday Tribune* Review, 25 November 2007.

324. Hug, *The Politics of Sexual Morality*, p. 213.

325. Katie Hannon, *The Naked Politician* (Dublin, 2004), p. 230.

326. NLI, IQA, Box 153, *Cork Examiner*, 17 May 1990.

327. NLI, IQA, Box 202, *Gay Community News*, 11 November 1998.

328. NLI, IQA, Box 234, *Irish Times*, 11 June 1984.

329. NLI, IQA, Box 228, NLGF, Young Fine Gael press release by Roy Dooney, 1 April 1979.

330. Ibid., Tom Redmond to Tonie Walsh, 11 November 1981.

331. Ibid., National H Block Committee to Norris, 13 May 1981.

332. NLI, IQA, Box 235, Gays against Imperialism meeting, 12 December 1981.

333. Ibid., undated account of involvement of Gays against Imperialism in march to mark the tenth anniversary of Bloody Sunday in 1982.

334. NLI, IQA, Box 228, Peter Barry to David Norris, 9 June 1981.

335. Ibid., Bernard Keogh to Michael D. Higgins, 24 May 1981.

336. Ibid., Bernard Keogh to Michael D. Higgins, 1 November 1980.

337. Ibid., Jim Kemmy press statement, 9 March 1983.

338. NLI, IQA, Box 228, NLGF, George Birmingham to Tonie Walsh, 15 May 1985.

339. Ibid., Tonie Walsh to Anne Colley, 7 March 1989 and Colley's reply, 14 March 1989.

340. NLI, IQA, Box 228, Gay and Lesbian Equality Network (GLEN), papers of Kieran Rose, 'Unite for Change'; report of seminar on lesbian and gay reform, 17 September 1988.

341. NLI, IQA, Box 228, GLEN, papers of Kieran Rose, 26 April 1989.

342. NLI, IQA, Box 143, *Gay Community News*, May 1998, p. 16, and Box 228, NLGF, Oliver Cogan to Bernard Keogh, 2 April 1981.

343. Family Solidarity, *The Homosexual Challenge: Analysis and Response* (Dublin, 1990), p. 10ff.

344. Hug, *The Politics of Sexual Morality*, p. 203.

345. NLI, IQA, Box 235, AIDS Action Alliance, *Irish Press*, 29 March 1990, and *Irish Independent*, 30 March 1990.

346. NLI, IQA, Box 130, memorandum from Monsignor Robert Lynch to all bishops, 25 June 1992.

347. Family Solidarity, *The Homosexual Challenge*, p. 15.

348. T. J. Flynn, '25 years of AIDS', *Sunday Tribune* Review, 1 October 2006.

349. NAI, 98/14/5/7, JCWSSW Minute Book 1980–89, 12 March 1987.

350. NLI, IQA, Box 130, memorandum on AIDS Alliance Forum, n.d.

351. Ardagh, *Ireland and the Irish*, p. 184.

352. NLI, IQA, Box 235, AIDS Action Alliance and *Irish Times*, 11 May 1987.

353. NLI, IQA, Box 130, September 1997; draft of articles by Stephen Meyler, health and lifestyle editor of *Gay Community News*.

354. *Magill*, March 1989, p. 14, and April 1989, p. 30.

355. Ardagh, *Ireland and the Irish*, p. 184.

356. *Sunday Tribune* Review, 25 November 2007.

357. NLI, IQA, Box 235, AIDS Action Alliance, *c.* August 1991.

358. NLI, IQA, Box 202, Gay Men's Health Project 1998: Report and Developments.

359. Colm Tóibín, *The Blackwater Lightship* (London, 1999).

360. See Eibhear Walshe, 'The Vanishing Homoerotic: Colm Tóibín's Gay Fictions', *New Hibernia Review*, vol. 10, no. 4, Winter 2006, pp. 122–37.

361. *Sunday Tribune* magazine, 16 December 2007, p. 15.

362. NLI, IQA, Box 228, GLEN, papers of Kieran Rose: David Harrad to Kieran Rose, 28 March 1991.

363. NLI, IQA, Box 235, Nigel to Martin and Charles, 17 March 1982.

364. NLI, IQA, Box 153, *Irish Independent*, 26 November 1990.

365. NLI, IQA, Box 228, GLEN, papers of Kieran Rose, business diary, 3 May 1993.

366. Eileen Battersby, 'The Novel TD', *Irish Times*, 14 March 1996.

367. NLI, IQA, Box 228, GLEN, papers of Kieran Rose, Suzy Byrne to Kerry Miller, 28 June 1993.

368. Ibid., minutes of GLEN meeting, 3 May 1993.

369. NLI, IQA, Box 202, GLEN to secretary of the Commission on the Family, 11 April 1996.

370. NLI, IQA, Box 143, *Gay Community News*, August 1998 commenting on *Irish Times* article of May 1998.

371. NLI, IQA, Box 202, 'OutYouth: A Report of the Dublin Gay and Lesbian Youth Group Pilot Project by Dr Carol-Anne O'Brien', October 1998.

372. Kilfeather and Walshe, 'Contesting Ireland', p. 1050.

373. Tom Lennon, *When Love Comes to Town* (Dublin, 1993), p. 103.

374. See also Jennifer Jeffares, *The Irish Novel at the End of the Twentieth Century: Gender, Bodies and Power* (London, 2002), pp. 85–8.

375. Kilfeather and Walshe, 'Contesting Ireland', p. 1069.

376. Ibid., p. 1118.

377. Colm Tóibín, 'Selling Tara, Buying Florida', *Éire-Ireland*, vol. 43, nos. 1&2, Spring/Summer 2008, p. 4.

378. *Sunday Tribune*, 23 July 2006.

379. Kilfeather and Walshe, 'Contesting Ireland', p. 1070.

380. *Evening Herald*, 24 April 2007.

381. *Irish Times*, 18 March 2006.

382. Quentin Fottrell, 'Dark Side of the Rainbow', *Sunday Tribune* Review, 23 July 2006.

383. NLI, IQA, Box 11, *Hot Press*, 'Bootboy' columns, vol. 21, no. 2, 5 February 1997, and vol. 20, no. 63, April 1996.

384. Máirtín Mac An Ghaill, 'Irish Masculinities and Sexualities in England', in Lisa Adkins and Vicki Merchant (eds.), *Sexualising the Social: Power and the Organisation of Sexuality* (London, 1996), pp. 122–45.

385. NLI, IQA, *Hot Press*, vol. 23, no. 13, 21 July 1999.

386. *Sunday Tribune* Review, 25 November 2007.

387. Kilfeather and Walshe, 'Contesting Ireland', p. 1068.

388. Hayley Fox Roberts, '"Always Keep a Lemon handy": A Skeletal History of Lesbian Activism in Late Twentieth-century Ireland', *History Review 12* (University College Dublin), 2001, pp. 113–27.

389. Ibid.

390. Ibid.

391. McCafferty, *Nell*, p. 422.

392. *Magill*, April 1979, p. 40.

393. Roberts, '"Keep a Lemon Handy"', p. 117.

394. NLI, IQA, Box 228, NLGF, press release, 19 June 1980.

395. McCafferty, *Nell*, p. 340.

396. Roberts, 'Keep a Lemon Handy', p. 118.

397. NLI, IQA, Box 153, Newsclippings: 1990s, *Sunday Independent*, 21 January 1990.

398. NLI, IQA, Box 228, NLGF, leaflet on 'Pink Economy', n.d.

399. NLI, IQA, Box 153, Newsclippings: 1990s, *Sunday World*, 4 March 1990 and 25 March 1990.

400. Roberts, '"Keep a Lemon Handy"', p. 121.

401. Emma Donoghue 'Lesbian Encounters', in Bourne *et al.* (eds.), *The Field Day Antholgy of Irish Writing*, vol. 4 (Cork, 2002), p. 1118.

402. Roberts, '"Keep a Lemon Handy"', p. 114.

403. NLI, IQA, Box 86, papers of Katherine O'Donnell, Women's Education and Research Resource Centre, 25 June 1999.

404. Donoghue, 'Lesbian Encounters', p. 1118ff.

405. Ardagh, *Ireland and the Irish*, p. 195.

406. NLI, IQA, Box 153, Newsclippings: 1990s, *Irish Times*, 12 February 1990.

407. Kilfeather and Walshe, 'Contesting Ireland', p. 1065.

408. Angela O'Connell, 'Patriarchy, Power and Pregnancy: Irish Lesbians on the Boat to England', *Irish Journal of Feminist Studies*, vol. 5, nos. 1&2, 2003, pp. 88–99.

409. Ailbhe Smyth, 'Feminism, Personal Political (or Ex-Colonized Girls Know More)', *Irish Journal of Feminist Studies*, vol. 2, no. 1, July 1997, pp. 37–55.

410. O'Carroll and Collins (eds.), *Lesbian and Gay Visions*, notes on contributors.

411. Donoghue, 'Lesbian Encounters', p. 1119.

412. NLI, IQA, Box 207, Women's Education and Resource Research Centre, Lesbian Archive.

413. NLI, IQA, Box 207, P.B. to Ailbhe Smyth, *c.* 1997.

414. Ali Bracken, 'It's about Justice and Equality, But in the End, It Comes Down to Love', *Sunday Tribune*, 29 April 2007.

415. *Irish Examiner*, 1 November 2007.

416. NAI, 98/14/5/6, JCWSSW Minute Book 1964–72, 20 April 1972, 18 May 1972 and 5 June 1972.

417. Ibid., 19 October 1972.

418. NAI, DT, 2003/16/34, Criminal Law Amendment Act 1935, George Byrne to DT, 18 September 1970.

419. Don Lavery, 'Irish Lady of the Night Brought Down British Lord in Sex Scandal', *Sunday Independent*, 7 January 2007.

420. Tóibín, 'A Brush with the Law', p. 14.

421. June Levine, 'A Woman in Gangland', *Magill*, December 1983.

422. Ibid.

423. Lyn Madden, *Lyn's Escape* (Cork, 2007).

424. Paul Reynolds, *Sex in the City* (Dublin, 2003), p. xiii.

425. Ibid.

426. *Irish Times,* 6 October 2005.

427. *Irish Times*, 29 September 2006.

428. *Irish Examiner,* 1 November 2007.

429. *Sunday Tribune*, 23 September 2006.

430. *Sunday Independent*, 8 October 2006.

431. Reynolds, *Sex in the City*, p. xv.

432. Evanna Kearins, *Rent: The Secret World of Male Prostitution in Dublin* (Dublin, 2000), pp. 13–39.

433. Dave Mullins, *Ladies of the Kasbah* (London, 1995), pp. 10–30.

434. *Magill*, January 1982, p. 9.

435. Hannon, *The Naked Politician*, p. 230ff.

436. *Magill*, June 1999, p. 2, and 'A Lover's Final Betrayal of Charles Haughey', *Sunday Independent*, 16 May 1999.

437. Hannon, *The Naked Politician*, p. 226.

438. *Magill*, February 1999, p. 40.

439. Ibid., p. 42.

440. Angela Macnamara, *Yours Sincerely* (Dublin, 2003), p. 99ff.

441. Kennedy, *Cottage to Crèche*, pp. x–xiii.

442. Hyde, 'Marriage and Motherhood', pp. 22–37.

443. Colm Tóibín, 'Gay Byrne: Irish Life as Cabaret', *Crane Bag*, vol. 8, no. 2, 1984, pp. 165–70.

444. Ardagh, *Ireland and the Irish*, pp. 178–9.

445. Fintan O'Toole, 'Still Failing to Protect Our Children', *Irish Times*, 23 July 2002.

446. *Irish Times*, 20 August 1998.

447. Paula Meehan, *The Man Who was Marked by Winter* (Oldcastle, 1991), p. 42.

448. Siobhán Kilfeather, 'Look Who's Talking: Scandalous Memoirs and the Performance of Gender', *Irish Review*, no. 13, Winter 1992/3, pp. 40–50.

449. McCafferty, *A Woman to Blame*, p. 11.

450. Ibid., p. 7.

451. Tom Inglis, *Truth, Power and Lies: Irish Society and the Kerry Babies Case* (Dublin, 2003), p. 3.

452. Ibid., p. 1.

453. Joanne Hayes, *My Story* (Dublin, 1985), quoted in Ursula Barry and Clair Wills (eds.), 'Republic of Ireland: The Politics of Sexual Morality', in Bourke *et al.* (eds.), *The Field Day Anthology of Irish Writing, Vol. 5* (Cork, 2002), pp. 1439–44.

454. See *Irish Times*, 2 and 3 June 2005.

455. McCafferty, *A Woman to Blame*, p. 31.

456. Ardagh, *Ireland and the Irish*, p. 163.

457. Ibid., p. 168.

458. Louise Fuller, *Irish Catholicism Since 1950: The Undoing of a Culture* (Dublin, 2003), pp. 251–3.

459. Bernard Canning, *Bishops of Ireland 1870–1987* (Donegal, 1987), p. 354.

460. Annie Murphy with Peter de Rossa, *Forbidden Fruit: The True Story of My Secret Love Affair with Ireland's Most Powerful Bishop* (London, 1993), p. 46.

461. Ferriter, *What If?*, pp. 65–76.

462. Ibid.

463. James Donnelly, 'A Church in Crisis: The Irish Catholic Church Today', *History Ireland*, vol. 8, no. 3, Autumn 2000, pp. 12–27.

464. Tom Inglis, 'Pleasure Pursuits', in Mary P. Corcoran and Michael Peillon (eds.), *Ireland Unbound: A Turn of the Century Chronicle* (Dublin, 2002), pp. 25–35.

465. *Magill*, 10 June 1986, pp. 16–36.

466. Fintan O'Toole, 'On the Side of Angels', *Magill*, February 1988, pp. 17–22.

467. Diarmaid Ferriter, 'Cardinal Lost His Way Somewhere Between Angels and Fallen Priests', *Irish Examiner*, 14 February 2008.

468. Mary Carolan and Andy Pollak, 'Bishop Reiterates Need for Debate on Celibacy', *Irish Times*, 2 September 1998.

469. Kevin Hegarty, 'Celibacy Falling Away in Practice if Not in Doctrine', *Irish Times*, 21 September 1996.

470. Ibid.

471. *Official Reports of the Debates of Dáil Éireann, 1922–2002*, 4 June 1970.

472. NAI, 98/14/5/6, JCWSSW Minute Book, 28 June 1979.

473. NAI, 98/14/4/1–17, JCWSSW, Children's Protection Society: Legislative Submission on the Video Recordings Bill, 1988; *Irish Times*, 11 February 1986; and *Irish Times*, 2 December 1985.

474. NAI, 98/14/4/1–17, JCWSSW, Kitty Shannon, Hon. Secretary, JCWSSW, to Minister for Justice, 7 March 1991.

475. Ibid., Children's Protection Society: Legislative Submission on the Video Recordings Bill, 1988.

476. Ibid., secretary to Minister for Justice to V. L. Crumplin, 5 November 1986.

477. Micheline McCormack, *Little Girl: The Lavinia Kerwick Story* (Dublin, 1997).

478. Mary Donnelly, 'The Calm of Reason: Judicial Sentencing in Sexual Offences Cases', *Journal of Irish Feminist Studies*, vol. 1, no. 1, March 1996, pp. 26–43.

479. *Irish Times*, 29 March 1995.

480. Ardagh, *Ireland and the Irish*, pp. 178–9.

481. Tom Inglis, 'Pleasure Pursuits', pp. 33–4.

482. Karen Sugrue, 'Sex in the City', in Corcoran and Peillon (eds.), *Ireland Unbound*, pp. 51–62.

483. *Irish Times*, 13 August 1999.

484. Ann Marie Hourihane, *She Moves through the Boom* (Dublin, 2000), p. 66.

485. NAI, 98/14/5/6, JCWSSW Minute Book 1973–80, 18 July 1974.

486. Tom Inglis, 'From Self-denial to Self-indulgence', *Irish Review*, no. 34, 2006, pp. 34–42.

487. McLaren, *Twentieth-century Sexuality*, p. 223.

488. Sheila O'Flanagan, 'New Man Must Learn Not to Cry So Publicly', *Irish Times*, 21 August 2001.

489. See Caroline Walsh (ed.), *Arrows in Flight: Short Stories from a New Ireland* (London, 2002), pp. 233–67.

490. See Anthony Clare, *On Men: Masculinity in Crisis* (London, 2000), pp. 5 and 213–21.

491. Roddy Doyle, *The Snapper* (London, 1990), p. 193.

492. Margaret Kelleher and Philip O'Leary (eds.), *The Cambridge History of Irish Literature, Vol .2, 1890–2000* (Cambridge, 2006), pp. 443–6, and Rüdiger Imhof, *The Modern Irish Novel: Irish Novelists after 1945* (Dublin, 2002).

493. Kelleher and O'Leary (eds.), *The Cambridge History of Irish Literature*, p. 451.

494. *Irish Times*, 26 September 2006.

495. Una Mullally, 'Generation Sex', *Sunday Tribune* Review, 31 December 2006.

496. Helen Murray, 'Sex and the Irish', *Sunday Tribune* Magazine, 24 April 2005.

497. *Sunday Tribune*, 9 July 2006.

498. *Sunday Tribune*, 8 October 2006.

499. Richard Layte and Hannah McGee, 'More Open Attitude on Sexual Matters Has a Downside', *Irish Times*, 17 October 2006.

500. *Sunday Independent*, 22 October 2006.

501. Tom Inglis, *Global Ireland: Same Difference* (London, 2008), p. 187.

502. Ali Bracken, 'Waking Up to the Uncomfortable Truth about Modern, Promiscuous Ireland', *Sunday Tribune*, 26 August 2007.

503. *Sunday Tribune*, 11 June 2006.

504. *Sunday Independent*, 29 October 2006.

505. Gene Kerrigan, 'Flawed Sex Law was Always a Time Bomb Just Waiting to Go Off on Us', *Sunday Independent*, 5 November 2006.

506. *Irish Times*, 16 January 2008.

507. *Sunday Tribune*, 30 March 2008.

508. Ali Bracken, 'No Sex Please, We're Irish', *Irish Times*, 29 August 2006.

509. Maurice Devlin, 'A Bit of the Other: Media Representations of Young People's Sexuality', *Irish Journal of Sociology*, vol. 12, no. 2, 2003, pp. 85–97.

510. Ibid., p. 97.

511. Inglis, *Global Ireland*, p. 186.

512. Patricia Redlich, 'Look Back at Anguish', *Sunday Independent*, 31 December 2006.

513. Catherine Heffernan, *Sexually Transmitted Infections: Sex and the Irish* (Maynooth, 2004), pp. 1–14.

514. Siobhán Kilfeather, 'Sexuality, 1685–2001' in Bourke *et al.* (eds.), *The Field Day Anthology of Irish Writing, Vol. 4* (Cork, 2002), pp. 756–8.

515. Ibid.

516. Tony Judt, *Postwar: A History of Europe Since 1945* (New York, 2005), p. 396.

517. Blake Morrison, *Things My Mother Never Told Me* (London, 2002), p. 27.

518. JJBL, Papers of Flann O'Brien, MS 97–27, Box 8, Section 7, 1–10, letter to 'Peggy', 16 April 1941.

519. Anthony Bradley and Maryann Gialanella Valiulis (eds.), *Gender and Sexuality in Modern Ireland* (Amherst, MA, 1997), p. 2.

520. Anna Clark, *Desire: A History of European Sexuality* (London, 2008), p. 220.

521. Ibid., p. 2.

522. Ibid., pp. 6–7.

523. Maria Luddy, *Prostitution and Irish Society* (Cambridge, 2007), p. 1.

524. Mark Finnane, 'The Carrigan Committee of 1930–31 and the "Moral Condition" of the Saorstát', *Irish Historical Studies*, vol. 32, no. 128, November 2001, p. 519.

BIBLIOGRAPHY

Archives

National Archives of Ireland (NAI)
Bureau of Military History (BMH)
Committee on Evil Literature (CEL)
Film Censor's Office (FCO)
Department of Health (DH)
Department of Justice (DJ)
Department of Local Government and Public Health (DLGPH)
Department of the Taoiseach (DT)
Crown Books at Quarter Sessions (CBQS)
Crown Files at Quarter Sessions (CFQS)
State Books at Central Criminal Court (SBCCC)
State Files at Central Criminal Court (SFCCC)
State Books at Circuit Criminal Court (SBCircCC)
State Files at Circuit Criminal Court (SFCircCC)
Papers of the Joint Committee of Women's Societies and Social Workers
    (JCWSSW)
Papers of Hilda Tweedy (including Papers of the Irish Housewives Association
    (IHA))

Public Record Office of Northern Ireland (PRONI)
Cabinet Secretariat (DCAB)

Department of Finance (DF)
Department of Health and Local Government (DHLG)
Department of Home Affairs (DHA)
Home Office (HO)
Crown Books at Assizes (CBA)
Crown Files at Assizes (CFA)
Papers of the Belfast Council of Social Welfare (BCSW)
Papers of the Belfast Women's Welfare Clinic (BWWC)
Diaries of Moya Woodside
Reminiscences of P. S. Callaghan

National Library of Ireland
Papers of the National Lesbian and Gay Federation (Irish Queer Archive (IQA))
Papers of Rosamund Jacob
Reports of the Catholic Protection and Rescue Society of Ireland (CPRSI)
Reports of the International Catholic Girls Protection Society (ICGPS)
Reports of the National Society for the Prevention of Cruelty to Children
     (NSPCC)

Dublin Diocesan Archives (DDA)
Papers of John Charles McQuaid

University College Dublin Archives, School of History and Archives (UCDA)
Papers of Desmond Ryan

John J. Burns Library, Boston College, Massachusetts (JJBL)
Papers of Bryan MacMahon
Papers of Flann O'Brien (Brian O'Nolan)
Papers of Frank O'Connor
Papers of Seán O Faoláin

St Patrick's College Drumcondra Archives, Dublin (SPCDA)
Papers of Christopher O'Reilly

Official Publications

Annual Reports of the Department of Local Government and Public Health, 1922–44 (in NAI)

Census of Ireland (1901) (in NAI)
Census of Ireland (1911) (in NAI)
Official Reports of the Debates of Dáil Éireann, 1922–2002
Official Reports of the Debates of Seanad Éireann, 1922–2002
Report of the Commission on Emigration and Other Population Problems (1956)
Report of the Commission of Inquiry on the Relief of the Sick and Destitute Poor (1927) (in NAI)
Report of the Committee on the Criminal Law Amendment Acts (1880–85) and Juvenile Prostitution (1930) (in NAI)
Report of the Commission to Inquire into Child Abuse (2009), available online at www.childabusecommission.ie
Report of the Committee on Evil Literature (1927) (in NAI)
Report of the Dublin Housing Inquiry (1943)
Report of the Interdepartmental Committee of Inquiry Regarding Venereal Disease (1926) (in NAI)
Report on Child Sexual Abuse (Law Reform Commission, 1990)
The Ferns Report: Presented to the Minister for Health and Children (2005)

Newspapers

Belfast Newsletter
Belfast Sunday News
Belfast Telegraph
Cork Examiner
Donegal Vindicator
Evening Herald
Evening Press
Examiner
Gay Community News
Guardian
Irish Catholic
Irish Examiner
Irish Independent
Irish Press
Irish Times
Limerick Leader
Mayo News
Northern Whig
Standard

Sunday Business Post
Sunday Independent
Sunday Press
Sunday Tribune
Sunday World
The Times (London)

Periodicals, Magazines and Academic Journals

Administration
American Mercury
Annalecta Hibernica
The Bell
Bullán
Christus Rex
Crane Bag
Dublin Review
Feminist Review
Freeman's Journal
Furrow
Hibernia
Holiday
Hot Press
History Ireland
History Review (University College Dublin)
Irish Archives
Irish Ecclesiastical Record
Irish Journal of Feminist Studies
Irish Journal of Sociology
Irish Historical Studies
Irish Monthly
Irish Review
Irish Studies Review
Irish University Review
Journal of Irish Economic and Social History
Journal of the History of Sexuality
Journal of the Social and Statistical Inquiry Society of Ireland
Magill
New Hibernia Review

Social History of Medicine Studies
University College Galway Women's Studies Review
Village
University of Limerick Women's Studies Collection

Books, Academic and Newspaper Articles, Chapters and Theses

Adams, Michael, *Censorship: The Irish Experience* (Alabama, 1968).

Adkins, Lisa, and Vicki Merchant (eds.), *Sexualising the Social: Power and the Organisation of Sexuality* (Basingstoke, 1996).

Alexander, Yonah, and Alan O'Day (eds.), *The Irish Terrorism Experience* (Dartmouth, Aldershot, 1991).

Allen, Nicholas, *George Russell and the New Ireland, 1905–30* (Dublin, 2003).

Andrews, C. S., *Man of No Property* (Cork, 1982).

Arensberg, Conrad M., and Solon T. Kimball, *Family and Community in Ireland* (Cambridge, MA, 1968).

Ardagh, John, *The New French Revolution* (London, 1968).

Ardagh, John, *Ireland and the Irish* (London, 1994).

Arthurs, Peter, *With Brendan Behan* (New York, 1981).

Bacik, Ivana, 'Tales of an Outspoken Woman', *Irish Times*, 27 November 2004.

Barry, Ursula, and Clair Wills (eds.), 'Republic of Ireland: The Politics of Sexual Morality', in Bourke *et al.* (eds.), *The Field Day Anthology of Irish Women's Writing, Vol. 5* (Cork, 2002), pp. 1409–75.

Bartlett, Thomas, and Keith Jeffery (eds.), *A Military History of Ireland* (Cambridge, 1996).

Bestic, Alan, *The Importance of Being Irish* (London, 1969).

Bestic, Alan, *Sex and the Singular English* (London, 1972).

Bew, Paul, *Charles Stewart Parnell* (Dublin, 1980).

Biever, Bruce Francis, *Religion, Culture and Values: A Cross-cultural Analysis of Motivational Factors in Native Irish and American Catholicism* (New York, 1976).

Birmingham, David, *A Concise History of Portugal* (Cambridge, 2003).

Bobbio, Noberto, *Ideological Profile of Twentieth-century Italy*, trans. Lydia G. Cochrane, (New Jersey, 1995).

Bohan, Harry and Gerard Kennedy, *Are We Forgetting Something?* (Dublin, 1999).

Bourke, Angela, *The Burning of Bridget Cleary* (Dublin, 1999).

Bourke, Angela, 'Rocks in the Road', *Dublin Review*, no. 21, Winter 2005–6, pp. 102–12.

Bourke, Angela, Siobhán Kilfeather, Maria Luddy, Margaret MacCurtain, Gerardine Meaney, Máirín Ní Dhonnchadha, Mary O'Dowd and Clair Wills, *The Field Day Anthology of Irish Writing, Vol. 4: Irish Women's Writing and Traditions* (Part 1) (Cork, 2002).

Bourke, Angela, Siobhán Kilfeather, Maria Luddy, Margaret MacCurtain, Gerardine Meaney, Máirín Ní Dhonnchadha, Mary O'Dowd and Clair Wills, *The Field Day Anthology of Irish Writing, Vol. 5: Irish Women's Writing and Traditions* (Part 2) (Cork, 2002).

Bracken, Ali, 'No Sex Please, We're Irish', *Irish Times,* 29 August 2006.

Bracken, Ali, 'It's about Justice and Equality, But in the End, It Comes Down to Love', *Sunday Tribune,* 29 April 2007.

Bracken, Ali, 'Waking Up to the Uncomfortable Truth about Modern, Promiscuous Ireland', *Sunday Tribune,* 26 August 2007.

Bradley, Anthony, and Maryann Gialanella Valiulis (eds.), *Gender and Sexuality in Modern Ireland* (Amherst, MA, 1997).

Breen, Suzanne, 'The House of Horrors', *Sunday Tribune*, 9 July 2006

Breen, Suzanne, 'Sex and Death with Mad Dog', *Sunday Tribune,* 29 October 2006.

Brennan, Pat, 'The Women's Movement in Ireland', *Magill*, April 1979, pp. 40–6.

Bromley, Michael, 'Sex, Sunday Papers and the Swinging Sixties: Cultural Consensus in Northern Ireland Before the Troubles', in Yonah Alexander and Alan O'Day (eds.), *The Irish Terrorism Experience* (Dartmouth, Aldershot, 1991), pp. 57–81.

Brophy, Brigid, *Don't Never Forget: Collected Views and Reviews* (New York, 1967).

Brown, Richard, *James Joyce and Sexuality* (Cambridge, 1985).

Browne, Alan (ed.), *Masters, Midwives and Ladies-in-Waiting: The Rotunda Hospital, 1745–1995* (Dublin, 1995).

Browne, Emma, Sara Burke and Vincent Browne, 'Child Rape Crisis', *Village*, 3–7 November 2005.

Browne, Ivor, *Music and Madness* (Dublin, 2008).

Browne, Noël, *Against the Tide* (Dublin, 1986).

Bruce, Steve, *Paisley: Religion and Politics in Northern Ireland* (Oxford, 2007).

Burke, Eimear, 'The Treatment of Working-class Children in Dublin by Statutory and Voluntary Organisations, 1889–1922' (MA thesis, UCD, 1990).

Butler, Hubert, *Grandmother and Wolfe Tone* (Dublin, 1990).

Byrne, Anne, Jane Conroy and Seán Ryder (eds.), *University College Galway Women's Studies Review, vol. 11*, 1993 (Galway, 1993).

Cafferky, John, and Kevin Hannafin, *Scandal and Betrayal: Shackleton and the Irish Crown Jewels* (Cork, 2002).

Callaghan, Mary Rose, 'Katherine O'Shea and C. S. Parnell', in Donal McCartney (ed.), *Parnell: The Politics of Power* (Dublin, 1991), pp. 137–48.

Candy, Catherine, 'Margaret Cousins 1878–1954', in Maria Luddy and Mary Cullen (eds.), *Female Activists: Irish Women and Change 1900–1960* (Dublin, 2001), pp. 113–41.

Canning, Bernard, *Bishops of Ireland 1870–1987* (Donegal, 1987).

Canning, Margaret, 'Black Belfast Catholic "Adopted" by His Mother Reunites with Father', *Irish Times*, 15 August 2007.

Carlson, Julia, *Banned in Ireland: Censorship and the Irish Writer* (Georgia, 1990).

Carolan, Mary, and Andy Pollak, 'Bishop Reiterates Need for Debate on Celibacy', *Irish Times*, 2 September 1998.

Cassidy, Colman, 'An Irishman's Diary', *Irish Times*, 10 January 2001.

Catholic Rescue and Protection Society of Ireland, *Report for the Year 1914* (Dublin, 1914).

Catholic Rescue and Protection Society of Ireland, *Report for the Year 1915* (Dublin, 1915).

Chrisafis, Angelique, 'Gays and Lesbians under Siege as Violence and Harassment Soar in Northern Ireland', *Guardian*, 6 June 2005.

Clare, Anthony, *On Men: Masculinity in Crisis* (London, 2000).

Clark, Anna, *Desire: A History of European Sexuality* (London, 2008).

Clear, Caitriona, *Women of the House: Women's Household Work in Ireland 1922–1961* (Dublin, 2000).

Cobb, Richard, *A Classical Education* (London, 1985).

Collins, Aongus, *A History of Sex and Morals in Ireland* (Cork, 2001).

Connell, K. H, *Irish Peasant Society: Four Historical Essays* (Oxford, 1968).

Connelly, S. J., 'Illegitimacy and Pre-nuptial Pregnancy in Ireland before 1864: The Evidence of Some Catholic Parish Registers', *Journal of Irish Economic and Social History*, vol. 6, 1979, pp. 5–23

Connery, Donald S., *The Irish* (London, 1968).

Connolly, Linda, *The Irish Women's Movement: From Revolution to Devolution* (Basingstoke, 2002).

Cooney, John, *John Charles McQuaid: Ruler of Catholic Ireland* (Dublin, 1999).

Cooney, John, 'McQuaid Has been Betrayed by His Own Voluminous Archive', *Irish Times*, 7 April 2003.

Cooney, John, 'Catholic Church Did Urge Doctors to Use Symphysiotomy Operation', *Irish Times*, 19 September 2003.

Copley, Anthony, *Sexual Moralities in France, 1780–1980* (London, 1992).

Corcoran, Mary P., and Michael Peillon (eds.), *Ireland Unbound: A Turn of the Century Chronicle* (Dublin, 2002).

Cosgrove, Art (ed.), *Marriage in Ireland* (Dublin, 1985).

Costello, Con, 'The Curragh Army Camp: "A Goodish Place, Sort of, in Dry Weather"', *History Ireland*, vol. 6, no. 3, Autumn 1998, pp. 33–8.

Cotter, David, *James Joyce and the Perverse Ideal* (New York, 2003).

Craig, Patricia (ed.), *The Oxford Book of Ireland* (Oxford, 1998).

'Crime Reporter', 'Crime in Dublin', *The Bell*, vol. 5, no. 3, December 1942, pp. 173–83.

Cronin, Anthony, *Dead as Doornails* (Dublin, 1976).

Cronin, Anthony, *Samuel Beckett: The Last Modernist* (London, 1997).

Crowe, Catriona, 'On the Ferns Report', *Dublin Review*, no. 22, Spring 2006, pp. 5–26.

Crowe, Catriona, review of Ray Kavanagh's *Mamie Cadden*, *Irish Times*, 19 February 2005.

Crowe, Catriona, review of Eibhear Walshe's *Kate O'Brien: A Writing Life*, *Irish Review*, nos. 36–7, Winter 2007, pp. 158–60.

Crowe, M. B., *Private Morals and Public Life* (Dublin, 1965).

Daly, Mary E., *Dublin: The Deposed Capital: A Social and Economic History, 1860–1914* (Cork, 1984).

Daly, Mary E., *The Slow Failure: Population Decline and Independent Ireland* (Madison, WI, 2006).

Daly, Mary E., 'Two Centuries of Irish Social Life', in National Gallery of Ireland, *A Time and a Place: Two Centuries of Irish Social Life* (Dublin, 2006).

D'Arcy, Brian, *A Different Journey* (Dublin, 2006).

Davis, Melissa Llewelyn, 'The Women in Collins's Life', *Irish Times*, 5 May 2007.

Dellamora, Richard, *Masculine Desire: The Sexual Politics of Victorian Aestheticism* (North Carolina, 1990).

Desmond, Barry, *Finally and in Conclusion* (Dublin, 2000).

Devlin, Maurice, 'A Bit of the Other: Media Representations of Young People's Sexuality', *Irish Journal of Sociology*, vol. 12, no. 2, 2003 pp. 85–97.

Dolan, Anne, ' Uncrowned Queen Stuck in History's Shadows', *Irish Times* Weekend Review, 3 May 2008.

Donnelly, Mary, 'The Calm of Reason: Judicial Sentencing in Sexual Offences Cases', *Journal of Irish Feminist Studies*, vol. 1, no. 1, March 1996, pp. 26–43.

Donnelly, James, 'A Church in Crisis: The Irish Catholic Church Today', *History Ireland*, vol. 8, no. 3, Autumn 2000, pp. 12–27.

Donoghue, Emma, 'Lesbian Encounters: 1745–1997', in Bourke *et al.* (eds.), *The Field Day Anthology of Irish Writing, Vol. 4* (Cork, 2002), pp. 1090–137.

Dougherty, Jane Elizabeth, 'Nuala O'Faoláin and the Unwritten Irish Girlhood', *New Hibernia Review*, vol. 11, no. 2, Summer 2007, pp. 50–66.

Doyle, Roddy, *The Snapper* (London, 1990).

Dudgeon, Jeff, 'Mapping 100 (and One) Years of Belfast Gay Life', www.// upstartpublishing.com/2007/05/25/mapping-100-years-of-Belfast-gay-life.

Duff, Frank, *Miracles on Tap* (Dublin, 1978).

Duffy, Patrick J. (ed.), *To and From Ireland: Planned Migration Schemes c. 1600–2000* (Dublin, 2004).

Dungan, Myles, *The Stealing of the Irish Crown Jewels: An Unsolved Crime* (Dublin, 2003).

Dunn, Joe, *No Tigers in Africa* (Dublin, 1986).

Dunne, Catherine, *An Unconsidered People: The Irish in London* (Dublin, 2003).

Dunne, Joseph, and James Kelly (eds.), *Childhood and Its Discontents* (Dublin, 2002).

Dunne, Lee, *Goodbye to the Hill* (London, 1965).

Dwyer, Ciara, 'The Heart of a Scandal', *Sunday Independent*, 15 July 2007.

Earner Byrne, Lindsey, *Mother and Child: Maternity and Child Welfare in Dublin, 1922–60* (Manchester, 2007).

Earner Byrne, Lindsey, '"Moral Repatriation": The Response to Irish Unmarried Mothers in Britain, 1920s–1960s', in Patrick J. Duffy (ed.) *To and From Ireland: Planned Migration Schemes c. 1600–2000* (Dublin, 2004), pp. 155–97.

Eder, Franz, Lesley Hall and Hekma Gert (eds.), *Sexual Cultures in Europe: National Histories* (Manchester, 1999).

Edwards, Ruth Dudley, *Patrick Pearse: The Triumph of Failure* (Dublin, 1977).

Elliott, Marianne, *The Catholics of Ulster: A History* (London, 2000).

Ellmann, Richard, *Oscar Wilde* (London, 1987).

Enright, Anne, 'Bad at History', in Colm Tóibín (ed.), *Synge: A Celebration* (Dublin, 2005), pp. 115–125.

Evans, David, *Sexual Citizenship: The Material Construction of Sexualities* (London, 1993).

Fagan, Terry, and the North Inner City Folklore Project, *Monto: Madams, Murder and Black Coddle* (Dublin, 2002).

Fahey, Bernadette, *Freedom of Angels: Surviving Goldenbridge Orphanage* (Dublin, 1999).

Fahey, Tony, 'Religion and Sexual Culture in Ireland', in Eder *et al.* (eds.), *Sexual Cultures in Europe* (Manchester, 2007), pp. 53–70.

Family Solidarity, *The Homosexual Challenge: Analysis and Response* (Dublin, 1990).

Fanning, Bryan, *The Quest for Modern Ireland: The Battle of Ideas 1912–1986* (Dublin, 2008).

Farmar, Tony, *Ordinary Lives: Three Generations of Irish Middle-class Experience, 1907, 1932, 1963* (Dublin, 1991).

Farmar, Tony, *Holles Street, 1894–1994* (Dublin, 1994).

Farmar, Tony, *Patients, Potions and Physicians: A Social History of Medicine in Ireland, 1654–2004* (Dublin, 2004).

Farrell, Michael, 'Inside the Marriage Tribunal', *Magill,* February 1984.

Fay, Liam, *Beyond Belief* (Dublin, 1997).

Ferguson, Harry, 'The Paedophile Priest: A Deconstruction', *Studies*, vol. 84, no. 334, pp. 247–57.

Ferris, Paul, *Sex and the British: A Twentieth-century History* (London, 1993).

Ferriter, Diarmaid, 'Suffer Little Children? The Historical Validity of Memoirs of Irish Childhood', in Joseph Dunne and James Kelly (eds.), *Childhood and Its Discontents* (Dublin, 2002), pp. 69–107.

Ferriter, Diarmaid, *The Transformation of Ireland, 1900–2000* (London, 2004)

Ferriter, Diarmaid, *What If? Alternative Views of Twentieth-century Ireland* (Dublin, 2006).

Ferriter, Diarmaid, *Judging Dev: A Reassessment of the Life and Legacy of Éamon de Valera* (Dublin, 2007).

Ferriter, Diarmaid, 'Women and Political Change Since 1960', *Éire-Ireland*, vol. 43, nos. 1&2, 2008, pp. 179–205.

Ferriter, Diarmaid 'Cardinal Lost His Way Somewhere Between Angels and Fallen Priests', *Irish Examiner,* 14 February 2008.

Finnane, Mark, 'Irish Psychiatry Part 1: The Formation of a Profession', in German E. Berrios and Hugh Freeman (eds.), *150 Years of British Psychiatry* (London, 1991), pp. 306–13.

Finnane, Mark, 'The Carrigan Committee of 1930–31 and the "Moral Condition" of the Saorstát', *Irish Historical Studies*, vol. 32, no. 128, November 2001, pp. 519–36.

Finnegan, Frances, *Do Penance or Perish* (Kilkenny, 2001).

Finnegan, Thomas, *Questions Young Girls Ask* (Dublin, 1965).

FitzGerald, Garret, 'Would Married Bishops Have Acted on Abuse?', *Irish Times,* 29 October 2005.

Fitzpatrick, David, *Harry Boland's Irish Revolution* (Cork, 2003).

Fitzpatrick, David, 'Marriage in Post-Famine Ireland', in Art Cosgrove (ed.), *Marriage in Ireland* (Dublin, 1985), pp. 116–31.

Fitzpatrick, David, 'Militarism in Ireland, 1900–1922', in Bartlett and Jeffery (eds.), *A Military History of Ireland* (Cambridge, 1996).

Fitz-Simon, Christopher, *The Boys* (London, 1994).

Flannery, Eoin and Angus Mitchell (eds.), *Enemies of Empire: New Perspectives on Imperialism, Literature and Historiography* (Dublin, 2007).

Flannery, Tony, *From the Inside: A Priest's View of the Catholic Church* (Cork, 1999).

Flynn, Mannix, *Nothing to Say* (Dublin, 1983).

Flynn, T. J., '25 years of AIDS', *Sunday Tribune* Review, 1 October 2006.

Foster, R. F., *W. B. Yeats: A Life: 1. The Apprentice Mage, 1865–1914* (Oxford, 1997).

Foster, R. F., *Luck and the Irish: A Brief History of Change, 1970–2000* (London, 2007).

Fottrell, Quentin, 'Dark Side of the Rainbow', *Sunday Tribune* Review, 23 July 2006.

Fottrell, Quentin, 'Having a Gay Old Time', *Sunday Tribune* Review, 25 November 2007.

Foucault, Michel, *The History of Sexuality, Vol. 1* (New York, 1980).

Foucault, Michel, *The Use of Pleasure* (London, 1988).

Fuller, Louise, *Irish Catholicism Since 1950: The Undoing of a Culture* (Dublin, 2002).

Gallagher, Ralph, 'Understanding the Homosexual', *Furrow*, vol. 30 no. 9, September 1979, pp. 559–68.

Garvin, Tom, *Nationalist Revolutionaries in Ireland, 1858–1928* (Oxford, 1987).

Garvin, Tom, 'The Strange Death of Clerical Politics in University College, Dublin', *Irish University Review*, vol. 28, no. 2, Autumn/Winter 1998, pp. 308–15.

Garvin, Tom, *Preventing the Future: Why was Ireland So Poor for So Long?* (Dublin, 2005).

Geoghegan, Patrick M., 'Setting the Liberator Free', *Irish Times* Weekend Review, 10 May 2008.

Golu, Chichi Ania (ed.), *In from the Shadows: The University of Limerick Women's Studies Collection*, vol. 3, 1997.

Green, Jonathan, *IT: Sex Since the Sixties* (London, 1993).

Grene, Nicholas (ed.), *J. M. Synge and Irish Theatre* (Dublin, 2000).

Grigel, Jean, and Tim Rees, *Franco's Spain* (London, 1997).

Grimes, Brendan, 'Carnegie Libraries in Ireland', in Library Commission of Ireland, *The University of the People: Celebrating Irish Public Libraries* (Dublin, 2003).

Grimshaw, Thomas W. (ed.), *Manual of Public Health for Ireland* (Dublin, 1875).

Gray, Paul and Liam Kennedy, 'A Sexual Revolution in the West of Ireland?', *History Ireland*, vol. 14, no. 6, November/December 2006, pp. 19–22.

Hackett, Francis, 'De Valera's Ireland', *American Mercury*, vol. 60, no. 253, January 1945, pp. 29–39.

Hall, Lesley A., *Sex, Gender and Social Change in Britain Since 1880* (London, 2000).

Hanley, Brian, 'Fear and Loathing at Coolacrease', *History Ireland*, vol. 16, no. 1, January/February 2008, pp. 5–7.

Hannon, Katie, *The Naked Politician* (Dublin, 2004).

Harmon, Maurice, *Seán O'Faoláin: A Life* (London, 1994).

Hart, Peter, *Mick: The Real Michael Collins* (New York, 2006).

Harte, Liam, 'History, Text and Society in Colm Tóibín's *The Heather Blazing*', *New Hibernia Review*, vol. 6, no. 4, Winter 2002, pp. 55–68.

Hayes, Joanne, *My Story* (Dublin, 1985).

Healy, Alison, 'Canon Lawyer Denies Code Silenced Sex Abuse Victims', *Irish Times,* 2 October 2006.

Healy, Dermot, *The Bend for Home* (London, 1996).

Hearn, Mona, 'Life for Domestic Servants in Dublin', in Maria Luddy and Cliona Murphy (eds.), *Women Surviving* (Dublin, 1989), pp. 148–80.

Hederman, Mary, 'Irish Women and Irish Law', *Crane Bag*, vol. 4, no. 1, 1980, pp. 55–9.

Heffernan, Catherine, *Sexually Transmitted Infections: Sex and the Irish* (Maynooth, 2004)

Hegarty, Kevin, 'Celibacy Falling Away in Practice if Not in Doctrine', *Irish Times*, 21 September 1996.

Henke, Suzette A., *James Joyce and the Politics of Desire* (London, 1990).

Hesketh, Thomas H., *The Second Partitioning of Ireland: The Abortion Referendum of 1983* (Dublin, 1990).

Hilliard, Betty, 'The Catholic Church and Married Women's Sexuality: Habits Change in Late Twentieth-century Ireland', *Irish Journal of Sociology*, vol. 12, no. 2, 2003, p. 42.

Holland, Kitty, 'Minister Advised to Close Dublin Run of Rose Tattoo', *Irish Times*, 4 January 2000.

Holland, Kitty, 'Many Unionists Bigoted against Gays, Says Leading Activist', *Irish Times*, 29 July 2008.

Holland, Mary, *How Far We Have Travelled: The Voice of Mary Holland* (Dublin, 2004).

Hooper, John, *The New Spaniards* (London, 1986).

Horgan, Goretti, 'Pro-Choice Lobby Served Important Purpose', *Irish Times*, 8 September 2003.

Horgan, John, *Noël Browne: Passionate Outsider* (Dublin 2000).

Horgan, John, *Irish Media: A Critical History Since 1922* (London, 2001).

Houlihan, Con, 'One of Our Own', *Evening Herald*, 9 July 2008.

Hoult, Norah, *Bridget Kiernan* (London, 1928).

Hourihane, Ann Marie, *She Moves through the Boom* (Dublin, 2000).

Hourihane, Ann Marie, 'They Travel to Knock to Hail Mary', *Sunday Tribune*, 13 August 2006.

Howell, Philip, 'Venereal Disease and the Politics of Prostitution in the Irish Free State', *Irish Historical Studies*, vol. 33, no. 131, May 2003, pp. 320–34.

Howes, Marjorie, 'Public Discourse, Private Reflection: 1916–1970', in Bourke *et al.* (eds.), *The Field Day Anthology vol. 4,* pp. 923–1035.

Hug, Chrystel, *The Politics of Sexual Morality in Ireland* (Basingstoke, 1999).

Humphreys, Madeleine, *The Life and Times of Edward Martyn: An Aristocratic Bohemian* (Dublin, 2007).

Hyde, Abbey, 'Marriage and Motherhood: The Contradictory Position of Single Mothers', *Irish Journal of Feminist Studies*, vol. 2, no. 1, July 1997, pp. 22–37.

Imhof, Rüdiger, *The Modern Irish Novel: Irish Novelists after 1945* (Dublin, 2002).

Inglis, Tom, 'The Constitution of Sexual Subjects in Irish Religious and Moral Discourse', paper presented to Theory, Culture and Society Conference, Berlin, August 1995, UCD Library photocopy 13743.

Inglis, Tom, 'Discourse and Practice: Mapping Changes in Irish Society', UCD Library photocopy 15449, 1995.

Inglis, Tom, 'Foucault, Bourdieu and the Field of Irish Sexuality', *Irish Journal of Sociology*, vol. 7, 1997, pp. 5–28.

Inglis, Tom, *Lessons in Irish Sexuality* (Dublin, 1998).

Inglis, Tom, 'Pleasure Pursuits', in Mary P. Corcoran and Michael Peillon (eds.), *Ireland Unbound: A Turn of the Century Chronicle* (Dublin, 2002), pp. 25–35.

Inglis, Tom, *Truth, Power and Lies: Irish Society and the Kerry Babies Case* (Dublin, 2003).

Inglis, Tom, 'Origins and Legacies of Irish Prudery: Sexuality and Social Control in Modern Ireland' *Éire-Ireland*, vol. 40, nos. 3 and 4, Fall/Winter 2005, pp. 9–38.

Inglis, Tom, 'From Self-denial to Self-indulgence', *Irish Review*, no. 34, 2006, pp. 34–42.

Inglis, Tom, *Global Ireland: Same Difference* (London, 2008).

Jackson, L.A., *Child Sexual Abuse in Victorian England* (London, 2000).

Jackson, Margaret, *The Real Facts of Life: Feminism and the Politics of Sexuality c.1850–1940* (London, 1994).

Jackson, Mark (ed.), *Infanticide: Historical Perspectives on Child Murder and Concealment, 1550–2000* (Aldershot, 2002).

Jeffares, Jennifer, *The Irish Novel at the End of the Twentieth Century: Gender, Bodies and Power* (London, 2002).

Jolas, Maria, 'The Joyce I Knew and the Women around Him', *Crane Bag*, vol. 4, 1980, pp 82–8.

Jones, Greta, 'Marie Stopes in Ireland: The Mother's Clinic in Belfast, 1936–1947', *Social History of Medicine*, vol. 5, no. 2, April 1992, pp. 255–77.

Judt, Tony, *Postwar: A History of Europe Since 1945* (New York, 2005).

Kavanagh, Ray, *Mamie Cadden: Backstreet Abortionist* (Cork, 2005).

Keane, Elizabeth, *Seán MacBride: A Life* (Dublin, 2007).

Kearney, Noreen, and Caroline Skehill (eds.), *Social Work in Ireland: Historical Perspectives* (Dublin, 2005).

Kearins, Evanna, *Rent: The Secret World of Male Prostitution in Dublin* (Dublin, 2000).

Kearns, Kevin, *Dublin Tenement Life: An Oral History* (Dublin, 1994).

Kelleher, Margaret, and Philip O'Leary (eds.), *The Cambridge History of Irish Literature, Vol. 2, 1890–2000* (Cambridge, 2006).

Kelly, James, and Daire Keogh (eds.), *A History of the Catholic Diocese of Dublin* (Dublin, 2000).

Kelly, James, 'The Operation of the Censorship of Publications Board: The Notebooks of C. J. O'Reilly, 1951–55', *Analectia Hibernica*, 40 (2004), pp. 223–369.

Kennedy, Finola, 'The Suppression of the Carrigan Report', *Studies*, vol. 89, no. 356, Winter 2000.

Kennedy, Finola, *Cottage to Crèche: Family Change in Ireland* (Dublin, 2001).

Kennedy, Finola, 'Inspirational Layman Who Brought Life to the Hostels', *Irish Times*, 7 November 2005.

Kennedy, Liam, 'Bastardy and the Great Famine: Ireland 1845–50', in Carla King (ed.), *Famine Land and Culture in Ireland* (Dublin, 2000), pp. 6–29.

Keogh, Dermot, Finbarr O'Shea and Carmel Quinlan (eds.), *The Lost Decade: Ireland in the 1950s* (Cork, 2004).

Keohe, Elisabeth, *Ireland's Misfortune: The Turbulent Life of Kitty O'Shea* (London, 2008).

Kenny, Mary, 'Forty Years On', *Studies*, vol. 92, no. 365, Spring 2003, pp. 7–13.

Kerrigan, Gene, *Another Country: Growing Up in '50s Ireland* (Dublin, 1998).

Kerrigan, Gene, 'Flawed Sex Law was Always a Time Bomb Just Waiting to Go Off on Us', *Sunday Independent,* 5 November 2006.

Kiberd, Declan, *Inventing Ireland* (London, 1995).

Kiberd, Declan, review of C. George Sandulescu (ed.), *Rediscovering Oscar Wilde* in *Irish Studies Review*, no. 14, Spring 1996, p. 56.

Kiberd, Declan, *The Irish Writer and the World* (Cambridge, 2005).

Kiberd, Declan, 'Synge's Opening Night to Remember', *Irish Times,* 26 January 2007.

Kilfeather, Siobhán, 'Look Who's Talking: Scandalous Memoirs and the Performance of Gender', *Irish Review,* no. 13, Winter 1992/3, pp. 40–50.

Kilfeather, Siobhán, 'Sexual Expression and Genre, 1801–1917', in Bourke *et al.* (eds.), *The Field Day Anthology of Irish Writing, Vol. 4* (Cork, 2002), pp. 825–94.

Kilfeather, Siobhán, 'Sexuality, 1685–2001', in Bourke *et al.* (eds.), *The Field Day Anthology of Irish Writing, Vol. 4* (Cork, 2002), pp. 755–1190.

Kilfeather, Siobhán, and Eibhear Walshe, 'Contesting Ireland: The Erosion of Heterosexual Consensus, 1940–2001' in Bourke *et al.* (eds.), *The Field Day Anthology of Irish Writing, Vol. 4* (Cork, 2002), pp. 1039–87.

Kinsella, Thomas (ed.), *Austin Clarke: Selected Poems* (Dublin, 1976).

Kirwin, Bill, 'The Social Policy of The Bell', *Administration*, vol. 37, 1989, pp. 99–119.

Lacey, Brian, 'Billy's Boys, or an Orangeman's Dilemma', *History Ireland*, vol. 16, no. 5, September/October 2008, pp. 18–19.

Lalor, Brian (general ed.), *The Encyclopaedia of Ireland* (Dublin, 2003).

Lalor, John, 'Vilification of Church Obscures Our Role in Ignoring Child Abuse', *Sunday Independent*, 6 November 2005.

Lavery, Don, 'Irish Lady of the Night Brought Down British Lord in Sex Scandal', *Sunday Independent*, 7 January 2007.

Lavin, Mary, *The Long Ago and Other Stories* (London, 1944).

Lavin, Mary, *Happiness and Other Stories* (Boston, 1970).

Lawless, Jo Murphy (ed.), 'Childbirth 1742–1955', in Bourke *et al.* (eds.), *The Field Day Anthology of Irish Writing, Vol. 4* (Cork, 2002), pp. 896–913.

Lawson, William, 'The Amendment of the Law in Ireland as to the Maintenance of Illegitimate Children', *Journal of the Social and Statistical Inquiry Society of Ireland*, vol. 13, December 1914, pp. 182–207.

Layte, Richard, and Hannah McGee, 'More Open Attitude on Sexual Matters Has a Downside', *Irish Times*, 17 October 2006.

Lee, Joe, *The Modernisation of Irish Society 1848–1918* (Dublin, 1973; this edn, 1992).

Lee, Joe, 'Women and the Church Since the Famine', in Margaret MacCurtain and Donncha O'Corráin (eds.). *Women in Irish Society: The Historical Dimension* (Dublin, 1978), pp. 37–46.

Leland, Mary, 'Prostitution in Cork', *Irish Times*, 28 November 1968.

Lennon, Hillary (ed.), *Frank O'Connor: Critical Essays* (Dublin, 2007).

Lennon, Tom, *When Love Comes to Town* (Dublin, 1993).

Levenson, Leah, *The Four Seasons of Mary Lavin* (Dublin, 1998).

Levine, June, *Sisters* (Dublin, 1982).

Levine, June, 'A Woman in Gangland', *Magill*, December 1983.

Levine, June, 'The Women's Movement in the Republic, 1968–80', in Bourke *et al.* (eds.), *The Field Day Anthology of Irish Writing, Vol. 5*, pp. 117–228.

Lewis, Brian, 'The Queer Life and Afterlife of Roger Casement', *Journal of the History of Sexuality*, vol. 14, no. 4, October 2005, pp. 363–82.

Library Council of Ireland, *The University of the People: Celebrating Irish Public Libraries,* (Dublin, 2003).

Lodge, David, *How Far Can You Go?* (London, 1980).

Luddy, Maria, *Women and Philanthropy in Nineteenth-century Ireland* (Cambridge, 1995).

Luddy, Maria, 'The Army and Prostitution in Nineteenth-Century Ireland: The Case of the Wrens of the Curragh', *Bullán*, vol. 6, no. 1, Summer/Fall 2001, pp. 67–85.

Luddy, Maria, 'Magdalen Asylums, 1765–1992', in Bourke *et al.* (eds.), *Field Day Anthology of Irish Writing, Vol. 5* (Cork, 2002), pp. 736–51.

Luddy, Maria, *Prostitution and Irish Society* (Cambridge, 2007).

Luddy, Maria, 'Sex and the Single Girl in 1920s and 1930s Ireland', *The Irish Review*, no. 35, Summer 2007, pp. 79–92.

Luddy, Maria, 'Unwitting Architect of Parnell's Downfall', *Sunday Business Post, Agenda Magazine*, 15 June 2008.

Luddy, Maria, and Cliona Murphy (eds.), *Women Surviving* (Dublin, 1989).

Luddy, Maria, and Mary Cullen (eds.), *Female Activists: Irish Women and Change 1900–1960* (Dublin, 2001).

Lyder, Hazel, 'Silence and Secrecy: Exploring Female Sexuality During Childhood in 1930s and 1940s Dublin', *Irish Journal of Feminist Studies,* vol. 5, nos. 1 & 2, 2003, pp. 77–88.

Lyons , J. B., 'Oscar Wilde's Final Illness', *Irish Studies Review*, no. 14, Spring 1996, pp. 24–7.

Lyons, F. S. L., *Charles Stewart Parnell* (Dublin, 1977).

Mac An Ghaill, Máirtín, 'Irish Masculinities and Sexualities in England', in Lisa Adkins and Vicki Merchant (eds.), *Sexualising the Social: Power and the Organisation of Sexuality* (London, 1996), pp. 122–45.

McAvoy, Sandra, 'Sex and the Single Girl: Ireland 1922–49', in Chichi Ania Golu (ed.), *In from the Shadows: The University of Limerick Women's Studies Collection,* vol. 3, 1997, pp. 55–67.

McAvoy, Sandra, 'Aspects of the State and Female Sexuality in the Irish Free State, 1922–49', University College Cork, PhD thesis, 1998.

McAvoy, Sandra, 'Before Cadden: Abortion in Mid-twentieth-century Ireland', in Dermot Keogh, Finbarr O'Shea and Carmel Quinlan (eds.), *The Lost Decade: Ireland in the 1950s* (Cork, 2004), pp. 147–64.

McAvoy, Sandra, 'Sexual Crime and Irish Women's Campaign for a Criminal Law Amendment Act 1912–35', in Maryann Gialanella Valiulis (ed.), *Gender and Power in Irish History* (Dublin, 2008), pp. 84–100.

McCafferty, Nell, *In the Eyes of the Law* (Dublin, 1981).

McCafferty, Nell, *A Woman to Blame: The Kerry Babies Case* (Dublin, 1985).

McCafferty, Nell, *The Best of Nell* (Dublin, 1984).

McCafferty, Nell, *Nell* (Dublin, 2004).

McCann, Eamonn, *War and Peace in Northern Ireland* (Dublin, 1998).

McCarthy, Áine, 'Hearts, Bodies and minds: Gender Ideology and Women's Committal to Enniscorthy Lunatic Asylum, 1916–25', in Diane Urquhart and Alan Hayes (eds.), *The Irish Women's History Reader* (London, 2002).

McCarthy, John P., *Kevin O'Higgins: Builder of the Irish State* (Dublin, 2006).

McClenaghan, Brendí, 'Letter from a Gay Republican', in O'Carroll and Collins (eds.), *Lesbian and Gay Visions of Ireland* (London, 1995), pp. 122–31.

McConvery, Brendan, 'Hell Fire and Poitín: Redemptorist Missions in the Irish Free State (1922–36)', *History Ireland*, vol. 8, no. 3, Autumn 2000, pp. 18–23.

McCoole, Sinéad, *Hazel: A Life of Lady Lavery, 1880–1935* (Dublin, 1996).

McCormack, Micheline, *Little Girl: The Lavinia Kerwick Story* (Dublin, 1997).

McCormick, Leanne, '"One Yank and They're Off": Interaction between US Troops and Northern Irish Women, 1945–45', *Journal of the History of Sexuality*, vol. 15, no. 2, 2006, pp. 228–57.

McCourt, Frank, *Angela's Ashes: Memoir of a Childhood* (London, 1996).

McCullough, Elizabeth, *A Square Peg: An Ulster Childhood* (Dublin, 1997).

MacCurtain, Margaret, and Donncha O'Corráin (eds.), *Women in Irish Society: The Historical Dimension* (Dublin, 1978).

MacCurtain, Margaret, 'Recollections of Catholicism, 1906–1960', in Bourke *et al.* (eds.), *The Field Day Anthology of Irish Writing, Vol. 4* (Cork, 2002), pp. 570–601.

Macdona, Anne (ed.), *From Newman to New Woman: UCD Women Remember* (Dublin, 2001).

MacEvilly, Sarah, '"A Match Made in Heaven?" A Woman's Perspective on Arranged Marriage in Ireland in the 1930s', in Chichi Ania Golu (ed.), *In from the Shadows: The University of Limerick Women's Studies Collection,* vol. 3, 1997.

McGahern, John, *The Collected Stories* (London, 1992).

McGahern, John, *Memoir* (London, 2005).

McGahern, John, 'An tOileanach', *Irish Review*, no. 6, Spring 1989, pp. 55–63.

McGahern, John, 'The Church and Its Spire', in Colm Tóibín (ed.), *Soho Square 6* (London, 1993), pp. 16–30.

McGarry, Fearghal, *Eoin O'Duffy: Self-made Hero* (Oxford, 2005).

McGee, Hannah, *The SAVI Report: Sexual Abuse and Violence in Ireland* (Dublin, 2002).

McGloin, Joseph, *What Not to Do on a Date* (Dublin, 1960).

MacGreil, Mícheál, *Prejudice and Tolerance in Ireland* (Dublin, 1977).

McHugh, Roger, 'Too Immoral for Any Stage', *The Bell*, vol. 15, no. 2, November 1947, pp. 60–64.

McInerney, Sarah, 'Banished: Fr McGinnity's 20-Year Punishment for Speaking Out', *Sunday Tribune*, 30 October 2005.

McKay, Susan, *Sophia's Story* (Dublin, 1988).

McKay, Susan, *Without Fear: 25 Years of the Dublin Rape Crisis Centre* (Dublin, 2005).

McKay, Susan, 'The "City for Everyone" Goes Back on Its Word', *Irish Times*, 7 July 2005.

McKeon, Jim, *Frank O'Connor: A Life* (London, 1998).

Mackey, Aidan, *What is Love?* (Dublin, 1964).

McLaren, Angus, *Twentieth-century Sexuality: A History* (Oxford, 1999).

McLoughlin, Dympna, 'Women and Sexuality in Nineteenth-century Ireland', *The Irish Journal of Psychology*, vol. 15, nos. 2 & 3, 1994, pp. 266–75.

MacMahon, Bryan, *The Master* (Dublin, 1992).

McMahon, Deirdre, 'John Charles McQuaid: Archbishop of Dublin, 1940–1972', in James Kelly and Daire Keogh (eds.), *A History of the Catholic Diocese of Dublin* (Dublin, 2000), pp. 331–44.

McMahon, Deirdre, 'Maurice Moynihan (1902–1999): Irish Civil Servant', *Studies*, vol. 89, no. 353, Spring 2000, pp. 71–7.

McMahon, Deirdre, 'Collins for the Celtic Tiger Cubs', *Irish Times*, 22 October 2005.

Macnamara, Angela, *Yours Sincerely* (Dublin, 2003).

Madden, Lyn, *Lyn's Escape* (Cork, 2007).

Maguire, Moira, 'The Carrigan Committee and Child Sexual Abuse in Twentieth-century Ireland', *New Hibernia Review*, vol. 11, no. 2, Summer 2007, pp. 79–101.

Malcolm, Elizabeth, 'Troops of Largely Diseased Women: VD, the Contagious Diseases Acts and Moral Policing in Late Nineteenth-century Ireland', *Journal of Irish Economic and Social History*, vol. 26, 1999, pp. 1–15.

Martin, Peter, *Censorship in the Two Irelands, 1922–1939* (Dublin, 2006).

Mason, Michael, *The Making of Victorian Sexual Attitudes* (Oxford, 1994).

Maume, Patrick, 'Between Fleet Street and Mayo: P. D. Kenny and the Culture Wars of Edwardian Ireland', *Bullán*, vol. 6, no. 2, Winter/Spring 2002, pp. 21–43.

Meehan, Paula, *The Man Who was Marked by Winter* (Oldcastle, 1991).

Meredith, Fiona, 'Dissenters Want Paisley Gone', *Village*, July 2007.

Milotte, Mike, *Banished Babies: The Secret History of Ireland's Baby Export Business* (Dublin, 1997).

Mira, Alberti (ed.), *The Cinema of Spain and Portugal* (London, 2003).

Moloney, Ed, *Paisley: From Demagogue to Democrat* (Dublin, 2008).

Moore, George, *The Untilled Field* (London, 1903).

Moore, Walter, *A Life of Erwin Schrödinger* (Cambridge, 1994).

Morash, Christopher, 'All Playboys Now: The Playboy of the Western World and the Audience', in Nicholas Grene (ed.), *J. M. Synge and Irish Theatre* (Dublin, 2000), pp. 131–51.

Morrison, Blake, *Things My Mother Never Told Me* (London, 2002).

Mosse, George L., *Nationalism and Sexuality: Respectability and Abnormal Sexuality in Modern Europe* (New York, 1985).

Muggivan, Tony and J. J., *A Tragedy Waiting to Happen: The Chaotic Life of Brendan O'Donnell* (Dublin, 2006).

Mulcahy, Risteárd, *Richard Mulcahy (1886–1971): A Family Memoir* (Dublin, 1999).

Muldowney, Mary, *The Second World War and Irish Women: An Oral History* (Dublin, 2007).

Mulholland, Marie, *The Politics and Relationships of Kathleen Lynn* (Dublin, 2002).

Mullally, Una, 'Generation Sex', *Sunday Tribune* Review, 31 December 2006.

Mullarney, Máire, *What About Me?* (Dublin, 1992).

Mullins, Dave, *Ladies of the Kasbah* (London, 1995).

Murphy, Annie, with Peter de Rossa, *Forbidden Fruit: The True Story of My Secret Love Affair with Ireland's Most Powerful Bishop* (London, 1993).

Murphy, C. B., 'Sex, Censorship and the Church', *The Bell*, vol. 2, no. 6, September 1941, pp. 65–76.

Murphy, John A., 'Human Side to a Demonised Dev', *Sunday Independent*, 21 October 2007.

Murray, Christopher, *Seán O'Casey: Writer at Work* (Dublin, 2004).

Murray, Helen, 'Sex and the Irish', *Sunday Tribune* Magazine, 24 April 2005.

Myers, Kevin, *Watching the Door: A Memoir, 1971–1978* (Dublin, 2006).

National Gallery of Ireland, *A Time and a Place: Two Centuries of Irish Social Life* (Dublin, 2006).

Newman, Jeremiah (ed.), *The Limerick Rural Survey, 1958–64* (Tipperary, 1964).

Ní Ghairbhí, Róisín, 'The Use of Hiberno-English as a Mouthpiece for Irish Identity in the Irish Theatre: Synge's *The Playboy of the Western World* and the Drama of Martin McDonagh', in Eoin Flannery and Angus Mitchell (eds.), *Enemies of Empire: New Perspectives on Imperialism, Literature and Historiography* (Dublin, 2007), pp. 142–60 .

Ní Ghlinn, Áine, *Unshed Tears: Deora Nár Caoineadh* (Dublin, 1996).

Ní Shúilleabháin, Brenda, *Bibeanna: Memories from a Corner of Ireland* (Cork, 2007).

Nic Eoin, Máirín, 'Maternal Wisdom: Some Irish Perspectives', *Irish Journal of Feminist Studies*, vol. 4, no. 2, 2002, pp. 1–16.

NSPCC, *Sixteenth Annual Report of the Dublin and District Branch 1904–5* (Dublin, 1905).

NSPCC, *Eighteenth Annual Report, 1906–7* (Dublin, 1907).

NSPCC, *Twentieth Annual Report, 1908–9* (Dublin, 1909).

NSPCC, *Twenty-first Annual Report 1909–10*, (Dublin, 1910).

NSPCC, *Twenty-second Annual Report, 1910–11* (Dublin, 1911).

NSPCC, *Twenty-fifth Annual Report, 1913–14* (Dublin, 1914).

O'Brien, John (ed.), *The Vanishing Irish: The Enigma of the Modern World* (London, 1954).

O'Brien, John, *A Chaste Courtship* (Notre Dame, 1965).

O'Brien, J. V, *Dear Dirty Dublin* (Dublin, 1978).

O'Carroll, Íde, and Eoin Collins (eds.), *Lesbian and Gay Visions of Ireland: Towards the 21st Century* (London, 1995).

O'Cathaoir, Brendan, 'An Irishman's Diary', *Irish Times*, 27 December 2001.

O'Connell, Angela, 'Patriarchy, Power and Pregnancy: Irish Lesbians on the Boat to England', *Irish Journal of Feminist Studies*, vol. 5, nos. 1 & 2, 2003, pp. 88–99.

O'Connor, Barbara, 'Ruin and Romance: Heterosexual Discourses on Irish Popular Dance, 1920–60', *Irish Journal of Sociology*, vol. 12, no. 2, 2003.

O'Connor, Frank, *The Saint and Mary Kate* (London, 1932).

O'Connor, Frank, *The Common Chord: Stories and Tales* (London, 1947).

O'Connor, Frank, *The Collar: Stories of Irish Priests* (Belfast, 1993).

O'Direáin, Mairitín, with Declan Collinge, 'J. M. Synge', *Irish Review*, no. 6, Spring 1989, pp. 63–4.

O'Doherty, E. F., and S. Desmond McGrath (eds.), *The Priest and Mental Health*, (New York, 1963).

O'Doherty, E. F., 'Sexual Deviations', in O'Doherty and McGrath (eds.), *The Priest and Mental Health*, pp. 124–35.

O'Dowd, Dinah, *Cry Salt Tears* (London, 2007).

O'Faoláin, Nuala, *Are You Somebody?* (Dublin, 1996).

O'Faoláin, Nuala, 'Failing to Face the Facts of Child Abuse', *Irish Times*, 19 March 1990.

O'Faoláin, Seán, *Midsummer Night's Madness* (London, 1932).

O'Faoláin, Seán, *An Irish Journey* (London, 1940).

O'Faoláin, Seán, *Vive Moi!* (Dublin, 1993; first edn 1963).

O'Faoláin, Seán, 'Answer to a Criticism', *The Bell*, vol. 1, no. 3, December 1940, pp. 5–7.

O'Faoláin, Seán, 'The Mart of Ideas', *The Bell*, vol. 4, no. 3, June 1942, pp. 153–8.

O'Flanagan, Sheila, 'New Man Must Learn Not To Cry So Publicly', *Irish Times*, 21 August 2001.

Ò'Gráda, Cormac, *Ireland Before and After the Famine* (Manchester, 1993).

O'Halpin, Eunan, *Spying on Ireland: British Intelligence and Irish Neutrality During the Second World War* (Oxford, 2008).

O'Hea, Jerome, *Sex and Innocence: A Handbook for Parents and Educators* (Cork, 1949).

Ò hÒgartaigh, Margaret, *Kathleen Lynn: Irishwoman, Patriot, Doctor* (Dublin, 2006).

O'Kane, Maggie, 'The Fairview Killers', *Magill*, April 1983.

O'Keefe, Michael, 'Case That Woke Us All Up to Sexual Scandal', *Sunday Independent*, 13 July 2008.

O'Kelly, Emer, *The Permissive Society in Ireland* (Cork, 1974).

O'Leary, Olivia, and Helen Burke, *Mary Robinson: The Authorised Biography* (London, 1998).

O'Leary, Olivia, *Party Animals* (O'Brien Press, 2006).

O'Loughlin, Michael, 'Those Glorious Seventies', *Sunday Independent*, 7 August 2006.

O'Malley, Thomas, *Sexual Offences: Law, Policy and Punishment* (Dublin, 1996).

O'Malley, Tom, 'Perceptions of Sexual Violence', in Byrne *et al.* (eds.), *University College Galway Women's Studies Review*, vol. 11, 1993, pp. 131–47.

O'Reilly, Emily, *Masterminds of the Right* (Dublin, 1992).

O'Rourke, Brian, *The Conscience of the Race: Sex and Religion in Irish and French Novels, 1941–73* (Dublin, 1980).

O Síocháin, Séamas, *Roger Casement: Imperialist, Rebel, Revolutionary* (Dublin, 2008).

O'Sullivan, Eoin, and Mary Raftery, *Suffer the Little Children: The Inside of Ireland's Industrial Schools* (Dublin, 1999)

O'Sullivan, Eoin, 'This Otherwise Delicate Subject': Child Sexual Abuse in Early Twentieth-century Ireland,' in Paul O'Mahony (ed.), *Criminal Justice in Ireland* (Dublin, 2002), pp. 172–202.

O'Sullivan, Michael, *Brendan Behan: A Life* (Dublin, 1997).

O'Toole, Fintan, *The Irish Times Book of the Century* (Dublin, 1999).

O'Toole, Fintan, 'The Sexual Politics of John B. Keane', *Magill*, February 1985, pp. 51–2.

O'Toole, Fintan, 'On the Side of Angels', *Magill*, February 1988, pp. 17–22.

O'Toole, Fintan, 'In a Cold Climate, a Heroic Stand', *Irish Times*, 19 November 2002.

O'Toole, Fintan, 'Still Failing to Protect Our Children', *Irish Times*, 23 July 2002.

O'Toole, Fintan, 'A Culture That Failed to See Evil', *Irish Times*, 1 November 2005.

O'Toole, Fintan, 'Picking the Lock of Family Secrets', *Irish Times*, 1 April 2006.

O'Tuama, Seán (ed.), *The Gaelic Laegue Idea* (Cork, 1972).

Parker, Andrew, Mary Russo, Doris Sommer and Patricia Yaeger (eds.), *Nationalisms and Sexualities* (London, 1992).

Pašeta, Senia, *Modern Ireland: A Very Short Introduction* (Oxford, 2003).

Pihl, Lis (ed.), *Signe Toksvig's Irish Diaries, 1926–37* (Dublin, 1994).

Pine, Richard, *2RN and the Origins of Irish Radio* (Dublin, 2002).

Plunkett, Horace, *Ireland in the New Century* (New York, 1908).

Prince, Simon, *Northern Ireland's '68* (Dublin, 2007).

Quiello, Rose, 'Borderline Women: The Heroines of Kate O'Brien's Novels', *Irish Studies Review*, no. 3, Spring 1993, pp. 8–10.

Quine, Maria Sophia, *Population Politics in Twentieth-century Europe* (London, 1996).

Quinn, Antoinette, *Patrick Kavanagh: A Biography* (Dublin, 2001).

Quinn, Cath, 'Images and Impulses: Representations of Puerperal Insanity and Infanticide in Late Victorian England', in Mark Jackson (ed.), *Infanticide: Historical Perspectives on Child Murder and Concealment, 1550–2000* (Aldershot, 2002).

Rapp, Dean, 'The Early Discovery of Freud by the British General Public, 1912–1919', *Journal of the Social History of Medicine*, vol. 3, no. 2, August 1990, pp. 217–45.

Rattigan, Cliona, '"Crimes of Passion of the Worst Character": Abortion Cases and Gender in Ireland, 1925–50', in Valiulis (ed.), *Gender and Power in Irish History* (Dublin, 2008), pp. 115–40.

Redlich, Patricia, 'Look Back at Anguish', *Sunday Independent,* 31 December 2006.

Reidy, Conor, 'Borstal Boys: The Institution at Clonmel: 1906–1914', *History Studies* (University of Limerick), vol. 6, 2005, pp. 64–78.

Reynolds, Paul, *Sex in the City* (Dublin, 2003).

Richards, Maura, *Two to Tango* (London, 1981).

Riddick, Ruth, *The Right to Choose: Questions of Feminist Morality* (Dublin 1990).

Riordan, Susannah, 'Venereal Disease in the Irish Free State: The Politics of Public Health', *Irish Historical Studies*, vol. 35, no. 139, May 2007, pp. 345–65.

Roberts, Hayley Fox, '"Always Keep a Lemon Handy": A Skeletal History of Lesbian Activism in Late Twentieth-century Ireland', *History Review, 12* (University College Dublin), 2001, pp. 113–27.

Robinson, Stephen, 'Bringing It All Back Home', *Gay Community News*, March 1998.

Rockett, Kevin, *Irish Film Censorship: A Cultural Journey from Silent Cinema to Internet Pornography* (Dublin, 2004).

Rohan, Dorine, *Marriage: Irish Style* (Cork, 1969).

Rose, Kieran, *Diverse Communities: the evolution of lesbian and gay politics in Ireland* (Cork, 1994).

Rothery, Brian, *What Europe Means to the Irish* (London, 1973).

Rouse, Paul, 'Law and Order', text of the National Archives of Ireland Dublin 1911 Census Project, www.census.nationalarchives.ie.

Rouse, Paul, 'Poverty and Health', text of the NAI, Dublin 1911 Census Project, www.census.nationalarchives.ie.

Ruane, Medb, *The Irish Journey: Women's Stories of Abortion* (Dublin, 2000).

Ruddock, Norman, *The Rambling Rector* (Dublin, 2005).

Ryan, Louise, 'The Massacre of Innocence: Infanticide in the Irish Free State' *Irish Studies Review,* no. 14, Spring 1996, pp. 17–21.

Ryan, Louise '"Drunken Tans": Representation of Sex and Violence in the Anglo-Irish War, 1919–21', *Feminist Review*, no. 66, Autumn 2000, pp. 73–95.

Ryan, Louise, *Gender, Identity and the Irish Press, 1922–1937: Embodying the Irish Nation* (New York, 2001).

Ryan, Paul, 'Coming Out, Fitting In: The Personal Narratives of Some Irish Gay Men', *Irish Journal of Sociology*, vol. 12, no. 2, 2003, pp. 68–86.

Rynne, Andrew, *The Vasectomy Doctor: A Memoir* (Dublin, 2005).

Saddlemyer, Ann (ed.), *The Collected Letters of John Millington Synge, Vol. 1, 1871–1907* (Oxford 1993).

Saint Vincent de Paul Society, *Social Workers' Handbook: For Catholic Social Workers in Dublin* (Dublin, 1942).

Sayers, Peig, *Peig* (Kerry, 1936).

Sheehy, Michael, *Is Ireland Dying? Culture and the Church in Modern Ireland* (London, 1968).

Sheridan, Kathy, 'Cynthia's Day of Vindication', *Irish Times*, 17 February 2007.

Sigel, Lisa Z, *Governing Pleasures: Pornography and Social Change in England, 1815–1914* (New Jersey, 2002).

Skehill, Caroline, 'Child Protection and Welfare Social Work in the Republic of Ireland', in Noreen Kearney and Caroline Skehill (eds.), *Social Work in Ireland: Historical Perspectives* (Dublin, 2005), pp. 127–46.

Smith, James M., *Ireland's Magdalen Laundries and the Nation's Architecture of Containment* (Notre Dame, ID, 2007).

Smith, James M., 'The Politics of Sexual Knowledge: The Origins of Ireland's Containment Culture and the Carrigan Report (1931)', in *Journal of the History of Sexuality*, vol. 13, no. 2, April 2004, pp. 208–33.

Smyth, Ailbhe, 'Feminism, Personal Political (or Ex-Colonized Girls Know More)', *Irish Journal of Feminist Studies*, vol. 2, no. 1, July 1997, pp. 37–55.

Smyth, James, 'Dancing, Depravity and All That Jazz: The Public Dance Halls Act of 1935', *History Ireland*, vol. 1, no. 2, Summer 1993, pp. 51–5.

Spreng, Jennifer, *Abortion and Divorce Law in Ireland* (London, 2004).

Stevens, Julie Anne, 'Mary Lavin (1912–1996): A Tribute', *Irish Journal of Feminist Studies*, vol. 1, no. 2, Winter 1996, pp. 25–36.

Sugrue, Karen, 'Sex in the City', in Corcoran and Peillon (eds.), *Ireland Unbound*, pp. 51–62.

Sweetman, Rosita, *On Our Backs: Sexual Attitudes in a Changing Ireland* (Dublin, 1979).

Sweetman, Rosita, 'The Blanket of Silence', in Mark Patrick Hederman and Richard Kearney (eds.), *The Crane Bag Book of Irish Studies* (Dublin, 1982), pp. 765–9.

Swift, Carolyn, and Gerard Whelan, *Spiked: Church–State Intrigue and the Rose Tattoo* (Dublin, 2002).

Synge, J. M. (edited by Robert Skelton), *The Aran Islands* (Oxford, 1979; first published 1907).

Tanner, Michael, *Troubled Epic* (Dublin, 2007).

Tifft, Stephen, 'The Parricidal Phantasm: Irish Nationalism and the Playboy Riots', in Andrew Parker *et al.* (eds.), *Nationalisms and Sexualities,* pp. 313–35.

Tobin, Fergal, *The Best of Decades: Ireland in the 1960s* (Dublin, 1984).

Tóibín, Colm, 'Gay Byrne: Irish Life as Cabaret', *Crane Bag*, vol. 8, no. 2, 1984, pp. 165–70.

Tóibín, Colm (ed.), *Soho Square 6* (London, 1993).

Tóibín, Colm, *The Blackwater Lightship* (London, 1999).

Tóibín, Colm, *Lady Gregory's Toothbrush* (Dublin, 2002).

Tóibín, Colm, 'A Brush with the Law', *Dublin Review*, no. 28, Autumn 2007, pp. 11–34.

Tóibín, Colm, 'Selling Tara, Buying Florida', *Éire-Ireland*, vol. 43, nos. 1 & 2, Spring/Summer 2008, p. 4.

Tracy, Honor, *Mind You, I've Said Nothing! Forays in the Irish Republic* (Washington, 1968; first published 1953).

Trench, Brian, 'The Contraception Backlash', *Magill,* January 1979.

Tyrrell, Peter, *Founded on Fear: Letterfrack Industrial School, War and Exile* (Dublin, 2006).

Ua Maoileoin, Pádraig, *Macadúna* (Dublin, 2001).

'Unemployed', 'Neutral Night', *The Bell*, vol. 4, no. 1, April 1942, pp. 37–40.

Urquhart, Diane, and Alan Hayes (eds.), *The Irish Women's History Reader* (London, 2002).

Valiulis, Maryann Gialanella (ed.), *Gender and Power in Irish History* (Dublin, 2008).

Valiulis, Maryann Gialanella, and Mary O'Dowd (eds.), *Women and Irish History* (Dublin, 1997).

Valiulis, Maryann, 'Engendering Citizenship: Women's Relationship to the State in Ireland & the United States in the Post-Suffrage Period', in Valiulis and O'Dowd (eds.), *Women and Irish History*, pp. 159–73.

Valiulis, Maryann, 'Virtuous Mothers and Dutiful Wives: The Politics of Sexuality in the Irish Free State', in Valiulis (ed.), *Gender and Power in Irish History,* pp. 100–15.

Viney, Ethna, *Ancient Wars: Sexuality and Oppression* (Attic Press, 1989).

Wall, Martin, 'Doctor with "Deep Fault Line" Which was Never Corrected, *Irish Times*, 1 March 2006.

Walsh, Caroline (ed.), *Arrows in Flight: Short Stories from a New Ireland* (London, 2002).

Walshe, Eibhear (ed.), *Sex, Nation and Dissent in Irish Writing* (Cork, 1997).

Walshe, Eibhear, 'The Erosion of Heterosexual Consensus', in Bourke *et al.*, *The Field Day Anthology of Irish Writing, Vol. 4* (Cork, 2002).

Walshe, Eibhear, 'The First Gay Irishman? Ireland and the Wilde Trials', *Éire-Ireland*, vol. 40, Fall/Winter 2005, pp. 38–58.

Walshe, Eibhear 'The Vanishing Homoerotic: Colm Tóibín's Gay Fictions', *New Hibernia Review*, vol. 10, no. 4, Winter 2006, pp. 122–37.

Walshe, Eibhear, *Kate O'Brien: A Writing Life* (Dublin, 2006).

Weeks, Jeffrey, *Sex, Politics and Society: The Regulation of Sexuality Since 1800* (London, 1981).

Weeks, Jeffrey, *Coming Out: Homosexual Politics in Britain from the Nineteenth Century to the Present* (London, 1977).

Weeks, Jeffrey, 'Foucault for Historians', *History Workshop*, no. 14, Autumn 1982, pp. 106–20.

Weeks, Jeffrey, *Making Sexual History* (Cambridge, 2000).

White, E., *States of Desire* (London, 1980).

Whyte, John H., *Church and State in Modern Ireland, 1923–70* (Dublin, 1971).

Wills, Clair, *That Neutral Island: A Cultural History of Ireland During the Second World War* (London, 2007).

Wohlgelerntner, Maurice, *Frank O'Connor: An Introduction* (New York, 1977).

INDEX